Colombia

LATIN AMERICAN HISTORIES

Thomas E. Skidmore, Series Editor

Colombia

Fragmented Land, Divided Society

Frank Safford
Northwestern University

Marco Palacios
El Colegio de México

New York   Oxford
OXFORD UNIVERSITY PRESS
2002

#4463299b

Oxford University Press

Oxford   New York
Athens   Auckland   Bangkok   Bogotá   Buenos Aires   Calcutta
Cape Town   Chennai   Dar es Salaam   Delhi   Florence   Hong Kong   Istanbul
Karachi   Kuala Lumpur   Madrid   Melbourne   Mexico City   Mumbai
Nairobi   Paris   São Paulo   Shanghai   Singapore   Taipei   Tokyo   Toronto   Warsaw

and associated companies in
Berlin   Ibadan

Published by Oxford University Press, Inc.
198 Madison Avenue, New York, New York 10016
http://www.oup-usa.org

Oxford is a registered trademark of Oxford University Press

Library of Congress Cataloging-in-Publication Data
Safford, Frank, 1935–
    Colombia : fragmented land, divided society / Frank Safford and Marco Palacios.
        p.   cm.—(Latin American histories)
    Includes bibliographical references and index.
    ISBN 0-19-504617-X (paper)—ISBN 0-19-514312-4 (cloth)
        1. Colombia—History.   2. Political violence—Colombia—History—20th century.
    I. Palacios, Marco.   II. Title.   III. Series.
    F2271 .S245   2002
    986.1—dc21
                                                                    00-058898

Printing number: 9 8 7 6 5 4 3 2 1

Printed in the United States of America
on acid-free paper

Contents

Maps and Tables

MAPS

TABLES

Introduction

This volume provides a history of Colombia from pre-Columbian times to the end of the twentieth century. Although many themes are treated in the book, several tend to predominate. The book emphasizes Colombia's fragmentation into regions and the development of distinct regional economies and cultural characteristics. It also analyzes the country's delayed economic development, in which geographic factors, including climate and topography, have played an important role. Finally, it stresses the relative weakness of the state and of state authority, to which both regional fragmentation and economic weakness have contributed.

Colombia's history has been shaped by its spatial fragmentation, which has found expression in economic atomization and cultural differentiation. The country's historically most populated areas have been divided by its three mountain ranges, in each of which are embedded many small valleys. The historical dispersion of much of the population in isolated mountain pockets long delayed the development of transportation and the formation of an integrated national market. It also fostered the development of particularized local and regional cultures. Politically, this dispersion has manifested itself in regional antagonism and local rivalries, expressed in the nineteenth century in civil war and in at least part of the twentieth century in intercommunity violence.

Wide cultural disparities were evident among Colombia's pre-Columbian populations. Under Spanish rule the topographically determined division between the country's eastern and western population groups was reinforced by political divisions stemming from the pattern of conquest. To these spatial and political divisions were added regional ethnic and cultural differences that were determined in part by the varying economic functions of the different regions. During the colonial period and afterward, an indigenous-mestizo population survived in the agricultural East, while on the Caribbean coast and in much of the gold-mining West African slaves played an important part in the formation of the population.

Status, power, and wealth, strongly concentrated in a social apex, acquired different meanings, depending on locality and region, ethnic identity, and culture, including the political culture. These differences have been somewhat attenuated with the economic growth of the country and its eventual integration through improved means of communication, changes that have become more and more palpable as the twentieth century has progressed. But longstanding social contrasts have persisted or have made a spirited reappearance. Despite the growth of urban middle classes during the twentieth century, profound social differences still can be observed in a continuing breach between the ideal of citizenship and political equality and the reality of continuing privileges and inequalities before the law and the justice of the state.

The themes outlined here are pursued, more concretely and less abstractly, in this book. It is a joint work, in which Frank Safford wrote the first ten chapters and Marco Palacios the last four.

This volume begins with an overview of some fundamental factors affecting Colombia's development, with particular emphasis on the economic consequences of Colombia's geography, viewed historically. A chapter on pre-Columbian cultures attempts, without going into great detail, to give a sense of the cultural variation existing before the European conquest. A chapter on the European conquest points out the ways in which the patterns of conquest reinforced the topographic division between East and West. Chapter 4 outlines the development of differentiated economic functions and cultural features of the eastern, western, and Caribbean coastal zones of the country. Chapters 5 and 6 focus on the colonial background to independence and the regional and political fragmentation that occurred in the struggle for independence itself. Chapters 7 and 8 deal with both efforts to create an integrated polity and the origins of the partisan divisions that have structured Colombian political life to this day. Chapters 8, 9 and 10 trace a movement from political centralization and economic stagnation (1831–1845) to a parallel evolution into political decentralization and the beginnings of a more pronounced external economic opening (1845–1876).

Colombia's integration into the world market was more difficult and prolonged than contemporaries supposed it would be. This may be seen in Chapter 11, which underlines the search for a functioning institutional order, a task made difficult by a fragile economic environment and aggravated by partisan conflict. The period 1875–1903 ends with prolonged and devastating civil war and the loss of Panama. Chapter 12 focuses on coffee, which finally permitted Colombia's incorporation into the world economic system. Coffee was the source of sustained economic growth, of the gradual formation of an internal market and of a relative political peace, accompanied by institutional reforms that strengthened political authority (1903–1946). Nevertheless, this period ended with the emergence of a populist movement, aborted and contained in the context of the Cold War, amid a political and social violence that occurred simultaneously with accelerated urban growth and a modest version of import substitution industrialization. This process covers the second half of the twentieth century, and to it are devoted the last two chapters of the book. Chapter 13 describes social, economic, and state political aspects of Colombia in the second half of the twentieth century, while Chapter 14 focuses on the different manifestations of violence in the country from 1946 to the present.

Please note that this volume refers to the capital of Colombia by the name appropriate to the time being discussed by the text. From its founding in the sixteenth century to 1819, the capital was known as Santafé de Bogotá, or often merely as Santafé. In 1819 it became simply Bogotá. The constitutional convention of 1991 restored the name Santafé de Bogotá. However, in common parlance, it is still called Bogotá. Therefore, in the text we continue to refer to the capital as Bogotá with reference even to events after 1991.

1

Continuity and Change in Colombia's Economic Geography: An Overview

Gabriel García Márquez's novel *One Hundred Years of Solitude*, with its depiction of the isolation of the village of Macondo, points to a salient feature of Colombia's physical and social geography. For most of its history Colombia's population has been relatively sparse and scattered in small, disconnected communities. As the relatively few travel accounts of the eighteenth century and the more numerous ones of the nineteenth make clear, historically large stretches of territory have been lightly inhabited, or even almost empty of people. The sparseness and dispersion of much of the population have tended to deter development of transportation, and hence economic integration, in Colombia.

Two other facts about Colombian geography are fundamental: Its more populated regions are both tropical and mountainous. The country lies across the equator. Parts of Colombia extend to 4 degrees south of the equator, although the bulk of the population lies between 3 and 11 degrees north. Because of its tropical location, temperatures in any given locality are more or less constant throughout the year. Temperatures vary primarily according to altitude. The largest city, Santafé de Bogotá, in the eastern highlands, at 2630 meters, or 8600 feet, has a generally cool temperature (an annual mean of 13° C, or 56° F), with daytime variations depending mainly on whether it is sunny or overcast and raining. In the relative chill of the Sabana de Bogotá, inhabitants tend to wear woolens or otherwise to dress warmly. The next largest cities, Medellín and Cali, are at lower altitudes and have noticeably warmer temperatures. Medellín, sprawling across the Valley of Aburrá, at about 1500 meters (4900 feet), enjoys equable shirtsleeve weather (annual mean of 21° C, 70° F). Cali, at 1002 meters (3300 feet) in the verdant Cauca Valley, is still warmer (annual mean of 25° C, 77° F). People on the Caribbean coast, as in the large modern city of Barranquilla or historically significant Cartagena, experience quite hot temperatures (annual means of 28–30° C, 82–86° F). The same is true of low-lying river valleys in the interior (as at Neiva, Honda, and Mompox on the Magdalena River) and in the Chocó, as well as on the eastern plains (*llanos orientales*) and in the Amazon basin.

Colombia's climate is tropical not only in the relative constancy of local temperatures but also in the abundance of rainfall in most of the national territory. The combination of constant temperature and ample rain produces a vigorous vegetation. This is true not only of the hot lowland areas but also

1

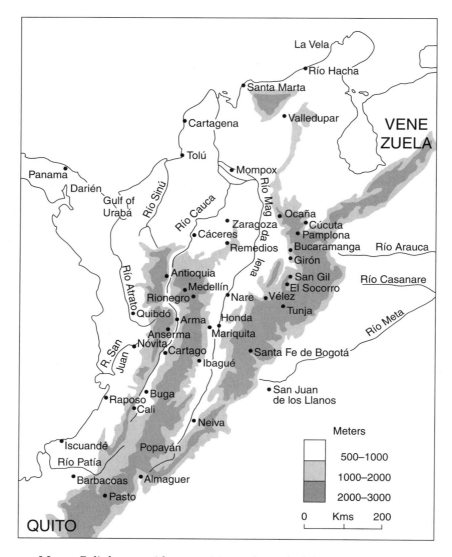

Map 1 Relief map, with some cities at the end of the colonial period.
From Anthony McFarlane, *Colombia before Independence*
(Cambridge, England, 1993).

of Colombia's mountains, which are generally an emerald green, in contrast
with the bleak and barren aspect of the west flank of the Andes in Peru. (See
Map 1.)

The Andes dominate the topography of the more peopled parts of the
country and, for most of its inhabitants, have established, historically, the

fundamental conditions of life. At least since the time of the Spanish conquest, the population in Colombia has clustered most densely in the highland regions, which provide an escape from heat and tropical diseases and where intermontane valleys offer favorable conditions for agriculture. About 9 percent of Colombia's national territory lies between 1000 and 2000 meters (3300–6600 feet), on mountain flanks or in intermontane valleys, where the climate is warm but comfortable. Only 6 percent of the land is higher than 2000 meters (6600 feet), where the temperature is relatively cool, or, at the higher reaches, even cold. Yet in the 15 percent of the country's territory that lies above 1000 meters (3300 feet) live the overwhelming preponderance of the population—in the nineteenth century about two-thirds of the people, in 1964 a little more than three-fifths.

By contrast, the tropical lowlands, which account for about 85 percent of the territory, have been more sparsely inhabited. Over the past century and a half the lowlands have possessed only a little more than a third of the national population. Colombia's eastern lowland plains (the *llanos*) and its southern Amazonian region historically have held very few people. Although these two regions make up more than half (56 percent) of the national territory, until recently they contained only a little more than 1 percent of the national population. The tropical forests of the Chocó in the northwest and the desert of Guajira in the northeast are also quite sparsely inhabited. However, over time there has occurred significant migration to lower altitudes, a process that has accelerated in the twentieth century.

Throughout Colombian history, the most peopled lowland area has been the Caribbean coast. Before the Spanish conquest, it apparently contained important population concentrations. After the conquest these indigenous cultures were decimated. But the Caribbean coast under Spanish domination assumed an important new role as an intermediary between the more populous interior and the outside world. Through the coastal ports—particularly Cartagena in the colonial period, then Santa Marta and Barranquilla in the nineteenth century—flowed imported and exported goods. For these port cities, effective connection to the Magdalena River, linking the coast to the interior, was a matter of the first importance. Another part of the Caribbean zone, the Isthmus of Panama, also functioned as a transit point for commerce, in this case between the Atlantic world and the Pacific coast of the Americas. Largely because of its closer linkage to external commerce, and the outside world in general, the Caribbean zone developed quite different characteristics from those of the more isolated interior. Its population has identified with the life and culture of the Caribbean, in contrast with the majority of the population in the more insulated Andean interior.

In Colombia's interior the Andean highlands have divided the country economically, culturally, and politically. The Andes in Colombia form not a single mountain range but three separate major *cordilleras*, which branch off from each other just north of Colombia's border with Ecuador and run more-or-less parallel in a north-northeasterly direction. The Colombian Andes do not attain the towering heights of the mountains in Peru and Bolivia. A few peaks in the Central and Eastern *cordilleras* reach more than 5100 meters (17,000 feet), but the mean altitudes of these two ranges are closer to 2700 meters (9000 feet). The much smaller Western Cordillera, running along the Pacific coast, has a mean altitude of little more than 1800 meters (6,000 feet). Nevertheless, these three ranges have presented considerable barriers to communication among the various regions of Colombia and between the interior of the country and the outside world.

The difficulties presented by these mountain barriers may be suggested by the fact that the Quindío pass, one of the principal routes across the Central Cordillera, through the middle of the nineteenth century, could be traversed on muleback only with difficulty. During the colonial era and, indeed into the nineteenth century, many travellers were carried across the Quindío pass in chairs borne on the backs of human porters, who were considered even more sure-footed than mules. Other routes across any of the three *cordilleras* were almost as difficult. Until the end of the nineteenth century all had to be traveled by mule or, in good conditions, by horse.

Travelers from the colonial era through most of the nineteenth century have left a vivid record of the horrors of ascending or descending the mule path connecting Honda, the principal upriver port of the Magdalena River, with the Sabana de Bogotá, the highland plain on which the capital city was established. Although the mule path from Honda to Santafé de Bogotá was the obligatory route to the capital for all travelers and commerce from the Caribbean coast or from much of the western part of the country, it remained hazardous for more than three hundred years. In its route from the river to the highland plain the path ascended and descended several subsidiary ridges before mounting the main trunk of the Eastern Cordillera; nonetheless, it gained a net of 2400 meters (7800 feet) in altitude within the short distance of about 77 kilometers (48 miles) of pathway. The problem of the steepness of the route was aggravated by the region's tropical environment, for heavy rainstorms frequently washed away parts of the pathway and left others extremely treacherous. A British traveler who journeyed down the path in the early 1820s described its upper stretches, descending from the Sabana de Bogotá to Villeta, as

> appalling, constantly mounting or descending on the rough pavement, torn up by the violence of the mountain torrent. . . . The mules with the utmost difficulty keep their footing, having to jump from one mass to another at the imminent risk of the rider's neck; on the other hand, where the road has not been paved, deep ruts are formed by the constant traffic in wet weather, in which at every step the animals are immersed to their girths.

But the upper part of the route just described was, by consensus, not the worst. The lower stretches were even more frightening. Thus, William Duane, a North American traveler, in the same years wrote:

> We had concluded at Villeta that nothing could be as bad . . . as the road descending to . . . that place: the road thence to Guaduas proved we were

mistaken; it was tremendous—down—down—down! rocks, ravines, precipices, steeps, swamps, thus again and again; free-stone ascents, which appeared to imbibe the moisture of a warm atmosphere, and crumble at the touch; hills under-worn at the foot, tilted into the ravine, and steep gulleys washed by the mountain floods, leaving the large rocks naked and tottering, over which, and over which only, lay the track for man and beast.

The trials of the path from Bogotá to Honda were such that owners of mule trains often refused to carry cargo over it during periods of heavy rain, because of the great risk to their animals. Even in relatively dry periods the cost of mule haulage on the trail was extremely high—24–38 cents per ton-kilometer (or 38–60 cents per ton-mile) in the mid-nineteenth century (1848–1861). And these freight rates came close to doubling in time of rain or when civil war made mules scarce. In the United States at this time overland freight costs by canal or rail were as low as 2–4 cents per ton-mile.

Although the path from Honda to Bogotá was much cursed and lamented because it was so much traveled by upper-class Colombians and foreign travelers, it was by no means unusual. Similar conditions obtained, although they were less frequently described, on almost any path traversing mountain flanks, including those connecting the Magdalena River with the population centers in the Boyacá and Santander regions to the east and with Antioquia and the Cauca Valley to the west.

The difficulty of transportation up the sides of the *cordilleras* historically kept the inhabitants of the interior separated into two clearly demarcated zones—an eastern zone, consisting of the intermontane valleys and the flanks and immediate watershed regions of the Eastern Cordillera, plus the upper Magdalena Valley, and a western zone, consisting of the Central and Western Cordilleras and the Cauca Valley between them. While transportation between the eastern and western zones was difficult until well into the twentieth century, within the two zones it was somewhat easier. Along the spine of the Eastern Cordillera a series of linked intermontane basins offered relatively flat terrain for travel from Bogotá in the south to Sogamoso to the north. Consequently, this region, incorporating much of the present departments of Cundinamarca and Boyacá, has been relatively integrated culturally and politically, from pre-Columbian times to the present. Directly to the north of the highland plains of Cundinamarca and Boyacá is the mountainous Guanentá region (currently the Department of Santander), deeply cut by ravines. This region has been culturally and politically connected to Cundinamarca and Boyacá yet has retained a distinctive identity because of its obstructive topography.

If linked intermontane valleys permitted a partial integration of the Eastern Cordillera from north to south, in the western part of the country the Cauca River Valley has played a similar role in aiding communications and thus cultural and political unification. The long, flat Cauca Valley made possible easy overland travel from Popayán in the south to Cartago in the north. To the south of Popayán, bordering Ecuador, lies the mountainous region of Pasto, difficult of access because of its broken terrain, yet nonetheless commercially, administratively, and politically linked to Popayán. Similarly, to the north of the Cauca Valley lies another difficult mountainous region, which the Cauca River cuts through deeply in its course to the Magdalena River and the Caribbean—the region of Greater Antioquia (now the departments of Antioquia, Caldas, Risaralda, and Quindío). The inhabitants of these northern mountains have been in an ambiguous relation to the rest of the West. In the pre-Columbian era the peoples inhabiting Greater Antioquia and the Cauca were culturally linked, yet distinctive, and politically independent. In the colonial period the inhabitants of Antioquia were culturally distinct from, yet for a time politically controlled by, Popayán in the Cauca Valley. And in the republican era the Cauca and Antioquia have been culturally different yet not infrequently allied politically.

Between the two population axes of the eastern and western highlands flow the muddy waters of the Magdalena River. Until well into the twentieth century the Magdalena was the principal link to the outside world for the great bulk of the population in the mountain fastnesses of the interior. It was along the Magdalena that Spanish conquerors first found their way into the mountain plains of the eastern highlands in the interior. It was on the Magdalena that Spanish administrators and imported consumer goods came to Santafé de Bogotá and the other towns in the interior where the Spanish colonial population was concentrated. And it was down the Magdalena that the interior sent its exports of tropical products—in small amounts in the late colonial era, in larger quantities after 1845.

The Magdalena River provided relatively rapid, easy transportation downstream. But, as a route into the interior, it presented obstacles. Entry into the river's mouth from the Caribbean was difficult and hazardous, and until the last decades of the nineteenth century travelers and goods usually came to the river by more indirect routes, via either Cartagena or Santa Marta. Many points along the river were obstructed by sandbars, while, in its middle course, particularly at the narrows around and above Nare, boats were challenged by swift currents and dangerous rapids. Still more rapids farther up the river made Honda the terminus for upstream navigation from the coast.

For travelers, the trip up the river, until the middle of the nineteenth century, was a purgatory for all those forced to experience it. Throughout the colonial period, and during most of the first half of the nineteenth century, the upstream journey from the Caribbean coast to Honda, through more than six hundred miles of damp, torrid tropics, had to be made in poled and paddled boats. The duration of this trip depended in part on the state of the river. A Spanish official in the eighteenth century reported that in the best conditions it took at least twenty-five days; if the river were rain-swollen, it might take as many as forty-five days, or at times two months. The time of the journey also depended on the type of boat. In the 1820s and 1830s, the mail canoe shot up the river in only fifteen days, but larger boats carrying freight often required more than two months—depending in part upon how cooperative the boatmen were. During this journey sweating travelers huddled wretchedly under a bamboo roof, at the mercy of mosquitoes, while the pounding feet of the boatman overhead shook dirt upon their heads. This was the only mode of river transportation available on the Magdalena until steamboat service became available—sporadically in the 1820s and 1830s, continuously after 1847.

Colombia's topography divided its population, from the pre-Columbian era onward, into three major regions: the East, the West, and the Caribbean coast. This topographic division of the more populated parts of the country into three major regions distinguishes Colombia from a number of other Spanish American countries. Mexico from pre-Columbian times has been mastered by the central valley of Mexico. In more recent periods, Santiago in Chile's central valley, and the coastal cities of Caracas in Venezuela, Buenos Aires in Argentina, and Montevideo in Uruguay, developed commanding power in those nations. Colombia, by contrast, has had no naturally centralizing topographic feature. Historically, Santafé de Bogotá has been dominant, but not unchallenged politically, and it has had to share economic power with important rivals in other regions.

In the pre-Columbian era, the three regions had clearly distinct cultures. The regional divisions were further confirmed by the pattern of Spanish conquest and settlement: the Eastern Cordillera was conquered and settled by Spaniards making their way south from Santa Marta up the Magdalena River, while other Spanish conquerors coming north from Peru and Ecuador and also south from Cartagena took over and settled western Colombia. Partly for this reason, much of western Colombia during much of the colonial era was not under the jurisdiction of Santafé de Bogotá.

In the colonial period the three major regions also developed different economic features. Gold mining was the motor of the economy of the West, and agriculture, along with attending to local markets, in a number of regions also supplied the miners. Gold mining was of transitory importance in the East; the foci of the eastern economy came to be agriculture and artisanal manufacturing, a part of whose product was supplied to the West, at least until the middle of the nineteenth century. Cartagena on the Caribbean coast focused upon the importation of slaves and consumer goods, the export of gold, and the supply of food and other goods to ships that called at the port as well as to other places in the Caribbean.

The three regions developed distinct racial and cultural profiles. The rapid decline of indigenous populations on the Caribbean coast and in gold-mining regions of the West led to their replacement with a largely African labor force. Accordingly, the Caribbean coast and parts of the West were marked by the cultural imprint of African slaves and their descendants. In the eastern highlands, by contrast, the indigenes survived in greater numbers and few African slaves were introduced. The East therefore retained a peasant population tinctured, in physiognomy and culture, with many traces of the pre-Columbian Muiscas.

The differences in the population bases of the regions have found expression in regional cultures and identities. Dominance by a largely Spanish-descended upper class has been evident in all three regions. But the tone of social relations between dominators and dominated has differed regionally. In the eastern highlands, relations between the upper class and peons and servants of partly indigenous descent historically featured a certain formality, and often arrogance, on the part of the former and an overt subservience and humility on the part of the latter. In coastal Cartagena or in the Cauca, aristocratic dominance was just as evident as in Santafé de Bogotá or Tunja. But on the Caribbean coast or in parts of the West, there has existed a greater ease and informality of relations between the dominant class and a spirited Afro-Colombian labor force.

In the nineteenth century the three major regions became politically antagonistic, with the West and the Caribbean region often joined by their common antipathy to the capital city in the East. One element underlying this regionalist rivalry clearly is the centuries-long tradition of independent importance of such cities as Popayán and Cartagena. That sense of regional importance had a foundation in economic power as well as in political tradition. Each of the three major regions held resources unique to it. In the colonial and republican eras alike, the principal resource of Santafé de Bogotá was its political power. But standing behind that power was the fact that the Eastern Cordillera possessed a total population much larger than that of either of the other two regions. The West, on the other hand, commanded the great bulk of the country's deposits of gold, the only important export in the colonial era and the first half of the nineteenth century. Upon gold were built the wealth and influence of Popayán in the Cauca Valley and Medellín in Antioquia. For its part, Cartagena in the colonial era controlled legal commerce with the outside world and a good share of the contraband trade.

Besides the economic, cultural, and political divisions among the three major regions, another kind of fragmentation has marked the history of Colombia—the fragmentation within each of these regions brought about by the dispersion of the population. During the sixteenth century and the early part of the seventeenth century Spanish settlers tended to concentrate in a few stable cities—Santafé de Bogotá, Tunja, and Pamplona in the Eastern Cordillera; Popayán and Pasto in the West; and Cartagena on the Caribbean coast. There were also a number of small, unstable communities founded by venturous Spaniards seeking their fortunes in outlying areas. Many of these settlements proved temporary, particularly in the West and in the Upper Magdalena Valley, usually because the Indian population either died off rapidly or was too implacably hostile to Spanish demands for labor, but also often because the local gold supplies were rapidly exhausted. Over the longer haul, however, there did occur a more enduring process of agricultural colonization.

From the seventeenth through the nineteenth centuries in the Eastern Cordillera and in Antioquia in the West colonists in search of land moved out from already established communities to form a host of new settlements in the many pockets of cultivable land that could be found in the rumpled *cordilleras*. More than seventy towns were founded in small niches in the deeply corrugated Santander region of the Eastern Cordillera. In Antioquia, from the core zone around Santa Fe de Antioquia colonists went forth in all directions, but their most notable thrust was southward along the Central Cordillera. Both Santander and Antioquia came to be among the more populated regions in Colombia, but their broken terrain tended both to limit the size and to increase the number of agricultural settlements.

Elsewhere, in the tropical lowlands of the Magdalena Valley, the Caribbean coast, and the eastern plains (*llanos orientales*) the population tended to be dispersed in even smaller communities—but for a different reason. Much of the land in these regions was used for raising cattle, which required only a small labor force. During the colonial period the flat lands of the lower Magdalena Valley supplied cattle, pigs, and grain to Caribbean coastal cities, the Spanish fleet, and, to a degree, the Caribbean islands. But seasonal floods during a large part of the year forced the transfer of cattle to high ground and often obstructed the supply of meat and grain to coastal consumers. Seasonal flooding also affected a good part of the eastern plains.

Small and scattered communities also characterized a quite different type of ecological zone, the forest lands of the Chocó and the Pacific Coast. Colombia's other great forested region, the Putumayo and Amazonia, was visited by few Spanish-speaking Colombians until the twentieth century. And even now these regions are only partly integrated into the national polity and economy.

Ultimately, as a result of the centrifugal colonization process, the Colombian population became quite dispersed. By the middle of the nineteenth century Colombia was a country with no very large cities but a congeries of many towns of middling or smaller size. As of 1851, only one city, Bogotá, had close to 30,000 inhabitants. But there were thirty municipal jurisdictions with 8000–15000 people, nearly 150 of 4000–8000, another 230 of 2000–4000, and more than 300 of less than 2000.

Rivalry among these towns has been a continuing feature of Colombian politics, from the colonial era into the republican period. Cartagena and Popayán, although distant from Santafé de Bogotá, were its rivals in the colonial era. During the nineteenth century Medellín, and after 1870 Cali and Barranquilla, emerged as other important cities. Besides a few large cities there were many smaller towns, often pitted against each other in intraregional rivalry. Because of economic change, cities and towns that were once regionally dominant over time gave way to newer contenders. In Antioquia, Santa Fe de Antioquia lost its ascendancy to Medellín after 1775, and Medellín was not able to secure a clear preeminence over Rionegro until the early republican era. Rionegro, in turn, had an emerging rival in nearby Marinilla, and so on. Popayán, the regnant city of the Cauca region in the colonial era, nevertheless had a long-term competitor in Cali, while Cali looked over its shoulder at Buga. On the Caribbean coast, during the eighteenth century, Cartagena, which controlled almost all legal trade with the outside world, had a rival in Mompox, an emporium for contraband goods brought from Santa Marta, Riohacha, and other points. In the republican era, with a more open trade system, Cartagena was superseded as a receiver of imported goods first by Santa Marta and then by Barranquilla.

Historically, there has been relatively little trade among the three major zones. This paucity of interregional trade may be attributed in part to the high cost of overland transportation, at least until well into the twentieth century. And the high cost of overland transportation in turn may be ascribed, at least partly, to the obstacles posed by a mountainous topography in a tropical environment, as mule paths and railroads alike were more costly to build and more difficult to maintain along mountain slopes seasonally washed by tropical rainfall than in more level and more temperate environs.

Another factor discouraging long-distance trade was the sparseness of the population and its dispersion into small pockets. In most of these niches most food and much of the clothing consumed was produced locally, with only a limited trade outside the immediate subregion. Transportation costs surely had much to do with this tendency to local autonomy. But it was also true that, in the conditions created by mountains within a tropical environment, exchange within the immediate areas was sufficient to provide a great variety of food. As in the tropics temperature varies according to altitude, in mountainous areas the vertical fall of the mountainsides creates climatic conditions permitting the cultivation of a great range of foods in nearby areas. Thus, in the highland plains of the Eastern Cordillera, farmers grew potatoes and certain kinds of grain (quinoa before the Spanish conquest, wheat and barley after the arrival of the Europeans); slightly lower on the flanks of the *cordillera* the temperature was ideal for maize; lower still tropical plants flourished, such as yuca (*manioc*), avocado, and cacao, before the Spanish conquest, and afterward also sugarcane and banana. This vertical complementarity therefore made it possible to obtain variation in diet without recourse to long-distance trade. Thus, while the tropics and the mountains together made interregional trade difficult, at the same time they made it less necessary. The possibility of satisfying a variety of wants through this vertical complementarity, and a consequent paucity of long-distance interregional traffic, together tended to delay improvements in interregional transportation. Few goods really had to be moved between the larger regions. Consequently, although Colombian elites in the nineteenth century constantly talked about the need for better overland transportation, in practice the sense of urgency may have been weakened by the comfortable realities of local complementarity. And, in any case, the possibility of depending on local exchange limited the traffic needed to sustain significant improvement in communications.

Even local trade was so restricted that many regions endured exceedingly primitive transportation conditions for many years. Bridges were uncommon except in the most populated areas. In the mountainous Socorro region, among other places, some rivers coursing through deep ravines were spanned by hide ropes, from which travelers and cargo on shaky platforms were suspended while they were pulled across. Meanwhile their mules and horses swam the torrent below. These rope traverses, known as *cabuyas* in Socorro province and as *tarabitas* in some parts of the Central Cordillera, were in use well into the nineteenth century.

The sparse and dispersed population offered few markets sufficiently concentrated to make transportation improvements economically viable or attractive. Furthermore, physical, economic, and political fragmentation retarded transportation improvements by making it difficult for Colombian politicians to establish national priorities in road building. The country's topography and the distribution of its population made only one project, the improvement of shipping on the Magdalena River, of immediate interest to all or even most regions. The construction of roads, or, later, railroads, from the populated highlands down to the Magdalena River, however, was a source of conflict among the various regions and localities—since whichever region succeeded in creating more efficient communications with the river would dominate the others commercially. And if such conflict existed among regions, so also there were smaller conflicts at the local level.

Given the country's topographic and political fragmentation, Colombian politicians at first simply refrained from confronting the problem of establishing priorities for improving overland transportation. From 1833 to 1844 the small amount of government funds available for public works was divided among the provinces strictly on a per capita basis—with the result that little progress was made on any single route. Attempts to concentrate the use of national funds on certain projects in the 1840s were brought down by a federalist reaction in the 1850s. For the next thirty years little effort was made to establish national priorities. One attempt in the 1870s to use most national funding for a railroad that would benefit the Eastern Cordillera alone stirred intense antagonism in the West and on the Caribbean coast and ultimately played an important part in provoking a radical reorientation of Colombian politics. Throughout most of the nineteenth century, however, Colombian politicians dealt with the problem of transportation priorities largely by ignoring it. The result was many small, underfunded, and often abortive projects and few major breakthroughs in overland transportation until the twentieth century.

While a sparse and scattered population, high transportation costs, and local self-sufficiency constrained long distance trade, some commerce did occur between the major regions, both in the pre-Columbian era and in more recent times. But such trade tended to be limited to a few items that were particularly scarce in certain regions and had a sufficiently high value to overcome the burden of high costs of haulage. The pre-Columbian Muiscas in the eastern highlands, for example, traded cloth goods and salt (the latter scarce in other regions) for gold and seashells from the Magdalena basin.

Similarly, the indigenes of what is now Antioquia traded part of their ample supply of gold to the peoples of the Caribbean coast, whose goods of exchange were slaves, peccaries, and cotton textiles.

During much of the Spanish colonial era, and indeed well into the nineteenth century, the Eastern Cordillera supplied gold-mining Antioquia with cotton and woolen textiles. Among other goods carried over fairly long distances in the colonial era and the nineteenth century were two highly valued commodities whose sale was monopolized by the government—tobacco and the salt produced in Zipaquirá and smaller salt mines in the Eastern Cordillera. Other than the exchange of these few products that were regionally scarce or were particularly valuable for some other reason, there was little in the way of long-distance trade to connect the three major regions.

Few foods were carried overland between the regions. Probably the most significant interregional movement of comestibles was that of cattle, which offered the advantage of being able to transport themselves. In the colonial era cattle raised in the upper Magdalena Valley supplied markets both in the eastern highlands and in the upper Cauca. Other than cattle, the food commodity most persistently carried in interregional trade was cacao, which was produced successfully in rather few regions and had a sufficiently high value to bear the cost of long-distance transportation by mule.

Because Colombia historically was so fragmented internally, the scale of internal commerce was too small to provide a stimulus to dynamic growth. Vigorous economic growth would have to be initiated by the pulse of external trade. However, for some two centuries, growing external trade tended to intensify the fragmentation of the internal market more than propelling its integration. This fragmenting effect of external trade first began to become evident at the start of the eighteenth century. During the seventeenth century wheat flour was shipped from the eastern highlands down the Magdalena River to coastal markets, and some of it reached Antioquia and other parts of the West. But from the early eighteenth century onward it increasingly became more feasible, and cheaper, for the Caribbean coast and the lower Magdalena Valley to obtain flour from overseas, for the most part from North America.

The loss of the flour markets in the lowlands to foreign producers was an early phase of a general process of further regional fragmentation that occurred most markedly in the nineteenth century. During the pre-Columbian era and most of the colonial period, interregional trade was limited by high transportation costs. But in the latter part of the eighteenth century and in the nineteenth century, the commercial links among the regions were further weakened by the increasing efficiency of the developing industrial economy of the Atlantic world. In the Colombian interior in the middle of the nineteenth century, farmers were still using wooden plows and were threshing wheat with running horses, artisans were spinning and weaving with techniques that were centuries old, and goods were moved overland by mule. Meanwhile, in Western Europe and the United States agriculture and industry were being transformed: Canals and then railroads were reducing overland transportation costs to a tenth or less of their former levels, and steam was increasing the speed and security of commerce first on rivers and then on the ocean. Because of these increased efficiencies, by the middle of the nineteenth century not only wheat flour from the United States but also a host of manufactured goods from Europe and the United States could be brought into the Colombian interior more cheaply than comparable goods that might be produced in another region of the country. As of 1850, it cost no more to move freight from Liverpool across the Atlantic and then by steamboat six hundred miles up the Magdalena River to the river port of Honda than for it to travel by mule down the mountain from Bogotá, less than a hundred miles away. Thus, a country already fragmented by topography further disintegrated economically during the nineteenth century because of its relative technological backwardness. This economic fragmentation paralleled, and undoubtedly contributed to, a process of political disintegration that, from 1840 through the 1870s, found formal expression in federalism.

Until well into the nineteenth century, the growth of external trade failed to help Colombia develop an integrated internal market because its exports were too slight to provide a basis for major improvements in overland transportation. During the first half of the nineteenth century Colombia lagged badly as an exporter by comparison with other Latin American countries. From the 1820s through the 1860s, a period first of economic stagnation and then of pronounced political conflict, Colombia struggled to find export commodities adequate to its needs for foreign exchange. Until the emergence of tobacco after 1845, gold remained the country's only substantial and reliable export. First the tobacco trade (1845–1865) and then, much more substantially, coffee increased the value of Colombia's exports per capita. But its relative position as an exporter in Latin America did not change very much. (See Table 1.1.)

Colombia's weakness in foreign trade meant that its government was able to collect little revenue, since in the nineteenth century customs duties were the chief source of state funds. Salvador Camacho Roldán in his treasury report of 1871 pointed out that Colombia's tax collections were one-sixth those of Argentina and Costa Rica, one-fifth those of Chile, one quarter those of Venezuela, and one-third those of Mexico. (Note that the relative order of these countries in revenue collections roughly corresponds to their position as exporters as shown in Table 1.1.)

Colombia's relative retardation as an exporter of tropical products is a puzzle requiring at least an attempt at explanation. It is possible that conditions for cultivation and transportation of such notable colonial exports as cacao were less favorable in the coastal lowlands of New Granada than in coastal Venezuela or Ecuador, both exporters of this commodity in the eighteenth century. New Granada's Caribbean coast was well situated for exports of tropical products, but the lower Magdalena River valley, which

Table 1.1 Exports per capita of selected Latin American countries, circa 1850–1912 (in U.S. dollars)

	1850	1870	1890	1912
Uruguay	54.9	46.6	44.6	50.3
Cuba	22.2	44.3	55.7	64.7
Costa Rica	11.4	21.2	37.9	27.1
Argentina	10.3	16.5	32.4	62.0
Chile	7.8	14.2	20.3	44.3
Bolivia	5.5	8.6	12.4	18.6
Latin America as a whole	**5.2**	**8.9**	**11.7**	**20.4**
Brazil	5.0	8.6	9.6	14.2
Peru	3.7	10.1	3.3	9.4
Venezuela	3.3	6.8	8.3	10.5
Mexico	3.2	2.3	4.4	10.7
Ecuador	2.0	5.0	8.1	15.5
Colombia	**1.9**	**6.6**	**5.7**	**6.4**
Guatemala	1.7	2.5	7.5	7.2
Paraguay	1.3	5.8	8.5	8.6

Source: Based on Victor Bulmer-Thomas, *The Economic History of Latin America since Independence* (Cambridge, England, 1994), Table 3.5.

dominated much of the region, was subject to seasonal flooding. However, other parts of the Caribbean coast were more usable for tropical agriculture, yet were not effectively exploited for exporting. It seems, therefore, necessary to turn to some other explanation for New Granada's retardation as an exporter of tropical agricultural products.

The existence of gold bullion as an export seems in various ways to have inhibited agricultural exports. From the sixteenth until the end of the eighteenth centuries, New Granada's success in extracting gold may well have induced local neglect of other export possibilities. Furthermore, because of the high value of gold in relation to its bulk and weight, it could be exported without requiring significant transportation improvements. Thus, gold exports did nothing to lay the groundwork for exporting other commodities. In the last decades of the colonial period, both elements of the New Granadan elite and some Spanish colonial administrators in New Granada did favor developing exports other than gold. They found, however, that merchants and government administrators in Spain had little interest in encouraging the export of tropical products from New Granada. Spanish merchants in the latter eighteenth century frequently resisted payment for goods in anything but gold, while policymakers in Spain in the last decades of the colonial era refrained from extending to New Granada trade advantages that they freely conceded to Cuba and Venezuela. So, in addition to a New

Granadan habit of relying on gold for exchange, there also appears to have existed in Spain a corresponding habit, if not a conscious policy, of viewing New Granada primarily as a supplier of gold, and not a source of tropical products. A possible further consequence of this colonial pattern of dependence on gold exports, reinforced by Spanish policy, was that New Granada entered the republican era without already-developed patterns of producing and exporting tropical commodities. This explanation of New Granada's retardation as an exporter of tropical products, emphasizing a path dependency initiated by its colonial role as an exporter of gold, is offered, it should be noted, as no more than a hypothetical clue to the puzzle.

After somewhat successful efforts to export tobacco (1845–1865), much more short-lived ventures in marketing cinchona bark, and brief and abortive experiments with indigo and cotton, Colombians from the mid-1860s onward increasingly began to turn to coffee as a potential export commodity. Coffee cultivation for export began in northern Santander and then spread to Cundinamarca, then to Antioquia, then south into Caldas, the Quindío, and the Cauca Valley. By the end of the 1880s, coffee had become the country's principal export. Its continued expansion helped Colombia to enter the railway era, belatedly, by providing some of the bulk freight, and the expanded import trade, needed to stimulate and sustain new railways. The growing coffee economy also indirectly increased government revenues, thus permitting the development of a stronger national government and greater government expenditures on transportation improvement.

Railroad construction nonetheless proceeded quite slowly at the beginning of the coffee era. As of 1904, after more than a quarter century of coffee expansion, the country still had only 565 kilometers (353 miles) of railway. Progress had been impeded by political instability, with major civil wars in 1876, 1885, and, most especially, 1899–1903, which siphoned revenues into military expenditures. In addition, the country's fragmented topography and dispersed population were still exacting a political cost in the inability to establish clear priorities in railroad construction.

More palpable progress in transportation improvement occurred after 1905, when notable coffee prosperity and political order permitted the pace of railroad construction to double. By 1909 the capital was connected to the Magdalena River by railway. Shortly thereafter Cali became effectively tied to world commerce by the completion of the Panama Canal (1914) and the railway from the Pacific port of Buenaventura to Cali (1915). But Medellín, the country's second city, did not become efficiently linked to the outside world until 1929, when the city completed its railroad connection to the Magdalena River after blasting a tunnel more than two miles long through the Central Cordillera. As of 1930, Colombia was still far from having an integrated transportation network, however, for even the two biggest cities, Bogotá and Medellín, still were not linked directly by rail.

Ultimately, the solution to Colombia's transportation problems, the key to national economic integration, lay less in the railroad than in highways.

The railroad, with its requirement of relatively low grades of ascent, was not well suited to Colombia's abrupt terrain. The development of automotive transportation in the twentieth century liberated Colombians from the constraints of the railroad, permitting them the greater flexibility and the steeper grades that were possible for trucks and automobiles. Highway construction was pursued seriously from about 1910 onward, although it too was hampered by the inability to establish priorities. Although the Colombian highway system was still extremely deficient as of 1950, it at least had permitted something approaching national economic integration.

The intensification of external trade during the second half of the nineteenth century, and the subsequent movement toward an integrated national economy in the twentieth century, brought some shifts in the pattern of urban development. A number of cities that had become important from the sixteenth through the eighteenth centuries because of their economic and political roles under the colonial system stagnated during the nineteenth and twentieth centuries. Their places as dominant urban centers were taken by cities better located to take advantage of a liberalized trade system focusing increasingly on international commerce.

In the Cauca region, for example, Popayán during the colonial era had ruled as the seat of political and ecclesiastical authority and the home of wealthy gold-mining entrepreneurs. But with the growth of tobacco exports from Palmira in the second half of the nineteenth century, both Palmira and the commercial center of Cali began to overshadow Popayán. After 1915, when railway connections to the Pacific coast finally connected Cali effectively to the outside world, the city emerged as the queen of the Cauca region. Over the next fifty years Cali was Colombia's fastest growing large city, its population multiplying by fourteen between 1918 and 1964.

Like Popayán in the Cauca, Cartagena dominated the Caribbean coast during the colonial era. Because of its unusually protected harbor and its proximity to the Isthmus of Panama, where Peru's silver waited, Cartagena became an obligatory point of support for Spanish treasure convoys. Cartagena provided the fleets with food and military protection. At the same time, it served as the focus for the legal exportation of gold and the importation of slaves for New Granada itself. Accordingly, Cartagena became a center of commercial activity and of military power to protect the commercial activity, as well as, with the establishment of the Inquisition, a seat of ecclesiastical authority. With the collapse of the colonial system, however, Cartagena's importance declined. The end of a controlled trade system reduced Cartagena's commercial importance and, by the same token, its military significance. In the republican era of free trade, efficient connection to the Magdalena River became the chief desideratum, and Cartagena, as a receiver of imported goods, fell behind Santa Marta in the 1830s, and both Cartagena and Santa Marta gave way to Barranquilla in the second half of the ninteenth century, particularly after Barranquilla became more fully able to exploit its position at the mouth of the Magdalena. While the population of Cartagena declined between 1850 and 1870, that of Barranquilla grew by 90 percent. After 1870 Barranquilla completely dominated trade on the Caribbean coast, as its ocean port and the Magdalena River became more efficiently linked by railway.

In a variation on the pattern, El Socorro and other towns in what is now the Department of Santander, during the second half of the eighteenth century had grown prosperous in part through the artisanal production of textiles, some of which were sold to Antioquia and other regions. By the middle of the nineteenth century, however, the weavers of Santander were losing markets in Antioquia and elsewhere to imported textiles. Efforts to substitute the manufacture of palm-fiber hats, both for export and for domestic consumption, temporarily sustained artisans in Santander, as well as other regions. But, ultimately, in the second half of the nineteenth century, a number of these artisan towns stagnated. After 1870 Bucaramanga emerged as the dominant city in the region, as a distribution center for imported goods as well as an exporter of coffee.

Thus, while a number of towns that had been important in the colonial period were stagnating or declining in the nineteenth century, cities more involved in the developing import-export trade, by contrast, grew notably. For some cities, like Medellín and Barranquilla, this growth was already evident between 1850 and 1870; for others, like Bucaramanga and Cali, notable development occurred somewhat later.

Despite the relatively rapid growth of the import-export centers after 1850, Colombia remained distinctively a country of many small cities until well into the twentieth century. This urban dispersal, reflecting the country's economic fragmentation, remained characteristic until railway and highway networks built in the first half of the twentieth century began for the first time to create something like a national market. With the increasing economic integration of the country, urban expansion began to become particularly evident in the four largest cities—Bogotá, Medellín, Cali, and Barranquilla.

2

Pre-Columbian Cultures

Given the fact that Colombia's topography has isolated its various regions from each other and the inhabitants of the interior from the outside world, it is perhaps surprising that it is sometimes called the "Gateway to South America." In Colombia's modern history the title seems not to fit. The Isthmus of Panama has served as a principal transit route from the Caribbean to the Pacific to the west coast of South America, but mainland Colombia itself over the past three centuries has been more a barrier than a gateway. The Panamerican Highway has yet to penetrate the jungle separating Panama from Colombia. In recent times Colombia could be said to have served as a South American gateway only in one way—as a center for refining and distributing narcotics.

Taking a very long historical view, however, Colombia has indeed served as a gateway, and an important one. Through the many centuries between the initial population of the Americas and their conquest by Europeans early in the sixteenth century, the land that is now Colombia served as a conduit through which peoples of many cultures flowed. The earliest migrations through the land are wrapped in the veils of prehistory, but it is probable that Colombia's Pacific coast served as an important intermediary point in the secular migration of peoples and cultures between Central and South America. Another important channel was the Magdalena River Valley, which linked Colombia's interior and the Amazon basin with the cultures of the Caribbean.

Archaeological artifacts offer mute testimony to the interweaving on Colombian ground of Caribbean, Central American, Amazonian, and Central Andean influences. Colombia's most renowned archaeological site, San Agustín, on hilly ground near the headwaters of the Magdalena River, developed as a cultural center as early as 300 B.C. A nearby opening in the *cordilleras* made it a natural point of exchange between the Amazon and the Magdalena basin. The stone cultures at San Agustín are in some ways similar to the lithic art of the Chavín culture of highland Peru; like that of Chavín, they exhibit themes that appear Amazonian in origin.

Another channel of communication and influence was the Cauca River Valley, which helped to link cultures from Nicaragua to Southern Colombia. Along this north-south axis a variety of tribal groups, while sustaining local peculiarities, shared similar modes of social and political organization, similar customs, religious beliefs, and material cultures.

Because of the recurrent flow of peoples through the land and the many contrasting ecological niches created by the country's dramatic topography, peoples of many different tongues and cultural attributes lived side by side. Among the many dialects spoken by the indigenes at the time of the European conquest, three linguistic families predominated—the Chibcha, the Carib, and the Arawak. But because the migration and settling of these peoples were channeled along lines established by the fragmented topography, these three language groups were not found in cohesive blocs but rather were interspersed. The Chibcha speakers, who were linked culturally and linguistically to Central America, at the time of the European conquest occupied several highland zones (the Sierra Nevada of Santa Marta, the Eastern Cordillera, and the southern part of the Central Cordillera), although some in the Chicbcha family, the Cuna and Cueva, lived in the lowland region bordering the Isthmus of Panama. The Caribs and Arawaks predominated in the lowlands: the Arawaks in the eastern plains (*llanos*), Amazonia, and the Guajira peninsula; the Caribs on the Caribbean coast, in the Magdalena Valley, and in the lower reaches of the Cauca Valley. The fearsome Caribs, generally distinguished by the Spanish by their use of bows and poisoned arrows, are thought to have invaded the lowland regions, driving out earlier Chibcha and Arawak inhabitants, possibly no more than two hundred years before the European conquest.

With some simplification, the pre-conquest peoples of Colombia may be divided into three regional groupings, more or less corresponding to the three topographic regions already discussed. Colombia's Caribbean zone was the site of some important early cultural developments, having given rise to the first sedentary villages that have been discovered in the country's territory. Coastal peoples that, as of about 3000 B.C., had depended upon the collection of mollusks, by about 2000 B.C. had developed a mixed economy exploiting abundant marine and river resources but also cultivating yuca (*cassava*) and other root crops. By about the time of Christ, maize, probably introduced from Central America, had begun to appear in villages on the Caribbean coast and in the lower Magdalena Valley. Maize was more productive and nutritive than yuca and permitted the growth of larger populations. But it also imposed new technical challenges, most particularly knowledge of cycles of growth and rainfall. This latter requirement may have encouraged the emergence of a class of priests with meteorological expertise. In any event, maize could be stored in a way that yuca could not. The possibility of accumulating surpluses and using them in trade also encouraged the emergence of dominant chiefs who controlled the surpluses and the commerce in them. Thus, with the arrival of maize culture, these villages evolved from egalitarian to more hierarchically ordered societies.

By the time of the Spanish conquest there existed significant political units on the broad flood plains of the rivers flowing to the coast. In the lower reaches of the Sinú, Cauca, and Magdalena River Valleys, some cultures had created large-scale systems of parallel ridges or embankments to sustain agriculture in conditions of periodic flooding. The construction of these works implied the development of elaborately hierarchical societies. One of the most striking of these at the time of the European conquest was the culture of the Sinú, San Jorge, and Cauca Rivers, near the Caribbean coast. The territory of the Sinú was divided among three related, more-or-less deified, regional rulers, whose authority was mutually recognized. One at least, the religious center of Finzenu, had streets and plazas and contained some twenty large multifamily houses, each with three or four smaller related buildings for servants and storage nearby. Its temple allegedly could hold a thousand people. The elites who inhabited these three towns were buried in mounds that, by the time of the Spanish conquest, had grown so large they could be seen for miles.

Perhaps the most impressive culture of the Caribbean zone at the time of the European conquest was that of the Chibcha-speaking Tairona, who lived on the northern and western flanks or foothills of the Sierra Nevada of Santa Marta, where they made use of different elevations to engage in complementary agricultural activities. More than forty Tairona community sites have been discovered, some with dozens of round wooden houses built on stone platforms. The Tairona are Colombia's only pre-Columbian peoples who constructed engineering works in stone; these included temple centers, stone roads, stairways, bridges, and irrigation and drainage works.

The Tairona were more able to resist the Spanish conquest than other coastal peoples in part because they were able to retreat into the abrupt Sierra Nevada and in part probably because some of them lived at altitudes high enough to make them less susceptible to some of the diseases, such as yellow fever and malaria, that were brought by the Europeans. The lowland peoples of the Caribbean zone, on the other hand, suffered demographic catastrophe with the arrival of the Europeans with new diseases.

The hierarchically structured Sinú and Tairona were not representative of the whole of pre-Columbian culture in the Caribbean zone. Mixed among these highly developed chiefdoms were peoples with only rudimentary social organization. The Sinú, for example, lived near the Chocó, a much more primitive forest people.

The gold that so excited the interest of the Spanish when they first ventured among the people of Colombia's Caribbean coast was not actually mined there. This gold was obtained in trade with peoples living in the Western and Central Cordilleras, in the region the Spanish came to call Antioquia. Gold was panned by the indigenes in various rivers, particularly the Cauca. But they also mined veins of gold in several places, with the richest mines at Buriticá, about twenty miles northwest of the present city of Antioquia. The gold of this region was sent north to the Gulf of Urabá and thence to Central America by one trade route, and by another northeast to the Sinú, the Tairona and present-day Venezuela. In return for the gold the peoples along these two routes sent in exchange sea salt, fish, cotton textiles, peccaries, and slaves. Other trade routes sent gold from Buriticá south along the Cauca River Valley and southeast to the Aburrá Valley (the site of the present city of Medellín), and from there to the Magdalena Valley.

The pre-Columbian societies of gold-bearing Antioquia formed part of a cultural matrix extending as far south as present-day Popayán. The population of this area—including those living in the Western and Central Cordilleras as well as the Cauca Valley between them—may have been rather large before the conquest. Estimates have varied from 600,000 to 1,000,000 inhabitants. But this population was divided into many tribal groups, speaking different tongues, ranging in size up to perhaps 40,000 people. Each of these tribes in turn was divided among many local chiefs who often made collective decisions about war but over whom there was little or no central control. Only in a few exceptional cases, such as that of the great lord Nutibara on the northwest flank of the Central Cordillera, did a single chief possess clear authority over a substantial area.

These tribal groups were chronically at war with each other. Some students of these cultures have assumed that the wars were fought to secure possession of land and may have reflected growing population pressures. Hermann Trimborn, however, sees the wars as having more symbolic and political motivations. He notes these were not total wars, in the sense that each group did not seek to annihilate the other. He argues that warfare occurred frequently because it provided local chiefs with their principal means of asserting and reinforcing their authority. Captives taken in war were killed and eaten in a ritual cannibalism that had a magical character, in that it was believed that the victors who consumed the vanquished thereby acquired their strength and courage. This acquired force was thought to be concentrated in the chiefs, a concept symbolized by the many heads, hands, and feet of sacrificed victims that decorated the external walls of the chiefs' houses. Cannibalism among these western groups, though probably magical in significance, may have extended beyond that motivation. The conquistador-chronicler Pedro Cieza de León describes the Páncara and Quimbaya, in present-day Caldas, as eating not only men but also women and children, from whom little power might be presumed to derive magically.

While political fragmentation, chronic warfare, and cannibalism were the general rule from the environs of present-day Cali northward, the highland groups from Popayán southward lived in a different manner. Such Chibcha-speaking peoples as the Coconucos, Pastos, and Quillacingas were, for the most part, docile farmers who were described by sixteenth-century Spaniards as not eating human flesh. By the standards of the Inca Empire, however, these peoples of the Pasto region were uncivilized and hard to dominate. Consequently, the northernmost reaches of the Inca Empire just before the Spanish conquest included the people of Tulcán on the present border of Colombia and Ecuador, but the Incas did not succeed in incorporating the Quillacingas farther to the north.

Although the Incas and their Spanish successors both considered the Quillacingas and Pastos uncivilized by comparison with the peoples of the

Central Andes, the indigenes of Pasto were much more settled peoples than their neighbors in the Cauca Valley. The indigenes of Pasto, therefore, accommodated themselves to the Spanish regime and survived in such numbers that at the end of the colonial era the Pasto region remained substantially indigenous in culture. By contrast, the less docile indigenes to their north declined drastically during the conquest period. In the Cauca Valley, for example, the peoples who cultivated the valley plain fled the area and refused to plant, in the hope that, without food, the Spanish would leave. The result, however, was that many of the indigenes in the Cauca Valley died of famine.

The peoples of the western zone who proved most difficult for the Spanish to subdue, however, were the inhabitants of the Central Cordillera, such as the Páez and the Pijaos. These peoples, with the aid of the difficult topography of their homeland, were able to defend their independence from Spanish control until early in the seventeenth century, when the Pijaos were virtually exterminated by the Spanish. The Páez survive today, although hardly flourishing, ensconced in small pockets of the rugged Central Cordillera.

The most renowned of Colombia's indigenous populations at the time of the European conquest were the Muiscas, or, as they are also commonly known, the Chibchas, who dominated the eastern highlands in the current Departments of Cundinamarca and Boyacá. The Muiscas occupied an area of roughly 10,000 square miles centering on the intermontane valleys atop the Eastern Cordillera, but also including the upper parts of the mountain flanks below these highland plains. Estimates of their population at the time of the conquest vary—from a low of about 300,000 to a high of 2,000,000, with most guesses hovering about the middle points of 800,000 to 1.2 million.

The Spanish conquistadores who first encountered the Muiscas were impressed by their great numbers, and some chroniclers said that they lived in large communities. Archaeological investigation, however, has discovered no indication of great urban centers. Muisca overlords inhabited elaborate household compounds, surrounded by stockades, but ordinary peasants lived dispersed amid their farmlands.

Along with the Tairona, to whom they were culturally and linguistically related, the Muiscas possessed the most hierarchically organized, territorially extensive social systems that the Spanish encountered in the territory of Colombia. At the lowest level was a territorial and kinship unit (the *uta*) composed of perhaps eight to twenty households. Several *utas* were grouped under intermediate chiefs, called "captains" by the Spanish, who in turn owed allegiance to a higher chief. These higher chiefs, for whom the Spanish used the Caribbean term *caciques*, headed regional groupings of perhaps ten thousand people or more.

Not long before the Spanish conquest, several of these higher chiefs came to dominate the others. Among the most powerful of these was the Zipa of Bacatá, whose area of hegemony centered upon the highland plain now called the Sabana de Bogotá. Several generations before the Spanish arrived, successive Zipas expanded their area of control, first by dominating the region of Fusagasugá on the mountain flanks to the southwest of the Sabana and then conquering a series of overlords in the highland plains to the north (Ubaté and Guatavita). By the time the Spanish appeared, the Zipas' domain covered an area extending perhaps 110 miles southwest to northeast at the farthest extremes, with a breadth of about 60 miles at the widest point.

While the Zipas' domain centered primarily on the basins of the Bogotá River and its affluents, a second important Muisca region, to the northeast, lay in the basins of the Chicamocha River and its tributaries. The most powerful lord in this northeastern zone was the Zaque of Hunza, whose region of primary control, in the area of what became the Spanish city of Tunja, apparently extended about 60 miles north and south and perhaps 30 miles east and west. To the northeast of Hunza, farther down the basin of the Chicamocha, were two other important lords, one whose seat was the Temple of the Sun (Sua) at Sugamuxi (now Sogamoso), the other ruling from Duitama to the northwest of Sogamoso. Judging from the testimony of indigenous community leaders in the sixteenth century, the authority of Sugamuxi and Duitama was recognized in areas forming parallel bands running for about 50 miles in a northeasterly direction, with the Chicamocha River dividing them. Although the indigenous communities within these zones paid tribute to the lords of Sugamuxi and Duitama, it may be, as some recent scholars have asserted, that one or both of these lords in turn accepted the dominance of the Zaque of Hunza. In any event, the boundaries of authority were not static, as the various lords sought to expand their territories at each others' expense or to incorporate previously independent communties.

The Muisca possessed an elaborate religious mythology, with some similarities to that found in the Central Andes. Although there was a residual belief in a creator god, the Muisca pantheon featured more prominently a sun god (Sua) and a moon goddess (Chia), who were connected in mythology with the chief overlords. The sun god had a particularly close connection with the northern confederations, as the chief temple of Sua was at Sugamuxi, while the family of the Zipa directly controlled the temple of Chia. (Chia is now a suburb of the city of Bogotá.) Many other gods were identified with natural occurrences (e.g., the rainbow, earthquakes) and with human needs, functions, or activities (e.g., pregnancy, dancing, drunkenness). Bochica, identified in myth with the sun, was the patron of artisans. Bachue, a fertility goddess, was conceived of as having emerged from a lake to people the earth and then returning to the lake, where she became a water snake. Accordingly, lakes and serpents were held sacred, and small gold totemic statues (*tunjos*) and other offerings were often deposited in lakes. Many other natural objects, such as mountains, rocks, and caves were considered sacred as the homes of supernatural beings. As in Peruvian cultures, the Muiscas also revered their dead leaders, whom they mummified and considered still to be present and powerful.

The Muiscas practiced human sacrifice, usually to the sun, with most of the victims being young boys captured in war or obtained in trade with the eastern plains. Although human sacrifice among the Muisca did not approach the scale of the sacral bloodbaths of Central Mexico, some features of these rituals bore similarities to Mexican patterns. The standard mode of sacrifice involved cutting the boy's heart out. Another ritual with Central Mexican counterparts called for the victim to be killed by throwing spears at him. Another common practice was to bury girls in the postholes of temples or other important structures. Unlike the peoples of western Colombia, the Muiscas apparently did not practice ritual cannibalism. In other words, they sought the aid of supernatural powers thorugh sacrifice to the gods rather than, as in the case of cannibals, by the direct assimilation of of the powers of the enemy.

Many aspects of Muisca life were ritually ordered. Collective work, such as the hauling of heavy objects, was performed to the cadence of rhythmic chants. The planting season (January through March) is said to have been accompanied by fertility rites, in which normal restrictions upon the use of *chicha* (at the time maize-based alcohol) and coca, as well as on marital fidelity, were temporarily relaxed. As among many indigenous cultures in the Americas, the consumption of alcohol and hallucinogens had a partly religious significance.

Muisca agriculture conformed to general Andean patterns, with digging sticks used for planting. The type of plant cultivated varied according to the altitude. In the highland plains, potatoes and quinoa predominated. Maize was the principal crop on the mountain flanks, where, because of the greater warmth, two annual crops were possible. Other plants of the lower, warmer altitudes included *arracacha*, cotton, guavas, pineapples, yuca, and coca. The highland Muisca had to trade with other groups in lower altitudes for some of these products, particularly cotton and coca.

The Muiscas had frequent markets—every four days in the most important trading centers. Goods traded over long distances were mainly those of high value that were totally lacking to a given group. As the Zipa possessed salt mines at Zipaquirá, salt was the principal commodity that his domains offered in trade, and salt from Zipaquirá was traded far down the Magdalena River. Among the valued commodities most lacking to the Zipa were gold, emeralds, and seashells. Emeralds were obtained in trade for salt with the Zaque, who controlled emerald mines at Somondoco. Gold came to the Muiscas from the region of Neiva and other points along the Magdalena River. The Magdalena Valley also provided coca and cotton, the latter also coming from the Guanes, a Chibcha-related people to the north, in what is now the Department of Santander. Slaves were obtained from the eastern plains.

Many of those with whom the Muiscas traded were peoples with relatively simple community structures. Some of their neighbors, such as the Laches and Tunebos in the eastern plains, may have been culturally related to the Muisca and had relatively peaceful relations with them. But the Muisca were frequently at war with the peoples on their western flank, many of them apparently Caribs, who were fierce antagonists. These Carib peoples (Muzos, Colimas, Panches) had small tribal groups, and their leadership was not hereditary but rather temporary and limited to time of war. Although the Muiscas and the Caribs were chronically at war, the division between them may have been maintained in part by environmental factors, with Muisca culture adapted to, and not venturing far beyond, the cooler high altitudes and the Carib tribes similarly limited to the hotter lowland forests.

During and after the European conquest many of the indigenous peoples suffered heavy population losses. This demographic catastrophe occurred for a number of reasons. First, the indigenes lacked antibodies to fight the new diseases brought by the Europeans and their African servants. Second, Spanish demands for food in the early stages of the conquest and settlement probably caused scarcities among those indigenes closest to Spanish settlements and travel routes. Finally, when the Spanish eventually shifted from simply pillaging the indigenes to more systematic exactions of labor tribute, labor demands brought dislocations to the indigenous economy. And, where spouses, male or female, had to work for long periods apart from their families, population recovery undoubtedly became more difficult.

The first to feel the advent of the Europeans were the peoples of the Caribbean coast. There special circumstances contributed to a particularly rapid and devastating population loss. By the time the Spanish established themselves on the north coast, they already had begun to enslave indigenes of the Caribbean islands for use in Hispaniola. This practice was extended to those the Spanish encountered on Colombia's north coast. In addition, the indigenes on the coast, like those in other lowland areas, must have been particularly affected by Old World diseases transmitted by mosquitos, such as yellow fever and malaria. As a consequence of these and other factors, the Sinú and other coastal peoples with relatively dense populations before the conquest were quickly reduced to negligible numbers.

Population losses were also rapid in lowland regions of the interior, such as the Magdalena and Cauca basins. Between 1537 and 1538, when the Spanish conquistadores first passed through the greater part of the Cauca Valley, and the 1570s, the populations along the Cauca River appear to have diminished in many places between 80 and 95 percent.

On the other hand, some lowland peoples in remote or heavily forested areas had little contact with the Europeans and thus have been able to survive, although not in great numbers. This was true of the peoples in Amazonia as well as the Motilones in northern Santander, the Cuna in the northwestern coastal area, and some indigenous groups on the Pacific Coast. It also has been true of the indigenes of the desert Guajira Peninsula.

In the colonial era, and still today, the major areas of readily observable demographic and cultural survival have been in the highland zones, most notably among the various groups in the Pasto region, the Páez in the southern part of the Central Cordillera, and the Kogui, relatives of the Tairona in the Sierra Nevada of Santa Marta. All of these peoples have been able to retain elements of their indigenous culture, in part because there was relatively little Spanish settlement in these regions.

The eastern highlands, by contrast, were one of the principal foci of Spanish colonization. There the Muiscas survived in substantial numbers, providing the demographic base of the peasant population of Cundinamarca and Boyaca. But, as the colonial period wore on, Muisca culture increasingly was diluted by the pressure of Spanish population and culture, as well as of Spanish policy. Elements of Muisca culture persisted in fragmentary, subtle, and subterranean ways, and through the nineteenth century, indigenes were clearly distinguished from other inhabitants of the region, both in the public mind and in parish records. However, the penetration of people of Hispanic culture into indigenous communities gave them an increasingly mestizo charcter, both racially and culturally, in the eighteenth and nineteenth centuries. Nevertheless, the indigenous presence remains evident today in the faces of the peasantry of Cundinamarca and Boyacá. And certain features of pre-Columbian economic patterns have hung on long after the disintegration of indigenous culture as a system of social meanings. In the nineteenth century, inhabitants of the Guane area in Santander who were no longer identifiably "Indian" were still growing and weaving cotton for sale to other regions, as they had in the pre-Colombian era. Weaving with wool has continued as an important peasant activity in Cundinamarca and Boyacá. Even in the twentieth century, Ráquira, the outstanding ceramics manufactory of the domains of the Zipa, has retained a specialty in pottery. And the diet of most Colombians, whether peasant or urban, continues to rely heavily on characteristic foods of the pre-Columbian era, especially yuca, potatoes, and maize.

3

European Conquest

Topography divided Colombia into three major zones—the eastern highlands; the West, centering on the basin of the Cauca River; and the Caribbean coast, including the basin of the lower Magdalena River. Pre-Columbian cultures varied among, and also within, these three zones. The European conquest perpetuated and reinforced these divisions—both during the epoch of conquest itself and over the long run—as Europeans penetrated the area of present-day Colombia from several different directions. Their claims to authority over various parts of the land tended to confirm the fragmentation already induced by the mountainous topography.

The first Spanish contacts occurred along the Caribbean coast. An initial voyage of exploration and trade by Alonso de Ojeda to the Guajira (1499) was followed by a second of Juan de la Cosa (1501), which identified the salient features of Colombia's northern coast, notably the bays of Santa Marta and Cartagena and the mouth of the Magdalena River. These early voyages of exploration, involving transitory contacts in the Guajira, the Cartagena area, and the Gulf of Urabá, led to two projects for permanent settlement in 1508—Diego de Nicuesa's province of Veragua, allotted by the Crown the territory from the Gulf of Urabá west, and a domain assigned to Ojeda called New Andalucía, originally stretching from the Gulf of Urabá east to Cabo de la Vela on the Guajira Peninsula. Ojeda and his associates, after fighting and enslaving Indians in the region of presentday Cartagena, moved down the coast to the Gulf of Urabá, where they were driven off by indigenes using poisoned arrows, the weapon most feared by the conquistadores. In 1510, the Ojeda group settled west of the Gulf of Urabá, among more easily subdued peoples in the Darien region. The Darien settlement became the foundation of the Spanish colony of Castilla del Oro on the Isthmus of Panama.

The colony in Panama provided a base from which the Spanish were able to establish more permanent control of the Gulf of Urabá and to explore the Chocó region in Colombia's northwest corner in the 1520s and 1530s. More notably, Panama was the jumping-off point for the Pizarro expedition, which, after subjugating much of Peru, sent a force back to the north under Sebastián de Belalcázar. Belalcázar's men entered southwestern Colombia (the Pasto highlands, the Pacific watershed, and the Cauca Valley) in 1535. In 1538 they established a Spanish presence in the Upper Magdalena Valley, and in 1539 they reached Antioquia.

While successive expeditions carried Spaniards in circular fashion from Panama to Peru and from Peru up through western Colombia, at the same

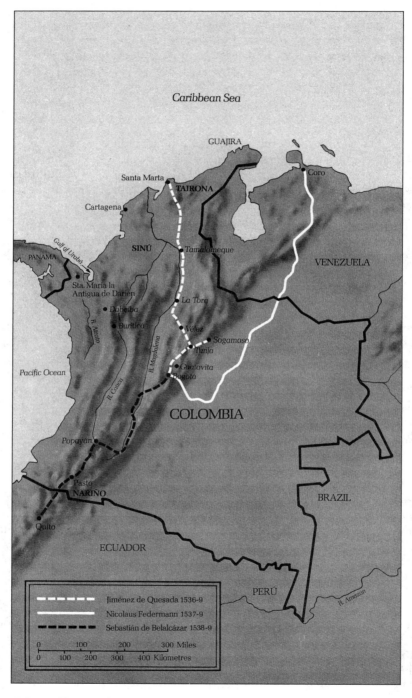

Map 2 Routes of conquest. From Warwick Bray, *The Gold of El Dorado*
(London, 1978).

time Colombian terrain was being explored from three different beachheads on the Caribbean. The first, dating from the middle of the 1520s, was the province of Santa Marta, whose limits came to be Cabo de la Vela to the east and the Magdalena River to the west. Soon thereafter, in 1529, a competing base of conquest was established to the east of Santa Marta, at Coro on the coast of Venezuela. This operation in western Venezuela was captained by Germans whose conquests were authorized by Charles V as a means of repaying debts to his bankers, the Welsers. In 1533 a third competitor on the Caribbean coast was established in Cartagena, under Pedro de Heredia. Heredia's authorized area of conquest covered the territory between the Gulf of Urabá and the Magdalena River.

Whatever the zone of conquest, initial European activity almost invariably amounted to little more than rapine. The conquistadores expected the indigenes to feed them as well as to enrich them with gold. If the indigenes had food and/or gold and were docile enough to provide them, relations between European and Amerind might be relatively peaceful for a time. But feeding the Europeans either maize or bullion only increased their appetites. As a result, whether they were peaceable or bellicose at first, many indigenous peoples ended up rebelling against or fleeing the Europeans' exactions.

The rapacity of the conquistadores must be understood not merely as a reflection of a general European cupidity but also as a function of the economic conditions of the conquest. Each of the beachheads of conquest was in a dependency relationship with the already settled areas that served as supply centers (Santo Domingo, Cuba, and Jamaica for the Caribbean coast; Panama for the conquest of Peru). Each of the conquest zones depended upon one or more supply centers to provide it with horses, munitions, clothing, and food, if the latter were not available in sufficient supply from local indigenes. Because of the scarcity of these goods, as well as because of price inflation encouraged by local bonanzas, prices in the conquest zones were extraordinarily high—sometimes eight or more times the levels in the more settled Caribbean islands. These expensive imports had to be paid for with a substantial exportable surplus: gold, pearls, Indian slaves—whatever might be available.

The economic organization of the conquest contributed to the general rapacity. Many conquistadores of the rank and file probably contracted debts to outfit themselves, and still larger liabilities often were assumed in the supply centers by the organizers of the expeditions to obtain the ships and other equipment needed by these enterprises. Because of the burden of these debts, as well as because of a generalized acquisitiveness, the leaders of the expeditions of conquest attempted to recoup by engrossing as much as possible of any treasure encountered and by selling goods to the rank and file at monopoly prices. The consequence was a general indebtedness and a general dissatisfaction among the soldiery, expressed in complaints against the leaders but also in demands for further expeditions of conquest so that they too might find their reward, repay their obligations, and, if possible, return to

Spain wealthy men. The burden of debt, as well as unsatisfied ambition, thus contributed to the dynamism of the conquest.

One example of this process occurred in the province of Cartagena. When gold objects were discovered in burial mounds in the Sinú, Pedro de Heredia, the governor of Cartagena, sent most of the Spaniards under him on long expeditions of exploration while he employed African slaves to dig up the bulk of the golden burial pieces. In addition, Heredia channeled scarce food acquired from the indigenes to feed his slaves, leaving many Spaniards to go hungry—allegedly two hundred starved to death. Food scarcity plus treasure-stimulated price inflation forced many Spaniards in the province deeply into debt. Those conquistadores who lost out in this process (but survived) pressed to continue exploration farther into the interior. The modes of operation in the various zones of conquest varied somewhat depending upon the specific conditions of each region. Along the Caribbean coast the principal economic activity of the discoverer-conquerors from a very early point had been the enslavement of Amerinds for sale to Santo Domingo, Cuba, and Jamaica, the agricultural supply centers for the conquest of the mainland. In each of the Caribbean zones of conquest—whether in Venezuela, Santa Marta, or Cartagena—the enslavement of indigenes for sale to the Caribbean islands remained a goal of the conquistadores, and often a salient activity, to the end of the 1530s.

Because the first Spaniards in Santa Marta and Cartagena depended primarily upon looting the Amerinds, these early settlements were extremely unstable. In Santa Marta, Spanish demands and violence caused many formerly peaceable indigenes by the end of the 1520s to rebel and to refuse to provide the Spaniards with food. The natives retreated into the mountain fastnesses of the Sierra Nevada, where the Spaniards could not effectively use horses. As the Spanish could not obtain food, or gold to buy imported food, from local Amerinds, the Spanish governors desperately turned to incursions farther inland, hoping thereby to occupy the discontented as well as to discover gold or enslavable Indians.

These expeditions by 1531–1532 had led the Spaniards in Santa Marta to begin moving up the Magdalena River. By 1532 they had found dense Indian populations upriver, most particularly at Tamalameque, the biggest Indian town they had yet seen in the region. These Indians reported that the river could be navigated farther on "for five months." This raised the hope that the Magdalena would lead to "very great secrets," stimulating preparation of a large expedition up the river.

At this point, news of the discovery of Peru completed the destabilization of Santa Marta. On the one hand, Francisco Pizarro's success moved many in Santa Marta, as well as in Cartagena and other settlements in the Caribbean, to decamp for Peru. On the other hand, the news of Peru permitted the governor of Santa Marta to raise the hope that further exploration of the Magdalena might offer a new route to Peru and the "South Sea." A second expedition up the river (1533–1535), however, proved disastrous; during an eighteen-month sojourn, many losses were sustained with little or no return in treasure. By 1534 the settlement in Santa Marta verged on total disintegration. Lacking food and torn by discord, it was rapidly losing men to Peru, to expeditions into the interior, or to the illness affecting all greenhorns in the Indies. By 1535 Santa Marta contained no more than nine horsemen and forty footsoldiers, and these few were unable to guarantee the security of the city against increasingly confident and aggressive assaults by Indian archers.

A dramatic change in the fortunes of conquest, although not in those of Santa Marta itself, occurred in 1535, when the Crown placed the province in the hands of Pedro de Lugo, the Adelantado of the Canary Islands, in return for a commitment from Lugo to make a major infusion of men and horses into the dying colony. With the increased resources invested by Lugo, Santa Marta mounted a major expedition up the Magdalena River. In April 1536, about six hundred men started south on land under the leadership of Lugo's chief judicial officer, Gonzalo Jiménez de Quesada, a Salamanca law graduate, with support from six or seven small ships that were to sail to a rendezvous with them in the lower Magdalena River. From the outset the expedition suffered heavy losses. In a storm two ships sank at the mouth of the Magdalena, while others were carried westward to Cartagena. Meanwhile, the main force trooping overland suffered from food scarcities; the indigenes' poisoned arrows; the hot, damp climate of the Magdalena; and mosquitos, ticks, and worms. Eventually, the land force hacked its way more than three hundred miles upriver to La Tora (now Barrancabermeja). When an exploratory party found the river above La Tora too swift to be easily navigable and the forest banks virtually uninhabited by indigenes, whose provisions were needed, some of Jiménez's men wanted to turn back, particularly as many were dying at the unhealthy site of La Tora. Hopes were roused in the leaders, however, by the fact that at La Tora they had found salt cakes apparently made by a different process than the sea salt they had encountered up to that point. This raised the possibility that some advanced and wealthy indigenous culture might lie farther on. In further reconnaissance up a tributary river, the Opón, a party came upon first an Amerind canoe, and then storehouses, both containing salt cakes and painted cotton mantles being used in trade. Their hopes thus apparently confirmed, Jiménez's men followed the Opón and the indigenous trade route and then cut their way through dense forests up the flanks of the Eastern Cordillera. Finally, early in March 1537, eleven months after leaving Santa Marta, some 170 men and 30 horses emerged on the mountain plains inhabited by the Muiscas.

After the trek up the hot Magdalena Valley, the highland domain of the Muiscas seemed practically a paradise to the Spaniards. The cool mountain valleys offered surcease from the discomfort and disease of the Magdalena. On the extensive green highland plains lived ample populations of sedentary cultivators, whose abundant food was left to the Spaniards as the Muiscas fled their homes. Even when the Muiscas ultimately did fight, it was with wooden swords and spear throwers, and not with the fearsome poisoned arrows of the Caribbean and the Magdalena Valley. And although these people did not yield gold in amounts that Spaniards had encountered in some places on the Caribbean coast, their possessions included the welcome novelty of emeralds.

Jiménez de Quesada was impressed by the density of the Muisca population and by the apparent splendor of their chiefs' homes. While these houses were constructed only of wood-and-daub walls, with thatched roofing, they were the largest, most complex, and most ornate indigenous dwellings that the expedition had seen. Their high, conical roofs were surmounted by poles, from which golden sheets wafted in the wind. The exotic splendor of these "palaces" prompted Jiménez to dub the Sabana de Bogotá "el Valle de los Alcázares" (the valley of the castles), in hyperbolic reference to the fortresses of his native Andalucía.

Recognizing that the Muisca culture represented something distinct, as well as physically separated, from the peoples of the Caribbean coast, Jiménez early on began to refer to the area of Muisca culture as "el Nuevo Reino de Granada" (the New Kingdom of Granada). This designation also had a political purpose. Jiménez hoped that the discovery of a new and different "kingdom" would provide substance for a claim that this new domain ought to be independent from his original base, the province of Santa Marta. Through most of the colonial period the eastern highlands retained a distinctive identity as "el Nuevo Reino," with the Spanish population of the region often called reinosos.

Despite the large numbers of the Muisca population, the conquest of the eastern highlands proved relatively easy. In addition to the advantages of a comfortable climate, abundant food, and an antagonist that did not use poisoned arrows, the mountain plains permitted the Spaniards to make effective use of cavalry charges against a population terrified by horses. The conquest of the highlands was also facilitated by political divisions among the Muiscas. In addition to the rivalries between two, and possibly among four or five, major chieftaincies, there were also internal divisions within these groups because of disputes over succession. These conflicts, particularly in the zone first encountered by the Spanish, that of the Zipa of Bogotá, enabled the conquistadores to gain Indian allies who helped them to subdue much of the rest of the Muisca area. Thus some 170 Europeans could conquer an area inhabited by probably more than one million indigenes.

Early in 1539, a year after Jiménez de Quesada effectively had conquered most of the Muisca territory, he got word of two other European expeditions approaching the New Kingdom of Granada. One had as its chief Sebastián de Belalcázar, whom Francisco Pizarro had sent north from Peru. Having founded Quito in October 1534, Belalcázar sent various lieutenants farther north into the territory of what is now southeastern Colombia (Pasto and the Cauca). Following them, Belalcázar in 1536 founded first Cali and then

Popayán. These ventures north of Quito began to get Belalcázar into difficulties with Pizarro, who was concerned that Belalcázar was seeking to create an independent domain in Quito and the Cauca Valley. In January 1538 Pizarro sent a new lieutenant to Quito to arrest Belalcázar. Both fleeing arrest and hoping to discover the land of "el Dorado," Belalcázar in March 1538 gathered together some two hundred Spaniards and a much greater crew of indigenous bearers from the Quito region and set forth for Popayán, from which he struck east across the Central Cordillera. After four months of struggle across the high, snowy mountains, unable to obtain much food from hostile indigenes and losing many horses and native bearers, his men finally emerged into the upper valley of the Magdalena River, where with considerable relief they found easily dominated peoples, food, and even some gold. Traveling north down the valley of the Magdalena, the Belalcázar expedition encountered a search party sent out by Jiménez de Quesada, who had heard that a European expedition was in the region.

Shortly after being told of the Spanish party going down the Magdalena Valley, Jiménez learned that still another European force was nearby, in the mountains south of Bogotá. This proved to be the expedition of the German Nicolás Federmann, who had left Coro, on the coast of Venezuela, in December 1536—by his own account with a force of 300 Europeans and 130 horses. After more than two years of great hardship, traveling south through the eastern plains, in which seventy Europeans, forty horses, and innumerable indigenous bearers died, Federmann finally had scaled the Eastern Cordillera.

The nearly simultaneous arrival of Belalcázar and Federmann was remarkable considering their diverse points and times of departure. The encounter of the three expeditions must also have been quite picturesque. Belalcázar's force corresponded to the conventional image of the conquistadores, as despite the wear of more than eight months' sojourn, they were fully equipped with European clothing and weapons, as well as being accompanied by Indian servants (*yanaconas*) from Quito and a goodly complement of pigs. The other two groups, however, appeared much less imposing. In the nearly three years since Jiménez de Quesada's men had left Santa Marta, their European clothing had almost completely rotted or worn away, and they were dressed in Muisca mantles and sandals. Federmann's men also had lost their European apparel in their more than two years on the eastern plains, and they were clothed in animal skins.

Elements of the picturesque aside, the occasion held a potential for violent conflict, given the ambitions of the conquistadores for wealth and of their leaders for lands to govern. In the end the three agreed to an arrangement by which thirty of Belalcázar's men and all of Federmann's might remain in the New Kingdom as beneficiaries of the conquest, while the question of the title to the newly conquered domain would be left to authorities in Spain to decide. Ultimately, the Crown confirmed Santa Marta's claim to the Muisca kingdom because of Jiménez's priority of conquest.

The accident that an expedition from Santa Marta reached the Muisca highlands before those from the Pacific coast or Venezuela gave political confirmation to the tendency, already established by topographical features, for Colombia to be divided east and west along two north-south axes. The high range of the Central Cordillera already had determined, in the pre-Columbian era, that Colombia would be divided into two distinct eastern and western zones. Jiménez de Quesada's priority in arriving on the Sabana de Bogotá reinforced that geographical division by making it a political reality. The fact that western Colombia was discovered and subjugated primarily by conquistadores coming from Peru, and secondarily from Cartagena and Panama, had a similar effect in confirming politically the physical separateness of the area to the west of the Central Cordillera from that to the east.

4

Colonial Economy and Society, 1540–1780

SPANISH SETTLEMENT

In the decades immediately following the conquest, the Spanish firmly controlled only islands of territory. In the interior they most clearly dominated the eastern highlands, in the same regions that were inhabited by the dense, sedentary Muisca culture. The Spanish also occupied frontier cities in the Upper Magdalena Valley but had little control of the surrounding country. They also established some settlements at the edge of the great eastern lowland plains, but their presence in this region was slight and would remain so to the end of the colonial period. In the West they clearly predominated in the immediate environs of Popayán and around scattered mining towns, but much of the countryside was effectively beyond their purview.

Even in regions that the Spanish completely controlled militarily, the areas outside Hispanic cities were inhabited almost exclusively by the indigenous population. If the Indians in the area were peaceable, Spanish authority was, for the most part, not challenged. If not, security was unpredictable.

The most important and durable of the scattered Spanish cities were established where there existed dense and docile Indian populations to provide food and labor for their Spanish conquerors, both of which initially were extracted through the institution of the *encomienda*. As docile indigenes were most numerous in the eastern highlands at the time of the conquest, Spaniards in the sixteenth century gathered in the greatest numbers in cities in that region.

There were four significant Spanish cities in the Eastern Cordillera. According to the survey of López de Velasco (ca. 1570), Santafé de Bogotá had an estimated 600 *vecinos* (adult male Spaniards), supported by some 40,000 tribute-payers (adult male Indians). In Tunja somewhat more than 200 Spanish male settlers were surrounded by more than 50,000 indigenous tributaries. Pamplona and Vélez, each with perhaps a hundred Spanish *vecinos*, were thought to have, respectively, roughly 20,000 and more than 5000 tributaries.

The other relatively large Spanish city at this time was Cartagena, with some 300 male Spaniards, supported by more than 7000 indigenous tribute-payers. However, in the upper Cauca region to the southwest, there were smaller communities of Spaniards, who also controlled substantial numbers of Indians. Pasto, with possibly less than thirty Spanish *vecinos*, enjoyed the service of an estimated 24,000 tributaries, while Popayán with Spanish citizenry in similar numbers had the support of some 9000 adult male Indians.

In the case of each of these cities most of the indigenous tributaries remained in the surrounding countryside. However, each of these cities did have large indigenous servant populations resident in, or adjacent to, the Spanish urban nuclei.

While the largest and most permanent of the early Spanish cities were established where there were dense, usable indigenous populations, many Spanish settlements sprang up because of the presence of precious minerals—generally gold, occasionally silver. Spaniards in Popayán were using Indian workers to take gold from nearby streams by the early 1540s, and Almaguer, some fifty miles south of Popayán, shortly thereafter was mining veins of gold. Gold found in streambeds and veins in the middle Cauca induced Spaniards to settle at various sites at about the same time (Cartago, Caramanta, Anserma, and Arma). Gold mined from veins at Buriticá in pre-Columbian times inspired the founding of Antioquia (1541), soon thereafter reestablished as Santa Fe de Antioquia (1546). Various areas near present-day Bucaramanga (but under the jurisdiction of Pamplona), in the Eastern Cordillera, were also early gold-mining sites. Much slighter gold deposits in tributaries of the Magdalena River played roles in the founding of Tocaima (1545), Ibagué (1550), Mariquita (1551), La Victoria (1557), and La Palma (1560).

Gold-mining towns were inherently unstable, as the gold deposits sooner or later ran scarce or the indigenous labor supply died out. Sometimes Spaniards left the depleted sites, but kept the names of the towns, which they would reestablish where they found new deposits, sometimes more than fifty miles away. The peripatetic mining town was particularly a feature of Antioquia. At least four towns there moved at least once. Remedios changed its location no less than four times between 1561 and 1594, covering more than a hundred miles in a series of thirty-mile leaps.

Some towns near gold deposits also became points of defense in regions where Indians were difficult to control. This was particularly true of Spanish communities in the upper Magdalena Valley, which were supposed to protect the chief routes connecting Santafé de Bogotá with the Spanish towns in the Cauca Valley. During the sixteenth century these frontier defense towns tended to be overrun by the Indians they were meant to control. Neiva was abandoned several times because of Indian attacks and was not permanently reestablished until after the defeat of the Pijaos and other marauders from the Central Cordillera early in the seventeenth century.

In the first decades after their founding the Spanish cities were at first quite primitive. At Santafé de Bogotá, Spaniards for a time inhabited *bohíos*, the Indian huts made of *bahareque* (reeds or branches sealed with dried mud). In time most Spanish houses in Santafé, Tunja, Popayán, and other significant towns in the interior were constructed in a mode brought from Spain—walls of *tapia pisada* (pressed earth), with tile roofs. As early as 1542 municipal authorities in Santafé ordered Spanish residents to build their homes with brick or stone, but walls of pressed earth remained the dominant mode for city homes for most of the colonial period, at least in the interior. Most urban homes in the colonial period were of one story. But by the early seventeenth century, the houses of the more affluent and well-placed tended to be of two stories; these larger homes were built around one or two patios, used in part for stabling mules and horses. In addition, such homes were likely to have adjacent plots, on which some Indian servants lived in their traditional huts.

On the Caribbean coast, there was a parallel transition from flimsy to more solid construction. In 1552 virtually the whole city of Cartagena burned down because all of the houses had wooden walls and straw roofs. This happened again when Francis Drake attacked the port in 1586. However, after this point Cartagena moved to the use of brick. The more substantial homes had brick walls also in the Magdalena River port of Mompox, in this case because the river periodically flooded the town and walls of pressed earth would not have held up. In these commercial port towns large storage rooms for goods in trade tended to take the place of the large patios of the cities in the interior.

Churches also evolved toward solidity, after a time. Santafé's first cathedral, constructed of wood in 1566, immediately fell down. Rebuilt in stone in 1572–1592, its roof collapsed again in 1601. During the seventeenth century, however, a number of monasteries and convents were built solidly of brick, often atop stone footings. But churches were much simpler, with walls of pressed earth, in the country towns that developed in the seventeenth century, inhabited first by Indians and then, by the eighteenth century, by many mestizos.

Although in the first decade after the conquest, the cities of the conquistadores in some ways retained an Indian look, in other ways they were developing European textures. In the early 1540s Spanish women were arriving in Santafé, many of them single women brought by Spanish authorities as potential mates for triumphant conquistadores. The basic elements of European material culture also began to be introduced at the same time. In the early 1540s, wheat, barley, chickpeas, green beans, and other garden plants reached Santafé de Bogotá. Not long thereafter wheat was being milled and baked into bread. By 1542 Santafé had its first tannery, and the next year it was producing brick and tiles.

A parallel development of European agriculture was occurring in parts of the West. By the 1540s wheat brought from Quito was being cultivated in Pasto, and during the 1560s and 1570s it spread to Popayán. Both Pasto and Popayán supplied some other parts of the West with European grains. During the last third of the century sugar cane cultivation was established around Cali and Buga.

In regions under clear Spanish dominance, the indigenes also were adopting elements of European material culture. Often at least part of the *encomienda* tribute owed by Indians had to be paid in gold; because in many places gold was not mined locally, Indians had to sell their products on the market to raise the necessary gold. They thus had to learn to adapt to the vagaries of the market. To make tribute payments they also often had to learn how to produce some European commodities, such as chickens and pigs on the Caribbean coast and wheat and barley in the eastern highlands.

Within a few decades, the Spanish and indigenous economies had become intertwined. In the highlands, sheep as well as pigs and chickens had become an integral part of the Indians' domestic economy. By the 1580s more than three thousand Indians were coming regularly to the market in Santafé with loads of coca, cotton, and textiles, which they exchanged for golden *tejuelos*, a kind of indigenous coin. Spaniards also used *tejuelos* as a means of exchange. Spanish landowners grew indigenous maize and potatoes, as well as European wheat and barley. On their haciendas the ground was broken, during the early seventeenth century, both by indigenous digging sticks and by European wooden plows. Indians served as drovers of Spanish-owned mule trains. By the early seventeenth century, if not before, some Indians had become small entrepreneurs, for example, renting out horses to Spanish travelers and merchants.

A similar integration of indigenous and European material cultures took place on the Caribbean coast. There, while pigs and chickens joined maize and cassava in the Indians' domestic economy, people of Hispanic culture incorporated cassava and maize into their farming and their consumption.

If the Indians were absorbing European material culture, they also were dying from European diseases. Santafé suffered major epidemics of smallpox in 1566 and 1587–1590; typhus in 1633, 1688, and 1739; and smallpox again in 1783. But lists of epidemics give no sense of the year-to-year Indian mortality that occurred because of Spanish exactions and the contexts in which they occurred. Among the indigenous populations most quickly decimated were those employed in gold mining. In 1582 an Augustinian friar surmised that in the course of two decades the Indian populations of Almaguer and Popayán had declined by 85 percent, while to the north, farther down the Cauca River valley, in present-day Caldas and Antioquia, the Indian population had been even more reduced. Other Indians who suffered particularly heavy losses were those forced to provide transportation services for the Spanish. Indian boatmen on the Magdalena River suffered a particularly heavy toll. Some Spanish officials asserted that over a period of two decades (1578–1596) more than 95 percent of the indigenous boatmen had died. Indigenes who carried cargos overland also suffered a high mortality, whether hauling goods from the Pacific coast to Cali or from the Magdalena River to the Central Cordillera or the eastern highlands.

Indians living in the cool highlands who were required to perform mainly agricultural labor were declining a bit more slowly—but still dramatically. According to the calculations of a modern scholar, in the Tunja district the number of indigenes dropped by close to 70 percent in the thirty-four years between 1562 and 1596. However, dying was not the only way that Indians might "disappear." By leaving their indigenous communities and becoming resident workers on haciendas, in mines, or in Spanish cities, they vanished statistically but not necessarily in the flesh.

REGIONS

The two chief centers of Spanish control in the interior in the sixteenth century, the eastern highlands and the upper Cauca region, were isolated from each other and would remain substantially disconnected long thereafter. They were separated physically by the Central Cordillera, which was often impassable by mule train and in which untamed Indians periodically attacked Spanish travelers. East and West were also separated administratively in large part because of the patterns of conquest—since the East was seized by men from Santa Marta, while the West was taken first by men from Quito and secondarily by conquistadores from Cartagena. Popayán and much of the rest of the Cauca region remained closely tied to Quito. The region was under the authority of Quito until 1549, when Santafé de Bogotá became the seat of an *audiencia*. However, when Quito also became an *audiencia*, much of the West, from Pasto to Buga, returned to the jurisdiction of Quito. East and West also were separated at first by the fact that they had similar, more-or-less self-sufficient economies.

By the beginning of the seventeenth century, however, East and West began to become more different economically. By this time only one gold-mining region in the Eastern Cordillera, between Pamplona and Bucaramanga, was producing significant amounts of gold. Most of the eastern highlands focused on the production of grains and the weaving of textiles. The East found at least a limited market for these in some mining regions of the West that continued to produce gold during the first half of the seventeenth century. Already by the 1580s gold dust from the West was paying for textiles woven by Indians in the Eastern Cordillera. Peasant-woven textiles from the eastern highlands continued to be sold in the West through most of the colonial period and into the nineteenth century. For a time in the early seventeenth century, the eastern highlands also sent preservable foods (hardtack, cheese, and hams) to some mining centers on the western side of the Magdalena River—to the Middle Cauca and to Remedios and Zaragoza. However, because of high transportation costs, these were in effect luxury products, so the volume of this trade must have been somewhat small.

Just as the East increasingly focused on agriculture and weaving textiles and the West became the chief source of gold production, the third major region of Spanish settlement, the Caribbean coast and the lower Magdalena River Valley, had its own special functions, all of which related to navigation and external trade. Cartagena was New Granada's official nexus with external commerce, with monopoly control of legal imports of European luxury products (particularly oil and wine) and African slaves. However, during the seventeenth century, and particularly in the eighteenth century, there also developed an active contraband trade along much of the Caribbean coast, from Riohacha on the east to the Atrato River on the west. Another function of the Caribbean coast was to supply foodstuffs to the armed Spanish fleet that brought European goods in exchange for American treasure. This fleet called at Cartagena from the latter half of the fifteenth century well into the eighteeenth century.

Cartagena also had a complementary relationship with the two major regions of the interior. It exchanged its imported slaves for gold from the western mines. It sent much of its luxury imports to Santafé de Bogotá, the chief consumption and distribution center in the eastern highlands. In turn the eastern highlands, at least during the seventeenth century, supplied the Caribbean coast with foodstuffs and manufactured consumer goods. As of 1610 Tunja was sending flour, hardtack, cheese, and hams, along with canvas cloth, *alpargatas* (canvas sandals), and rough woolens to the Caribbean ports of Cartagena and Santa Marta and the Magdalena River ports of Tenerife and Mompox.

However, by the end of the seventeenth century the Eastern Cordillera was losing its markets in the Caribbean coastal region. In the 1690s wheat disease ruined harvests in Villa de Leiva, one of the principal wheat producers in the interior; in the first decade of the eighteenth century the Eastern Cordillera provided only one quarter of the flour in the Cartagena market. From that time on, British flour, mostly produced in English North America, took over the Caribbean markets. In the eighteenth century wheat flour from the interior was unable to compete in part because of high transportation costs—flour from the eastern highlands cost five to six times much in Cartagena as it did in its areas of production. The flour also tended to spoil during the long, hot, moist journey down the Magdalena River to the coast.

The three regions also developed distinctive racial features. In the agrarian eastern highlands, the dense indigenous population died less rapidly than in mining regions, and by the eighteenth century its inhabitants were largely mestizo (Hispanicized indigenes, or progeny of Spanish-Indian miscegenation). In much of the West (particularly in regions associated with mining) and on the Caribbean coast, on the other hand, the Indians died off more rapidly and African slaves came to provide much of the demographic base.

Because of their differing economic functions and differing population profiles, each of the regions developed in distinctive patterns and faced somewhat varying issues.

The East

In the Eastern Cordillera one central theme was organizing, exploiting, and Christianizing the indigenous population. One problem was economic. By the latter part of the fifteenth century the Indian population had so declined, and the Spanish population had so grown, that *encomienda* tribute was no longer an adequate mechanism for supplying food to the Spanish urban population. Consequently, Spaniards had moved from simply receiving tribute to direct agricultural production. But control of Indian communities by Spanish *encomenderos* tended to block access of other Spanish farmers to indigenous labor.

There were also questions of religious acculturation and political control. Indian peasants in the Eastern Cordillera in the latter part of the sixteenth century lived dispersed on individual plots or in relatively small communities. This pattern was contrary to a Spanish cultural disposition to live in agglutinated villages and towns. In the 1590s this Spanish urban inclination was reinforced by a wave of hysteria among Spanish clerics over discoveries that Indians, despite formal conversion to Christianity, were continuing pre-Columbian religious practices. Spanish authorities saw the problem in the dispersion of the indigenous population, which made clerical supervision difficult. Since inculcation of religious belief was a form of social control, this also was a political question.

Between 1590 and 1620 Spanish administrators found a solution for the problem of supervision in concentrating the indigenes in larger Indian towns. In 1601 some 83 indigenous communities in the jurisdiction of Santafé de Bogotá were merged into 23, and in 1602 another 104 Indian communities were reformed into 41 larger ones. In these larger towns, the Indians were to be civilized, as Spaniards saw it, as well as Christianized. The new towns were to be laid out in a grid pattern, with the church dominating a central plaza. On the other hand, while the indigenes were supposed to live according to prescribed European norms, they were to be isolated from corruption by the Hispanic population at large by limiting the presence of Europeans to clergy and Spanish administrators.

Although many Indians resisted this process of concentration, ultimately Spanish administrators succeeded in reducing many indigenes to the prescribed towns. The Indian towns in Hispanic form established at this time left an enduring imprint on the region. Many of these towns have survived to the present, although many of them had become more mestizo than Indian by the middle of the eighteenth century.

In addition to permitting closer Spanish supervision and control, the concentration of the Indians into larger towns also had the advantage of removing the indigenes from the plots they had formerly occupied, thus freeing up large amounts of land for Spaniards to claim. The declining numbers of Indians provided a rationale for the reduction of their land. In any case, in the view of Spaniards, Indians did not need as much land as Spaniards did. A close study of the Sabana de Bogotá concludes that the land assigned to newly concentrated Indian communities averaged between 2.7 and 3.6 acres (or roughly 1 to 1.5 hectares) per family; in some communities the allocation amounted to little more than an acre. With the later growth of the peasant population and the division of land among heirs in successive generations, the remaining plots clearly were not sufficient to sustain families.

By reducing peasants to small plots and opening up large areas of prime land for acquisition by Spaniards, the concentration of Indian communties in the early seventeenth century greatly facilitated the developing disparity between small numbers of large landowners of Spanish descent and large numbers of peasants with tiny plots of land.

The reduction of Indian peasants to very small plots moreover was an effective mechanism for generating a greater supply of Indian labor for Spanish farms. In order that this labor would be more broadly allocated, the Indians were removed from *encomendero* control—although to compensate the *encomenderos* the Indians were required to provide them with a larger commodity or monetary tribute. This exaction, of course, put the Indians under still greater pressure to enter the labor market. Finally, to make sure that indigenous labor was used for desired purposes, Spanish authorities further imposed upon members of Indian communities a series of overlapping labor obligations. In the Santafé de Bogotá region they had to provide designated terms of service to cities and their residents (the *alquiler general*), to work in the silver mines of Mariquita (the *mita minera*), and to provide labor to Spanish farmers (the *concierto*). Because of these multiple labor obligations, an adult male Indian might spend half the year away from home, which meant that the indigenes often could not effectively farm their plots. Further, although the Indians were paid in these various forms of draft labor, their pay was set so low as to require half a year to earn the money required to make their tribute payments.

Of the various draft labor obligations, the most onerous in the district of Santafé was the *mita minera*, which by the 1620s required as many as 1500 men per year to work in the mines for periods varying from four months to a year. Further, Indians from the cool highlands had to descend to the tropical clime of Mariquita, where they often had to work half submerged in water in the mines. Many died in Mariquita; others fled to escape the labor draft. As a consequence, the highland communities supplying the labor drafts steadily shrank. Thus, in New Granada, as in Mexico and Peru, labor drafts for the mines tended to be self-liquidating. The mining *mita* in the eastern highlands began to decline in the 1640s, although it was not finally abolished until 1729. The labor draft for the cities began to break down around 1670. But the agricultural *concierto* remained important until the first decades of the eighteenth century.

Under the pressure of the labor drafts, many Indians left their communities to become wage workers on Spanish haciendas or in Spanish cities. As of the 1680s, some 10,000 Indians were thought to be living in Santafe de Bogota along with the city's 3000 Hispanic residents. Many of these indigenes, particularly women, were servants in Spanish households. Some Indian males became urban artisans and lived in barrios largely populated by indigenous and mestizo craftsmen. In the process many changed their socioracial identities, so that some Indians redefined themselves as mestizos and not a few mestizos came to be thought of as whites ("blancos de la tierra").

The mestizo population also was increasing through other social mechanisms. Indian or black slave women who were domestic servants were exposed to sexual predation by males both in and outside the household. Further, because there were many more women than men in the cities, particularly among Indians, blacks, and mestizos, women living independently often fell into informal unions, in the process swelling the mestizo or mulatto population.

Mestizos were also growing in number in rural areas. As the indigenous populations in Indian towns declined, people of Hispanic culture, most of them probably mestizos, moved in to farm Indian community land. Although Spanish regulations forbade the Indians to sell their land, they were permitted to rent it in order to raise money for tribute payments. Rental must have been an obvious recourse for Indians whose labor obligations outside the community made it difficult for them to farm their own plots. In addition, although it has not yet been quantitatively established, it seems likely that many mestizos or poor Spaniards married or mated with Indian women. By these various mechanisms substantial mestizo populations developed in supposedly Indian towns. In 1755–1757 a survey of indigenous communities in the jurisdictions of Tunja and Vélez discovered that in most supposedly Indian towns, the majority of the inhabitants were now mestizos. And in Tunja, where the largest concentration of indigenes had lived, three-fifths of the residents in "Indian" towns were non-Indian.

Another measure of the transition from Indian to mestizo in the Eastern Cordillera may be found in the first systematic census (1776–1778). At that time people defined as Indians constituted less than 36 percent of the province of Santafé, people of mixed race (mostly mestizos) accounted for more than 34 percent, and "whites" made up another 29 percent.

At the end of the eighteenth century, the highland plains of the Eastern Cordillera still dominated the East demographically. But during the seventeenth and eighteenth centuries important satellite zones emerged on the warmer flanks of the mountains. Settlers who moved down the mountain flanks south and west of Santafé grew such warm country plants as plantains, cassava, and maize, but the principal commercial crop was sugar cane, molasses from which was made into cane liquor and unrefined sugar (*panela*).

The most significant area of subtropical colonization from the Eastern Cordillera in the colonial era was in the Guanentá basin, north of Vélez. Hispanic colonists from Vélez began to move into the region in small numbers in the latter half of the sixteenth century, but the population at that time remained largely indigenous. Only during the seventeenth century did the Hispanic population become large enough for some formerly indigenous pueblos to be transformed into Hispanic parishes and *villas* (small towns). Once the Guanentá had developed a significant Hispanic population, it appears to have been colonized in part by a process of cellular division. Numerous mountain spurs divide the Guanentá into many small pockets. When a town began to press upon the resources afforded by its mountain niche, some of its residents would hive off to form a new community in another small pocket nearby. The Guanentá therefore developed as a region of many small towns, though two, el Socorro and its rival San Gil, tended to dominate.

In contrast with Tunja, which was in a long-term decline, the towns of the Guanentá were growing dynamically in the eighteenth century. By the latter part of the eighteenth century, the region had become particularly notable as a producer of raw cotton and cotton textiles. Much of its cloth went to Santafé de Bogotá, the commercial emporium from which it was distributed to markets as far away as the mining regions of western Colombia.

The Guanentá, despite being broken into small mountain pockets, was among the more densely populated regions in the eastern zone. But it was more productive, in relation to both population and area, than the eastern highlands. Some contemporaries attributed the productivity and prosperity of the area to the division of its land into relatively small units, something practically dictated by its broken topography. Pedro Fermín de Vargas, writing circa 1790, noted that in the Guanentá most people owned their own modest plots, so they took a particular interest in the land and its cultivation. Furthermore, as women and children did much of the spinning and weaving, everyone was productively employed.

In contrast with the densely populated mountain valleys of the Guanentá, two other regions, the upper Magdalena Valley and the eastern Llanos, offered extensive, relatively flat plains that came to be used principally for raising cattle and thus remained sparsely populated. The two political capitals of the interior, Santafé de Bogotá in the Eastern Cordillera and Popayán in the West, competed to secure for their citizens the supply of cattle raised on the plains of the upper Magdalena.

The West

Like their counterparts in the Eastern Cordillera, Spaniards in the Cauca were amassing large landholdings, on parts of which they grew food crops and raised cattle. But gold mining was the motor of the economy in the Cauca as well as in Antioquia to the north. In the seventeenth century, however, that motor was running down. Gold deposits discovered in the later sixteenth century were declining or giving out in the early decades of the seventeenth century. By the end of the 1630s the value of legally registered gold in the West was less than half the levels at the end of the sixteenth century. And production continued to decline for some time after that. (See Table 4.1.)

Meanwhile, however, new mining areas in the West were developing that would carry production to much higher levels during the eighteenth century. In the 1630s Antioqueños were discovering new deposits in the highland regions of Rionegro and the valley of the Osos (valley of the Bears), and after 1640 men from Popayán were beginning to mine gold north of that city in Caloto. Hispanic goldminers were also attempting to exploit gold deposits in tributaries of rivers along the Pacific coast—the Atrato and San Juan

Table 4.1 Legally registered gold in the districts of Santafé, Antioquia, Cartago, and Popayán, 1595–1644 (in gold pesos of 22.5 carats)

	Santafé	Antioquia	Cartago	Popayán	Total
1595–1599	1,349,705	1,748,526	n.d.	344,823	3.443.054
1600–1604	927,255	1,621,168	n.d.	n.d.	2,548,423
1605–1609	744,345	1,423,588	54,390	283,564	2,505,887
1610–1614	675,930	1,294,291	92,280	221,775	3,028,621
1615–1619	705,735	1,172,140	34,995	189,400	2,102,270
1620–1624	503,125	1,156,150	55,305	134,410	1,848,990
1625–1629	451,180	1,122,994	n.d.	179,396	1,753,570
1630–1634	294,370	821,310	n.d.	159,850	1,275,530
1635–1639	329,090	717,331	n.d.	85,400	1,059,821
1640–1644	96,910	437,414	n.d.	n.d.	524,324

District of Santafé = Santafé, Remedios, Pamplona
District of Antioquia = Antioquia, Zaragoza, Cáceres, Guamocó
District of Cartago = Toro, Anserma
n.d. = no data
Source: Germán Colmenares, *Historia económica y social de Colombia, 1537–1719* (Bogotá, 1973), pp. 228–229.

rivers in the Chocó and various rivers in the region of Barbacoas, south of Buenaventura. Indians living in both of these regions fought off Spanish incursions for decades. But by the 1680s, Hispanic entrepreneurs had gangs of slaves panning gold in both areas. Men from Popayán tended to dominate mining in Barbacoas and the San Juan basin, while Antioqueños were involved in the Atrato.

By the 1730s, the combined production of Antioquia, the Chocó, Barbacoas, and Caloto and other sites near Popayán had reached levels surpassing those at the end of the sixteenth century. By the 1790s, these mining regions were producing three times as much gold as in the 1590s. Among these regions, the Chocó and Popayán were strong producers through most of the eighteenth century, with Antioquia and Barbacoas coming on strong after 1760. (See Table 4.2.)

Gold mining was extremely important to the Hispanic elite because throughout the colonial period gold was New Granada's only significant export, and hence the chief means of paying for imported luxuries. As important as gold was to New Granada, its production of precious metals was modest compared with that of other mining areas in colonial Latin America. While New Granada was the largest single producer of gold in colonial Spanish America, the industry generated nothing like the wealth of silver mining in Mexico or Peru. Between 1735 and 1800, the gold registered in New Granada's western mining regions represented less than one-thirteenth of the value of Mexican bullion mined in the same years.

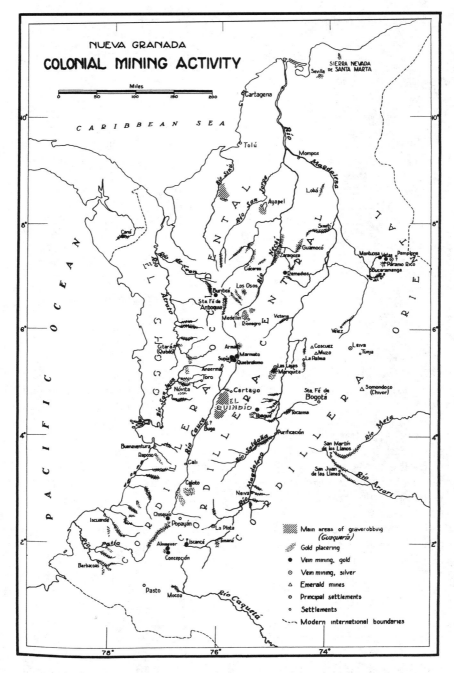

Map 3 Colonial mining sites. From Robert C. West, *Colonial Placer Mining in Colombia* (Baton Rouge, LA, 1952).

Table 4.2 Legally registered gold production in four regions of the West, by
five-year periods (in thousands of silver pesos)

	Popayán	Barbacoas	Chocó	Antioquia	Five-Year Totals	Annual Means
1735–1739	1391	613	2366	256	4626	925.2
1740–1744	1124	317	2323	348	4112	822.4
1745–1749	792	326	2312	316	3746	749.2
1750–1754	564	243	1747	544	3098	619.6
1755–1759	944	461	1498	559	3462	692.4
1760–1764	1020	921	1687	820	4448	889.6
1765–1769	1055	952	1678	751	4436	887.2
1770–1774	1483	995	1808	1125	5411	1082.2
1775–1779	1360	893	1639	1684	5576	1115.2
1780–1784	1908	1361	1940	1987	7196	1439.2
1785–1789	1731	1688	2158	2655	8232	1646.4
1790–1794	1616	1767	2667	3281	9331	1866.2
1795–1799	1541	1783	2581	3662	9567	1913.4
Totals	16,529	12,320	26,404	17,988	73,241	

Source: Jorge Orlando Melo, "Producción de oro y desarrollo económico en el siglo XVIII," in Jorge Orlando Melo, Sobre historia y política p. 68.

Given the more modest scale of wealth produced in New Granada, it did not develop a class of titled aristocrats that was so evident in eighteenth-century Mexico or, to a lesser degree, in Lima. Gold mining did create an aristocracy of a lesser, untitled, sort in Popayán, but in Antioquia it generated a dominant class that by the end of the colonial period was more in the mold of a commercial bourgeoisie. Indeed, in Antioquia the men who became most wealthy were those who engaged in commerce with the mines more than those who were mining entrepreneurs.

In the early phase of New Granadan gold mining, in the second half of the sixteenth century, the labor force was primarily indigenous or involved both Indians and African slaves. In the vein mines of Almaguer in the upper Cauca, where Indians were relatively plentiful, both indigenous workers and African slaves were used between 1575 and 1600. On the other hand, circa 1590–1610, at Remedios and Zaragoza, in what is now Antioquia, African slaves did the mining, presumably because much cheaper Indian labor was not available. In the Chocó in the seventeenth century entrepreneurs used Indians as part of their mining force because African slaves were expensive. But after the use of Indian labor in mines was prohibited early in the eighteenth century, there developed a division of labor, in which the indigenes produced food for consumption by an African slave mining force.

African slaves in the Chocó and the rest of the West were expensive, double their cost in the port of Cartagena, because those brought legally had to come by a round-about route—up the Magdalena River and then across the Central Cordillera. It would have been much cheaper to bring them from Cartagena up the Atrato River. But because the Atrato had become a route for contraband exports of gold and imports of slaves, Spanish authorities closed it to trade.

Slave gangs were used in mining veins in underground shafts, as well as in sluice mining, which involved digging up ore-laden earth and washing it in a constructed water course. However, in places where gold was simply panned in streams, much of the labor was performed by individual free agents, known as *mazamorreros* in Antioquia, where they were particularly common. In the 1780s the chief Spanish official in Antioquia thought that *mazamorreros* were producing two-thirds of the gold in the province, and a later estimate in 1808 raised that proportion to five-sixths.

The Caribbean Coast

In contrast with the insulated interior, the northern coast turned outward to the Caribbean. Maritime trade, legal or illegal, gave the tonic to coastal life. Throughout the colonial period, Cartagena was the region's dominant city. Its protected harbor and its location close to the Isthmus of Panama established it as an important port of call for Spain's convoyed treasure fleets, and thus as the chief port for the extraction of gold and the importation of slaves and other goods. These activities, however, also made Cartagena a target of attacks by foreign privateers and naval forces from the 1540s to the 1740s. Such assaults induced the Spanish crown to make heavy investments in fortifying the port from the 1620s through the 1650s and again through most of the eighteenth century.

Because of the importance of defending Cartagena, the largest contingent of military forces in New Granada was stationed at the port. Cartagena also was a significant ecclesiastical center: It had four monasteries and two convents and was the site of an episcopal see and, after 1610, of the Inquisition. With its various commercial, military, and ecclesiastical functions, it was by far the largest city on New Granada's Caribbean coast, with about 10,000 inhabitants in the 1690s, perhaps 12,000 in the 1770s. However, the town population fluctuated considerably, dropping drastically during and after foreign attack, swelling when the Spanish convoy fleet arrived, as people from the hinterland rushed in to sell provisions.

Though Cartagena's well-protected bay gave it great advantages as a port, its development as an emporium for imported goods was impeded by the lack of good connections to the Magdalena River, the natural artery to markets in the interior. Until 1650, goods were brought from Cartagena to the Magdalena either by a hazardous sea route or overland by mules, at considerable expense. In 1650 Cartagena's governor led a project to dig canals linking navigable swamps so as to permit freight to be carried from the river to the city by a much cheaper all-water route. The opening of this Canal del Dique, by providing cheaper transportation to the Magdalena, enhanced Cartagena's ability to supply food to visiting Spanish ships and imported goods to the interior. However, the canal was not maintained and became virtually unusable between 1679 and 1724. Reopened in 1725, by 1789 it again had deterioriated. Maintaining the Canal del Dique was of vital interest to Cartagena; nonetheless, it remained closed for long periods of time, ultimately bringing the decline of Cartagena as a commercial port in the nineteenth century.

Because of distance and transportation difficulties, Cartagena was substantially disconnected from the interior. Most of its food requirements were provided by a broad hinterland in the coastal zone itself. Initially Cartagena was supplied by indigenes, but as their population declined drastically in the sixteenth century, farmers of Hispanic culture took over this function—growing beans, cassava, and plantains on plots near Cartagena and maize in the Sinú region. Large estates on the sabanas of Tolú and in the regions of Mompox and Valledupar supplied Cartagena with beef and crews of visiting ships with salted beef and pork. With the decline of the Indian population, African slaves provided most of the labor force on these large holdings.

SOCIAL CHANGE

Over the nearly three centuries of the colonial period, one of the chief social changes was the drastic decline of the indigenous population. In the Eastern Cordillera, a very large Indian population evolved over time into a predominantly mestizo one, substantially Hispanic in culture. In contrast, in the southwest, in the regions of Pasto and, to a lesser degree, Popayán, people with indigenous cultural identities hung on in larger proportions and for a much longer time. Elsewhere in the West, from Cali northward to Antioquia, the Indian population rapidly declined and was largely replaced by African slaves and their descendants. The same was true, to a lesser degree, on the Caribbean coast and in its hinterland in the lower Magdalena valley.

Importations of African slaves occurred on a relatively small scale for most of the sixteenth century, picking up in pace from 1590 to 1630 with the mining booms of Remedios and Zaragoza. Slave imports and gold mining then declined together until toward the end of the seventeenth century, when the development of mining in the Chocó, Barbacoas, the Cauca, and Antioquia renewed demand for slaves. During the first half of the eighteenth century, slave importations greatly increased as a French contractor brought in 4250 (1703–1714), the British South Sea Company 10,300 (1714–1736), and Spanish contractors 13,000 (1746–1757).

In the last decades of the eighteenth century, demand for slaves declined—surprisingly, given the notable growth in mining production in the Chocó, Antioquia, and Barbacoas at this time. In the 1780s and 1790s Spanish authorities tried to encourage the growth of gold-mining by permitting more slaves to be imported. But goldmining entrepreneurs showed little interest in buying them. At the end of the eighteenth century slave prices in the Cauca and the Chocó were only half what they had been at the beginning of the century. What was happening?

It seems unlikely that the slaves imported before 1757 would have satisfied labor needs some thirty years later. It appears rather that New Granada was becoming less dependent on imported slaves because of a growing population of homegrown slaves. In addition, increasing numbers of free blacks and mulattos provided an alternative work force. The emergence of numbers of native-born slaves reflected a significant change in the sex ratio of the slave population. Slave importations had tended to favor young males as more useful for heavy labor than females. Slave reproduction was hindered in the seventeenth century by an imbalance in the sex ratio, aggravated by the fact that slave women tended to be placed in the cities, while men were predominantly in the mines or on haciendas. However, during the eighteenth century natural birth processes were beginning to produce a more equal sex ratio among slaves. The first systematic census, in 1776–1778, indicates that women made up more than 45 percent of the slave population in every important slave-holding area (Antioquia, the Chocó, the Caribbean coast, and lowland regions in the West). With more women in the slave population, more male slaves could have mates and larger numbers of slave children were born.

At the same time, the numbers of free blacks and mulattos were growing. According to the 1776–1778 census, *libres* (free blacks, mulattos and others of mixed race) already made up close to three-fifths of the population of Antioquia, while slaves constituted one-fifth. In Cartagena free blacks and people of mixed race represented more than three-fifths and slaves less than one-tenth of the population.

There were various routes to freedom. Slave rebellions had occurred sporadically, more frequently in the late sixteenth century than afterward. Rebellion, however, was more likely to lead to death than freedom. Usually slaves, whether on haciendas or mining, simply escaped into the wilderness. Such escaped slaves, known as *cimarrones*, often formed communities called *palenques*, most of which were relatively small. Few contained as many as a hundred escapees. On rare occasions escaped slaves might dare to attack Spanish mining settlements; more frequently they raided plantations to enlist other slaves as recruits. Occasionally they attacked Spanish commerce along the Magdalena River or overland trails in the mining districts. Escaped slaves also preyed upon Indians. Most escaped slaves were male, and they often raided indigenous communities to obtain mates. Spanish authorities periodically sent military expeditions to destroy *palenques*, execute their leaders, and reenslave the rest. But Spanish policy toward communities of escaped slaves was inconsistent, alternating between toleration and repression. During nonrepressive periods, haciendas and *palenques* often maintained peaceful relations.

A more peaceful route to liberty was for slaves to purchase their freedom. This was possible for urban slaves, who, by renting out their services, might acquire savings. Some slaves in gold-mining areas were also able to accumulate enough money to buy their freedom. The declining value of slaves in the late eighteenth century may have facilitated freedom through self-purchase.

Those blacks who reached "freedom" were by no means fully accepted as citizens. Many continued to live in a gray area between slavery and freedom. Often masters manumitted slaves only on condition of continued service. Besides, the dominant Hispanic population feared free blacks as a source of social disorder. After an abortive attempt of slaves to escape in Cali in 1771, an array of social controls was imposed on free blacks—including restrictions on moving about freely and carrying arms and prohibitions against marrying outside their racial group. Perhaps to avoid such restrictions, many former slaves moved out of areas of Hispanic control. Former slaves from the mines of the Chocó, for example, tended to migrate to the Pacific coast, where, remote from Spanish authority, they lived by fishing, hunting, and subsistence agriculture. On the other hand, in Antioquia free blacks and mulattoes continued to farm in areas settled and dominated by whites and played an important role in gold panning as independent *mazamorreros*.

By the latter part of the eighteenth century people largely of mixed race, but completely in Hispanic in culture, had become more numerous in most regions than any of the other socioracial groups—whites, Indians, or black slaves. In the 1776–1778 census 46 percent of the population of New Granada was classified as *libres* (free blacks, mulattoes and mestizos), 26 percent were deemed "white," 20 percent Indian, and 8 percent slaves. There were, of course, regional variations within this general patterns. Slaves and Indians remained the largest categories in the Chocó, and Popayán and Antioquia still had relatively large slave populations. In the province of Pasto, 58 percent were still considered Indian, and only 3 percent were "libres." It must be borne in mind that census-takers varied a good deal in the way they applied these socioracial categories. A given individual might be classifed as white by one census-taker and as mestizo or mulatto by another.

The *libres* formed the greater part of the society's underclass. Some whites were poor also, but they were generally less impoverished than poor mestizos and mulattoes. However, some mestizos and mulattoes did accumulate enough wealth to aspire to claims of higher status. During the last decades of the eighteenth century, the growing number of aspiring mestizos and mulattoes created evident social tensions.

Since the latter part of the sixteenth century Spanish regulations had aimed at keeping mestizos and mulattoes out of positions of honor. Documentation of legitimate birth and "purity of blood" was required to become a university student or to hold a public position, including even that of notary. The system of discrimination was reinforced by recording the birth status and "caste" identity of an individual in parish records at the time of

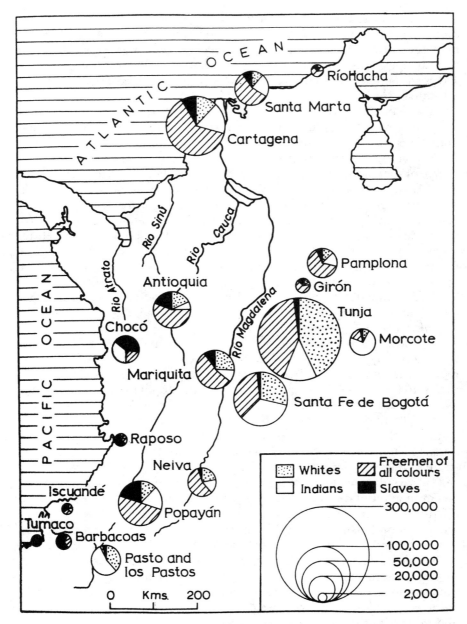

Map 4 Population distribution, with proportions of socioracial groups by region (ca. 1778). From Anthony McFarlane, *Colombia before Independence* (Cambridge, England, 1993).

baptism. Throughout the colonial period the status assumptions embedded in these regulations were internalized in lived social values. That is, from the point of view of the established elite, the status of mestizo or mulatto implied a lack of public honor.

However, over time the lines of socioracial discrimination became eroded and lost clarity. A mestizo who had accumulated wealth, who already had occupied a prestigious position (e.g., as a councilman in a *cabildo*), or who was connected to a socially prestigious family might claim to be effectively white and eligible for positions of honor. During the eighteenth century, as the numbers of people with indeterminate racial origins increased and as some attained relative wealth, conflicts over the status of individuals in the legally established and socially embedded socioracial hierarchy became particularly evident. When individuals of unclear socioracial identity sought to enter the social elite, some in the elite, or at its edges, viewed such pretensions as a threat to their own status and vigorously resisted the incorporation of mestizos or mulattoes into the ranks of respectability. Elite families remained preoccupied with retaining the distinction of "purity of blood" and resisted marriages that might throw that status into question. This resistance was stiffened by authorities in Spain, who in 1778 issued a Royal Pragmatic on Marriage, which gave parents increased legal power to prevent their children from contracting "unequal" marriages. Even among people of lesser social status, who could not prove their own "purity of blood," not a few strenuously defended their families' status by opposing marriage with those they considered of inferior socioracial rank. The second half of the eighteenth century was particularly notable for lawsuits over the public reputations of individuals—that is, whether they should be considered mestizo, mulatto, or white.

While attempts of mestizos or mulattoes to occupy positions of honor met some resistance, their growth as a social category was viewed with equanimity by some in the elite—perhaps as long as they kept their place as peasants and artisans. Mestizos, some asserted, represented a positive step toward the Europeanization of the Indian population. In an essay on the economic problems and possibilities of New Granada, Pedro Fermín de Vargas (ca. 1790) condemned Indians as lazy and stupid and proposed their elimination through miscegenation.

5

Crises of Authority, 1700–1808

During the greater part of the eighteenth century, royal officials in the New Kingdom of Granada sought to strengthen the effective authority of the state. They were moved to do so in part by the exigencies of war. After the Bourbons took control of Spain early in the eighteenth century, they fought wars with England (1739–1748, 1762–1763, 1779–1783), with revolutionary France (1793–1795), and again with England (1796–1802 and 1805–1807). The military challenge, from England in particular, stimulated the Spanish royal government to attempt several more-or-less linked reforms. Spain's rulers understood that greater military strength required increased government revenues, and that larger revenues demanded more administrative efficiency and greater economic production. The need for a more effective economy in turn stirred concerns to reform economic structures and institutions and encouraged efforts to appropriate scientific and technical innovations from more advanced European competitors. Beyond the linked efforts to increase military strength, collect more revenues, and achieve greater administrative effectiveness, Bourbon administrators also sought social order for its own sake.

The Spanish Bourbon reforms succeeded in expanding trade within the empire, revenue collections, and military forces in the American colonies. In New Granada the results were much more modest than in Mexico or some other parts of Spanish America. Nonetheless, in New Granada military forces also were augmented, and administration and revenue collection were strengthened. Although wars with Great Britain frequently disrupted trade between Spain and New Granada, exports were diversified slightly and expanded during brief periods of peace.

Ironically, innovations under the Spanish Bourbons helped sow the seeds of colonial rebellion. Administrative reform in the colonies meant, to many Spanish officials, a conscious policy of preferring Spaniards to creoles in filling high positions, a policy that further intensified colonials' irritation with the system. Attempts to increase tax collections provoked popular insurrection and tended to undermine the authority of Spanish officials, whom many Spanish Americans increasingly considered arrogant, arbitrary, and unconcerned with the welfare of their American subjects. Experiments with new agricultural exports increased creole frustrations, as the products of New Granada's forests and farms found scant markets in Spain while Spanish administrators established government monopolies over some export products that did prove relatively successful. Spain's opening to contemporary science was accompanied by the penetration of Enlightenment political ideas and, in the wake of the English-American and French Revolutions, of republican influences.

If the Bourbon reforms stimulated a Spanish American appetite for more change than Spain's rulers intended, international warfare, which had played such an important role in prompting the Bourbon reforms, also ultimately undid the Spanish Bourbon regime. The fiscal demands of war stirred substantial tax riots in New Granada in the 1760s and full-scale rebellion in 1781. Spain's inability to protect oceanic shipping in time of war caused substantial losses to New Granadan exporters and thus made palpable to them the disadvantages of political connection to Spain. Finally, in 1808–1810 French forces took over Spain and removed the Spanish crown, thus sequestering the ultimate authority underlying Spanish government.

THE VICEROYALTY OF THE NEW KINGDOM OF GRANADA

Throughout the sixteenth and seventeenth centuries the Spanish state had only a weak presence in New Granada. Authority over the area was fragmented. The Audiencia in Santafé de Bogotá had jurisdiction over the eastern highlands, most of the Magdalena Valley, the Caribbean coast, and, after 1576, Antioquia. Difficulty of travel and communications, however, hampered effective control over these areas. Provincial governors remained effectively independent of the authority of the Audiencia. And Santafé de Bogotá lacked even formal authority over much of what is now western Colombia. During much of the sixteenth and seventeenth centuries the greater part of the West and also the upper reaches of the Magdalena Valley were under the governor of Popayán, who was subordinate to the Audiencia of Quito after its creation in 1563. But the ecclesiastical jurisdictions did not correspond to the civil ones; the bishop of Popayán was suffragan to the archbishop of Santafé de Bogotá. And, in matters of heresy, the Inquisition in Cartagena ruled the whole region. In addition to the problem of the spatial fragmentation and intersection of authority, each of the governing bodies was, in one way or another, weakened by internecine conflict. In New Granada, there had been many examples of such conflicts—among church authorities, within the Audiencia, and between the Audiencia and church authorities.

The Bourbons attempted to strengthen the state and amplify its scope, both in Spain and in its overseas dominions. The first expression of this Bourbon intent in northern South America was the creation in 1717 of the Viceroyalty of el Nuevo Reino de Granada (the New Kingdom of Granada), with Santafé de Bogotá as the viceregal capital and western Colombia as well as present-day Ecuador and Panama and much of Venezuela under its governance.

The newly created viceroyalty did not last long, as Spanish authorities soon concluded that New Granada was too unpopulated, poor, and short of revenues to be able to sustain a viceregal establishment. In 1723 the viceroyalty was suppressed and the president of the Audiencia once again became the chief administrative authority. Renewed threat of war with England, however, brought the restoration of the viceroyalty in 1738. Indeed, the War of Jenkins' Ear broke out in 1739, six months before the new viceroy, Sebastián Eslava, arrived in Cartagena, where he stayed to direct the defense of that port. Eslava was on hand in 1741 when a British fleet of 180 ships and 23,600 men under Admiral Edward Vernon attacked, but failed to take, Cartagena. Because war with Great Britain continued until 1748, Eslava found it necessary to remain in the fortified port throughout the nearly nine years he served as viceroy. Later, two subsequent viceroys, Manuel Flores (1776–1782) and Antonio Caballero y Góngora (1782–1789), also spent much of their time of governance in Cartagena, as Spain was once again at war with Great Britain (1776–1783).

The re-created viceroyalty covered a large territory, including what is now Colombia, Ecuador, Panama, most of Venezuela, and the islands of Trinidad and Margarita. In fact, the viceroy could not possibly govern this farflung expanse. He had very little contact with Ecuador and had almost no idea what was going on in Venezuela. In 1777, after nearly four decades of ineffective governance from Santafé de Bogotá, the coastal areas of Venezuela were removed from the viceroyalty and placed under the jurisdiction of the captain-general of Caracas, although the Orinoco River basin in the interior continued under the viceroy in Santafé. Ecuador also remained effectively autonomous, under the Audiencia of Quito.

CREOLE ELITES

In the viceregal government, European-born Spaniards dominated the highest positions. American-born Spaniards (creoles) also played a role in administration, but generally at middle to lower levels. Creoles tended to be subordinated for a number of reasons. It was a general principle of Spanish administration that royal administrators should not govern in the lands of their birth. (Municipal officers were a different matter.) Spanish rulers believed that men governing outside their homelands would be more loyal to the Crown and less entangled in local interests. Further, Spanish royal administrators, both in Spain and America, naturally were more inclined to trust men born in Spain than those from America. Spaniards also tended to have better connections at the Spanish court than did their American competitors.

As a consequence, the highest administrative positions always were dominated by Spaniards. All of New Granada's viceroys were Spanish-born, as were also a large majority of the judges in the royal Audiencia. Between 1687 and 1810, four-fifths of the Audiencia judges in Santafé were European Spaniards. Although creoles played a somewhat larger role in the Audiencias during the first half of the eighteenth century, between 1759 and

1788 their numbers shrank. At all times creole judges generally came from other regions of Spanish America, particularly from Lima. The few New Granadans who had high positions in the Audiencia of Santafé for the most part served as fiscales (Crown attorneys) and did not become judges. The most notable exception was Joaquín Mosquera y Figueroa, son of a Popayán family that had grown rich in gold mining in the West, who served as a judge in the Audiencia of Santafé between 1787 and 1795, in a notable career that later led to high position in Mexico, Caracas, and finally Spain itself. Mosquera's brilliant career, however, was the aberration that proved the rule. On the other hand, while the Crown avoided the appointment of local men to the Audiencia, the judges frequently became linked to the creole aristocracy by marriage, so that interests of well-connected creoles did find representation. Although creoles generally were denied the highest political positions, some high-status creoles became administrators of revenue and treasury offices or as lawyers practicing before the Audiencia. Some also served as provincial administrators (*corregidores*), lieutenant governors, or advisers to governors. Although prospects of rising to the top of viceregal administration were slight for the American-born, educated creoles nonetheless aspired to government posts because of the social honor that attached to such positions.

Study of the law was the usual creole channel to government positions, except for a relative few who won office by virtue of family ties or political connections in Santafé de Bogotá. For upper-sector creoles from the provinces, in particular, education in the two *colegios* in Santafé—San Bartolomé and Nuestra Señora del Rosario—provided a possible avenue to government office and thus to upward mobility. Access to university education, however, remained restricted largely to creoles who already were of relatively high status.

Until the first decades of the eighteenth century San Bartolomé and el Rosario had served primarily to educate creoles for the priesthood. During the eighteenth century, however, the number of law students multiplied, particularly in el Rosario. The expansion of university studies after 1770, and in particular the growth in the number of lawyers, greatly increased the supply of creole aspirants for government office. The emergence of a larger corps of creole lawyers over the long term created a legally trained elite, some of whom came to resent the fact that the higher government positions often were given to less-educated Spaniards rather than to creoles with law degrees. A number of these creole lawyers later played critical roles in leading the independence movement, once the imperial crisis began in 1808. The contacts they made with students from other provinces enabled them to form networks making possible an at least somewhat coordinated movement toward autonomy in 1809–1810. Further, the men trained as lawyers in the last decades of the colonial period had the intellectual formation necessary to articulate justifications for independence and to organize the initial republican governments.

The universities also produced creole ecclesiastics. Until well into the eighteenth century, the Church was a more general career option for creoles than was the law. By the latter part of the seventeenth century, creole friars were clearly more numerous than Spanish ones in the Dominican and Augustine religious orders. Among the secular clergy, parish priests were creoles in overwhelming numbers. The more able, educated, or well-connected creoles in the secular clergy might aspire to a few scarce places as dignitaries in cathedral chapters. Those who arrived at such positions became visible ornaments in the ecclesiastical hierarchy. Nonetheless, despite the numerical predominance of creoles in most strata of the colonial church, Spaniards continued to control the very top of the ecclesiastical hierarchy, just as they did the apex of the civil state. Of the fifteen men who served as archbishop of Santafé between 1704 and 1810, only three were American-born, and only one (from Tunja) was from the immediate region. When the independence era began in New Granada in the first decade of the nineteenth century, all of New Granada's prelates (the archbishop of Santafé and the bishops of Cartagena, Santa Marta, and Popayán) were Spaniards. A sense of class difference between creole priests in poor parishes, on the one hand, and wealthy Spanish bishops, on the other, may well have existed. But if such resentment existed in some, most were more bound by piety and faith in the hierarchical structure to which all were committed.

A third institutional lodging for creoles, the military, became increasingly important during the eighteenth century, and particularly during the last two decades of the colonial era (1790–1810). Creole appointments as military officers were enhanced by Bourbon efforts to expand the colonial military, initially in response to foreign threats but later also to cope with potential internal disorder. Because of the need to cope with European exigencies, the Spanish Crown in the last third of the eighteenth century increasingly relied on creole officers to staff military units in the colonies, both in the regular army units and in the militia. The growing importance of creole officers in the last decades of the colonial era is exemplified by the infantry officers in the regular army in Cartagena. As of the 1770s and 1780s, creoles made up only about a third of all officers, and Spaniards virtually monopolized the senior positions. By 1800, Spaniards and creoles were nearly equal in total number of officers and at the senior positions. By 1807 creoles were numerically dominant overall and held some of the highest positions. The same trend occurred with militia units in Cartagena, except creole numerical dominance came earlier (during the 1790s) and was much more marked. These trends were less true in Santafé de Bogotá, however. Whether because of concern to protect the viceregal capital or because Spaniards preferred postings there, Spanish officers remained dominant in Santafé de Bogotá to the end of the colonial period.

Still another activity in which creoles increasingly competed with Spaniards during the last decades of the eighteenth century was overseas wholesale commerce. Through much of the colonial period trans-Atlantic commerce (primarily the exchange of gold for imported goods) was dominated by Spanish merchants. But toward the end of the eighteenth century some creole merchants became increasingly effective competitors in commerce, including contraband trade. Contraband was common throughout the eighteenth century. But it probably increased when war interrupted normal commerce. Between 1790 and 1810, because the British navy effectively blocked Spanish shipping during two Anglo-Spanish wars (1796–1802 and 1805–1807), creole merchants, and Spanish ones as well, were actively pursuing illicit trade with Jamaica, as well as with other foreign-owned islands in the Caribbean. It is not evident that creole merchants regarded their Spanish competitors with antagonism. The important fact, rather, was that creole merchants, although relatively few in number, represented a developing interest group.

In sum, by the first decade of the nineteenth century there existed a significant body of creoles who, while not occupying the topmost positions in civil government, the Church, the military, or commerce, were close to the top and in frequent contact with the Spaniards in supreme authority. Normally these creole elites were loyal collaborators with Spanish colleagues. However, in time of crisis, when Spanish officials expressed distrust of creoles, relations between Spaniards and creoles could turn tense and hostile.

ORDER AND INNOVATION UNDER THE BOURBON VICEROYS

Certain concerns perennially preoccupied those who governed the viceroyalty of el Nuevo Reino de Granada: the need to produce more gold and get it to Spain and, in service to the latter aim, to maintain the defenses of Cartagena, the port through which legal exports of gold flowed back to Spain. To these concerns, which were also priorities of the predecessor Hapsburgs, new ones were added in the last quarter of the eighteenth century, among them the aims of cutting the leakage of bullion through contraband trade by opening more avenues of legal trade and the expansion of colonial exports other than bullion. In New Granada, however, while gestures were made toward increasing colonial exports of tropical fruits and other economic improvements, in fact these aims frequently were subordinated to, and sometimes conflicted with, the long-established priorities of producing bullion, defending its shipment to Spain, and preventing its leakage from the system through contraband trade. Defense of bullion shipments, as well as the realm as a whole, involved the Spanish Crown in enormous investments in the improvement and maintenance of fortifications of the port of Cartagena during the eighteenth century.

Defense against contraband was connected to the establishment of control over untamed Indians on the frontiers. The indigenes living in the Guajira Peninsula were perennially engaged in contraband, as were the Cunas in the Darien region. In the 1770s and 1780s military campaigns attempted, without much success, to subdue the Indians in both places. But the Bourbon concern for social order went beyond suppressing contraband. In general they made efforts to bring people dispersed in the forests—like escaped slaves, mulattoes, and Indians in the Magdalena basin—into settlements where they would be under political control and religious supervision. As one common phrase of the day put it, officials and churchmen wanted these people to live within earshot of the church bell (*al son de campana*).

Viceregal administrators also focused on several perennial economic problems. By comparison with silver-producing Mexico and Peru, New Granada was a relatively poor colony. In the eighteenth century Spanish officials rarely failed to comment upon the poverty of the country and its lack of much domestic or external commerce. Antonio Manso, president of the Audiencia of Santafé, reported that on his arrival in 1724, Santafé and its environs were in "ultimate desolation: the principal and noble residents living out of town, commerce inactive, public offices vacant, all depressed and in a lamentable poverty." Manso noted that New Granada had many unexploited, or underexploited, resources. Gold was being mined, particularly along the Pacific coast. But other resources seemed more-or-less neglected: emeralds at Muzo in the eastern highlands, copper deposits, as well as a variety of forest products, such as dyewoods, balsams, and fine hardwoods. And the Eastern Cordillera's traditional grain agriculture was suffering from competition from imported flour.

These themes echoed through the reports of the viceroys from the middle of the eighteenth century into the first decade of the nineteenth. Creole spokesmen began to articulate the desire to exploit New Granada's untapped economic possibilities at least by the 1770s, and creole commentary, particularly on the desirability of developing nonbullion exports, became particularly notable from about 1790 onward.

Viceroys in New Granada began to emphasize this theme as early as the 1760s. Viceroy Messía de la Zerda (1761–1772) and his creole adviser, Francisco Antonio Moreno y Escandón, both pointed out in 1772 that the coastal provinces could export cattle hides, cattle, mules, dyewoods, cotton, indigo, and cacao. But Santa Marta and Riohacha could neither export these products to Spain nor obtain legally imported goods because Spanish ships rarely visited these ports. For this reason, the people of Santa Marta and Riohacha had no alternative to engaging in contraband trade with the British, Dutch, and French. And, while more Spanish ships came to Cartagena, Spanish merchants were interested in taking only gold in payment for imported goods. So if Cartagena wanted to export its crops and animal products, it too had to resort to contraband trade with the Caribbean islands.

The promulgation of Spain's "free trade" policy of 1778, which authorized trade among a greater number of Spanish and Spanish American ports, aimed to bring contraband trade into legal channels and to expand the overall volume of trade. This measure seemed to suggest the possibility that New Granada might now expand its legal exports of tropical products. However, the "free trade" policy brought only the most modest returns to New Granada. At the time that it was implanted, Spain was at war with Great Britain (1779–1783), and the British fleet virtually closed down trade between the Spanish Caribbean and Spain until the end of the war. A period of peace with England (1783–1795) brought some increase in New Granadan legal exports to Spain. However, in 1796–1802 and again 1805–1807 Spain was again at war with Great Britain. The high point of legal New Granadan exports of agricultural and forest products to Spain occurred during the brief window between 1802 and 1804.

During periods of war, maritime commerce did not stop. Rather, it continued as contraband or, when Spain permitted legal trade with neutrals, with the United States. Nonetheless, the instability and unpredictability of trading conditions after 1795 brought economic losses and frustration to creole merchants. A source of particular irritation to creole elites wishing to expand New Granadan exports was the inconsistency of Spanish policy. José Ignacio de Pombo, of the Cartagena merchants' guild, in 1807 pointed out that Spanish authorities more readily extended the benefits of neutral trade and the elimination of export taxes to Cuba and Venezuela while denying these advantages to New Granada. Although Pombo himself did not infer this, it might be concluded that Spanish merchants and policymakers conceived of Cuba and Venezuela as sources of agricultural exports but still viewed New Granada's role primarily as a source of gold bullion. Whether or not this was the case, New Granada reached the end of the colonial period without having developed, unlike Cuba, Venezuela, or Guayaquil, a strong pattern and tradition of exporting tropical crops.

New Granada thus remained to the end of the colonial period an ineffective exporter by comparison with most other parts of Spanish America. Between 1785 and 1796 Cartagena, the principal port of New Granada, took more than 8 percent of the goods exported from Cádiz, the principal Spanish port trading with Spanish America. But during the same years New Granada provided only a little more than 3 percent of Spanish American exports to Cádiz. By contrast, Venezuela, with a much smaller population than New Granada, supplied more than 9 percent of Spanish America's exports to Cádiz and absorbed more than 10 percent of Spanish America's imports from Cádiz.

Many of the Bourbon administrators' economic concerns involved the improvement of overland transportation. Whether the question was sending flour from the interior to the Caribbean coast, supplying the mines, or increasing exports, the opening up and maintenance of mule trails over the viceroyalty's mountainous terrain was widely recognized as central to its development. But, despite discussion of the need for better communications, the viceregal government did little to improve the mule trails—understandably, perhaps, taking into account the fiscal burden imposed by sustaining the military strength of Cartagena. From about 1790 onward, educated creoles increasingly found fault with the Spanish regime for not doing enough to improve internal communications and for obstructing the development of external trade.

NEW GRANADA'S ENLIGHTENMENT

In the belief that it might aid economic improvement, the Spanish viceroys sponsored the introduction of contemporary natural science. An early, and probably the most important, agent of the scientific Enlightenment in New Granada was José Celestino Mutis, who came to Santafé in 1761 as the personal physician of Viceroy Pedro Messía de la Zerda. Mutis had studied botany at the new botanical garden in Madrid, but, as was typical of the age, his scientific interests ranged quite broadly. In Santafé he taught mathematics and Copernican astronomy at the Colegio del Rosario. Mutis's teachings, particularly the Copernican cosmology, represented a radical departure from the Ptolemaic notions then still entrenched in the Spanish world, and the heliocentric cosmology he taught soon came under attack by the Dominican order, the institutional guardian of Thomist thought. The struggle to control the content of secondary education went on for at least four decades, with the "philosophy" course required of all secondary students sometimes being given by those in the Scholastic tradition, sometimes by adherents of the new natural science. As late as 1801 teachers of the new physics had to defend themselves against clerical charges of impiety. Later, when the Spanish regime began to collapse after 1808, some educated creoles blamed the Spanish regime for keeping their American subjects in scientific backwardness, even though various viceroys had sympathized with and supported the cause of scientific enlightenment.

Under the stimulus of Mutis, and despite the resistance of some clergy, there emerged a clutch of upper-sector creoles committed to the study and propagation of modern science. From the 1780s onward New Granadan elites—both royal administrators and creole intellectuals—began increasingly to emphasize the practical applications of science to the economy. One expression of this were attempts to found "Sociedades de amigos del pais"—"patriotic" societies—whose primary interest was economic improvement. Such societies, modelled on similar bodies then emerging in Spain, were attempted in Medellín and the province of Cartagena in 1781 and in Mompox in 1784. (The Cartagena and Mompox societies both were aimed primarily at encouraging the cultivation of cotton.) During these same years, the Spanish government was making efforts to improve mining production by sending mining engineers and technicians to New Granada. And in 1782 Archbishop-Viceroy Caballero y Góngora sponsored Mutis's proposal for a natural history survey. Although the survey was called the Botanical Expedition, its participants actually interested themselves in much more than botany—including astronomical and meteorological observations and the elaboration of a map of New Granada. The Expedition for a time also came to be charged with supervising the collection and export of cinchona bark and cinnamon and the planting of indigo and nutmeg.

The Botanical Expedition had several effects beyond collecting information on New Granada's plants and encouraging some vegetal exports. A corps of creoles who worked with Mutis on the Expedition became interested in natural science. Further, in the process of their investigations into New Granada's natural resources, they developed both a stronger identification with their homeland as a country and a belief in its economic possibilities. The Botanical Expedition, by fostering scientific and economic patriotism among the creole elite, provided part of the attitudinal foundation for the eventual move toward independence from Spain.

Along with stimulating more interest in economic progress, the growth of creole interest in the natural sciences may also ultimately have facilitated the introduction of Enlightenment political ideas. This is harder to establish than the development of scientific and economic patriotism, as during the 1790s it became risky for colonial elites publicly to espouse unorthodox political ideas. Nonetheless, it does appear that at least some of the standard Enlightenment writings with political implications were borne into New Granada on the same tide and by the same channels as modern works of natural science. The men who conducted research in natural history and meteorology also tended to know something about Enlightenment writers on economic, social, and political topics. Many of the participants in the Botanical Expedition were active later in the movement for independence from Spain.

REVENUES AND REBELLION

While Bourbon administrators wanted to foster economic improvement and, to that end, the introduction of modern science, their chief preoccupation was to increase revenue. Revenues were needed in part to pay for the more elaborate administrative establishment of a viceregal government, as well as to help sustain the frontier missions. But war in various ways multiplied these needs. Because of the constant threat of war, even in peacetime troops and patrol ships on the Caribbean coast had to be supported, and fortifications constantly had to be improved and repaired. In time of war all of these expenses increased. Through the 1770s the viceregal government of the New Kingdom of Granada was not able to meet all of these demands. It could pay administrative salaries and more or less attend to the defense of Cartagena, but the much richer Viceroyalty of Peru had to sustain the fortification of the Isthmus of Panama, while the Viceroyalty of New Spain (via its Cuban dependency) took care of the coast guard. Focusing their attention on war, royal officials in New Granada invested very little in basic development projects, such as the improvement of overland transportation.

In the 1750s viceregal administrators began to push seriously for more effective revenue collection. A government monopoly of the sale of cane liquor, initially established on a rather loose basis in 1736, was tightened in the 1750s and soon became a significant revenue earner. In the 1760s the royal government established monopoly control of the sale of tobacco, which also became an important source of income. Later, between 1776 and 1780, in time of war, officials tightened up the cane liquor and tobacco monopolies, raised prices for both liquor and tobacco, and doubled existing sales tax exactions, among other impositions.

These innovations did help to increase revenues. Greater fiscal resources enabled the Viceroyalty of New Granada to become less dependent upon the richer viceroyalties in Peru and Mexico for military expenditures. By the middle of the 1780s New Granada could assist the defense of Panama and sustain the coast guard, and by the 1790s was aiding Venezuela. Nonetheless, the viceroyalty generally was unable entirely to support the costs of its own administration and defense.

Although the Bourbon administrators succeeded in increasing revenues in the latter half of the eighteenth century, new exactions came at the price of stirring widespread revolt. Riots against the fiscal monopoly of cane liquor (*aguardiente*) began to occur as early as 1752, and in 1764–1767 a rash of protests spread through the viceroyalty. In Quito in 1765, crowds of perhaps ten thousand clamored against the liquor monopoly and a tightened collections of the sales tax. The Quito upheaval soon was followed by lesser disturbances in the Cauca Valley (Popayán, Cali, and Cartago), in some of the principal gold-mining regions of the West (Raposo and the Chocó), and in the upper Magdalena Valley. The riots of the 1760s frightened royal officials, who became painfully aware of their lack of military power to suppress popular rebellion. Viceroy Pedro Messia de la Zerda, who had to weather the 1760s upheavals, reported at the end of his term in 1772 that he lacked the military forces required to control the situation even in case of local rebellion. Except in a few places, like Cartagena, where military units were concentrated, he reported, governmental authority depended entirely upon the good will of the inhabitants:

> Without their consent there is no force, there are no arms or faculties with which the authorities can make themselves respected and obeyed; . . . ruling is very risky and the good result of government measures is exceedingly contingent . . . [One is obliged] to operate with fear and at times without entire freedom, accommodating oneself by necessity to the circumstances.

The pattern of war-induced tax exactions followed by rebellion was repeated, on an even larger scale, in 1776–1781. In 1779 Spain once again was at war with Great Britain and was in need of increased revenues for the war effort. In this case the drama was intensified by a more centralized approach to colonial administration in Spain, carried out in a ramrod spirit under the leadership of José de Gálvez, who became minister of Marine and the Indies in 1776. Gálvez, who had served as a special emissary of Bourbon centralism in Mexico (1765–1771), was a firm believer in tightening the administrative system, which to him meant, among other things, trusting important colonial positions to Spaniards rather than creoles, particularly to

Spaniards as zealous and uncompromising as he. In pursuit of his reformist, centralizing goal, Gálvez created the new office of regent, a royal officer who was supposed to serve as the viceroy's chief administrative officer. In fact, as Gálvez's regents were his creations, they had his ear and thus, in effect, more power than the viceroys. Gálvez's chosen agent in New Granada was Juan Francisco Gutiérrez de Piñeres, a Spanish bureaucrat who had no previous experience in the New World but who was, like his chief, amply supplied with arrogance. Gutiérrez de Piñeres's single-minded pursuit of revenue provoked the Comunero rebellion of 1781, which for a time brought the authority of Spanish administrators close to total collapse.

Although Gutiérrez de Piñeres's actions sharpened the crisis, it had its origins before his arrival in Santafé de Bogotá in 1778, with protests against the actions of the royal tobacco monopoly. Tobacco was an ideal crop for small farmers because it could be grown on a small plots yet generate a product of relatively high value. In the 1770s, poor farmers in many parts of the Guanentá region cultivated tobacco on their tiny plots. From 1776 through 1778, however, the government tobacco monopoly progressively restricted the areas in which the leaf might legally be grown. By 1778 legal cultivation of tobacco was limited to only one parish in the Guanentá. Further, the monopoly police vigorously enforced the restrictions, ripping up all tobacco plants outside permitted areas and arresting and imprisoning violators. All of this occurred in the context of a period of food scarcities and a smallpox epidemic in the Guanentá, in which some six thousand are said to have died. In 1778 the Guanentá began to react against the restriction of tobacco cultivation. In February 1778 people in Mogotes drove off the monopoly guards; in October 1780 there were riots in Mogotes and Simacota, in December in Charalá.

Meanwhile Gutiérrez de Piñeres was conceiving new ways to raise revenues. In May 1780, he doubled the retail prices that consumers paid to the government monopolies on tobacco and *aguardiente*. In August 1780, to cut down on contraband imports, he reenforced an elaborate system of checks on commerce known as the *guías* and *tornaguías*. He then proceeded to increase sales taxes and tighten their collection. Toward this end he resurrected the Armada de Barlovento, a sales tax exacted in the seventeenth century to support the Caribbean fleet, but which long ago had been merged with another sales tax, the *alcabala*, and forgotten. Resurrecting the Armada de Barlovento exaction in effect doubled the sales tax. The Armada de Barlovento was particularly grievous to people in the Guanentá, as raw cotton and cotton yarn were among the commodities affected, and the Guanentá was the chief center of cotton weaving in the viceroyalty. For poor people in the Guanentá, these measures eliminated one of their chief bases of support, tobacco, and endangered a second, cotton weaving.

The conjunction of the new exactions provoked a series of riots, usually on market days, which brought crowds to the towns. In Socorro, on March 16, 1781, people protested against the Armada de Barlovento tax, but in later demonstrations in surrounding towns in the Guanentá, the protests expanded to include the tobacco and *aguardiente* monopolies as well as the sales tax. Initially the most visible participants were the poor, women as well as men, who, in crowds sometimes numbering two thousand or more, destroyed government stocks of tobacco and cane liquor, released those imprisoned for cultivating tobacco illegally, and even on occasion stoned symbols of royal authority. If the poor were throwing the stones, men of somewhat more middling fortune—butchers, weavers, cattle traders, and small farmers—appear to have organized the rebellion. Throughout a month of assaults upon government revenue offices most local notables attempted to steer clear of the ruction. Ultimately, however, these men of substance came to accept formal positions of leadership.

Gutiérrez de Piñeres reacted to the Guanentá upheaval in two ways. First, he attempted to remove some of the impetus for the movement by suspending collection of the Armada de Barlovento on cotton and cotton yarn. Immediately thereafter he moved to repress the insurrection. The fact was, however, that the viceregal government had pitifully little force with which to oppose the rebels. The available regular military consisted of only seventy-five halberdiers. Fifty of these, along with some twenty monopoly police, were sent north to repress the rebellion. This small force proved ludicrously inadequate to the task. The Comuneros organized village militias, which, upon receiving news of the military expedition coming north from the viceregal capital, early in May 1781 marched south and frightened into submission the puny royal force sent to subdue them.

Meanwhile, the upheaval had spread beyond the Guanentá. During the month of May assaults on royal revenue offices or other forms of rebellion occurred in at least twenty towns in the eastern highlands, and corresponding movements occurred in the principal towns of the eastern lowland plains. Ultimately the tax rebellion extended through much of the upper Magdalena Valley and found occasional echoes as far away as some gold-mining settlements in Antioquia. More than sixty towns and villages took part.

By the end of May 1781 the Comuneros, variously estimated at 15,000 or 20,000 in number, were camped just north of the capital, which was virtually defenseless before this mass of aroused insurgents. The regent had fled the capital, seeking safety first in the river port of Honda, and then on the coast in Cartagena. The remnants of government in Santafé de Bogotá, with Archbishop Antonio Caballero y Góngora the leading effective authority, averted the insurgents' seizure of the capital only by acceding to a list of thirty-five Comunero demands. Although the list was composed by upper-sector leaders, many of the demands clearly welled up from the angry mass of the Comuneros. They called for a host of taxes to be ended or reduced. The Armada de Barlovento was to be abolished forever and the regular sales tax limited; fiscal monopolies of tobacco and playing cards were also to be ended, and the *aguardiente* monopoly was to lower the price of cane liquor to former levels; a wartime headtax donation levied on all subjects was to be revoked. The implementation of all of these provisions would have meant the abandonment of virtually all of the new Bourbon revenue measures of the previous two decades.

Still other articles expressed a generalized hostility toward Spanish colonial administrators. In addition to insisting upon the expulsion of Gutiérrez de Piñeres, the Comuneros stipulated that future administrative appointments should go preferentially to creoles rather than to Spaniards. The wording of this demand clearly expresses colonial anger at their Spanish overlords, while also asserting creole equality and a sense of at least incipient national identity:

> in government positions of the first, second, and third level the nationals of this America are to be preferred and privileged above the Europeans, since the latter daily show the antipathy which they maintain against the people here . . . [and since] they ignorantly believe that they are masters and the Americans are all, without differentiation, their inferior servants; and so as not to perpetuate this blind practice, only in case of necessity, according to their ability, good inclination and sympathy for the Americans, can they be equally appointed, as all of us are subject to the same King. . . .
>
> [W]e ought to live in a brotherly fashion; and he who attempts to dominate and advance himself more than is suitable to equality . . . will be separated from our community.

This insistence on the appointment of creoles to some extent represented a reaction of high-born creoles to the Spanish practice of keeping *criollos* out of the most important administrative positions. But the anti-Spanish reaction reflected more than the defense of the interests of upper-class creoles. In the Comunero riots even poor mulattoes, who clearly were not potential candidates for administrative office, expressed resentment against Spanish functionaries, whom they considered arrogant and insensitive. The poor, after all, were those most likely to be harassed and jailed by tax collectors and the monopoly police.

The archbishop, having acquiesced in the Comuneros' demands to avoid seizure of the capital, persuaded the rebels to return to their homes. After the fervor of rebellion cooled somewhat in the Guanentá, and reinforcements of royal troops arrived from Cartagena, the archbishop was able to restore order. Once the rebels were demobilized, the royal government carried out exemplary punishments. José Antonio Galán, who had persisted in rebellion after the capitulation of June 1781, and three other Comuneros were hanged in January 1782; their heads, hands, and feet were placed on poles in public squares of the capital and the towns that had figured notably in the rebellion. Others among the more active rebels were sentenced to two hundred lashes, public shame, and imprisonment in Africa. Landless peasants in the Guanentá were sent as colonists to the Isthmus of Panama, where many doubtless died in its hot, tropical environment. The penalties levied upon more affluent participants were less horrendous; some were simply impris-

oned in Cartagena. Years afterward, it was said, some people in the Guanentá still lived scattered in the forests, fearing possible retribution.

Once the most severe punishments had been administered, royal officials felt safer and in March 1782 revoked the agreement with the Comuneros
on the ground that it had been obtained under threat of force. Subsequently,
in August 1782, Caballero y Góngora, now as viceroy as well as archbishop,
conceded a general amnesty to the Comuneros. The troubles were not entirely over in Socorro province, however. In October 1783 the archbishop-
viceroy reported to the minister of the Indies that some forty men "of low
extraction" had entered the town of Charalá, allegedly with the intention of
killing the local authorities, robbing the more well-to-do and starting an uprising. Although this venture was easily put down, viceregal officials remained uneasy. Caballero y Góngora had further heard that the respect and
"subjection" in which he had been held in the province was turning to
hatred. The archbishop-viceroy was convinced that both the Comunero
rebellion of 1781 and the present unease were the work of discontented
upper-sector creoles in the capital, who had poisoned the minds of the country folk. He concluded that New Granadans needed to be restrained by a
strong hand.

Not all Spanish officials agreed, however, that an iron hand was the best
solution. Francisco Silvestre, the governor of Antioquia at the time, believed
that colonial administrators should follow a policy of conciliation to diminish distrust between Spaniards and creoles. He called for banishing "the enmity between European Spaniards and American Spaniards," by placing
them "reciprocally" in political, military, and church positions. Without such
a policy, Silvestre predicted, there would be constant "envy, disunion, and
rivalry," which some day could cause Spain to lose New Granada.

Scholars who have studied the Comunero rebellion have disagreed on
its significance. Some Colombian historians have considered it a precursor
of the movement for independence from Spain. Others have depicted it as
simply a protest against new taxes, with no connection to the struggle for
independence nearly thirty years later. Several considerations support the
latter view. The social character of the Comunero rebellion was rather different than the movement for independence proved to be. The Comunero
rebellion seems to have been a protest welling up from the masses, over
which local notables initially had slight, if any, control. (Some subsequent
interpretations have followed Archbishop Caballero y Góngora in believing
that the rebellion was fostered by creole elites in Santafé. However, creoles
in the capital appear to have seconded the movement only after it already
had been initiated by the common people in the Guanentá.) Further, many
in the creole elite were frightened by the mass rioting of the Comunero rebellion, aided in its containment, and either acquiesced in or supported its
repression. By contrast, local notables led, and for the most part controlled,
the movement for independence that occurred as a consequence of the imperial crisis that began in 1808. Furthermore, the Comuneros did not actually call for independence from rule by the Spanish monarch. With the

occasional exception of some crowd attacks on the royal coat of arms, the rebels invariably pledged their loyalty to the king, blaming Spanish colonial administrators for the hated taxes. The Comunero movement largely conformed to the traditional formula for rebellion in the Spanish world—"Long live the king, and death to bad government."

On the other hand, the Comunero movement can be seen as foreshadowing independence in its manifestation of anger toward Spanish administrators and in a correlative desire for government by locals. Colonial hostility to Spaniards had been expressed in various ways through most of the eighteenth century. Now, for the moment at least, there occurred an explicit demand that the royal government have a more creole face. This was far from a cry for independence. But it represented a step toward something like the development of nationalist sentiment. Furthermore, in later years neither the New Granadan populace nor their Spanish colonial rulers forgot the Comunero revolt. The events of 1781 resonated strongly in 1793–1797, when, once again in time of war, the viceregal government faced what it took to be another crisis, and also in the imperial crisis of 1808–1810, which precipitated the movement for independence.

THE CRISIS OF THE 1790s

The crisis of the 1790s in New Granada occurred in the context of the successful establishment of republican government in the United States and the dramatic events of the French Revolution. Spanish colonial officials who in the 1780s had encouraged scientific aspects of the Enlightenment in the 1790s now began to see in the English-American and French revolutions the spreading poison of those currents of contemporary political thought that questioned monarchy and fostered republican government.

This shift in focus became evident during the rule of Viceroy Josef de Ezpeleta (1789–1797). It was manifest in the newspaper Ezpeleta sponsored, the country's first regularly published periodical, the *Papel Periódico de la Ciudad de Santafé de Bogotá* (1791–1797). When the *Papel Periódico* first appeared, its editor, the viceroy's Cuban protégé, Manuel del Socorro Rodríguez, placed himself in the ranks of the modernists by supporting rationalism and taking the side of contemporary natural science against the defenders of old Scholastic notions. He, like other educated creoles, was a scientific and economic patriot. He printed essays that defended American capacities, as against European assertions of American degeneration. Other essays depicted Muisca culture before the Spanish conquest in a positive light. Rodriguez took an interest in encouraging exports of agricultural products, among other things devoting many issues to a discourse on cinchona by José Celestino Mutis. And he encouraged the establishment of patriotic societies to promote economic progress.

By July 1791, however, Rodríguez had become alarmed by the French Revolution. Without abandoning his commitment to modern science or to scientific and economic patriotism, he condemned the Revolution's assaults on monarchy and the Church, for which he blamed, in part, the works of Voltaire and Rousseau. Soon Rodríguez was worrying about the influence of both the French and English-American revolutions. Although Rodríguez did not express hostility to the English-American Revolution in the newspaper, in a private letter to Spain in April 1793 Rodríguez lamented the advance of its republican influences. "Since the erection as a free republic of the Angloamerican provinces," he said, things had taken a different turn in Spanish America. "All those who pride themselves on being enlightened are enthusiastic eulogists" of the North American revolutionists, and Santafé's literary gatherings were discussing, "and even forming plans," to emulate North American independence. More recently, the French Revolution had given "a new vigor to these pernicious reasonings," and Rodríguez was alarmed by "the spirit of infidelity" that he saw everywhere. In *tertulias* (social gatherings) republican enthusiasm had reached such a point that people were "praising the rights of nature and humanity, forgetting that there are sovereigns, laws, and religion." Such anxieties became still more acute after June 1793 when news that Spain was at war with revolutionary France reached Santafé de Bogotá.

In this context the political crisis of 1794–1795 broke over Santafé de Bogotá. Most of the actors in that drama were of the colonial elite, in contrast with the popular upheaval of the Comuneros. A central figure in the events was Antonio Nariño, the creole son of a Spanish royal administrator, who was married to the daughter of another high-ranking Spanish official. Aided by his families' social rank and political position, he was appointed treasurer of the tithe in Santafé. He also was exporting sugar and cinchona bark to, and importing cloth from, Spain. A man with an active mind, he possessed a library of some 2000 volumes. Nariño in some ways typified the late colonial Enlightenment in having a gentleman's interest in the natural sciences; nearly sixty of the tomes in his library dealt with physics, botany, and other scientific topics. He also gravitated to modern social and political philosophies; it was later discovered that seventy-eight of his books were on the Inquisition's list of condemned titles. Among the authors in his library were Voltaire, Diderot, Mably, and such critics of Spanish colonialism as Raynal and Robertson. By 1789 Nariño had written an essay clearly influenced by Rousseau. About the same time he was hosting *tertulias*, in which the most select of Santafé's intellectuals, including several enlightened priests, would read and discuss Spanish newspapers. Nariño planned to decorate a room he called his "sanctuary" in a mode that might be termed "Enlightenment kitsch." The walls were to celebrate Liberty, Philosophy, Reason, and Minerva, goddess of wisdom and invention. Each of the walls was to be bedizened with linked representations of classical and modern figures, attended by appropriate inscriptions. Among the groupings were Socrates and Rousseau, representing "truth, solitude, disinterest" and "the study of the hearts of men in all nations;" Pliny and Buffon, the study of nature; Tacitus and Raynal, the knowledge of nations and men; Xenophon and Washington, as "intrepid philosophers and warriors;" and Cicero, Demosthenes, and William Pitt, orators and philosophers who loved their countries. Some, like "the divine Plato" and Newton, merited individual citations. The image of Benjamin Franklin was to bear the legend: "With his hands he took the lightning from the heavens and the sceptre from the tyrants."

Nariño's political enthusiasms proved to be his undoing. In 1793, in another detail typical of the late colonial Enlightenment, Viceroy Ezpeleta's nephew, who was captain of the viceregal guard, lent Nariño a copy of a history of the French Constitutional Assembly, a book that Nariño later said came from the library of the viceroy himself. In it Nariño found the Declaration of the Rights of Man, which he translated and had secretly printed at his press, for private distribution. For months this went unnoticed. But ultimately Nariño paid dearly. His printing of the Declaration of the Rights of Man came at a time when Spain had joined the European alliance fighting against the French Revolution. In 1794 anything French appeared especially dangerous to royal officials.

In February 1794 the viceroy was told that a French physician, Luis de Rieux (a close friend of Nariño), had asserted in a Santafé *tertulia* that it was time to "shake off the yoke of despotism and form an independent republic after the example . . . of Philadelphia." The viceregal government, of course, was alarmed by this news. But it became truly hysterical only in August 1794, when three students at the Colegio del Rosario posted a pasquinade that both recalled the Comunero protest against tax exactions and threatened the end of Spanish rule:

> If they don't remove the revenue monopolies,
> If the oppression does not cease,
> What was robbed will be lost,
> The usurpation will meet its end.

This message, along with another lampoon mocking the judges of the Audiencia, stirred the latter to panic, further exacerbated by reports of Nariño's edition of the Declaration of the Rights of Man. The judges' investigations of these events quickly escalated when a Spaniard, who may have initiated the pasquinades prank, tried to improve his standing with the judges by informing on his youthful collaborators, spicing his testimony with the claim that they were part of a conspiracy to start an uprising against Spanish rule. Readily believing these charges, Viceroy Ezpeleta immediately called upon the clergy to preach against heresy and infidelity, while sending out warnings to Spanish governors as far away as Venezuela and Cuba.

The crisis of 1794–1795 revealed the sense of weakness and vulnerability of those who ruled the viceroyalty and the extent of the antagonism and distrust that had built up between "European Spaniards" and "American Spaniards." Fearing an uprising, the viceroy put his troops on alert and gave orders not to permit the entry of creoles into military barracks. In conducting their investigations of the supposed conspiracy, the Audiencia judges trusted the assistance only of European Spaniards. They searched the homes of creole residents for weapons and of creole intellectuals for dangerous books. One of those whose books were inspected suspiciously was Camilo Torres Tenorio, then a professor of law in the Colegio del Rosario, and later one of the principal leaders of independence in Santafé.

The royal officials' general suspicion of all creoles offended the creole-dominated cabildo of Santafé, which complained that the viceregal government was attempting systematically to impugn the reputations of the most respectable Patricios, as upper-class creoles often preferred to call themselves. The fears and resentments between creoles and Spaniards soon found further expression when the viceroy, acting at the behest of the Spaniards in Santafé, annulled the cabildo's election of two creoles as alcaldes and inserted a Spaniard into one of the positions. The Audiencia judges asserted that they could not trust creole alcaldes to provide them with the police assistance they needed.

Meanwhile, the judges of the Audiencia—in the prosecution of Nariño, the students of the pasquinades, and the supposed insurrection conspiracy—were subjecting suspects to all manner of arbitrary treatment. Nariño in his trial defended his printing of the Declaration of the Rights of Man by pointing out that the principles of popular sovereignty had been published in Spanish newspapers, some of them in articles by one of the judges of the Audiencia itself. Worse, the judges learned that Nariño's defense was being copied and handed about among the creole elite. The judges responded by sending Nariño's defense counsel, his brother-in-law José Antonio Ricaurte, to prison in Cartagena, without trial. Not surprisingly, no one wanted to take Ricaurte's place in Nariño's defense. (Years later Ricaurte died in his Cartagena prison, still not having been tried or even charged.) Nariño himself was sentenced to ten years in prison in Africa, perpetual exile, and the confiscation of all his property. His printer was condemned to three years' prison in Cartagena and was prohibited from working again as a printer.

At the same time, in the pasquinade and insurrection cases, the judges of the Audiencia imprisoned many young creoles without charge, subjecting them to intimidation and stretching one on the rack. After two years in prison in Santafé, the three students of the pasquinades were condemned to six to eight years in prison in Spanish Morocco, to be followed by perpetual exile. As late as 1806, having completed their sentences, they were still seeking permission to return to New Granada. Ten others, suspected of conspiring to rebel, were never tried but nonetheless were sent to prison in Spain on the grounds that, because of their local connections, they could not be held securely in Santafé and that their conversations might corrupt the troops guarding them. Also, because of conflicts in the suspects' testimony, the judges thought it necessary to use torture, which if performed in Santafé could "exasperate" the locals and provoke a reaction. (They blamed the "lack of suitable instruments" for the failure to elicit damning evidence in torture already applied.) The judges sent one of the ten, Francisco Antonio Zea, to prison in Spain even though they admitted there was no real evidence against him. "Considering his education and his intimate friendship with Nariño and Rieux" and the fact that he was "clever and restless," they believed his presence in New Granada to be "noxious and harmful." Zea spent five years in prison, followed by years of exile in Spain.

The alleged conspiracy was, in fact, just talk, and the evidence all hearsay. But the talk, as revealed in investigative testimony, gives a glimpse of the mental furniture of New Granadan university students in the 1790s. They apparently lacked much reading material to nourish their thoughts. The notion that the Spanish conquistadores were usurpers who had treated the Indians cruelly was circulating among them. They were aware that the writings of Bartolomé de Las Casas were considered dangerous because of his condemnations of the Spanish conquest, but claimed that none had ever seen any of his works. The students evidently were stimulated by the French Revolution and vaguely hoped for the implantation of a republican system, but unlike Nariño they showed no clear sign of acquaintance with the political philosophers of the Enlightenment. And they wondered whether there might be a repetition of the Comunero upheaval.

The Comunero rebellion had an even stronger resonance in the mind of Antonio Nariño. Nariño escaped his captors upon reaching the port of Cádiz in Spain and went to Madrid to see if he might obtain a royal pardon. Having learned that a pardon was unlikely and fearing capture, he traveled to France, where he talked with Hispanic American conspirators. Then, in England, he discussed with the British government possible aid for an independence movement, but lost interest when he concluded that the British wished to take the place of the Spanish as colonial masters. By 1797, he secretly had returned to New Granada. There his behavior indicated a continuing ambivalence toward the authority of the Spanish Crown. He still hoped for a royal amnesty. But, while he waited for that good news, he studied the possibilities of an uprising—to start in the Guanentá, the land of the Comuneros. Nariño, in disguise (sometimes as a priest) and taking back roads, traveled around the northern provinces, taking the political temperature of people in general but talking most particularly to priests, whose influence he deemed of critical importance. He found that the *alcabala* (sales tax) still vexed the common people, who considered it a nuisance particularly because it was collected rigorously, even on items of very small value. The betrayal of the Comuneros by the local upper class, who saved themselves at the expense of the poor, still burned in popular memory. So also did the post-rebellion repression—most particularly the fate of those condemned to colonize the Isthmus of Panama. Nariño found the people of the Guanentá "generally discontented," although too ignorant to begin a rebellion on their own.

Nariño had worked out in some detail a plan for insurrection. It was in many ways a late colonial version of the kind of caudillesque scheme that sprouted now and again in the republican era. Nariño believed that a rebellion would have to begin in the countryside, not the capital. Country folk could be recruited because an uprising would bring a welcome interruption to the tedium of rural life. City people, he thought, would not be so easily aroused; anyway, there were royal troops in Santafé de Bogotá, and, as his own experience had shown, any kind of plotting in the capital would be easily discovered. Nariño planned to go to Palogordo, in el Socorro province, where there were "gangs of dangerous men" who could be won over with "promises." With these men he would present himself in a town on market day, where he expected to recruit more adherents. Then he would write to cabildos and priests of other towns to gain still more support. Nariño intended to finance his rebellion by seizing local revenue offices. And the Socorro region offered a population of some 70,000 that might be mobilized. Further, there were few troops in the capital, and aid could not come quickly from the Caribbean ports, if at all, because Spain was again at war with England at the time. Finally, the troops in Santafé de Bogotá were completely unfamiliar with, and could not cope with, the difficult terrain of the northern provinces. Nariño believed that, even without firearms, his recruits could hold off royal troops by seizing control of the leather traverses that were the only means of crossing the deep gorges of the Guanentá.

In the end, however, after his elaborate reconnaissance, Nariño remained ambivalent. He could not bring himself to insurgency, in part perhaps because he did not sense enough support from local priests. (Only two were clearly sympathetic—one of these was willing to cooperate as long as religion were not attacked. However, some others accepted the tracts proffered by Nariño, including Rousseau's Social Contract and a copy of the French constitution.) After reconnoitering the Guanentá, Nariño returned to Santafé and confessed all, first to the archbishop, who promptly reported the confession to the viceroy. Nariño had hoped through a full confession to receive clemency, but Spanish authorities considered him too dangerous to free and he remained imprisoned in Santafé until 1803, when he was released only because he seemed to be dying.

Antonio Nariño was an unusual man, hardly typical of the creole elite. But his dramatic activities throw light on the temper of colonial society as the eighteenth century neared its end. The crisis of 1794–1797 clearly reminded creole elites of the Comunero rebellion of 1781 and deepened the antagonism of some educated creoles toward their Spanish colonial rulers. The common people, at least in the northern provinces, as Nariño discovered, remained discontented with colonial taxes and, with creole leadership, could be induced to rebel. Royal officials also were vividly aware of the Comunero precedent and remained worried that they could not contain another rebellion, not only because royal armed forces were weak but also because, in case of emergency, they feared they could depend on few creoles to rally to support the government.

The growing alienation between Spanish authorities and creole elites is reflected in two differing responses to the crisis of the 1790s. In September

1796, Manuel del Socorro Rodríguez, the Cuban protégé of Viceroy Ezpeleta, wrote an earnest letter to Manuel Godoy, then the power behind the Spanish throne. Rodríguez, at that time still a fervent royalist, again warned that in New Granada "the spirit of independence and licentiousness" was "sinking ever deeper roots" and that the example of U.S. independence and their republican system had become compelling. Rodríguez attributed American alienation from the Spanish system to many ills, including the "contempt" that the clergy demonstrated for the poor and the behavior of provincial administrators who sought only to enrich themselves. He particularly stressed, however, the exclusion of Spanish Americans from high government positions. He noted much "exasperation" in "American spirits" because of the harshness with which they were treated, "and much more when they [know] that various European magistrates have advised, and continue to advise" that Americans not be appointed to government posts. Many educated and meritorious Americans, Rodríguez asserted, were capable of filling responsible positions, but the Spanish government disdained them. When ignorant Spaniards were given preference over well-educated American lawyers, these Spaniards became the object of American ridicule and Spanish Americans lost faith in Spanish royal government. If Spain wished to regain and hold the loyalty of Spanish Americans, it must appoint the best of them to higher office.

The alienation between Spanish governors and the Spanish Americans they ruled was further underlined by a contrasting letter, also written to Godoy in 1796, this one by Rodríguez's patron, the Spanish Viceroy Ezpeleta, speaking also for the judges of the Audiencia and the archbishop. Ezpeleta argued that, in order to keep its American colonies, the Spanish government should continue its policy of favoring Spaniards over Spanish Americans, on the ground that the peninsulares were more loyal to the government. Thus, in the 1790s alienation of a number of educated creoles already was clearly evident, but creoles and many Spanish administrators reached quite contrary conclusions about what should be done about it.

THE EVE OF INDEPENDENCE

The crisis of 1794–1797 brought to the surface creole discontent with the Spanish regime and a more generalized anger at Spaniards; however, in placid times these feelings tended to recede as ties of family, friendship, and business or professional relations between creoles and Spaniards once more came to the fore. To what degree did there exist as of 1800–1808 a basis for a movement for independence, beyond temporary crisis-induced mutual distrust between Spanish officials and Spanish immigrants, on the one hand, and creole elites, on the other? Did there also exist a positive basis for nationalism, in the sense of some shared sense of identity with New Granada as a place and a people? Events of 1810, and afterward would make clear that local and provincial identities remained strong; nonetheless, among at least some educated creoles there does appear to have emerged a nascent sense of a New Granadan identity before the end of the colonial era.

Benedict Anderson's much-cited *Imagined Communities* argues that late colonial newspapers, published in New Granada from 1791 to 1810, helped to develop a sense of shared community among creole elites in the various regions of New Granada. Newspapers, however, were not the only basis of interconnection among the various regions. University studies in Santafé's two colegios brought together students from various provinces and established relationships that were later maintained through private correspondence. As a medium of communication the newspapers had a limitation in that, as long as viceregal authority remained intact, they refrained from political commentary that might be regarded as questioning the existing order. Such political conversation does appear to have occurred, principally in *tertulias*, where European newspapers, in which political commentary was less restricted, were read and discussed. Probably to some extent, although the evidence is not ample, the ideas exchanged in *tertulias* reached other localities through private correspondence, including the mailing of foreign newspapers and books. However, New Granada's late colonial newspapers did serve an important function in serving as media for expression of a growing interest among the creole elite in their country as a land and as a land of economic potential.

One aspect of that sense of identification with the land was a glimmering of interest in indigenous culture, manifested in various articles in the *Papel Periódico* in 1793. Much more important in providing content for a nascent patriotism, however, was the role of the Botanical Expedition, which both recruited educated creoles from various provinces in a common project and stimulated their interest in the geography of New Granada, its resources and economic potential. This interest was already evident in articles in the *Papel Periódico*, but it found its maximum expression in Francisco José de Caldas's *Semanario del Nuevo Reino de Granada* (1808–1810), which featured geographical descriptions of various provinces, as well as articles on exploitable agricultural crops and forest products. Caldas himself emphasized New Granada's commercial as well as agricultural potential, predicting that, with coasts on both the Atlantic and the Pacific, it was destined to make the country an emporium of trade between Asia and Europe.

In response to the "free trade" policy of the 1770s and 1780s, as well as the initiatives of the Botanical Expedition, New Granada's interior became more attuned to exporting, first shipping relatively small quantities of cinchona bark beginning in the 1780s and then cotton and indigo from Socorro and the end of the 1790s and the first years of the nineteenth century. These exports from the interior reinforced an already existing trade in cattle hides and dyewood from the Caribbean coast and cacao from the lower Magdalena valley.

This period of modest growth in agricultural exports was accompanied by the emergence of a conscious economic liberalism. Pedro Fermín de Vargas, formerly the creole corregidor of Zipaquirá, around 1790 wrote essays promoting New Granadan economic development, in which he criticized colonial taxes and monopolies that constrained exports. Vargas's friend, Antonio Nariño, in 1797 also counseled Viceroy Pedro de Mendinueta that such taxes were inadvisable. Two of the late eighteenth-century viceroys were relatively liberal in economic policy—Ezpeleta (1789–1796) and his successor, Mendinueta (1797–1803). Both advised against government monopolies on exportable crops and supported tax remissions for them. Liberal economic tendencies, which in the 1790s were suggested by colonial self-interest, were reinforced during the first decade of the nineteenth century by the circulation of the ideas of Adam Smith among at least some in the elite. The most notable of those influenced by Smith in this decade was José Ignacio de Pombo, the leading intellectual force in the merchants' guild of Cartagena. But Smith's ideas were also penetrating into the provinces in New Granada's interior.

Developing interest in exporting tropical products and the oxygen of liberal economic ideas ultimately proved an explosive mixture, particularly when New Granada's hopes for commercial development were frustrated by chronic war between Great Britain and Spain (1796–1802, 1805–1807). Spain's inability to protect Spanish American commerce was made particularly evident during the war with England in 1805–1807. The brief period of peace between Spain and Great Britain in 1802–1804 had permitted exports of cotton, cacao, cattle hides, and dyewood to triple over previous years. Merchants in the interior, as well as on the coast, apparently took part in this commercial expansion. Because of the hopes raised by this experience, the renewal of war in 1805 had a particularly devastating impact on New Granadan exporters. The consequences of the interruption of trade by the war of 1805–1807 were dramatized in a letter written by José Acevedo y Gómez, a Santafé merchant and city councillor, on July 19, 1810, the day before he led the people of the capital in a decisive break with the Spanish regime. Acevedo recalled that during the war he had lost 120,000 pesos, the fruit of twenty years of work. The government, he said, had made him lose this money because he could not get his shipments to Spain and the viceroy would not permit trade with neutrals in the Caribbean. Acevedo lost his shipments of cinchona bark, his cacao spoiled, and the cotton, which the Spanish government required him to send to Cádiz, was captured by "an enemy powerful at sea." Thus, Acevedo said, "this barbarous Government has let my family perish." He concluded that he would consider his remaining funds in Spain well lost if thereby "my country [could] cut the chain with which it finds itself bound to the Peninsula," which by 1810 he considered a "perennial fountain of its tyrants."

This letter, written in the agitated days of July 1810, reflects the heated emotions of that time. But all was not frustration for creoles in the decades before 1810. In a number of respects it was a time of relative economic prosperity. Gold mining was expanding during the last decades of the eighteenth century. Economic growth in Antioquia, in particular, had a positive effect on the Guanentá region of the eastern highlands, which supplied Antioquia with cotton textiles. Population grew notably in the Guanentá, and tithe collections there more than tripled between 1780 and 1810. Somewhat more gradual, locally varied, economic expansion occurred in the other relatively settled and populated parts of New Granada's eastern zone.

By the beginning of the nineteenth century the relative prosperity fueled by the growth of the domestic economy and the modest expansion of export activity had become noticeable, at least in some parts of the viceroyalty. Viceroy Pedro de Mendinueta, on concluding his term in 1803, wrote that the somber picture of New Granada painted by Archbishop-Viceroy Caballero y Góngora in 1789 was no longer true. Caballero y Góngora had described a country that was "absolutely depopulated, without agriculture or industry, without commerce or communications . . . and abounding in impoverished people, idlers, and criminals." Less than fifteen years later, Mendinueta perceived a markedly different country. Mendinueta's New Granada had many flourishing towns—most notably the Magdalena River ports of Mompox and Honda; Medellín, the commercial center for Antioquia's flourishing gold mines; the weaving towns of San Gil and Socorro in the Guanentá; and San José and Rosario de Cúcuta, where cacao was grown for export as well as internal consumption. New Granada, Mendinueta reported, had not suffered any scarcities of basic foods for a long time. And because of its prosperity, revenues had increased.

Despite the frustrations brought by wartime interruptions of trade, creole elites in the decade before 1810 do not appear to have been markedly discontented with Spanish rule. A sense of the temper of the more politically alert of New Granada's creole elites in the decade preceding the outbreak of independence may be glimpsed in the letters of Miguel Tadeo Gómez of el Socorro, a cousin of the Santafé merchant, José Acevedo y Gómez. Miguel Tadeo Gómez in 1810 emerged as one of the most fiery leaders of the independence movement in the province of el Socorro, but the tone and content of his correspondence between 1801 and 1808 was far from revolutionary. Born in San Gil in 1770, the descendant of early colonizers of the Guanentá, Gómez had studied at the Colegio del Rosario in Santafé before moving on to appointments in revenue offices first in Popayán and then in el Socorro. In addition to his duties as a revenue administrator, Gómez pursued commercial speculations, including both the sale of cloth woven in el Socorro to markets within New Granada and the export of dyewoods and cinchona bark. Acutely aware of his isolation in provincial Socorro, he nonetheless participated in colonial intellectual life of the time. In 1803 he accompanied José Celestino Mútis on one of his botanical surveys, taking particular interest in the discovery of an alleged hybrid of a goat and a deer. (Could such a hybrid procreate, or was it like a mule?) From his friend José Joaquín Camacho, the creole corregidor of Pamplona, Gómez borrowed the works of such eighteenth-century French Enlightenment figures as Condorcet and

Condillac, as well as Gaspar Melchor de Jovellanos's report on agrarian reform, about which Gómez was so enthusiastic that he copied the whole thing. He evidently was also familiar with the ideas of Adam Smith, as in 1807 he spoke of having proposed to the viceregal government a reform plan based in part upon the doctrines of Jovellanos and Smith. Gómez's brush with Enlightenment thought, however, left his religious faith unimpaired. Fearful of smallpox and other illnesses and having lost his sons to disease, he sought to ward off danger through the fulfillment of religious vows at the shrine of Chiquinquirá.

By 1807, however, some notes of frustration shadow begin to shadow Gómez's aspirations. He now felt that "the royal officials [were] his opponents," preferring to "fill offices with their friends." He also warned his friend José Joaquín Camacho (recently removed from his position as corregidor in Pamplona) that if, as he expected, the intendancy system were implanted in New Granada, creoles' opportunities for government positions would become still more limited. As a private entrepreneur engaged in small-scale exporting of tropical products, Gómez by 1807 was anticipating the possibility of a regime of completely free trade—he asked Camacho to report to him on the commercial possibilities of Pamplona province, in particular the growth that would occur if there were complete freedom to send New Granadan products from any port in exchange for foreign goods. Unfortunately, like his cousin in Santafé, José Acevedo y Gómez, by July 1808 Miguel Tadeo Gómez had lost the fruits of ten years of effort in his export ventures.

In the first decade of the nineteenth century, hunger for unrestricted foreign trade and the influences of economic liberalism were becoming more evident, as was creole irritation at the preferment in office of less qualified Spaniards. But dramatic change in the system had to await events in Spain. In 1808 Napoleon seized the Spanish king and much of Spain, thereby ultimately bringing into question the source of authority of the Spaniards who governed the colonies. With the crisis of the empire, colonial administrators once again became tense, and the acute distrust between Spaniards and creoles that had been evident in 1781 and 1794–1797 again emerged.

6

Independence, 1808–1825

THE COLLAPSE OF THE SPANISH REGIME

Between 1780 and 1808 creole elites had developed increasingly critical attitudes toward the Spanish regime. Creoles trained in the law were conscious that Spaniards were preferred over them in appointments to government positions. Further, creole lawyers often considered the Spanish appointees arrogant, ill-educated, incompetent, and insufficiently concerned about local welfare. In effect, there were strains of mutual contempt between some Spanish administrators and creoles whose training and aspirations oriented them to government employment. Merchants, for their part, by 1808 were deeply aware of the disadvantages of operating within an imperial system too weak to defend the commerce of its citizens. Although the viceregal government had sponsored the Botanical Expedition, some educated creoles had come to believe that Spanish rule had kept New Granada in scientific and technical backwardness. And they successively noted, and were inspired by, the examples of the American and French revolutions. A few at least aspired to emulate what was generally known as the system of Philadelphia. Further, creoles, in Santafé at least, held in their memories Spanish distrust and arbitrary oppression during the crisis of 1794–1795.

Creole discontent with Spain and Spaniards, however, usually remained latent. Although historical sources point to some antagonism between creoles and Spanish immigrants, many upper-status creoles had Spanish fathers, uncles, or brothers-in-law, and Spaniards and creole notables both formed part of the dominant class. It was usually only in moments of crisis that mutual suspicion between Spanish officials and creole elites surfaced. When royal officials turned to Spanish immigrants as allies against creole elites, creole anger against the regime could be extended to Spaniards in general.

Nonetheless, decisive movement for independence awaited external events. The independence of New Granada, as well as the rest of Spanish America, was precipitated by the crisis, and then the disappearance, of the Spanish monarchy. For some years there had been clear signs of debility and corruption at the heart of the Spanish monarchy. Charles IV was widely considered a weak king, dominated by Manuel Godoy, his chief minister since 1793. In 1801 and again in 1807 Godoy had involved Spain in alliances with Napoleon to despoil Portugal. Both of these schemes provided excuses for Napoleon's armies to invade the Iberian peninsula, and in the latter case temporarily to dominate it. In November 1807 the Spanish Crown agreed to permit French armies to cross Spanish territory to conquer Portugal. After seizing Portugal, however, French troops stayed in Spain and by March 1808 more than 100,000 occupied the area north of the Ebro, which Napoleon demanded be ceded to France. In the context of this threat to Spanish sovereignty, a noble-directed popular upheaval at Aranjuez brought the arrest of Godoy, the renunciation of the throne by Charles IV, and the accession of his son Ferdinand. Soon, however, Napoleon induced both Charles IV and Ferdinand VII to come directly under his control, and in May 1808 he required both to cede the throne of Spain to him. Napoleon's attempt to appropriate Spain provoked widespread Spanish guerrilla resistance, led by local juntas.

Some well-informed creoles, from European newspapers and discussion at *tertulias*, had become aware that all was not well with the Spanish monarchy even before Napoleon struck his blow. Nonetheless, creole notables, as well as the rest of the populace, were shocked by the news of the captivity of the Spanish monarchs, which reached Santafé in August 1808. In early September Viceroy Antonio Amar y Borbón convoked a meeting of Spanish and creole notables to recognize the authority of the junta of Seville, in the absence of the captive Ferdinand VII. The creole elite, as much stunned by these events as their Spanish governors, joined in recognizing the Seville junta and pledged 500,000 pesos in financial aid to the junta's fight against the French. The Santafé cabildo, led by its alcalde, José Acevedo y Gómez, incorporated the emissary from Seville into its ranks as a regidor. And notables, creole and Spanish, wore silver medals to demonstrate their allegiance to Ferdinand VII.

But already there were some indications of stress between Spanish officials and creole elites. Some of the creoles who attended the September meeting later said they were irritated by the Seville junta's assertion of authority over Spanish America, by the perceived arrogance of the Sevillano representative, and by the viceroy's call for a vote without permitting them to speak. However, as of September 1808, creoles in New Granada appear to have been primarily concerned to support Spain and its royal family against the French enemy.

The various juntas in Spain could not long hold creole loyalties. If the disappearance of the king justified the creation of juntas in Spain, why should autonomous juntas not also be established in Spanish America? Furthermore, the authority of the ad hoc governments in Spain was undermined by their precariousness. Despite some significant Spanish victories against the French in mid-1808, toward the end of that year French armies, now 300,000 strong, began to dominate much of the peninsula. The credibility of the Junta Central was still further damaged by its efforts to prevent news of Spanish defeats from reaching Spanish America and to depict defeats as victories. To Spanish Americans during 1809 the surviving Spanish junta increasingly appeared both weak and prevaricating. Creole notables, not trusting the news they were getting from Spain, tended to believe the worst— that the French were about to wipe out the last vestiges of Spanish authority in the peninsula. And if the French succeeded in eliminating the last surviving Spanish junta, creole notables wondered, would their colonial governors not then recognize the French regime, just as they had recognized the Spanish juntas, in order to retain their positions?

Ironically, the efforts of successive juntas in Spain to bolster their own authority tended to undermine that of colonial officials. In self-justificatory propaganda sent to the colonies, Spanish juntas stressed the corruption of Manuel Godoy and the connivance with Napoleon that had occurred in the years preceding the imperial crisis. This propaganda emanating from Spain opened the way for creoles to question the authority of colonial officials, many of whom had been appointed by Godoy or during his period of primacy. New Granadan creoles came to denigrate the viceroy in Santafé and many Spanish provincial governors as "creatures of the vile Godoy."

As Spanish control over Spain dwindled, the importance of Spanish America in the empire ballooned. The huge colonial tail now was barely attached to an almost imperceptible metropolitan dog. Attempting to hold the loyalty of the people inhabiting its gigantic colonial appendage, the negligible ad hoc government in Spain adopted an increasingly conciliatory rhetoric. By January 1809, it was declaring that it did not consider Spanish dominions in America to be colonies, but rather integral parts of Spain. At the same time it invited the Spanish American colonies to elect representatives to a government that would govern Spain and Spanish America.

Such blandishments ultimately failed to persuade the more unquiet creole notables. For all the rhetoric of equality, it was clear that, in the minds of the Spanish junta, Spanish Americans were not really equal to Spaniards. Under the plan proposed by the junta, Spanish America would be grossly underrepresented. All of Spanish America, with a population at least equal in size to that of Spain, would have no more than a third as many representatives. New Granadan creoles cooperated in the process of electing their single delegate. But the underrepresentation of Spanish America increasingly signified to them an inequality of treatment that paralleled their exclusion from the highest colonial offices.

The disappearance of legitimate authority in Spain, the uncertainty about the future fate of Spain, and the insecurity of colonial officials activated and intensified the mutual distrust of Spaniards and creole elites. Tensions between Spanish governors and resident Spaniards, on the one hand, and creole notables, on the other, first burst into open conflict in Quito in 1809. In January 1809 the creole-dominated Quito cabildo broke with custom by electing creoles to both alcalde positions, rather than choosing a Spaniard for one of them. Spaniards in Quito responded by insisting that government officials arrest prominent creoles, whom they accused of engaging in a conspiracy to displace the colonial regime and form a junta. Quito's creoles, for their part, contended that local Spaniards were plotting to murder the creole nobility. Whether this plot was real or a creole invention, Quito's creole notables in August 1809 used it as ground for removing the Quito Audiencia and establishing an autonomous junta. The Quito notables also justified their action by alleging that they feared colonial authorities would embrace the French regime in Spain. If the disappearance of the monarchy warranted the resumption of sovereignty by local juntas in Spain, they further argued, Spanish Americans also should be able to establish similar self-governing juntas.

The creole revolution in Quito proved a defining event in New Granada, as, in their reactions to it, Spanish governors and Spanish residents came into conflict with the most outspoken creole leaders. The Spanish governor in Popayán, apparently with local support in Popayán and Pasto, collaborated in suppressing the Quiteño revolution. But in regions farther from Quito—in the Eastern Cordillera as well as the Magdalena valley—many creole notables were more sympathetic to the Quito movement. In two emergency meetings in Santafé de Bogotá in September 1809 the Spaniards present wanted to repress the Quiteño junta, while the creoles, although their views varied, generally urged conciliation. According to one of the *oidores* present, "almost all of the Santafé cabildo, supported by a swarm of lawyers, who with pretensions to wisdom, [wanted] to direct everything," urged following the example of Quito by forming juntas in all the provincial capitals in New Granada. Two lawyers, José Gregorio Gutiérrez Moreno and Frutos Joaquín Gutiérrez, proposed the formation of a junta in Santafé, presided over by the viceroy, suggesting that colonial officials were no longer widely trusted and therefore only with the incorporation of creole notables into a junta could New Granadans have confidence in the government and respect its orders. (The call to establish juntas found an echo some weeks later in the cabildo of the Magdalena port of Mompox, according to that city's outraged Spanish governor.)

The September 1809 meetings accentuated the mistrust between Spanish governors and creole notables in Santafé de Bogotá. Those creoles who had urged establishing a junta in Santafé were now suspect. The viceroy issued an edict threatening to punish anyone posting subversive placards or circulating news of French victories in Spain. And he sent a military expedition to put down the Quiteños. Some creole notables meanwhile apparently plotted to subvert or detain the military force bound for Quito, seize the viceroy, and set up an independent junta in Santafé. Among the apparent principals in the plots were the canon Andrés Rosillo, a son of Socorro; Luis Caicedo y Flórez, a wealthy landowner and alcalde in the Santafé cabildo; Pedro Groot, who as a royal treasurer in Santafé held one of the highest government positions enjoyed by a creole; the lawyers Ignacio Herrera and Joaquín Camacho (previously corregidor of Pamplona and at the time corregidor of el Socorro), and Antonio Nariño. Allegedly Nariño was to bribe the local garrison, and the creole military officer Antonio Baraya, while on guard in the viceregal palace, was supposed to arrest the viceroy. Domingo Caicedo, the son of Luís Caicedo y Flórez, was to mobilize black slaves from the family's immense landholdings in the Upper Magdalena valley, promising them freedom, while Miguel Tadeo Gómez, the administrator of the *aguardiente* monopoly in el Socorro, was expected to enlist volunteers from that region. Although a number of creoles were identified as participants in the aborted conspiracy, the Audiencia imprisoned only three, among them Andrés Rosillo, a canon in the cathedral, and Antonio Nariño. Nariño was arrested, one official source indicates, for attempting to go to Socorro to get support for establishing a creole junta. In the reaction to the events in Quito, if not before, we see evidence of coordinated action among creole elites in different provinces.

Some of those alleged to be involved in the conspiracy of 1809 also had been suspects in the crisis of 1794—notably Antonio Nariño and Sinforoso Mutis. Those who spoke out and/or plotted to act against the colonial regime in 1809 represented the advance guard of the movement for independence. As a group they were in many ways representative of the more educated part of the *criollo* elite. Of fifteen of the more visible, all but one had studied at the Colegio del Rosario or San Bartolomé. Those whose principal role was to speak tended, predictably, to be lawyers. Some of these held posts in the viceregal government (as *fiscal del crimen* or adviser to the mint, for example), but their principal political base was the Santafé cabildo. Among the alleged plotters, seven held positions in the colonial apparatus (three revenue or treasury officials, a corregidor, a military officer, a canon in the cathedral, and a section leader in the Botanical Expedition). Some of the fifteen were descendants of conquistadores or families that had lived in New Granada for several generations, much of whose wealth was in land; but eight had Spanish fathers who had come as merchants or royal officials. In either case, their social background was such that, as well born, highly educated creoles, they could well feel both a basis of authority to act in behalf of their compatriots and a sense of frustration at the limits of their position and authority within the colonial regime.

During and after the Quito crisis, several lawyers, all born in provincial towns, but educated and practicing in Santafé, played prominent roles in articulating creole grievances. They were Ignacio Herrera, born in Cali; Camilo Torres of a Popayán family; and Frutos Joaquín Gutiérrez from Cúcuta. Although their screeds were written under somewhat differing circumstances, they shared certain common themes. Spain had kept Spanish America in economic and cultural backwardness, and the Spanish regime had denied colonials acquaintance with modern science. The Spanish system had obstructed commerce and through revenue monopolies and outright prohibitions had denied freedom of industry. Two of their memorials mentioned Spain's "enslavement" or tyrannical treatment of the Indians. They complained of the corruption of the "vile Godoy" and extended their criticism to existing colonial officials, many of whom were the "creatures of Godoy." All objected to Spanish contempt for creoles and the unequal treatment of creoles, who were denied high office in Spanish America and would be underrepresented in the proposed government in Spain.

Torres's "Representación del Cabildo de Santafé" of November 1809, widely known as the "Memorial de Agravios," addressed the issue of representation most directly and fully. Only Spanish Americans, Torres argued, could represent Spanish American interests. He made the point in a way that permitted him to indict the whole of Spanish colonial governance. Spanish governors had come to America with the idea of making their fortunes and returning to government careers in Spain. Consequently, they took no deep and abiding interest in American problems:

> The ills of the Americas are not for them, they do not feel them. . . . A bad road is improved provisionally for their passage; they do not have to pass it a second time, and thus it does not matter to them that the unhappy farmer, who carries his products on his shoulders, must shed his sweat or his blood.

The Spanish governor, "in sum, does not know the problems of the people he rules. . . . [H]e only makes haste to gather riches to return with them to the land where he was born." Torres concluded that, since only Spanish Americans could know their own interests, it was not merely necessary to increase Spanish representation in Spain; beyond that, Spanish America should establish its own autonomous juntas like those in Spain.

In a context of growing distrust between Spaniards and creoles after the abortive revolution in Quito, the Audiencia in Santafé worried that the creole-controlled cabildo of Santafé might also attempt a revolution against viceregal authorities or in other ways behave disloyally. On the advice of the Audiencia, the viceroy in December 1809 inserted six trustworthy Spaniards into the cabildo and appointed another Spaniard as the cabildo's *alférez real*. The sharpening distrust between Spaniards and creole notables later found expression in a tiff in the cabildo between between the creole lawyer Ignacio Herrera and the Spanish *alférez real*.

The growing sense of crisis was intensified by the apparent collapse of the last remnants of authority in Spain itself. By February 1810, a newly formed Council of Regency governed little more of Spain than the port of Cádiz. With French forces controlling almost the whole of the Iberian peninsula, already-existing creole fears that Spanish colonial administrators would collaborate with French rule were further confirmed. Meanwhile, the Council of Regency inadvertently was doing its part to undermine both its authority and that of colonial officials. Desperate to retain Spanish American loyalty, the Regency, in calling for more American delegates to be incorporated into Spanish government, imprudently announced:

> From this moment, American Spaniards, you see yourselves elevated to the dignity of free men; you are no longer the same men bent under a yoke made . . . heavier by being . . . distant from the center of power; looked upon with indifference, harassed by greed, and destroyed by ignorance. . . . [Y]our destinies now depend neither upon ministers nor viceroys, nor governors; they are in your hands.

Such rhetoric, when combined with the Regency's tenuous toehold in Spain, further encouraged creoles to think of really removing the yoke and achieving the dignity of free men by establishing their own independent juntas. The thinking of at least one creole leader is reflected in a letter of May 29, 1810, from Camilo Torres to his uncle, an *oidor* in Quito. Torres noted that, with Spain apparently about to be engulfed by the French, the *oidores* in Santafé proposed to reestablish Spanish royal government in the Americas, with an American Cortes electing as regent some member of the Spanish royal family. Torres, however, rejected this solution. Either the Spanish monarchy existed or it did not. If it did not, then the contractual ties binding Spanish Americans to the Spanish Crown had ceased to exist, and sovereignty had returned to its origins, to the people, and Spanish Americans now were free and independent. They now had recovered the rights assigned to them by nature, reason, and justice. Nor would Torres accept the continuance of Spanish governors. Outraged by the recent appearance in Santafé of the heads of two creole youths executed after only a simulacrum of a trial (for having tried to start a rebellion in Casanare), Torres now was emboldened to denounce all Spaniards sent to rule New Granada. "Born and nurtured in ancient despotism, imbued with perverse maxims and accustomed to consider the people as vile slaves, these chiefs . . . are not fit for governing free men." In Torres's view, New Granadans should "imitate the conduct of the North Americans, let us follow the steps of this philosophical people, and then we will be as happy as they. Let us work, then, to form a government similar, and if possible, equal to that of those republicans."

Torres surely was not completely representative of creole notables as a class; doubtless he was more certain and more outspoken than most in his commitment to republicanism. But men sharing his vision in various parts of Spanish America were at this time reacting to the crisis in Spain by establishing independent juntas that quickly moved toward republican forms. On April 19, 1810, the cabildo of Caracas formed an autonomous government and other Venezuelan towns soon did the same. Evidently encouraged by the Venezuelan initiative, creole notables in Cartagena soon followed suit, in a two-step process on May 22–23 and June 14, 1810. In the decisive displacement of the Spanish governor on June 14, creole military officers, commanding largely American-born units, played a decisive role. Cartagena elites on June 14 also mobilized people from the relatively poor barrio of Getsemaní, using Pedro Romero, an artisan living in the barrio, as one of their chief agents. According to one retrospective account, Romero, whose family depended for its subsistence on work at the royal arsenal, at first was alarmed by the idea of trying to remove royal officials. However, once the process had begun, Romero and his Lancers of Getesemaní became important forces in the movement for independence in Cartagena. They subsequently were mobilized to press creole notables in Cartagena to declare absolute independence on November 11, 1811.

News of the establishment of juntas in Caracas and Cartagena helped to prompt similar actions in towns in New Granada's interior. Their acts were not entirely isolated. José María Castillo y Rada, who was born in Cartagena but was educated in Santafé and had practiced law there, linked elites in those two cities. Another cross-regional link was Antonio de Villavicencio, an aristocratic creole naval officer, who had been born in Quito, educated in Santafé, and at the time of the independence crisis was in Cartagena. Creole notables in other towns also were in communication with each other. In June and July 1810, Joaquín de Caycedo y Cuero, an aristocratic creole in Cali, was writing friends in Santafé and elsewhere, anticipating the establishment of a creole Junta Suprema in Santafé and the need for supporting provincial juntas. Similarly, at the end of June 1810, José Acevedo y Gómez in Santafé de Bogotá wrote a friend in Cartagena that it was necessary to establish a junta in the capital, with representatives from the various provinces. He seemed confident that the provinces would collaborate with such a junta. Creoles in Socorro, Pamplona, and Tunja had written the cabildo in Santafé complaining of the oppression of their Spanish corregidores and opposing recognition of the Regency in Spain. Shortly thereafter, these towns removed local Spanish governors and established juntas as provisional governments: Pamplona on July 4, el Socorro on July 10, and, finally, the capital on July 20.

Events in el Socorro were typical of the movements in 1810. As in Quito in 1809, a rumor spread that the corregidor in Socorro was planning to arrest and/or murder local creole leaders, most notably Miguel Tadeo Gómez. Demonstrations by Socorro's citizenry provoked gunfire from the local garrison, followed by a mass upheaval and the surrender of the corregidor and all of his forces. The Socorro elite then formed a junta, which pledged its allegiance to the absent Ferdinand VII, while vowing to resist both the "favorites of Godoy" (i.e., the current colonial officials) and any possible "emissaries of Bonaparte." The Socorro junta also wrote Santafé that it would send a force of two thousand men to demand the formation of a junta in the capital.

Creole leaders in Santafé apparently had been constrained by fear of the viceroy's military forces. But the formation of the juntas in Cartagena, Pamplona, and Socorro enabled them to act. The pattern of creole elite manipulation of the populace in Cartagena and el Socorro was repeated in the capital. With news of the juntas in Pamplona and el Socorro, they first spread a rumor that Spaniards intended to kill nineteen notable creoles, with Camilo Torres and José Acevedo near the top of the list. Having mobilized the *populacho* to defend the homes of the supposedly threatened creoles, on July 20, 1810, they provided the spark for a general explosion by deliberately provoking a dispute with a Spanish merchant known to be hostile to creoles.

As elsewhere, the revolution evolved from a movement for limited autonomy to a clear break with Spanish authority. On July 20, the creole leaders contended that they were merely creating an emergency government in the absence of the king. Initially they claimed loyalty not only to Ferdinand

VII but also to the Regency in Cádiz. At first, also, the creole leaders asked the viceroy to preside over their junta.

These formulas did not last long, however. Some creole agitators rallied the popular masses in Santafé to insist on a clearer break with the past. (The most visible of these agitators was the thirty-five-year-old José María Carbonell, the son of a Spanish merchant.) Under popular pressure the creole notables in the junta first arrested the most hated judges in the Audiencia and then on July 25 confined still more Spanish officials, including the viceroy. The following day the Santafé junta, while still protesting its loyalty to Ferdinand VII, took the significant step of disavowing the authority of the Spanish Regency, thus, in effect, breaking with the entire existing apparatus of colonial government.

While the creole notables of Santafé initially found it useful to mobilize the common people, junta leaders soon worried that the activated masses would escape their control. For at least a month following the displacement of the viceroy and the Audiencia, the *populacho* in the capital, prompted by creole agitators, periodically pressed the new junta to rougher measures than it intended. The junta sought to treat displaced royal officials with some decorum, but creole populists and their popular followers insisted on putting the judges of the Audiencia in shackles, and they attacked some Spanish private citizens in the streets. Later they demanded that the viceroy and his wife be put in common prisons.

As in the Comunero riots in the province of Socorro in 1781, and as would also occur at later stages in the independence period, women played a prominent role in the Santafé crowds in 1810. On August 13, José María Caballero, a tailor, noted in his diary with horror, "the vile rabble of women" demanded that the wife of the viceroy be put in the women's prison. As she was being taken to the prison, hundreds of women lined the route, broke through her elite protectors, shredded her clothes, and cursed her. "The insolences that they were saying," Caballero added piously, "were enough to make one cover his ears." (Later, creole women of notable families escorted the virreina back to the viceregal residence.)

The junta struggled to control the *populacho*. It sought to still rumors of counterrevolution by the Spanish garrison and other royalist forces and encouraged friendly behavior toward "good Spaniards." As popular agitation against the imprisoned viceroy and his wife mounted, the junta quickly sped them out of town and imprisoned José María Carbonell and others who were agitating the crowds. Later, the junta declared that anyone gathering people in the plaza would be accused of lèse-majesté.

The revolution of 1810 in several ways echoed the crisis of 1794. One of the Audiencia judges displaced in 1810 noted that many of the creole leaders on July 20 were among those who had been arrested in 1794. And the most hated of the Audiencia judges in 1810 was the senior judge, Juan Hernández de Alba, one of the chief prosecutors of the alleged conspiracy of 1794.

THE PATRIA BOBA, 1810–1816

While the creole revolution in Santafé was not the first in New Granada, it was the most important because of Santafé's role as the viceregal capital. The movements in Cartagena, Socorro, and Pamplona had involved simply the overthrow of governors or corregidores. The revolt in Santafé displaced the central government of the whole viceroyalty. And, since Santafé was the viceregal capital, its leading citizens inevitably assumed that it was their responsibility to organize a new overarching government to preside over New Granada. In the initial act forming the Santafé junta, they envisioned forming a national government, federal in structure, with representatives from each province. And they soon invited the various provinces to send representatives to form such a constitution.

Some provincial capitals proved unwilling to cooperate with the Santafé junta, however, as the collapse of the viceregal regime unleashed a host of regional rivalries. Cartagena took the lead in opposing Santafé's scheme to organize a new central government in the viceregal capital. A manifesto from Cartagena denied that the Santafé junta had any authority to organize a new government. It further proposed that delegates meet in Medellín, with the suggestion that deliberations could be carried on there more peacefully than in Santafé. An article possibly written in Popayán, but printed in Cartagena, also warned that the West, which (at least in gold production) was wealthier than the East, would never accept rule from Santafé.

Beyond the split between Cartagena and Santafé, there occurred a more general fragmentation. Wherever a junta in a provincial capital thrust aside colonial authorities, they proclaimed their province a sovereign state, so that such provinces as Tunja, Socorro, Pamplona, and Antioquia became independent entities. The juntas almost invariably justified their actions by referring to natural rights and social contract doctrines. (With the king gone, they were "reassuming" their natural rights.)

Historians have disagreed as to whether the social contract doctrines employed in 1810 reflected Enlightenment influences or, rather, drew on sixteenth-century Spanish political theory. In some cases the declarations of 1810 could admit either interpretation or both. In others, however, the mark of the Enlightenment is clear. For example, both in el Socorro and in Santafé de Bogotá the initial declarations of July 1810 were founded on the people's "imprescriptible rights," language taken directly from Rousseau's *Social Contract*. From 1810 onward, as the break with Spanish authority became more complete, creole political rhetoric increasingly made use of Enlightenment and Anglo-American or French revolutionary formulas.

The mix of French Enlightenment writings, Anglo-American institutions, and Spanish colonial traditions can be seen in the early provincial constitutions of 1811 and 1812. The influence of Rousseau and/or the French Revolution is most evident in the constitutions' statements of their philosophical bases. The first constitution, that of Cundinamarca (formerly the province of Santafé) in April 1811, combined the rhetoric of Rousseau and the French Revolution in stating that its purpose was to guarantee the "the impre-scriptible rights of man and the citizen." Later constitutions such as that of the Republic of Tunja (December 9, 1811) or the State of Antioquia referred to the "general will" and otherwise echoed Rousseau's *Social Contract*, de-claring for example that the sovereignty of the people "is indivisible, im-prescriptible, and unalienable." Montesquieu, Rousseau, and Anglo-American practice were reflected in the constitutions' strict adherence to the division of legislative, executive, and judicial powers. On the other hand, the mark of the Spanish colonial tradition was also evident in the perpetuation of the *residencia* (the review of the conduct of officials at the end of their terms of office) and in an unqualified commitment to the Roman Catholic Church, not only as the state religion but also as the only acceptable one.

In addition to the establishment of autonomous governments in such provincial capitals as Tunja and Cartagena, further fragmentation occurred as secondary towns sought to split away from provincial capitals and es-tablish themselves at the head of new provinces. The Magdalena River port of Mompox for a time defied the authority of Cartagena, asserting that the existing ties of authority having been broken, each locality had regained its sovereignty. In the eastern zone, in a like spirit, Girón separated from Pam-plona, San Gil and Vélez from el Socorro, Sogamoso from Tunja, and Am-balema from Mariquita. In the Cauca Valley, Cali headed a confederation including Anserma, Toro, Cartago, Buga, and Caloto that was pitted against the old provincial capital of Popayán, which was controlled by the Spanish governor of the province and in which royalist sentiment predominated. Some of these splits reflected rivalries deeply rooted in the colonial period. Cali and Popayán, for example, had disputed preeminence in the Cauca re-gion since the earliest Spanish colonization of the region. And San Gil and el Socorro had been rivals from their early years. In all of these cases deeply rooted local ambitions to imbue their towns with power and prestige, in competition with nearby rivals, motivated these attempted separations. But Santafé, in its effort to establish central authority, reinforced this tendency to intraprovincial conflict. When provincial capitals refused to collaborate with Santafé, the junta in the capital for a time encouraged provincial se-cessionists, in some cases sending troops to support their independence against the existing regional capital.

In April 1811 Santafé formed the new state of Cundinamarca, a clear at-tempt to reassert the city's authority over much of the former viceroyalty. Its first president, Jorge Tadeo Lozano, took the view that a federation of many small provinces could not survive, as some of the provinces were too small to be self-sustaining. Lozano proposed a federation of four large de-partments. By far the biggest and most populous department under Lozano's plan, however, would be Cundinamarca, which would encompass all of present-day Colombia east of the Magdalena River. This proposal served only to alarm elites outside Santafé itself.

Santafé's intent to reconstitute its authority over a large part of the former viceroyalty found still stronger expression later in 1811, when Antonio Nariño, released from prison in Cartagena in 1810, seized control in Santafé and attempted to establish a centralist government. While Nariño was consolidating his authority in Santafé, representatives of various provinces (Cartagena, Antioquia, Tunja, Pamplona, and Neiva) in November 1811 attempted to lay the foundation for a federal government. Nariño's Cundinamarca refused to cooperate. Nariño, probably correctly, believed a federal system would be too weak. But he and his supporters in Santafé de Bogotá also fought the federalist scheme because they did not want to weaken the city's colonial powers and prerogatives. Accordingly, late in 1811 there began a conflict between Nariño's Santafé and a federalist coalition, a contest that endured until the end of 1814, when Santafé finally was defeated by the federalists.

During these internecine struggles, many creoles seemed to behave as if effective royal authority would not be restored in Spain, and therefore it was not imperative to organize for defense against royalist forces. In fact, however, even while Spain herself remained under Napoleonic control, local royalist forces controlled substantial parts of the country and posed significant threats. In the lower Magdalena valley and the Caribbean coast, Cartagena, itself rent by factional conflict, fought against royalist forces controlling Riohacha, Santa Marta, and the Isthmus of Panama. Until 1815 Cartagena and royalist Santa Marta remained at a standoff, with the Magdalena River the disputed frontier between them. One consequence of the struggle between Cartagena and Santa Marta was a substantial interruption of commerce on the river to the interior.

In the meantime, the total defeat of patriot forces in Venezuela by July 1812 raised a new threat from the north. The Venezuelan, Simón Bolívar, vanquished in his mother country, arrived in Cartagena in November 1812. Bolívar soon established himself as the commander of Cartagena's forces in the Magdalena Valley. By March 1813 he also had defeated Spanish forces in the eastern highland province of Pamplona, and, with aid from both Nariño and the Congress of the United Provinces, in May 1813 he once again invaded Venezuela. But once Bolívar had moved on to the core region of Venezuela, however, royalist forces reappeared in the Venezuelan-Colombian borderlands and remained a danger.

The third region in which royalist forces threatened was the Cauca region to the south. From the latter part of 1810 patriot forces in Cali and the towns to its north in the Cauca Valley were pitted against the regions from Popayán to the south, where royalist control was sustained in part by regular soldiers from Peru but more significantly by local Indians from the region of Pasto and Afro-Colombians from the Patía Valley, both of whom were effective guerrilla fighters. Pasto's Indians were rallied to the Spanish cause by the appeals of royalist priests, who depicted the creole patriots as atheists. The Patía Valley blacks were drawn to royalism in part by the Spanish governor's promise to free slaves who fought for the Spanish cause. But the Patianos' royalist loyalties were also energized by antagonism toward the patriot creole elites. When some Patianos seized a merchants' mule train and killed the merchants, patriot leaders responded by burning the town of Patía. From that time (if not before) Patianos and creole elites viewed each other with deep distrust. Royalist power in the region was further strengthened by the annihilation of republican government in Quito by royalist troops from Peru and southern Ecuador in November 1812. By June 1813 royalist forces had taken control of the entire Cauca Valley.

As royalist reaction began to threaten the divided and fragmented creole governments, patriot leaders broke more decisively with Spain. In November 1811 a factional revolution in Cartagena had moved that province to declare absolute independence from Spain. After the defeat of Nariño at Pasto and the seizure of the whole of the Cauca Valley by royalist forces, the government of Cundinamarca at Santafé also declared absolute independence from Ferdinand VII in July 1813, and Antioquia followed suit in August.

At the time they declared absolute independence, creole leaders sought to rally support and legitimate their authority through symbolic expression of revolutionary motifs of American independence. As early as the 1790s, some creoles had begun to take an interest in, and a positive attitude toward, the preconquest Muisca culture. At the same time, some were beginning to take a more critical view of the Spanish conquest, as an act of violent injustice to the indigenes—even though the creoles themselves were descendants of the dominating Spaniards. After 1810 these themes now came more to the fore. Creole leaders now explicitly rejected the conquest as a legitimate basis for Spanish authority. Early independence period political catechisms, written by patriot priests to rally popular support for the new creole regime, refuted the Spanish right to rule by virtue of conquest. At the same time creole leaders sought to bolster the authority of their governments by identifying them symbolically with that which was not Spanish but authentically American—the indigenes. The region dominated by Santafé was renamed Cundinamarca (derived from a Muisca name) and Cartagena in 1811 linked itself with the indigenous Calamarí. During 1812 creoles in Cundinamarca and Cartagena began to use representations of young Indian women as their symbol of liberty. Such symbolic expressions became particularly evident with the declarations of absolute independence in 1813. At this time Cundinamarca issued a new coin, on which the image of the king was replaced by that of a young Indian woman, accompanied by the inscription "American liberty."

At the time of declaring absolute independence creole leaders were also making use of symbols associated with the French Revolution. At this time the French Revolutionary Frigian cap began to be used as a symbol. And, in 1813 creole leaders began ceremonial plantings of "trees of liberty." In Nariño's Cundinamarca, American Indian and French revolutionary symbolism were merged: In April 1813 Indian maidens in feathered headdresses presided over the planting of trees of liberty. The ceremonial planting of trees of liberty (often followed by the surreptitious uprooting of the trees by royalists) continued until practically the conclusion of the Spanish reconquest early in 1816.

Also in accord with French revolutionary patterns, creole gentlemen began to address each other in letters as *ciudadano*, rather than the more traditional *don*. This change seems to have had a political significance beyond simply copying forms of the French Revolution. Consciously using the term "citizen" meant rejecting their former identity as subjects of the king, in favor of republican modes. Furthermore, the adoption of the term "citizen" was intended to signify a new assertion of a degree of civil equality. As early as 1810 the government of Santafé extended the right to vote to Indians, and at least in some places Indians actually did vote and elect their own representatives to electoral bodies. Furthermore, during the early republican years (1810–1815), there was a conscious concern to eliminate the caste system that had ordered colonial society, replacing it with a formally undifferentiated citizenship.

By July 1813, the danger of royalist forces clearly was reinforcing such revolutionary propensities. Royalists were threatening the northern provinces. The Spanish general Juan Sámano now controlled all of the Cauca Valley, which directly menaced Antioquia. Antioquia itself responded by putting itself under a dictator as well as declaring absolute independence. The eastern provinces were so alarmed that Cundinamarca and the federalist congress collaborated in sending one military force under Bolívar into the northern provinces and another under Nariño into the Cauca Valley. Bolívar was so successful that he was able to push to the center of Venezuela, before again being defeated by royalists there in 1814. In the Cauca, Nariño, after some initial successes, was totally defeated in Pasto and captured by the royalists in May 1814.

The destruction of Nariño's army in the Cauca threw creole leaders into a panic. Their fears were further intensified by the threat of royalist forces from Venezuela. Soon came the news that Napoleon had fallen and Ferdinand VII had returned to power, raising the prospect of strong military forces being sent from Spain to suppress the creole patriot governments. Prompted by these accumulating dangers, the New Granadan Congress, formerly committed to a weak federal structure, in July and August 1814 belatedly began to attempt more centralized control at least of finances and military operations. The Congress also sought to draw Cundinamarca into a more united system. Despite the looming peril of Spanish reconquest, however, the man that Nariño had left behind as governor of Cundinamarca, his uncle Manuel Bernardo Alvarez, refused to cooperate. Faced with Alvarez's stubborn refusal, the Congress once again decided to force Santafé into a general union by conquest. This time, the forces of the Congress, under the command of Simón Bolívar, in December 1814 succeeded in taking Santafé. Recognizing the importance and prestige of the former viceregal capital, the Congress immediately moved from Tunja to Santafé de Bogotá. Santafé, however, was far from receptive to the Congress. Alvarez, facing Bolívar's attack, had imprisoned and persecuted patriot federalists while placing arms in the hands of Spaniards and creole royalists in the belief that they could be depended upon to defend Santafé's independence and prerogatives. At the same time, many of Santafé's clergy had attacked Bolívar and his Venezuelan troops as atheist fiends. After Bolívar took Santafé de Bogotá, many of its residents—at least a third, according to a contemporary, José Manuel Restrepo—became covert royalists. Periodically during 1815 royalists and the former adherents of Cundinamarca conspired in Santafé against the Congress.

After Bolívar's conquest of Santafé, the badly divided patriots quickly succumbed to royalist forces. Early in 1815 Bolívar took a force down the Magdalena River to subdue the royalists in Santa Marta. But the patriot government of Cartagena, under the influence of a rival of Bolívar, viewed him as a threat and refused to cooperate. Believing Bolívar would attack Cartagena, its government withdrew all its forces from the Magdalena River to defend the city, leaving the river undefended against the Santa Marta royalists. Finally, Bolívar, his men ill and dying in the hot and humid lower Magdalena, resigned in disgust and went into exile in Jamaica. As a consequence of this fiasco, the patriot forces completely lost control of the lower Magdalena to the royalists of Santa Marta.

Meanwhile, the Spanish General Pablo Morillo had brought a force of 10,000 from Spain to Venezuela. By July 1815 Morillo was sailing to Santa Marta with some 8500 of these, and in August he laid siege to Cartagena. Its citizens held out heroically for 108 days, but finally, after more than a third of its population of 18,000 had died of hunger and disease, Cartagena capitulated on December 5, 1815. The conquest of the remaining free areas of New Granada followed quite rapidly. Royalist forces from western Venezuela in February and March 1816 swept south through Pamplona and Socorro provinces on their way to Santafé de Bogotá, while others, starting from Cartagena, moved to take Antioquia and the Chocó.

By this time many who had once supported New Granadan independence were totally demoralized. Even Socorro province, once among the most ardent in supporting independence, gave a triumphal reception to the royalist troops. Patriot military units disintegrated and fled. And when the patriot government in Santafé called for a general enlistment as royalist forces approached, only six men stepped forward. José Fernández Madrid, the new emergency president, tried to flee south to the Cauca Valley to take a stand there. But this was a hopeless cause, as royalist troops converged on the Cauca from four directions (Pasto, the Chocó, Antioquia, and Neiva).

By July 1816 all of the more populated regions of New Granada were completely under Spanish control. After 1816 guerrilla groups operated for a time in some regions of the Eastern Cordillera. But the remnants of patriot forces were able to hold out continuously only in the broken terrain of el Socorro and, more importantly, in the hostile environment of the lowland plains of Casanare. Some patriots sought to take refuge in the forests. Many, however, remained in the cities, encouraged by amnesties proclaimed by some of the conquering Spanish generals. General Morillo, however, overruled these amnesties and proceeded to execute large numbers of the creoles who had participated in the republican governments. At least 125 of those notable enough to be counted and remembered were shot in 1816. Morillo certified the importance of some of these by displaying their bodies after death. Camilo Torres, who had played leading roles from 1809 through 1815, and Manuel Rodríguez Torices, one of the leaders in Cartagena, had the further distinction of having their decapitated heads exhibited. Some ninety-five priests accused of sympathizing with independence were forced to march to exile across the hot, humid eastern lowlands, many dying along the way. Uncounted ordinary citizens died, or were killed, while being sent to prison or into exile. Innumerable artisans, peasants, and others too modest to merit historical notice were also executed between 1816 and 1819. At least two women were among those shot down by royalist firing squads, both for aiding patriot guerrillas. The more famous of these was Policarpa Salavarrieta, the daughter of a corregidor of Guaduas, who was executed in Santafé de Bogotá for her role as an agent for guerrillas in the eastern plains. The other was Antonia Santos Plata, who financed one of the various guerrilla groups in the province of el Socorro. At the same time Spanish authorities seized the property of many creoles, executed or not, leaving their families in misery. Such atrocities, it should be noted, did not begin in 1816. Through much of the fighting between royalists and patriots from 1811 onward, it had been common for both sides to execute officers and even footsoldiers taken prisoner in battle. But the many executions of notables, as well as common people, in 1816 and subsequent years simply served to harden New Granadans' bitterness toward Spain and their desire for independence.

The first, abortive period of attempted independence in New Granada, from 1810 to 1816, has long been known as the Patria Boba, the time of the Foolish Fatherland. The name is well deserved. The disaster of 1810–1816 must be ascribed above all to the naivete and narrow vision of many of New Granada's creole leaders. Throughout the period the elites of the various regions were able only sporadically to collaborate with each other in forming a unified government and a coordinated defense against royalist forces. José Manuel Restrepo, an actor in the events, blamed the widespread elite belief in the federalist system for much of the weakness and divisiveness of the Patria Boba. Because the leaders of New Granada's Congress, and of many of its various regions, were committed to a weak federal system, Restrepo said, they were unable to raise adequate revenues and armies from the provinces or to develop a coordinated defensive strategy. Modern interpreters, by contrast, stress less the weaknesses of the formal system of federalism and emphasize more the underlying regional preoccupations and rivalries among segments of the elite.

Both ways of understanding the problem have merit. Regional divisiveness was evident on all sides. And Spanish colonial tradition undoubtedly contributed to regional divisions. Unlike the English American colonies, colonial Spanish America had no experience of cooperation among widespread localities in regional legislatures. Beneath the Spanish bureaucratic hierarchy there existed only city governments, with no formal linkages between them. And during the colonial period neighboring cities were riven by long-term rivalries that were carried into the 1810–1816 period, and indeed became more evident then. But contemporary commitments to a federal system did mean that there was no effective institutional counterweight to narrow regional interests.

Because of the many rifts within the provinces, as well as between regional governments, between 1810 and 1815 creole energies, money, and blood were spent to a considerable degree on internal conflict among various patriot forces rather than on defense against royalist threats. These internecine struggles exhausted the economic resources and literally drained away the lifeblood of the common people. By 1816, Restrepo says, many people in almost all the provinces were tired of internal war and in the restoration of Spanish rule hoped for the return of order, peace, and tranquility.

It is impossible to say with assurance in what proportion various segments of the population supported the patriot or the royalist causes between 1810 and 1815. It seems likely that in most regions—other than in Santa Marta, Popayán, and Pasto—the majority of civilian elites were sympathetic to the patriot cause. Most creole priests may have been patriot sympathizers, but not a few priests were strongly royalist. The royalist clergy, by tying religion to monarchy, insisting that to deny the king was to deny God, undoubtedly played a role in undermining popular support for independence during the Patria Boba. The role of the royalist clergy was most evident in Pasto, but it seems to have had some importance in Santafé de Bogotá and other places. It may be true, as José Manuel Restrepo contended, that between 1810 and 1815 the movement for independence was principally a concern of the educated elites and aroused scant popular enthusiasm. However, after the brutality of the Spanish reconquest of 1816–1819, the desire to be rid of Spanish rule became much more general.

PATRIOT RECOVERY, 1819–1825

From 1816 to 1819 Spanish military officers and their local royalist collaborators almost completely controlled New Granada as well as neighboring Venezuela and Ecuador. Patriot guerrillas offered sporadic resistance in a few areas, but they operated continuously only on the lowland plains of Casanare. In August 1819, however, creole patriots suddenly, and decisively, regained the upper hand with Simón Bolívar's defeat of royalist forces at the Battle of Boyacá. After Boyacá, Spanish authorities in panic abandoned the viceregal capital, and their provincial counterparts were quickly driven from the greater part of the more populated regions of New Granada.

Nonetheless, significant royalist resistance continued on the Caribbean coast until late in 1821 and in the rock-ribbed royalist province of Pasto into 1825, and royalist guerrillas operated in neighboring Venezuela to the end of the 1820s.

Throughout the period of patriot dominance (1819–1825), as in earlier periods, the struggle was marked by several common features. In this later stage, as earlier, there continued a pronounced tendency for both royalists and patriots to shoot prisoners—particularly military leaders but sometimes also common soldiers, many of whom had been impressed into service. Another common feature was the notable impact of climate and other geographic factors on both sides.

One example of the impact of environment was in the relationship between the cool eastern highlands and the *llanos*, the hot lowland eastern plains. After the Spanish reconquest of 1816, royalist forces in the eastern highlands were not able to subdue patriot guerrillas in the *llanos* in part because horses from the highlands were not able to adapt to the different grasses of the lowland plains. And, without mounted troops, the royalists could not function effectively on the plains against native *llanero* horsemen. Furthermore, royalist operations in the eastern lowlands were hampered by the fact that the *llanos* were flooded during more than half the year. Consequently, the lowland plains remained an effective patriot refuge throughout the years of Spanish dominance between 1816 and 1819.

Because Spanish forces could not operate effectively in the eastern plains, Simón Bolívar was able in 1819 to use the *llanos* as a base for attacking royalist forces controlling the more densely populated highlands. In this case the environmental challenge was reversed. Remarkably, Bolívar began his march from the *llanos* to the highlands at what might seem the most difficult time, in May, during the long rainy season, when the lowland plains were flooded. This, however, increased the element of surprise, as an attack from the lowlands, especially during the rainy season, seemed almost inconceivable. Indeed, Bolívar's troops did suffer terribly. The main body of his forces were *llaneros*, and neither they nor their horses were accustomed to the cold highlands. Many *llaneros* lacked the clothing need to resist the cold and fell ill, some dying, soon after the climb into the highlands. Many of their horses were lamed by the rocky mountain terrain (horses in the *llanos* did not need, and thereore did not have, horseshoes). Bolívar's expedition appears to have succeeded in large part because, after he reached the highlands, the Spanish allowed him enough time to reequip his surviving *llaneros* with highland horses, food, and clothing and to augment his forces with local recruits.

Bolívar's defeat of royalist forces at the battle of Boyacá on August 7, 1819, decisively changed the course of the struggle for independence in northern South America. Before the battle of Boyacá, Spanish authorities dominated all of the more populated regions of Venezuela and New Granada and were unchallenged in Ecuador. After Boyacá, the Spanish viceroy fled in panic, and patriot forces were able quickly to take control of most of the more densely peopled regions of New Granada—the eastern highlands from Santafé to Pamplona, the gold-mining regions of Antioquia and the Chocó, and the Upper Magdalena Valley. From this base in New Granada, Bolívar was able to attack and defeat royalist forces in Venezuela, Ecuador, and, ultimately, Peru and Bolivia. Although there remained significant royalist resistance on the Caribbean coast through 1821 and in southwestern Colombia until 1825, patriot leaders between 1819 and 1822 were able to begin to construct an independent republic.

External events aided in this process. The final triumph over Napoleon in 1815 had enabled Ferdinand VII to send a large army to repress the patriots in Venezuela and New Granada in 1815–1816, but victory over Napoleon also had meant that the British could move away from alliance with Spain and more freely encourage Spanish American independence. The end of the fight against the French brought the demobilization of the British army, and almost six thousand of these soldiers came to serve the patriot cause in northern South America. British soldiers of fortune formed part of Bolívar's army at Boyacá, as well as in many subsequent battles. British merchants also aided Colombian independence by financing the provisioning and transportation of these soldiers as well as supplying, on credit, substantial amounts of military equipment to the patriot forces.

Events in Spain also helped to strengthen the forces for independence. Spanish military units that were about to be sent to Spanish America to put down the independence movements in January 1820 revolted and forced Ferdinand VII to restore constitutional government. The revolution of 1820 in various ways aided the cause of independence. Conflict between constitutionalists and absolutists kept Spain in turmoil until April 1823, when the king of France intervened to restore absolutist rule. Thus, for more than three years (1820–1823) Ferdinand VII could not send significant military reinforcements to Spanish America. Forced to adopt a less intransigent policy, in 1820 he instructed colonial authorities to negotiate with the insurgents. In northern South America a temporary, partial armistice was negotiated. The process of negotiation itself represented a kind of recognition of the insurgents, thus strengthening their legitimacy. During the negotiation and the armistice itself (August 1820–April 1821) significant defections from royalism, of regions and creole royalist military leaders, occurred, and patriotic enthusiasm at this moment became more general.

At the same time, other foreign governments were moving to legitimize Spanish American independence in more positive ways. The United States took the lead in this. In 1820 the United States House of Representatives passed a resolution favoring the recognition of the emerging Spanish American republics, and the president of the United States received Colombia's first diplomatic agent. In 1822 the United States formally recognized Colombia, as well as other Spanish American states. The British government delayed its recognition until January 1825, but in the meantime played an important role in restraining the French monarchy from intervening directly in Spanish America.

Meanwhile, within Colombia itself patriots moved to consolidate independence by establishing a constitutional government. In May 1821 delegates from New Granada and Venezuela gathered at Cúcuta to form a new constitution for the emerging Republic of Colombia, and in September 1821 the delegates predictably elected Simón Bolívar that republic's first president.

Despite these positive developments, the war for independence was not over in Colombia. Early in 1820 the royalists still controlled the entire Caribbean coast, the Lower Magdalena Valley, and the Cauca region. As long as they held the port cities of Cartagena and Santa Marta and the Magdalena River artery to the interior, they could block the supply of arms and other foreign goods to patriot-held regions. And, without foreign trade, the patriots could not collect customs duties. By July 1820 the patriots had succeeded in taking much of the Lower Magdalena and had the royalists in the port of Cartagena under siege. But the royalists in Cartagena were able to hold out for fifteen months, until October 1821. Elsewhere in the Lower Magdalena region and on the Caribbean coast—in Ocaña, Valledupar, and Santa Marta— royalist guerrillas continued to operate until late in 1821. And as late as 1823 royalist rebellion broke out again in the Santa Marta region, with royalist Indians in the town of Ciénaga the focus of the rebellion.

The struggle to defeat the royalists on the Caribbean coast and in the Lower Magdalena was costly in human life. Many of the patriot soldiers fighting on the coast came from the mountainous interior and were not accustomed to the hot, humid coastal lowlands. Many were felled by dysentery and the "black vomit." Most of these troops from the interior either died or deserted. In a single year one battalion lost 90 percent of its troops.

In addition to royalist resistance on the Caribbean coast, the Cauca Valley was also a source of concern. In January 1820, Spanish troops took Popayán, the administrative capital of the region, and then swept north through the flat Cauca Valley. Patriots in el Valle had to flee across the Quindío pass to safety. Over the longer haul, however, patriot forces were able generally to control the Cauca Valley. The principal patriot concern in the Cauca zone was the region of Pasto, in Colombia's mountainous southwest. Royalists continued to hold Pasto until June 1822, and royalist guerrillas periodically rose up temporarily to seize control of the province until 1825. Royalist strength in Pasto was worrisome for a number of reasons. First, it threatened the integrity of the new nation as envisioned by Simón Bolívar. In 1819 at Angostura, and once again in 1821 at Cúcuta, constitution-makers had envisioned a Republic of Colombia including Venezuela, New Granada, and Ecuador. But royalist Pasto blocked the way to the liberation of Quito from Spanish control. Even after Quito was freed from Spanish rule in May 1822, royalist Pasto continued to stand between liberated Quito and the rest of the Republic of Colombia. In part because royalists blocked or threatened patriot communications through Pasto, Ecuador went virtually unrepresented in the earliest Colombian congresses. In addition to the menace that royalist Pasto presented to the integration of the Republic of Colombia, it also threatened Simón Bolívar's dream of driving the Spanish from Peru. As long as royalism had a strong following in Pasto, Bolívar had to worry about Pasto as a continuing threat at his rear, a threat both to his base in the young Republic of Colombia and to the supply of arms and men to the Colombian forces seeking to liberate Peru.

The Pasto region was hard to conquer for several reasons. First, the Spanish bishop of Popayán and most of the region's parish priests had succeeded in inculcating the notion that supporters of independence were enemies of religion. (The doctrine of popular sovereignty, generally accepted by New Granada's patriot elites, by denying the divine right of royal rule, was, from their point of view, clearly irreligious.) The mass of the people in Pasto, many of whom were Indian peasants, were deeply traditionalist and apparently believed that they were fighting in defense of their religion quite as much as for their king. With its people harboring such convictions, Pasto became Colombia's Vendee, the center of counterrevolutionary resistance to a new, independent, republican government.

Second, because of its topographic and climatic features, the Pasto region presented formidable obstacles to invasion by outsiders. Moving south from Popayán, the first barrier to patriot progress was the Patía River basin, which had to be crossed even to get to Pasto proper. The Patía and its tributaries were hot, low-lying river valleys, in which, experience had proven, outsiders were likely to fall ill. In addition, those who traveled south had to pass through narrow gorges, which offered many opportunities for ambush by guerrillas. And the largely Afro-Colombian populace of the Patía, committed to the royalist cause since 1810, had become skilled in guerrilla warfare. If an invading force were able to pass through the Patía, there remained the prospect of further ambushes in narrow mountain defiles everywhere in the Pasto region. There also was the problem of Pasto itself. The city of Pasto, resting high on a volcanic hill and surrounded by deep gorges, was itself well situated for defense. Even harder to penetrate, however, were its ring of outer defenses, formed by the converging Juanambú River north of Pasto and the Guáitara River to its south. Each of these rivers sends turbulent rapids through deeply cut, steep, rocky river channels. The city of Pasto and its immediate surroundings were easily defended by placing troops at the difficult crossing points across these rivers. As patriot forces had learned in 1812 and again in 1814, if these river crossings were well defended, attempts to traverse them could be very costly, if not impossible. Repeatedly in 1821–1822 patriot efforts to subdue the Pasto region failed. Ultimately, it proved much easier to take Quito with troops setting out from Guayaquil than to try to push through Pasto.

After Bolívar's most trusted lieutenant, General Antonio José de Sucre, took Quito in May 1822, Pasto stood between patriot forces to the north in the Cauca Valley and to the south in Quito. At this point Pasto's elites, even though royalists, decided it would be prudent to surrender to the patriots.

The mass of Pastusos, however, were determined to fight on, no matter what the odds. Only the revered Spanish bishop of Popayán was able to persuade them to capitulate. But the battle for Pasto was far from over. In October 1822 royalist guerrillas once again took the city of Pasto, and, although they were driven out again the following December, they continued to operate freely in the mountains and remained a serious threat until the middle of 1824, when several of the remaining guerrilla leaders were captured and executed.

By early 1823 Bolívar and other republican leaders had concluded that the only solution to Pastuso resistance was virtual extirpation. Repressive measures included the impressment of a thousand Pastusos into the army for service in Peru, the exile of three hundred to Quito, and a general confiscation of Pastuso property, as well as the killing of captured troops, executions of leaders, and some spectacular atrocities. In March 1823 José Manuel Restrepo noted in his diary that only women remained in the city of Pasto and remarked, matter of factly, that it would be necessary to "change" the population of Pasto because of the "tenacious and destructive" war it had made on the republic. Four months later, Restrepo added, "It is necesary to destroy the Pastusos and this is very difficult in such a . . . craggy terrain."

The repressive measures, however, hardened, rather than destroyed, Pastuso resistance. In September 1823 General Bartolomé Salom, left by Bolívar to stamp out rebellion in Pasto, reported:

> It is not possible to give an idea of the obstinate tenacity and rage with which the Pastusos operate; if before it was the majority of the population which had declared itself our enemy, now it is the total mass of the villages which make war on us with a fervor that cannot be expressed.

Salom noted that among the prisoners taken by his troops were nine- and ten-year-old boys. The Pastusos "are persuaded," he said, "that we are carrying on a war to the death, and they don't believe us at all."

Although the endemic Pastuso rebellion was quieted for a moment by the executions of some of the principal leaders in June 1824, it would reappear from time to time. Even after the Spanish army in Peru was decisively defeated at the Battle of Ayacucho (in December 1824), effectively ending royalist resistance in its most important center in South America, royalist insurgency continued to erupt in Pasto. In April 1825 a royalist priest, claiming that Bolívar had been killed, prompted a rebellion that sprouted in localities throughout the region. By this time the province had been completely laid waste, its crops, cattle, and sheep and the woolen textile industry the sheep had supplied all destroyed. The struggle to subdue and control Pasto and the Patía from 1810 to 1825 created among elites elsewhere in the republic an enduring image of these regions as sources of trouble, with unreasonable populations whose resistance to outside control had to be dealt with by repression.

In most other parts of New Granada the wars of independence appear to have been less destructive than in Pasto. Nonetheless, the long conflict took its toll. Wherever armies passed, during the fight for independence as in subsequent civil wars, localities suffered heavy losses of livestock. The eastern part of the country, with the Eastern Cordillera at its center, where roughly 60 percent of the population lived, had enjoyed a notable economic growth in the last three decades of the colonial period. Between 1810 and 1816, during the Patria Boba, agricultural production appears to have declined in most localities in the eastern zone. In some places production increased somewhat during the Spanish Reconquest of 1816–1819, but then remained more or less flat during the early 1820s when the patriots recovered dominance of the region. While the populated eastern zone, like Antioquia in the West, did not experience significant fighting after 1819, both were bled of men and financial resources to sustain the fight elsewhere. In 1820–1821 Cundinamarca had sent some 35,000 men to fight in Venezuela, the Caribbean Coast, or Pasto. In this brief time Socorro province alone supplied eight thousand recruits, about 5 percent of its total population, in addition to more than a thousand horses and mules, considerable clothing, and 200,000 pesos. Gold-mining Antioquia, with greater funds at its disposal, provided twice as much money as Socorro but only two thousand recruits, nearly half of whom were slaves. Loss of slaves, either by escape or recruitment to armies, adversely affected gold mining, less probably in Antioquia than in the Cauca, where use of slaves in mining was much more general. The heavy cost of sustaining armies, not only on the Caribbean coast and in Pasto but also in Ecuador and Peru, combined with a collapsing tax system, put the finances of the new republic deeply in deficit. Its foreign debt, accumulating since 1817 because of war expenditures and a poor bargaining position vis-à-vis British lenders, by 1824 stood at £6,750,000 (or 33,750,000 in dollars or Colombian pesos), an unsustainable burden on the Republic of Colombia as it emerged into independence.

The wars of independence brought some significant social changes to New Granada, yet the creole aristocracy was able to retain a virtually unchallenged monopoly of power. At the base of the society the most notable change was the movement of uncounted numbers of Afro-Colombians from slavery to freedom. Both royalists and patriots, as a matter of wartime necessity, filled out their military ranks by recruiting slaves, to many of whom they promised freedom. The royalists appear to have taken the lead in this, sometimes identifying the royalist cause with a fight against creole slaveowners. But the incorporation of slaves into the army also became a deliberate policy of Simón Bolívar, who in 1820 ordered the recruitment of five thousand slaves (later scaled down to three thousand) from the gold mines and farms of Antioquia, the Chocó, and the Cauca.

Bolívar's policy provoked controversy within the patriot elite. Creole slaveowners protested that they, and their mining and agricultural enterprises, would be ruined. Bolívar, however, held that the slaves would make strong and committed soldiers. Further, he noted that the incorporation of slaves into the republican army, and their subsequent freedom, was in various ways necessary to the political order. Citing Montesquieu, Bolívar contended that slavery could endure in a despotism but not in a free society, where the evident freedom of others would turn slaves into enemies of the system. Furthermore, using blacks in the army would reduce their numbers. If only whites served in the army, blacks would soon outnumber them. "Is it not useful," Bolívar asked, "that the slaves should acquire their rights on the battlefield and that their dangerous number be lessened by a process both necessary and legitimate?" Bolívar's argument thus interestingly combined enlightened political philosophy with fear of racial conflict.

7

Bolívar's Colombia, 1819–1831

In 1819, under the leadership of the Venezuelan General Simón Bolívar, Venezuela and New Granada were joined as the Republic of Colombia; Ecuador was later incorporated when it was liberated from Spanish control in 1822. The Republic of Colombia had to confront two severe tests simultaneously—to free itself, and then Peru and Bolivia, from Spanish royalist forces and at the same time to lay the institutional bases for a new polity. While Bolívar directed the war effort, the New Granadan General Francisco de Paula Santander, as vice president of Colombia, attended to the construction of the new republic. Colombia succeeded in its military task of ending Spanish control of Andean South America. But once this strategic aim was achieved, the union of Venezuela, New Granada, and Ecuador began to fail as a polity. In 1826 the union entered into a prolonged political crisis—involving concurrent, and often interconnected, conflicts between clergy and university-educated liberal politicians, between military officers and the same liberal civilian politicians, between the central government in Bogotá and elites in Venezuela and Ecuador, and ultimately between Bolívar and Santander and their respective adherents. The crisis continued to 1831, by which time the Republic of Colombia had fragmented into its original constituent parts—Venezuela, New Granada, and Ecuador.

FOUNDING COLOMBIA

With the decisive victory over Spanish forces at the battle of Boyacá in August 1819, if not before, Simón Bolívar became the preeminent leader of the independence movement, politically as well as militarily, in both Venezuela and New Granada. In 1819 his signal importance was recognized in the title by which from that time he was generally known—the Liberator. It was Bolívar's vision, will, and leadership that brought Venezuela, New Granada, and Ecuador together in the single Republic of Colombia—retrospectively called "Gran Colombia," to distinguish it from the present Republic of Colombia. Bolívar seems not to have been the first to conceive of the union of Venezuela, New Granada, and Ecuador as an independent nation; Francisco Miranda, the precursor of Venezuelan independence, proposed this in 1808. But Bolívar conceived of the union of Venezuela and New Granada as early as 1813, and by 1815 he was including Quito in this conception. And it was his leadership that made the union an at least temporary reality.

The notion of placing Venezuela, New Granada, and Quito under a single government undoubtedly was inspired initially by the fact that during part of the eighteenth century all three had been joined, at least technically, under the viceroyalty of New Granada. There thus existed at least a figment of an administrative tradition uniting the three regions. However, as has been noted, neither Venezuela nor Quito had ever been effectively governed from Santafé de Bogotá. The fundamental basis of the union lay in Bolívar's experience in the struggle to liberate Venezuela, which evolved into a conscious strategy. The movement for independence having been defeated in Venezuela in 1812, Bolívar had fled to Cartagena, where he soon became a military leader. By 1813 Bolívar was taking New Granadan troops into Venezuela in what proved to be an unsuccessful attempt to liberate it. Later, in 1819, Bolívar led troops from the *llanos* of Venezuela and New Granada into New Granada's eastern highlands to establish a base for trying once again to liberate Venezuela. Thus, during the struggle for independence, Bolívar came to believe that the fates of Venezuela and New Granada were intertwined. The independence of the one depended upon the liberation of the other. But Bolívar conceived of Venezuela and New Granada as being joined in more than a tactical military alliance necessary to end Spanish rule. He hoped to create of Venezuela and New Granada, and the Audiencia of Quito as well, a republic large enough to defend itself against foreign powers.

Others came to share Bolívar's vision of joining Venezuela and New Granada, but some worried that regional rivalry between New Granadans and Venezuelans would threaten the survival of this larger republic. In June 1819, before Bolívar led his forces from the *llanos* to attack royalist forces in New Granada's eastern highlands, the New Granadan General Francisco de Paula Santander, then the Liberator's chief lieutenant in the *llanos* of Casanare, wrote the Venezuelan Colonel Pedro Briceño Méndez, expressing his fear that regional antagonisms could tear Venezuelans and New Granadans apart. The union would survive, Santander thought, if elites in both regions wanted to make it work. But, he continued, the leadership of Bolívar was critically important—only he had the confidence of both New Granadans and Venezuelans.

After the victory over Spanish forces at Boyacá, Bolívar returned to the temporary patriot capital at Angostura, on the Orinoco River, where in December 1819 a predominantly Venezuelan Congress formally proclaimed a Republic of Colombia, including Venezuela and New Granada, as well as Ecuador—when liberated from Spanish control. The Congress, not surprisingly, elected Bolívar as the republic's first president and a New Granadan civilian, Francisco Antonio Zea, as its vice president. In addition, the congress provided for vice presidents to govern Venezuela, New Granada (now called Cundinamarca), and, eventually, Ecuador. The Congress, in a rhetorical gesture of independence from Spain, also declared that the capital of the Department of Cundinamarca henceforth would be no longer be called Santafé de Bogotá but simply Bogotá.

Immediately after the battle of Boyacá Bolívar had appointed General Santander to govern patriot-controlled New Granada; Santander's subsequent election as vice president for Cundinamarca by the Angostura Congress simply confirmed Bolívar's decision. Born and raised in the Cúcuta region bordering Venezuela, Santander had studied law in Santafé de Bogotá (1805–1810) but had not really practiced that profession, as he enlisted in the local patriot military as a lieutenant in October 1810. As Santander rose through the ranks to become a general, he came to think of himself as a military man. Yet as vice president, Santander proved to be as lawyerly as military in his inclinations. His frequent insistence on adhering to the letter of the law caused him to be known as *el Hombre de las Leyes* (the Man of the Law)—a label that for Bolívar came to be tinged with sarcasm, for Santander's legal-mindedness often irritated, and sometimes enraged, the Liberator, who often had little patience with legal niceties. For more than two years (1819–1821) Santander ruled New Granada under a provisional government. In 1821 Santander was elected vice president of the Republic of Colombia as a whole. As vice president he governed the republic while Bolívar was absent from the capital, prosecuting the war for independence, until the Liberator's return to Bogotá in November 1826.

Throughout the 1820s civil authority was divided between civilians and military officers. Santander was aided by civilian ministers in Bogotá, but military officers predominated in the provinces. The transition toward a greater civilian role in governance began, however, in May 1821, when delegates from Venezuela and New Granada met in the border town of Rosario de Cúcuta to form a constitution for the new Republic of Colombia.

The constitutional convention at Cúcuta marked a generational change in political leadership. Many of the leaders before 1819 had been executed or had died during the Spanish reconquest. Some had survived and continued to play leading roles, most notably, of course, Bolívar. Antonio Nariño, who had been such a prominent actor in 1793–1795 and again in 1808–1814, had returned from prison in Spain. Bolívar, in recognition of Nariño's role as a precursor of independence, appointed him interim vice president of Colombia, in which position he inaugurated the Congress of Cúcuta as its first president. Two Antioqueños, José Manuel Restrepo and José Felix Restrepo, who had been visible leaders in the earlier phase of the independence period, also were important at Cúcuta and afterward. But many of the leading New Granadans at Cúcuta and in subsequent years were men who had functioned mostly in subaltern roles between 1810 and 1819. Such men as Vicente Azuero, Francisco Soto, and José Ignacio de Márquez emerged as salient figures at Cúcuta and continued to play important political roles in New Granada into the 1840s.

Discussion at Cúcuta over whether and under what form Venezuela, New Granada, and Ecuador might join under a single government reflected regional sensitivities, and insensitivities, that later found expression in overt hostility. The delegates generally agreed that some kind of union was necessary to defeat the Spanish and secure independence. But some New Granadans feared that under a united government New Granada might become a "colony" of Venezuela. However, Vicente Azuero of el Socorro, who played a leading role in crafting the constitution of 1821, moved from distrust of Venezuela to support for New Granadan–Venezuelan union. Before the convention Azuero had opposed tying New Granada and Venezuela too closely together, in part because he feared New Granada would be contaminated by the "social disorder" then evident in Venezuela, in part because of the "concentrated hatred and rivalries" between the people of the two regions. However, at the convention he concluded that union was the only means of overcoming these regional rivalries.

Regional differences also were evident in discussion over whether the convention might declare Ecuador part of the union—even though Ecuador, not yet having been liberated from Spanish control, had no delegates at Cúcuta. Venezuelan delegates, who had little or no experience with or knowledge of Quito, were inclined to incorporate Ecuador forthwith, while the New Granadans, particularly those from the Cauca region, which historically had been linked to Quito, insisted that Ecuadoreans be invited, rather than obliged, to join.

Proponents of union emphasized the strategic necessity of defeating Spain and the likelihood that a larger republic would more readily win recognition from, and be able to defend itself against, European and other foreign governments. There was, however, little or no consideration of whether the union might actually function as an integrated economic entity. Indeed, the one comment that focused on economic factors suggested a lack of commercial ties that militated against union: A Cauca delegate asserted that Ecuador had more trade relations southward along the Pacific coast than with New Granada.

Although the delegates, with a single exception, ultimately agreed on the desirability of union, the question continued to be debated in another form when they discussed whether the government should be centralized or more loosely federative. Some New Granadan delegates, taking the United States as their model, argued that a federal system would more effectively guarantee individual liberty than a centralist one. But a majority of the delegates favored a unitary or centralist system. The need for a strong government to carry on the fight against Spain was probably the most immediately persuasive reason for supporting centralism. Many contemporaries, including Bolívar, attributed creole failure to sustain independence in Venezuela and New Granada between 1810 and 1816 to the weaknesses of the federalist governments of that time.

For those who were most committed to centralism, however, the rationale for it went beyond the exigencies of the war for independence. Many delegates at Cúcuta believed that a centralist system was better adapted to Colombian realities. The country lacked enough educated people and financial resources to operate the provincial legislatures implied by a federalist regime. Finally, some contended, while the U.S. government was admirable, it could not be made to work in Spanish America. According to the more committed centralists, Spanish Americans lacked the North Americans' political experience and "civic virtue" (that is, a culture of active civic responsibility) necessary to make the cumbersome federalist system work. Nonetheless, some New Granadans who favored a centralist system in 1821 held out hope that Colombia's citizens might ultimately attain sufficient political maturity to make possible the eventual adoption of federalism.

The constitution adopted in Cúcuta in 1821, which in many ways set the pattern for Colombian constitutions until the 1850s, was clearly centralist. Formally it followed the U.S. pattern. It established a president and vice president with four-year terms, a bicameral legislature, and a judiciary whose members were to be determined jointly by the executive and the legislature. But in its emphasis on centralized authority the Colombian Constitution it was far different from the U.S. federalist model. The intendants, who governed very large regions, and their subordinate provincial governors were appointed by the president and were considered his direct agents. Also, there were no autonomous state legislatures.

Control of the government by the educated elite was more or less assured by an electoral system that restricted suffrage and also muffled it through indirect elections. The vote at the parish level was limited to males who were either twenty-one years of age or married and who either owned property worth a hundred pesos or independently exercised a craft or profession. The constitution also required that voters be literate, although that provision was suspended until 1840, when, it was expected, more citizens would be able to read and write. The voters at the parish level were to choose cantonal electors who would elect the president, vice president, and legislators.

The Congress of Cúcuta decided to place the capital of the republic at Bogotá, probably in part because of its established role as viceregal capital. Bogotá also seemingly would be a central location if Ecuador became a part of the republic as intended, although, in fact, it was more difficult to reach from Venezuela or Ecuador than would have been a site on the isthmus of Panama. Some Venezuelans were not happy with the choice of Bogotá, preferring a capital near the New Granadan–Venezuelan border. Thus, from the moment of its birth, the republic was affected by the conflicting Venezuelan and New Granadan regionalism that ultimately led to the collapse of Bolívar's Colombia.

In addition to the constitution, the Congress of Cúcuta in 1821 also adopted legislation intended to start Colombia on a genuinely republican course. Believing that the republican system depended upon freedom of expression, the delegates abolished the Inquisition and proclaimed freedom of the press. They also sought to liberate black slaves and Indians and incorporate them as citizens. Following the precedent of a law of 1814 in the State of Antioquia, the congress enacted a "law of free birth," which declared that henceforth children born to slave mothers would become free, although in fact they remained under the control of the mother's master until the age of eighteen. The number of slaves in New Granada at this time actually was relatively small, making up possibly no more than 4 percent of the total population, although in some western gold-mining provinces slaves constituted much larger proportions (Buenaventura, 38 percent; the Chocó, 28 percent, Popayán, 14 percent).

Following a pattern already initiated by the provisional government in Bogotá in 1810, the Congress also sought to incorporate Indians into the general body of citizens. It abolished the Indian tribute as demeaning to the Amerindian population and called for the division of Indian community lands into individual plots. Further, it enacted various measures intended to elevate the Amerindians, at least symbolically, from their colonial degradation. Henceforth they were no longer to be called "Indians" but rather "indigenes," and they were to be considered citizens like any other New Granadan. The congress specifically declared that indigenes could hold government office.

The Congress of Cúcuta also repeated the intentions of the patriots of 1810 in trying to lay the foundations for a broad-based educational system, which was generally believed necessary for the success of republican government. Schools would serve to inculcate loyalty to the system as well as to increase the number of literate citizens. The Congress of 1821 called for the establishment of a secondary school in every province and at least one primary school in every town or village that had at least one hundred adult males. This latter law was a worthy expression of republican aspirations, but many communities, which had to finance the primary schools, did not have the resources required to make the ideal effective. In many places they also lacked the necessary local leadership, particularly as in the immediate post-independence era many of the young men of influential provincial families gravitated to Bogotá in pursuit of higher education, political careers, and other advantages offered by the capital. Furthermore, it was hard for many localities to obtain teachers. Republican government opened many opportunities for political office for the few educated people in the country; by comparison, the low salaries and negligible status of primary school teachers held little attraction. In the early republican decades Colombia sought to compensate for the scarcity of school teachers by making use of the Lancasterian system, in which the more advanced students would help to teach other pupils. Despite the lack of funds and teachers, during the 1820s there occurred a notable increase in public primary education over that available at the end of the colonial period. School statistics for the period are fragmentary, but one example is suggestive. In 1810 the province of Pamplona had one public primary school; in 1822, it had thirty.

While Colombian elites supported primary education as necessary to the success of the republic, secondary and higher education was of much more importance to them personally; obtaining a law degree would provide their sons not only social and economic status but also the foundation for a political career. Upper-sector Colombians in provincial towns therefore were particularly anxious to establish secondary schools in provincial capitals. This concern was reflected in the expansion of the number of secondary schools in the republic from five in 1821 to twenty-two in 1827. In addition, to make it easier for provincial youths to obtain law degrees, there was considerable pressure in the 1820s, as well as afterward, to offer some instruction in jurisprudence in provincial colegios.

The Congress of Cúcuta attempted major reforms of the revenue system inherited from the colonial period. By 1821 liberal economic principles had spread widely among the civilian elite, and the delegates sought to reform the tax system in accord with those principles. Antonio Nariño in his initial speech at Cúcuta outlined the liberal principles that ought to govern revenue policy: Taxes ought to be levied on income not property, the government should avoid the colonial practice of raising revenue through government monopolies over the production and sale of such products as tobacco and cane liquor, and the legislators should also take care that indirect duties (like sales taxes) not impede private economic activities. Nariño's advice on revenue legislation was in accord with the general sentiment of the Congress. But as a matter of fiscal prudence some important traditional revenues were retained—most notably, the tobacco, salt, and gunpowder monopolies and the *diezmo* (the 10 percent tax on gross agricultural production). However, the Cúcuta congress did eliminate sales taxes on domestic products and reduced them on imported goods. And it ended the state monopoly on cane liquor. It sought to replace the lost revenues by establishing a new direct tax (*contribución directa*) on income (10 percent on income from land and capital and 2–3 percent on salaries).

This new *contribución directa*, however, proved hard to collect, and government officials did not want to arouse the hostility likely to be provoked by energetic tax collection. The government lacked the means to enforce honest declarations of income. For landowners it could make rule-of-thumb assumptions about the amount of income likely to be earned by a given capital value of land. But merchants could and did hide their capital. Many feared to make honest declarations because of the danger of having their funds taken in forced loans—which had become the standard means of raising funds during the post-1810 conflicts. But the inability to collect regular direct taxes simply meant that the government had to continue to resort to forced loans. So it was a vicious circle. Government officials finally concluded that, while the old colonial taxes were disliked, people were accustomed to them and they were easier to enforce. Consequently, some of the colonial taxes that had been abolished or reduced in 1821 were restored later in the decade.

Although revenues from some traditional taxes fell, income from customs duties increased with expanded importations of manufactured goods. The right to trade freely with nations other than Spain had been a creole aim from the very beginning of the independence era. The opening of Colombian ports to unrestricted foreign trade permitted the release of pentup demand for foreign consumer goods. Importations to New Granada were somewhat obstructed until 1821 by Spanish military control of much of the Caribbean coast. But after that time imports, primarily of British goods, swelled, greatly increasing income from customs duties. By 1825–1826, admittedly an exceptional year, when imports from Great Britain reached a temporary peak, revenues from customs collections appear to have been perhaps six times as great as before 1810. Whereas customs collections made up only about an eighth of total revenues in the last years of the colonial era, by 1825–1826 duties on foreign trade probably accounted for more than half of all tax income.

Despite increased revenues from customs duties, the new republic was far from being able to meet its expenses. It had more people on the payroll than the colonial regime—it had to sustain a national congress as well as diplomatic representatives—and it had more judges and provincial administrators than had existed before 1810. The expense of sustaining large military forces in the fight for independence, however, was overwhelmingly the greatest fiscal burden during the 1820s. Although patriot forces had gained the upper hand in New Granada in 1819–1820, the Colombian army went on fighting until 1825—in struggles against the royalists on the Caribbean coast of New Granada and in Venezuela, Pasto, Ecuador, and ultimately in Peru and the territory that became Bolivia. Even after the actual fighting stopped, the Republic of Colombia still had a large army that somehow had to be paid. As of 1825, when the fight for independence ended, Colombia had possibly 25,000–30,000 men under arms, and military expenditures were absorbing more than five million pesos, roughly three-quarters of government revenues. During the 1820s, consequently, the Colombian government struggled under heavy deficits.

To reduce expenditures the government in 1822 ultimately withheld two-thirds of the salaries of civilian employees and one-third of those of the military. To sustain itself the republic during the early 1820s also resorted to issuing paper currency, whose value was backed by the products of the government salt monopoly. And it turned to internal borrowing—much of it in the form of more or less forced loans. But the government also looked to England for financing. By the time Colombia was proclaimed by the Congress of Angostura in December 1819 and more formally created by the Congress of Cúcuta in 1821, British and other creditors already were making substantial claims stemming from sales of military supplies to various patriot forces before 1819. Colombian agents in London between 1819 and 1822 may have recognized some illegitimate debts. But the fact was that the new republic, desperately in need of funds for a struggle it might well not win, was not in a good bargaining position in its dealings with British merchant-capitalists. Ultimately, in 1824, the Republic of Colombia recognized a debt totaling £6,750,000 (or, at five pesos to the pound sterling, 33,750,000 pesos).

This amounted to about five times the republic's annual revenues. Of that total, £2,000,000, roughly 30 percent, represented previously accumulated debts from 1810 to 1824. A new loan of £4,750,000 was expected to tide the republic over its fiscal crisis, but military expenditures quickly ate up much of it.

Furthermore, because of discounts and advance interest payments, Colombia actually received far less than the face value of the loan. And after financial crisis hit the London market in November 1825, Colombia lost some £400,000 that had been left in the hands of its British bond merchant, who went bankrupt early in 1826. With the collapse of the British bond market in 1825–1826 and the discovery that Colombia (like most other new Spanish American states) could not pay the interest on its foreign debt, the republic's credit was destroyed, and the flow of foreign funds came virtually to a halt. The republic was left with an external debt far too large for its meager resources to cope with. Subsequently, after the collapse of the Republic of Colombia in 1830, the successor state of New Granada periodically sought to establish its credit by reaching settlements with its European creditors on its share of the Colombian debt. But New Granada was not able to sustain any of these agreements for very long. In part because of its inability to service the debt, but probably even more because it seemed to offer very limited economic possiblities, New Granada was able to attract little foreign investment for much of the rest of the nineteenth century. Meanwhile, within Colombia, opponents of the Santander administration laid down a heavy barrage of criticism, accusing the government and its agents of incompetence and corruption in handling the foreign loans.

When British funds stopped flowing after the financial crisis of 1825–1826, Colombia's fiscal emergency intensified. By late 1826 civilian government employees were not being paid at all, and the military were being paid very little. The authority of the government seemed to be disintegrating, and its leaders increasingly feared military rebellion. Chronic fiscal crisis provided part of the context for the political strife that rent Colombia in the late 1820s and ultimately led to its breakup in 1830.

CONFLICTS

During the 1820s there emerged several conflicts that were important either because they portended the breakup of Colombia or because they found long-term expression in national politics. Among the latter was the developing contention over the power and privileges of the Church. The aspirations of the country's small, university-educated elite (particularly lawyers) to introduce liberal ideas and institutions into Colombia generated much of this controversy. Many clergy perceived the incursion of such ideas as likely to undermine the traditional authority of the Church. Clerical sensitivity probably was intensified by a sense of relative decline in the strength of Church. Even before the beginning of the independence era, Enlightenment influences appear to have begun to discourage the entry of members of elite families into the clergy. After 1810 interest in clerical careers further declined because political leadership opened up new career possibilities for the elite. Further, during the struggle for independence, papal support for the Spanish Crown and disagreement between the Vatican and the republican government over authority to nominate bishops had impeded the consecration of new clergy. By 1825, the number of secular priests in New Granada had dropped by one-third from those existing in 1776, and there were one-sixth fewer friars. Undoubtedly a sense of decline in numbers and authority intensified the antagonism of many clergy to the introduction of Enlightenment-inspired ideas as well as to government measures tending to weaken the Church as an institution.

The clergy were not completely unified in attacking elite liberalism, as some priests themselves advocated liberal ideas and policies. But certain aspects of the liberal project of the university-educated elite met noisy opposition from a number of clerics, who were able to stir anti-liberal hysteria among the mass of the country's less-educated citizens. The gulf between the secularizing goals of the university-educated liberal elite and the traditional piety of the country's common people proved a source of political vulnerability for Colombian liberalism from the 1820s through the nineteenth century and beyond.

Partly because of deliberate restraint on the part of both lay liberals and clerical delegates, the Congress of Cúcuta avoided major disputes over Church issues. Even so, there were hints of problems to come. The Congress's abolition of the Inquisition provoked some murmuring among the clergy. But the Cúcuta decision that raised the biggest outcry was the decision to shut down monasteries and convents inhabited by less than eight religious. This decision, as well as one in 1826 to raise the age of taking religious vows to twenty-five, in part reflected a belief that religious orders were unproductive and, as a burden on the economy, should be scaled down. The Colombian legislators intended to put the resources of the convents to more productive use—supporting secondary education. Understandably, the regular clergy felt threatened, still more so when some laymen proposed suppressing religious communities altogether.

After the Congress of Cúcuta other Church-related issues emerged. The Colombian government had to settle its relations with the Vatican, including papal recognition of the Republic of Colombia and resolving the question of whether the republican government would exercise the *patronato real*, that is, whether it would play the same role in selecting bishops and parish priests as had the Spanish monarchy. Vice President Santander and many in the lay elite argued that the selection of clergy was an inherent right of government, while the Vatican and some Colombian clergy contended that it was a privilege specifically granted by the Pope to the Spanish Crown and did not automatically apply to the republican government. This conflict was settled through a de facto compromise in 1827, when the Vatican began to confirm bishops and priests nominated by the Colombian government. Some other issues had to do with Church property rights, most particularly whether Church rights to quit-rents (*censos*) might be in any way altered. But these issues, while of great interest to the clergy and to the political elite, did not inspire anxiety among the mass of the population. The *patronato* issue was more a matter of diplomatic negotiation with the Vatican than of internal politics. Church property issues directly affected the economic interests of many people, but in the 1820s at least they did not stir widespread public passion.

On the other hand, political liberals pressed some innovations that affected deeply held traditional beliefs and thus could be used by resistant clergy to arouse strong hostility among those less-educated people who had remained untouched by the Enlightenment. The issues that provoked the most heated discussion in the 1820s involved the introduction of new foreign ideas that appeared to conflict with church doctrines.

To some degree the problems posed by newly imported beliefs were prompted by the Colombian political elite's desire to encourage European immigration. The chief public justification for seeking European immigrants, and one of its real motivations, was to bring to the country people with capital, education, and technical skills that would aid Colombia's economic development. Encouraging Europeans to immigrate, however, required creating an atmosphere of greater religious toleration, of openness to new ideas and secular practices already current in Europe. Some clergy reacted bitterly to the intrusion of small numbers of Europeans and to the gestures toward religious toleration that were meant to encourage immigration. In October 1823, Secretary of the Interior José Manuel Restrepo, a man touched by the Enlightenment but of conservative disposition, noted in his diary the appearance of "a multitude of writers . . . who, affecting zeal for the Catholic religion, preach absolute intolerance, that we not admit any foreigner, and that Colombia return to the darkness that covered it in 1800." These fanatical preachments, Restrepo observed, "stem from the fact that, as the people become more educated, the ecclesiastics begin to lose their influence and defend the terrain inch by inch." (He also claimed that these aroused clergy were opponents of independence and were using the pretext of religion to discredit the republic.) Restrepo worried about the impact of their preachings on the uneducated: "the lower class will be capable of committing murders."

The clerical reaction against the incursion of foreigners and foreign impieties found expression, as early as 1822, in vigorous attacks upon the spread of Freemasonry among the political elite. Freemasonry first came to New Granada as an outgrowth of its external trade; the first lodge was founded in Cartagena in 1808, with a patent issued by a Masonic lodge in Jamaica. Early in the 1820s not a few upper-class Colombians—including Vice President Santander, several cabinet ministers, and even some clergy—became Masons. Some of the early members later denounced Freemasonry when they became more fully aware of the Roman Catholic Church's hostility to it. But Masonry remained a common tie among many men in the political current that ultimately emerged as the Liberal Party.

Another issue that aroused some clergy was the founding of Bible societies, whose aim was to spread knowledge of Holy Scripture among the people. Such societies were promoted by an agent of the British and Foreign Bible Society, who entered the republic late in 1824. Many in the Bogotá elite, including cabinet officers and some high ecclesiastics, in 1825 joined in forming a Bible society in the capital. Subsequently, when it became clear that the Bible societies were instruments of Protestant penetration, many clergy turned against this innovation.

In November 1825 the Santander administration ordered the use of Jeremy Bentham's treatises on civil and penal legislation in the university law course on principles of legislation. Clergy and pious laymen objected to Bentham because he called for social decisions to be made according to a utilitarian calculus rather than in light of Christian doctrine. They also chose to interpret Bentham's pleasure–pain calculus as an encouragement to sybarritic, amoral behavior. On another level, Bentham's philosophy was based upon a sensational epistemology—that is, upon the idea that experience, rather than divine inspiration, is the source of truth. Denouncing Bentham as a "materialist," clergy and proclerical laymen campaigned to remove his text on legislation from the law curriculum. Liberals in the Santander administration counterattacked, not only with defenses of Bentham in the press but also by urging sanctions against particularly outspoken priests. The controversy over Bentham periodically resurfaced during the nineteenth century.

In addition to clashing with clergy, liberal lawyers conflicted with military officers. In part it was a contest for power between two groups with different claims to authority, the military on the strength of having liberated the country, the lawyers by virtue of their legal preparation. They also differed in ideology and culture. The lawyers were committed by profession, at least formally, to the rule of law and tended to condemn military officers as acting arbitrarily and violently. The military, for their part, tended to view the lawyers as pompous and self-important and their laws as unrealistic obstacles to effective action.

To the civilian elite it was important to bring the military under the rule of law. According to José Manuel Restrepo, some military officers objected even to having a constitution, which inevitably would restrict the military's arbitrary authority. Military men were angered when civilian legislators at Cúcuta in 1821, as well as subsequently, sought to cut back the juridical privileges of the military. Some civilians also held that soldiers should not be allowed to vote. On some occasions enlisted men were denied the vote because they did not fulfill the property qualifications. Beyond that, some civilian legislators contended that military men in general should be denied the vote because, as they had to obey their superiors, they could not exercise independent judgment. Meanwhile, in the fiscal crisis of the 1820s, the military, like civilian government employees, often went unpaid or only partially paid. At the same time civilian legislators, particularly in 1825, when the fight for independence was coming to a close, were voicing criticisms of extravagant military expenditures. Considering all of these things, military officers felt that civilian political authorities did not sufficiently appreciate their liberators. For their part, civilians in public life feared violent reprisals by military officers.

The conflicts between military officers and civilians in public life in part reflected class and cultural differences. Many of the military officers, particularly among the Venezuelans, were uneducated men of humble social origins. By contrast, civilian political leaders generally came from relatively high-status families and had university educations, usually with degrees in law. Some civilian lawyer-politicians both condemned the capricious actions of military officers and mocked their lack of education and culture. Criticisms of and sarcasms about the military, uttered in Congress and even more in the press, aggravated the irritation of army officers toward civilian politicians. The officers particularly disliked lawyers, who, in the eyes of the military, were masters of intrigue. Further, the lawyers, with their legal locutions, both flaunted their literary education and befuddled those who were less educated. In a characteristic military complaint against lawyer-legislators, General José Antonio Páez from Caracas in October 1825 reminded Bolívar that the Spanish General Pablo Morillo had once told the Liberator that the Spanish had done Bolívar "a favor in killing lawyers." Páez regretted that the patriot military had not completed the extermination. The lawyers, he added, "are in open war with an army to whom they owe their very existence."

In February 1826, Vice President Santander, whose politics often allied him with liberal lawyers, summed up the situation:

> The discontent of the military is spreading because everywhere they are treated with distrust, and even with scorn, the effect on the one hand of the bad conduct and worse manners of some of our officers, and on the other of the fact that the ambitious lawyers want to destroy anyone that can oppose them.

The rancor between civilians and military officers was intensified in New Granada by the fact that a large proportion of military officers were Venezuelans, while the lawyers who dominated the judiciary, legislative, and central executive positions were New Granadans. Thus, the division between civilians and military became intertwined with regional tensions between New Granadans and Venezuelans.

Rivalry between Venezuelans and New Granadans was most acute in the former colonial capitals of Caracas and Bogotá. In the colonial era Caracas had been the seat of government for the captaincy-general of Venezuela, and the Caracas elite did not take well to their role as a provincial dependency under Bogotá. In 1821 the *caraqueños* had objected when the Congress of Cúcuta chose Bogotá as the national capital. They also denied the legitimacy of the 1821 constitution on the ground that Caracas had not been adequately represented at Cúcuta and that the constitution had not been properly ratified. Further, they complained that New Granadans were monopolizing government positions in Bogotá, making Venezuelans semicolonists. (In fact, it was inevitable that *granadinos* would dominate the civil government in Bogotá, because distance tended to diminish the representation of both Venezuelans and Ecuadoreans.) Soon after the adoption of the constitution of 1821, some dissidents in Caracas began to call for a federalist structure that would place Caracas at the head of a more autonomous Venezuela.

Relations between Bogotá and Caracas and between New Granadan civilians and Venezuelan military officers were worsened by a series of events beginning with the murder trial of Colonel Leonardo Infante, a black Venezuelan *llanero* who allegedly had terrorized the Bogotá neighborhood in which he resided and in 1824 was convicted of killing another black Venezuelan officer in the capital. When a Bogotá court-martial, in a divided decision, voted a death sentence for Infante, the president of the court, Miguel Peña, a Venezuelan, refused to sign the sentence. In response, the Colombian Senate in 1825 suspended Peña from his court duties. Peña retaliated by complaining to Bolívar that the Santander government was hostile both to Venezuelans and to military officers as a class. Afterward, he joined those in Caracas already agitating for the separation of Venezuela from the government in Bogotá. The death penalty ultimately carried out against Infante alienated Venezuelan military officers, while the treatment of Peña provided more fuel for attacks in Caracas on the central government.

Peña and other Venezuelan dissidents found in General José Antonio Páez the strong man they needed to lead the departure of Venezuela from the Republic of Colombia. Páez was a tough *llanero* chieftain who had played a leading role in the military liberation of Venezuela. But when the task of fighting Spanish forces gave way to that of constructing a new government, Páez found himself subordinated to other officers of greater refinement but less military achievement. His New Granadan rival, Francisco de Paula Santander, had become vice president of the republic. To this irritation was added the central government's interference in matters of public order in the region under Páez's command, made worse by the fact that some political leaders in Bogotá questioned his loyalty. In 1825 Páez wrote Bolívar denouncing the civilian legislators in Bogotá who sought to reduce the military heroes of the independence "to the condition of slaves."

Páez's anger at the government in Bogotá intensified when the Chamber of Representatives in March 1826 brought charges against him for abuse of power in military recruitment in Caracas. The complaints against Páez actually were initiated by rival authorities in Caracas, including the municipal government, and were pressed in the national Congress by Venezuelan congressmen. Vice President Santander, for his part, tried to discourage the

Congress from taking action against Páez, anticipating a violent reaction from the Venezuelan general. The Congress, however, intent upon demonstrating civilian authority over the military, pressed ahead. Ironically, Páez blamed Santander and his government, more than his fellow Venezuelans, for bringing the charges. The congressional accusation against Páez in 1826 prompted him, with the encouragement of both civilian and military dissidents in Venezuela, to lead a movement to separate Venezuela from Colombia. This movement burst forth in the city of Valencia at the end of April 1826 and spread quickly to Caracas and other cities in central Venezuela.

The Venezuelan crisis was one of several important sources of conflict between Vice President Santander and his allies, on the one hand, and Simón Bolívar and his followers on the other. The breach that developed between these leaders and their adherents between 1826 and 1828 may be thought of as establishing the magnetic field that has oriented a substantial part of Colombian political history. The rupture between groups supporting Santander and Bolívar marks the first of several points of division between the two political constellations that ultimately came to be known as the Liberal and Conservative parties. And just as the parting of the Liberator and Santander marked the first dividing point between two long-term political traditions, so also has it established a dominant framework for conventional Colombian political historiography. Bolívar loyalists and opposing adherents of Santander developed two contrasting narratives, each explaining the break in ways that blamed the other side. Since then these diverging narratives have been perpetuated and developed by historical writings representing Colombia's Conservative and Liberal party traditions, with Conservatives exalting the Liberator and denigrating Santander, while the Liberal tradition has tended to defend Santander.

Tensions between the vice president and the Liberator had surfaced while Bolívar was in Peru from 1823 through 1825. Bolívar was angered by the slowness with which Santander's financially strapped government provided support for his troops in Peru. Bolívar also was infuriated when Santander questioned whether the Liberator might legally exercise his "extraordinary faculties" as president of Colombia, or whether his orders were binding on officials in Colombia, while he was in Peru. The Colombian Congress in July 1824 responded by declaring that Bolívar could not exercise any power at all in Colombia while he was in Peru. The furious Liberator responded by resigning his direct command of the Colombian army in Peru—even though the decision of the Colombian Congress did not require Bolívar to give up his command. This incident not only soured relations between Bolívar and Santander but also increased Venezuelan military officers' resentment of Santander, both because he had questioned Bolívar's authority and because he had cast doubt on the validity of their own promotions. Despite these conflicts, Bolívar supported Santander's reelection as vice president in 1825, and in May 1826 proposed to resign the presidency so that Santander might replace him.

Relations between the Liberator and his vice president began to deteriorate to a point of no return only during the latter half of 1826. Several intertwined issues fed a conflict that led to an obsessive mutual antagonism. One source of division was Bolívar's attempt to implant in Colombia a new constitution that he had conceived late in 1825 for the new republic of Bolivia. The other had to do with the Liberator's manner of dealing with Páez's separatist rebellion in Venezuela.

After the decisive defeat of royalist forces at Ayacucho in December 1824 effectively had liberated Peru and Upper Peru, Bolívar was lionized as a conquering hero throughout the region. In August 1825 leaders in Upper Peru decided to become an independent state, to name that state after Bolívar, and to ask the Liberator to write its constitution. This invitation, along with honors showered on Bolívar in Peru and elsewhere, induced in the Liberator a belief that he could serve as the supreme state-builder of the Andes. At the time that he drafted the constitution for Bolivia (November–December 1825), Bolívar was receiving reports of agitation in Colombia, particularly in Venezuela, for widely differing kinds of regime change. Some in the Venezuelan elite for years had advocated more federalist autonomy, but others were said to be inclined to monarchy. Bolívar endeavored to incorporate both of these extremes in his constitution. He sought the stability and permanence of monarchy by putting at the head of his ideal state a president who would serve for life and who, in nominating his vice president, could choose his successor. Further, one of three legislative bodies, the censors, also would serve for life. On the other hand, a college of electors, consisting of one individual for each ten adult male citizens, at least in the Liberator's mind, would provide representation of local interests, thus, he hoped, appealing to federalists. Bolívar, aflame with the pride of authorship, viewed the constitution for Bolivia as the ideal remedy for the political ills of Spanish America. As the constitution was being adopted in Bolivia and Peru during the Liberator's presence there, Bolívar, while still in Peru, also sought its establishment in Colombia.

The Liberator's dedication to the propagation of his constitution was reinforced by word that the existing government in Colombia was functioning badly. The Peruvian delegate to the Congress of Panama of 1825, José María Pando, on his return from the isthmus in May 1826, informed Bolívar that he had been told that Colombia was suffering a host of ills: The government's revenues were inadequate, there were too many government employees, the administration of justice was too complicated, there were too many laws and people did not understand them. The Liberator readily accepted the truth of Pando's report. (The fact that Pando enthusiastically praised the Bolivian Constitution tended to confirm Bolívar's trust in Pando's judgment.) Pando's message, that the Colombian government was dysfunctional and disliked, provided further justification for implanting Bolívar's new constitution.

When the Liberator passed on Pando's report to Santander, the vice president at first denied its truth, claiming that it was at least exaggerated. Two weeks later (July 19, 1826), however, the vice president confessed a host of afflictions to the Liberator. Excessively liberal laws made prosecution of crimes difficult. And, it was true, most people did not understand the laws. Press attacks on men in public office made them reluctant to serve in the government. Government expenses did outrun revenues. The abolition of some colonial imposts by the Congress of Cúcuta in 1821 had reduced government income, a problem further aggravated by widespread tax evasion. At the same time the republic had to bear the heavy burden of the foreign and domestic debt and the cost of the military expedition to Peru. Santander denied that the government had too many employees: The cost of civilian employees, including those engaged in revenue collection, was less than two million pesos; the biggest difficulty was sustaining the military, at an annual cost of eight to twelve million pesos. While Santander may have intended to suggest to Bolívar that military costs were the principal problem, the vice president's recital of woes must have confirmed the Liberator's belief that a radical change in the system was necessary.

Even before receiving this litany of troubles, however, Bolívar was drumming up support for his constitution in Colombia. In February 1826, when the Liberator received a letter from Páez, proposing that Bolívar establish a Napoleonic regime, Bolívar rejected this imperial vision, urging Páez instead to support the Bolivian constitution. At this time, the Liberator envisioned the adoption of his constitution in Colombia as occurring in 1831, as the existing constitution of 1821 provided that it could not be reformed for a decade. But a regime change became more urgent in July 1826, when the Liberator learned of Páez's move to separate Venezuela from Colombia the previous April. Bolívar responded to this crisis by encouraging military pronouncements favoring emergency rule by the Liberator, to be quickly followed by the establishment of the Bolivian constitution. In August 1826 Bolívar was commending his constitution to various senior military officers, including the intendants in Guayaquil and Cartagena. These messages were borne by Antonio Leocadio Guzmán, whom Páez had sent to Peru to urge his Napoleonic project on Bolívar, and whom the Liberator sent back to Venezuela, via Guayaquil, Panama, Cartagena, with the evangel of the Bolivian constitution. In most places on Guzmán's itinerary, his arrival prompted a military-organized popular pronouncement in favor of a Bolivarian dictatorship and/or the Bolivian constitution.

Santander, along with other liberals in New Granada, disliked several aspects of this process. The vice president held that there was no legal way to reform the constitution before 1831. The vice president also condemned the military-organized pronouncements as unconstitutional. (Attempting to avoid further such pronouncements, Santander ordered that the Liberator's agent, Guzmán, be detained in Cartagena—an order that the staunch Bolivarian intendant, General Mariano Montilla, chose to ignore.) Finally, Santander voiced his anguish that Bolívar was using his influence to overthrow the existing order when his authority was such that a single word from him would be sufficient to maintain it. And, indeed, Bolívar's decision to pursue his constitutional dream by encouraging a series of military-driven pronouncements did have a profoundly disorganizing effect upon the republic. Instead of bringing the order he sought, Bolívar destabilized the system by encouraging the further reopening of the constitutional question.

In addition to the unconstitutional procedures that the Liberator had fostered, Santander, like other New Granadan liberals, objected to the Bolivarian constitution itself. Bolívar's code would establish, in effect, a constitutional monarchy in republican dress; in so doing it would violate the fundamental republican principle of alternation in power. The Vice President, however, refrained from making this criticism in his letters to the Liberator. Rather, Santander quietly supported publication, at the time of Bolívar's arrival in Bogotá, of a brief against the Bolivian constitution penned by Vicente Azuero.

When Bolívar passed through Bogotá in November 1826, on his way to dealing with the Páez rebellion in Venezuela, his relations with Santander were strained but peaceable. Santander believed that he had convinced Bolívar not to attempt a constitutional reform before 1831. Accordingly, he and his liberal supporters undertook a press campaign to turn national opinion against the Bolivarian constitution. It was the agitation of the Bogotá press, after the Liberator left the capital, against Bolívar's constitution as well as his approach to the rebellion in Venezuela, that finally brought a complete rupture in his relations with the vice president.

For his part Santander became still more upset at the Liberator because of the way he handled the crisis in Venezuela. Throughout the 1820s Bolívar had considered Páez to be among a small number of generals whose commanding influence, and therefore whose good opinion, was essential to maintain the system. In 1825, when Venezuelan federalist, or separatist, agitation appeared increasingly threatening, the Liberator had sent Peruvian troops northward for the purpose of keeping Venezuela under control. But Bolívar's assumption at that time was that Páez would command those troops, using them to restrain the Venezuelan separatists. Now that Páez was leading the separatist movement, the Liberator proved unwilling to challenge him militarily, ultimately turning to conciliation. During the first half of 1827 the Liberator was able to persuade Páez to end his rebellion, but at a cost of conceding Páez effective control of a virtually independent Venezuela. Bolívar granted Páez complete amnesty and confirmed him as the ruling chief in Venezuela. Such an amnesty, Santander and his New Granadan supporters protested, was really a capitulation. Bolívar also promoted military officers who had joined Páez's rebellion while not rewarding those Venezuelan officers who had stood with the government. Further, the Liberator praised Páez for "saving the republic." Bolívar's exaltation of Páez and those who had joined him in rebellion was taken as a slap in the face by Santander and others who had sought to bring Páez and Venezuela under the control of constitutional processes and the authority of the national government.

During the crises of 1826–1827 two contending parties developed. A Bolivarian party believed that only the Liberator could save the country, and many of his adherents were prepared to do whatever Bolívar ordered—for which reason their opponents called them *serviles*. Many of the most unrestrained Bolivarians were military officers, for the most part Venezuelans but also some New Granadans. Some British officers who had fought under the Liberator were also highly visible among the Bolivarians. In March 1827 General Rafael Urdaneta voiced both these officers' unconditional allegiance to the Liberator and their distrust of lawyers. The liberal lawyers, Urdaneta wrote,

> who are so ostentatious about knowing much, . . . entangle us in their theories, when we don't need . . . written theories, having . . . the talent of Bolívar, to tell us what we ought to do. . . . If opinion is free in Colombia, mine is for the Liberator, and I will serve no one but him, I do not recognize any government but his.

Venezuelan generals in New Granada were particularly active in encouraging a Bolivarian dictatorship. In mid-1827 military units in Cartagena, where the Venezuelan General Mariano Montilla was in command, offered to march to suppress the liberal critics of the Liberator. And agents of General Urdaneta were inducing towns in the northern provinces (Socorro, Pamplona) to adopt proclamations favoring dictatorial faculties for Bolívar. The Liberator himself took such military-inspired public acts as substantial justification for exercising dicatorial powers. In Bolívar's view the army was in fact the people in arms, whereas his liberal lawyer opponents represented only a tiny university-educated elite.

While many military officers were among the most unconditional supporters of Bolívar, the Liberator also had a following among New Granadan civilians. Some of these were Colombian aristocrats who were willing to concentrate authority in the Liberator's hands, as the surest bulwark against the onset of political, and perhaps also social, disorder. Among the most notable of these civilian Bolivarians were aristocratic elements in Popayán, Cartagena, and Bogotá.

If some of Bolívar's unconditional supporters looked with favor upon extraconstitutional rule by the Liberator, his liberal opponents as early as July 1827 contemplated attempting a revolution against his rule. The Liberator's critics, many of whom looked to Vice President Santander as their leader, called themselves constitutionalists (because they upheld the constitution of 1821) or liberals. New Granadan lawyers from the northern provinces of the Eastern Cordillera—such as Vicente Azuero, Francisco Soto, and Diego Fernando Gómez—were the ideological spearheads of this party. These relatively uncompromising liberals had strong support from some men from various parts of the Magdalena Valley, from Mompox to Neiva, and more moderate allies in Antioquia and various parts of the Eastern Cordillera. Some New Granadan army officers from the Socorro region provided military support for Santanderista liberalism, but two of the preeminent liberal caudillos, Colonels José María Obando and José Hilario López, hailed from the Cauca.

THE END OF GREATER COLOMBIA

As the simultaneous conflicts between Venezuelans and New Granadans, military and civilian elites, Bolivarians and Santanderistas became acute during 1825–1827, Colombian notables struggled with the problem of devising a political future for the nation. Thoughts about how the polity might be reconstructed were stimulated in part by Bolívar's call for an early constitutional convention, but also by the apparent possibility, if not likelihood, that Venezuela, New Granada, and Ecuador might go their separate ways. By 1827 each of the three regions in many respects already was operating in de facto autonomy.

Colombia's cabinet ministers, among others in the political elite, feared that if the republic dissolved into separate Venezuelan, New Granadan, and Ecuadoran units, the resulting states would be too small and weak to be viable. European ambassadors concerned about the repayment of the huge Colombian debt to foreign creditors particularly prompted some Colombian notables to worry that the collapse of the union would bring the smaller states into conflict with Great Britain and with each other over the settlement of the foreign debt.

The Liberator hoped that a constitutional convention, by adopting the Bolivarian constitution or some similarly stabilizing instrument, would provide the basis for Colombian union. But the convention, held in the northern mountain town of Ocaña, from March to June 1828, proved a great disappointment to the Bolivarians, for the Santanderistas proved more successful in getting delegates elected than the Bolivarians had anticipated. The Bolivarians attributed the Santanderista success to ungentlemanly politicking to get their men chosen. In fact, however, the Bolivarians also worked to manipulate the selection of delegates in areas where they had effective influence. The result was a virtual deadlock between two angry, intransigent parties, with a group of moderates, among them Joaquín and Rafael Mosquera of Popayán and José Ignacio Márquez of Boyacá, standing between them.

The Bolivarians hoped to implant some variant of the Bolivian constitution, or at least a centralized system featuring a strong executive with ample emergency powers. On the other hand, Santander, Vicente Azuero, and other liberal leaders, who had been centralists up to the time of the Ocaña convention, were now seeking a more federal structure as a check against a Bolivarian dictatorship. Although both sides were highly polarized on these points, each faction modified its proposals in the hope of winning moderate support. The Bolivarian project at Ocaña called for an eight-year term for the president, with no restriction on reelection—an attempt at reducing the number of destabilizing elections that approached, but obviously fell short of, Bolívar's life-presidency. The Santander party, by contrast, proposed a four-year presidential term and forbade reelection. To create further barriers to a Bolivarian dictatorship, the liberals also sought to reduce the extraordinary emergency powers granted to the executive in the constitution of 1821 and to create departmental assemblies permitting the development of greater provincial autonomy.

While the Bolivarians modified their constitutional proposal to win moderate votes, they were not happy about doing so. Many of them thought they were conceding too many limits on the executive powers they wished to grant the Liberator. Well before the convention the Bolivarians had decided that, if they could not get their way, they would walk out of the convention and, in effect, establish a regime of force. As the Liberator himself wrote to the Bolivarian delegate General Pedro Briceño Méndez, in March 1828, before the Ocaña convention began its sessions,

> Tell the federalists that they cannot count on the country if they triumph, since the army and the people are resolved to oppose them openly. The national sanction is in reserve to impede that which the people do not like.

Bolívar added that his supporters "ought to leave rather than signing . . . what is not in accord with their conscience." On May 6 José María Castillo y Rada, the leader of the Bolivarian delegation at Ocaña, echoed these views: If the liberals obtain any part of their program, he wrote Bolívar, "a considerable number of us are resolved to leave, so that the Convention cannot continue its work, . . . and denounce their crime to the Nation, and persecute them to death." Two days later, Castillo y Rada reiterated that if the liberal constitution prevailed, the Bolivarians would dissolve the convention and the Santander party "would not enjoy their triumph, because we will carry out a war of extermination until we annihilate their race." Accordingly, on June 10, 1828, the Bolivarians left the convention, denying it a quorum—thus, in their minds, opening the way for unconstrained rule by the Liberator.

As the Ocaña convention sputtered toward collapse, Bolivarians moved to proclaim the Liberator dictator. By June 7, before the convention actually broke up, General Rafael Urdaneta, the secretary of war, with the agreement of the rest of the cabinet, was planning a public meeting in the capital that would reject the acts of the convention (whatever they might be) and would confer on Bolívar an absolute dictatorship. Urdaneta took particular pleasure in having Bogotá as the site of this act, since he viewed the capital as a center of Santanderista constitutionalism. On June 13 Colonel Pedro Alcántara Herrán, the intendent of Cundinamarca, carried out Urdaneta's plan to the letter. In the meeting of Bogotá notables the few who dared to dissent were intimidated into silence. Urdaneta's next step was to have the local garrison endorse the action of the Bogotá meeting. ("The troops tomorrow will take an oath to recognize the will pronounced by the people and to sustain the wishes of the Liberator. After this act all opposition will be overcome by sheer force.") The Bogotá initiative was quickly seconded by similar pronouncements elsewhere. Taking such public meetings, and the failure of the convention at Ocaña, as sufficient justification, the Liberator proceeded to rule by decree. Despite this apparent triumph, some Bolivarians remained uneasy about the continued presence of Santander and his adherents in the country. When Santander received demonstrations of support in Pamplona and Cúcuta, his native province, Urdaneta concluded that that region "never will be decidedly ours, if we don't clean out those gentlemen."

To shore up the new regime, the Liberator made a deliberate appeal for Church support. Bolívar was schooled in Enlightenment secularism, and his explicit opposition to an established Church in his introduction to the Bolivian constitution in 1826 had irritated clergy and pious laymen. But in July and August 1828 he courted the clergy. He abrogated some of the legislation of the early 1820s that had irked some churchmen—for example, the 1821 law that had suppressed monasteries and convents with fewer than eight members and a subsequent law that had prohibited the taking of religious vows before the age of twenty-five. Further, he invited the Archbishop of Bogotá to propose to the government any additional changes that might be desirable. And when Bolívar issued his decree of August 27, 1828, outlining the organization of his dictatorship, he included a promise to sustain and protect the Roman Catholic Church. Bolívar already could count on overwhelming support from the military. Nonetheless, he appealed to army officers by restoring full military privileges enjoyed under Spanish rule, which had been trimmed back earlier in the decade.

Bolívar and his advisers in August 1828 contemplated decreeing the establishment of a regime that would combine features of the Cúcuta and Bolivarian constitutions, including, as General Rafael Urdaneta put it, "a legislative body like that of England, although without lords and without a nobility." But the Liberator finally desisted when cautioned by the moderate Joaquín Mosquera, a Popayán aristocrat whom Bolívar particularly respected. Instead, Bolívar's organic decree of August 27, which served in effect as a dictatorial constitution, simply claimed for himself, as "Liberator President," both legislative and executive powers until a new constitution could be written by a convention to meet in January 1830. The organic decree established an advisory council of state of eighteen men, all appointed by Bolívar himself. To remove Santander from the scene, Bolívar abolished the office of vice president and appointed him Colombian envoy to the United States.

In reaction to Bolívar's dictatorship, young liberals in the capital plotted to seize the Liberator and his ministers, with the aid of a New Granadan military unit then in the Bogotá garrison, and proclaim Santander as the constitutional chief of Colombia. When one of the plotters, the young lawyer Florentino González, consulted Santander about this plan, Santander expressed sympathy for their cause, but opposed executing the plot while he was in the country. When González countered that the plan depended upon having Santander present as the constitutional leader, Santander (according to González's later testimony) fell silent, which González interpreted as tacit assent. The conspirators were young lawyers or university students, joined by some junior and mid-level military officers. González claimed that their initial intention was not to murder Bolívar, but, when the plot was discovered and they had to act with precipitation, that in effect appeared to become their aim. In a hasty and ill-organized action, the conspirators attempted to assassinate (or seize) Bolívar in the presidential palace on the night of September 25, 1828. However, with the aid of his mistress Manuela Saenz, the Liberator managed to escape by leaping from a palace window and hiding under a bridge until military forces loyal to him could regain control of the capital. Many of the conspirators were arrested and tried summarily by a military court, and fourteen were executed. Among those shot was General José Padilla, one of the few blacks who had attained the rank of general in Colombia. Padilla, being held in the capital on an accusation of mutiny in Cartagena, had been selected by the conspirators as the man to take military command of Bogotá after their coup, although Padilla himself may well have known nothing of the plot.

After the assassination attempt Bolivarians redoubled their efforts to eliminate Santander and his partisans from Colombian politics. Bolívar temporarily moved his minister of war, the steely General Rafael Urdaneta, to the post of military commander of Cundinamarca so that Urdaneta might preside over the prosecution of the conspirators. Santander was among those condemned to death by the court martial. But Bolívar's council of state, to the disgust of Urdaneta, urged the Liberator to commute Santander's death sentence. Santander was imprisoned in Cartagena and then sent into exile. Many liberals who had nothing to do with the conspiracy also were exiled and/or imprisoned. Among those exiled were Vicente Azuero, who had served in the supreme court, and Francisco Soto, a perennial legislator. At the time of the plot both were living far from the capital—Azuero in el Socorro, Soto in Pamplona—and learned of the attempt on Bolívar's life only when soldiers came to arrest them.

The Bolivarians sought to eliminate not only liberal leaders but also the germ of subversive principles. Noting that many of the participants were young lawyers and university students, the Bolivarians concluded that Colombian youths were being corrupted by the university curriculum. Bolívar already had prohibited the use of Bentham in March 1828; after the September conspiracy he also suspended study of the principles of legislation, public law, constitutional law, and administrative science and added required courses on the foundations of the Roman Catholic religion.

The assault on the Liberator coincided with a developing threat of war with Peru and a Peruvian-encouraged rebellion against the Bolívarian regime in the Cauca region, led by the Santanderista caudillos José María Obando and José Hilario López. The Cauca rebellion, beginning in October

1828, centered on the Patía Valley, between Popayán and Pasto, where Obando had a following. Bolívar, who had marched to the Cauca to attend to the war with Peru as well as to put down the rebellion, extended an amnesty to Obando and López, tacitly accepting their de facto control of Pasto and Popayán—rather than try to fight local guerrillas in the formidable terrain of these places, where so much blood had been shed during the war for independence. Meanwhile, the rebellion in the upper Cauca and the war with Peru temporarily revived separatist agitation in Venezuela.

At this juncture, while Bolívar remained in the south, both he and his council of ministers in Bogotá were growing increasingly anxious about the future of Colombia. As of April 1829 Colombia enjoyed domestic peace. But by this time Buenos Aires, Chile, Guatemala, and Mexico, as well as Peru and Bolivia, had experienced substantial turmoil, reinforcing the Bolivarians' pessimism about political order in Spanish America. The council of ministers worried that the union of Venezuela, New Granada, and Ecuador would not survive the death of Bolívar. The Bolivarians therefore had to begin to contemplate how to bind Colombia together and conserve order once the Liberator had died.

In April 1829 Bolívar proposed to his ministers that they explore with Great Britain the possibility of establishing a British protectorate over Colombia. The council of ministers doubted that the British would take on such a responsibility if Colombia appeared about to dissolve. To consolidate internal order they proposed a life-presidency for the Liberator, to be followed upon his death by a monarch drawn from a European dynasty. The council of ministers recognized some evident political problems in proposing the establishment of an outright monarchy. For almost two decades Colombian leaders had proclaimed the virtues of republican government and condemned monarchy as tyrannical. The very mention of a plan for a monarchy was likely to expose them to attack from university-educated republicans. But the ministers saw several advantages in a constitutional monarchy headed by a European prince. It would make Colombia more respectable in the eyes of the European monarchies, thus helping to assure Colombia's external security. And it would avoid national presidential elections, which were likely to incite "ambitious" men to carry the nation into civil war. A constitutional monarchy, they hoped, would restrain both the arbitrary actions of military officers and (in their view) the demagoguery of the university-educated. Thus, in various ways they imagined it would bring order and stability to the country.

The ministers and others in on the plan set about developing support for monarchy among Colombian notables, European diplomats, and, most critically, Bolívar himself. The ministers assumed that Colombian generals and the Church hierarchy would approve, and they claimed enthusiasm among the elite in Bogotá. Some in the aristocracy of Popayán endorsed it, although Joaquín Mosquera opposed the idea. But military officers outside the capital proved far from unanimous in backing a constitutional monarchy. General Páez in Venezuela was cool to the project, saying he first wanted to know what Bolívar thought about it, and General Mariano Montilla, the Venezulan commander in Cartagena, considered it desirable but impracticable.

Bolívar, after several months of appearing to be sympathetic to the project, in July 1829 writing from Guayaquil, pronounced firmly against it. The Liberator now thought it was hopeless to try to continue to hold Venezuela and New Granada together. The rivalry between New Granadans and Venezuelans made their separation inevitable, particularly as they were no longer forced into alliance by a threat from Spain. This, Bolívar noted, was one point upon which both Páez and Santander could agree. As long as the Liberator lived, he might be able to hold the two regions together; but he could not last much longer. The separation might occur more peacefully if it occurred while he was still alive.

Bolívar also rejected the idea of a European monarch. Colombia was too poor to sustain a monarch and his court, and, in any case, many Colombians would object to the titled aristocracy and the formalized inequality that a monarchy implied. Nor would Colombian generals and others ambitious for power accept a monarchy. Furthermore, it was extremely unlikely that they actually could obtain a European prince: What prince would care to come to Spanish America to preside over anarchy? Bolívar also noted that "European obstacles" were likely. Although he did not spell the point out, he probably suspected what proved to be the case: that the British would not accept a French prince on an American throne.

Undoubtedly the Liberator was correct in most of the points of his analysis. However, his frustrated ministers also suspected that Bolívar's views were conditioned by concern for his historical reputation. In a republican era, he might advocate a constitutional monarchy in republican dress, but he was not prepared to let his name be linked to an overtly monarchical project. Bolívar was particularly sensitive to such imputations, as at the time the eminent constitutionalist Benjamin Constant and other notables in Europe were condemning his dictatorship of 1828–1829.

Bolívar's refusal to cooperate killed the monarchy project. It had, nonetheless, several negative consequences. Although Bolívar had opposed the project, opponents blamed him for the scheme and his reputation suffered. General José María Córdoba, who in June 1828 had fiercely supported dictatorship by the Liberator, in September 1829 attempted a rebellion in his native province of Antioquia, with opposition to monarchy as one of his slogans. The plan for a monarchy also provided ammunition for Venezuelan separatists to attack both Bolívar and the government in Bogotá. The monarchy project and Córdoba's abortive rebellion in Antioquia together provided both excuse and occasion for a definitive movement for Venezuelan secession in November 1829, culminating in General Páez's announcement of separation in January 1830.

While Páez was confirming Venezuela's departure from Greater Colombia, in Bogotá delegates were gathering for a constitutional convention that, it was hoped, might somehow save the Colombian union. Bolivarians dominated the convention, but some liberal constitutionalists from Antioquia and Socorro were present. However, with the chief liberal leaders (Santander, Azuero, and Soto) absent, Bolívar was so pleased with the composition of the congress that he termed it "admirable." The constitution confected by the Congreso Admirable was a compromise between the Bolivarian and liberal projects presented at the conflicted Convention at Ocaña. Its features, however, are of little more than symbolic interest, as at the time it was promulgated, May 5, 1830, the republic for which it was intended was in the process of collapsing.

In March 1830 an abortive mutiny of militia in Bogotá had denounced Bolívar's rule, proclaiming the separation of Venezuela and New Granada. In April General Juan Nepomuceno Moreno seized power in Casanare and declared the province part of an already effectively independent Venezuela. In Pamplona Venezuelan officers rebelled, demanding to return to their homeland. Before the constitution was completed many in the New Granadan elite had concluded that writing a new constitution for the Colombian union was pointless if a separatist Venezuela would reject it.

Those who still held out hope that greater Colombia might be saved looked to Bolívar as its indispensable savior. For liberals as well as Bolivarians, Bolívar and Colombia were bound together. For the Bolivarians, saving Colombia provided justification for keeping Bolívar in power, something they also desired because they saw him as a guarantor of order. For many New Granadan liberals it was just the reverse. The breakup of Colombia would eliminate the principal justification for the Liberator's continuance in power, as well as relieving them of their Venezuelan military antagonists. For supporters of secession in Venezuela Bolívar by 1830 had become the enemy precisely because only the Liberator might conceivably have detained Venezuela's departure from the union.

In the early months of 1830, as Colombia was collapsing, Bolívar also was clearly in decline. He was physically wasted, visibly approaching death. His prestige, at its zenith in 1825, was also damaged by the events of the succeeding years—among New Granadan elites by his handling of Páez in 1826, in Venezuela by the monarchy project (which he had opposed), and in many minds by his identification with military power and privilege. By April 1830, many, including Bolívar himself, doubted that even he could hold the republic together. Gravely ill and depressed, the Liberator had repeatedly told his followers that he did not wish to return to the presidency. Many passionate Bolivarians, however, insisted that he remain in power, some civilians because they viewed the Liberator as the key to political order, and many military officers, particularly Venezuelan ones, because they saw him as protector of their power and privileges. Responding to the pressures of some Bolivarians, the Liberator in April 1830 proposed that he be elected president but leave the work of governing to a vice president. To his surprise and hurt, some of his most faithful adherents, including General Rafael

Urdaneta and José María Castillo y Rada, opposed this. Bolívar once again urged the Congress not to elect him and prepared to leave Bogotá.

The Congress elected two moderates, Joaquín Mosquera, whom Bolívar favored, as president, and General Domingo Caicedo as vice president. Both figured among the most aristocratic of New Granada's upper class— Mosquera as the son of a rich and influential gold-mining and landowning family in Popayán, Caicedo as the heir of an equally established family in Bogotá with immense cattle lands in the Upper Magdalena Valley.

The election of political moderates and the Liberator's departure worried the more ardent Bolivarians, particularly Venezuelan military officers, who feared for their safety without the presence of Bolívar. Alarmed by the threats of liberals, who were reemerging in Bogotá, two Venezuelan military units in the capital mutinied immediately after the election and soon departed for Venezuela. The misgivings of the Bolivarians were soon realized when President Mosquera, seeking to conciliate New Granadan liberals, began to appoint Santanderistas to high positions. The selection of the most combative liberal leader, Vicente Azuero, as minister of the interior, was particularly threatening. Soon Azuero revoked decrees issued by Bolívar during the reaction of 1828, including some that had expanded the juridical privileges (fueros) of the military.

In June and July 1830, with the emergence of liberals and liberal policies, the political atmosphere in Bogotá grew increasingly conflictive. Disputes were occurring between a Venezuelan battalion and a liberal-oriented New Granadan battalion, whose members wore ribbons with the motto "Liberty or Death." Fearing a possible coup by the Venezuelan unit, the government in August ordered it to march to Tunja. However, ardent Bolivarians and leaders of cavalry militia in the Sabana de Bogotá (who had been affected by the recent restriction of military privileges) persuaded the officers of the Venezuelan battalion to defy the government. Their crushing defeat of the defenders of the constitutional government at the battle of Santuario left the Venezuelan officers completely in control of the capital. Unable to govern, President Mosquera and his cabinet resigned. The Bolivarian General Rafael Urdaneta took over as a provisional president, to rule, he said, only until Bolívar returned to govern. But Bolívar, then in Cartagena, discouraged and quite ill, declined. Not long thereafter, in December 1830, the Liberator died on a hacienda near Santa Marta.

Since Urdaneta described his regime as an interim government pending Bolívar's return, the death of the Liberator undermined the rationale for the regime. In the early months of 1831 New Granadan forces advanced against Urdaneta from the Cauca and the Upper Magdalena valley under the leadership of Generals José María Obando and José Hilario López and from Casanare under General Juan Nepomuceno Moreno. Meanwhile, military rebellions dissolved Bolivarian control of Antioquia and much of the Caribbean coast, while guerrilla groups sprang up in Ibagué, in Socorro, and near Bogotá. In April 1831, after negotiations, Urdaneta resigned in favor of the constitutional vice president, General Domingo Caicedo, with a guaranty that there would be no reprisals against those who had supported the Urdaneta regime. Both armed Bolivarians and their liberal antagonists resisted compromise. But, with the aid of General López, a coalition government under Caicedo provided a more or less peaceful transition to a post-Bolivarian era. Most of the Venezuelan military who had formed the core of the Liberator's support soon returned to their homeland.

With the departure of the Venezuelans and the removal of notorious local Bolivarians from the military, the swollen officers' corps was greatly reduced in New Granada. Partly for this reason, from 1832 through the end of the nineteenth century the military as a corporate group had less weight in New Granada's politics than in Mexico, Peru, or Venezuela. The country still had its share of civil wars and generals as national presidents, but the latter were generally elected. To a greater degree than some other Spanish American countries, New Granada, and later Colombia, in the nineteenth century operated in some approximation of constitutional rules.

And so ended Bolívar's Colombia, a little more than a decade after its founding. The collapse of greater Colombia was inevitable. The union of Venezuela, New Granada, and Ecuador had been driven by the need for a coordinated fight against Spanish royalist forces. Once Spanish royalist forces had been defeated, the need for union lessened. Several other facts contributed to the demise of the union. The independent administrative authority enjoyed by Caracas and Quito during the colonial period made it difficult for elites in those cities to accept being governed from Bogotá. Further, the time and difficulty of travel from Venezuela and Ecuador to Bogotá inhibited their representation in the Congress or in other parts of the national government. A relative lack of representation in civil government contributed to the sense of regional rivalry in both Venezuela and Ecuador.

Regional economic and social differences also played a role. The dominant class in highland Ecuador complained that the abolition of the Indian tribute by Colombian legislators had made it less necessary for Indian peasants to work on landed estates. As a weaving region, highland Ecuador also wanted protection against imported foreign cloth. But Venezuela, which specialized in the export of tropical products, insisted on free trade. The dissimilar interests of the various regions of Colombia made difficult, if not impossible, the formulation of coherent, nationwide fiscal legislation—a fact recognized by Bolívar, who, while in Ecuador and Venezuela, decreed regional exemptions from existing trade and tax laws. Beyond the difficulty of fashioning a single national economic and fiscal policy, there was also the fact that Ecuador, New Granada, and Venezuela were not bound together effectively by internal trade connections. With the decline of Bolívar's prestige and health, the fate of Gran Colombia was sealed.

8

The Formation of New Granada as a Polity, 1831–1845: Origins of the Two Traditional Parties

Although the Bolivarian regime collapsed in 1830–1831, memories of its political battles hung on, affecting the shape of politics in New Granada in the 1830s and 1840s. During the years 1831–1845, the two rival parties that have dominated the country's subsequent history emerged.

ASSEMBLING THE NATIONAL TERRITORY

With the dissolution of Bolívar's Colombia, one early challenge was to secure the territory of the emerging republic of New Granada. During the uncertainties of 1830–1831, Casanare threatened attachment to Venezuela and the Cauca region to Ecuador, and the Isthmus of Panama contemplated independence. Casanare was quickly reincorporated, as Venezuela showed no interest in absorbing it. Panama was a more difficult case, as local notables in 1831 envisioned a brilliant future for an independent isthmus as a tropical version of the Hanseatic cities. However, this dream was damaged, at least in 1830–1831, by the intervention of some Venezuelan military officers who, having been driven out of Ecuador, sought to establish for themselves an independent state in Panama. After the Panamanian Colonel Tomás Herrera defeated the Venezuelans in September 1831, the isthmus rejoined New Granada. But the possibility of an independent Panama remained a recurrent anxiety of authorities in Bogotá throughout the nineteenth century.

The allegiance of the greater Cauca region was a more complicated matter. Venezuelan General Juan José Flores, who dominated Ecuador from its independence in 1830 to the mid-1840s, throughout these years tried to incorporate Pasto into his new republic. New Granadan leaders feared the loss of Pasto might mean the separation of the Cauca region, which would have been intolerable. What remained of New Granada would not be a viable nation, not only because of diminished population and territory but also because the West produced the great bulk of the country's gold, at the time New Granada's only significant export.

Various facts favored attaching Pasto, and even Popayán, to Ecuador. Pasto, in particular, was closely linked to Quito. Pasto and Popayán were more connected commercially to Quito than to Bogotá, while the Pacific coastal regions traded with Guayaquil. The religious orders in Pasto were under superiors in Quito. Young men of notable families in Pasto, and some in Popayán, had studied in Quito. Some migrants from Ecuador in Pasto and its coastal regions served as agents of Flores's designs. In Popayán some notables also supported linkage with Quito rather than with Bogotá.

Elites in Popayán were particularly susceptible to tactical alliances to the south when they felt threatened by political forces elsewhere in New Granada. Colonels José María Obando and José Hilario López in 1828–1829, to bolster their resistance to Bolívar's dictatorship, temporarily allied themselves with a Peruvian attempt to seize Ecuador. Similarly, during the crisis of 1830–1831, while leading men in the principal towns of the Valle del Cauca chose to cast their lot with Urdaneta's government in Bogotá, their counterparts from Popayán rejected the Urdaneta regime, which had overthrown the constitutional government of which their own Joaquín Mosquera had been president. Noting also that neighboring Pasto already had annexed itself to Ecuador, Popayán's notables in November 1830 temporarily declared allegiance to the government in Quito.

However, probably uneasy about being ruled by the scheming General Flores, some in Popayán, and elsewhere in the West, advocated an alternative separate "fourth state," which would incorporate all of the West from Pasto through Antioquia, possibly also including the Isthmus of Panama. Although José María Obando was widely rumored to be the source of this scheme, in fact its principal proponents in Popayán were some aristocrats concerned with preserving order and social peace, which were threatened, they feared, by *castas* who had access to arms.

A fourth state never fully took form. But much of the Cauca region remained effectively independent of Bogotá's authority, and Popayán and Pasto were formally linked to Ecuador from November 1830 to January 1832. During 1831 Generals José María Obando and José Hilario López, both natives of Popayán, were nominally Ecuadoran officers but nonetheless played central roles in New Granadan politics, as the military leaders most responsible for ending the Urdaneta regime and reestablishing constitutional government in Bogotá. In June 1831 these two "Ecuadoran" officers became, respectively, New Granada's minister of war and general-in-chief. Obando, as minister of war in Bogotá, in October 1831 sent López to Popayán to reincorporate the Cauca into New Granada, a process that López initiated with a *pronunciamiento* of the Popayán garrison in January 1832. Although Ecuador lost control of Pasto and Popayán at this time, Flores's ambition to control Pasto, and perhaps the Cauca also, continued to affect the region into the 1840s.

General Obando, first as minister of war and then as vice president, seems to have played an especially important role in fostering the reintegration of New Granada in 1831–1832. Beyond his military prestige, Obando had some credibility with potentially separatist leaders because he himself, on two occasions, had led the temporary separation of the Cauca. He could present himself to potential separatists as someone sympathetic to their desires but also committed to the reintegration of New Granada. To those who aspired to a separate fourth state, whether in the Cauca, Antioquia, or Panama, Obando wrote that he too once had supported such an idea. But now the constitutional convention that began its work in 1831 was creating a new charter that would be truly republican and would satisfy provincial concerns. Further, it was important to construct a republic big enough to defend itself.

Aside from the question of territorial definition of the republic, there were other uncertainties in the early 1830s. The Caribbean coast was unsettled politically. During the late 1820s, Cartagena's military commander, the Venezuelan General Mariano Montilla, backed by civilian devotees of the Liberator, had made the city a center of particular support for Bolívar and authoritarian political projects. But with the death of Bolívar in December 1830, the existing regime began to lose authority. After the Urdaneta regime collapsed, military officers in Cartagena, organized as a club of "veterans of liberty," sought to establish an independent Caribbean state, with Cartagena as its capital. This and other schemes for dominance of the Caribbean coast by Cartagena were foiled by the resistance of other coastal towns (notably Mompox, Santa Marta, and Riohacha). Their objection to rule from the departmental capital in Cartagena undoubtedly played a role in the elimination of the large departments of the 1820s, leaving the provinces of which the departments had been composed as the regional governing units in the constitution of 1832.

After January 1832, the isthmus, the Cauca, and the Caribbean coast were incorporated into New Granada, but maintenance of control over these provinces remained a concern in Bogotá. Accordingly, Francisco de Paula Santander, as president (1832–1837), made sure that in each of these places he had strong, reliable military leaders.

ORIGINS OF THE LIBERAL AND CONSERVATIVE PARTIES, 1830–1842

The division between the political factions that became Colombia's Liberal and Conservative parties may be understood from several different perspectives. Most contemporaries comprehended it as a master political narrative. That narrative, which remains valid as a description of political evolution over time, depicts the developing party divergence as a sequel to the conflict between liberals and Bolivarians in 1826–1830. Beginning in 1831 the victorious liberals began to split into two factions, liberal *exaltados* ("extremists" or "purists"), who wanted permanently to exclude Bolivarians from political office, versus moderate liberals, who sought a broader political peace through the reincorporation of the Bolivarians. While differences between these two groups reflected varying political dispositions, they also corresponded to previously established political friendships. Conflict between the two liberal factions became more explicit in the presidential election of 1836 and hardened in its aftermath, in part because of election-induced antagonisms and bitterness over subsequent distribution of political office. Finally, the civil war of 1840–1842 brought a virtually unreconcilable antagonism between liberal dissidents and a moderate-Bolivarian government party that afterward (in 1848) took the name of the Conservative Party. While contemporaries usually described the developing division in terms of this master political narrative, historians over the past six decades have interpreted the developing divisions in provinces and localities from varying socioeconomic perspectives. The remainder of this chapter first presents the master political narrative, reconstructed in accord with currently available historical information, and then summarizes some recent explanations or hypotheses about the socioeconomic bases of political alignments in the first half of the nineteenth century.

THE MASTER POLITICAL NARRATIVE

During the first half of the nineteenth century, most of the more visible participants in politics were gentlemen, men who were born into the upper class and/or whose social position was confirmed by marriage, through achievement in education and at the bar, in economic enterprise, or by rising through the ranks of the military or the clergy. Most were university-educated professionals or had military careers; in either case, they were likely also to own land and quite possibly also engage in commerce. These members of the political class were not, however, the only participants in politics. Relatively obscure parish priests could be highly influential in rural communities. And in the larger cities some elements of the lower strata, particularly artisans, played active roles as voters and supporters of the gentlemen who figured as visible political leaders.

As of the early 1830s there had not yet developed clear party organizations, but there did exist networks of friends who recognized in each other shared values and orientations. During the 1830s elections could be competitive, but most candidates for office still adhered to a gentlemanly code that required them decorously to feign lack of ambition for political office. Those who were most openly active politically attempted to maintain personal loyalties through extensive correspondence and to sustain factional positions through newspaper articles, often published anonymously

The 1830s were a time of emerging conflict between two wings of the liberal opposition to the Bolivarian military authoritarianism of the late 1820s. On one side were those liberals who saw the presence of Bolivarians in government as incompatible with the survival of a republican system and therefore sought to eliminate every vestige of Bolívarian presence in the government and the military. These more intransigent liberals were called *exaltados* (extremists) by their critics; they usually called themselves simply "liberals" or "patriots." In the late 1830s they also called themselves *progre-*

sistas. Diverging on some points from the *exaltados* were the moderate liberals, who tended to favor conciliating the Bolivarians, and ultimately, between 1836 and 1842 moved into political alliance with them—although some *exaltados* believed that some moderates were allied with the Bolivarians as early as 1831 or, in some cases, were covert Bolivarians masquerading as moderates.

A striking aspect of the developing conflict between *exaltados* and moderates was the relative lack of ideological differences between them in the 1830s. The discord between the two factions was rather over how to respond to memories of the political battles of the 1820s, in which moderates and *exaltados* had been allied in opposition to Bolivarian authoritarianism. In effect, during the 1830s they divided over issues that were ceasing to have more than symbolic significance.

During the 1820s there was a substantial consensus between these two flavors of New Granadan liberals. Before 1831 those who came to be identified as *exaltados* and moderates both were committed to the rule of constitutional law. And the experiences of the 1820s had taught civilians in both groups to fear the arbitrary power of the military. Both moderate and "extreme" liberals objected to Bolívar's constitutional project of 1826–1828, considering it a constitutional monarchy in republican guise. And when Bolivarian military officers overthrew the constitutional government of President Joaquín Mosquera in 1830 and installed the Urdaneta regime, moderates as well as *exaltados* were driven from government. At that time some men who later came to be identified as moderate leaders, such as José Ignacio de Márquez, were sent into exile along with notable *exaltados* like Vicente Azuero and Francisco Soto.

Beyond these shared political commitments and experiences, *exaltado* and moderate liberals agreed more generally in their cultural and political orientations. Both wanted New Granada to become an enlightened society following Western European models. Moderates and *exaltados* read the same books. Both were likely to be familiar with and espouse the ideas of Montesquieu, Benjamin Constant, and Alexis de Tocqueville (after the latter's *Democracy in America* reached New Granada, ca. 1836). Civilians in both groups disliked the dominance and disruptive actions of military officers and sought to reduce the size of the military. Many moderates, like most *exaltados*, during the 1830s also objected to, and feared, religious fanaticism and intolerance.

Despite these shared views, during the 1830s *exaltados* and moderate liberals began to divide into two contending groups. To a degree these two groups may have represented differing social identities. But they also had differing political temperaments—the *exaltados* championed change at the risk of conflict, while moderates gave order a much higher priority. Moderates and *exaltados* differed on the most effective tactics for bringing the military under civilian control and on the degree and rapidity with which religious practices and clerical preoccupations might be leavened by enlightenment. *Exaltado* liberals, of whom Vicente Azuero and his younger colleague Florentino González were among the most active and intransigent spokesmen, favored confrontational policies that would exclude Bolivarians from the military and politics and that would weaken the financial position or juridical privileges of the Church. Moderates, although they might agree with these goals, considered such a conflictive approach imprudent and counterproductive. Where the *exaltados* from 1831 onward sought to eliminate from military and political positions those who had supported Urdaneta in 1830, the moderates sought to reunify the polity through conciliation. Where *exaltados* sought to break the political power of the Church, moderates tried to avoid direct conflict with it, some because they valued the Church as a pillar of social order, others because they feared the power of the clergy to arouse the masses against the enlightened society sought by moderates and *exaltados* alike. These differences became magnified and accentuated by personal rivalries and hostilities among the leaders of these two groups of liberals as they competed in elections to public office.

The divergence between moderates and *exaltados* began to become apparent the moment General Rafael Urdaneta was forced out in April 1831. Urdaneta and the moderate liberal Vice President Domingo Caicedo had avoided a full-scale military conflict, achieving a relatively peaceful transfer of power through the agreement of Apulo (April 28, 1831), which, among other provisions, had guaranteed that all military officers on both sides would retain their positions and promotions and the command of their existing military units. Intransigent liberal leaders, notably the lawyer Vicente Azuero and Generals José María Obando and Juan Nepomuceno Moreno, who had not been present at the negotiations at Apulo, strenuously objected to the concessions Caicedo had made there. These *exaltado* liberals insisted that government officials and military officers who had collaborated in the Urdaneta regime be purged.

When Vice President Caicedo refused to remove former collaborators with Urdaneta from the army and the government, the most forceful *exaltados* in Bogotá at the time, Vicente Azuero and General Moreno, proposed to overthrow Caicedo in favor of General José María Obando. They were stopped only by the intervention of Obando's friend and ally, General José Hilario López, who had been a party to the Apulo agreement. Ultimately, however, the intransigent liberals got their way. Under *exaltado* pressure, Caicedo replaced the Bolivarians in his cabinet with two of the most prominent intransigent liberals, Vicente Azuero and General Obando. Obando—first as minister of war, and then as vice president after Caicedo was harried into resignation in November 1831—proceeded to carry out part of the *exaltado* agenda by expelling many of Urdaneta's collaborators from the army. During 1831 Obando removed 298 regular military and militia officers who had supported the Urdaneta regime. Some of these "dictatorials" were ordered into exile, particularly those among the thirty-five Venezuelan and twenty-five British officers whom Obando ejected from military service.

These measures made it possible to reduce the heavy financial burden of the military—although, even with these reductions, the armed forces still consumed half the national budget. However, men of prudent temperament feared a reaction by military officers who had been dismissed—a reaction that proved not long in coming.

Meanwhile, even before Caicedo's resignation in November 1831, José Ignacio de Márquez had become the effective leader of the moderate liberals in the constitutional convention that began to meet on October 15, 1831. Márquez, from the relatively tradition-bound highlands of Boyacá, had been a highly visible participant in the Congress of Cúcuta in 1821 and at the Convention at Ocaña in 1828. He had been the minister of finance of the constitutional government both before and after the Urdaneta regime. In the constitutional convention of 1831 Márquez led the moderates in contention with an *exaltado* group headed by Vicente Azuero of Socorro and Francisco Soto of Pamplona.

Differences between *exaltado* and moderate delegates appeared at various points in the constitutional convention of 1831–1832. The first division occurred over the name of the republic being reconstituted. Azuero and Soto, in accord with Santander (still in exile), now believed, with Bolívar dead, that the government in Bogotá should attempt to reconstitute greater Colombia, but as a confederation of New Granada with Venezuela and Ecuador, rather than as a centralized regime as had been the case in the 1820s. They believed, as Bolívar had, that such a larger political entity would command more respect from the great powers. Because Santander, Soto, and Azuero wanted to reconstruct Colombia, although in a looser form, they favored the name New Granada for the polity to be governed in Bogotá, leaving the name Colombia for a possible future larger confederation. By contrast, Márquez, who had argued against too close a union with Venezuela at the Congress at Cúcuta in 1821, now opposed any political connection with Venezuela whatsoever. Accordingly, Márquez and his supporters believed the territory still under the governance of Bogotá should appropriate the name Colombia, thereby discouraging the idea of a larger confederation. The constitutional convention debated this issue for eighteen days before voting narrowly (31–30) for the Azuero–Soto position, to call the renewed republic New Granada. The vote largely followed factional lines, the *exaltados* supporting Azuero and Soto, the moderates Márquez. In regional terms, men representing the established centers of the colonial era (Tunja, Bogotá, Cartagena) voted for the most part with Márquez for Colombia and absolute separation, while those from less "aristocratic" provinces (Socorro, Neiva, Mariquita) mostly voted for the *exaltado* position.

Another closely contested issue was the election of General José María Obando as provisional vice president in competition with Márquez, a decision reached only after the delegates had cast seventeen ballots. Soon after Obando's election, the slight *exaltado* majority granted extraordinary faculties to Vice President Obando to exile civilians and military officers who had supported the overthrow of the constitutional government in August 1830 and the subsequent Urdaneta regime. These measures passed in a series of close votes, over the resistance of the moderates led by Márquez. At this time Vicente Azuero and Francisco Soto became convinced that Márquez was trying to attract support from Bolivarians in order to challenge Francisco de Paula Santander in the next presidential election. Pursuing this ambition, Azuero alleged, Márquez had become the "protector of the perverse and egoist" (i.e., Bolivarians) and was defending religious "fanaticism."

Later, in March 1832, the convention elected Márquez as provisional vice president over General Obando in another long series of closely contested votes. After his election Márquez proceeded to reincorporate into the army a number of the Urdanetista military officers that Obando had removed in preceding months. General Obando, as well as other anti-Bolivarian military officers, particularly resented Márquez's restoration of these "dictatorial" officers. The issue of exclusions and reincorporations of Bolivarian civilians and military officers continued to resonate periodically through the 1830s. Márquez's "betrayal" in restoring the Bolivarians in 1832 later became one of General Obando's justifications for rebellion against Márquez's presidential administration in 1840.

General Francisco de Paula Santander, although personally partial to the *exaltados*, while in exile (1829–1832) maintained a correspondence with moderates, and even some Bolivarians, as well. Such diplomacy, as well as Santander's stature as chief executive between 1819 and 1826, prompted most New Granadan notables to believe that Santander was the preeminent national figure whose leadership was indispensable for the reconstitution of the republic. In March 1832 the constituent congress, known as the Convención Granadina, overwhelmingly elected the exiled Santander as the provisional president of New Granada. In the subsequent national election, Santander received 80 percent of the electoral votes for president.

When Santander returned from exile and assumed the presidency in October 1832, he spoke of reconciliation. However, like the *exaltados*, he intended to exclude from the government those who had supported Urdaneta. While still in exile in Europe Santander had written Vicente Azuero that those who had usurped the constitutional government ought not to be persecuted, but "neither should the future of the country be confided to notorious enemies of freedom." Santander seems implicitly to have distinguished between the Bolivarians of 1828 and those implicated in the Urdaneta regime of 1830. Although Santander remained suspicious of men who had supported Bolívar in 1828, as president he did make some effort to win over and make use of some former Bolivarians who had not taken part in usurping the constitutional government in 1830.

After the restoration of a constitutional regime in 1831–1832, some former supporters of Urdaneta who had lost their military positions continued to conspire against the government. When they attempted to seize control of the Bogotá garrison in July 1833, the government moved quickly to seize and prosecute the plotters. President Santander executed eighteen of those convicted, sending thirty-four to prison. In addition, the highest ranking conspirator, the former General José Sardá, who had escaped from jail, was tracked to his hiding place and murdered preemptively.

The deaths of the conspirators, particularly of those who were well connected socially in Bogotá and Cartagena, earned Santander the enmity of some influential families in those cities. However, notables in Antioquia and the Cauca considered these executions blows well struck on behalf of order. For his part, General Obando blamed the conspiracy not on the exclusion of Bolivarians but rather on their reincorporation into the military by Vice President Márquez. Obando complained that, after his efforts to "purify" the army, Márquez in 1832 had "set himself to respond to grievances, . . . brought in perverse officers, reinscribed villains who had not washed off the blood" of the overthrow of constitutional government in 1830. Márquez had done this, Obando thought, to build an opposition to Obando within the army, as a check on the latter's control of the military and his presumed ambitions.

In addition to the status of the Bolivarian military, various Church-related issues entered into controversy in the 1830s. Inherent in all the Church questions was the conflict between some educated laymen, who sought to establish the dominance of the secular state and to develop a modern, institutionally liberal, society, and many clergy and large numbers of pious followers, who clung to established religious beliefs, practices, and institutions. It is not surprising that clergy would have reacted with hostility to liberal secularizing projects because they implied reductions of Church power, resources, and ideological authority. Moreover, clerical uneasiness probably was intensified by a relative loss of institutional strength of the Church since the end of the colonial period. With the winning of independence, the opening of elite careers in politics contributed to making the Church a less attractive career option. And, while by 1835 the number of parish and other secular priests had rebounded somewhat from the sharp decline that had occurred during the independence era, there had occurred an absolute reduction in the number of friars and a relative decrease of secular priests in relation to the growth of the population. On the other hand, clergy were aware that they still had great moral authority with the population as a whole.

Santander was acutely aware of the sensitivities of the clergy and their power to stir up the mass of the populace in defense of the Church. He also knew that, because of the controversies of the 1820s, many clergy tended to be hostile to him and his closest political friends. In 1834, in a letter to a former Bolivarian, General Pedro Alcántara Herrán, Santander noted that many clerics and pious laymen feared that his government was "going to finish off religion, the friars, the tithe, etc.," in contrast with Bolívar, who had "protected and sustained them." Santander, however, like the moderates, wanted to avoid unnecessary confrontations with the clergy. While still in exile, in 1831, Santander counseled Vicente Azuero to go slow on reforms touching upon religion. "Let us secure peace and political liberty, establish a firm and respectable national government . . . put in use freedom of the press and wait for time to do the rest. Religious freedom is the daughter of political freedom, of order and of a government founded on indestructible bases."

Despite Santander's hope of avoiding conflict with the clergy, various Church-related controversies did emerge in the early 1830s. One such issue was primarily of concern to the religious orders. In 1828 Bolívar had revoked laws of the 1820s that had required the closure of monasteries with fewer than eight friars and had forbidden taking vows to enter religious orders before the age of twenty-five. After these laws were restored by the Granadan convention in 1832, friars in Bogotá began to publish papers contending that both the legislature and the executive were attacking religion. In May 1833 there were fears of a friar-inspired revolution in the capital.

While the friars sought to defend their orders, secular clergy and their many pious followers in the mass of the population were more aroused by government efforts to establish limited forms of religious toleration. To encourage foreign immigration, the Congress in 1835 decreed that non-Catholics might be granted land to establish cemeteries. In Antioquia, this measure became one motive of a popular upheaval in defense of religion. In Marinilla, already roiled by clerical agitation in 1833–1834, one priest, José María Botero, in 1835 published attacks on the cemetery decree, denounced the government as impious, and encouraged the populace to rebel. While some opponents of the Santander government in Bogotá were sending Botero money to publish his writings, many in the political class, moderate as well as *exaltado*, were alarmed because Botero had widespread support among the people of Antioquia. When Botero was jailed in Medellín on charges of sedition, a mob (said to have numbered from 600 to 800) liberated him.

Moderate liberals, as well as *exaltados*, strongly disapproved the agitation of the friars in Bogotá and of Botero in Antioquia. Moderates in the early 1830s joined *exaltados* in seeking to constrain the growth of the religious order. Liberals of both types viewed religious orders as outdated institutions that lured into unproductive lives individuals who might otherwise make useful contributions and that held in mortmain properties that otherwise would put to better use. Similarly, moderates agreed with *exaltados* in favoring at least some movement toward religious toleration as a means of encouraging immigration. Moderates, however, resisted pressing for radical reforms that were likely to move the clergy to arouse a pious populace. In 1834, when Florentino González in his newspaper, *El Cachaco*, published proposals for complete religious toleration as well as the suppression of religious orders and seizure of their property, President Santander, on the advice of the moderate Vice President Joaquín Mosquera, denied responsibility for these ideas and had González shut his newspaper down.

Although Santander shared the *exaltados'* rationalist orientation and even admonished the rebellious Botero to become more attuned to "the spirit of the century," in general he agreed with the moderates on the need to rein in the *exaltados'* more provocative anticlerical projects. In 1836 Santander cautioned the Chamber of Representatives against attempting to restrict Church juridical privileges, on the ground that public opinion was not prepared for this innovation. Santander feared this measure would provoke an extreme reaction, providing an opportunity for opponents of the government to undermine its authority.

While Santander tried to avoid ecclesiastical reforms that he considered provocative, he reacted angrily when he believed that religious agitation was being used as a weapon to undermine the government. An example of this was Santander's response to the second great controversy over the use of Jeremy Bentham's treatise on principles of legislation as a required text for law students. The adoption of Bentham's text for the university curriculum in 1826 had provoked furious criticism from clergy as well as pious laymen, and in March 1828 Bolívar had forbidden its use in the universities. In May 1835 the Congress restored the 1826 curriculum, including Bentham's treatise on legislation, despite contrary petitions from high-ranking clergy and many respectable laymen. All of these opponents believed that Bentham's utilitarian doctrines would subvert religious beliefs and morality.

Santander at first attempted to conciliate critics of the legislation text, but he took a much harder stance when he became convinced that the criticisms of Bentham actually had the purpose of attacking his government. Not long after the administration made clear that instructors would be free to teach Bentham critically, the friars of the order of the Candelaria nonetheless proposed to deny absolution to university students studying the Bentham text. President Santander interpreted this as outright defiance of the government's authority. In a letter to Vice President Mosquera, he threatened to ask the Congress to suppress the Candelario monastery, which he described as "full of royalist, ignorant, Bolivarian and insolent friars." "There cannot be a republic," he added, "with such swine."

By December 1835 Santander was construing widespread press attacks on Bentham as a concerted effort to discredit the government by using the "terrible weapon" of religion, and accordingly became more intransigent. Santander explained that he had published an aggressive defense of Bentham, to which Vice President Mosquera had objected, because "it was necessary . . . to make the enemies of the government understand that we were resolved to remain firm." "I am capable of becoming a heretic or Mahommedan," he added, "in order not to cede a bit of ground to the stubborn enemies of the present government."

In March 1836, while the controversy over Bentham was still in full cry, the Santander government confronted another challenge when the Chamber of Representatives voted against an agreement with Venezuela on the division of the Colombian debt—on the ground that the secretary of foreign relations had negotiated the agreement without congressional authorization. The intent of this vote, at least on the part of some legislators, clearly was to express opposition to the government itself, and not simply to express an opinion on the content of the agreement. Ominously, in the view of the *exaltados*, General Tomás Cipriano de Mosquera, a notorious Bolivarian in the 1820s, led the Chamber opposition, consisting mostly of moderates, in defeating the debt agreement. This vote was construed by *exaltados* as one more indication of a developing Bolivarian-moderate alliance.

THE PRESIDENTIAL ELECTION OF 1836

The presidential election in June 1836 proved an important further step in the developing definition of New Granadan party alignments. In the previous election in 1832, potential party differences had been masked by near-consensus support for Santander. In 1836, however, two political constellations, still somewhat inchoate but in the process of becoming more clearly identified, were pitted against each other.

Santander chose as his candidate General José María Obando, who shared his anti-Bolivarian commitments, yet would not arouse the hostility of religious fanatics. Desire to avoid inflaming religious traditionalists was one reason that Santander did not opt initially for Vicente Azuero, who was inclined to champion reforms that would anger the clergy and arouse the pious. Santander also thought a strong military chief like Obando was still needed in the presidency to maintain control of the army, particularly considering the danger of military conspiracies like those that had occurred in 1830 and 1833–1834. In addition Santander worried about possible regional dissidence and rebellion, particularly on the Caribbean coast and in the West, where Obando could command support.

Many men committed to republican principles who had supported Santander in the late 1820s and in the election of 1832 turned away from his candidate in the election of 1836. Some were alienated from Santander by his exclusion of Bolivarians, his commitment to Bentham, and/or his propensity to acrid newspaper polemics. Aside from their feelings about Santander, many rejected Santander's chosen candidate, General Obando. Many liberals, moderate as well as *exaltado*, seeking to diminish the military's role in politics, wanted to elect a civilian. There was also a widespread perception that Obando was too ambitious. This judgment seemed to be confirmed by Obando's publication before the presidential election of a statement of his principles, a clear departure from the requirement of the existing political culture that gentlemen not publicly express overt interest in political office. To some degree the criticisms of Obando by civilians of established, more or less aristocratic families also may have reflected an implicit class perspective. Although Obando's illegitimate origins were not discussed publicly, this may well have been a subtext for notables who decried his alleged "ambition."

While Obando was distrusted by anti-military republican gentlemen, he was resolutely opposed by former Bolivarians. Obando had led military resistance to Bolívar's dictatorship in 1828 as well as to the Urdaneta regime of 1830, and he had been the person chiefly responsible for removing supporters of Urdaneta from the military. Many Bolivarians, viewing Obando as an arch-enemy, also chose to believe that Obando had been responsible for the murder of General Antonio Jose Sucre in 1830.

While many Santander loyalists lined up for Obando or, in el Socorro and some other liberal centers championed Vicente Azuero, as a civilian and principled liberal, most who found both Obando and Azuero unacceptable turned to José Ignacio de Márquez. Even Márquez's supporters feared, however, that the army might not obey a civilian. There was a question whether Márquez, if elected, might be thrown from the presidential saddle.

In the national vote in the 1836 election there occurred a substantial unification of the votes of moderates around Márquez and of *exaltados* around Obando—despite the existence of other notable candidates, particularly General Domingo Caicedo on the moderate side and Vicente Azuero for the *exaltados*. Márquez won 73.6 percent of the electoral ballots for known moderates, while Obando, with President Santander clearly supporting him, had 71 percent of the electoral votes for Santanderistas.

What determined how electoral votes were cast? It often was alleged, at least into the 1850s, that the executive branch of the national government, through its appointed governors, and the local influence of the governors' appointees, could control community electoral boards (juntas), which by disqualifying opposition voters, could guarantee victory for those sympathetic to the existing administration. In 1836 there were some instances of manipulation of elections by the executive branch. Opponents of the government's candidates particularly objected that in Bogotá the local garrison had been permitted to vote, presumably as their commanders instructed. However, government efforts on behalf of Obando so antagonized moderate notables in the capital that they were able to mobilize and largely neutralize the government in the election. Some of the beginnings of party organization may be traceable to the electoral battle in Bogotá province in 1836.

Aside from government actions in Bogotá, it appears there was no general control of the election by agents of the national executive. Márquez, whom President Santander clearly did not want to win, gained a plurality of the electoral votes and enough supporters of Márquez were elected to Congress to guarantee his election there. Furthermore, the electoral patterns varied a great deal not only among provinces but from one canton to another. In many cantons, it seems, elections were controlled by small groups of locally influential men who came to a consensus. In 25 of the country's 110 cantons all of the electoral votes went for a single candidate. In another 13 cantons the ballots were lopsidedly for one candidate. But these concentrations of votes could differ a great deal from one canton to another. In Casanare province, all of the electoral ballots of one canton went to Vicente Azuero, all in a second went to Obando, and all in a third went to Márquez. Vigorous competition among supporters of more than two candidates within a single canton occurred only in thirteen cases. Five of these were cantons in the province of Bogotá, and all of the rest occurred in the capitals of provinces. Clearly, electoral competition was most likely to occur where the opinions of more than a few notables were in play.

Most of the cantons and provinces in which both moderate and *exaltado* votes were strongly represented were among those that became particularly conflicted in subsequent years. Two of the highly competitive cantons, Vélez and Neiva, became the sites of fierce party battles between 1837 and 1841. And a number of others (Cartagena, Mompox, Pamplona, Cartago, Popayán, and Pasto) also became particularly volatile and conflictive during the civil war of 1840–1842.

In the presidential election of 1836 some regions revealed partisan commitments with which they became perennially associated. Socorro province, the Barranquilla region, and the Isthmus of Panama already showed clear liberal orientations. Most of Tunja province was already inclined to be conservative, but some persisting liberal pockets, as in Soatá, were also evident.

The political interests in play behind the vote varied regionally. In Antioquia by the mid-1830s there was already a well-established antagonism toward Bogotá. Antioqueños resented Bogotá's restrictions on the exportation of gold dust, on the management of the province's colegio, and on the development of an ironworks in Antioquia. But these issues seem unlikely to have prompted a vote for Márquez, long a resident in the capital and associated with its centralist policies. Rather, it appears that Antioquia's notables made up their minds largely on the same basis as their counterparts elsewhere—on local assessments of the personal qualities and liabilities of the leading candidates. In Márquez they saw moderation, in Obando an unpredictable military caudillo.

If Antioquia was solidly for Márquez, the Cauca region was sharply divided. Popayán and Pasto, Obando's home turf, supported him, despite his dangerous popularity among rural folk in the region, which made him a potentially uncontrollable caudillo. Nevertheless, he also had put his sword at the service of the local aristocracy in 1830–1831. By contrast, the Cauca Valley, often at odds with Popayán, and in 1830–1831 with Obando, voted heavily for Márquez.

Because Márquez had won a clear plurality, but not an absolute majority, of electoral votes in 1836, the Congress of 1837 had to decide the election. Although the electoral votes in the presidential election had been relatively close between moderate and Bolivarian candidates, on the one hand, and Santanderistas, on the other (52.7 percent to 47.3 percent, respectively), a clear majority of the Congress of 1837 were moderate or Bolivarian. Only the delegations from Socorro, Vélez, and Panama were strongly Santanderista. The Congress therefore easily elected Márquez.

THE MÁRQUEZ ADMINISTRATION

Márquez as president at first sought to remain above faction. He asked Santander's cabinet to stay on (only one did), and he left *exaltados* in the governorships of two important provinces, Antioquia and el Socorro. Despite Márquez's efforts to be conciliatory, Santander and his collaborators displayed an unconstrainedly bitter partisanship. Two of Santander's adherents, Florentino González and Lorenzo María Lleras, while holding positions in the Márquez government, nonetheless acted as members of the Santanderista opposition. The Santanderistas then professed to be shocked when Márquez in August 1837 sacked González and Lleras.

Santander and his lieutenants began to publish an opposition paper, *La Bandera Nacional*, which focused on Márquez's appointments, looking for signs of backsliding away from liberalism. At first they could find rather little about which to complain. By December 1837, however, they were accusing the Márquez administration of Bolivarian sympathies—because writers who defended the Márquez government had spoken favorably of Bolívar and critically of Santander. The fact was, however, that the Márquez administration was in policy not visibly different from that of Santander. Precisely because there was little substantive basis for criticism, the Santanderistas dwelled on political symbolism, raising the specter of Bolivarianism.

Santanderistas found some justification for their fears of a moderate-Bolivarian alliance with the entry into the Márquez government of two military officers who had been visible Bolivarians in the 1820s—Generals Tomás Cipriano de Mosquera and Pedro Alcántara Herrán. Particularly alarming was the appointment of Mosquera as secretary of war in July 1838. Mosquera cherished a personal grudge against General Obando, who had subjected him to ignominious military defeat in 1828. Obando and others feared that Mosquera would Bolivarianize the army; by October 1838 Obando claimed that General Mosquera was removing liberal officers from the military. Obando expected Mosquera soon to be reincorporating supporters of the Urdaneta regime, which indeed did begin to occur in 1839. So the Santanderista charges of a Márquez alliance with Bolivarians were premature but ultimately were confirmed.

The Santanderistas also charged that the Márquez government was in league with the religious fanatics, although in fact Márquez had given the ultrareligious little comfort. In August 1837 Márquez strictly enforced a law forbidding religious vows before the age of twenty-five, in doing so bringing down upon himself the condemnation of the fanatics. Also, Márquez took no action to end the use of Bentham in university classes, saying this was a matter for the Congress to decide.

Religion became a significant force in elite politics at the time of the vice presidential election of 1838, when a "Catholic Society" was created, with the overt goal of promoting an ultrareligious agenda and electing proclericals. (It has been suggested that there also was a covert monarchist agenda.) The liberal press claimed that Márquez was allied with the Sociedad Católica. In fact, neither Márquez nor his moderate supporters were sympathetic to the Catholic Society. The Católica was a political competitor of the moderates, and many moderates were disturbed by its fanatical tenor.

CIVIL WAR, 1839–1842

The irony of the Santanderista charge that Márquez was allying himself with the religious fanatics became fully evident in 1839, when during the Márquez administration the suppression of four understaffed monasteries in Pasto sparked a rebellion by the ultrareligious Pastusos. Because of strong traditionalist religious sentiment in Pasto, that province had been exempted from the 1821 and 1832 laws calling for the elimination of understaffed convents. In 1839, however, on the initiative of a Pastuso legislator, the Congress voted overwhelmingly to suppress the Pasto convents. The religious rebellion that began in Pasto in July 1839 was largely, although not completely, suppressed by the end of the year. But in January 1840 there erupted not far away, just south of Popayán, a quite different revolt, led by General José María Obando.

At the time of the initial religious revolt, government officials had been nervous about Obando, and not a few suspected (incorrectly) that Obando was in some way involved in Pasto's religious rebellion. In any case, Obando's reputation as a caudillo was for many sufficient reason for anxiety. The anticipated revolt by Obando, however, was prompted by the unexpected reemergence of accusations that he had ordered the murder of General Antonio José Sucre in 1830. These accusations, made by a Pasto *guerrillero* who had been captured by the government, actually alarmed some in the Márquez administration. Government authorities believed they had to investigate the accusations, but they did so with the foreboding that the investigation might lead Obando to rebel, as indeed occurred. However, within the government there were striking differences about how to handle Obando. General Pedro Alcántara Herrán sought to avoid a major rebellion by conciliating Obando, while Herrán's close friend, the secretary of war, General Tomás Cipriano de Mosquera, clearly hoped to destroy Obando through the criminal process.

General Herrán had been sent to Pasto to suppress the religious rebellion and so was on the scene when Obando first rebelled in January 1840. As Herrán later explained, he wanted to do what he could "to save Obando" by persuading him to desist from rebellion. He also bore in mind that he could not defeat Obando decisively, among other reasons, because Obando had a following among the people of the region and he would have had the support of many guerrillas scattered across its mountainous landscape. If Obando's rebellion were not stopped quickly, it would be "interminable." Accordingly, Herrán convinced Obando that he would be treated fairly and got him to lay down his arms, accept an amnesty, and go to Pasto to submit to the process of a criminal investigation.

Although Herrán's amnesty succeeded in ending the rebellion and persuading Obando to cooperate in the judicial process, Herrán nonetheless was the target of much criticism, and indeed abuse, from armchair generals in Popayán and Bogotá (including President Márquez), for conciliating the rebel rather than seeking to destroy him. Among those upset by the amnesty was General Mosquera, who resigned as secretary of war to go to Popayán in order to make sure that Obando was treated with all the rigor the law required (or might permit).

Obando, who had begun the judicial process confident of his innocence, and therefore his eventual acquittal, became alarmed in April 1840 when he learned that his arch-enemy, General Mosquera, had arrived in Popayán—for the purpose, as Obando immediately perceived, of persecuting him. By May, Obando was becoming convinced that his enemies were manipulating the judicial process against him—through a propaganda campaign and the suborning of testimony, as well as by continuing to hold him after a judge ordered him freed. Seeing himself surrounded by enemies apparently determined to destroy him, in July 1840 Obando escaped his place of confinement and declared himself again in rebellion.

While Obando was growing desperate about his plight, Generals Mosquera and Herrán worried that the government lacked sufficient military forces to suppress the guerrillas already operating in Pasto, not to speak of dealing with possible revolts in other parts of the republic. Mosquera therefore got the president of Ecuador, General Flores, to send Ecuadoran troops to help put down the guerrillas, in return for a commitment from Mosquera and Herrán to try to persuade the New Granadan government to let Flores have Pasto—his long-sought prize. The troops promised by Flores did provide some assistance in defeating Obando in September 1840.

After the defeat of Obando, Ecuador's troops in Pasto enabled Generals Herrán and Mosquera to leave the region with the hope that it would remain secure while they attended to rebellions elsewhere in the country. But military aid from Ecuador was bought at some moral cost. Opponents, as well as friends, of the Márquez government were aware of the judicial persecution of Obando. And, while not knowing exactly what Mosquera had promised Flores, they objected to Ecuador being permitted to intervene in New Granada. These acts of dubious integrity and patriotism provided additional excuses for liberal rebellions in various parts of the country—although these doubtless would have occurred anyway.

On the occasion of his second rebellion, Obando pronounced in favor of various causes, including the freedom and integrity of both New Granada and Ecuador, the protection of religion, and "federation." The adoption of a federal system had been advocated by some representatives in the Congresses of 1838 and 1839. As of May 1839 Obando had objected to these proposals, believing that the liberal opposition, out of spite, was pressing for a change that would weaken the nation. When he rebelled in July 1840, however, a desperate Obando included "federation" in his motley collection of justifications.

Obando's revolt was seconded by rebellions in most of the populated areas of the country. In Vélez two attempts at revolt actually had preceded Obando's pronouncement of July 1840, as had one abortive movement in Casanare. Subsequent rebellions in the provinces of Tunja, el Socorro, Antioquia, Santa Marta, Cartagena, Mompox, and Panama for the most part proclaimed "federation" as their theme. The visible leaders of many of these upheavals were regionally based military caudillos, and the rebellions were presented as if they were locally generated. At least some of the provincial revolts, however, were encouraged and manipulated by Vicente Azuero and other *progresista* civilians in the capital. According to some accounts, the death of Francisco de Paula Santander in May 1840 freed these *exaltados* from his restraint, enabling them to pursue a more aggresssive assault on the Márquez administration.

At the time friends of the national government claimed that these provincial revolts lacked popular support, that they represented simply the actions of ambitious military officers and other local bosses (*gamonales*), whom the civilian population was afraid to oppose. However, some regional caudillos, in the effort to hold their local power bases against government forces, in fact mobilized mass elements. General Obando began his revolt in 1840 with a following among blacks in the Patía Valley. And, after suffering several decisive defeats by government units, in early 1841 he tried to recover by offering freedom to slaves who would join his forces. Obando's appeal to Afro-Colombians in the greater Cauca zone made him particularly fearsome to the region's aristocracy, which, in any case, worried about the specter of race/class warfare.

The rebellion on the Caribbean coast was quite variegated, socially and regionally. General Francisco Carmona and others who initiated the coastal revolt began by mobilizing the largely Indian population of Ciénaga, a transit point for boats traveling between Santa Marta and the Magdalena River. The rebellion on the coast later was joined by some politicians at the margins of the traditional aristocracy of Cartagena—notably Juan José Nieto, a man of humble mestizo birth, whose fortunate marriages brought him upward social mobility but who was frustrated by, as he believed, having been counted out of an election to Congress by Cartagena's establishment. Such emerging elites in turn mobilized support among poorer folk—in Cartagena among artisans and the poor Afro-Colombian population of the barrio of Getsemaní. Thus, in Cartagena as in the Cauca the movement reflected elements of class division. In other regions, such as Antioquia and Santander, class dimensions of the revolt are less clear.

Intraregional tensions also were at work in some places. Sabanilla, Sabanalarga, and other secondary towns on the Caribbean coast traditionally dominated by Cartagena supported the revolt, believing it might win more independence from the provincial capital. One of the demands of the revolution was the opening of Sabanilla-Barranquilla to foreign trade, a development that clearly conflicted with the interests of the established port of Cartagena. However, General Carmona and other leaders of the rebellion on the Caribbean coast also clearly sought to draw together the region as a whole, in opposition to rule from Bogotá. Carmona proclaimed himself the leader of the "United State of the Federal States of the Coast."

The "War of the Supremos" was long and devastating. The "federalist," as distinct from the initial "fanatical," part of this conflict, in its various regional manifestations, lasted some twenty-nine months, from January 1840 until its final defeat in May 1842. And the war directly involved all of the more populated areas of the country. The pattern of the rebellion took a particular toll on the hapless folk who were dragooned into the national army. Because the rebellions were widely scattered and the government's military strength limited, its few dependable battalions had to march long distances, from south to north to south again, through varyingly hot and humid or cold climates. Consequently, mortality rates in government units were high. General Mosquera learned that on long marches he could expect to lose nearly half of his men from desertion and disease. In Popayán and Pasto army ranks were decimated by a smallpox epidemic in the first half of 1840. When much of the government force marched to the northern provinces later in that year, they must have carried smallpox with them, for this disease was still wreaking havoc in the ranks in el Socorro and Pamplona in 1841. The marching armies also spread smallpox among the civilian population. As for the effects of climate change, General Herrán in 1841–1842 reported very high mortality among the highland recruits that he took with him to pacify the Magdalena Valley.

The war also devastated the economy. Between 1835 and 1837 a relative optimism about the country's economic prospects had emerged; efforts were being made to develop exports of tropical products, as well as modern manufacture of iron, paper, glass, textiles, and porcelain, and there were plans to put steamboats on the Magdalena River. The war ruined much of that. Those most directly affected were landowners, who could expect to lose virtually all of their cattle, horses, and mules to armies passing through. The war, of course, also sapped an already weak national treasury. In 1841 exports and imports dropped to less than half their former levels, and in fighting on the Magdalena the only steamboat on the river was destroyed. Toward the end of the war, an orgy of speculation in real estate and government bonds in Bogotá ended in a crash in January 1842, which brought ruin to many established families.

The war proved a defining moment in the development of political allegiances. In the Cauca slaveowners could not forgive the disruption and the threat to social order brought by Obando's recruitment of slaves and attacks on their haciendas. And men of order in Antioquia, Bogotá, and elsewhere were outraged by an upheaval that was so destructive and, in their view, so unjustified. In the war itself deaths on both sides, including executions of prisoners, usually by firing squads but sometimes by lancing, hardened the political division between liberals on the one hand and the moderate-Bolivarian coalition on the other. The political loyalties, and animosities, that were confirmed and cemented in this civil war found enduring expression in the conflict between two parties (after 1848 known as Liberal and Conservative) that dominated the country's politics throughout the remainder of the nineteenth century, as well as the twentieth century.

Several ironies are embedded in the process of party formation between 1835 and 1842. The strident Santanderista opposition to the Márquez government, and the subsequent civil war, propelled moderates into the very alliances with Bolivarians and clergy about which the Santanderistas had worried. In 1837–1838 *exaltado* complaints against the Márquez government alienated moderate liberals who had loyally served Santander (such as Juan de Dios Aranzazu, Rufino Cuervo, Lino de Pombo, and Joaquín Acosta), pushing them toward a moderate-Bolivarian coalition. Many of these moderate liberals formed the backbone of what later came to be known as the Conservative Party. Further, under attack from the Santanderistas, Márquez looked to, and received, the support of such former Bolivarians as Generals Pedro Alcántara Herrán and Tomás Cipriano de Mosquera. The moderate liberals and former Bolivarians now fused and came to be known as *ministeriales*, that is, supporters of the administration. When the liberal rebellion broke out, Bolivarian military officers became indispensable to the defense of the ministerial government—so much so that the former Bolivarian General Herrán, one of the military saviors of the government, in 1841 became Márquez's successor in the presidency. General Mosquera, another former Bolivarian who won critical victories for the government, succeeded Herrán as president in 1845. So the *exaltado* assault on Márquez, on the charge that he was in league with the Bolivarians, backfired, seemingly accelerating the elevation to power of those who remained loyal to the memory of the Liberator.

Similarly, the Santanderista charge that Márquez was seeking to use religion as a political weapon also turned out to be a self-fulfilling prophecy. Moderates and former Bolivarians, some of whom had been in varying degrees either religious skeptics or anticlerical in the 1830s, became convinced by the civil war of 1839–1842 that younger generations were being corrupted by secondary education that was too lax and misled them with dangerous ideas (i.e., those of Bentham). The rebellion stimulated a plan to bring back the Jesuits, who had been expelled by the Spanish Crown in 1767. The Jesuits promptly were put in charge of various secondary schools to instill a reverence for social order in potentially wayward elite youth.

SOCIOECONOMIC INTERPRETATIONS OF POLITICAL ALIGNMENTS

The fundamental division between two parties that came to be known as Liberals and Conservatives emerged during the years from 1826 to the end of the civil war of 1839–1842. Up to this point the developing party division has been depicted more or less as it was seen by many contemporaries, with the critical issue being the attitudes and policies toward the Bolivarians, exclusion or conciliation. Twentieth-century interpreters, however, have sought retrospectively to understand the political alignments that emerged by 1842 as an expression of social division. What social features, then, underlay this division?

Conventionally, conservative elites in Spanish America have been identified as landowners, clergy, and military officers, while liberal elites were considered mostly to be lawyers and merchants. But this simple formula cannot withstand scrutiny; both parties were diverse in social composition and occupation. Many visible conservatives were lawyers and/or merchants, and many liberals were landowners and military officers. There were even some liberal clergy, particularly before 1850. In any case, such categorizations by occupation or economic interest inevitably fail because, through most of the nineteenth century, a single individual in the active political elite was likely to have several occupations—for example, landowner and lawyer or military officer and merchant. And if an individual did not encompass such varied occupations, members of his family probably did.

If the long-conventional scheme pitting conservative landowners, clergy, and military against liberal lawyers and merchants is now recognized as offering an inadequate understanding of the socioeconomic bases of political alignments, what alternative formulations may be put in its place? One formulation has proposed that conservatives were likely to come from cities that were important administrative centers in the colonial period, while liberals hailed from towns that were more marginal in the colonial era but were of growing importance in the republican era. Important cities in the colonial period offered greater access to university education and connections to colonial administrators, thus facilitating the entry of youths from these centers into the political elite, in contrast to young men from subsidiary provinces who, as relative outsiders, had a harder time entering the political establishment. Further, some cities that were important in the colonial period suffered relative economic decline in the republican era, thus reinforcing their conservative orientation. For New Granada this formulation fits to a degree. Popayán, Cartagena, and Tunja, all important in the colonial period and in relative decline in the early republican era, were predominantly conservative in the first half of the nineteenth century, in contrast with the provinces of el Socorro, Vélez, and Neiva, which were marginal in the colonial era and emerged as centers of liberal strength.

This scheme, however, is inadequate for a number of reasons. It does not account for the conservatism of Antioquia, which, like typically liberal provinces, was not important administratively in the colonial era. Furthermore, it does not explain political divisions within regions or even within cities. Several other formulations address these local divisions. One sees descendants of colonial administrators, as social and political insiders, defending centralized and more authoritarian government, while those of less well-connected families in the same localities tended to be liberals. An alternative way of understanding local divisions describes a conservative establishment not in relation to colonial administrative offices but rather with relation to economic power in general and large landholdings in particular. The latter analysis, persuasively applied to Cali, finds that conservatives and liberals in that city had similar kinds of occupations but that conservatives began with better social locations, primarily with regard to family wealth.

Scattered contemporary comments do seem to suggest a sense of differentiation between a recognized establishment and socially emergent individuals. Men of conservative orientation, in 1839–1840, as well as later in the 1850s, often thought that those who favored a federalist system were men of lesser social position who, being unable to reach high national office, aspired to magnify their power in a smaller theater on the local level. In 1839 General Tomás Cipriano de Mosquera wrote that federalism was supported by those who, having discovered "that the highest positions are reached with difficulty without merit, and without precedents of honor and virtue, want to be leaders in miserable provincial governments." José Manuel Restrepo also occasionally dismissed rebels as men who were trying to reach too far beyond their social origins or educational attainments. When the Gaitán brothers turned against the government in Febuary 1840, Restrepo explained that "they want to rise to a level beyond what their personal qualities and their humble origins permit." In these quotations, however, it should be noted that "merit" or "personal qualities" are mentioned along with social origins. And, in fact, individuals of provincial, less than aristocratic, origins, who were intelligent and well-educated, rose to the top as Bolivarians or, later, as *ministeriales* or Conservatives. Restrepo himself is a notable case of ascent by a man who became distinctly conservative.

In some other cases, the differentiation between establishment and socially emergent is described more specifically in terms of cities. Francisco Soto of Pamplona, like José Manuel Restrepo of Antioquia, was a provincial who rose through merit. Born in San José de Cúcuta, he studied law in Santafé de Bogotá in the late colonial period with the leading lights of the time (Camilo Torres, Frutos Joaquín Gutiérrez). Although he became an important minister, legislator, and jurist, he nonetheless resented the haughtiness of men from established colonial centers. In July 1831, Soto ascribed the political reaction under Urdaneta, in part, to "the exalted aristocracy of some sons of Bogotá, Pamplona, Tunja and other towns who dreamed of marquessates and earldoms." A few months later he blamed Popayán's threat to join Ecuador on that city's "aristocrats (because they do exist in New Granada)." And he complained of the tendency of Bogotanos "to suppose themselves infallible, and for that reason to disregard the ideas of those of us who live in the provinces."

The division between provincials and established people in the colonial centers may be seen in the development of a heated political conflict over higher education policy that emerged in the 1830s and 1840s. During the late colonial period, the route to government appointments for *criollos* predominantly lay in the study of law at Bogotá's two colegios—San Bartolomé or Nuestra Señora del Rosario. With the effective independence of New Granada after 1821, the new government sought to make secondary education more widely available by founding provincial colegios. During the 1820s, furthermore, the government responded to provincial desires by permitting the study of law at these establishments, thus facilitating the entry of provincial youths into political careers and government positions. In 1826, however, a reaction began, and authorities in Bogotá, in the name of standards, began to try to restrict legal and other professional instruction to the three universities established in the chief centers of the colonial aristocracy (Bogotá, Cartagena, and Popayán). This effort reached its culmination under the ministerial governments of 1837–1845. In the aftermath of the civil war of 1839–1842, the ministerials tended to blame political disorder on a supposed superabundance of university-educated lawyers. The ministerials in the early 1840s claimed that young lawyers, because they were underemployed, turned to political careers, and the pursuit of their ambitions fueled the country's political upheavals.

While the ministerials saw more restricted access to higher education as necessary to public order, the policy was perceived by gentry in lesser provincial towns as a deliberate attempt to frustrate the careers of their sons. The policy provoked so much resistance that the government of General Tomás Cipriano de Mosquera (1845–1849) softened the restrictions on professional education in the provinces. After the election of Liberal General José Hilario López in 1849, the Liberals, many from modest provincial backgrounds, moved in 1850 to demolish the whole system of centralized control of higher education.

Conflicts over higher education policies from 1821 through 1850 thus seem to illustrate a contest for power between descendants of the colonial aristocracy in Bogotá, Cartagena, and Popayán on the one hand and men of lesser provincial origins on the other. But the same issue also points to the need to modify and complicate this interpretation of Colombian politics in the period when the two traditional parties began to emerge (1827–1842). First, not all of those who supported a strong central government (including centralized control of education) were descendants of the colonial aristocracy in Bogotá, Cartagena, and Popayán. José Manuel Restrepo, born in the town of Envigado in Antioquia but sent to be educated in Santafé de Bogotá at the Colegio de San Bartolomé (1799–1806), was not a son of the colonial bureaucracy. Yet as secretary of the interior (1821–1830), with other cabinet members of more clearly aristocratic origins, he supported Bolívar's dictatorship of 1828 and was one of the chief proponents of the monarchy project of 1829. Restrepo also was the architect of the more centralized and restrictive higher education policy in 1826 and one of its principal advocates in the 1830s and 1840s.

Mariano Ospina Rodríguez, the dominant force in the centralizing reaction that occurred after the civil war of 1839–1842, also was a provincial not connected to the colonial aristocracy. Born in Guasca, a small farming town north of Bogotá, to a family with middling landholdings, Ospina came to the capital to study at the Colegio de San Bartolomé. As a university student he was a Santanderista liberal and indeed took part in the conspiracy against Bolívar in September 1828. When the conspiracy failed, Ospina escaped to Antioquia, where, because of his evident capability, he soon emerged as a political leader in the province, in the process seemingly assimilating its predominantly conservative values. After the civil war of 1839–1842, Ospina as secretary of the interior (1841–1845) championed bringing the Jesuits back to the country and inserting them into secondary education. Ospina also was the most vigorous and visible champion of restricting professional education to the three universities in Bogotá, Cartagena, and Popayán. He also pushed for a constitutional reform that would strengthen the hand of the government; the resulting constitution of 1843 was perceptibly more centralist, giving more power to the executive and reducing that of the Congress and provincial legislatures. Subsequently Ospina became the dominant figure in the Conservative Party.

The cases of José Manuel Restrepo and Mariano Ospina Rodríguez illustrate the point that some of those who founded the political group that came to be known, after 1848, as the Conservative Party had provincial origins that were sociologically similar to those of the men who founded the Liberal Party. Further, since neither Restrepo nor Ospina nor others in the ranks of the moderates and *ministeriales* came from families with colonial bureaucratic traditions, they could hardly be viewed as acting to defend preexisting political privilege. Their predominant concern was preserving political and social order.

Desire for order surely was the most important factor drawing the elites of Antioquia into an identification with political conservatism. Antioquia as a region had no important administrative centers in the colonial era and thus in many ways corresponded to the sociological makeup of the largely liberal province of el Socorro. Indeed, from the 1820s through the 1850s, some towns in Antioquia, among them Rionegro and Santa Fe de Antioquia, were identified with liberalism. However, from the 1830s onward Antioquia as a whole increasingly became a bastion of conservatism. Presumably the capital accumulation generated by gold mining and commerce based on gold exports encouraged the development of a regional upper class that for the most part gave a very high priority to social order and the security of property rather than to the pursuit of political ambitions, which tended to find expression in civil war. The religious piety of the Antioqueño poor further provided a social base for elite conservatism in the region.

Intraregional conflicts also played an important part in the development of partisan political identities. In the northern provinces, the towns of el Socorro and San Gil developed antagonistic partisan identities in part because of their competition to dominate Socorro province and its financial and economic resources. Similarly, in Antioquia the growing dominance of political conservatives in Medellin may have encouraged some of the elite in its commercial rival, Rionegro, to adopt a liberal party identity. Neighboring Marinilla, a smaller rival of liberal Rionegro, in turn became a conservative town. On the Caribbean coast, the ports of Santa Marta and, even more, Sabanilla-Barranquilla in the early republican era emerged as liberal challengers to the established but declining port of Cartagena.

Ideologically, the two parties that emerged in the 1830s and 1840s did not divide clearly over economic policy. Although elite economic ideas and policies varied over time, from the early 1830s until 1880 they tended to move within an overall bipartisan consensus—leaning toward protectionism in the early 1830s but evolving toward free trade from the late 1840s until 1880. On the subject of political organization, those in the Santander stream (usually known as liberals) after 1837 tended to be more sympathetic to more regional autonomy, while their conservative rivals favored a more centralist structure. But on the question of federalism versus centralism, both parties changed their views opportunistically, and on this subject also there was often an elite consensus, albeit one that changed over time.

The two parties most consistently divided on attitudes toward the power and influence of the Church, most clearly after the civil war of 1839–1842. Liberals, while often Catholic in belief and practice, generally thought that the Church as an institution was too powerful and tended to restrain economic productivity and public enlightenment. Most political conservatives, by contrast, came to believe that the Church must play a central role in preserving the social and moral order; accordingly, they were willing to concede to the clergy a tutorial role in educating the young and guiding poor, less educated people. Political conservatives also viewed the Church as a political ally and as an instrument for mobilizing support for conservative causes. The influence of the clergy on the population at large tended to give conservatives an important advantage in their competition with liberals, whose notions, often imported from abroad, were likely to be incomprehensible and threatening to their less educated compatriots. The Church-related political and ideological differences between conservatives and liberals, already evident in a muffled way in the late 1830s, became sharp and strident in the 1850s and 1860s.

9

Economy and Society, 1821–1850

DEMOGRAPHIC TRENDS: STILL A VACANT LAND

In the 1820s and 1830s New Granada retained many of the economic patterns of the late colonial era but in some ways was in a worsened condition. Warfare from 1810 through 1825 had taken a heavy toll. Although population estimates for 1810 and the census of 1825 are both considered unreliable, local censuses indicate substantial demographic decline. Data for Cali indicate that the number of people in that city dropped by nearly 19 percent between 1809 and 1830, and accounts of the 1820s refer to substantial population losses in many other places.

Between 1835 and 1870 New Granada's population grew by roughly 74 percent. Growth was much higher than the average in Antioquia, the Cauca, and Panama; lower than the average in the Eastern Cordillera; and lowest in the Magdalena Valley and on the Caribbean coast other than Panama. Over the period as a whole, the population of Antioquia grew almost twice as fast as that of the eastern belt, more than three times as fast as that of the Caribbean coast (excluding Panama). But the eastern belt (the Eastern Cordillera plus the Upper Magdalena Valley) remained the most populous region, with 48 percent of the national population in 1835 and 46 percent in 1870, while in the West, Antioquia and the Cauca together made up 22 percent of the population in 1835 and more than 27 percent in 1870. During these years the share of the population on the Caribbean coast (excluding Panama) fell from 14 to 11 percent. (See Table 9.1.)

New Granada, as described by travelers, whether European, North American, or New Granadan, was a rather vacant land. In many areas, large expanses of territory between small towns, taking hours of journey by horse, seemed virtually uninhabited. New Granadans were conscious that their land was vast, their numbers few. During the greater part of the nineteenth century this consciousness encouraged lavish distribution of large tracts of public land for various needs of the state or kinds of perceived public good. Rights to public land were granted as compensation to soldiers of the independence wars and as one of several means of backing public debts. Grants of public land were made in largely futile efforts to attract European immigrants. Public land grants, along with rights to toll collections, also helped to encourage entrepreneurs to open up new trails, whether to facilitate trade or to develop previously unpopulated regions. Grants of public lands en-

Table 9.1 New Granada's population by region, 1810–1870, in thousands
(numbers rounded to the nearest thousand)

	1810	1825	1835	1843	1851	1870	Percent Growth, 1835–1870
The West	*311*	*254*	*368*	*479*	*567*	*801*	*118*
Antioquia	111	104	158	190	243	366	132
Cauca	200	150	210	289	324	435	107
Eastern Cordillera	*447*	*399*	*807*	*917*	*1057*	*1346*	*67*
Cundinamarca	189	189	256	279	317	414	62
Boyacá	231	209	289	332	380	499	73
Santander	237	201	262	306	360	433	65
Upper Magdalena	*100*	*98*	*157*	*183*	*208*	*231*	*47*
Tolima	100	98	157	183	208	231	47
Caribbean coast	*332*	*278*	*354*	*373*	*412*	*555*	*57*
Bolívar	170	122	178	192	206	242	36
Magdalena	71	56	61	62	68	89	46
Panama	91	100	115	119	138	224	95
Totals	*1309*	*1229*	*1686*	*1932*	*2244*	*2933*	*74*

Regional territories are those of the states that existed after 1863.

Sources: Fernando Gómez, "Los censos de Colombia," in Miguel Urrutia and Mario Arrubla, eds., *Compendio de estadísticas históricas de Colombia* (Bogotá, 1970) pp. 9–30, and Jorge Orlando Melo, "La evolución económica de Colombia, 1830–1900, Cuadro 1," in *Manual de historia de Colombia*, Jaime Jaramillo Uribe, ed., II (Bogotá, 1970), pp. 138.

abled trail-builders to settle colonists along new routes, providing both users of the trail and a labor force to maintain it. Land grants and colonization thus functioned together—more to open up new trails than to improve the quality of existing ones. Grants of public land, colonization and cutting new routes was a particularly notable pheonomenon in the Antioquia region after 1830.

Most of the population lived in small rural pockets. There were myriad little farming communities scattered across New Granada's broken terrain; most towns were little more than locations for local weekly markets, and most cities were still only small towns. Bogotá, the political and educational capital as well as a center for the distribution of domestic and imported goods, had an urban population officially counted, in 1835 and 1843, at 40,000. As of 1851, no other town in the country approached 20,000 people. Medellín was developing relatively rapidly as the dominant commercial center in Antioquia, Cali much more slowly in the Cauca.

Several cities that had been significant in the colonial period—Cartagena, Tunja, and Popayán—were no longer among the larger towns. In part because of the silting up of the canal connecting Cartagena to the Magdalena River, Cartagena during the 1830s and 1840s lost its dominance as a receiver of imported goods, and Santa Marta emerged as a more effective competitor, to be succeeded after mid-century by Barranquilla. At mid-century Cartagena, with fewer than 10,000 citizens, was not even among the larger dozen cities. Popayán with 7000 and Tunja with 5000 were far from being among the top twenty municipalities. These established colonial towns, however, remained important as centers of provincial governance and higher education. Popayán and Cartagena, along with Bogotá, boasted the three designated national universities of the 1830s and 1840s, and Tunja had one of the best-endowed secondary schools. Thus these established colonial cities that were now relatively static retained a political weight exceeding the size of their populations or their economic significance.

BOGOTÁ

Bogotá, as the capital, was the New Granadan city most described by visitors. It was not a particularly impressive place. The Sabana de Bogotá surrounding the city appeared to have rich land, but, as it had been largely denuded of all trees except willows, it seemed to some a bit dreary. Agricultural techniques remained backward; farmers still tilled their fields with wooden plows. The city, although the largest in the country, nonetheless was still relatively small. Its narrow, cobbled streets did not have to accommodate much wheeled traffic, except for an occasional cart, as the capital in the 1830s boasted only three closed carriages, plus a few gigs. The Calle de Comercio was the only street with both lamps and sidewalks, the latter only two feet wide. With the aid of rainfall or water from springs, channels in the center of the streets were supposed to carry off sewage, especially in streets that ran downhill from east to west. But the city's sanitation, as a colonial viceroy is alleged to have said, depended more on the appetites of burros, pigs, and vultures. Two rivers running through the city also carried off refuse. Women washed clothes somewhat upstream from the points where the garbage was dumped in. Many homes depended on *aguadoras* (female water-carriers) to bring water from fountains in pottery jugs.

Most houses were of one story. The walls of most dwellings still were built of adobe brick or rammed earth. Bogotá's more august houses, of two stories, still were constructed around patios, in the Spanish Mediterranean tradition. In the 1820s and 1830s the houses, with few exceptions, were poorly furnished by European standards. In the early 1820s the more affluent were installing glass windows; by the middle of the 1830s glazed windows had become more common but still were to be found in less than half the homes. In the 1820s families with pretensions to elegance were covering their floors with carpets, but lesser folk still used straw mats.

The ground-floor street fronts of many houses were occupied by small shops. The shops were generally windowless, with light and air entering only through a single door to the street. Many were occupied by artisans. Others carried on a desultory retail trade, enlivened by a much more active commerce in gossip and political discussion. Few of these shops could have been profitable, since a considerable number were competing for a modest amount of trade. In the 1860s there were said to be more than three thousand shops in Bogotá—one for every thirteen inhabitants!

Although Bogotá was a poor place by European standards, for the university-educated elite the city held many attractions. It was the center of political controversy and the chief arena of political careers. And it was the only city in the country with something like an urban culture. Bogotá had a theater of sorts, as well as a public library, a natural history museum, and at least the remains of an astronomical observatory. Provincials who came to Bogotá for university education and perhaps some initial experience in politics often pined for the political and cultural activity of the capital once they had returned to the land of their birth.

Foreign visitors to Bogotá were struck by the dominant presence of its ecclesiastical structures. The imposing cathedral looming over the east side of the main plaza well represented the power and influence of the Church. However, to many upper-class males the most important feature of the cathedral might be its *altozano*, the terrace in front of the cathedral where gentlemen gathered to gossip about politics and events of the day. While English and Anglo-American visitors tended to admire the cathedral, they often took a dimmer view of the city's monastic establishments, which in their eyes, and also in those of some in the New Granadan elite, represented simply a dead weight on the society's productivity. As of 1810 eight large buildings were occupied by male religious orders and five by nunneries. By 1835 there were fewer friars but more nuns than in 1825. Nonetheless, the 215 friars in the province of Bogotá in 1835 represented almost half of the total in the nation, and the province's 161 nuns made up more than a third of the national total.

Bogotá as a political center was represented much less imposingly than was the Church. The presidential "palace" was described by J. Steuart (1836–1837) as "a shabby affair," with nothing to distinguish it from the houses around it—although President Santander sought to enhance its dignity by receiving official visitors sitting on a throne under a crimson canopy. The chambers of the Congress, Steuart said, consisted "simply of two common rooms . . . over some low 'aguardiente' shops."

If Bogotá's political function was not gloriously represented, neither was its commercial one. As modest as the shops of its merchants were, however, Bogotá was a center of distribution for manufactured goods in New Granada's most populated interior provinces. Hand-woven textiles made in many parts of the Eastern Cordillera came through Bogotá to be sold in the Magdalena Valley and in Antioquia. Imported textiles and other consumer goods also came up the Magdalena River to Bogotá, from whence they were distributed to the eastern highlands as far north as Pamplona—although at least as of the 1850s the regions between Pamplona and Tunja were also receiving foreign goods from the Magdalena River via Ocaña and/or from Maracaibo via Cúcuta. Bogotá at that time was also distributing some foreign merchandise to the Upper Magdalena Valley and to the Cauca Valley.

REGIONAL ECONOMIES AND INTERREGIONAL TRADE

Aside from shipments of textiles and some specialty goods, trade among the various regions of the country was relatively limited. Foods, in particular, tended not to be sent to very distant markets because most provinces, at least in the interior, produced most of the basic consumption goods. Geographic studies of the Corographic Commission in the 1850s indicate that all of the most populated provinces in the mountainous interior grew at least two of the standard starches (potatoes, maize, plantains, rice, and yuca); most grew all, or almost all, of these crops. Beans, peas, arracacha, and a variety of fruits were also widely cultivated, as was sugar cane.

Similarly, a number of the manufactured goods in common use were made in many regions, although artisan manufacture was much more generalized in the eastern highlands and in Pasto than in the the rest of the West, from Popayán to Antioquia. Products made of fique (the fiber of the agave), such as rope, sacks, or *alpargatas* (sandals used by most of the people who used footwear at all), were produced throughout the Eastern Cordillera and, to a lesser degree, in much of the West. A wide array of textiles of cotton and/or wool also were woven in most provinces of the eastern highlands as well in the Pasto region. North of Pasto, from Popayán to Antioquia, only a limited number of textile specialties were made in any province. Leather goods, such as riding gear, shoes, and shoe soles, also were widely produced in the Eastern Cordillera; once again, in the West the variety of leather goods that were locally produced tended to be more limited.

Interregional trade thus was limited by the fact that many regions produced many of the same products, particularly basic foods but also some kinds of manufactured consumer goods. The high cost of overland transportation further restricted internal trade. In the nineteenth century, as in the colonial period, mules carried most overland freight, even over principal trade routes. In the Eastern Cordillera at mid-century mule haulage over level ground cost 23 to 38 cents per ton-mile (about ten times the cost of moving freight by railway in the United States at that time). On the trails over mountain slopes, like those that connected the highlands to the Magdalena River, freight costs were far higher. On one of the most traveled of these routes, the one from the river port of Honda to Bogotá, between 1820 and 1860 freight cost 38 to 102 cents per ton-mile, depending whether it was rainy, a time of war, and/or mules were scarce. Generally, mule-owners would not risk their animals on mountain trails in the rainy season. Some mountain trails were too difficult to use mules at all, and human bearers transported cargo and passengers, at costs 70 to 100 percent higher than for mule haulage. In the 1820s and probably for some time afterward, both cargo and affluent travelers were borne by peons from the head of navigation in the Nare River, in the Magdalena basin, to the highlands of Antioquia where most of its population lived. At least until the 1840s human bearers also carried freight and passengers through the Quindío pass, which connected the Cauca Valley to the Magdalena basin.

Despite the heavy freight costs of carrying cargo from the eastern highlands to the Magdalena and from the Magdalena into the Central Cordillera, some goods with high value for weight or specialty items traveled from the East to the West. Trade over some distance did occur, not only in textiles but also in salt, cacao, and animals on the hoof (cattle, horses, and mules). Bogotá in the 1850s sent some mules, iron, and riding gear, along with national textiles, to Antioquia, and Ocaña provided the Antioqueños with anise, sugar products, wheat flour, and *alpargatas*—in both cases in exchange for gold. But still it could not be said that the country had a national market for any product, and that would remain true throughout the nineteenth century.

A much broader commerce occurred within regions, particularly between complementary high, cool areas and lower, warm ones. In the region of Bogotá, for example, the town of La Mesa, in the warm country south of the capital, served as a point of exchange of lowland products, like cacao from Neiva, *panela* (crude brown sugar), maize, and rice, for highland commodities like the salt of Zipaquirá, potatoes, and textiles. In Boyacá, at the highland town of Sogamoso, lean cattle and raw cotton from the *llanos* of Casanare were exchanged for textiles made in the highlands. However, high freight costs must have imposed some limit on the distance to which goods that were heavy and of low value might be traded. As of 1834, if a muleload of potatoes were transported more than 32 miles over flat land or 20 miles over sloping mountainside, the freight cost would have exceeded the value of the potatoes at their point of origin.

No important improvements in overland transportation occurred before 1870, for various reasons. The fact that most regions were able to supply most of their basic needs through local or immediate regional exchange tended to diminish the scale of trade and thus the incentives to invest in major improvements. In addition, given the slow rhythms of its internal economy and its weakness in foreign trade, the national government lacked the fiscal resources to undertake significant projects. The government's fiscal weakness was such that it could afford to do little more than pay the military and other government employees. Further, the slight government funds available for investment in overland communications during the 1830s were distributed among the provinces on a per capita basis. This eliminated political conflict over the distribution of such funds, but it also made major breakthroughs unlikely. In the 1830s and 1840s, therefore, most repairs of overland routes were performed by local labor drafts, to which poor people provided obligatory labor and the more affluent contributed funds to buy the work of others. These projects, directed by local authorities with no technical preparation and employing a reluctant work force, did little more than remedy some of the damage done to mule trails by traffic and rain (particularly traffic in time of rain). New mule routes generally were opened by private entrepreneurs in return for grants of public lands and the right to collect tolls. As mentioned, such efforts made significant contributions in Antioquia, both in colonizing new areas and developing new trails connecting the interior to the outside world. Such efforts in the Eastern Cordillera, however, were generally less successful, possibly because competition among rival projects undermined all of them, perhaps because there simply was not enough traffic to sustain the new trails in any case. Before mid-century there occurred little qualitative improvement in overland transportation, such as the construction of wagon roads. To achieve important advances in internal transportation, New Granada needed the stimulus of vigorous foreign trade to provide a greater volume of traffic that would encourage investment in the improvement overland routes.

FOREIGN TRADE, DEPRESSION, PROTECTION, AND MANUFACTURING ENTERPRISE

From at least the 1790s an opening to foreign commerce had been a concern of some New Granadan elites, and more trade with Europe had been one of the goals, and one of the achievements, of independence. Unfortunately, in the republican period, as in the colonial era, New Granadans proved to be more able to expand consumption of imported goods than to develop exports other than gold.

There was no lack of desire to consume imported goods. Some Colombians had taken refuge in Jamaica, Europe, or the United States during the Spanish Reconquest of 1816–1819, and in those places became more aware of new standards of consumption. These notions were reinforced by the many British soldiers and merchants, as well as other foreigners, who sought their fortunes in New Granada after 1815. Further, independence had brought much easier access to foreign goods. Colonial contraband trade with Jamaica became legalized and liberated with independence. In the 1820s and the 1830s most British and other foreign goods came to New Granada by way of Jamaica; as of the end of the 1830s close to half of the country's imports still were coming from intermediaries in Jamaica. By mid-century, however, direct trade with England and France had become the standard mode.

The appetite for imported goods became evident as soon as free and secure foreign trade became possible at the end of 1821. From 1822 to 1823 the value of British goods imported into Colombia nearly tripled, and by 1825 importations from Great Britain reached a peak more than six times the level during 1822. The increased volume of importations between 1822 and 1826 was paid for in part by British loans, in part by British investments in mining and other enterprises. The flow of British money to Colombia, particu-

Table 9.2 Estimated annual Colombian gold production,
1801–1890, in millions of pesos (rounded off)

1801–1810	3.1	1851–1860	2.2	1882–1884	2.8
1811–1820	1.8	1861–1864	2.0	1885–1886	2.4
1821–1835	2.4	1865–1869	2.3	1887–1890	3.5
1836–1850	2.5	1879–1881	2.5		

Source: Vicente Restrepo, *Estudio sobre las minas de oro y plata* (Bogotá, 1952), p. 199.

larly in 1825–1826, fueled a temporary boom in imports, stimulated commercial activity, and encouraged new standards of consumption.

However, with the collapse of Colombia's bond broker and the British bond market in 1826, British bounty disappeared as a means of financing imports. After 1826, Colombia had to depend exclusively on its own exports as a means of generating foreign exchange. Unfortunately, during the independence period, the country's capacity to export had declined. Gold production was disrupted by the war for independence, particularly by the escape of slaves or their induction into military service. Loss of slave labor especially hampered the recovery of gold mining in the Cauca and on the Pacific coast. In contrast, Antioquia, which depended more on free labor, recovered as a gold producer during the 1820s and 1830s. Nonetheless, according to the estimates of Vicente Restrepo, annual gold production in Colombia did not regain the levels of the end of the colonial period at any time before the 1880s. (See Table 9.2.)

Despite the relative decline in gold production, gold bullion remained the country's overwhelmingly predominant export. During the independence period, New Granada had lost ground in its foreign sales of tropical products. After independence the market for its cinchona bark disappeared, and its exports of cacao appear to have been negligible. Cotton in the late 1830s still represented nearly 5 percent of New Granada's exports, but its volume was tiny by Atlantic world standards, equivalent to less than 0.3 percent of the value of cotton shipments from the U.S. South at the time. By the 1840s U.S. competition had driven New Granadan cotton almost completely from world markets. Of the late colonial exports cattle hides and dyewoods remained the most viable, if still minor, commodities in the early 1840s. During the 1830s experiments were made with exports of tobacco from the region of Ambalema, along the banks of the upper Magdalena River. Some hope for the future of New Granadan tobacco developed in the 1830s and more markedly in the 1840s. But tobacco remained a relatively slight factor in New Granada's exports before 1845, in part because production was controlled by a government monopoly, and the government, often short of funds, failed to invest enough to expand production substantially. (See Table 9.3.)

Table 9.3 Most significant New Granadan exports by value, 1834–1845
(mean annual value in thousands of gold pesos)

	1834–1835/1838–1839		1840–1841/1844–1845	
	Value	Percent of Total	Value	Percent of Total
Gold	2413.0	74.0	2413.0	73.0
Cotton	155.3	4.8	52.9	1.6
Dyewoods				
Palo brasil	115.4	3.5	133.7	4.0
Palo mora	35.9	1.1	45.4	1.4
Hides	101.9	3.1	149.8	4.5
Tobacco	86.6	2.7	118.5	3.6
Total	3261.6		3306.5	

Source: José Antonio Ocampo, *Colombia y la economía mundial, 1830–1910* (Bogotá, 1984), Cuadro 2.7, p. 100.

Hoping to develop sources of foreign exchange other than gold, the successive governments of Colombia and New Granada offered tax exemptions for tropical crops that, it was hoped, might be exported. In 1821 coffee, cotton, and sugar products were granted exemptions from export taxes for ten years; in 1824 Colombia reimposed some export taxes but exempted new plantations of coffee, cacao, and indigo from paying the tithe. In 1833 New Granada ended export taxes for all tropical fruits and in 1835 offered export premiums to cotton, sugar, and rice.

Such measures, however, brought little result. During the 1830s New Granada's exports remained at low levels, somewhat below those obtained during its brief period of relative success exporting tropical products in the last decade of the colonial period. New Granada at this time, and for a considerable period thereafter, remained one of the least successful exporters in Latin America. At the end of 1820s and in the 1830s New Granada's exports were insufficient to provide the exchange required to sustain its increased flow of imports. One reflection of this fact: Upper-class women in Bogotá were selling their jewelry to pay for imported goods. Payments for imports were draining the country of coin, and, in the absence of banks to expand means of payment through banknotes, the drainage of coin, it was believed, was causing price deflation, economic stagnation, and depression.

As means of payment shrank, prices of locally produced goods, cultivated and manufactured, dropped. In Bogotá prices of basic foods fell by a third to a half between 1830 and 1834. At the same time, scarcity of currency along with a loss of confidence in the country's economic prospects made it difficult to get credit. Those who could get loans paid 12 to 36 percent per annum; some borrowers were said to be paying 60 percent. High interest rates and the crisis of confidence that accompanied them discouraged attempting new enterprises.

Contemporaries generally blamed the depression on the trade imbalance, and many in turn attributed the trade deficit to New Granadans' developing taste for imported refinements, particularly among townspeople of the middling and upper class. (Peons in the interior, in town and country, were still wearing tough cotton cloth made on handlooms in the Eastern Cordillera.) As of the 1830s, most of the imported goods were textiles or clothing; at least in Bogotá there was not yet much sign of consumption of imported luxuries that were cumbersome and costly to transport. The chief exception seems to have been mirrors, which in upper-class homes were the principal adornment—in as much profusion as possible, according to one foreign visitor.

Although imported luxuries were still rather modest by comparison with later decades, contemporary newspapers condemned the increased consumption of foreign goods. Some editorialists inveighed against a new luxury in dress among young women in particular. José Manuel Restrepo, on the other hand, took a more sanguine view of New Granada's transition from the innocence of colonial simplicity to the anguish of republican underdevelopment. In 1834 Restrepo noted that "the poverty of the citizens is felt even more because the people are learning of necessities that previously were unknown to them." "Little by little," he continued, "better taste in dress, furniture and adornment of houses is being introduced. This presages progress in the civilization of the people." But, he added more darkly, "if there is not a corresponding improvement in the industry and wealth of the citizens, they will be more unfortunate because they will not be able to obtain the new pleasures that they have known."

The economic crisis of 1830–1834 provoked a protectionist reaction throughout much of New Granada. José Ignacio de Márquez, as secretary of finance in 1831, argued that the sources of the depression lay not merely in the import-induced contraction of the currency but also in the destructive effect of increased imports on the base of the domestic economy. Competition from imported goods was ravaging artisan manufactures in the eastern highlands. As local manufacturing declined, Márquez pointed out, so also did demand for locally produced wool and cotton. The impact on both artisanry and agriculture was evident throughout the Eastern Cordillera: The provinces of Pamplona, Socorro, Tunja, and Bogotá, once productive, were being impoverished. Márquez also asserted, as did other New Granadans at the time, that the import trade in New Granada was being monopolized by British merchants. Unable to compete with British importers, who had established connections in England, New Granadan merchants, along with artisans and farmers, were also being ruined. Márquez called for prohibiting the importation of goods that competed with New Granadan productions, high duties on luxury products, and the reimposition of restrictions on foreign merchants.

Proposals for protection from foreign imports stirred a debate between free traders and protectionists that continued throughout the period of most acute crisis, 1830–1834. The leading spokesman for free trade was a British immigrant, William Wills, who brandished the standard arguments of liberal political economy: England's dense population and concentrated capital destined it to become an industrial nation; New Granada, with its sparse population and abundant land, must specialize in the export of tropical agriculture. Wills, and like-minded New Granadan free traders, argued that the solution to the commercial crisis was to improve the country's capacity to import by developing its tropical exports. (Wills practiced what he preached, during the 1830s sending experimental shipments of New Granadan tobacco to test the London market.)

The protectionists' response confronted liberal economic theory with practical experience: Given the concentration of New Granada's population in the interior and its extraordinarily poor transportation conditions, how could it effectively export? In any case, no one seemed to want New Granada's tropical products. Liberal trade theory might have behind it the weight of authoritative writers in England and France, but it did not seem to work for New Granada. New Granada imported a great deal from Great Britain, but England bought very little produced by New Granada. While an already-industrialized England now preached free trade, it in fact had pursued and still continued protectionist policies itself (particularly in giving preferential treatment to tropical products from the British Caribbean as against their Latin American competitors). If the British pressed their goods on New Granada but refused to buy New Granadan products, what was New Granada to do? For many, particularly in the eastern highlands, the answer was a turn toward autarchy, toward an economy in which domestic agriculture and domestic manufactures would feed on each other.

The division between protectionists and free traders, however, did not strictly follow regional or party lines. Support for protection probably was strongest in the eastern highlands, whose artisans and agriculturalists were most damaged by free trade. But while elites in Santa Fe de Antioquia in 1830 stood firmly for free trade, their counterparts in Medellín and Rionegro—by that time the leading commercial towns in Antioquia, but where some artisans were also present—favored prohibiting the imports of finished goods produced by urban artisans. And, while merchants in the port of Cartagena opposed import prohibitions, they nonetheless supported protective customs duties.

Similarly, individual opinions on the issue did not correspond to political factions. Free trade views were espoused by the former Bolivarians José María Castillo y Rada and José Manuel Restrepo, the moderate Lino de Pombo, and various *exaltado* liberals. But liberals, as well as other political factions, split over this question. Francisco de Paula Santander while in exile in 1831 found validation for protection in New Granada in the protectionist tariffs in the United States at the time. Francisco Soto, who had been the first professor of liberal political economy in New Granada in the 1820s, as Santander's secretary of finance (1832–1837), also adhered to Santander's moderately protectionist line—high duties but not import prohibitions.

The protectionist movement reached its zenith in 1833. The Chamber of Representatives in that year voted to prohibit the importation of a number of items by an overwhelming margin. However, this measure was beaten down in the Senate, and ultimately both houses accepted a policy of high tariffs, but not prohibitions. Wheat-growers in the interior were protected with 100 percent tariffs in a doomed attempt to recover coastal markets lost to North American flour for more than a century. Urban artisans, who were at least subordinate political actors in cities like Bogotá and Medellín, also were given protection against the importation of ready-made clothing, the tariff for which rose from 30 percent of value in 1831 to 100 percent in 1833. The legislators, however, gave much less protection to hand-weavers, who were for the most part women in provincial towns, and thus politically voiceless. Duties on common cloth went up only to 25 percent of value.

After 1833 the protectionist wave began to subside. The heavy tariff on wheat flour had so discouraged importation that it had become practically unavailable on the Caribbean coast. In 1834 the Congress cut duties on flour in half and also began to trim duties on common cloth. Tariffs remained high on ready-made clothing, perhaps because they were not such a large proportion of imports as common cloth, as well as because of the political leverage of urban artisans.

In any case, the tariffs established by gentlemen politicians in Bogotá were unlikely to affect the great mass of artisan manufacturers in the Eastern Cordillera or the Pasto region. The high cost of transportation up the Magdalena River in poled boats, when added to even moderate customs duties, already provided a substantial barrier that imported goods had to overcome. (By contrast, high overland freight rates cut both ways: They restricted the radius of trade in locally made goods as much as those of imported ones.) Since the cost of upriver transportation was a significant protective factor for artisan manufacturers in the interior, the effective establishment of steamboats on the Magdalena River at mid-century probably had as an important impact on local artisans as did any change in the tariff. The most important factor negatively affecting artisan manufacturers in the interior was the growing difference in production costs between factory-made goods in Europe and the handmade ones of local artisans. Fortunately for New Granadan consumers, but unfortunately for the artisan weavers of the interior, the prices of imported textiles declined continuously in the first half of the nineteenth century. As of 1860 the prices of imported cotton goods were less than a third of their levels in 1820. Nonetheless, artisan manufacturers in the interior hung on in large numbers at least through the 1870s, aided in part by deeply established habits of consuming certain kinds of goods not made in Europe (e.g., ruanas and *alpargatas*). Artisans in the interior also adapted to import pressure by increasing and improving production of a variety of types of straw hats, some of which were exported effectively from the 1850s into the 1870s.

More or less at the time of the protectionist burst of the early 1830s, several companies in Bogotá were attempting to establish modern factories. However, these enterprises were related to the protectionist thrust only in the general sense that both reflected a desire to develop the economy. The first of these manufacturing companies, the ironworks at Pacho, was incorporated in 1823, a time of optimism about the new republic, before the onset of the depression and anxiety that pervaded the early 1830s. The other enterprises—a chinaware factory (1832), a paper mill (1834), a glass factory (1834), and a cotton textile mill (1837)—were launched in the context of the depression of the 1830s. But none of these enterprises sought any protection from import competition. (Some of the entrepreneurs, indeed, were confirmed anti-protectionists, José Manuel Restrepo, long active in the Pacho ironworks, being a notable example.) Rather, they asked for, and received, monopoly privileges that protected them from competitors within the country using modern technology, but not from foreign imports. Only one of the privileges granted to these manufacturing companies stirred much protest—interests in Antioquia objected that the privilege granted to the Pacho enterprise prevented them from developing their own ironworks in Antioquia. (The most notable and prolonged protest against such privileges focused on a monopoly in the use of steamboats on the Magdalena River, held by a German merchant from 1823 to 1837, which, critics complained, had kept steamboats off the river for most of that time.)

Bogotá's manufacturing enterprises were of modest size. In the middle 1830s three of them were valued at between 15,000 and 20,000 pesos. Ultimately the ironworks, the pottery factory, and the cotton textile mill each appear to have absorbed 100,000 pesos or more. Yet by the standards of the Atlantic industrial world they were not large operations. The cotton textile mill by 1840 was said to be able to process 300,000 pounds of cotton per year; this was much larger than the smaller mills of Puebla in Mexico at the time, but half to a third the size of Puebla's two largest mills.

The organizers and investors in these factories were distinctly upper class. Many were active in national or provincial politics. Their motivations in establishing the factories seem to have reflected both their class positions and the fact that a number of them were prominent in public affairs. Although they clearly hoped to make a profit, establishing factories to them also represented a step toward becoming a modern nation.

The small factories attempted in and around Bogotá were at worst dismal failures, at best modest successes. The largest and most important of these ventures, the ironworks at Pacho, took a long time to go into effective production. Early failures discouraged the initial investors. But by mid-century iron produced at Pacho was being sold through much of the Eastern Cordillera, where it was made into agricultural implements and nails in the provinces of Tunja and el Socorro and even as far north as Pamplona

and Cúcuta. Pacho iron also was an item in trade with Medellín and Rionegro in Antioquia, where it was used to make agricultural and mining
tools. The chinaware factory in Bogotá also, after burning down, came back
into production and served New Granadan consumers for decades. However, the other enterprises did not last long. The glass factory was effectively
dead by 1838; the paper mill lasted apparently until 1840; the cotton mill
hung on until 1845, when its American technical director died.

The difficulties of these early factories are not hard to explain. None of
the New Granadan entrepreneurs had any previous experience with manufacturing enterprise, nor did they have any prior knowledge of the technical processes involved. They therefore had to rely heavily on foreign
technicians, who were not always dependable. Bogotá's early industrial entrepreneurs imported most of their machinery, some of it very heavy and
costly to transport. They invested most of their capital in plant (in at least
one case with superfluous attention to decor) and underdestimated their
need for later working capital. After initial difficulties, they found it hard to
raise additional funds. Further, these were isolated enterprises, attempted in
a context in which there was not a community of mechanics to lend support. When the imported machinery broke, skilled artisans might not be
readily available to do the repairs. Last but not least, given a sparse, generally poor population, a stagnant regional economy, and high transportation
costs, the potential market was limited. These relatively small and isolated
manufacturing enterprises are interesting primarily as an expression of dominant class intent to modernize the country economically.

The four manufacturing enterprises that still survived as of 1840 undoubtedly were affected by the civil war of 1839–1842 and the chain of bank-
ruptcies and the tangle of subsequent legal suits that hit Bogotá early in 1842.
The civil war of 1839–1842 contributed to the financial crisis of 1842, but ultimately the roots of the crisis lay in the profound depression that had settled on the eastern highlands by 1830. Extremely high interest rates probably
contributed to the development of the crisis, as contemporaries and later an-
alysts have noted. However, the high cost of capital should not be attributed
to the elimination of legal restrictions on interest rates in 1835, as some have
suggested. Very high interest rates, even if technically illegal, prevailed years
before the enactment of the 1835 law.

PAISAS: THE RISE OF ANTIOQUIA

While the Eastern Cordillera endured depression during the early 1830s, the
gold-mining province of Antioquia was prospering. Antioqueños and others, both at the time and later, ascribed their region's economic success in
part to the qualities of the region's people: From at least the 1820s onward,
contemporaries described the people of Antioquia as notably hard-working
and enterprising.

Although nineteenth-century testimony about the industrious Antioqueño is too abundant to be denied, most contemporaries also understood that the presence of gold differentiated the economies of Antioquia, the Chocó, and the Pacific coast from those of the rest of the country. Gold was New Granada's biggest source of exchange until the end of the 1850s, and its most consistent one to the end of the nineteenth century. Access to gold meant that, during the 1830s, when the Eastern Cordillera was suffering from a shortage of means of payment for imported goods, Antioqueño merchants had significant advantages over their counterparts in expanding their importing activities, including the establishment of direct ties with suppliers in Europe.

Antioquia between 1810 and 1850 appears to have produced half of all of the country's gold (after 1850 more than half), with the Chocó and the Pacific coast responsible for most of the rest. Antioquia had several advantages over these other regions in continuing and expanding gold production. During the latter part of the eighteenth century much of the gold panning in Antioquia was already being performed by free workers rather than slaves. As of about 1780, free blacks, mulattoes, and mestizos were more than three-fifths of the population, slaves less than a fifth. And during and after the independence period, Antioquia made a smooth and rapid transition from slave to free labor. In 1835 slaves accounted for only about 2.2 percent of the population of Antioquia, as contrasted with 15.4 percent for Buenaventura and the Chocó and 12.2 percent for Popayán. Antioquia's gold industry was therefore much less affected by the decline of slavery after independence than were the mines of the Chocó, the Cauca, and the Pacific coast. Antioquia also had better agricultural resources than the Chocó and thus could better supply its miners with food. Further, Antioquia's more or less independent gold washers, its *mazamorreros*, often mined on a seasonal or part-time basis, growing at least some of their own food. Antioquia's gold mining also was aided, over the long term, by technical improvements. Beginning in the 1820s, French, British, and Swedish mining engineers and entrepreneurs introduced ore mills, which in subsequent decades facilitated exploitation of vein mines.

Antioquia's gold economy fueled the development of a regional bourgeoisie with considerable accumulations of capital. A number of these emerging capitalists were involved both in mining enterprises and in commerce. From colonial times investments in gold mines were divided among various shareholders because of the risks of mining. Commercial activities, buying gold dust and supplying goods to the miners, as well as to the rest of the province and to the Cauca Valley, were more dependable sources of income and savings. Some of Antioquia's wealthy men began as retail merchants near mine locations but, with capital accumulations, ultimately migrated to Medellín or Rionegro, where they became wholesale merchants dealing with much broader markets.

In the last decades of the colonial period the larger Antioqueño merchants typically obtained Socorro textiles from Bogotá and imported goods from Cartagena or Mompox. During the independence and immediate post-independence periods, however, a number of Antioquia's merchants established direct contact with the British commercial entrepot in Jamaica, thus enabling them to bypass intermediaries on the Caribbean coast. Antioquia's merchants had one striking advantage as importers. They had direct access to the region's gold dust, which was not only New Granada's chief source of foreign exchange but was also the means of payment preferred by their suppliers in Jamaica.

By 1820, if not before, elites in other parts of New Granada perceived Antioquia's merchant-capitalists to be unusually wealthy. Further, whereas in other regions much of the wealth of the dominant class was tied up in land, Antioquia's emerging merchants had at their disposal more liquid, easily mobilized wealth, an important advantage in an economy in which there were no banks to facilitate capital mobilization.

Antioquia's relative financial strength was already visible during the fight for independence, when the region was the leading source of internal financing for the patriot cause. New Granada's dependence on Antioquia for financing continued in the post-independence period. After the civil war of 1839–1842, for example, when the government was once again strapped, the president turned to four Antioqueño merchant-capitalists for 200,000 pesos to help recapitalize the operations of the government tobacco monopoly.

The accumulated wealth of Antioquia's merchant-capitalists gave them several advantages that enabled them to extend their activities beyond Antioquia. Their loans to the government put them in possession of large bond-holdings, and these, if not also a sense of gratitude in the national government, tended to give them a special claim on government contracts as well as on purchases of public lands. The strong capital position of Manuel Antonio Arrubla and Francisco Montoya and their reputations as businessmen were surely among the reasons they were put in charge of negotiating the large British loan of 1824, with its attendant commissions. Further, the Antioqueños' liquidity enabled them to mobilize capital resources to take advantage of opportunities outside of Antioquia. From the 1820s well into the 1840s navigation on the Magdalena River was dominated by a firm in which two of the three principals were Antioqueños. In the 1840s and 1850s Antioqueños were the leading merchants in the tobacco trade in Ambalema, and later in the century they also controlled the exploitation and export of cinchona bark (for quinine) in the upper Magdalena Valley.

Although Antioquia's wealthy merchant-capitalists were very visible in Medellín, as well as elsewhere in the country, they constituted a minority within the province's upper class. The 1853 tax rolls for Medellín indicate some twenty-two men whose incomes would be considered very large by Bogotá standards. Beneath them, however, were another five hundred whose annual earnings of about 1000 pesos would be more characteristic of New Granada's upper sector elsewhere.

In *paisa* lore Antioquia's magnates of the nineteenth century are described as self-made men, born in poverty, who triumphed through application of the standard capitalist virtues—hard work, self-discipline, honesty, foresight, calculation, punctuality, and so on. According to the same lore, after they became wealthy they continued to dress plainly and live simply. A mid-nineteenth-century Antioqueño writer, Juan de Dios Restrepo, depicted the region's bourgeoisie as having little use for the finer cultural graces, instructing the young not to waste their time with novels or poetry. Restrepo satirically contrasted the hard-working austerity of the *paisa* patriarchs with the more cultured and political, and less work-oriented, tone of life among the elite in Bogotá.

Some accounts of Antioquia, however, suggest that Restrepo's picture of the austerity of its merchant-capitalists may have been exaggerated. A Swedish visitor in 1825–1826, Carl August Gosselman, was astonished by the luxuries he found in the home of Pedro Sáenz, one of the chief merchants of Rionegro. "To encounter a salón of such exquisiteness, . . . furnished and decorated with a nearly European pomp," embedded in the interior of South America, "was truly unexpected." Gosselman was struck by the "innumerable mirrors, hanging lamps, tables, chairs, and [even] a grand piano," all of which, as he pointed out, had to be carried from the Magdalena River to the highlands on the backs of peons. Further, Gosselman concluded, since no one in the household could actually play the piano, it represented what would now be called conspicuous consumption. On the other hand, Gosselman was also impressed that Sáenz was in other ways truly cultured; his library contained many books in English and French, both languages that the Rionegro merchant understood quite well.

Accounts of the austerity of Antioquia's merchant-capitalists probably had some basis in reality, but it is also probable that this picture of the regional bourgeoisie was a useful myth. Depicting Antioquia's magnates as self-made men who retained and propagated the values of self-discipline and work served both to justify their wealth and to make them appropriate exemplars of the regional ideology that Antioquia was a poor land made rich through energetic effort and enterprise.

The mass of Antioqueños undoubtedly were poor, at least relative to the merchant-capitalists of Medellín or Rionegro. And they were growing in number. The standard explanation for Antioqueño population growth is that *paisas* as a rule married early and had a lot of children. There seems to be a good deal of truth in this. In the 1850s a national geographic survey reported that in rural Antioquia men married at 15–18 years of age and women at 11–14. According to the census of 1835, 67 percent of adult free males in Antioquia were married, as contrasted with a national average of 55 percent. And children (under the age of 16) made up 51 percent of Antioquia's free population, whereas the national average was 44 percent.

High marriage rates probably did foster population growth in Antioquia, although the latter could have occurred in the absence of this proclivity to marriage. The importance of high marriage rates in Antioquia may lie

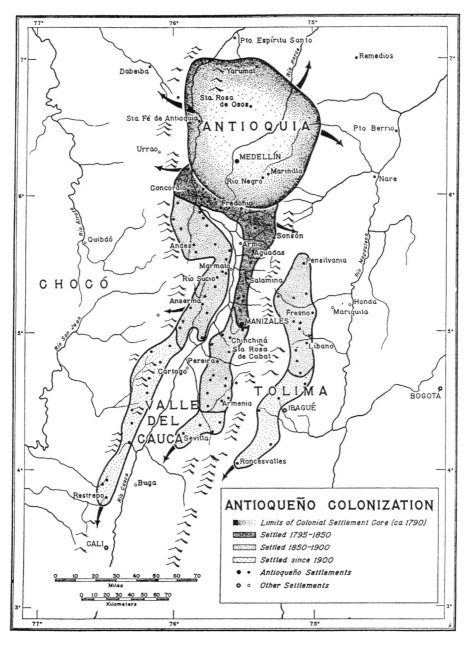

Map 5 Antioqueño colonization (ca. 1950). From James J. Parsons,
Antioqueño Colonization in Western Colombia (Berkeley, CA, 1968).

just as much in helping to consolidate a social order that placed a high value on hard work as part of a strong sense of responsibility to family. One should add here, so as not to gild the Antioqueño lily overmuch, that, although the *paisa* poor were generally thought of as hard-working and honest, they also could be, perhaps particularly outside the social controls within Antioquia itself, hard drinkers and fearsome fighters.

Growth of population powered the *paisas'* vigorous territorial expansion. During the nineteenth century Antioqueños pushed in all directions from the core cities of Santa Fe de Antioquia, Medellín, Rionegro, and Marinilla. Although some notable colonization occurred toward the east, north, west, and southwest, the Antioqueños at first occupied a much greater territory to the south, colonizing all of what is now Caldas, Risaralda, and the Quindío, and penetrating into the Cauca Valley and parts what became the State of Tolima.

Antioquia's population growth had placed increasing pressure on the land in the parts of the region that had been colonized in the seventeenth and eighteenth centuries. Around Medellín and Rionegro by the end of the eighteenth century farmland was being divided into increasingly small plots and its fertility was decreasing. And in some places land was monopolized by large owners. Land scarcity and sterilization may have pushed individual Antioqueños into spontaneous colonization. But to some degree the colonization process also was organized by the merchant-capitalists of the larger towns. Sometimes it was a coercive process. In the last decades of the eighteenth century Spanish administrators pressed people considered to be vagrants into colonizing new areas. And some coercive colonization continued in the nineteenth century—with vagrants, prisoners for debt, or convicts in general placed at the disposal of private entrepreneurs. But not all those who colonized new areas were vagrants, convicts, or even poor; the wealth of some colonists is suggested by the fact that they brought slaves or servants as part of their labor force.

Some colonization projects aimed to further gold mining by providing food to known mining sites. Whether near gold mines or other potential markets or not, the process of colonization followed certain common patterns. In the Cauca basin merchant-capitalists in Medellín, took over large expanses of land in the flatter valleys, on which they fattened cattle. Poorer colonists found themselves obliged to occupy higher, hilly land. There, after clearing the forests with ax and fire, they planted maize, beans, yuca (cassava), *plátanos* (plantains), and sugar cane. And they raised pigs. If markets for their crops were not reachable profitably, part of the surplus was fed to the pigs, which could move themselves to market.

The colonization process was often conflictive. Poor colonists often began to farm new areas, only to find that the land formed part of large blocks of land to which title had been obtained by wealthy men in Medellín, Rionegro, or other established towns. Some titles stemmed from royal grants in the colonial period; others derived from purchases of public land, at very low prices and with depreciated government bonds, in the republican era. In both cases, the colonists represented an economic resource to the large title-holders, since the colonists by clearing and farming the land gave it a value it had not previously had. However, disputes often developed between the colonists and the title-holders over who would profit from the increased value produced by the labor of the colonists.

Some colonizing entrepreneurs who had obtained large grants of land appear to have perceived colonization as a more or less collaborative process. In the Cauca Valley southwest of Medellín, large landowners encouraged the development of the new areas by making plots available to colonists in return for working on opening and maintaining mule trails linking the region to markets. In other cases, however, prolonged altercations over land rights occurred between magnates who claimed legal title to immense expanses and the many squatters who had settled on the land. Often disputes over titles ultimately boiled down to a disagreement over the price squatters would pay the title-holders for their land. In such fights the wealthy men who claimed legal title to the land were able to make use of their connections to legislators, provincial governors, and others in the political elite, while the claims of poorer colonists were backed only by the simple fact of occupation.

A notable struggle between land magnates and colonists occurred in the area of the present Department of Caldas, which was claimed by the Aranzazu family of Rionegro on the basis of a late colonial grant. This conflict, which was fought out from the early 1820s into the 1850s, had the politically well-connected Juan de Dios Aranzazu representing the family interests in Medellín and Bogotá, while his uncle, Elías González, took command in the colonization area itself. Arrayed against them were colonist leaders in such settlements as Salamina (founded 1827), Neira (1843), and Manizales (1848). González was murdered in 1851, apparently in retaliation for burning colonists' farms. The national government settled the issue in 1853 by ordering the distribution of a sizeable amount of land to squatters in the Aranzazu tract.

In addition to disputes between colonists and holders of titles to large blocks of land, there also were divisions between colonist oligarchies and poorer, less favored colonists. Wealthier colonists or those who first came into an area and entrenched themselves dominated the *juntas de pobladores* (colonist committees) and the city councils and used these positions to distribute land in ways that favored their relatives and friends and dealt out those who were poorer or less well connected. Those colonists who failed to obtain adequate plots of land found it necessary to become renters, hire themselves out as wage workers, or move on to a new colonization site. Thus, the unequal distribution of land at each stage of the colonization process contributed to the ceaseless dynamism of Antioqueño expansion into Caldas and beyond, into the Quindío and the upper Cauca Valley.

Colombian elites outside Antioquia were enchanted with the *paisa* colonists. As Antioqueños came into the Quindío, political authorities in the Cauca region were eager to concede them land so that they might establish permanent communities. Caucano leaders, it has been argued, welcomed Antioqueño migrants as a "white" alternative to the region's existing Afro-Colombian and indigenous populace. This may well be true, but the Cauca elite also valued the Antioqueño migrants as hard workers. Jorge Juan Hoyos, the governor of Cauca Province, believed Antioqueño settlements would help to develop overland communications to Antioquia as well as across the Quindío pass to the Magdalena Valley and would have a positive effect on agriculture in the Cauca Valley itself. "One Antioqueño peon is worth three from here," he reported to President Herrán in 1844. "These men do not rest: no sooner do they finish sowing crops on their possessions than they come to contract themselves for . . . the rainy season." Later Hoyos reported that he had made more progress on clearing the Quindío trail than he had expected, "aided by the Antioqueño peones, who up to now have shown only one bad quality, that of not stopping."

THE CAUCA: ARISTOCRACY AND STAGNATION

During the nineteenth and twentieth centuries Antioqueños have been wont to compare themselves to, and to have a sense of rivalry with, people in Bogotá. But perhaps a more interesting comparison is of Antioquia with the Cauca region to its south. Antioquia boasted important gold-mining sites at various points throughout the colonial period, but its period of overwhelming dominance came late, beginning to build toward the end of the eighteenth century and becoming particularly evident in the nineteenth century.

By contrast, the Cauca region was important throughout the colonial period. The region had been a leading gold producer practically from the time the Spanish had established themselves in Popayán in 1536. Furthermore, in contrast with the agricultural limitations of the rugged Antioquia, both the Popayán region and the flat expanse of the Cauca Valley to its north offered evident potential for the production of food. The agricultural and mineralogical bounty of the Cauca made it an attractive focus of Spanish settlement, and Popayán emerged early in the colonial era as the political and ecclesiastical, as well as the economic, capital of the West. Popayán in the colonial period thus developed an aristocracy that came to be based on gold mining powered primarily by black slaves and agricultural estates making use of the labor of both slaves and the surviving Indian population in the western flank of the central cordillera.

By the 1820s and 1830s Popayán, and the region as a whole, had lost much of its economic weight, in large part because of the effects of the struggle for independence. Pasto had been devastated, mainly by republican repression, during the 1820s. Both around Popayán and in the Cauca Valley, contending armies had recruited much of the available labor force, including not a few slaves, while many other slaves escaped during wartime disorder. Warring armies also stripped haciendas of cattle, horses, and food. During the independence war food became so scarce in the Cauca Valley that it was no longer able to supply the mines in the Chocó and slave gangs there tended to disintegrate. Recurring regional conflict in the early 1830s brought further disruptions, and in his rebellion of 1840–1841 General José María Obando, along with all of the other predations that attended civil war, filled his ranks with slaves. The mobilization of slaves and free blacks by Obando and others brought not only the further erosion of slavery but also some cases of slave rebellion during the 1840s. Racially configured class antagonism and violence continued a central feature of the Cauca's society and politics in subsequent decades.

The continuing decline of slavery until its abolition in 1852 further weakened gold mining in parts of the Cauca region, whereas Antioquia, more dependent on free labor, recovered quickly after the independence crisis. Estimates at mid-century by the Comisión Corográfica suggest that the per capita value of Antioquia's regional trade may have been more than five times that of Popayán and the Cauca Valley.

Yet aristocratic Popayán remained significant politically, far beyond its size or its economic strength, for much of the nineteenth century. The Mosqueras, the Arboledas, and others in the Popayán elite with whom they intermarried retained their distinction among the political leadership of a society that was at once republican and aristocratic. During the nineteenth century, four Mosquera brothers occupied eminent positions in New Granada. Two were presidents, Joaquín (1830) and Tomás Cipriano (1845–1849, 1861–1863, 1863–1864, 1866–1867). Manuel María Mosquera was a perennial ambassador in Europe (1838–1849), and his twin brother, Manuel José, became archbishop of Bogotá (1834–1853).

Despite the damage wreaked in the independence period, Popayán in the 1820s still retained some of the glow of its colonial glory. A British visitor, Colonel J. P. Hamilton, was dazzled by Popayán and its aristocracy. He found the city's buildings "much superior to those of Bogotá," particularly the mansions of the "few very rich families." He was especially impressed by the homes and estates of the Mosqueras and the Arboledas. Joaquín Mosquera had been in England and "tried to imitate [English] habits and customs as much as possible." And at Japio, José Rafael Arboleda's estate near Quilichao, everything was beautifully ordered. The bedrooms were decorated "completely in the French style" and were stocked with French and British toiletries found only "among rich families in Europe." Even the slave women who panned the gold, according to Hamilton, were "neatly dressssed in white petticoats with blue ornaments."

There was, however, a grittier side to the Mosqueras and Arboledas that Hamilton did not notice. A hint of the less idyllic: The much respected Joaquín Mosquera, considered in the political class the very emblem of judgment and moderation, in 1824 severed a tendon in his finger, with subsequent gangrene and amputation, from "a blow to the tooth of a Negro." And while some in these families lived in style in Popayán, others might be found in crude huts in the depressingly primitive Chocó, looking after family mining enterprises.

In any event, if the Mosqueras, Arboledas, and their kind were the elegant ornaments of the Cauca, they were not completely representative of even the upper class in the rest of the region. Particularly in the Cauca Valley north of Popayán, some landowners with large tracts of land lived among their slaves and tenants in a relatively simple manner, and even in rude conditions, whether in town or country, their relative wealth visible mainly in the quantities of their land and cattle. They occupied a beautiful valley, fertile and well-watered, but whose economic possibilities were constricted by the surrounding mountains that walled them off from potential markets. In the first half of the nineteenth century the region's only products that could reach farther markets were its gold and cinchona bark, to which tobacco was added after mid-century. Improved transit across the Isthmus of Panama by an American railway constructed in the 1850s began to strengthen the incentive to link Cali more effectively to the port of Buenaventura on the Pacific. But fuller integration of the region into world markets had to await the construction of the Panama Canal.

THE CARIBBEAN COAST

New Granada's Caribbean zone, including the Isthmus of Panama, contained about a fifth of the country's population in the 1830s and 1840s. Remote from the population in the mountainous interior, and living in very different circumstances, the people of the Caribbean Coast tended to feel distant from the rest of their compatriots, not only spatially but also culturally. This sense of alienation went beyond the rivalry between Cartagena and Bogotá. While the people in the interior were isolated in mountain pockets, the people of the coast were much more connected to the outside world. They were part of the Caribbean, culturally as well as commercially. In speech and in cultural style, the coast was strongly Afro-Caribbean. And the *costeños'* lives were shaped not by mountainous constriction but by water-borne commerce.

Of the various subregions of the coast, the most distant from the interior, and the most isolated from its political currents, was the Isthmus of Panama. As a point of transit between the Atlantic and the Pacific, Panama was more marked by the passage of foreigners than were other parts of the country. Already in the 1830s and 1840s Britons, Frenchmen, and North Americans, sometimes in league with New Granadans, were proposing schemes for roads, railroads, or canals to speed the isthmian crossing. After the discovery of gold in California, hordes of North Americans traversed the isthmus on their way to the gold fields. At mid-century, Panama had more foreign residents among its population than any other place in the country. Panama's role as an increasingly active transit point strengthened its sense of difference from the rest of the country and awakened in its elites the possibility of a separate future as a commercial emporium.

Elsewhere in New Granada's Caribbean zone the preoccupations of the elite were differently focused. While the life of Panama was in the Atlantic-Pacific crossing, in the coastal belt from Cartagena to Santa Marta the critical goal was to become the chief transit point for trade between the Atlantic world and the New Granadan interior. During the colonial period the capacious and protected port of Cartagena had been officially privileged and the rest of the coast had depended mostly on contraband trade. However, the clogging of the Canal del Dique, linking Cartagena to the Magdalena River, made it impossible for Cartagena to hold its dominance and in the 1830s and 1840s Santa Marta took Cartagena's place as New Granada's chief port for the receipt of imported goods. During these years the ocean port of Sabanilla and the nearby river port of Barranquilla remained insignificant. Indeed, Cartagena and Santa Marta, rivals in every other respect, combined their political weight to keep the port of Sabanilla closed to international traffic from 1824 to 1842. Ultimately, however, in 1871, when Barranquilla and Sabanilla became linked by railway, Barranquilla emerged as the dominant port on the Caribbean Coast.

SLAVES AND INDIANS

The Congress of Cúcuta in 1821 had established as a national goal the incorporation of black slaves and Indians into the republic as citizens. Although New Granadan elites intended to end the colonial period's legal distinctions among racial *castas*, it cannot be said that the dominant class considered either blacks or Indians to be their equals. But the upper class did have rather different conceptions of these two subordinated groups. The submissive Indian population of the Eastern Cordillera did not appear to be a threat to elite control. Rather, from the perspective of the dominant class, they remained passively in the abjection to which they had been reduced under Spanish colonial rule and were too inclined to resist elite invitations to integration and progress. The black population, however, was another matter. In contrast with the passivity of the indigenes, blacks were likely to assert their freedom, and that relative assertiveness frightened the dominant class.

New Granadan slaveowners, particularly in the Cauca, resisted freeing their slaves. Many Caucano slaveowners felt that the 1821 law of free birth, which promised them the labor of the children of slaves until the age of eighteen, did not provide them with adequate compensation. Furthermore, they worried that, once manumitted, blacks would no longer be willing to work; owners of mines and haciendas would lose their labor force, and they would confront the specter of a possibly unoccupied, vagrant, and uncontrolled free black population.

There also was a nagging anxiety about what would happen during the slow transition from slavery to freedom. If some slaves were being freed by the 1821 law, either by birth or by purchase of their manumission, would this not make the condition of slavery more intolerable for those who remained in it? These tensions could lead to race warfare. To avoid such an explosive situation, one delegate at Cúcuta in 1821 had proposed that all slaves be freed simultaneously. And in 1822, Jerónimo Torres of Popayán, fearful that increasing numbers of free blacks would lead to racial conflict, proposed eliminating the black population through miscegenation—by sending vagrants and prostitutes to live with manumitted slaves.

Fear of the free black population was most intense where blacks were most concentrated. During the 1820s anxiety about race war was expressed most often with regard to Venezuela, but it became a public concern in Cartagena in 1828, when Bolivarians accused General José Padilla of rallying the *pardos* of that city in support of his mutiny. In July 1831 authorities in Mompox complained that the city's *pardos* had become "insolent" and feared a rebellion; later in 1831 and 1832 similar elite anxieties surfaced in Santa Marta and Cartagena, and some of those accused of conspiracy were shot. These supposed conspiracies were thought to be linked to anti-slave agitation in Jamaica, and some in the New Granadan elite worried about the likely impact on their country if Great Britain should abolish slavery in the British West Indies. Anxieties about race war also agitated the Cauca. Both to avoid losing their property and labor and because of dread of losing social control, slaveowners in the Cauca region became the focus of resistance to the gradual emancipation envisioned by the 1821 law.

There was a clear division of sentiment over the manumission of slaves between the Eastern Cordillera, where there were relatively few slaves, and the Cauca, where slaves were relatively numerous. The eastern provinces of Vélez, which had 637 slaves in 1835, and of Tunja, which had only 133, manumitted more slaves between 1835 and 1839 than either the Province of Popayán or Cauca Province, each of which contained more than 5000. In 1839, the year that the first slave children would have been freed under the law of free birth, it was reported that slaveowners in the Cauca were asking parish priests to change the birth records of the children of their slaves. And when slave children reached the age of freedom, some Cauca owners continued to try to hold them, contending they were still owed the cost of feeding the slave children for eighteen years. In other cases they simply refrained from reporting that the slave children had come of age.

Slaveowner resistance to manumission in the Cauca in the 1830s gave way to violent social conflict in the early 1840s. During his rebellion against the national government in 1840–1841, General José María Obando first mobilized free blacks from the Patía Valley, among whom he had long had a following. Later, attempting to recoup from a series of defeats, Obando in February 1841 also began to recruit slaves from mines and haciendas elsewhere, promising them freedom. With his slave and free black recruits, Obando was able temporarily to seize Popayán, Cali, and virtually the whole of the Cauca Valley. Although Obando ultimately was defeated by government forces, his mobilization of free blacks and slaves continued to leave aftershocks in the region. In April 1843 bands of free blacks and slaves in the Caloto region, claiming that Obando was returning to free the slaves, assaulted various haciendas. Local whites fled from the countryside to the town of Caloto, and a general panic spread throughout the Cauca.

During Obando's mobilization of free blacks and slaves in 1840–1841 and its more limited sequel in 1843, a strong slaveowner reaction occurred in the Cauca. The first response of the Congress in Bogotá to growing anxiety in the Cauca was to require slave children, whom the 1821 law had declared free at eighteen, to bind themselves to labor contracts to the age of twenty-five. Discussed in 1840, the idea was enacted in 1842, under the argument that a period of continued forced labor would help to prepare the children of slaves for responsibility in freedom. In the minds of slaveowners in the Cauca, however, another fundamental reason for prolonging forced labor was to prevent the collapse of the slave system by reducing the disparity of conditions between slaves and their free children. To slaveowners it seemed that the growing number of free blacks was making more intolerable the condition of those still in slavery, and putting the young freedmen to forced labor would minimize the difference between slavery and freedom.

The reaction in the Cauca became much more extreme after the events in Caloto in April 1843. In a petition to Congress some three hundred Popayán notables, as well as some from Cali, complained that their capital invested in slaves, essential to the regional economy, had been extinguished by the law of 1821 without compensation. Secondly, the law of free birth, by freeing some slaves but not others, had created havoc. Freed slave children had become vagrants, while escaped slaves infested the forests and were a threat to society. The Popayán petition urged repeal of the law of free birth, arguing that its promise of eventual freedom was responsible for the upheaval. And, if slaves engaged in sedition, they, *and their children*, should be denied the right of manumission.

The Congress in Bogotá refrained from embracing these extreme proposals, but it did enact several other slaveowner demands. In 1843 it declared that leaders of "bands of malefactors" who used force to commit robbery would suffer the death penalty. The Congress further established punishments for encouraging slave rebellion and offered freedom to slaves who reported conspiracies to rebel. And it permitted slaves to be exported (which had been prohibited in 1821). The exportation of slaves was justified by slaveowners as necessary to get rid of "incorrigible" or dangerous slaves. However, the measure also opened a way for owners to recover part of their capital invested in slaves at a time when the end of slavery was visibly approaching. The concern not to lose money invested in slaves is evident in the fact that, even before the 1843 law permitted exportation of slaves, Cauca slaveowners were already doing it illegally in the 1830s. Thus, fear of black rebellion in 1840–43 moved the Congress to make legal what some slaveowners already had been doing illegally for largely economic reasons.

Despite the draconian measures enacted in 1843, many in the Cauca elite still resented the government in Bogotá, dominated by men from provinces where slavery was marginal, who did not understand the problems of slaveowners in the Cauca. General Eusebio Borrero of Cali, angry that the Congress had not repealed the law of free birth, in 1843 threatened to resurrect the 1831 proposal to have the Cauca secede from New Granada and form a "fourth state."

Despite resistance of slaveowners in the Cauca, the slave population was declining in that region, as everywhere else in the country. (See Table 9.4.) Given the slow pace of manumissions before 1846, it seems unlikely that manumission explains the decline before that time. The decrease of slavery in the Cauca probably reflects the mortality of slaves, the continuing escape of some, and, to a degree, the exportation of slaves. During the late 1840s, and particularly after 1849, with Liberals in power and anti-slavery sentiment rising, the pace of manumission accelerated. Finally, in 1851, during the Liberal administration of General José Hilario López, the Congress de-

Table 9.4 Number of slaves and proportion of population by region, 1835–1851 (provincial data grouped into the regions that became states between 1857 and 1880)

Region	1835		1843		1851	
	Number of Slaves	Percent of Population	Number of Slaves	Percent of Population	Number of Slaves	Percent of Population
The West						
Cauca	21,599	10.3	15,212	5.7	10,621	3.3
Antioquia	3455	2.2	2730	1.4	1778	0.7
Caribbean Coast						
Bolívar	4867	2.7	3012	1.6	1695	0.8
Magdalena	1960	3.2	1495	2.4	860	1.3
Panama	1461	1.2	1187	1.0	496	0.4
Eastern Belt						
Tolima	1504	0.9	908	0.5	345	0.2
Cundinamarca	1245	0.5	802	0.3	216	0.07
Boyacá	311	0.1	125	0.04	37	0.01
Santander	2439	0.9	1307	0.4	420	0.1
Nation	38,840	2.3	26,778	1.4	16,468	0.7

Source: Fernando Gómez, "Los censos en Colombia," Tables 6,7,8, in Miguel Urrutia and Mario Arrubla, eds., *Compendio de estadísticas históricas* (Bogotá, 1970).

creed the complete abolition of slavery as of January 1852. At this time slaves made up less than 1 percent of the national population and only a little more than 3 percent in the Cauca.

Dealing with the Amerindian population was also a somewhat vexing, if generally less threatening, question for the political elite. The surviving Indian population was of several types. Some, like the forest peoples in Chocó or the Putumayo, were rather distant from the principal areas of Hispanic settlement and tended to be forgotten. Others, like the inhabitants of the Guajira peninsula, tended to be a problem because in the republican period, as in the colonial era, they were active in contraband and sometimes violent; still, they also were at the margin. When elite policymakers thought about Indians they had in mind the sedentary indigenous populations, particularly in the Eastern Cordillera and in Pasto and Popayán, which by the eighteenth century were already somewhat integrated into the Hispanic economy and culture.

Both at the end of the colonial era and in the early republican period New Granadan creoles sought to bring this partially integrated Indian population more thoroughly into Hispanic society. The Hispanic dominant class both in late colonial times and in the nineteenth century considered even sedentary and somewhat Hispanicized indigenes to be inferior and stupid. In the view of the Hispanic elite, Indians were unenterprising economically and tended to hold back the development of the country. From the latter part of the eighteenth century onward, elites believed the solution to the "Indian problem" lay in homogenizing the indigenes with the Hispanic population—economically, culturally, and genetically. In the late colonial period this meant opening up Indian community lands for use by white and mestizo farmers. In the early republican years these goals continued but another aspect also came to the fore at least temporarily—that of political integration. The goal of political integration was particularly reflected in the Congress of Cúcuta in 1821, which declared that henceforth the indigenes were to be considered citizens. However, this declaration that Indians were to be citizens proved to be empty rhetoric; soon creole elites lost interest in involving Indians in the political system. For the bulk of the nineteenth century, the emphasis was on the economic integration of sedentary Indian populations through the division of Indian community lands.

Spanish policy for the greater part of the colonial period had insisted that Indian lands be held in common by the community as a means of protecting these lands from alienation to the dominant Hispanic population. Toward the end of the colonial period but still more clearly in the nineteenth century, Hispanic elites increasingly believed that the isolation of Indian communities (resguardos) was harmful to the indigenes themselves. As long as the Indians held their land in common and were not permitted to sell it, they could not participate actively in, and be stimulated by, the free market. This prevented individual indigenes from becoming enterprising and restrained the development of the national economy.

On this theory, the first republican government in Santafé de Bogotá in 1810 had called for the division of the *resguardos*—although with a twenty-year period when the indigenes could not sell their individual plots to protect them from Hispanic manipulation. In the confusion of the Patria Boba, nothing was done to implement this policy. The Congress of Cúcuta in 1821, however, took up the idea again, decreeing that Indian lands would be divided among members of the community, now with a protective period of only ten years during which they could not sell their plots. During the 1820s some efforts were made to divide Indian community lands, but in the struggle for independence and the distractions of post-1826 politics not much was done.

The first big push to divide the *resguardos* occurred in the 1830s and 1840s. Dividing the Indian lands proved to be much more difficult than creole elites had imagined. Few trained surveyors were available. There were also complications in determining who had right to the divided land. Many mestizos lived in Indian communities, and determining who should be considered an "Indian" was problematic. Many Indians also no longer resided in their communities: What were their rights? But beyond such legal complications was the fact that many Indian communities did not want their land divided and did their best to stall the process. For the most part creole elites were unsympathetic to this Indian resistance and pressed ahead. In Popayán, however, local elites, apparently satisfied with their existing labor arrangements with neighboring Indians, took the side of the Indian communities. Many Indians in the Central Cordillera bordering the Cauca Valley were able to retain their community lands until toward the end of the nineteenth century.

During the 1830s and 1840s the division of *resguardos* occurred most actively in the Eastern Cordillera. During the 1830s the two major political factions, the *exaltados* and the moderates, agreed in pursuing the policy. By the end of the decade, however, it was becoming evident that, despite the prohibition against Indians' selling their new properties for ten years, many Indians in fact were losing their land to Hispanics. Becoming alarmed, the Márquez and Herrán governments began belatedly to try to prevent the Indians from alienating their land. In 1843 the protective period during which they could not sell their land was extended to twenty years. However, in 1850 this gesture at a protective policy was reversed when the Congress authorized provincial legislatures to divide and permit the sale of Indian community lands. During the 1850s, the pace of alienation of Indian plots accelerated.

By 1845, and increasingly in later years, some in Bogotá's elite, even some who had played an active role in dividing Indian lands, began to recognize the negative economic and social consequences of this policy. Before the division of *resguardo* lands around Bogotá, Indian farmers had been the chief cultivators of vegetables for the Bogotá market. As these indigenous cultivators lost their plots, the Hispanics who took over the land used it for the most part to graze livestock. Local production of vegetables declined, and food prices rose in the city. At the same time, since little labor was needed to tend the livestock, the Indians who had lived on the land were expelled from it. The resulting labor surplus tended to hold wages down both in agriculture and in urban occupations. And many Indians found it necessary to move elsewhere in search of survival. Many were believed by contemporaries to have migrated from the eastern highlands to the hot country of Tolima to work as cultivators of tobacco as exports of that product to Europe began to develop toward the end of the 1840s. We do not know how many people may have migrated from the highlands to the Upper Magdalena Valley. But anecdotal contemporary evidence indicates that migrants from the highlands were particularly susceptible to disease and their mortality rate may have been quite high.

PRIMARY EDUCATION

Interest in the development of primary education, a theme of the 1820s, continued in the 1830s and 1840s, with only moderate success. Primary schooling depended heavily on local leadership and support, and that was quite variable. The statistics are incomplete and haphazard, but there does appear to have been a growth in primary instruction during the 1830s. As of 1833 there were 17,000 primary students. By 1838 more than 27,000 children were in primary school, possibly a little more than 11 percent of the school-age

Table 9.5 Primary school statistics, selected provinces, 1835

Province	Province Population (1835)	Number of Primary Schools	Number of Students	Primary Students as Percentage of Population	Primary Students as Percentage of Population under Sixteen
Antioquia	158,017	86	2836	1.8	3.6
Cauca	50,420	31	1296	2.6	6.0
Cartagena	130,324	36	1308	1.0	2.6
Mompox	47,557	126*	1088	2.2	5.5
Santa Marta	46,587	43	1250	2.7	6.4
Bogotá	255,569	64	2594	1.0	2.4
Tunja	236,983	56	2071	0.9	2.1
Socorro	114,513	26	1157	1.0	2.4
Nation	1,686,038	690	20,123	1.2	2.8

*Mompox data include private schools; all others public schools only.
Sources: School statistics: Lino de Pombo, *Memoria del Interior y Relaciones Exteriores*, 1836, Cuadro #2 (Bogotá, 1836); Population: Fernando Gómez, "Los censos de Colombia," Table 6, in Miguel Urrutia and Mario Arrubla, eds., *Compendio de estadísticas de Colombia* (Bogotá, 1970).

population. The republic had more schools than parish districts, although it did not have a school in every parish.

In the 1830s and 1840s, as later in the century, Antioquia took the lead among the larger provinces in establishing primary education. However, some smaller provinces, like Mompox, Santa Marta, Cauca, and Popayán, appear to have done better on a per capita basis. (See Table 9.5.)

More attention was being paid to the education of young women. By 1838 girls made up about a sixth of the primary students. Most must have been the daughters of relatively high-status families. Of the girls receiving primary education, nearly two-thirds were in private schools. Primary education seems to have been reaching boys of more varied social strata: Nearly 90 percent of the boys receiving primary education were in public schools. In the case of both sexes, however, the development of a two-track, public and private school system was already apparent, with more than a fifth of all primary students in private schools.

After the 1830s, the growth of primary education appears virtually to have stopped, if it did not go into reverse—although the statistics are too incomplete to be certain. During the 1840s the official total numbers of students in school remained at about the top levels reached in the 1830s. Furthermore, while public schools declined in number, the number of private schools increased. In the late 1840s close to three-fifths of the schools were now private, although less than 30 percent of the students were in private schools. To some degree the growth of private schooling reflects the fact that more girls were receiving primary instruction, but the pattern also suggests that primary education was no longer reaching quite as broadly into the society.

10

The Liberal Era, 1845–1876

Between 1845 and 1876 Colombia's foreign trade grew and the country became increasingly oriented to the external economy. In these years also Liberals became politically dominant. The growth of external trade and the political hegemony of the Liberal Party so coincided that there has been a tendency to see them as inextricably intertwined. Contemporary Liberals themselves tried to claim credit for the growth of the external economy. But in fact men of both parties shared much the same economic vision. Besides, the growth of foreign trade after 1845 was shaped by external economic factors as well as by Colombian policy. Although there was not as tight a connection between political liberalism and foreign trade expansion as is sometimes assumed, it can be said that the growth of exports did create an atmosphere of optimism that may well have fostered the Liberals' willingness to undertake a good deal of institutional experimentation.

During these years partisan conflict was intensified by the Liberal revolution of 1849–1854, featuring institutional and political democratization and mobilization of elements of the popular classes, followed closely by the emergence of open class warfare. Tense disputes developed over the power and position of the Church and an overt alliance between Roman Catholic clergy and the Conservative Party. Coinciding with this party conflict was a more or less bipartisan movement to a federalist political structure, culminating in the formation of nine autonomous states.

TOWARD AN EXPORT ECONOMY

Aspirations to develop exports other than gold first began to sprout in the late colonial period among Spanish officials as well as creole elites. But attempts to diversify exports in the last two decades of the colonial era were frustrated by various obstacles—the reluctance of Spanish merchants to accept payment in anything but coin or bullion, the propensity of even export-oriented viceroys to put potentially exportable products under fiscal monopolies, the restraints of other colonial taxes, the apparent tendency of the Spanish government to favor other colonies producing tropical products (notably Cuba and Venezuela), and, ultimately, the disruption of commerce by maritime warfare. In the early republican era, creole political leaders sought to encourage exports of tropical products through tax exemptions but achieved slight success before the 1840s. Among the visible obstacles to the growth of New Granadan exports was the fact that Great Britain, the leading source of the country's imports at the time, discriminated in favor of its British colonial suppliers of tropical products. However, other Latin American producers of tropical products were exporting more successfully than New Granada, so other factors must have been at work. Contemporaries lamented that the concentration of the country's population in the mountains of the interior placed them at a competitive disadvantage because of transportation costs. One obvious solution was to develop production of tropical exports in the Magdalena Valley, which would permit relatively easy transportation down the Magdalena River to the Caribbean coast. However, a noticeable migration of capital or labor to the Magdalena Valley did not occur until after 1845, perhaps in part because until that time New Granadan entrepreneurs were not entirely sure of the opportunities there, perhaps also because of an unconscious tendency to continue to rely on gold as the chief source of foreign exchange. In addition, Colombian critics later noted, there was a tendency for Bogotá merchants to focus simply on importing, letting others concern themselves with generating foreign exchange.

From the early 1830s onward it was thought that tobacco might prove to be a successful export product. Development of tobacco exports was hampered, however, by the fact that the industry remained under the government fiscal monopoly established during the late colonial period. In 1821, at the time of the effective establishment of the republic, legislators had abolished, reformed, or reduced a number of colonial fiscal devices. But the legislators of 1821 did not dare to touch the tobacco monopoly because it was too important a source of revenue. The tabaco *estanco* had been the biggest revenue earner in the late colonial period, and it remained the second largest, after customs duties, in the first decades after independence.

The tobacco monopoly, however, presented serious obstacles to the successful exportation of New Granadan leaf. First, production under the monopoly was restricted. To facilitate vigilance against contraband, the government permitted cultivation in just a few small areas. Limited production under the monopoly also had the effect of constricting the supply, which permitted government offices to sell tobacco with a high markup. The ability to charge high prices in domestic sales made the tobacco *estanco* a cherished source of revenue, but also made it difficult for New Granadan tobacco to compete in external markets. In the 1830s entrepreneurs, both national and foreign, who attempted to export tobacco bought from the government monopoly often lost money on these ventures. In part this was because tobacco prepared in rolls by the monopoly for New Granadan consumers was not suitable for foreign markets, which preferred flat leaves. But the greater problem was a lack of a clear place in the market. Cuban tobacco dominated the high end of market, while tobacco from the United States sold at prices too low for tobacco from the New Granadan tobacco *estanco* to be able to compete. Among the advantages of North American tobacco was its cheaper cost of transportation, accentuated by the great flow of European immigrants to the United States, who by providing cargo westward helped lower shipping costs for vessels returning from the United States to Europe. While the United States in 1836–1840 exported more than 50,000 tons of tobacco per year, New Granada's shipped out less than 350 tons in its peak year of the late 1830s.

New Granadan elites debated several alternatives to the government-run tobacco monopoly. In the early 1830s various provincial legislatures urged ending the monopoly, and the national Congress discussed the idea. But the Santander, Márquez, and Herrán administrations all opposed ending the *estanco* on the ground that the government could not do without its revenues. An alternative to abolishing the monopoly was to turn production of tobacco for the *estanco* over to private companies. In 1828 Bolívar authorized renting out tobacco production areas to private entrepreneurs, whose product would be sold to the *estanco* and marketed by it. Advocates of private operation of the production areas argued that private companies could expand production by raising the capital needed to advance money to cultivators, or even to pay them at all—something the government was not always able to do. But the proposal for private companies to produce within the framework of the monopoly was vetoed by Vice President José Ignacio Márquez in 1832.

In the early 1840s, however, the idea of putting tobacco production for the monopoly in the hands of private entrepreneurs revived. The civil war of 1839–1842 had left the government unable to advance money to cultivators and unable to stem contraband in tobacco. Furthermore, rising tobacco prices in Europe intensified the allure of expanding production for export— although some administrators continued to believe that the monopoly should continue to focus on the dependable, high-margin domestic market rather than plunging into the risks of producing for variable, competitive foreign ones.

Despite these divided counsels, in 1841–1842 the Herrán administration invited offers for contracts for the private administration of the tobacco monopoly, with a view to producing more tobacco for export. Although the first proposals came to nothing, ultimately a contract for the private administration of tobacco production at Ambalema was made with the Antioqueño firm of Montoya, Sáenz in 1845, during the first year of the presidency of General Tomás Cipriano de Mosquera (1845–1849). In 1846, the Mosquera administration made additional contracts for the private operation of the already-established producing area at Girón and in the region of San Gil, where tobacco cultivation had been shut down before the Comunero rebellion.

General Mosquera, the man who presided over the first phase of tobacco expansion (1845–1849), was a central actor in New Granada's nineteenth-century politics, and one of its more singular personalities. The second son of an aristocratic Popayán family, he was driven by ambition for achievement and honor. In 1826, as intendant of Guayaquil, he was the first of the military leaders to organize local support for a Bolivarian order. Not long thereafter the moderate liberal Juan de Dios Aranzazu described him as untrustworthy and "fickle," a man "who changes opinions frequently, who to-day kisses the dictatorial whip and tomorrow entones hymns to liberty." Later, while fighting the rebellion of 1839–1842, he appalled even some government supporters by summarily executing rebel leaders. Although most political moderates who supported the government thought the civil war a complete disaster, Mosquera himself considered the war, and apparently his executions, glorious. In an 1841 letter reporting on the most notable executions, he wrote: "The Republic has taken on a beautiful outlook, and although we are impoverished, there is now much moral force. . . . An internal war militarizes the Nation and prepares it for great deeds." Before he assumed office, the prospect of General Mosquera in the presidency was viewed with alarm even by his brothers. Yet in his presidential term (1845–1849) Mosquera's ambitions found expression not in violence but in efforts at material improvement.

Many of Mosquera's initiatives directly bore upon the advancement of commerce, both domestic and external. Mosquera made strenuous efforts at improving overland communications. Earlier governments had taken the politically easy course of dividing funds for public works among the provinces on a per capita basis, with the result that each province might make minor repairs on mule trails but no significant work could be undertaken. Mosquera concentrated public works on routes that were construed as having national rather than merely local importance. This meant particularly routes that would facilitate exports by helping to connect the interior with external markets. Among the projects in which his government took a particular interest was helping the Cauca Valley break out of its isolation by improving its connection to the Pacific port of Buenaventura. He also initiated surveys for a cart road from Bogotá to the Magdalena River, put army units to work on overland routes, and contracted construction by a U.S. company of a railway across the Isthmus of Panama. He also founded a military college to train civil engineers. A number of Mosquera's projects were so grand that they took many years to finish, if they were completed at all. They also put the government into fiscal difficulties with which his successors had to struggle.

In addition to Mosquera's efforts at improving overland transportion, his second secretary of finance, Lino de Pombo, in 1846 attempted to regularize commerce by standardizing weights and measures and reforming the currency. He also won approval of legalizing the exportation of gold dust, a measure of great importance to Antioquia's merchants. Before this reform all gold was supposed to be sent to the government mint and taxed, a requirement that encouraged contraband exports of gold dust.

The Mosquera administration developed a sharper focus on the development of tropical exports with the appointment in September 1846 of Florentino González as secretary of finance. Mosquera's choice of González surprised contemporaries. While General Mosquera had been a devoted Bolivarian, González had been one of the chief conspirators against Bolívar in

September 1828. And during the civil war of 1839–1842 Mosquera had been the most notably ferocious warrior for a government that had imprisoned González as (in its view) a dangerous liberal.

Toward the end of the war, González had gone into voluntary exile in Europe, spending much of his time in Great Britain, precisely at the time that British trade policy was being liberalized. He returned in 1846 with a shipment of imported goods and many ideas about how to invigorate New Granada's economy. Soon after his return he published a series of articles in which he laid out an integrated program emphasizing the development of the export economy. Some of what he advocated, particularly the cultivation of tobacco for export in the Magdalena Valley, was already in process. But González articulated his ideas with such focus, force, particularity, and perspicacity that they captured the imagination of many contemporaries. His program and his rationale for it soon became the mantra of much of the upper class. González emphasized that the country's future lay in tropical exports, for which new opportunities now existed because England recently had repealed the tariffs that favored tropical commodities produced in the British empire. He stressed the need to concentrate on the Magdalena Valley because at the time only the Magdalena River could provide reasonably cheap transportation of tobacco or other products to the Caribbean coast and foreign markets. González believed therefore that putting steamboats on the Magdalena rather than the improvement of overland trails had to be the country's highest transportation priority. The government should encourage steamboat navigation on the Magdalena by investing in private steamboat companies. He also assured more cautious doubters that they need not fear the fiscal consequences of ending government control of the tobacco industry: As tobacco exports expanded under private enterprise, they would finance increased imports, bringing larger collections of customs duties.

But increasing tobacco and other exports also required a more general expansion of trade. If New Granada were going to be a more successful exporter, it had to bring more ships into its ports, and that meant increasing its importation of foreign goods. To encourage more foreign ships to enter New Granadan ports, González called for the elimination of differential duties that had discriminated against goods brought in ships of some countries, most notably the United States. He also urged that import duties as a whole be lowered, even though this would adversely affect domestic artisans. González, and others who later echoed him, believed that artisan weavers in the interior were wasting their time trying to compete with foreign factories: They would be better off cultivating tropical crops for export.

As secretary of finance González made good on much of his program for expanding foreign trade. According to contemporaries in 1847 customs duties were lowered by an average of 25 percent. But on some commonly used consumer goods (cotton cloth, boots, and shoes) duties appear to have dropped to one-third or less of the rates of 1844. At the same time the Mosquera administration offered to aid steamboat companies on the Magdalena with government investments, with the consequence that two competing companies based in Santa Marta and Cartagena were founded and began to provide the first effective and continuous service on the river. González also moved to expand tobacco exports by making contracts with merchant-capitalists to develop production in new areas of the Upper Magdalena Valley in addition to the long-established site of Ambalema. These later contracts reflected, and reinforced, the spreading enthusiasm for tobacco as an export product and increased pressure to end all restrictions on tobacco cultivation.

González's appointment had been cheered by those wanting to end the tobacco *estanco*, but, to their surprise, as secretary of finance he now sang a different tune. Two months after entering the administration González urged delaying the end of the monopoly until the companies of merchant-capitalists who had been given control of designated production areas could develop larger foreign markets for New Granadan tobacco. Small operators who would swarm into the industry once it were freed, González believed, could not expand New Granada's markets because they lacked the larger merchants' capital and experience. Furthermore, only substantial companies, with monopoly control over production in their areas, could enforce the quality controls necessary for success in foreign markets. Accordingly, he urged that the *estanco* be retained, with a few companies controlling production, until New Granada's tobacco exports reached 50,000 quintales (roughly 2500 tons)—a level that, as it turned out, was not reached until 1855.

Pressures for free cultivation became irresistible, however, and in 1848 the Congress declared that tobacco cultivation would be completely freed in 1850. To compensate for the loss of the nation's second largest revenue source, the legislators proposed a heavy tax on exported tobacco, a tax so burdensome that it would have made exporting the leaf impossible. The tax therefore was quickly abandoned. Cautious men still feared the fiscal consequences of ending the monopoly. But President Mosquera, both a progressive autocrat and a politician with an eye to the popular, was undeterred by such anxieties and signed the measure, characteristically declaring that no one was "going surpass him in liberality of principles nor in daring to decree important measures."

As the tobacco industry moved from government monopoly to private management of production under the monopoly, to the complete liberation of the industry, tobacco exports rapidly expanded. Partly this represented an increase in production, but at first it was even more a matter of shifting tobacco sales from the domestic market to foreign ones. Mean annual production rose by 31 percent between 1844–1846 (when the monopoly was still largely under government control) and 1847–1849 (when the private companies were in charge), but in the latter years exports nearly tripled while domestic consumption declined. When free cultivation was permitted, exports expanded still more. In 1852–1855, annual mean exports were double those in 1847–1849. By this time no one knew how much tobacco

Table 10.1 Colombian and U.S. exports of tobacco, 1851–1870 (annual averages, in tons)

	Colombia	United States	Colombian Tobacco Exports as Percentage of U.S. Tobacco Exports
1851–1855	1306	66,900	2.0
1856–1860	3570	76,877	4.6
1861–1865	5351	63,900	8.4
1866–1870	5968	95,000	6.3

Sources: Colombia: José Antonio Ocampo, *Colombia y la economía mundial,* Cuadro 5.1 (Bogotá, 1984) pp. 207–208; United States: *Historical Statistics of the United States* (Washington, DC, 1975), p. 899.

was being consumed in the domestic market, as the disappearance of the government monopoly meant the end of statistics on domestic sales. In effect, with the extinction of the fiscal monopoly and the new orientation toward exporting, domestic consumption of tobacco dropped from view as a policy concern.

The tobacco boom that began in Colombia in the late 1840s was never large by world standards. For the period of rapid growth (1850–1870), the volume of Colombia's exports represented a small percentage of those of the United States in the same years. (See Table 10.1.)

But within the country the boom had an important impact. Tobacco was the first notably successful New Granadan export other than gold. Its relative success dramatized for a significant segment of New Granada's dominant class, as never before, the possibilities of exporting tropical products. Capital and labor from Antioquia and the eastern highlands flowed together into the upper Magdalena Valley to join landowners, merchants, and workers native to the region in exploiting these potentialities. Encouraged by the palpable success of tobacco in the 1850s and 1860s, New Granadan elites for the first time developed an energized commitment to the export of tropical products, a commitment that carried them through various abortive experiments with other commodities before they finally began to explore seriously the possibilities of coffee in the mid-1860s.

During the early 1850s tobacco exports were supplemented by reemerging exports of cinchona bark (used for making quinine), which at that time was extracted mostly from the forests of the Cauca region and the Upper Magdalena Valley. New Granada's cinchona bark was judged in foreign markets to be of lower quality than that of Bolivia or Peru; its success in exporting cinchona bark was made possible in part by constrictions in the supply of superior bark from these other sources. Nonetheless, until about

1883 New Granada remained, with some ups and downs, a leading supplier of cinchona bark, and the bark was a significant contributor to the country's exports.

The combination of continued exports of gold with those of tobacco and cinchona bark greatly expanded New Granada's capacity to import. As a consequence upper-class consumption of European luxuries grew in the 1850s, and rose still more with further increases in exports in the 1860s and 1870s. But the upper class was not the only beneficiary of foreign trade. Through most of the years 1850–1875 slightly more than a fifth of New Granada's growing imports came from France. French goods were largely luxury products (silks, woolens, finished clothing, leather goods, wine, and cognac), mostly consumed by the upper sectors. However, Great Britain was by far the biggest source of imports, with more than half of total imports for the period from the 1850s through the 1870s. During that time more than four-fifths of British imports were textiles, and more than three-fifths were cotton cloth. During the 1850s and 1860s increasingly larger proportions of the population were using imported cotton cloth, in part because it was cheaper (although apparently less durable) than locally made goods. Women of the popular classes, first in the cities and then in rural areas, appear to have begun dressing in imported cottons before males of the same class, many of whom continued to wear tougher New Granadan cloth for some time. But during the 1850s and 1860s, coarse drill cloth, used for men's work clothes, increasingly became an important component of importers' shipments, indicating that manual workers were beginning to use imported drill.

To the degree that imported cloth was cheaper than New Granadan textiles the greater part of the population benefited from the trade expansion of the 1850s. On the other hand, increased importations of foreign cloth accelerated the century-long decline of the handweavers in Socorro and elsewhere in the Eastern Cordillera. The difficulties of the handweavers of the eastern highlands already had become noticeable in the 1830s, and the greater flow of imports after 1845 reduced their markets still further. But textile weavers by no means disappeared from the northern provinces after 1850. However, at least some of those who formerly had woven textiles turned to making palm-leaf hats, both for domestic consumption and for export.

Among the positive consequences of the tobacco boom and the general expansion of foreign trade at mid-century was the definitive establishment of steamboat transportation on the Magdalena after 1847. Increased tobacco exports helped make this possible by providing more freight going downstream—in 1852 more than 70 percent of tobacco shipments down the Magdalena went in steamboats. The increased flow of imported goods also supplied a greater quantity of freight for the upstream return. Steamboat service provided speedier and more secure haulage than poled boats and ultimately lowered upstream rates. (See Table 10.2.) Steamboats continued

Table 10.2 Freight rates on the Magdalena River, 1823–1868, between the Caribbean Coast and Honda (cost per carga [250 pounds], in pesos.)

	Upstream		Downstream	
	Poled Boats	**Steamboats**	**Poled Boats**	**Steamboats**
1823–1842	9.00–16.00		1.50–6.50	
1848–1850		6.25–7.25	2.25	1.75–2.75
1855–1856	6.00–8.00	7.00–10.00		
1857	5.60	3.20–6.30	3.60	2.00–3.60
1858		4.00–4.80		2.80–4.20
1859		4.50–5.80		
1863		6.00		
1865		3.50		
1867		3.00–5.00		
1868		5.00		

Source: Frank Robinson Safford, "Commerce and Enterprise in Central Colombia, 1820–1870," Ph.D. dissertation, Columbia University, 1965, Table II, pp. 464–467.

to encounter difficulties on the Magdalena: The river in many places was obstructed by sandbars, parts of the river could not be navigated in dry seasons, and some of the steamboats brought from the United States were not able to operate at all on stretches of the river that were very shallow. Nonetheless, expanded trade on the river provided the freight needed to encourage more or less continuous service.

Tobacco production and cinchona extraction combined to set the regional economy in movement. Demand for labor to grow tobacco and cut cinchona caused wages to rise in the upper Magdalena Valley in the early 1850s. Contemporary writers believed that peasants from the eastern highlands, including Indians who had lost community lands, were among those who migrated to the Upper Magdalena. As mountain valley land formerly farmed by peasants was turned to cattle grazing, food production failed to keep up with growing demand. Prices of basic foods roughly doubled in Bogotá between 1852 and 1854. Rising food prices may be attributable in part to growing demand from, and higher wages in, the tobacco and cinchona industries and in part to food scarcities caused by the transfer of rural labor from food production in the highlands to the lowland tobacco region and by the conversion of Indian community lands in the highlands from vegetable-growing to cattle-grazing under their new latifundiary owners. New artificial grasses (guinea and *pará*) for fattening cattle were also replacing cultivated food crops in the warm country regions southwest of Bogotá.

The tobacco boom that began in the 1840s, with its brief complement of cinchona bark exports in the early 1850s, provided an important part of the context for the liberal revolution that occurred after 1849. The expansion of exports and imports that became perceptible in the late 1840s seemed to bear out the prophecies of Florentino González, and it confirmed the New Granadan elite as a whole in its commitment to a focus on external trade. The need to concentrate on exports of tropical products became the economic watchword for the political generation that emerged in the 1840s. And the export expansion, and concomitant rising prices, fostered a new atmosphere of exuberant optimism among the upper class in Bogotá and elsewhere in the previously stagnant interior, an optimism that encouraged an enthusiasm for innovation, particularly in younger elements in New Granada's political elite.

At the same time the fulfillment of González's program produced an opposite reaction among Bogotá's artisans, who strenuously objected to the lower tariff on finished goods of 1847 and who had to suffer the rising food prices of the 1850s. Soon after the enactment of the lower tariff, in October 1847, Bogotá's tradesmen formed an artisans' society, which initially campaigned for a return to tariff protection but during the early 1850s also protested rising food prices. The mobilized artisans were important actors in the Liberal revolution of 1849, but soon came to oppose both some aspects of the Liberal program and the elite politicians who espoused it. While Bogotá's artisans agitated for protection, there was no similar mobilization among the handweavers of the northern provinces, nor did Bogotá's artisans show any interest in protecting the weavers. Most of the cloth used by urban tailors must have been imported.

THE LIBERAL REVOLUTION, 1849–1854

In the presidential election of 1848, the moderates of the 1830s, called *ministeriales* in the 1840s and known as Conservatives after 1848, split their votes among several candidates, enabling the chief Liberal contender, General José Hilario López, to win a strong plurality—42.9 percent of the electoral vote, versus a combined total of less than 41 percent for his two principal Conservative opponents. As no candidate had a majority of the total electoral vote, however, the election had to be decided by Congress, in which Conservatives outnumbered Liberals. Nonetheless, on March 7, 1849, when the Congress met in the church of Santo Domingo to elect the president, after several close votes, López won by a narrow margin.

The manner of that election immediately became a subject of partisan controversy. During the initial ballots, masses of people of varying social classes crowded into the church to witness the congressional votes. When the press of the crowd broke the barrier separating the public from the legislators, the general public was removed from the church to avoid disorder. At the time Conservatives claimed that the popular-class supporters of López threatened them with knives, inducing some Conservatives to vote for López. With the clear intent of delegitimizing a Liberal presidency, the steely Conservative Mariano Ospina Rodríguez wrote on his ballot that he voted for López so that the deputies would not be murdered. Liberals answered that, while the crowd was somewhat disorderly, those in it were not armed and that the only ones who displayed arms were some of the Conservative legislators. The unresolvable partisan dispute over what happened on March 7 underlines a central fact: The López government of 1849–1853 began on a note of extreme partisan feeling. And Liberals were conscious that, although they held the presidency, they were still a minority, while Conservatives believed the Liberal government was illegitimate.

The Liberal revolution that began with the election of López actually was several overlapping revolutions. It was first a partisan conflict for political dominance between Liberals and Conservatives, in which both parties striving for hegemony engaged in a considerable amount of popular mobilization, with some attendant violence. That conflict was particularly concentrated between 1849 and 1852. It was secondly an institutional revolution, in which a number of Liberals and Conservatives came to agree on some important changes (seeking to expand foreign trade while weakening the central government and strengthening provincial autonomy), but disagreed strongly about others (particularly many affecting the Roman Catholic Church). It also was a partial, or incomplete, social revolution, which illuminated, and provided political expression of, class divisions within New Granadan society. Unusually overt class conflicts appeared— most notably between the landed aristocracy and the poor in the Cauca Valley and between the artisans of Bogotá and part of the army, on the one hand, and an alliance between the upper-class dominated Liberal and Conservative parties, on the other (1853–1854).

The Liberal revolution really began before the election of General López to the presidency. For each of the groups in conflict, events of the previous decade had provided a context. First there were the established politicians who had become political actors during the 1820s and 1830s. Both liberal *progresistas* and more conservative *ministeriales* of the late 1830s and early 1840s shared as a formative drama the civil war of 1839–1842, which confirmed in the *ministeriales* a fear of disorder and the need to keep control and which inspired in liberals a corresponding desire to reclaim control of the national government. For both groups General José María Obando was a focal symbol—a demon of disorder for *ministeriales*, a victim of *ministerial* repression for liberals. Although to some of the older generation of liberals Obando was the chief surviving symbol of their party, it was not possible to consider him as a presidential candidate when the campaign began early in 1848, for Obando, in exile in Peru, was considered by many a dangerous man and was still forbidden to return to the country. Ultimately most liberals turned to General José Hilario López as their candidate, precisely because, a steady man who had not taken part in the civil war of 1839–1842, he seemed not to threaten the standing order. The program put forward for López, written by Ezéquiel Rojas, another veteran liberal, was also reassuringly safe—calling for the protection of individual liberties, the rule of law, impartial justice, strict economy, and the appointment of public employees for their capacity rather than their political affiliation. The statement most nearly approaching the inflammatory asserted that religion should not be used as an instrument of government.

If veteran liberals sought not to frighten the electorate, other, more combustible, elements were entering the political process. One was the emergence of popular classes as a more active political force, with the initial leadership of Bogotá's artisans. Artisans occupied a social position somewhere between the upper class and the mass of poor and illiterate unskilled workers, and in politics they played a role, at least as voters, but a subordinate one. Although Lorenzo María Lleras had attempted to mobilize artisans in support of the *progresista* liberals in the late 1830s, artisans neither in Bogotá nor elsewhere were particularly identified with liberalism. But the lowering of the tariff on finished goods in 1847 under the Mosquera government changed the situation. In October 1847 Bogotá craftsmen formed a Society of Artisans to press for tariff protection as well as other aspects of artisan welfare. Artisans were its most active founders, but two of its first members were sympathetic lawyers, one of whom was the society's first vice director. Initially, the society did not have clear political commitments; its early activities focused on literacy instruction to expand the ranks of their voters. However, sometime before June 1848, young university-educated liberals persuaded the artisans' society to support the presidential candidacy of General López—although some artisans preferred the putative conservative Joaquín José Gori, who was an avowed protectionist.

The Society of Artisans, transformed into the Democratic Society of Bogotá after the election of López in March 1849, became the model for liberal political mobilization of the popular classes in many other towns across the country. These Democratic Societies, which usually had some elite direction, energized mass support for the López government and became a means of intimidating the opposition in areas where Liberals were not dominant. Such violence was particularly evident in the Cauca Valley, where a struggle between *hacendados* and small farmers over community common land in the jurisdiction of Cali in 1848 evolved into the mobilization of armed bands of the popular classes, who late in 1850 first attacked haciendas owned by Conservatives, and then assaulted their persons. Later on these attacks spread to Buga, Tuluá, Cartago, and elsewhere in the Cauca Valley. From the point of view of Liberal leaders these assaults helped weaken the dominance of Conservatives of the region. Accordingly, when Conservatives criticized the Liberals' use of mobs, some Liberal officials airily dismissed the violence as "democratic frolics."

Another element in the process of polarization was a new generation of upper-sector liberals, for the most part born in the 1820s, who were finishing their university educations and entering politics in the middle to late 1840s. Some of these young men had experienced the death, execution, or persecution of a father or uncle in the war of 1839–1842. More directly, in their own persons, they had lived the postwar reaction as secondary or university students and had rebelled against an ideological conservatism that tried to deny students exposure to some of the philosophical consequences of the Enlightenment. They were moved, however, by more than irritation with the conservative reaction of the early 1840s. Like others of the post-independence generation in Spanish America, from Mexico to Chile, they believed that the earlier generation that had founded the nation had set forth republican ideals but had failed to fulfill them. The founders had won independence from Spain, but the colonial heritage was still present in the continuance of slavery, in the revenue system with its fiscal monopolies and the tithe (*diezmo*), in continuing religious "preoccupations" and cultural domination by a traditionalist church, and in the degradation of the mass of the people. These young men, born in the 1820s and early 1830s, believed that their generation must banish all vestiges of the colonial era and establish a truly democratic republic.

Many of these young liberals were influenced by political and ideological currents in France. A bitter debate over the role that the Jesuits might play in higher education was raging in France during the 1840s. Eugene Sue's anti-Jesuit novel *The Wandering Jew* (1845) colored and reinforced hostility to the Jesuits among younger men in New Granada's political class. With their own suspicions of the Jesuits legitimated by French assaults, New Granadan liberals, in concert with young conservative Julio Arboleda, condemned the presence of the Society of Jesus soon after the Jesuits' return to New Granadan soil in February 1844. In 1845 the Jesuits were strongly attacked in the Chamber of Representatives, and they continued to be subjects of controversy until they were expelled by the López government in 1850.

The Revolution of 1848 in Paris intensified the influence of French impulses, particularly on some of the younger generation of the New Granadan elite. The Revolution of 1848 helped bring the first French Revolution more into elite consciousness, making its rhetoric and symbols more vivid and relevant. In 1849 New Granada's Liberal government decided that government officials, as in the Patria Boba, should be addressed in the French Revolutionary egalitarian mode as "citizen." European egalitarian-communitarian writers, such as Lamennais, Proudhon, and Louis Blanc, influenced some in the younger generation of New Granada's political class at mid-century, although in the end the young Granadan radicals proved more committed to liberal individualism in the Anglo-Saxon mode.

At the outset the young generation of Liberals embraced all three principles of the first French Revolution—equality and fraternity, as well as liberty. Equality and fraternity seemed to be represented in their alliances with Bogotá's artisans and popular classes in Democratic Societies elsewhere. The young Liberals saw themselves as constructing a true democracy by incorporating poorer compatriots previously at the margins of the political process—although it was also clear from the outset that they had the less noble aim of co-opting social subordinates as a political arm to aid in sustaining the Liberal regime. In the early years the joint efforts of younger Liberals and the Democratic Societies did have a socially meliorative impact, most notably in the campaign for the immediate abolition of slavery in 1850–1851. The spirit of equality and fraternity may also be seen in young Liberals' objection to imprisonment for debt and their lack of enthusiasm for the coercion of vagrants (one of the conservatives' chief panaceas). Democratic principles also were clearly manifest in their affirmation of universal suffrage for literate adult males.

Over time, however, it became clear that, while espousing democratic and egalitarian aims, the Liberals of the new generation were ultimately controlled by their class identities and remained unconsciously elitist and paternalist in their attitudes toward the poor. Upper-class Liberals had assumed that the lower orders they were redeeming from ignorance would gratefully follow young elite leadership. When their popular-class tutees dared to disagree with them, younger Liberals were quick to dismiss their less-educated protégés as brutish and incapable of thought. As their relations with the artisans of Bogotá soured, equality and fraternity became less evident in the goals of the new generation, while liberty of various kinds remained enshrined in their ideology—freedom of speech and the press, freedom of religion, freedom of instruction, free trade, free enterprise.

The new generation's desire for radical institutional change and the development of organized mass politics were not the only elements in the political polarization of the 1850s. There also was a conscious effort by some Conservative leaders to develop a clear party identity and a militant party ideology. In May 1848, as the presidential election season was reaching a climax, Mariano Ospina Rodríguez and José Eusebio Caro for the first time gave the name "Conservative" to the political party of which Ospina had been a leader for nearly a decade. Ospina and Caro also sought to give the Conservative Party an ideological definition, contrasting its commitment to religion, order, and morality with, in their view, the irreligious anarchism of the Liberal "reds." Ospina quite consciously chose the Church and Christianity as emotionally powerful symbols that would attract broad support for the Conservative Party. And, as the Liberals sought to mobilize a mass base with its Democratic Societies, Ospina and others emulated them with parallel Conservative mass organizations with varying names. The one in Bogotá was called the Popular Society for Mutual Instruction and Christian Fraternity; in Cali, the Society of Friends of the People; in Popayán, the Popular Society of Republicans. Violent encounters were occurring between the artisans of the Democratic Society and those of the Popular Society in Bogotá by January 1850 and only a few months later between the Democratic Society and the Friends of the People in Cali.

In addition to trying to mobilize mass support through popular organizations, Liberals and Conservatives also formed new elite political clubs. In 1850, university-educated Liberals in Bogotá established the Escuela Republicana, in which young professionals and university students advocated advanced or utopian projects, many of them imported from France. Following the French writers Lamennais and Lamartine, members of the Escuela Republicana called for a return to the democracy and egalitarianism of Christ, condemning the attachment to property and power of the established Roman Catholic Church. A speech by José María Samper expounding such themes, in which he identified the young radical Liberals with the hill of Golgotha, prompted their opponents to ridicule them as the *gólgotas*.

The formation of the Escuela Republicana was an act laden with political symbolism. It was inaugurated on September 25, the date of the assassination attempt on Bolívar by an earlier generation of university-educated liberal youth. Almost immediately Conservative youths formed a counterpart group, the Sociedad Filotémica, also symbolically inaugurated in Bolívar's former country house. Conservatives also organized an upper-class women's auxiliary, the Society of the Christ Child.

Both Liberals and Conservatives heated up the temperature of partisan mobilization in strident newspaper combat as well. During the early 1850s partisan newspapers proliferated in great numbers across the country. Party feeling was further aroused when the López government began to dismiss Conservatives from government jobs after May 1849—at first particularly those who, like José Eusebio Caro, were publishing fierce newspaper attacks on the government that employed them.

While partisan accusations were frequently exchanged and some political coercion occurred rather early in the López administration, there were nonetheless few radical institutional changes during its first two years. In 1849 Conservatives held a clear majority in the Senate and a slight edge in the House of Representatives, so only measures with which Conservatives agreed could be enacted. By 1850 the balance had swung somewhat more in the Liberal direction, but still in the Senate Liberals and Conservatives were evenly balanced. Accordingly, no legislation could occur without at least some bipartisan support.

Both parties for the most part continued committed to developing external trade. Before 1849, when the Conservatives held executive power, some of them had objected to abolishing the government tobacco monopoly because of the likely loss of government revenue, while Liberals took the lead in pushing for the end of the monopoly. After López's election, their positions reversed. In 1849 López's minister of finance, Ezequiel Rojas, a veteran liberal, now resisted ending the tobacco monopoly for fiscal reasons, while Conservative congressmen supported abolishing the monopoly in 1850 in order to further tobacco exports. In another measure that aimed at expanding New Granada's foreign trade, the Conservative-dominated Congress of 1849 also agreed to make the Isthmus of Panama a free-trade area. Also in accord with dominant liberal economic precepts, petitions for protection from artisans in Bogotá and Cartagena won little support in the Congress. In 1850 a proposal to raise duties on finished goods by 25 percent was endorsed by at least nine Liberals and a few Conservatives in the Chamber of Representatives but was firmly rejected by their fellow legislators in both parties.

Both parties also supported a movement toward fragmentation of regional government into ever smaller provinces and the concession of greater authority to provinces and municipalities, which had been evident already in the 1830s and 1840s. The movement toward fragmentation into smaller provinces partly reflected deeply rooted local rivalries within provinces. But there also existed a more or less bipartisan desire to develop more capacity for self-government at the provincial and municipal level. This aspiration may have been encouraged by Alexis de Tocqueville's *Democracy in America* (1835), which attributed the success of democracy in the United States in part to the vitality of local government. At this time there appears to have existed a belief that effective regional government would be more possible with smaller provinces. Accordingly from 1849 through 1852 some thirteen new provinces were created by subdividing larger ones.

The push for greater authority in the provinces also obviously was motivated in part by resentment of decisions made in Bogotá. Despite the efforts of the Herrán administration (1841–1845) to reassert centralist control after the federalist rebellion of 1840–1842, and the strongly centralist thrust of the succeeding Mosquera government (1845–1849) as well, federalist aspirations continued to bubble up from the provinces. During the latter 1840s, political leaders of various political hues argued that the provinces knew their own needs better than the national government in Bogotá and that they needed both more autonomy and greater fiscal resources to attend to local development. Under the Mosquera administration, in 1848 the Congress granted provincial legislatures increased authority to levy taxes, contract for public works, supervise the division and sale of Indian community lands, and generally promote economic development. And in the subsequent presidential campaign of 1848 all of the principal candidates called for more provincial autonomy.

The movement to shift authority to the provinces continued under the Liberal government. A key measure was the decentralization of revenues in 1850, proposed by a new secretary of finance, Manuel Murillo Toro. Murillo, a man of modest origins, was born in the small community of Chaparral in the province of Mariquita. True to these humble beginnings, Murillo was, among Liberal leaders of the period, the most consistently social democratic in spirit. Confronting a seemingly unmanageable fiscal deficit, aggravated by the end of the tobacco monopoly and smaller customs collections because of lower tariffs, Murillo proposed to escape the problem by handing over to the provinces some of the central government's responsibilities as well as part of its taxing authority. Murillo hoped by turning some of the more hated colonial taxes over to the provinces that the latter would destroy the colonial fiscal regime piecemeal. He hoped the provinces would replace the tithe, a 10 percent tax on gross agricultural production, as well as various sales taxes, with some type of direct tax. The latter had been tried in the 1820s unsuccessfully. But Murillo claimed that the earlier experiment with direct taxes had failed because, as formulated by the national Congress, the taxes were not sufficiently sensitive to local interests. He argued that, if much of the fiscal responsibility were turned over to the provinces, they would find modes of taxation that better fit local wishes. As Murillo saw it, the decentralization of revenues was not merely a fiscal measure. This was also a way to democratize the country. By weakening the powers of the central government, Murillo hoped, it would undercut the chief cause of partisan strife—the passion to get control of the offices and patronage of the national government. And giving more responsibility to the provinces to tax and provide government services would help create a more vigorous and effective democracy at the local level. Murillo admitted that the provinces through inexperience might make mistakes at the outset, but, like the supporters of federalism in Cúcuta in 1821, he argued, that they would learn to govern themselves in the process. This vision of fostering local democracy formed a part of the ideological substrate underlying the Liberals' push for a federalist structure in the 1850s.

Other than the decentralization of revenues and expenses in 1850, probably the most radical legislative departures in these two years were the decisions to supplement the standing army with an organized national guard and to declare that university degrees would not be necessary to exercise professions. Both of these seemingly democratic measures apparently had some bipartisan support.

Despite the moderation of legislative activity, Conservatives found an issue to chew on with the López government's decision to expel the Jesuits in May 1850. Many Liberals were hostile to the Jesuits in part because the sons of Loyola were seen as a political instrument of the Conservative Party. However, President López himself, as well as some of the older Liberals in his administration, resisted ejecting the Jesuits, in part from fear of an angry popular reaction. Indeed, thousands signed petitions opposing the expulsion, and upper-class ladies in Bogotá pleaded with the president not to commit this sacrilege. Ultimately, however, López bowed to Liberal pressure and expelled the Jesuits by executive order—on the dubious legal ground that Charles III's order of expulsion of 1767 was still in effect. Considering the agitation that preceded the ejection of the Jesuits, the reaction to the act itself was surprisingly mild.

In 1851 the Liberals for the first time had large majorities in both houses of Congress. (Conservatives claimed, probably with some justice, that government intimidation and control of elections had made possible the Liberal majorities.) Unquestioned dominance of the Congress permitted the Liberals to adopt more radical measures. One of these was the decision to abolish slavery immediately. In April 1849, at the start of the López administration, some younger Liberals began a campaign for the immediate abolition of slavery. Neither the Congress nor the López administration was ready for such a decisive act, although the process of compensated manumissions did accelerate. In late 1850 and early 1851 petitions for immediate abolition were sent by provincial legislatures, where slavery was not important, and by Democratic Societies in the Cauca, where it was. These petitions now found a willing audience in a Congress dominated by Liberals, and a law of May 1851 declared that slavery would be completely ended as of January 1852.

Of greater political consequence than the abolition of slavery was the 1851 legislation affecting the status of the Church. The more important of these terminated the ecclesiastical *fuero* (the priests' privilege of being tried in ecclesiastical courts) in civil and criminal matters (May 14), granted to municipal councils a role in choosing parish priests and made the church financially dependent on provincial legislatures (May 27). Owners of properties burdened by quit-rents (*censos*) held by the church were permitted to free themselves of these obligations by paying the government half of their capital value (May 30).

Each of these measures in some way expressed an important element of Liberal ideology. The more radical Liberals believed the Roman Catholic Church, with its hierarchical structure, was incompatible with democracy; more moderate Liberals shied away from such an absolute position but nonetheless believed that church power and privileges needed to be reduced, for both political and economic reasons. The abolition of the *fuero* represented an assertion of the principle of equality before the law. Laws giving municipal councils a role in choosing parish priests and making the church dependent on provincial legislatures were efforts both to weaken the hierarchical structure of the church and to localize control over it. Finally, the redemption of the *censos* was above all an economic measure aimed at facilitating the exchange of land in an open market. Conservatives, however, did not see the liberal actions as matters of principle; from their perspective liberals simply were engaged in an assault on the Church as an institution.

The ecclesiastical innovations of 1851 were among the events that provided a motive for the Conservative rebellion of that year. As these measures made their way through Congress, Conservatives in Bogotá planned to start a revolution, possibly a coup d'etat in the capital, when the anti-Church laws were actually enacted—to take advantage of the shocked reaction of a pious populace. Meanwhile, however, a junta of Conservatives in Popayán had concocted a different plan, involving insurrection throughout the western provinces. In April 1851 Conservative revolutionary movements began in Pasto and in various parts of the Cauca Valley. Although the Conservative insurrection in the Cauca Valley was quickly crushed, the revolution spread to Antioquia in June and to the eastern part of the country (the Bogotá region, Mariquita, Tunja, and Pamplona) in July and August.

The Conservative rebellion of 1851 at the time was depicted by Liberals as an act of resistance to the complete abolition of slavery, and that idea appears in more recent interpretations also. It is probable that anger over the abolition of slavery provided some emotional energy for the revolution in the Cauca. But even slaveowners there realized there was little hope of reviving that dying institution. In fact the expressed motivation for the rebellion differed depending on the region. Julio Arboleda, the most visible leader of the Cauca uprising, while surely embittered by inadequate compensation for freed slaves, also denounced the Liberals' mobilization of the popular clases, many of whom were free blacks, against conservative elites in the Cauca Valley in 1850–1851: "Who are those armed men, almost all blacks, who walk the streets of Cali? They are freedmen whom the government has armed. . . . They are agents of the government." Conservative revolutionaries in Antioquia warned that Liberal-sponsored social disorders of the Cauca Valley could spread to Antioquia. But Antioqueño Conservatives were at least as disturbed by Liberal attacks upon the Church, and a number of clergy were active in the revolution there. In Medellín and smaller towns around it Conservatives also objected to the Liberals' recent division of Antioquia into three provinces, an attempt to break Conservative hegemony in the region by creating Liberal-dominated new provinces with capitals in the relatively liberal cities of Rionegro and Santa Fe de Antioquia. One of the first acts of General Eusebio Borrero, the leader of the Antioqueño revolution, was to proclaim the reunification of the former large province of Antioquia as a federal state. Significantly, the slogan of the rebellion in Antioquia was "God and Federation."

Conservatives in other provinces provided still other rationales for rebellion. In Pasto insurgents proclaimed the expelled Jesuits as their cause; in Mariquita they waved the flag of federalism. The most frequent Conservative banners, other than hostility to the Liberal government, were the defense of the Church and security of property. But the most common denominator among the Conservative rebels, whether guerrillas in Bogotá province or magnates in Medellín, was a desire to break the political hegemony of the Liberal Party and restore Conservative control of the national government.

Defeat of the Conservative rebellion and the consequent consolidation of Liberal hegemony freed the Liberal regime to continue to put pressure on the Church. Because Archbishop Manuel José Mosquera refused to cooperate with the 1851 law giving municipal councils a role in choosing parish priests, the Congress brought charges against him in May 1852 and ultimately expelled him from the country. On the same grounds, formal accusations also were brought against others in the Catholic hierarchy, including the bishops of Santa Marta and Cartagena.

The Liberal revolution of 1849–1852 consolidated the alliance between political Conservatives and most politically active Roman Catholic clergy. Mariano Ospina Rodríguez had laid the foundations for this alliance in the early 1840s through the reintroduction of the Jesuits as an instrument of order. When the Conservatives lost control of the government in 1849, Ospina again turned to the banner of the Church as a means of mobilizing political support as well as an instrument of social order. In June 1852—after the failure of the Conservative rebellion of 1851 and at the time of the expulsion of

Archbishop Mosquera—Mariano Ospina in a letter to José Eusebio Caro, co-founder of the Conservative Party, coolly analyzed the possible banners that might be used to rally support for the Conservative cause. In Ospina's view the principal elements in the Conservative credo were political liberty, security of person and property, and the Christian religion. But experience had shown that those Conservatives who were most concerned about security of person and property would not fight for the cause. Only the banner of religion could mobilize fervent popular support for the Conservative Party. While Ospina and other Conservatives saw the Roman Catholic Church as their ultimate political weapon, many of the clergy, for their part, embraced the Conservative Party as the chief defender of the Church against radical Liberal innovations.

While Liberals were consolidating their hegemony in 1852–1853, they were also in the process of dividing among themselves. Often the fractures were between older Liberals like Ezequiel Rojas, Lorenzo María Lleras, and López himself, on the one hand, and younger, more utopian, radicals, whose recognized senior leader was Manuel Murillo Toro. From 1849 to 1852 Murillo was perceived as the chief promoter of radical reform within López's cabinet. Murillo ultimately proved too radical for López. Murillo was remarkable among the Liberal elite in the nineteenth century in his serious and sustained concern about the inequality that was so evident in New Granadan society. He perceived that the root of this inequality lay in the unequal distribution of land. To begin to reduce this inequality, in 1851 and 1852 Murillo strongly advocated establishing strict limits on the amount of public land that a single person might acquire and requiring that title to public land be denied to anyone who did not cultivate the property he claimed. President López opposed this egalitarian measure—grants of public land were an important means of compensating army officers, and rights to large blocks of public lands provided one of the chief supports of public credit. In April 1852 Murillo resigned from the cabinet in part over his differences with López over the public lands issue. Murillo's insistence on limits on public land grants at this time was an exceptional stance for the time. Most Liberals of the time were liberal individualists, for whom the solution to social inequality was simply the unimpeded operation of the free market. Murillo was unusual in attempting to give liberal egalitarian rhetoric concrete, practical expression. Even many of the younger, more radical, liberals who supported Murillo, like José María Samper, while egalitarian in self-concept, were more believers in the free market than practical egalitarians.

Murillo's principal supporters outside the cabinet were recent university graduates, some of whom had begun their political lives by giving classes to, and indoctrinating politically, the Bogotá artisans' society and its successor the Sociedad Democrática. Early in 1850, however, the young upper-class radicals and the artisans began to come to a parting of the ways. Their differences became baldly apparent when Bogotá's artisans in 1850 were agitating for protection for finished artisan products like clothing and leather goods. When the artisans called for protection, university-educated youths lectured them on the principles of political economy and the virtues of free trade, angering the artisans. There it was, suddenly apparent: the class differences between craftsmen and the university-educated, between those who made objects for upper-class consumption and those in the upper class who preferred to import foreign versions of those same goods. From early 1850 onward Bogotá's artisans increasingly became aware, and resented, that they had been manipulated by the young upper-class Liberals.

The founding in September 1850 of Bogotá's Escuela Republicana as an elite youth organization separate from the artisans' Sociedad Democrática may be viewed as symptomatic of the growing alienation between the artisans and their erstwhile young upper-class mentors. Perhaps because they now felt uncomfortable in the Sociedad Democrática, Bogotá's elite youth withdrew to form their own separate organization, the Escuela Republicana. In Escuela meetings young upper-sector Liberals indulged in a good deal of rhetorical preening and expounded such advanced proposals as religious liberty, civil marriage, and the abolition of the army. Some of these notions had little resonance among the artisans and indeed were abhorrent to many of the craftsmen.

Class difference between most of the political and economic elite, on the one hand, and the artisans and other subalterns, on the other, was the fundamental fact underlying their increasing alienation from each other (1850–1852) and subsequent violent antagonism (1853–1854). The differences found expression in various ways. In 1851, the popular classes in the Democratic Societies, organized as militia units, had provided part of the military force used in repressing the Conservative rebellion in the Cauca as well as elsewhere, and units composed largely of Bogota's artisans had been sent to Antioquia to put down the revolution there. Yet after the Conservative rebellion, the López government, clearly worried that the popular classes in the Democratic Societies might become an uncontrollable political force, stopped encouraging the societies. Leaders among Bogotá's artisans were growing increasingly resentful that the López government, having used them to repress the Conservatives, now was neglecting them and making no effort to reward them.

In particular, Bogotá's artisans were angered by the failure, in their view, of the López government to provide them with protection from foreign competition. In 1849 the Congress had raised customs duties 10 percent, and in 1852 boosted them again by 25 percent. However, these measures aimed primarily at increasing revenues. They did not protect urban artisans because the legislation provided across-the-board increases that raised the cost of imported textiles used by urban artisans and gave no special protection to finished goods such as clothing, saddles, or furniture. A notable aspect of the urban artisans' pressure for protection was its narrow focus on their own particular interests as makers of finished goods; their democratic vision did not much extend to the welfare of the peasantry or of textile weavers in the northern provinces.

Throughout the period from 1849 through 1853, Bogotá's artisans continued to press the Congress for special protection, at times winning small concessions but often being spurned with scorn and condescension by many, although not all, upper-class legislators. Already, by 1850, a pattern was becoming observable in the Congress of Conservatives and young radical Liberals voting together against protection for the artisans while some older Liberals like Lorenzo María Lleras of Bogotá and Juan José Nieto of Cartagena supported the artisans' clause.

Another element in the growing antagonism of Bogotá's artisans toward the political and economic elite was the rise of food prices from the middle of 1852 through early 1854. In the Bogotá region the increase in prices probably was attributable in part to the loss of land by Indian peasants who had grown vegetables and in part to the drain of some highland labor to tobacco cultivation and cinchona extraction, which had raised wages and increased demand for food in the Magdalena basin. But the situation apparently was also aggravated by the monopolization of beef supplies to the Bogotá market by a few large landowners. Outrage at monopolists became a part of the litany of artisan protest in the capital.

During 1853, artisan anger over the tariff, rising prices, and upper-class disdain began to find expression in violence on the streets of Bogotá, involving pistols and revolvers as well as rocks and clubs. The principal antagonists, their class identities made evident by their dress, were ruana-wearing artisans and frock-coated upper-class youths. On May 19, 1853, the artisans staged a mass demonstration to persuade the Congress to provide more protection from foreign goods. When the Congress failed to satisfy the artisans, a melee occurred in which artisans assaulted some congressmen and an artisan was killed. Other violent confrontations between elite youth and artisans ensued.

As the division between Bogotá's artisans and university-educated radical youths deepened, so too did the rift between some in the older generation of Liberals who came to politics in the 1820s and 1830s and the younger cohort that was coming to the fore in the 1850s. This conflict within the Liberal elite, already evident from the beginning of the López administration, became more pronounced after the defeat of the Conservatives in 1851. The divergence between Liberal factions had as its focal point the person of General José María Obando, whom everyone expected to be the Liberal candidate for the presidency in 1852. As of 1849 Obando was the sentimental favorite of most rank-and-file Liberals. Obando clearly represented the "old" liberalism rather than the new radical model, but even the young radicals of the Escuela Republicana in March 1851 voted overwhelmingly to support him for the presidency in 1852. After the defeat of the Conservative rebellion in 1851 and the consequent decision of the Conservatives not to present a presidential candidate, however, radical Liberals began to turn against Obando as a man insufficiently enlightened to preside over the continuation of the Liberal revolution. In the 1852 presidential election many radical Liberals supported General Tomás Herrera of Panama, who had led the defeat of the Conservative revolution of 1851.

Despite the defection of the radical minority, Obando won overwhelmingly in a presidential election that the Conservatives did not contest. But Obando's administration was riven by intra-Liberal conflict from its inception. Despite Obando's objections, radical Liberals, joined by Conservatives, adopted a federal constitution in the 1853 Congress, with provincial governors to be elected rather than appointed by the president. The powers of the president, and the national Congress, were further weakened by having the judges of the Supreme Court elected and by giving the judges a role (with the president) in determining whether a state of disorder required emergency measures. The constitution also was broadly democratic, in that all elected officials from the president down were to be chosen by direct, secret ballot with suffrage extended to all adult males without any property or literacy restriction. At the same time radical Liberals adopted many other innovations, such as civil marriage and divorce, the separation of Church and State, the drastic reduction of the standing army, and the end of the death penalty.

Obando and the old-line Liberals who supported him disliked many of these radical measures, which they believed would so weaken national government controls as to invite revolution and an early return of Conservative hegemony. Obando so objected to the enervation of presidential powers by the independent election of governors that even before taking office he threatened to resign if this change were adopted. He and those closest to him also worried that the separation of Church and State, by removing government control over clerical appointments, would free the clergy to do their utmost to undermine the Liberals politically. Finally, the Obandistas opposed ending the death penalty and further weakening the national army, prompting radical Liberals to call them the "Draconians."

Obando's forebodings were realized in the elections of 1853, when almost as many Conservatives as Draconian Liberals were elected as provincial governors and Conservatives and radical Liberals predominated in the Congress, with only slight representation of traditional Liberals of Obando's stripe. In reaction, Obando ultimately acquiesced in, and appears to have encouraged, a military coup d'etat. As early as April 1853, even before the radical program had been adopted, there was already talk among the Draconians of making Obando a dictator. And from that time onward rumors of an impending coup surfaced sporadically.

During 1853 and 1854 army officers on active duty increasingly came to the fore as a political interest group and a likely instrument of dictatorship. New Granada's senior officers were divided, in this respect, between those who came from aristocratic families or who, through distinction and rewards earned in the struggle for independence, had entered the aristocracy and those whose livelihoods depended upon military pay. The latter became increasingly alienated during the 1850s as both radical Liberals and Conservatives sought to shrink the army. For reasons of economy, as well as to secure civilian authority, every government since the fall of the Bolivarians in 1831 had sought to keep the size of the standing army to a minimum, although internal disturbances periodically caused its ranks temporarily to be increased again. In 1848, the administration of General Tomás Cipriano de Mosquera had reduced the standing army from 3400 to 2500 men. In 1849, the first of the administration of General López, the Congress shrank the army to 1500. Nonetheless, these curtailments of the number of men in the ranks had not directly attacked army officers on active duty, whose numbers had remained relatively constant (three or four generals and eight colonels, from 1849 through 1852). Only in 1852, after the defeat of the Conservative rebellion of 1851, did there begin a movement drastically to weaken, and perhaps eliminate, the army as an institution.

The publication, beginning in November 1852, of *El Orden*, a newspaper supported by collections from army officers, is an indicator of their growing fear of antimilitary legislation. Earlier in 1852 the Chamber of Representatives had discussed reducing or suspending military pensions. But in 1853 radical Liberal and Conservative congressmen began a much more general attack on the standing army. In that year the Congress rejected increases in compensation to military officers on active duty and threatened to reduce or eliminate military pensions.

By 1853 General José María Melo, the commander of the army garrison at Bogotá, had become the most visible champion of military interests. In contrast with such aristocratic generals as Mosquera and Eusebio Borrero or those like José Hilario López, whose military service had brought substantial properties, Melo's fortunes depended upon his military career.

As the future of the standing army emerged as an issue, an alliance between Bogotá's artisans and the military garrison in the capital began to develop. President Obando and General Melo both had become members of Bogotá's Sociedad Democrática. And not a few military officers, including President Obando, had homes in Bogotá's predominantly artisan barrio of Las Nieves. A shared social status at the margin of the upper class and a shared hostility toward Conservative and radical Liberal political elites brought the military and elements of the popular classes together not merely in Bogotá but also in some provinces. In May and June 1853 this feeling of mutual sympathy between the artisans and the military garrison in Bogotá was expressed by a tendency of the military to take the side of the artisans in their street fights with upper-class youths.

Upper-class fear of both the military and the artisans found expression in the Congress of 1854. Radical Liberals and Conservatives voted to reduce the standing army from 1500 to 800, with only one colonel and no generals on active duty—with the clear intent of removing General Melo from the scene. (Reportedly all of the generals not then on active duty approved this reduction.) The same legislation, for good measure, called for immediately dissolving the Bogotá garrison. Obando vetoed this measure, meanwhile promising Melo a place in his cabinet if it came to be enacted.

Beyond Melo and the Bogotá garrison, the radical Liberals and the Conservatives worried about the National Guard, which was composed mainly of artisans and others of the popular classes in the Democratic Societies. In the 1854 Congress various Conservatives proposed replacing the army with newly formed "municipal guards," which presumably would be firmly under upper-class control. At the same time, both radical Liberals and Conservatives pressed for a law for "free commerce in arms"—in order to enable the upper class to arm itself against the standing army or the national guard, should it prove necessary.

Upper-class civilian politicians' fear of General Melo also was manifest in charges brought against him for allegedly having killed a soldier in the Bogotá garrison. The desire of radical Liberal civil authorities to use the case to bring him down was evident. Ultimately, this case, along with the accumulated hostility of Melo and many other military officers toward Conservative and radical Liberal politicians, helped to precipitate the coup of April 17, 1854.

The coup was staged by General Melo, with the support of both the military garrison and many of the artisans of Bogotá. Melo and others apparently expected Obando to head the new order created by the coup, but Obando suffered a failure of will and adopted the role of helpless bystander. So Melo became Bogotá's military dictator, with the active support of many Bogotá artisans and some Obandista Liberals. Melo's views echoed those of Obando: The new constitution of 1853 left the central government impotent; radical Liberals had insulted the Church and destroyed the army. Melo reversed policy on all three fronts: Governors under his regime would be appointed, not elected; Roman Catholicism would again be the state church; and an expanded army once again would enjoy the *fuero militar*.

The seizure of the capital city by General Melo, backed by the Bogotá garrison and many artisans, quickly stirred a reaction from leaders of both the Liberal and Conservative parties. Conservatives and many upper-class Liberals joined together in an alliance, which they called "constitutionalist," to defeat the Melistas, whom they called the "dictatorials."

General Melo facilitated his ultimate defeat by following a passive strategy of maintaining control of the region around Bogotá and awaiting the attack of his establishment opponents. A successful attack by the constitutionalists on the capital was delayed for months, however, in part because the elite coalition found that the revolution in Bogotá had significant support in the Cauca and the Caribbean coast and some sympathy even in Antioquia and el Socorro. In much of the Cauca, in some places on the Caribbean coast, many in the popular classes, who were organized in Democratic Societies and National Guard units, backed the revolution. In these regions also some upper-sector Liberals whose political fortunes were closely tied to popular mobilization of the Democratic Societies either sympathized with the Melo revolution or maintained an ambiguous stance in order to conciliate their political clients in the popular classes. In addition, particularly in regions in which Conservatives had been dominant before 1849, like the Cauca, Antioquia, and Cartagena, some Liberals distrusted the Conservatives and believed (it turned out with good reason) that the alliance against Melo was being used by Conservatives as an excuse to persecute Liberals and return these places to Conservative control.

In the Cauca region military units (regular army and/or National Guard) pronounced for Melo in Popayán and Quilichao, as well as in Cali, in mid-May, a month after the Melo coup in Bogotá. There also was widespread backing for the revolution in Palmira and many other places in the Cauca Valley. In the Cauca popular support for the Melo revolution probably reflected in part loyalty to General Obando, the regional hero of the poor. For this reason General López insisted that the constitutionalists say that Obando was being held prisoner by Melo, rather than collaborating with him as was generally believed by constitutionalist leaders. López warned other constitutionalist leaders that, if they publicly condemned Obando, they would completely lose the Cauca to rebel forces.

Beyond popular loyalty to Obando, however, lay the history of class warfare in the region. Fear of, and repression of, rebellion by slaves and free blacks in the early 1840s and attacks on Conservative landowners by Liberal mobs, from Cali to Cartago, in 1850–1851, had left a heritage of violence and hatred between property-owners and the popular classes. General López reported that the resistance to the constitutionalists in the Cauca represented not so much sympathy for Melo as popular fear and hatred of local Conservatives. These fears were amply confirmed as, once the rebels in the Cauca were defeated, Liberals from Pasto to Cartago were persecuted; in Cali they were subjected to severe repression. After a Conservative victory at Palmira, many rebels who had surrendered were killed, some lanced to death while kneeling and begging for mercy. Liberal Vice President José de Obaldía, who was firmly committed to alliance with the Conservatives, chose to view this slaughter as simply an expression of Cauca landowners' outrage at the violence they had suffered at the hands of Liberal mobs in 1851. But this Conservative vengeance also enabled Conservatives to destroy Liberal control of the Cauca Valley.

Conservative violence and repression continued in the Cauca after Melo was defeated. Antonio Matéus, the Liberal governor of Cauca province in 1854, was viewed by Conservatives as a covert supporter of the Melo revolution because he resolved to defend rebels in Cali against attack by Manuel Tejada, an intransigent Conservative. Matéus ultimately led a military unit from his province against the Melo regime in Bogotá. General López and other Liberals believed that Matéus had temporized at first because of the strong support for Melo in his province and viewed him as a hero who had played a key role in preventing the Cauca Valley from falling under Melista control. But Conservatives could not forgive Matéus for the Liberal violence of 1851 or his ambiguous behavior in 1854. Two months after the constitutionalist victory over Melo in December 1854, Matéus was suspended as governor of Cauca province, and within a year he was murdered in Palmira.

In Antioquia, where Conservatives had been dominant until 1851, some Liberals distrusted the Constitutionalist alliance of Conservative and Liberal leaders, believing this would lead to a restoration of Conservative hegemony. Accordingly, some Liberals in Sopetrán and Rionegro attempted rebellions against Conservative Constitutionalist authorities. On the Caribbean coast, as well as in Ocaña, the fight against Melo was seen by Conservatives and Liberals alike as, in reality, another phase in the struggle for local dominance between the two parties. On the Caribbean coast, General Mosquera was deeply suspicious of the Liberal governor of Cartagena, Juan José Nieto, and had him removed. In fact, wherever General Mosquera went, Conservatives replaced Liberals in political authority. From the Conservative point of view, all Liberals were considered inherently suspect of collaborating with Melo or with those in the populace that sympathized with the revolution.

After the defeat of Melo in Bogotá in December 1854, some Liberals considered too sympathetic to artisans, like Lorenzo María Lleras, were imprisoned for a time. But in Bogotá the constitutionalists were particularly severe with the artisans themselves. Those considered most dangerous were exiled abroad, to Panama or other provinces. By contrast, a number of upper-sector politicians in Bogotá who had collaborated with Melo soon were reincorporated into political activity.

It was in the provinces that the constitutionalist victory had the greatest impact. Conservative local and regional governments imposed by Conservative military officers in 1854 then proceeded to maintain their hegemony in the Cauca Valley, parts of the Caribbean coast, and Ocaña. The exclusion of ballots from areas of Liberal strength further aided the perpetuation of Conservative control. Reports of such arbitrary measures raise questions as to the degree to which Conservative electoral victories from 1854 through 1856 represented popular support for Conservatism in the only national elections with universal male suffrage in the nineteenth century or a consequence of a successful Conservative counterrevolution in 1854–1855. In 1855 the Conservatives captured a majority in the Senate and a narrow edge in the Chamber of Representatives. Conservative electoral dominance became still more clear in 1856, when the Conservative candidate for the presidency, Mariano Ospina Rodríguez, with 95,600 votes, decisively defeated the Liberal standard-bearer, Manuel Murillo Toro (79,400), despite the third-force candidacy of General Tomás Cipriano de Mosquera (32,700).

Whatever the degree to which it was affected by arbitrary actions at the local or regional level, the 1856 presidential election revealed clear regional political tendencies. Conservatives were dominant in Antioquia and in the highland regions of Cundinamarca and Boyacá. Liberals retained bases of support in the Caribbean zone, in the warm country on the flanks of Cundinamarca's Eastern Cordillera, and majority control of Santander, although that state was contested by the Conservatives. Liberals and Conservatives also competed for control of the Cauca Valley and the Upper Magdalena Valley. But a significant new force emerged in the followers of General Mosquera, who showed particular strength in parts of the Caribbean zone (the state of Panama and the provinces of Cartagena and Mompox) and in his home turf of Popayán. Many of Mosquera's supporters in the Cauca and the Caribbean coast during the 1850s and 1860s transferred their allegiance to Rafael Núñez of Cartagena during the 1870s and 1880s.

THE CLIMAX OF FEDERALISM

Despite the return of Conservative dominance of the national government after 1855, the trend that had begun in the late 1840s—the redistribution of power away from the central government and to provincial governments—continued. Because of the decentralization, and the elimination, of many sources of national revenue, the income of the national government dropped precipitously during the 1850s. As of 1848–1849 gross national revenues amounted to more than 3.3 million pesos; from 1851 through 1858 the national government's annual income averaged less than 1.7 million pesos. Partly because of increasing fiscal penury, but also from a conviction that a large army represented a potential threat to constitutional government, legislators, after 1854 as well as before, continued to scale down the national military. By 1857, the standing army had been reduced to a third of its size in 1853 (from 1500 troops to 500), and the military budget was less than a third the amount in 1853.

The practical movement toward federalism had begun in the early 1850s with the decentralization of revenues, the continuing reduction of the standing army, and the provision for the election of governors in the constitution of 1853, but in 1855–1857 the federalist movement developed still more momentum. In 1855 most provincial legislatures across the country supported further movement toward federalism. All of the northern provinces, from Vélez through Pamplona, were enthusiastic, as were those in the upper Magdalena basin (Neiva, Mariquita, and Tequendama); Antioquia, Popayán, and the Chocó also endorsed it. The clearest opposition to further regional autonomy came from the provincial legislatures of Bogotá and parts of the Cauca region (Cauca, Buenaventura, and Pasto provinces). Cartagena also was cool to the idea and abstained. A number of leading Conservatives, with *El Porvenir* of Bogotá as their voice, opposed a federal government as too weak to preserve order. However, some Conservatives, particularly in Antioquia, saw regional autonomy as a way of preserving at least their part of the republic from the contagion of liberal nostrums. As of 1855–1857 support for federation was so general, with even some Conservatives supporting some version of the idea, that Mariano Ospina, the chief party leader, as well as other Conservative notables, had to mute their public opposition.

If some Conservatives endorsed the movement toward federation, it was nonetheless clear that Liberals were most generally committed to it. *El Tiempo* of Bogotá, founded in 1855, was the chief advocate for a highly decentralized system. Manuel Murillo Toro led the constellation of Liberal writers for *El Tiempo* who elaborated an ideology in support of a more decentralized structure. But among the Liberal phalanx advancing arguments favoring federalism was Rafael Núñez, twenty-five years later a severe critic of political decentralization.

The Liberals of *El Tiempo* in 1855 announced, with some satisfaction, that many of their earlier aims had been achieved—the lowering of tariff barriers, the destruction of most colonial taxes, the separation of Church and State, the end of slavery and imprisonment for debt, the implantation of universal suffrage. But the Liberal program, they believed, would reach its culmination with the establishment of a completely federal system. Liberals identified centralist systems with absolute authority, backed by large standing armies and an established Church. Centralized government had meant oppression and civil wars inspired by the desire to seize control of the resources of the national state. A federal system, by reducing the power and resources of the central state, would reduce incentives to control it and thus end civil wars. Conflict also would be eliminated by forming regional units that were homogeneous culturally and economically. If each regional entity had homogeneous economic interests, each could develop those interests to the maximum without fear of arousing conflict. Each regional unit could experiment with differing institutional solutions in accord with its particular interests, thus achieving a harmonious diversity.

Liberal federalists confronted a dilemma in the question as to whether autonomous regional political units should be large or small. The notion that regional units were to have homogeneous economic interests suggested that regional polities should be small—otherwise they were likely to contain some conflicting interests. For this reason, Manuel Murillo supported having small regional units. However, many others believed that the subdivision of provinces that had occurred between 1847 and 1853 had created regional governments too small to be viable. In 1855, therefore, the Congress began to reintegrate the recently divided provinces of Bogotá, Antioquia, Pamplona, and Pasto. Further, in February 1855 the Congress declared the Isthmus of Panama a "sovereign federal state." The creation of the State of Panama stimulated representatives of other regions to solicit statehood. In 1856 Antioquia also became a state, and in 1857 the congress created the new states of Santander, Cauca, Cundinamarca, Boyacá, Bolívar, and Magdalena. The creation of these larger states threw into doubt the Liberal assumption that regional governing units might truly have homogeneous interests.

The existing constitution of 1853 made no provision for "federal states," so their creation between 1855 and 1857 was a legal anomaly. It therefore became necessary to write a new constitution to provide a framework for the new states that already had come into being. The Constitution of 1858, in which the national state was renamed the Confederación Granadina, was supposed to supply this want. The constitution, however, was vague about the relations between the national government and the states. Ambitious politicians and competing political parties seeking to secure party hegemony, in the states and nationally, interpreted the constitution in tendentious and contrary ways. Conflicting interpretations of the relationship between the central government and the states proved to be one source of the political conflicts that began in various states during 1859 and after 1860 consumed most of the nation in civil war. Indeed, the question of the appropriateness of central government intervention in the states remained a troublesome issue until at least 1880.

PANAMA AND NATIONAL INTEGRITY

The creation of a "sovereign federal state" of Panama was an indicator of the growing importance of the Isthmus of Panama and a portent of its future independence from New Granada. From the 1820s onward, British, French, North American, and New Grandan entrepreneurs had proposed schemes for roads and canals across the isthmus. The establishment in 1843 of steamship service connecting Valparaiso in Chile and el Callao in Peru to Panama both reflected and reinforced development of the Pacific coast of Spanish America and hence of the growing importance of the isthmian link to the Atlantic.

The developing economic significance of the isthmus for world trade raised the question for political leaders in Bogotá of whether and how New Granada might retain possession of Panama in the face of the growing interest of such world powers as Great Britain, France, and the emerging United States. Until 1845, Bogotá looked principally to Great Britain as a guarantor of New Granadan sovereignty in Panama. Subsequently, however, New Granadan leaders came to recognize that they would have to deal primarily with the United States—a realization made palpable by the U.S. conquest of Mexico in 1846–1848 and the activities of the North American filibusters in Nicaragua in the 1850s. Growing U.S. interest in Panama and New Granada's implicit dependence on the United States was reflected in the Mallarino-Bidlack Treaty of 1846–1848, under which the United States guaranteed the neutrality of the isthmus and freedom of transit over it.

Soon after the treaty was approved, the discovery of gold in California and the consequent rush of North Americans made the Yankee presence in Panama a sudden reality. In 1849 a New York company contracted to build a railway across the isthmus, superseding an earlier contract of 1847 with a French enterprise. With the aid of workers brought from China, India, and various parts of Europe, but more successfully from Jamaica and Cartagena, the 47-mile railway was finished by January 1855. But the flow of North Americans across Panama did not await the construction of the railway. During 1849, before the railroad was even started, close to 8000 crossed the isthmus, mostly California-bound, and the following year the number more than doubled. By 1853, when the railway was still less than half complete, it already was carrying more than 32,000 passengers.

The avalanche of North Americans crossing the isthmus brought problems. Frictions between North Americans and Panamanians led to outbreaks of violence as early as February 1850. North Americans often disregarded local Panamanian authorities, going so far as to form their own de facto local governments in the port cities, which issued decrees applying even to New Granadan residents. Already by 1850 North American warships were intervening during moments of particular conflict.

Political elites in the New Granadan interior viewed these isthmian developments with alarm. José Manuel Restrepo, having already been disturbed by the U.S. seizure of much of Mexico, in March 1850 predicted that the North Americans eventually would grab all of Mexico and Central America down to the Isthmus of Panama. By July 1850 Restrepo concluded that the prosperity of Panama would bring the loss of the isthmus and its incorporation into the United States. In 1855, the Panamanian Senator, Justo Arosemena, argued that New Granada would be able to keep Panama only by making it a more autonomous state. But others in Bogotá believed that the creation of a "sovereign state" on the isthmus actually was the first step toward Panamanian independence.

Fear of U.S. expansionism increased in 1855 with the activities of North American filibusters in Nicaragua. The rather optimistic response of Bogotá's Liberal federalists to this threat was to imagine the formation of a larger Colombian federation, including not only Venezuela and Ecuador but also all or parts of Central America and possibly even the Dominican Republic. It was hoped that joining these republics in a large confederation might give North American expansionists pause. This was an unusually utopian Liberal pipedream. Neither Venezuela nor any of the other potential components of this grand confederation was likely to want to take part. Further, even if if had come into being, given the loose confederative structure that Liberals envisioned, it is hard to see how this grand confederation could have responded effectively to foreign aggression against any of its members.

The inadequacies of Liberal federalism in dealing with challenges from foreign powers were made clear in 1856–1858, in a serious conflict with the United States over events in the Isthmus of Panama. On April 15, 1856, after a North American killed a melon salesman in Panama, a riot ensued. Panamanians stormed the railway station in which North American passengers sought refuge and from which the Yankees rained rifle fire on the Panamanians. Two Panamanians and as many as fifteen North Americans were killed. Responding to this "Panama melon" incident, the United States claimed an indemnity of $400,000. Worse, the United States also demanded the creation of independent, self-governing municipalities in the two railroad terminus points of Colón and Panama and the cession of 10 miles of territory on each side of the railway plus two islands in Panama bay to be used for a U.S. naval station.

The Panama melon crisis evoked various responses from the New Granadan upper class, some of which cast light on deeper social and political attitudes. Many in the political elite considered the U.S. demands unacceptable. But New Granada had little capacity to resist. With effectively no navy and the national army reduced to less than 500 men, it could not defend the isthmus. Furthermore, New Granada already was being threatened with a British naval blockade because of a dispute over repayment of an earlier loan (the Mackintosh loan).

Many in the interior nonetheless responded to the North American challenge with bravado, calling for defense of the national honor. Veterans of the independence wars offered their aging bodies for the cause. Many who inclined to patriotic bluster, including members of the New Granadan Congress, could not have expected to do any fighting themselves. Matilde Pombo de Arboleda of Popayán, the mother of two prominent Cauca Conservatives, expected heroic resistance to the invaders. In any case, she added, war with the United States might have the benefit of doing away with the country's political parties and raising up a dictator, which the country needed anyway, to moderate "our very exaggerated democracy."

The reactions of many Colombians were highly conflicted, expressing simultaneously outrage at the North Americans trampling across the isthmus and the demands of the United States, pique at the Panamanian population and authorities for getting the republic into this jam, and a sense of helplessness in dealing with the power of the United States. Some inclined to heroic gesture proposed to resist the North Americans with guerrillas— although elites in the interior doubted that adequate guerrillas might be found among the populace of Panama.

Liberals were among those most conflicted. For many years, and particularly during the federalist enthusiasm of the 1850s, New Granadan Liberals had looked to the United States as a model republic. Now the model republic was making unreasonable demands and might well seize Panama. *El Tiempo*, the tribune of New Granadan Liberalism, now discovered many negative aspects of the United States: Despite its republican virtues, it was an aggressive, slave-owning society, materialist and soulless, and crude and uncouth to boot. *El Tiempo*'s advice to the government was fractured. It urged the government to stand strong and refuse to cede anything to the United States. However (and this went unmentioned by the Liberals), since the federalist binge of the 1850s had effectively weakened and disarmed the central government, New Granada actually could not effectively resist. *El Tiempo* in the end found its escape in a federalist posture: The government of New Granada should disclaim any liability, since the failure to protect the transient North Americans was the responsibility of the authorities of the Sovereign State of Panama.

Those responsible for government policy could not take refuge in such a facile solution. Like others in the interior, the men in the Mallarino and Ospina administrations recognized that isthmian authorities had been at fault for not restraining the Panamanian mob, and worse, for joining in the attack on the North Americans in the railway station. But, as Conservatives, they were not given to Liberal federalist illusions, and therefore recognized that to deny responsibility was to concede the right of sovereignty over the isthmus. Their pessimistic conclusion was that, one way or the other, New Granada would soon lose the Isthmus of Panama. One of their chief concerns was to milk as much as possible from Panama before it either became independent or was seized by a foreign power. In particular, they focused on the idea of selling off or otherwise alienating public lands in Panama before New Granada lost the isthmus. One bright idea was to settle the current controversy with Great Britain by repaying the Mackintosh loan with Panamanian public lands.

Lino de Pombo, New Granada's secretary of foreign relations in 1856, combined bravado with the government's desire to cash in quickly on Panama as a fiscal resource. Pombo's plan was to goad the United States into seizing Panama and then collect an indemnity from the Yankees. Pombo very nearly succeeded in provoking U.S. military action. By lodging a counterclaim of $150,000 against the U.S. government he so infuriated both the North American public and politicians in Washington that flotillas were dispatched both to Colón and Panama while private enterprise filibusters prepared to invade the isthmus.

Other leaders in Bogotá were more cautious. Mariano Ospina, who became president in April 1857, hoped that Great Britain or France might intervene on New Granada's behalf. (Ospina was particularly partial to the idea of British protection: During the civil war of 1839–1842 he had supported making New Granada a British protectorate.) But the hope of British intervention was soon dashed. Great Britain made it clear that its relations with the United States were more important to it than the fate of either New Granada or Panama. Indeed, British officials said they considered the U.S. demands entirely appropriate. Once Ospina realized that European support was not forthcoming, he tried another tack: He proposed to annex not merely Panama but all of New Granada to the United States.

Incorporating all of Colombia into the United States was not a completely new idea. After the failed Conservative revolution of 1851 in Antioquia, when the radical Liberals were riding high, some conservative Antioqueños had discussed becoming part of the United States as a means of obtaining political stability and security of property to Colombia. To this idea that annexation to the United States would bring stability there was now the added consideration, in Ospina's mind, that the energetic Yankees ultimately would take over most of Spanish America anyway—why uselessly expend money and blood trying to avoid the inevitable? As it turned out, the U.S. government was not interested in absorbing New Granada and quietly spurned Ospina's offer.

Ospina was not alone among the Bogotá elite in conceiving that New Granada might be gobbled up by a horde of Yankee filibusters or in entertaining the advantages of incorporation into the United States. After the Panama melon dispute was settled (on terms not so onerous to New Granada as had been feared), Florentino González, at the time New Granada's attorney general, continued to speculate on the consequences of a filibuster invasion. The North American invaders, González imagined, were likely to bring slavery back to the Caribbean states and the Cauca Valley. But for the interior highlands a Yankee conquest could have positive effects. In Santander, Boyacá, Cundinamarca, and Antioquia, "the white race is . . . numerous, and they can maintain their preponderance" as part of the United States. In these states, González concluded, the North Americans "would marry our daughters," bringing about a "fusion of the two races that would be advantageous." "This, far from alarming me, pleases me; and thus . . . my efforts to avoid annexation are inspired by a disinterested sentiment of philanthropy in favor of the Africans and mestizos that populate the other states."

CIVIL WAR, 1859–1863

As the Panama melon crisis was coming to an end in 1858, a more serious internal conflict was developing into the civil war of 1859–1862. When the federal states evolved between 1855 and 1858, it could be supposed that the new system would reduce partisan warfare. With power fragmented among a weak national government and more or less autonomous states, the stakes of power, and hence the motivation for rebellion or coup d'etat, would be reduced. Unfortunately, the fragmented federal system rather than diminishing partisan conflict, generalized it. Minority parties in the states could not accept the prospect of permanent powerlessness and soon staged revolutions against the locally dominant party. In the State of Santander, the majority Liberals adopted a state constitution under which representatives to the state assembly were to be elected at large, with the result that Liberals monopolized the state legislature. This provided an excuse for Conservative rebellion in Santander beginning in February 1859. With somewhat less reason, the Draconian Liberal, Juan José Nieto, overthrew the Conservative government in Bolívar in July 1859.

While these conflicts reflected local and regional rivalries, the national government also was a participant. Conservative rebels in southern Santander, who had invaded the state from the Conservative-dominated State of Boyacá, used arms belonging to the Confederation government. Further, Mariano Ospina, the Conservative national president, made no effort to discourage Conservative incursions into Santander. The involvement of the national government in regional revolutions soon became more active. In May 1859 the national government established in each state an inspector of the public force, who was to supervise the armed forces of each state. Liberals feared that these and other national agents sent into the states by the Ospina government would be used to undermine state governments not controlled by Conservatives. Their fears proved justified, as in 1860 the national military inspector in the Cauca led an abortive rebellion against the state government headed by General Tomás Cipriano de Mosquera.

Relations between the national government and the states were complicated by the fact that the Constitution of 1858 left important aspects of that relationship undefined. In 1855 Panama had been created as a "sovereign" state, but the legislation subsequently erecting the other states did not refer to them as "sovereign." In 1858, when the national Congress wrote a constitution to clarify the situation, General Mosquera proposed that the states be given the status of "sovereign," but the Constitution of 1858 did not concede them sovereignty. However, in Mosquera's Cauca, Liberal-controlled Santander, and Panama, where federalist opposition to Ospina's national government was particularly strong, state leaders nonetheless asserted state sovereignty. The issue of state sovereignty developed particular importance when a national law in April 1859 specified that elections of the president and national congressmen were to be administered in the states by boards appointed by the national government. Dissident leaders in the states understandably interpreted the law as an attempt by Conservatives to obtain and preserve their hegemony in all of the states through control of elections.

In addition to local partisan conflicts, the intervention of the national agents in state politics, and the lack of constitutional clarity about the relationship of nation and states, New Granada also was moved to civil war by the conflicting personal ambitions, political projects, and rivalries of General Mosquera and President Ospina. General Mosquera as president in 1845–1849 had not entirely conformed to conventional conservative policies. Subsequently, while he held the loyalty of some military officers, many civilian Conservatives distrusted him. In 1855, when General Mosquera was flaunting anticlerical attitudes, he was conspicuously excluded from the Conservatives' directing junta in Bogotá. Mosquera retaliated by initiating the formation of a third party, intermediate between the Conservatives and Liberals, sustaining elements of the policies of each. In 1856, after wooing first Liberals and then Conservatives, he was disappointed not to be chosen as the Conservative candidate for the presidency. After running unsuccessfully as a third-party candidate in 1856, Mosquera in 1857 played a leading role in the politics of the Caribbean coast, where he had a strong following, before returning to his native Cauca, where he was elected the first state governor. As governor of the Cauca, Mosquera in 1859 stepped forward as the chief champion of the states' autonomy as against all assertions of national authority by President Ospina. At the same time, while challenging the Conservative president, he once again moved to establish in the Cauca a third party, now called the National Party, a coalition of men personally loyal to Mosquera with some Liberals and Conservatives.

While General Mosquera openly displayed his personal ambitions, Mariano Ospina's aspirations were expressed in the quest for dominance by the Conservative Party, the political entity he had nurtured over nearly two decades. Both Ospina and Mosquera since 1840 had changed their political tunes according to prevailing trends. Both men had been firm centralists in the early 1840s. Between 1855 and 1858 both swam in the federalist stream, although in Ospina's case uncomfortably. (Ospina in 1856 did strongly support creating the state of Antioquia, his adopted region, a place that Conservatives would dominate.) As national president (1857–1861), however, he resolutely asserted the authority of the national government as against Mosquera, who as a state leader insisted on state autonomy.

After the passage of the national election law in April 1859, Mosquera began to push for the independence of the Cauca and, allegedly, the formation, with Panama, of a separate nation. Confronting Mosquera's threats of rebellion, the national government in 1860 declared that any state governor who defied national laws would be held criminally accountable. This "law of internal order" became the occasion for outright warfare between General Mosquera and the national government.

Before and during the outbreak of large-scale war in 1860, some Liberals and Conservatives alike sought conciliation, but they were overwhelmed by the intransigents on both sides. On the Liberal side, Manuel Murillo and some other Radical civilians urged peace in their newspaper, *El Tiempo*, but other Liberals, including those who had been Draconians or Melistas in 1854, supported Mosquera's rebellion. On the Conservative side, General Pedro Alcántara Herrán, who had been chosen the Conservative candidate for the presidency in the 1860 election, encouraged conciliation, in which he was supported by merchants in Bogotá and the State of Antioquia. But Herrán was too conciliatory for the intransigent Conservatives around Mariano Ospina. For this reason, just before the election Ospina's hard-line Conservatives dumped Herrán as the party candidate, replacing him with the more fiery Julio Arboleda. As Ospina wrote to the governor of Antioquia in explanation of the last-minute removal of Herrán, "[W]e all understand that it is necessary to exterminate the contrary party at all cost; this reason tells us, this public concience teaches us."

Ospina's insistence on asserting the authority of the national government and on destroying those who opposed him brought catastrophe to the party he had created. Outmaneuvering Ospina and his forces at every turn, Mosquera's armies took Bogotá in July 1861. The war continued, both in the Eastern Cordillera and in the West, however, and Conservative forces were not completely subdued until February 1863.

As Mariano Ospina's term as president ended April 1, 1861, and the civil war prevented a normal succession, he handed over executive authority to the elected attorney general. Subsequently, Ospina, seeking to flee Bogotá, was captured by Mosquera, who ordered his execution. Mosquera was prevented from having Ospina and others high in his administration shot only through the intercession of foreign diplomats and some prominent Liberal leaders. Nonetheless, Mosquera did summarily execute three other prominent Conservatives without trial, to the horror of many. Mosquera clearly intended the executions both to intimidate the political class and to demonstrate his own personal authority. Subsequently, Mosquera's nephew, Julio

Arboleda, who had become the Conservatives' chief standard-bearer, retaliated by arbitrarily executing some two dozen men in Popayán and elsewhere in the Cauca. Arboleda was later assassinated, allegedly by a son of one of the men whom he had executed.

General Mosquera followed his executions in Bogotá with a still more sweeping assertion of his authority, a series of decrees drastically attacking the Church. On July 20, 1861, two days after taking the capital, Mosquera declared that henceforth the president would exercise the "right of tuition" with regard to all religions; that is, no "higher ministers," presumably meaning bishops, could exercise their functions without the president's permission. This decree, asserting state control of the Church, represented a reversal of the earlier bipartisan policy of separation of Church and State adopted in 1853. Six days later Mosquera expelled the Jesuits, who had returned during Ospina's presidency. And in September he declared that all real estate held in mortmain, that is, in perpetuity, by Church or other corporations would be sold at public auction. When church leaders protested these decrees, Mosquera in November imprisoned Archbishop Herrán and other prelates who had objected and extinguished all religious communities for resisting the order to turn over their property.

General Mosquera's anticlerical decrees were acts of vengeance for clerical support of Mariano Ospina in the election of 1856 as well as during the civil war. Mosquera, as well as many of his Liberal allies, wanted to bring the Church under control and neutralize it politically. The decrees also were affected by the exigencies of the war itself. The sale of Church-owned real estate was prompted in part by the need to raise money to carry on the war effort. But the sale of Church properties also had a longer-range rationale of making these properties circulate freely in the market, which according to liberal economic theory ought to guarantee their more productive exploitation. In all of these respects, Mosquera's sale of Church property in many ways was consciously patterned after a similar measure in Reforma Mexico in 1856–1857.

Some subsequent interpretations of this period have argued that Mosquera, like his Mexican predecessors, intended that sales of church lands be carried out in such a way that they could be bought by small farmers rather than being monopolized by large estate owners. However, the motives announced in the original decree of 1861 say nothing about furthering smaller landholdings. Further, much of the Church property was actually urban. In any event, as in Mexico, fiscal necessities induced the New Granadan government to sell Church properties quickly and in large units, with the result that most were bought up by already-affluent men.

RIONEGRO AND AFTER, 1863–1876

As the fighting ended in February 1863, representatives of the country's nine states (Mosquera had created the new State of Tolima in 1861) gathered in

Rionegro to write a new constitution, which it was hoped would remedy the defects of the 1858 charter. The convention of Rionegro was an assembly of the victors, in which there was no Conservative representative. Nonetheless, the victors were divided, with the Radical Liberals holding a slight edge over the followers of General Mosquera. Mosquera's authoritarian tendencies frightened the Radicals. They feared he would use nearby troops to intimidate and control the convention, and indeed Mosquera attempted to bully opposing delegates, casually suggesting that he might shoot some of them. The Radicals recognized that Mosquera, as the military leader of the victorious coalition, was the dominant figure of the hour, but they resolved to thwart him in symbolic as well as substantive ways to keep him within constitutional constraints.

It is often affirmed that the Radicals' fear of Mosquera's dictatorial propensities prompted them to draft a constitution that limited the term of the national president to two years and forbade immediate reelection. While fear of General Mosquera probably was a motivation at Rionegro, radical Liberals in 1855 already were proposing presidential terms of only two years. A weak national executive formed an integral part of the Radicals' program for federal democratization. Clearly, the Radicals, in addition to fearing General Mosquera, also differed with him on principles of government. Mosquera in 1845–1849 was a strong centralist and a strongly directive president. In 1857–1858, having lost the presidency to Ospina, he became an opportunistic federalist, defending his turf in the Cauca. But, as he showed during the civil war in 1861 and at Rionegro in 1863, in essence he remained an authoritarian caudillo. Leading Radicals, by contrast, sought to check concentrated power in defense of individual liberties. Hence they supported the reduction of executive authority, in relation to the Congress, as well as regional autonomy.

Among the issues over which General Mosquera and the Radicals disagreed was the appropriate relationship between Church and State. While the Radicals shared Mosquera's dislike of clerical support for the Conservative Party, they were much less given to punitive policies toward the Church. Radicals approved of many of General Mosquera's anticlerical decrees of 1861 as necessary wartime measures. But they continued to believe in the ideal of a free Church within a free State—that is, in the separation of Church and State. General Mosquera, however, wanted a return to the kind of government control over the Church that had been exercised in the colonial period and in the republican era until the separation of Church and State in the Constitution of 1853. General Mosquera also adopted a strongly punitive attitude toward Church leaders who resisted swearing allegiance to the Rionegro Consitution of 1863, while Radicals tended to be more conciliatory, particularly toward the more moderate prelates.

The difference between Mosquera and the Radicals on state autonomy was clear both at Rionegro and subsequently. At Rionegro, moved by bitter experience with Ospina and fear of Mosquera, as well as by liberal principles, the delegates refrained from giving the national government a clear right to guarantee public order in the states. The 1863 constitution ambiguously announced that it was the duty of the national executive to "velar por la conservación del órden general," which could mean variously that it was to "watch over," "guard," or "protect" the general order. Whether, or in what ways, the national government might have a right to intervene in the states remained a point in contention throughout the life of the Rionegro Constitution (1863–1886).

The differences on this question between General Mosquera and an often-principled Radical, Manuel Murillo Toro, were made clear in 1864, when a Conservative revolution in Antioquia removed the state governor implanted there by General Mosquera. At the time of the revolution in Antioquia, President Mosquera could not respond immediately as he was leading New Granadan troops into battle with Ecuador. On his return to Bogotá, Mosquera intended to suppress the Conservative government in Antioquia. However, Murillo, his successor in the presidency, chose to accept Conservative control of Antioquia—particularly as the new Conservative regime there promised to adhere to the 1863 constitution. Murillo also undoubtedly was not displeased that the governor overthrown in Antioquia was a Mosquerista. But Murillo's decision to accept Antioquia's Conservative revolution was consistent with his pronounced pacifism and his belief in state autonomy.

The appropriate response of the national government to upheavals in the states again became an issue in 1867 during another presidency of General Mosquera. At that time, a series of arbitrary acts by Mosquera, ending with the closing of Congress and the imprisonment of leading Radicals, led to a coup d'etat against the Caucano caudillo. Among General Mosquera's sins, in the eyes of his opponents, was military intervention in the State of Magdalena, which prompted Radicals and Conservatives to enact a law declaring that the national government must observe strict neutrality regarding upheavals in the states.

The Radicals themselves, however, were far from adhering consistently to the principle of federal nonintervention in the states. After the Radical coup d'etat removed Mosquera in 1867, Carlos Martín, a Radical secretary of the interior, asked Congress to repeal the neutrality law in 1868. Martín sought legislation modelled on the U.S. Constitution's federal guarantee of order in the states. The Radical-dominated Congress, however, insisted on the strict neutrality of the federal government with regard to internal conflicts in the states. Ironically, not long after the national Congress insisted on the neutrality of the central government, the Radical national president, Santos Gutiérrez, forcibly removed the Conservative government of the State of Cundinamarca. It should be noted that, in this case, Radicals in Bogotá believed that if the Radical national government did not displace the Conservative state regime, the latter, backed by irregular forces streaming into the capital from the surrounding area, might overthrow the government of the Union.

Throughout the years from 1864 to 1876, maintaining control of the national government trumped the principle of state autonomy as the Radicals' governing rule, at least when it came to elections. Under the constitution of 1863, the national president was elected by a majority of the nine states, with each state having a single vote. The Radicals' retention of the central government therefore required obtaining victories in at least five states in the biennial elections for the national presidency. Radicals generally sought to obtain such electoral victories by more or less peaceable means—by mobilizing the votes of army garrisons, by local intimidation, or by other standard modes of electoral manipulation. Occasionally, however, it proved necessary for the national army, known during this period as the Guardia Colombiana, to intervene more forcefully in selected states—usually in states that were lightly populated and relatively marginal politically, like Magdalena or Panama. The most flagrant abuses occurred in the presidential election of 1875–1876, precisely because, at that time, Radical hegemony came under serious threat. The challenge came from the combined forces of independent Liberals and many Conservatives, with particular strength on the Caribbean coast and in the Cauca, regions that had come to resent the unremitting control of the national government by Radicals hailing in large part from the Eastern Cordillera.

FISCAL ASPECTS OF THE FEDERAL SYSTEM

Under the federal system, the national government retained customs duties and the national salt mines as its chief sources of revenue. As of 1873–1874 customs duties accounted for four-fifths of national government revenues. Most other taxes were ceded to the states. As a consequence of the decentralization of revenues, the revenues of the regional governments increased greatly in relation to those of the national government. Nonetheless, the combined revenues of the nine states remained lower than those of the central government. In 1873–1874, the net revenues of the national government amounted to 3.3 million pesos, those of the states 2.1 million. In the division of labor at that time, the states spent more than the central government on public works and somewhat less on armed forces. National government investments on public education were roughly equal to the combined expenditures of the nine states.

Advocates of the federal system favored the decentralization of revenues in part because it would enable the various regional states to choose the revenues they preferred and would allow them greater freedom to adopt economic policies most of interest to their regions. However, under the federal system the various states were not equally able to pursue their regional interests, because their capacity to raise revenue varied greatly. Panama, Antioquia, and Cundinamarca were far stronger fiscally than the other states. (See Table 10.3.) Consequently, Antioquia and Cundinamarca were able to spend much larger sums on public works than any of the other states. In 1873 to 1874, Antioquia's 293,000 pesos and Cundinamarca's 162,000 pesos

Table 10.3 State populations, state revenues, and state revenues per capita, circa 1870–1874 (revenues in Colombian pesos)

State	Population* (1870)	State Revenues (1873–1874)	State Revenues per Capita
Antioquia	365,974	396,564	1.08
Bolívar	241,704	201,800	.84
Boyacá	472,475	122,100	.26
Cauca	435,078	158,400	.36
Cundinamarca	409,602	440,626	1.08
Magdalena	85,255	78,801	.92
Panama	205,221	318,000	1.55
Santander	425,427	235,957	.56
Tolima	230,891	151,000	.65
Totals	2,871,627	2,103,247	.73 (mean of state revenues)

*Population totals are for the states; they exclude the populations of the territories.
Source: *Anuario estadístico de Colombia, 1875* (Bogotá, 1875), pp. 48, 220.

together made up 75 percent of the total spent by the nine states on public works. Indeed, at that time the expenditures on public works of these two dominant states exceeded those of the national government. The effect of the federal system, then, was to favor the development of a few strong states to the neglect of the weaker ones.

ECONOMIC CULTURE AND ECONOMIC POLICY, 1845–1876

The expansion of tobacco exports that began after 1845 had a dramatic impact on New Granadan society and culture. The upper class was visibly affected. Long accustomed, during the colonial period and the early republican decades, to a somnolent economy, many gentlemen in Bogotá and much of the rest of the country had lived largely off low rents from rural estates and urban property, and perhaps also occasional government employment. With the tobacco boom in the upper Magdalena Valley, not a few were suddenly energized by the perception of new opportunity. Entrepreneurs and workers migrated to the Upper Magdalena to clear land and plant tobacco, while others in the dominant class became export merchants.

New Granadan society after 1845 became more markedly oriented toward external commerce, and the upper class became more bourgeois in attitude. Newspapers reflected this cultural change. Before 1845, they were devoted largely to political themes—partisan ideology, argumentation, attacks. After 1845, and particularly after 1847, the political themes continued, but leading newspapers increasingly carried commercial statistics, domestic and foreign market reports, and articles about the production methods and potential marketability of exportable products.

In the 1850s much of this information was about the tobacco industry, and to a lesser degree, such secondary exports as cinchona bark and palm-fiber hats. But New Granadan elites before 1876 were never content to rest with a single export crop, or even a few. The volume of the country's exports, even of tobacco, was relatively small; their position in Atlantic markets was marginal, and they were much affected by fluctuations in external demand. Upper-sector entrepreneurs, therefore, were constantly experimenting with various alternatives—most of which proved to be of modest scale and rather slight dependability. During the 1850s efforts were made to export indigo, and for a time in the 1860s and early 1870s indigo formed part of the country's varied array of export crops. Civil war in the United States raised hopes for cotton exports in the 1860s, hopes that were quickly dashed by the unexpectedly rapid postwar recovery of cotton production in the U.S. South. Forest products also attracted entrepreneurial attention. Cinchona bark was the most significant, from the 1850s into the 1880s. Dyewoods were a well-established export from the colonial era, although of relatively minor importance in the republican era. Still other forest products too insignificant to get much notice in the press were experimented with by merchants constantly seeking new sources of foreign exchange—among them vegetable ivory and such medicinals as sarsaparilla and ipecac. Coffee, long cultivated on a small scale in Santander and elsewhere, began to attract significant attention in the 1860s. By the 1870s coffee had become one of the three most important tropical exports, along with tobacco and cinchona bark, of a fairly broad array of tropical exports. Coffee, however, did not reach its position as the dominant tropical export until the late 1880s. (See Table 10.4.)

Given the newly aroused enthusiasm about the possibilities of exporting tropical products, those who developed, planted, and marketed tropical commodities came to be viewed, at least in some sectors of the society, as heroic pioneers. Francisco Montoya, who led the development of tobacco exporting in the late 1840s, was resented as a monopolist by smaller competitors during his period of dominance, but after his bankruptcy in 1857 he was regarded as a tragic hero of national enterprise. Toward the end of the century Medardo Rivas wrote *Los trabajadores de tierra caliente*, a paean of praise to those upper-class gentlemen who, from mid-century onward, left the comforts of Bogotá to descend into the Upper Magdalena valley, risking disease and death in the hot climate to seek their fortunes as planters of various tropical crops.

While pioneers in the development of export products were the most visible economic heroes of the period, those who most profited from the expansion of exports were the less heroic merchants who concentrated on the import trade. In the first decades of the nineteenth century the import trade did involve some heroism. At that time it was common for merchants to the

Table 10.4 Colombia's six most important exports, 1834–1891 (mean annual values, in thousands of gold pesos, and percentage of total exports)

Before 1845: continued overwhelming dependence on gold

1834–1839			1840–1845		
Gold	2413.0	74.0	Gold	2413.0	73.0
Cotton	155.3	4.8	Hides	149.8	4.5
Brazilwood	115.4	3.5	Brazilwood	133.7	4.0
Hides	101.9	3.1	Tobacco	118.5	3.6
Tobacco	86.6	2.7	Live animals	63.7	1.9
Live animals	80.8	2.5	Coffee	60.7	1.8

1850s and 1860s: tobacco emerges; cinchona bark and palm hats appear, then decline

1854–1858			1864–1870		
Gold	2113.8	33.3	Tobacco	2757.3	37.3
Tobacco	1769.0	27.8	Gold	2227.8	30.1
Cinchona bark	620.4	9.8	Coffee	595.6	8.1
Palm hats	605.0	9.5	Cotton	426.5	5.8
Coffee	258.5	4.1	Cinchona bark	350.8	4.7
Hides	253.6	4.0	Palm hats	232.2	3.1

1870s: tobacco declines; coffee emerges; cinchona bark again becomes significant

1870–1875			1875–78		
Gold	2218.5	22.2	Gold	2423.7	24.0
Tobacco	2115.7	21.2	Coffee	2252.5	22.3
Coffee	1637.1	16.4	Cinchona bark	1765.2	17.5
Cinchona bark	1466.6	14.7	Tobacco	1341.1	13.3
Hides	456.3	4.6	Hides	580.3	5.7
Silver	370.7	3.7	Silver	376.9	3.7

1880s: cinchona bark booms and busts; coffee begins to dominate

1881–1883			1888–1891		
Cinchona bark	4763.4	30.9	Coffee	4170.4	34.1
Gold	2886.0	18.7	Gold	3275.0	26.9
Coffee	2607.4	16.9	Silver	993.2	8.2
Hides	1200.8	7.8	Hides	855.9	7.1
Silver	766.2	5.0	Tobacco	833.4	6.9
Live animals	546.3	3.5	Rubber	325.8	2.7

Source: José Antonio Ocampo, *Colombia y la economía mundial, 1830–1910* (Bogotá, 1984) Cuadro 2.7.

interior to journey to Jamaica to buy shipments and then to accompany them on the long, uncomfortable, often frustrating, journey by poled boat up the Magdalena River—a trip that might take heavily loaded boats anywhere from six to twelve weeks. The costs and difficulties of the import trade under these conditions limited entry into the import trade.

In the middle decades of the century these features of the import trade changed. By 1840, while a large proportion of New Granada's imports still came from Caribbean entrepots, much of it now came directly from England and France, indicating that at least some of the more substantial merchants in New Granada now had commercial relations with the supplying countries in Europe. A radical change occurred, however, between 1845 and 1855, when growing exports of tobacco, and secondarily cinchona bark and palm-fiber hats, began to fuel increased imports, and growing exports and imports supplied a flow of freight permitting the definitive establishment of steamboats on the Magdalena River.

From this time onward increasing numbers of importers in the interior were able to establish credit relationships with commercial houses in England and France. By 1848, at the port of Santa Marta, the value of goods coming directly from England was five times as great as that of those coming from the British Caribbean. Direct relations with commission houses in England and France meant that New Granadan importers could operate on a greater volume and with lower costs. The definitive establishment of steamboat transportation on the Magdalena did not end all problems with river transportation; steamboats ran aground and now and again exploded and burned, and frustrated importers often had trouble getting, and keeping, space on the steamboats. Nonetheless, steamboats permitted the carriage of goods with greater security and speed, and lower costs, than was possible with poled boats. With these increased efficiencies, the threshold for entry into the import trade was lowered and competition among importers increased.

Importers also became a stronger interest group in Bogotá, Medellín, and other commercial centers. In the early 1850s merchants began to complain about the existing ad valorem system of customs duties. The assessment of duties by value required that every package be opened for evaluation of the contents. This meant all imported goods had to be repackaged after passing through customs, which was costly to merchants and increased the chance of damage to goods in transit up the Magdalena River and over boggy mule trails in the interior. Merchants in the early 1850s campaigned for the adoption of a "gross weight" collection system, under which goods of the same category (e.g., textiles) but different qualities would all pay the same tax, the amount to be determined by the gross weight of the package. This method of taxation, by making it unnecessary to open packages in the customs house, would reduce the costs to merchants. It also offered advantages to the state, as this simpler system would reduce collection costs and would encourage more goods to be brought in legally rather than as contraband, thus improving the revenue yield of customs duties. The gross weight system had the support of merchants and the commerce-oriented bourgeoisie of all political colors. It was proposed in 1851 by Juan Nepomuceno Gómez, later secretary of finance under President Obando in 1854. In 1853 many Conservative or politically-colorless merchants in Antioquia and Bogotá were its most visible adherents. One of the more vigorous advocates of the gross weight system in 1853 was Leopoldo Borda, of a Conservative family, which at the time was responsible for one-quarter of all imported goods brought to Bogotá. Later, after General Mosquera decreed the establishment of the gross weight system in 1861, it was defended by the Liberal economic writers Aníbal Galindo and Miguel Samper.

While it is true that the gross weight system decreased the costs of customs collections both to merchants and the government, its adoption also implicitly reflected the contemporary bourgeoisie's devotion to commercial advantage at the expense of the interests of the poor. The gross weight system afflicted urban artisans by lowering duties on finished clothing. Contemporary critics also pointed out that by placing all textiles in the same category, and taxing them by weight, the gross weight system placed much higher duties by value on cheap cotton goods consumed by peasants than the finer textiles bought only by the affluent. In the late 1870s common cotton cloth might be taxed at 50 or 75 percent of its value, and machetes and other agricultural tools at more than 50 percent, while duties on silk might amount to as little as 4 percent of its value. Aníbal Galindo defended this anomalous situation with the seemingly cynical argument that, after all, the affluent purchased more imported luxuries than the poor did cheap clothing, so in the end the rich would pay their share. The collection of customs duties by gross weight continued in place well into the twentieth century, although with increasing refinements to reduce the inequities that were so characteristic of the era of Radical domination.

Commercial growth after mid-century sparked increased interest in developments directly related to the expansion of foreign trade, most particularly the establishment of commercial banks and the improvement of communications. From the 1820s onward Colombian leaders had promoted projects for a national bank, which might help to stabilize the government's credit position. None of these projects came to fruition, precisely because the government's fiscal condition and credit were so weak. The first enduring banking institutions, issuing credit-based bills, were private houses founded in Antioquia in the 1850s (Restrepo & Compañía of Medellín, 1854, and Botero Arango e Hijos of the city of Antioquia, 1858). The region's gold economy and commercial activity, as well as the economic culture of the region, undoubtedly contributed to the relative success of these firms. In 1864–1865 Bogotá's first incorporated commercial bank appeared, a branch of the British Bank of London, Mexico, and South America, one of whose palpable functions was the sale of letters of exchange on England to importers. This bank closed after two years, however, allegedly because of a pronounced propensity of its Colombian clients not to repay loans. Commercial banking became a widespread phenomenon in Colombia only in the 1870s, a decade in which note-issuing banks appeared in virtually all of the country's significant commercial centers. The Banco de Bogotá, which opened its doors in 1871, devoted much of its activity to the sale of letters of exchange to importers; indeed, in 1874 it was accused of monopolizing this activity in the capital. By 1876, two new banks had been established in Medellín (1873 and 1874); one each in Bucaramanga, Barranquilla, Cartagena, and Cali (1873–1874), two more in Bogotá in 1875; and another in Neiva (1875). On the one hand, the rapidity with which these banks sprang up testifies to a certain optimism about the country's economic future during a period of relative political peace. On the other hand, most of these banks suffered in the late 1870s from crises of confidence generated by a combination of civil war (1876–1877) and the decline of key export products, particularly tobacco. The Banco de Bogotá, one of the strongest of these institutions, had to suspend payments for at least five months because the civil war of 1876 prevented it from moving funds freely among its regional branches. Despite such contretemps, commercial banks continued to multiply after the civil war of 1876. In 1883 there were some two dozen note-issuing banks (not counting savings banks and branches of the Banco de Bogotá)—eight in Cundinamarca, seven in Antioquia, two each in Boyacá and Tolima, and one each in the states of Bolívar, Cauca, Magdalena, Panama, and Santander. Private banks as a whole went into crisis, and many closed, when, in the context of civil war, the Núñez government in 1885 issued a series of measures progressively requiring the use of bills issued by the National Bank and restricting the usability of those issued by the private banks.

The years of Radical dominance (1864–1880), in addition to initiating banking, were also a period of aspiration to major improvements in communications. Public concern focused primarily upon the development of routes, overland or by water, that would facilitate foreign trade. The Magdalena River remained the principal artery to the outside world, and in the interior highlands improving links with the river was a high priority. In Antioquia the trail from Medellín, through Rionegro and Marinilla, to Nare, established at the end of the colonial period, was the predominant route to the Magdalena during most of the nineteenth century. However, in the eastern highlands no single route served the interests of the various population centers strung along the mountain chain from Bogotá north into the State of Santander, and each subregion championed a route that most favored its development. In Santander, as of 1864, five different routes to the Magdalena had been projected. Similarly, at this time five distinct routes from Bogotá to the Magdalena were competing for public support. These two examples of competing projects in the Eastern Cordillera were reflective of a more general problem of developing a national policy establishing clear priorities among the various regional interests in the country as a whole.

Despite the Radicals' commitment to state autonomy, the central government under Radical control from 1864 to 1880 sought to develop a national policy for communications development. Manuel Murillo Toro, among the most committed of liberal federalist ideologues, as president of the State of Santander in 1857–1858 had gone so far as to proclaim that road construction and education should be left completely to private enterprise. But as national president in 1864 he recognized that improvements in transportation required the leadership and support of the central government. In that year the Congress formulated a national plan, authorizing the central government to borrow eight million pesos abroad, to be used either to buy stock in companies executing public works considered to be national priorities or to guarantee these companies a 7 percent return on the capital they invested. The 7 percent guaranty proved to be the standard formula adopted.

Although some contemporaries emphasized the need for developing priorities in transportation development, the Radicals of the 1860s and 1870s could not bring themselves to exclude the claims of any important region of the country. The national priorities proclaimed by Congress in 1864 called for, among other things, central government investment in projects connecting the Cauca Valley to the Pacific, Cúcuta to the Zulía River, Cundinamarca and Boyacá to the Meta River, and Bogotá, Santander, and Antioquia to the Magdalena River, as well as improvements in navigation of the Magdalena and Meta and in the ports of the Caribbean coast.

By 1871 the assemblage of projects had changed in several respects. Whereas in 1864 constructing wagon roads had been the goal for improvement in overland routes, by 1871 railways had become a conceivable alternative, at least in some places. Secondly, the legislators of 1871 sought to roll into one project a number of the competing regional schemes for linking the Eastern Cordillera to the Magdalena. The solution was a proposed Northern Railway (Ferrocarril del Norte), which would link Bogotá to the population centers of highland Boyacá and Santander before plunging down to the Magdalena Valley. This resolution of the problem proved excessively heroic. While it conciliated competing local aspirations, the projected Northern Railway proved too large and costly to be realized. Over the next three decades no more than 47 kilometers were constructed over the relatively flat plains north of Bogotá. Furthermore, although the Northern Railway totally failed in its object—to connect the greater part of the Eastern Cordillera with the Magdalena—the project was sufficiently grandiose to foster resentment on the Caribbean coast and in the Cauca Valley against the Radical leadership, most of whom were from the Eastern Cordillera. It is true that Radical-era legislation on transportation development paid some regard to favored projects of the Cauca and the Caribbean coast, and national funds, significant in the case of the Cauca, were expended on these projects. But Caucanos and Costeños could not help noticing that in the 1871 law 67 percent of the national funds for transportation priorities were to be committed to a single project, the Eastern Cordillera's Northern Railway.

Although some improvements were made in mule trails and wagon roads between the Magdalena and Bogotá in the 1870s, very little railway construction occurred. There were two significant advances in communications between 1864 and 1876. A telegraph network, which by comparison with railway construction required relatively little capital investment, was initiated. And a short railway, constructed from the Magdalena River port of Barranquilla to the ocean port of Sabanilla (1869–1870), by facilitating the movement of goods between the river and ocean ships, quickly established Barranquilla as Colombia's chief commercial port. Even as late as 1885, Colombia had only 286 kilometers (179 miles) of railway. Of this total, the longest single route, the Panama railway (80 kilometers), had been built long before (1850–1855) by a North American company because of a pressing U.S. need for an effective link to California. Colombia in 1904 still had only 465 kilometers (291 miles) of rail (now subtracting the Panama line, which was no longer part of Colombia).

Various problems contributed to the laggard pace of railway construction in Colombia. Construction costs were relatively high in the country's mountainous, tropical conditions. Whereas the cost of construction in the United States and Canada was about 18,000 dollars per kilometer, over largely mountainous routes in Colombia the cost was closer to 30,000 dollars per kilometer. Topography was not the only geographical challenge. Torrential rains made both construction and maintenance difficult. And disease and mortality among workers tended to be high in tropical lowland zones.

But Colombia's railways could have been constructed more quickly had these enterprises been able to win more ample financing. Colombia's weak revenues and its history of nonpayment of foreign debt obligations made it a poor candidate for foreign loans. But substantial foreign money would have been invested directly in railway construction if the country had some important resource in which world markets were vitally interested. A relative lack of external investment appears to reflect, above all, that there was little in the Colombian economy to attract foreign interest. Foreign capital constructed railways much more rapidly in Argentina and northern Mexico, not only because the terrain was more favorable but also because these places had resources that compelled extraction. Ultimately, in the first decades of the twentieth century, coffee helped to supply the freight necessary to get at least a fragmentary national rail network constructed. But, to the degree that there now exists a national market in Colombia, it is primarily because of automotive transportation.

Along with a burst of commercial banking and at least the beginnings of railway construction, the years of Radical dominance (1864–1880) were also a period of renewed efforts in public education, both at the university level and in primary instruction. The Liberals of mid-century, like the earlier generation of the 1820s, believed strongly in the importance of education as the foundation of republican politics as well as a fount of civilization. Between 1849 and 1853, however, Liberals were somewhat distracted from the mission of education by the revolutionary reforms they were undertaking. Indeed, radical Liberal policies of the early 1850s tended to undermine earlier attempts to strengthen higher education. During the 1830s and 1840s government policies had sought to acquaint educated men with the natural sciences by requiring the study of scientific subjects as a prerequisite to university study of law or medicine. Also, in 1848, under the first presidency of General Tomás Cipriano de Mosquera, a military college offering polytechnical education was established; during its brief existence (1848–1854) this institution produced the country's first small corps of civil engineers.

After the Liberals captured the presidency, their early efforts at democratization weakened the thrust toward science in higher education and interrupted the training of engineers. In 1850 the Liberals struck a blow against elitism by declaring that university degrees were not necessary for practicing professions. As this reduced the incentive for degrees, enrollment in secondary schools and universities declined. Further, because of the fiscal crisis produced by the decentralization of revenues in 1850, the national government was not able adequately to finance the three *colegios nacionales*, with which the Liberals replaced the universities, with the result that scientific instruction suffered. Many Liberals were also suspicious of the Colegio Militar; they regarded it as an elitist institution and saw it as strengthening the military at a time that Liberals, as well as many Conservatives, were bent on reducing or even eliminating the standing army. Accordingly, they allowed the Colegio Militar to die in 1854.

Renewed efforts to strengthen public higher education began in January 1867, when General Mosquera, during his last presidency, decreed the establishment of the Instituto Nacional de Ciencias y Artes, through which he aimed to resurrect the military school as well as the academic study of the natural sciences. The Radical-led coup that overthrew President Mosquera in May 1867 ended this initiative, but the following September the Radicals themselves moved to establish a National University with a good deal of emphasis on the natural sciences and engineering. The National University as conceived by the Radicals included instruction in the traditionally established faculties of law and medicine. But the university also created new faculties in the natural sciences, engineering, and the manual arts and crafts and encouraged students to enroll in these programs. The several dozen students who came with scholarships allotted to the various states were required to specialize in one of these scientific or technical programs. Other students in the university were not restricted to the scientific or engineering faculties. Nonetheless, during the 1870s and early 1880s large proportions of students were enrolled in natural sciences and engineering. The totals in these two fields exceeded those in law and medicine together in the early years, and subsequently remained comparable. Presumably the choice of these new careers reflected a perception of increased opportunities in science and engineering as Colombia entered the railway era. As the numbers of students in the university increased in the 1880s and 1890s, the proportion studying law and medicine also increased. However, as of 1890, 62 were enrolled in mathematics, civil, or mining engineering, with 144 in a merged faculty of medicine and natural sciences. (There were some 118 in the more traditional, more politically oriented faculty of law.)

Paralleling the establishment of the National University by the Liberal-dominated government in Bogotá, the Conservative government of the State of Antioquia in 1871 turned its provincial colegio into the University of Antioquia. In 1874 this university created a school of civil engineering, which in 1887 became an independent National School of Mines, which, despite its name, produced civil as well as mining engineers.

Along with the reconstruction of university education in the 1870s, the Radical governments also attempted major improvements in the quality and quantity of primary education. When Manuel Ancízar toured the northern provinces with the national geographic survey in 1850–1851, one of his principal concerns in each community was the state of primary education, in his view the key to "civilizing" New Granadan society. Although Ancízar was pleased to find some good local schools, he often was discouraged by the lack of effective primary education in rural communities. (Among other things, Ancízar noted that peasant fathers resisted sending their sons to school, believing formal education would ruin them for farm labor.)

In 1870, the national government began to promote the establishment of normal schools in each of the nine states—the first systematic attempt at teacher training. This effort was supplemented by various publications providing helpful materials to teachers and students alike, and authorities tried to supply schools with the texts and maps that they generally had lacked. School enrollments nearly doubled between 1871 and 1876, but sagged again after that time.

The school reform movement came a cropper in large part because of religious objections. The Organic Decree of Public Primary Instruction, issued by the government of President Eustorgio Salgar in November 1870, aroused proclerical anger from the outset by declaring that the public schools themselves could not provide religious education, although provision might be made by parents for priests to provide religious instruction. Such an arrangement, apparently treating religion as marginal to primary education, offended many clergy and Conservatives. The issue of religious instruction in the schools was further inflamed when the assembly of the State of Cundinamarca actually prohibited clergy from teaching religion in the schools. Archbishop Vicente Arbeláez, supported by five other bishops, sought to avoid conflict over the issue by encouraging clergy to teach classes in religion within the framework established by the government. But some other clergy, most notably Bishop Carlos Bermúdez in Popayán, opted for intransigence. Bishop Bermúdez in 1872 declared that he would excommunicate any parents who sent their children to public schools. Two years later he forbade students in the normal schools from taking part in processions in Holy Week. Pious laity organized in Catholic Societies vowed resistance to the government schools and established primary instruction by loyal Catholics. Catholic hostility to the Radicals' school reform was further inflamed when the national government, with remarkable lack of foresight, brought German teachers, seven of whom were Protestant, to staff the state normal schools. Religiously inspired resistance was so strong that the German normal school directors soon had to return to Germany.

The conflict between the government and clergy in the Cauca over religion in the schools became the banner under which Caucano Conservatives marched in rebellion against the national government in 1876. Other tensions also underlay this conflict. Liberals at this time had become deeply divided between Radicals and Independents, the latter supporting Rafael Núñez for the presidency against the Radical Aquileo Parra. In the Cauca, as in some other places, Independent Liberals formed an alliance with Conservatives in support of Núñez. Conservatives were angered when the Radical governor of the State of Cauca nullified the state's vote for the presidency, thus sealing the manipulated victory of the Radical candidate, Aquileo Parra. But religion provided the emotional energy for the Conservative rebellion. As Liberals said at the time, they knew that Conservatives were readying for civil war when they began to wave the flag of religion. Although Radicals succeeded in "electing" their candidate and defeating the Conservative rebellion in 1876, their regime in effect was morally broken. In 1878 General Julian Trujillo, a Núñez sympathizer who had crushed the Conservative rebellion in the Cauca, was elected president. His two-year term proved merely a way station to the triumph of Núñez in 1880, which marked the definitive end of the Radical regime.

11

Neither Liberty nor Order, 1875–1903

In the last decades of the nineteenth century enduring symbols of the Colombian nation finally were adopted: the national anthem, the coat of arms, and the constitution of 1886, which although often reformed, was not replaced until 1991. In the national coat of arms the tricolored national flag, which dates from the time of independence, is wrapped around the shield, over which the Andean condor poses with the legend "Liberty and Order" held in his claws. The shield itself is divided horizontally into three sections representing, from top to bottom, two cornucopias, a Frigian cap, and the Isthmus of Panama.

But the country has been poorer than the cornucopias suggest, and poverty has restricted the liberty symbolized by the Frigian cap. The loss of the Isthmus of Panama in 1903 revealed the debility of the state, which also has restrained the broadening of constitutional liberties. In this period neither liberty, fervently defended by federalist, Radical Liberals, nor order, supported by centralist, Catholic Conservatives, were obtained, nor liberty and order together, as hoped for in the constitution of 1886.

The period opened with the irreparable division of the Liberal Party in the presidential election of 1875–1876 and ended with Liberal defeat in the War of the Thousand Days (1899–1902), whose most important consequence was the loss of Panama. A civil war in 1885 made possible a radical change in the constitution in 1886 and Colombia moved from a federal to a centralized republic.

The periods between the wars were characterized by extreme factionalism within each of the two parties, particularly in the governing party. The Liberals were most divided between 1875 and 1886, when the party passed from Radical hegemony to the rise of rival factions that came together with the name Independents. In 1878, for the first time since they had overthrown General Mosquera in 1867, the Radicals lost the presidency. In this year the Independent Liberals and the Conservatives formed an alliance, which reached its zenith during the civil war of 1885 and the elaboration of the new constitutional system in 1884–1887. At that point there emerged a "national party," which the Conservatives ended up dominating.

In the 1890s many Independents returned to the Liberal fold, and the Conservative Party divided into two groups—the governing Nationalists and the dissident Historical Conservatives. The Historical Conservatives formed tactical alliances with the Liberals, who themselves suffered both old divisions and some new ones, the latter stemming from a generational

Map 6 Colombia, political divisions (1861–1903). From Helen Delpar,
Red against Blue: The Liberal Party in Colombian Politics, 1863–1899
(Tuscaloosa, AL, 1981).

breach. One point of agreement between the Historical Conservatives and Liberals was their opposition to the "virus of socialism," which they saw in government policies, principally that which required acceptance of the National Bank's paper money.

The period from 1878 to 1900 is known as the Regeneration. The name derives from a phrase of Rafael Núñez, the arbiter of Colombian politics from 1874 until his death in 1894, although his influence would weigh heavily decades afterward. In 1878 Núñez summarized his criticism of the Radical period, saying it had left the country with the choice of either "fundamental regeneration or catastrophe." In the following years he elaborated: Federalism and and doctrinaire liberalism had carried the country to catastrophe, from which it could escape only by establishing "scientific peace." The country would need a centralist constitution that would recognize Catholicism as a core element of social cohesion. But the Regeneration itself ended catastrophically in the War of the Thousand Days. In 1900, amid the conflict, the Historical Conservatives carried out a coup d'etat that ended the Regeneration.

Underlying the factionalism and the instability were the violent fluctuations in demand for the principal export products, except for gold. The fall of tobacco exports (1878–1882), the decline of the market for cinchona bark (1876–1877) and its complete collapse after 1883, and the coffee depression after 1896 caused unemployment, discontent, and instability, particularly in the regions that produced these products.

In this setting there occurred an alteration in the relative importance of the various regions of the country. Antioquia, the center of gold mining and dynamic colonization in the nineteenth century, in the twentieth century developed as a prosperous coffee belt. Its elite from an early point had become concentrated in Medellín and its gold provided stability. By contrast, the upper Cauca region centering on Popayán and the State of Bolívar headed by Cartagena declined. Popayán and its surrounding region were overshadowed by the rise of Cali and the Cauca Valley, while Barranquilla now eclipsed both Cartagena and Santa Marta as the most efficient transfer point between the Magdalena River and the Caribbean. Santander, the heartland of Liberalism, also descended in the nation's politics. There, with a declining economy in the southern part of the state and dynamism in the north, a notable movement of population occurred, from the southern regions of Vélez, San Gil, and El Socorro northward to Bucaramanga and Cúcuta. Bogotá, however, maintained, and perhaps reinforced, its position as capital city.

TO BECOME CIVILIZED

The *Anuario Estadístico de Colombia, 1875* and the *Estadística de Colombia* (1876) testify to the hopes of the educated upper classes for the effective establishment of liberal constitutionalism and the growth of foreign trade, the two faces of the coin of progress. The authors of these reports emphasized their effort to achieve some statistical rigor, a characteristic of "the great civilized nations." The latter were the countries that figured most notably in Colombia's export and import trade—Great Britain, France, the United States, and Germany. From these countries radiated the spirit of the time. To these same nations the larger merchants, as well as not a few politicians and literati, traveled at least once in their lives, sometimes accompanied by their families. There merchants had their agents; there, principally in Paris, Colombian literati had their books printed.

By underlining the deficiencies of the statistics they presented, the authors of the republic's first ample statistical summaries made clear the enormous distance that, in their belief, separated Colombia from the civilized nations. This was palpable in matters of justice, public order, schools, and transportation. The backwardness was immediately recognizable in the precariousness of public administration and in the difficulty of collecting, compiling, and presenting statistical information. They noted, for example, that no local or national government had managed to organize a system of civil registry that, according to the law, ought to replace parish records of baptisms, marriages, and deaths. But they blamed this latter failure on popular religiosity rather than state inefficiency. The country's division into nine states, uneven in economic strength, size of population, and population density, perhaps accentuated this fragility. (See Table 11.1.)

The economic strength of the states affected their stability. Santander was destabilized in the 1870s and 1880s by fluctuations in the international market for cinchona bark, while gold provided Antioquia with a steady and

Table 11.1 The nine states of the United States of Colombia, circa 1870

State	Population	Populated Areas, sq. kms	Population Density*	Unsettled Areas, sq. kms	Employees of States
Antioquia	365,900	33,000	11.1	26,000	493
Bolívar	241,704	40,000	6.0	30,000	407
Boyacá	498,541	30,500	16.3	55,800	268
Cauca	435,078	63,000	6.9	603,800	474
Cundinamarca	413,658	23,100	17.9	183,300	313
Magdalena	88,928	25,000	3.9	44,800	146
Panama	224,032	36,100	6.2	46,500	303
Santander	433,178	18,500	23.4	23,700	555
Tolima	230,891	36,300	6.4	11,400	192
Total	2,931,910	305,500	9.6	1,025,300	3,151

*Inhabitants per populated square kilometer.
Source: *Anuario Estadístico de Colombia, 1875* (Bogotá, 1875).

rising income. The states' various political systems also had an effect on stability. The state constitution of Antioquia was exceptional in providing the state president with a four-year term, with the possibility of reelection. In almost all the other states the president or governor had a two-year term and could not be reelected. Partly for this reason Antioquia enjoyed greater continuity than other states. It had a single president, Pedro J. Berrío, between 1864 and 1873, and six between 1873 and 1885, including brief periods of three Radicals (1877–1880) imposed on Conservative Antioquia after its capitulation in the civil war of 1876. By contrast the State of Bolívar had twenty-four changes of government from 1873 to 1885, and Magdalena ten.

There were only about 4500 government employees, national and state. Such a small number could not administer the country effectively. Power flowed through traditional, informal networks. The national State could not be, above all at the local level, more than one of the expressions of these familial and clientelistic networks. By 1916 the number of public employees had increased to 42,700. But, even then, in the overwhelming majority of the municipalities there were not enough "personnel for the municipal council, the mayor, the district judge, the revenue administrator . . . and even less for committees to oversee road construction, nor anyone to grab for the collection and distribution of revenues, nor anyone who dared to collect the property tax nor any other tax from powerful people with political influence, [such as] the hacienda owner who lives in the capital of the Republic or of the Department," as Rufino Gutiérrez wrote in his survey of the country's localities conducted in 1917.

THE FEDERAL SYSTEM GIVES WAY TO CENTRALIST REGENERATION

In the 1870s the federalist system and the libertarian tonic of the 1863 constitution had begun to show their limitations and contradictions, even for the very Radicals who had consecrated them in constitution and law. In 1870 the Radicals sought to fulfill the republican ideal through a nationally organized program to improve primary education. But under the federal system, in states that had no effective center of power and were divided regionally, as was the case in the Cauca and Santander, it was easier for the clergy, brandishing Pius IX's encyclical *The Syllabus* (1864), to instigate war.

In the case of the railways, the regionalist conflict was more complex: The Liberal bulwarks of the coast and the Cauca could not accept a policy that gave 67 percent of the national budget for transportation development to the Northern Railway, a costly plan to connect Bogotá, across a long mountainous trajectory, to Bucaramanga before descending to the Magdalena River. This project, they thought, disproportionately rewarded the loyalty of the states of Cundinamarca, Boyacá, and Santander, dominated by the "oligarchy of the Radical Olympus."

This regionalist feeling divided the Liberals in the electoral campaign of 1875, in which Rafael Núñez of Cartagena was pitted against the official candidate of the Radicals, Aquileo Parra of Santander, a strong proponent of the Northern Railway. The electoral campaign ended in a civil war among Liberals on the Caribbean coast. Panama and Bolivar declared for Núñez and against the government in Bogotá. Finding a deep division among the Liberals of the State of Magdalena, the national president, Santiago Pérez, sent troops there to make sure that the Radical candidate Parra won that state's electoral vote. As neither of the candidates received a majority of the votes of the states, the election had to go to the national Congress, where Parra was elected. Meanwhile, Núñez, having been denied the presidency, in 1876 was elected governor of the state of Bolívar.

In 1876 conflict over public education led to a religiously inspired Conservative rebellion, called in some places "the war of the parish priests." The Liberals temporarily united to defeat the Conservatives, which they did after eleven months of combat. But for the Radicals it was a Pyrrhic victory. During this war began the uncontainable rise of a Liberal coalition that brought together Mosqueristas of the Cauca, Independent Liberals from Santander, and Núñistas from the coast. This coalition would end up headed by Núñez. In 1878 the coalition brought General Julian Trujillo, a Cauca Mosquerista and the victorious leader of Liberal forces in the 1876 war, to the national presidency. The decline of the Radicals, aggravated by the death of their long-time leader, Manuel Murillo Toro, in 1880, eased the way to the end of the federation. In 1880 Núñez, who would lead the way to a new, more centralized, system, was elected to his first term as national president.

It is said that when Victor Hugo learned of the constitution of Rionegro, he exclaimed that it was conceived for a country of angels. Perhaps for this reason, the constitution had not been in place for four years before one of the principal Radical leaders asked for its reform. One of the inconsistencies of the angelic document had to do with maintaining public order. The Rionegro Constitution was frequently compared with the United States Constitution, which stipulated the obligation of the Union to protect the states in case of any domestic violence. But in the United States of Colombia, an 1867 law declared that in case of civil conflict within a state, "the Government of the Union will maintain relations with the constitutional government [of the state in question] until its authority was no longer recognized in the territory of the state, and it will recognize the new Government and will enter into official relations with it, as soon as it has organized itself according to the principles of the popular, elective, representative, alternating and responsible system." Núñez, soon after becoming the national president, proposed a law to the Congress that would authorize the central government to intervene in the states in grave cases of public order that could threaten national peace. In that same year (1880), the Congress approved this measure.

Núñez's fundamental criticisms focused on the political culture, characterized by violence, inflexibility, intransigence, and intolerance. One of the distinguishing marks of the Independents in this period was their change of tone on religion. Little by little they gained the confidence of Conservatives and the Church. In a peculiar version of the positivism that pervaded much of Latin America at the time, Núñez concluded that popular religiosity was an instrument of cultural integration and social cohesion, so that the anticlerical rhetoric of earlier Liberalism was obsolete. The Independents believed that the Regeneration project was an advanced form of Colombian Liberalism. Santander had established the bases for administrative organization of the republic. Under the leadership of Murillo Toro, Radicalism had undertaken the final struggle against the vestiges of the colonial socioeconomic order. Without renouncing these legacies, the Regeneration would bring a new order of tolerance and concord, necessary to embark upon the material development of the country.

On assuming the presidency in 1880 Núñez appointed Conservatives to significant positions and slowly began to form an unusual bipartisan alliance. To succeed him in 1882 Núñez chose Francisco J. Zaldúa, a prestigious septuagenarian jurist of moderately Liberal antecedents, in the belief that Zaldúa would continue his policies in harmony with a Congress that had Independent majorities. The Radicals, however, tried to seduce Zaldúa with the hope that, under his presidency, Radical and Independent Liberals might reunite. The death of Zaldúa aggravated the problem because his successor, José E. Otálora, succumbed to the temptation of a possible Radical candidacy. Thus, during the two-year term of Zaldúa and Otálora the relations between Independents and Radicals became poisoned. The denouement came with the election of Núñez to a second presidential term (1884–1886) as a candidate of the National Party.

In 1884 Núñez confronted the kind of regional conspiracy that he knew quite well and had taken part in when he was a federalist. A muddled succession to the presidency of the State of Santander at the end of 1884 led to an armed uprising by Radicals against a new bipartisan regional alliance that was imposing its candidate. This episode, which was being watched by politicians all over the country, culminated in Liberal rebellions in various states, particularly on the Caribbean coast. At the beginning of 1885, Núñez and the Conservatives agreed upon the creation of a national reserve army, which eventually would deal with these revolts. Once the Radicals had been defeated, Núñez announced that the constitution of 1863 had died and began a new constitutional process, which concluded with a new constitution in 1886.

The war of 1885 convinced the Regenerator of the need to give a new turn to constitutional government. He found a partner in Miguel Antonio Caro, one of the most combative of the doctrinaire Catholic-Conservative writers. Now Núñez could repudiate federalism: ". . . [I]n addition to an external boundary we created nine internal boundaries, with nine different constitutions, nine costly bureaucratic hierarchies, nine armies, nine agitations of all kinds." The federalist Liberals had consecrated maximum liberties without considering minimum means of protecting them. The Liberals' absolute freedom of the press was a parody of liberty. The laxity of the penal system encouraged crime. The ideological disputes of the Radical oligarchy consumed the nation's energies in anachronistic conflicts like those relating to the Church.

The dramatic defeat of the Liberals in the 1885 war left the way open for a drastic change in the structure of the State. In September 1885 the government convoked a Council of Delegates to draft a new constitution. The council was composed of eighteen delegates—each state having two, one Conservative and one Independent, appointed by the state president. In November 1885 the council approved the bases of the reform, which were then submitted to the municipalities for ratification. Finally it was issued in August 1886 and the council unanimously elected Núñez president for the period 1886–1892.

The constitution, although often reformed, had a long life. Issued "in the name of God, supreme source of all authority," it declared the Catholic religion to be the essential element of nationality and social order, while at the same time recognizing religious toleration. The constitution sought to centralize power in the national government and to strengthen the hand of the president. The president's term was lengthened to six years, and the Congress was authorized to grant special powers to the president, in addition to the extraordinary powers permitted by the norms of states of siege. The sovereign states were converted into departments, with governors appointed by the president. The nation recovered control of mines, saltworks, and those public lands it had ceded to the states. The 1886 constitution reestablished the death penalty and prohibited commerce in or bearing firearms, while a series of laws restricted freedom of the press and public assembly.

One of the fundamental aspects of the new system was the alliance of Church and State. The Concordat of 1887 and the additional covenant of 1892 brought the restoration of full privileges to the Catholic Church. The Church obtained financial compensation for the seizure and sale of Church properties. The legal monopoly of Catholic marriage, affecting the persons and properties of all married persons, was restored. Through its educational activities, its control of school texts, the press, the confessional, and the pulpit, the clergy inculcated political and social values that would weaken the effects of liberal secularization. As a consequence, in some provinces local conflicts intensified.

The Church was beginning to recover after the blows suffered from the Mosquera decrees of 1861. In 1891 there were 542 parish priests in the archdiocesis of Bogotá. Religious communities, both male and female, had increased notably. There were 469 friars and 731 nuns, a substantial proportion of whom were foreigners—two-fifths of the friars, one-fifth of the nuns. Most members of religious orders were educating the progeny of the elites, although some religious communities focused on the popular classes. A number of male religious worked in frontier missions, while some nuns were dedicated to work in hospitals.

In the 1890s foreign priests who arrived under the agreements of the Concordat had a decisive influence in defining the political profile of the Church. These foreign clergy had lived through and survived, variously, the Bismarckian Kulturkampf, the anticlericalism of Italian unification, French republicanism, the crusading spirit of the Carlist wars in Spain, and the secularist campaign of Eloy Alfaro in Ecuador. The reactionary attitudes of these foreign clergy fell on fertile ground. The anti-Catholic affronts of the Liberals were alive in the collective memory of many Colombian Conservatives.

Not all the immigrant religious were so politically oriented. The Sisters of Charity of Tours, who arrived in 1873, at the height of the Radical period, dedicated themselves preferentially to the poor and the sick, a mission that tended to distance them from political passions. Nevertheless, in a country so politicized, political wars on occasion compelled their charitable attentions. In the two weeks of the decisive Battle of Palonegro, near Bucaramanga (May 1900) in the War of the Thousand Days, these nuns attended the wounded of both sides, Liberals as well as Conservatives. After the battle, hundreds of bodies lay on the field decomposing; the wounded abandoned by the Liberals in their precipitous flight could be heard moaning; women, children, and the aged wandered about looking for family members; and the nuns aided everyone.

The Regeneration inspired a conservative nationalist current with a markedly anti-liberal and anti-Yankee tenor. Applying the corporativist principles of Leo XIII's encyclical *De Rerum Novarum* (1891), this nationalism had an anticapitalist tint. This ideological bent had a long-term influence, carrying through the first half of the twentieth century.

The Regeneration could not resolve the problem of regional inequalities and the conflicts that ensued from them. In 1888 the government sought to reorganize the national territory, with the purpose of weakening the states (newly turned to departments.) It proposed dividing the Cauca, Bolívar, and Antioquia. It found support for this idea from Conservatives in Manizales and Santa Fe de Antioquia (in the case of the department of Antioquia), in Barranquilla with regard to Bolívar, and in Pasto with respect to the Cauca. However, elites in Medellin, Popayán, and Cartagena vigorously resisted, and the issue threatened the unity of government supporters. This question remained alive and finally was resolved in the first decade of the twentieth century. By 1912 the eight departments remaining after the secession of Panama had been split into fourteen. (See Table 11.2.)

Government centralization made the fiscal deficit more acute and aggravated conflict over the distribution of public expenditures. The national government, for example, assumed the obligation of guaranteeing public order and thus had to sustain a larger national army, which rose to 6500 men on average, and had to be reequipped. It also took charge of the judicial branch, the development of navigation and railways, and the payment of

Table 11.2 Political-administrative division, 1886–1912

Departments, 1886	Departments, 1912	Intendencies	Comisarías
Antioquia	Antioquia, Caldas	—	Urabá
Bolívar	Bolívar, Atlántico		
Boyacá	Boyacá		Arauca
Cauca	Cauca, Nariño, Valle	Chocó	Caquetá, Putumayo, Juradó, Vaupés
Cundinamarca	Cundinamarca	Meta	
Magdalena	Magdalena		La Guajira
Santander	Santander, Santander del Norte		
Tolima	Tolima, Huila	—	—

Source: *Censo de población* (Bogotá, 1912).

compensation to the Church as required by the Concordat, as well as responsibility for the foreign debt.

To provide for "administrative decentralization," the national government permitted the departments to have various taxes rather similar to those enjoyed by the previous states. However, the central government prohibited the departments from collecting duties on goods transferred across their boundaries (as the states had done). To compensate the departments for consequent decreases in revenue, the national government for a time agreed to distribute among the departments 25 percent of all increases in import duties. (In 1896, because of its fiscal penury, the central government had to renege on this commitment.)

If the national government provided some revenues to the departments, it also redistributed expenses. Thus in 1892 the basic costs of primary instruction were transferred to the departments; the Nation retained responsibility only for secondary and university education.

As the Regeneration became increasingly conservative, with the centralized constitution of 1886 and the embrace of the Church in the Concordat of 1887, Independent Liberals increasingly became alienated from the regime. With Independent Liberals no longer active in the government, political problems after 1888 stemmed from divisions among Conservatives. The death of Núñez in 1894, followed a few months later by that of the able Carlos Holguín, left the ultra-Conservative Vice President Miguel Antonio Caro in charge. Caro's rigidity, the instability of the export economy, and fiscal pressures contributed to the regime's misfortunes and its final collapse amid the civil war of 1899–1903.

Elections marked the rhythm of public life of the Regeneration, even though only supporters of the government took part in them. With the exception of the delegation from Antioquia, Liberals had no representation in Congress. Elections ritualized disputes within the government party, disputes that were of the same types as in earlier times—personalist, regionalist, generational; tactical skirmishes with little substance. Nonetheless, electoral activity continued to absorb the attention of political elites. The Porfirian regime in Mexico was a model for many in the Regeneration, but the Porfirian ideal of "less politics and more administration" had no place in the mentality of local political machines. As under the federation, electoral campaigns occurred continually. Every two years there were elections of municipal councillors and deputies to assemblies; every four years members of the Chamber of Representatives were chosen, and every six years the electors who would designate the president and the vice president. Departmental assemblies elected senators every two years. If the Regeneration, with its centralism and its concentration of power in the hands of the president, deliberately sought political demobilization, the electoral laws, which fostered an unending succession of campaigns, and the customs of municipal political machines had a contrary effect. Consequently, the stability so much desired by the Regenerators proved impossible to attain.

During the 1890s, disputes between Historical Conservatives and Nationalists became accentuated. The Historical Conservatives shared with many Liberals a mutual commitment to foreign trade. The Liberals also split. A peace-oriented faction, mainly the remnants of the old Radical oligarchy, looked to alliance with the Historical Conservatives. Younger, more aggressive Liberals, however, pressed for war against the Nationalist regime. However, the differences between the two Liberal factions were not clear-cut: The older group also prepared for war, while the younger one did not completely reject the idea of coalitions with dissident Conservatives.

For many government supporters the principal issue was the continuation of Caro in the presidency. With crises in the coffee market and in the government's fiscal situation in the background in 1896, the question of the presidential succession deepened divisions between the Historical Conservatives and the Nationalists. The Historical Conservatives formed tacit alliances with the peace-oriented Liberals, in the hope of showing that the liberal constitutionalist ideal of alternation of power could be fulfilled in Colombia.

The play of tactics produced a comedic finale. Caro renounced the idea of reelection and pulled out of his sleeve, as candidates for the presidency and vice presidency, two venerable lawyers, Manuel A. Sanclemente and José Manuel Marroquín, whose combined ages totaled 155 years. The country duly elected them for the period 1898–1904.

Amid an acute commercial depression, the political elite moved irreversibly down the road to war. The Liberals' war faction rebelled in October 1899. The next day, the government followed the established routine for such occasions. It gave departmental governors both civil and military authority, with the power to decree forced loans and expropriations, which were levied on the more affluent Liberals and in the Liberal localities where the "authors, accomplices, supporters and sympathizers" of the revolution lived. This pattern, common in Colombia's civil wars, reinforced party identities; it divided Colombians along party lines more than along those of socioeconomic classes. All shared the costs of the war, although perhaps the powerful, whose property and income were affected by party enemies, were more intensely resentful than the poor.

The conflict lasted three years. It confirmed the saying that war is the continuation of politics by other means. In this case, factional politics continued during the war among both Liberals and Conservatives. In 1900, Vice President Marroquín, urged on by the Historical Conservatives, carried out one of the few coups d'etat in Colombian history.

After six months of conventional warfare, the war broke up into a series of guerrilla skirmishes. In 1902, when the Liberals had been defeated in the rest of the country, their fortunes revived in Panama, whose interior they dominated. Accordingly, the unconditional surrender of the Liberals occurred in Panama somewhat later than in the rest of the country.

The war provided more anecdotal texture to the mythology of the two parties in the twentieth century. The economic elites exaggerated its disastrous effects. The most important consequence was the loss of Panama. That story is simple. First, Panama had a special status within Colombian federalism because the isthmus was physically separated from the rest of the nation. And because of its importance as a potential transit point between the Atlantic and the Pacific, it was the one part of Colombia that was of great interest to the most powerful nations in the Atlantic world. Federalism in Panama took flight in the middle of the nineteenth century when the isthmus became an important route from the east coast of the United States to California at the time of the gold rush. The Panama Railway and the arrival of hundreds of North American adventurers and businessmen gave the white oligarchy of Panama City a feeling of their own importance. There were, however, ties of other Colombians with Panamanians—notably the influence of Liberals among blacks in the slums of Panama City and the influence of Colombian Conservatives among the landowners of the interior.

These Colombian equilibria were broken by the announcement in 1879 of a contract to construct a canal across the isthmus and the formation of a French company directed by Ferdinand de Lesseps, already famous for his creation of the Suez Canal. De Lesseps began construction in 1882. However, he proceeded on the basis of the fatal assumption that a canal over the Isthmus of Panama could and should be cut through at sea level, as had been the case at Suez. In addition to this mistake, the company was ruined in 1889 by the worst political scandal of the Third Republic. In 1890, 1893, and 1900 the Colombian government made successive ten-year extensions of the contract with the appropriately named New French Company. The third occurred at a time when the War of the Thousand Days had reached the isthmus. At this time separatist sentiments and international interests in an autonomous Panama were circulating with increasing intensity.

Meanwhile in 1899–1900 the government of the United States decided to build the canal. It acquired the rights from the New French Company and signed a treaty with Colombia in 1903. The Colombian Senate rejected the treaty on the ground that several clauses violated national sovereignty. What followed was a conspiracy of diverse interests, which ended with the declaration of Panamanian independence, under the protection of the United States navy, and the recognition of the new republic by the United States in November 1903.

The men of the Regeneration called themselves Nationalists. Nationalism had at this time a peculiar meaning. The nationalists were men of order. The mentality of the Colombian elite could not subscribe to a nationalism based on the mestizo populace, or on an appreciation of its values. It could not conceive an image of a national culture compatible with modernity or the changes occurring in the broader world. Conservative nationalism tended to mean either a return to Hispanic foundations or, a little later, the affirmation of patrimonial rights. The Hispanicist nationalists stressed the importance of Roman Catholicism, the Spanish language, and the institutions implanted by the Spaniards in the colonial period. The other conservative nationalists asserted the preeminent rights of the state to subsoil mineral rights as against foreign mining and oil interests. But neither variant of nationalism proved able to prevail in Colombia's difficult relations with the United States regarding Panama and, somewhat later, oil.

EXPORTS AND COLOMBIAN DEVELOPMENT

At the beginning of the twentieth century Colombia's development lagged behind even much of Latin America. Whether measured in literacy; in the construction of railways, roads, and bridges; in the improvement of ports; or in urbanization or the number of banks, Colombia remained among the less developed countries of the region.

Exports had grown significantly in percentage terms between 1850 and 1882, but starting from a very low base. According to calculations of José Antonio Ocampo, between 1835–1838 and 1905–1910 Colombia's exports per capita increased by 110 percent and their purchasing power by 170 percent. For the years 1874–1910 Ocampo establishes five subperiods: (1) recession and crisis (1874–1877), (2) bonanza (1878–1882), (3) severe depression and recuperation (1883–1892), (4) bonanza (1893–1898) and severe depression (1898–1910).

The data in Table 11.3, which, for the years 1875–1891 present figures for annual averages of exports and imports, suggest that there were continuous positive trade balances. However, these average figures mask the considerable instability of the year-to-year values of imports and exports. (See Table 11.4.) In any case, the volume of imports inevitably responded to changes in the volume of exports. Declines in sales of exports forced the volume of imports down, which in turn brought a drop in collections of customs duties. And when customs duties fell, fiscal crisis ensued because customs col-

Table 11.3 Colombian exports and imports, 1875–1910 (mean annual values in thousands of gold pesos)

	1875–1878	1878–1881	1881–1883	1888–1891	1898	1905	1906–1910
Exports	10,105	13,689	15,431	12,165	19,154	17,216	15,542
Imports	7923	10,755	11,930	12,119	11,052	12,282	12,942

Source: Based on José Antonio Ocampo, *Colombia y la economía mundial, 1830–1910* (Bogotá, 1984), pp. 100–101, 143.

lections were overwhelmingly the most important source of revenue for the national government. Two other significant revenues (from salt and the Panama Railway) did not represent more than a quarter of central government income. And other revenues had high collection costs, in contrast with customs duties. The critical importance of customs duties to government revenues was generally recognized—to the extent that seizing customs houses was the first goal of any group rebelling against the government.

When customs collections, and thus total revenues, fell, the government's alternatives were limited and disagreeable. It could suspend payments of salaries of government employees or fail to make payments to holders of the internal debt—in either case weakening loyalty to the government. Or the government might try to borrow money, under onerous terms, mortgaging future customs duties as a guarantee on the loans.

Given the instability of the values of Colombia's exports, and hence of its imports, and given the national government's heavy dependence on the taxation of foreign trade, it can be readily seen how fluctuations in the ex-

Table 11.4 Composition of Colombian exports, 1875–1910 (percentages of total value of exports)

Products	1875–1878	1878–1881	1881–1883	1888–1891	1898	1905	1906–1910
Gold*	24.0	19.1	18.7	26.9	17.4	14.1	20.4
Coffee	22.3	21.4	16.9	34.3	49.0	39.5	37.2
Tobacco	13.3	7.5	1.2	6.9	8.3	3.3	3.0
Cinchona	17.5	25.4	30.9	0.3	—	0.1	—
Other agricultural products†	13.3	19.1	17.8	19.1	16.6	35.0	24.0
Other‡	8.6	7.5	14.5	12.5	8.7	8.0	15.4

*Actual gold exports were likely to have been greater because contraband exports of gold were common.

†Includes cotton, animal skins, live animals, wood, indigo, rubber, cacao, bananas, and sugar.

‡Includes silver, platinum, and palm-fiber hats.

Source: Based on José Antonio Ocampo, *Colombia y la economía mundial, 1830–1919* (Bogotá, 1984), pp. 100–101, 143.

port trade could weaken the government, thus encouraging political instability. In addition, trade fluctuations affected the common man. Imported textiles had become an item of basic consumption for even the poor, so any constriction of imports brought a higher cost of living. Further, export crises threatened unemployment in the producing areas, creating uncertainty and discontent. The vicissitudes of foreign commerce were one of the most important causes of the vicious circle of export depressions–fiscal crises–civil wars.

Alterations of demand for Colombian products in world markets played roles in all three of the significant civil wars of this period—in 1876–1877, 1885, and 1899–1902. Civil wars tended to break out, or to be prolonged, in regions that were most deeply affected by loss of demand for their products in foreign markets. The complete collapse of demand for cinchona bark in the world market in 1882–1883 brought fiscal crisis to the national government. But the direct economic effects were most felt in Santander, at the time the chief producing area, and it was in Santander that the war of 1885 broke out. Antioquia, by contrast, with a steady income from its gold exports, remained relatively unaffected. Santander, once again, was the region most affected by a severe crisis in coffee markets that extended from 1898 to 1910, and Santander was the epicenter of the War of the Thousand Days (1899–1902). (See Table 11.4.)

TRANSPORTATION AND COMMUNICATIONS

From the 1840s, when Colombia began to enter actively into the exportation of tropical products, it was recognized by the elite that poor transportation conditions in the country limited its competitiveness in international markets. Since the 1840s elite plans for transportation development had focused overwhelmingly on improving routes to the outside world. This propensity was confirmed when they sought the aid of foreign firms for transportation improvement, as foreign interests also were interested primarily in international trade. Unfortunately, Colombia had no primary product of compelling interest whose extraction required major improvements in transportation. Colombia's most important resource, from the point of view of foreign investors, was precious metals, and these could be taken out by mule. Consequently, little improvement in overland transportation had been achieved as of the 1870s, and not much more by the end of the nineteenth century. Almost everywhere goods still were hauled by mule over trails, a mode of transportation that was both costly and hazardous.

For most of the country the Magdalena River remained the chief channel for exporting and importing. There were two exceptions. Santander carried on much of its external trade through Lake Maracaibo in Venezuela. And the Cauca Valley hoped that an improved route to Buenaventura would improve its chances of entry into international markets—however, that hope would be largely frustrated until the opening of the Panama Canal in 1914.

Because of the central importance of the Magdalena River for international trade, many plans for transportation development focused on improving haulage on the river or on connecting the highlands to the river. Aside from the railway across the Isthmus of Panama built in the 1850s, the single most important railroad in the country was the short route of 17 miles connecting the Magdalena River port of Barranquilla with its sea port on the Caribbean, completed in 1870. This line greatly aided foreign trade by providing a safe and relatively efficient link between the river and the ocean. In addition, other railway projects aimed to connect the highlands in the interior with the Magdalena River. These lines were not conceived as part of a unified national system. They were a series of local lines, with differing track widths and other technical specifications. Even in 1945, when Colombia had 2125 miles of track, transporting coffee from market to ocean port might require nine or ten transshipments.

In any event, railway construction before the twentieth century was extremely slow. Between 1867 and 1910 an average of only a little more than 13 miles of track per year was laid among all of the various projects in the nation.

Many explanations may be adduced for Colombia's slow rate of railway construction. Because of Colombia's poor nineteenth-century record in maintaining interest payments on the large foreign debt acquired in the independence period, the national government had trouble raising funds in European capital markets. Colombia was not completely closed out, but it could obtain foreign capital only at high cost—with heavy initial discounts and high interest rates.

Colombia also was able to induce foreign companies to undertake railway construction projects. In the late 1870s Francisco Cisneros, an energetic Cuban entrepreneur, contracted to build three major rail lines (from Medellín to the Magdalena River, from Buenaventura to the Cauca Valley, and from Girardot on the Magdalena River toward Bogotá), plus a host of lesser projects. Cisneros's progress was slow by comparison with rates of construction in the United States; by 1885 he had laid 85 miles of line. But all of this was over difficult terrain. In any event, Cisneros gave up when the civil war of 1885 and the change of government structure in 1886 paralyzed his work. Political wars and instability thus also obstructed railway construction.

As of 1918 British companies were in charge of seven of the country's sixteen railway projects. But their progress was no faster than that on projects under the supervision of the government or Colombian private companies. All had to cope with difficult routes, torrential rains, climates that endangered the health of workers and thus raised labor costs—in short, high construction costs. And since there was little immediate prospect of profitable operations, progress depended upon the availability of government subsidies—in a country whose capacity to collect revenues was severely limited.

Table 11.5 Development of the national telegraph network

Year	Kilometers (miles)	Lines	Offices
1865	50 (31.3)	3	5
1875	2500 (1562.5)	4	53
1880	3430 (2143.7)	6	102
1892	9619 (6011.9)	9	350
1913	20,000 (12,500)	10	500
1935	35,000 (21,875)	14	900

Sources: 1865–1892: *Colombia (Consular) Report for the Year 1891* (London, 1893), p. 4. 1913–1935: *Anuario General de Estadística* (Bogotá, 1937), p. 137.

Ultimately the fundamental problem was the lack of freight generated by Colombia's weak export economy. After 1905, expanded production of coffee helped provide freight for the lines connecting the highlands to the river. And political peace provided a better environment for construction.

If Colombia was extremely slow in developing overland transportation, it was able to move more quickly on the less challenging task of integrating the country by telegraph. The telegraph system radiated outward from Bogotá. The first three lines went toward Cartagena, Medellín, and Popayán. Later they reached northward to Cúcuta, and more branches were extended. But as of 1912 the cities of the Caribbean coast still had no submarine cable ocean connections; telegraphic messages from Europe had to come by way of the Pacific port of Buenaventura. In 1912 the United Fruit Company established the country's first wireless communications in the banana zone of Santa Marta. (See Table 11.5.)

The telegraph was of great importance in linking merchants in foreign commerce to different localities. They could operate in various markets almost simultaneously, accept and discount letters of exchange in minutes, know instantly the prices of coffee or cattle in different markets. Now news and private communications; electoral results; quotations from the markets of London, Paris, and New York; and orders from political chiefs and ecclesiastical authorities circulated instantaneously through the country. But the telegraph lines were frequently damaged and repairs were delayed, particularly in distant and isolated places. According to one joke, a husband sent his wife in the provinces the following wire: "When this reaches you, I will be in your arms."

MONEY AND BANKING

Since the colonial period, the monetary system had operated on the basis of coin, with silver and gold at parity. But modes of exchange varied regionally. In gold-mining Antioquia, gold dust as well as gold coin were in common circulation; in other parts of the country silver coin was in more frequent circulation. In Colombia, as elsewhere, the devaluation of silver in relation to gold in 1873–1876 had an important impact. Despite the increased relative value of gold, in Colombia gold and silver coins officially were considered at parity. As a consequence the more valuable gold coin rapidly was exported, leaving silver as the only coin in circulation. Although there were complaints of monetary scarcity at this time, the supply of money actually was being increased during the 1870s by the rapid spread of commercial banks issuing banknotes, which, at least for a time, seem to have had fairly widespread acceptance.

In the 1870s more than forty-two banks opened and functioned without any control other than that of stockholders. In 1881 their paid capital was 2.5 million pesos, distributed among no more than one thousand shareholders. This gives an idea of the small size of the commercial elite. One of the initial motivations for establishing the first commercial banks was to facilitate foreign trade; one of the banks' chief functions was the sale and discounting of bills of exchange. Accordingly, banks were most concentrated in the most commercially active states—twelve in Cundinamarca, eleven in Antioquia, five in Bolívar, four in the Cauca, three each in Santander and Boyacá.

The banks' credibility was greatly aided, at first, by substantial government backing. During the 1870s banknotes issued by private banks in Bogotá were accepted in payment of taxes by the national government, which also used them to pay its creditors. Further, the national government kept deposits in these banks. State governments also accepted private bank bills in their transactions, thus in effect making them partial guarantors of the banks' credit.

Soon after the election of Rafael Núñez as national president in 1880, the trajectory of Colombian banking began to change drastically. Before 1880, all banks were private, albeit aided importantly by government acceptance of their banknotes. Núñez, from the beginning of his presidency, wanted to establish a government-owned bank. Using the revenues of the Panama Railway as a guaranty, he borrowed three million dollars in New York. When private merchants and bankers refused to invest in a state-operated bank, Núñez used one million dollars of the New York loan to found the National Bank, which opened in January 1881. In order to retain their right to issue their own banknotes, private banks were obliged to accept those of the National Bank.

Some believed that Núñez's motive in establishing the National Bank was to debilitate his political opponents in the "Radical oligarchy," who were closely linked to private banking. There is reason to question this proposition, however, as many of the Conservatives and Independent Liberals who supported Núñez in 1875–1876 and again in 1880 were leaders in the private banks. It is much more likely that he saw the establishment of a National Bank as a means of strengthening the central government and making it more independent of the private banks. By 1892 thirty of the forty-two banks existing in 1881 had disappeared. But this death rate is more attributable to the hazards of the market than to government regulation.

The fiscal crisis engendered by the civil war of 1885 led the Núñez government in the following years to reinforce the circulation of National Bank notes by granting it monopoly power to issue banknotes, prohibiting the issue and circulation of notes of the private banks. In fact, however, the requirement that the private banks take their notes out of circulation was delayed in enforcement until nearly the end of the nineteenth century.

A central issue after 1885 was the amount of paper money the National Bank was putting into circulation. In order to bolster confidence in the government's banknotes, a series of laws and decrees fixed ceilings on the amounts the National Bank might issue. In 1887 the government committed itself not to circulate more than twelve million pesos in banknotes. But in 1889 fiscal bankruptcy, induced in part by bureaucratic expansion and military expenditures, brought issues of National Bank notes well above the twelve million peso limit.

The government strove to amortize its paper money, and in 1892 tried to establish parity between its banknotes and gold coin. In 1894, however, the fact that the government had gone over the promised twelve million peso limit in banknote issues became known. In the ensuing scandal the National Bank was liquidated at least formally. It became a dependency of the Ministry of the Treasury, thus leaving the issue of paper money directly at the discretion of the government. Accusations by the political opposition and some bankers that the Regeneration would use the national bank to make up its budget deficits initially were exaggerated. However, in 1898, at the time of a coffee depression, and even more during the War of the Thousand Days, the government issued twenty-one times as much paper money as it had between 1886 and 1899. By printing money that became increasingly devalued the government was able to finance its military operations and smash its Liberal opponents. But the hyperinflation during the war still frightened people twenty years later.

In 1903, with the civil war concluded, the government decreed the end of paper money and began to return to the gold standard. The banking policy of the Regeneration was the subject of one of the most impassioned ideological polemics of the second half of the nineteenth century; only the religious agitation over the educational reform of 1870 was comparable. The issue was framed in terms of the fundamental opposition between the statism of the Regeneration and the economic liberalism of its opponents. In the debates various kinds of arguments were mixed indiscriminately. Opponents saw signs of statism in the centralist and presidentialist character of the constitution of 1886, in the National Bank, and in the "protectionist" increases of import duties introduced in 1880. To these indications of statism opponents added government monopolies over cigars, cigarettes, and matches.

Today it seems clear that increases in customs duties under the Regeneration aimed in large part to raise more revenue, and the issues of banknotes by the Banco Nacional did not affect international transactions, since these continued to be carried on in convertible international currencies. Moreover, credit paper other than the banknotes of the Banco Nacional also circulated in the country.

The acts of the Regeneration have been used to legitimate various economic policies of the second half of the twentieth century. Devaluation of the paper money under the Regeneration provided fodder for a mid-twentieth-century polemic about the virtues and defects of statism versus economic liberalism. In his biography of Rafael Núñez (1944), Indalecio Liévano Aguirre launched a fierce attack upon the free trade commitments of the Radical Olympus. Writing at a crucial time in the nation's industrialization, Liévano concluded that Núñez was the father of modern economic nationalism in Colombia. The pillars of his policy, according to Liévano, had been government management of customs duties, banks, and money.

Since that time, as a hundred years ago, this question has been debated, but now with increasing economic refinements. It has been argued that Núñez's devaluation of paper money represented a coherent policy to encourage coffee exports by lowering the costs of production, thus favoring not only large producers and exporters but also smaller cultivators. It is also said that, in this way, devaluation helped create the internal demand needed to sustain the development of light industry. However, it may be suggested that paper money issues played less of a role in coffee expansion than did international prices. Another factor in the growth of the coffee industry was the use of labor systems in which monetary payments to workers were limited, which kept labor costs low and isolated them from the effects of changes in the value of money.

It also has been pointed out that the Regeneration really did not have a monetary policy, that Núñez in establishing the National Bank did not conceive of it as a central bank, and that exchange rates and interest rates continued to be determined by external markets and, in fact, the gold standard. It also should be noted that the National Bank and its paper money often helped private banks to deal with serious liquidity problems. And many bankers and merchants took advantage of the differentials between internal interest rates and the rates of devaluation.

Nor was the National Bank used to "buy up internal debt," as critics of the time alleged. Internal debt paper, according to Núñez, was a mechanism to fuse private interests with those of the state. For this reason in the monetary debates of 1892 Núñez emphatically opposed a proposal that the National Bank buy up the internal debt with paper money.

It also may be doubted whether government policy could actively encourage the creation of demand to support domestic industry, given the country's low income per capita and its unequal distribution. As for Núñez's tariff policy, apart from his concern to increase revenues, his clearest political intention was to gain the support of urban artisans.

POPULATION AND COLONIZATION

In the last decades of the nineteenth century, the overwhelming majority of Colombians still lived scattered in more or less self-sufficient peasant communities. In 1870, of 760 municipal districts in the country (excluding Panama), only 21 had more than 10,000 inhabitants.

The government's statistical compilation of 1876, after noting that as of 1870 Colombia had a population of 2.9 million, stated that in its area of more than 1.3 million square kilometers, more than 50 million could live and prosper. That the country was underpopulated is made clear by the data in Table 11.1. Three-quarters of the national territory was virtually uninhabited, and even in the most densely populated eastern zone immense areas remained unsettled. Meanwhile the high plains and fertile valleys were underused by large landowners for such purposes as grazing cattle. Colombia continued to fit Jovellanos's description of Spain in the eighteenth century: "land without men, and men without land."

The landless men of the highlands were forming a new country by clearing and settling unexploited public lands. Because of migration within the country during the second half of the nineteenth century, the regional distribution of the population was changing. Historically, the largest concentration of people was in the Eastern Cordillera; while the population of this region remained the largest, over time its relative weight diminished by comparison with other areas, as population growth lagged particularly in Boyacá and Santander. By contrast population growth was faster in provinces of the Caribbean coast and those in the West, with the fastest growth occurring in Antioquia. (See Table 11.6.)

In discussing the peculiarities of the Colombian people, the educated elite, in various degrees, revealed a deeply rooted pessimism, with a certain racist tint. Many of the negative characteristics that they noted could be attributed to ignorance, a consequence of the precariousness of the school system. An economy based on agriculture and the export of primary products was compatible with an illiterate populace. No modern technology substituted for human energy in clearing the forests for farming; in maintaining and harvesting tobacco or coffee; in the extraction of chinchona bark, rubber, or other forest products; and very little even in mining.

An example of the dominant racial stereotypes was the idea that the "Antioqueño race" was of Basque or, according to some in Bogotá, Jewish origin. With such conceptions the Antioqueño elite could erect a mythical ethnic boundary between their region and the rest of the country. The notion that Antioquia's entrepreneurial energy was based on a single unique racial heritage contrasts with the reality that its population, as in much of the rest of the country, stems from a tri-ethnic mix. The typical Antioqueño, as imagined in the regional stereotype, apparently did not include the blacks and mulattoes living along the Cauca River valley running from south to north through Antioquia. Such exclusive racial conceptions underlie the as-

Table 11.6 Percentage distribution of population by regions, 1851–1951

Regions*	1851	1870	1912	1938†	1951†
Antioqueño	11.6	13.5	21.3	23.3	23.9
Cauca	14.9	16.1	17.1	17.0	19.1
Caribbean coast‡	11.9	12.2	14.5	16.4	16.2
Bolívar	8.7	8.7	10.5		
Magdalena	3.2	3.5	4.0		
Eastern	61.5	58.2	47.0	43.3	39.5
Boyacá	18.2	18.1	11.6		
Cundinamarca	15.2	14.9	14.7		
Santander	18.2	15.4	12.0		
Tolima	9.9	8.2	8.7		
Total population (in millions)	2.02	2.71	5.47	8.70	11.45

*The regions refer to the areas of the sovereign states of the federal period, so that the Antioqueño and Cauca regions refer to the areas of the states of Antioquia and Cauca between 1863 and 1886.
†The political-adminisitative divisions of 1938 and 1951 have been adjusted to the scheme of this table.
‡Excludes Panama.

sertions of the Manizales elite that they are "improved Antioqueños," in that the proportion of blacks in their region is lower than in Antioquia. The racial-ethnic data of the censuses of 1851 and 1912, while fallible in that they depend on the subjective and variable views of the census-takers, nonetheless show that Antioquia's population historically was more variegated than Antioqueño legend would suggest.

Comparing the data for 1851 (Table 11.7) with that for 1912 (Table 11.8) also suggests the manifest anxiety to "whiten" the society during the second half of the nineteenth century. In the sixty years between the censuses of 1851 and 1912 the percentage of "whites" in the population doubled (from 17 to 34.4 percent). By contrast, the percentage of "Indians" in the population halved and the proportion of "mixed" dropped by a quarter.

In general the racial distribution of the population in the various regions of the country maintained similar patterns to those of the late colonial period. Blacks formed a larger proportion of the population in parts of the West (Cauca, Valle, and Antioquia) and on the Caribbean coast than in the eastern belt. The surviving Indian population was particularly concentrated in the south (Narino and the upper Cauca). In the eastern highlands, where a relatively dense indigenous population had lived at the time of the Conquest, most of their descendants had become hispanicized during the eighteenth and nineteenth centuries. Blacks and indigenes continued to be stigmatized.

Table 11.7 Percentage distribution of population by "race," 1851

Sovereign States	Whites (1)	Indians (2)	Blacks (3)	Mestizos (4)	Mulattos (5)	Zambos (6)	Total Mixed (4 + 5 + 6)
Antioquia	20.5	2.9	3.7	42.2	29.5	1.2	72.9
Bolívar	13.7	5.5	5.5	25.3	22.0	28.0	75.3
Boyacá	3.0	38.4	0.7	48.1	4.7	5.1	57.9
Cauca	19.4	7.9	13.0	37.3	21.8	0.6	59.7
Cundinamarca	24.5	29.4	0.3	45.0	0.6	0.3	45.9
Magdalena	6.7	10.7	6.7	26.7	29.3	20.0	76.0
Panama	10.1	5.8	3.6	65.2	7.2	8.0	80.4
Santander	23.1	0.0	1.1	69.8	5.6	0.5	75.9
Tolima	17.4	15.8	1.6	48.9	15.8	0.5	65.2
Colombia	**17.0**	**13.8**	**3.8**	**47.6**	**13.1**	**4.7**	**65.4**

POPULATION AND ECONOMY

For entrepreneurs the populace at large represented essentially a factor of production. The growth of the population in the nineteenth century, estimated at an average annual rate of 1.5 percent, and its geographic mobility permitted the elites to hope for progress in agricultural and other exports. Judging from the census of 1870, some 82,000 people, or 5 percent of the economically active population, were engaged in exploiting tobacco, cinchona

Table 11.8 Percentage distribution of population by "race," 1912

Departments	Whites	Blacks	Indians	Mixed
Antioquia	34.5	18.3	2.2	45.0
Atlántico	21.1	11.5	4.9	62.6
Bolívar	19.6	21.0	10.3	49.1
Boyacá	25.8	0.0	8.0	66.2
Caldas	36.9	5.0	2.3	55.8
Cauca	25.3	19.8	34.5	20.4
Cundinamarca	47.5	3.5	5.1	43.9
Magdalena*	—	—	—	—
Valle	48.2	13.7	3.9	34.2
Huila	29.7	3.9	8.5	57.8
Nariño	45.4	7.7	26.3	20.5
N. Santander	43.4	6.0	0.3	50.2
Santander	36.0	6.2	0.8	57.0
Tolima	25.1	5.0	8.8	61.0
Colombia	**34.4**	**10.0**	**6.3**	**49.2**

*The 1912 census for the Department of Magdalena does not provide data by "race."

bark, and coffee and in mining. In this period these activities represented at least 80 percent of the value of exports, and perhaps 10–15 percent of gross domestic product. This indicates that the levels of productivity of the population not engaged in producing for export were quite low. It further suggests the importance of rural artisanry, employing 350,000, mostly women in the eastern highlands and the South (Narino and the Cauca), as an aid to the domestic economy of peasant families in these regions.

THE FRONTIER OF "OPEN RESOURCES"

During the second half of the nineteenth century there were three principal currents of migration. In Santander the population shifted from the southern part of the region (Socorro-San Gil) northward to Bucaramanga, Cúcuta, and the Venezuelan provinces of Táchira and Zulia. Second, peasants from the highlands of eastern and central Boyacá and eastern Cundinamarca migrated westward to the slopes of western Cundinamarca, to central and southern Tolima, and to some degree into the Middle Magdalena, while others moved eastward to the piedmont of the eastern *llanos* and the plains of Casanare and San Martín.

The third major migration was that in Antioquia, which fanned out in all directions. Part of the movement to the north and northeast was associated with mining, but colonization also went into tropical areas north in Urabá and west into the Chocó. Antioqueño colonization to the south first went into present-day Caldas and southwestern Antioquia, but when public lands in these places became scarce, it continued farther south along the Central Cordillera, toward the Cauca Valley. Meanwhile migrants from the Cauca Valley joined Antioqueños on the fertile mountainsides of the Quindío and in the present Department of Risaralda. Still other Antioqueños crossed the Central Cordillera and established themselves in northern Tolima, from there continuing farther south. Some colonists who advanced along the river valleys were unable to obtain land, as entrepreneurs in Medellín already had established title to it for cattle-raising. The conflict over public lands was much more acute in these places, and in the forests of Urabá, than in the south and southwest of Antioquia.

The movement of these people from the cool highlands toward the warmer zones of the mountain slopes and valleys was the most important social phenomenon of the century from 1850 to 1950. Although colonists of these warmer zones were threatened with malaria, tropical anemia, and yellow fever, which particularly affected infants, the menace of disease could not overcome the hunger for land. To live on the frontier was to live at hazard. A North American physician, Hamilton Rice, who in 1912 traveled through the eastern plains and rain forests, was amazed by the prevalence of malaria. In San Martín, of the three hundred people Rice examined, all were infected, adults and children, men and women. Rice, who had been in charge of hospitals in Russia, Turkey, and Egypt, said he had never seen such suffering. In Villavicencio, the only place where quinine could be obtained, the cost of medicine was exorbitant. Such descriptions could be extended to the warm areas of many parts of the country, and they are documented for the coffee zones colonized by the Antioqueños.

Peasants emigrated from their places of birth because the level and fertile land had been taken by families of landowners and merchants, and with the increase of the peasant population they could not sustain their families on their small plots of land. So they pushed vigorously to the frontiers of colonization that had opened by 1850, and as these became saturated they went farther on into new territory.

In the period 1870–1905 more individual titles to public land were granted than in any previous or later period. Official statistics show a pattern of concentration of public land grants. While they were establishing coffee plantations or opening pastures for cattle-raising, entrepeneurs offered employment to migrating peasants, who could cultivate their own plots in return for clearing the land. Thousands of poor peasant families who do not appear in the official statistics could subsist for several generations on such plots, without titles or protection of the law.

THE EXPANSION OF COFFEE

By the last decade of the nineteenth century coffee had become Colombia's principal export product, and the economies of Santander and Cundinamarca depended heavily on coffee exports. Coffee-growing developed first in Santander as an extension of coffee culture in Venezuela. The reports of the Corographic Commission in the middle of the nineteenth century indicate that coffee was already notable in Santander. Somewhat later it reached Cundinamarca and then crossed the Magdalena River into Tolima and Antioquia.

In Santander, the first major region of cultivation, and in many parts of the West, where it arrived later, coffee-growing was initiated by small and medium-sized farmers; in these regions, however, the success of coffee soon attracted the interest of merchants who began to establish it on large holdings. By contrast, in Cundinamarca and Tolima the establishment of coffee was pioneered by large haciendas and smaller cultivators emerged later.

In the last third of nineteenth century some six hundred coffee haciendas were founded, particularly concentrated in Northern Santander, Santander, Cundinamarca, Tolima, and southwestern Antioquia. The coffee haciendas in all of these regions were small by comparison with those in Guatemala, El Salvador, and Brazil.

The coffee hacendados tended to plant coffee in virgin land, but with titles, some dating from the colonial period. The fact that they owned titles meant that they were opening a frontier of "closed resources," as distinguished from a frontier of "open resources," in which occupying the land provided the basis for title, as occurred, for example, in some phases of Antioqueño colonization.

Coffee hacendados sought to limit their initial costs as much as possible. Monetary wage costs were minimized by having the land cleared and coffee planted by workers who were compensated by being allowed to grow food crops on part of the land they cleared. When the first harvest approached, four or five years after planting, the merchant-hacendados got advances from foreign commercial houses at interest rates lower than those current in Colombia. In this way they were able to finance the purchase of machinery and buildings needed for drying the coffee beans and preparing them for market.

In no coffee-growing region did wage labor predominate. In the coffee haciendas established mostly in the Eastern Cordillera and the center of the country, as well as in the smaller coffee farms that predominated in the West, coffee culture maintained aspects of the structure of colonial agrarian society. Whether on large haciendas or on small farms, the labor of whole families was employed in planting, maintaining, and harvesting coffee. Also, in both cases, the cultivators tended to be self-sufficient in food production.

However, the specific labor arrangements on haciendas tended to differ among the three production zones of Santander, Cundinamarca-Tolima, and Antioquia. The chief differentiating element was the perceived ethnic difference between the hacendado and the worker families, whether resident or seasonal. In Cundinamarca and Tolima, most workers probably were mestizos, but owners apparently thought of them as "Indians." By contrast, in Santander and Antioquia, hacendados considered their workers to be "white," even though they also were likely to have been mestizo.

In zones where there was a greater perceived cultural difference between owner and worker, as in Cundinamarca and Tolima, a precapitalist arrangement called *arrendamiento* prevailed. The *arrendatario*, in return for the use of a plot on which he could grow food, was obliged to provide for the hacienda a certain number of days of work. Included in this obligation was the work of the family of the *arrendatario* and even of peons who worked for him.

By contrast, in Santander and Antioquia, where the perceived cultural difference between hacendado and cultivator was less, other arrangements were characteristic. In Santander, the prevalent mechanism was sharecropping, in which the cultivator and his family attended to a given number of coffee bushes, and then divided the harvest with the owner according to a prearranged agreement.

In Antioquia the *agregado*, or service tenant, predominated. This arrangement may be thought of as midway between the sharecropper system of Santander and the pre-capitalist *arrendatario* system of Cundinamarca. The *agregado* in Antioquia received monetary wage payments. But he had a smaller plot for cultivating food and it was farther away from his home. In all three cases it was assumed that the food grown by the worker formed part of his total compensation. (A typology of these regional variations is presented in Table 11.9.)

The systems outlined here changed over time, so that the labor institutions of coffee haciendas in the 1930s and 1940s were quite different from those of the earlier "traditional" world of the late nineteenth century.

Table 11.9 Typology of coffee haciendas (at the end of the nineteenth century)

	Cundinamarca-Tolima	Santander	Antioquia
Social origin of landowner	Merchant	Merchant	Merchant
Dominant labor system*	Pre-capitalist, *arrendamiento*	Sharecropping (*aparcería*)	*Agregados*
Pattern of settlement of resident workers	Diffuse; dispersed plots	Diffuse; dispersed plots	Concentrated; nucleated villages
Relations of class and "race"	Owner and worker of different "race"	Mixed	Owner, worker, racially homogeneous
Owner's diversity of activities	Low	n.d.	High
Land tenure pattern in area of hacienda	Large estates	Large estates, and peasant smallholdings	Large estates and peasant smallholdings

*Within each of these systems there were a variety of contractual possibilities, which, nonetheless, retained the dominant characteristics.
Source: Marco Palacios, *Coffee in Colombia* (Cambridge, England, 1980) p. 79.

Available hacienda accounts suggest that monetary wages (which represented a fraction of the total compensation) diminished during the period of coffee's takeoff in Cundinamarca, Tolima, and Antioquia. The haciendas served as precursors, establishing and spreading coffee cultivation, but later came under competition from small and medium-sized cultivators, who could hold their own with big operators because coffee-farming is very labor intensive and it is virtually impossible to mechanize production. During the twentieth century small cultivators in Antioquia and the Cauca, because of the greater fertility of their soil and better climatic conditions, were able to compete advantageously against the large coffee hacendados of Cundinamarca and Tolima.

After the War of the Thousand Days many haciendas, however, did survive and prosper. In the first half of the twentieth century capitalist enterprise again concentrated on foreign commerce, although expansion of city populations and economic growth also propelled urban speculation, transportation enterprises, and the establishment of protected manufacturing—opportunities favored by political peace.

12

The Republic of Coffee, 1903–1946

The period from 1885 to 1930 often is called the "Conservative hegemony." Such a periodization, however, overemphasizes the Church and its alliance with the Conservatives. The Catholic hierarchy indeed was considered part of the government between 1886 and 1930 and in the opposition from 1930 until 1946, when a Conservative once again became president. But the years from 1886 to 1930 should not be considered a single period, as the loss of Panama initiated a new era. Between 1903 and 1945 the country became fully integrated into the world market as coffee became consolidated. Civil war was delegitimized by the elites as a form of political competition. New political actors, such as workers' unions, appeared and the broadening of political and social rights became inevitable. Unions and workers' rights were particularly important themes during the "Liberal Republic" of 1930–1946. All of these changes implied a profound transformation of the State. The problems of the state began with the importance of U.S. power and influence, demonstrated dramatically with the separation of Panama. Problems of national sovereignty also emerged in the first half of the twentieth century regarding the boundaries with Venezuela, Brazil, Peru, and Ecuador and the status of the border territories. This period, which ends after World War II, is that of the Republic of Coffee.

Coffee, whose principal market was in the United States, provided the basis for the development of transportation and communications, for the flow of foreign investments and international credit. But Western Europe retained cultural prestige. The continuing authority of the Church may be considered one aspect of a broad, sustained European influence.

The country was ruled by the constitution of 1886, although it was reformed in some respects in 1910, 1936, and 1945. Long-established political practices persisted. If, after the War of the Thousand Days, an elite consensus supported a turn toward peaceful politics, the inertia of partisan factions still shaped alliances and conflicts. Table 12.1 reveals the persistence of both two-party confrontation and internal divisions within each party. Paradoxically, divisions within the parties strengthened two-party politics. Each party had a moderate wing that eventually allied itself with the moderates of the contrary party, the two together forming an ad hoc centrist coalition.

Until 1950 all changes of government occurred within the framework of the constitution. The elections of 1904 and 1910 were indirect. After the constitutional reform of 1910 there were ten presidential elections by direct vote, and after 1936 all adult males could vote. In four (1926, 1934, 1938, and 1949) the opposition party abstained, alleging lack of guaranties of a fair election. In three (1914, 1918, and 1942) the voters' choice was largely limited to the candidate of one party, supported by elements of the adversary party. Of the three most contested elections, that of 1922 brought the country to the brink of civil war, and in those of 1930 and 1946 the government party fell from power because it divided in the election, permitting victory by a moderate candidate of a minority party. Table 12.1 illustrates these variations and the

Table 12.1 Presidential elections by direct vote, 1914–1950

Year/President Elected	Party of President	Vote Opposition Candidate	Total[†]	Percentage for Winner	Participation* A	B
1914/José Vicente Concha	Historical conservative	N. Esguerra, Republican	331	89	6.4	n.d.
1918/Marco Fidel Suárez	Nationalist conservative	G. Valencia, Historical Conservative	405	53	6.9	n.d.
1922/Pedro Nel Ospina	Historical conservative	B. Herrera, Liberal	656	62	10.5	n.d.
1926/Miguel Abadía Méndez	Historical conservative	Abstention	370	99	5.4	n.d.
1930/Enrique Olaya Herrera	Moderate liberal	A. Vásquez, National Conservative; G. Valencia, Historical Conservative	824	45	11.1	n.d.
1934/Alfonso López Pumarejo	Radical Liberal	Abstention	942	99	11.5	61
1938/Enrique Santos	Moderate Liberal	Abstention	514	99	5.9	30
1942/Alfonso López Pumarejo	Radical Liberal	C. Arango, Liberal	1148	59	12.1	56
1946/Mariano Ospina Pérez	Conservative	G. Turbay, Moderate Liberal; J.E. Gaitán, Radical Liberal	1366	41	13.2	56
1950/Laureano Gómez	Radical conservative	Abstention	1140	99	10.3	40

*Column A is the percentage of the total population that voted; column B is the percentage of the male population over age twenty-one that voted.

[†]In thousands.

Sources: Based on Registraduría Nacional del Estado Civil, *Historia electoral colombiana, 1810–1988* (Bogota, 1991), pp. 151–159; statistics of participation, column A, and those for the 1926 election of Abadía from *Statistical Abstract of Latin America*, James W. Wilkie and David Lorey, eds., vol. 25 (Los Angeles, 1987) p. 874.

tendency to greater participation—with the predictable exception of elections in which one party abstained.

Colombian economic and political historiography considers 1930 to mark one of the important points of change in the twentieth century. In this year, amid the Great Depression, the Liberals, for the first time in half a century, won the presidency. Nevertheless, as we will see, the socioeconomic and political effects of the Great Depression were much briefer and less severe in Colombia than in most Latin American countries. Moreover, the change in government in 1930 occurred with the election of a moderate Liberal whose regime was a de facto centrist one.

COFFEE

From the last third of the eighteenth century until the present, coffee has been one of the principal export products of Latin America. Its centers of production moved from Haiti, the principal world producer until the great uprising of 1791, to Jamaica, Cuba, and Puerto Rico. After the abolition of slavery in Haiti, coffee production slowly recovered at the beginning of the nineteenth century, with cultivation by independent peasants. At this time the French established coffee in Guayana, and it was also taken up in Venezuela and Brazil. Since the middle of the nineteenth century, Brazil has dominated the world supply.

Mexico and Central America also began to grow coffee, their industries taking off by the middle of the nineteenth century, somewhat before the crop became centrally important in Colombia. During the mid-nineteenth century the commercial cultivation of coffee advanced imperceptibly from the Venezuelan Andes into the Eastern Cordillera of Colombia. By the end of the nineteenth century, coffee cultivation had spread geographically and its structures of production varied. The abolition of slavery in Brazil ended slave production of coffee. In the post-slavery period, various types of large coffee estates prevailed in some places, notably Brazil, El Salvador, Guatemala, and Chiapas in Mexico. But in Costa Rica, Venezuela, Colombia, and the Mexican state of Veracruz small and medium-sized cultivators emerged, survived, and often prospered alongside coffee haciendas. It was possible for small producers to compete with large estates because with coffee, which is labor intensive, significant economies of scale cannot be obtained.

The market for coffee also changed. At first a luxury product, coffee became widely consumed in continental Europe and in the United States. During and after the U.S. Civil War, the United States emerged as one of the most active consumers. And in the twentieth century it has been the most important buyer. U.S. predominance as a consumer led for a time to North American control of the coffee market in Colombia. When the big Medellín coffee exporters went bankrupt in New York in the 1920s, North American coffee companies swept into Colombia and dominated purchases of coffee until the 1930s. In 1927 a leading businessman in Antioquia referred to the

American companies as "the claws of Yankee imperialism." Since the 1930s, the internal coffee market once again has come under Colombian control.

Once the consumption of coffee had become popularized, it began to take on the market characteristics of a basic product, with low elasticity of demand. That is, only if there were enormous increases in price would consumers abandon it. It is also true that coffee has very low elasticities of supply. Because it takes four or five years for coffee bushes to mature, and they then may produce steadily for several decades, once a farmer has invested in coffee, he is unlikely to abandon it even in times of sharp declines in prices.

Since the middle of the nineteenth century, big variations in the coffee market have depended on variable climatic conditions in Brazil. Periodic, but unpredictable, freezes in Brazil bring sudden reductions in its production, causing world prices to rise substantially. Stimulated by high prices, growers elsewhere plant many more bushes; when these new plants mature, after four or five years, a greatly increased supply once again sharply lowers prices.

Beyond the cycles produced by variations of weather in Brazil, other features make coffee a highly speculative commodity. Unlike sugar, tobacco, and cotton, coffee can only be grown in the tropics. Unlike wheat or petroleum, it is not an essential commodity. And it can be stored for long periods. Thus, it generates speculation that contributes to a notable instability of prices, not only year to year but even day to day. The unpredictability of the coffee market has induced in Colombians a fatalistic syndrome, expressed in popular sayings, such as coffee is in reality Colombia's minister of finance or that Colombia's instability is a consequence of freezes in Brazil.

This fatalism conceals a pair of central problems in Colombian economic development that probably are shared in various degrees with other Latin American countries. In the nineteenth century, when there was no significant industrial sector, the diminution of exports had severe impact on government revenues and on the consumption of the upper class. As the twentieth century advanced, industrial development has depended on income from exports to pay for imports of machinery and raw materials. Until the 1970s this income came fundamentally from coffee.

The second problem is one of ideological masking. Colombian elites have been reluctant to recognize explicitly that between 1906 and 1989 the world coffee market was a political market. The market was shaped successively by the Brazilian government (1906–1937), the United States government (1940–1948), and a series of agreements among coffee producers and consumers (1962, 1968, 1976, and 1983). In each case the explicit objective was to raise and stabilize coffee prices at levels above those that would have resulted from the free market.

The political management of the international market became linked to political protection within the country. The Federation of Coffeegrowers, founded in 1927, emerged as a powerful interest group. Although a private entity, it came to be a kind of cogovernment with regard to matters affecting coffee. Placing itself above partisan conflicts, the leadership of the coffee federation has been one of the nuclei of an ad hoc centrist political coalition. However, for twentieth-century Conservatives the small coffeegrowers in western Colombia have played a role analogous to that of urban artisans for the Liberals: They are an electoral base and symbol of democratic participation. But there is an important difference: The local organizations of the coffee federation provide a network of political patronage for small coffee cultivators that has not been characteristic of relations between upper-class Liberals and urban artisans.

Before the creation of the Federation of Coffeegrowers, in Antioquia and Caldas the *fondero* (a kind of combination innkeeper and country-store owner) served as the first intermediary in the chain of commercialization. Through advance payments on the harvest, the *fonderos* developed clienteles of small and medium cultivators. A key person both for the growers and for the commercial houses, national or foreign, the *fondero* often became a discreet or open electoral broker. When the Federation of Coffeegrowers intervened in the coffee-buying process, limiting the profits of intermediaries, classifying and certifying qualities of coffee, establishing depositories, fixing prices, and organizing the cultivators, informal political structures emerged that complemented or displaced the *fondero*, depending on the time and the place.

The Federation of Coffeegrowers changed significantly in 1940 with the creation of the National Coffee Fund as a consequence of the First Interamerican Quota Pact. The pact required the producing countries to hold back a part of their harvest in order to reduce the quantity exported. Established by the government but administered by the federation, the fund was supported by two coffee taxes, which financed the purchase of the entire national harvest. Through the fund, the federation controlled the marketing of coffee within Colombia and monopolized its export. Particularly during the 1950s the federation also created an assemblage of enterprises and institutions that financed, insured, and stored coffee, as well as transported it within the country and abroad. In addition to establishing the Banco Cafetero in 1953, the federation, acting for the Coffee Fund, refinanced the Caja de Crédito Agrario (the government's chief institution for lending to farmers) and was the chief partner in the Flota Mercante Gran Colombiana, Colombia's government-owned shipping corporation.

The coffee federation became in effect a government agency, which negotiated and administered for Colombia the various international coffee pacts. It thus enjoyed a monopoly position—with regard to information as well as the control of the entire stock of Colombian coffee—in its relations with the big international coffee buyers. It also was in a strong position to negotiate the internal price of coffee and tax rates, as well as credit, exchange, and monetary policies, with each successive government administration. Since 1937, only three men have served as chief executive of the coffee federation, during which time some twenty presidents and fifty ministers of finance have passed before them.

In the 1930s the Federation of Coffeegrowers began to take the place of the big United States coffee companies in the Colombian market. With its control of the Coffee Fund, for a time it displaced all coffee exporters, negotiating directly with the multinational companies that since the 1960s have controlled the processing, marketing, and sales of coffee. The end of the international coffee pacts in 1989 weakened the federation; nonetheless, it continues to buy and store coffee as well as to support research and the diffusion of technology and statistics. The Federation has played a positive role in many coffee areas, constructing aqueducts, schools, and roads—a source of much of its social legitimacy. However, recently, operating in a free market and at a time when coffee exports have lost their former importance, the federation has been criticized as bureaucratic and inefficient.

If coffee gave life to Colombia's modern economy, the United States was its umbilical cord. The United States displaced Western Europe as the chief market for coffee at the beginning of the twentieth century, and its importance increased still more during the two world wars. In the 1960s, as coffee was losing importance in Colombia's economy, the balance of its coffee sales shifted back toward Europe. (See Table 12.2.)

Since Colombia's imports from the United States were not increasing as much as its coffee exports to that country between 1918 and 1940, the United States government sporadically put pressure on Colombia, pointing out that Colombian imports from Great Britain were being paid for with dollars earned from sales to the United States. In a system of free convertibility of

Table 12.2 Markets for Colombian coffee, circa 1863–1969 (percentage distribution of value of exports)

Five-year Periods	United States	Europe	Other
1863–1867	26	74	—
1873–1877	40	60	—
1883–1887	65	35	—
1893–1897	44	56	—
1903–1907	72	28	—
1915–1919	91	7	2
1925–1929	92	7	1
1935–1939	77	19	4
1939–1943	93	4	3
1944–1948	92	3	5
1955–1959	81	17	2
1965–1969	47	49	4

Source: Marco Palacios, Coffee in Colombia (Cambridge, England, 1980), p. 212.

currencies, this would not have been a problem, except from a political point of view.

The continuous growth of the production of coffee is the most decisive phenomenon in Colombian economic history in the twentieth century. As the economy diversified, however, coffee's relative importance in time declined. In 1920–1925 coffee represented 70 percent of Colombia's exports, in the 1950s 80 percent. (See Table 12.3.) But by 1990–1998, it made up only 17 percent. Similarly, in 1925–1935 coffee contributed 16 percent of the gross domestic product (GDP); in 1950–1952 its contribution dropped to 10.3 percent, and by 1991–1998 it was only 2.0 percent.

The development of transportation in twentieth-century Colombia can be understood only in the context of the growth of the coffee economy. In the first decades of the twentieth century, coffee was expanding with particular dynamism in the West (Caldas, Risaralda, the Quindío). But this region, enclosed in the Central and Western Cordilleras, lacked an adequate channel to external markets. The opening of the Panama Canal in 1914 had a decisive effect in integrating this coffee zone into the world market. Cali, given its location between the coffee areas and the Pacific port of Buenaventura, became the transportation node of western Colombia. And the possibility of exporting coffee via Buenaventura accelerated railway construction. As the Panama Canal opened up possibilities for the port of Buenaventura, the Magdalena River began to lose its near-monopoly as a channel for exports from the interior. Until the middle of the 1930s the Magdalena remained the chief route for exported coffee, and Barranquilla the principal port. But since that time Buenaventura has been the predominant exporter of coffee.

Table 12.3 Some socioeconomic indicators, 1900–1950

	1900	1910	1920	1930	1940	1950
Economic						
Coffee exports, as percentage of total exports	49	39	62	64	62	72
GDP per capita*	118	146	172	230	291	360
Social						
Population (in thousands)	3998	4890	6213	7914	9147	11,946
Life expectancy (at birth)	n.d.	31	32	34	38	49
Literacy[†]	34	39	44	52	57	62

*GDP per capita: absolute values. $U.S. at 1970 parity purchase prices.

[†]Percentage of population over fifteen years of age.

Source: Rosemary Thorp, *Progress, Poverty and Exclusion. An Economic History of Latin America in the 20th Century* (Baltimore, 1998), Statistical Appendix.

In 1931 the government's priorities in transportation shifted from railways to highways. In good part under the stimulus of coffee, rapid progress occurred. During the next twenty years Colombia constructed an annual average of 850 kilometers (531 miles) of highway. By 1950, 21,000 kilometers (13,125 miles) of highway integrated the country in a way that would have been unimaginable at the end of the nineteenth century. Despite regionalist pressures for special attention, the national transportation plan advanced.

First small two-ton trucks, and then after World War II much larger trucks, were decisive in moving products to the seaports. In the 1940s automotive transportation was about to surpass the railways, whose rolling stock was obsolete and labor costs were high. At that time the railways and highways each carried about a third of all freight; by 1990 the highways carried 80 percent and the railways only 3 percent.

The development of commercial aviation had no direct link to coffee, but it paralleled automotive transportation as an especially important advance for a mountainous country with a widely dispersed population. The first airline, initially established by Germans living in Colombia, began operations in 1919, with flights up the Magdalena River Valley. By 1950, air transport annually was carrying 150,000 tons of cargo and 800,000 passengers. In Colombia's broken and farflung topography, air transportation has been used for quite diverse types of cargo, including cattle. Banks have used airplanes as branches to provide service to remote areas.

It is said that Colombia leaped from the mule to the airplane. Despite this dramatic change, the infrastructure of land transportation remained uneven in the 1950s. Traffic density was very high in the Bogotá region and, to a much lesser degree, around Medellín and Cali, in contrast with the rest of the country. Although highway traffic now predominated, the supply of automotive transport was limited and freight rates were high. Many roads were not safe because of bad weather, geological instability, and the corruption of public works contractors. Colombians became more aware of these problems as they listened to radio broadcasts of the Vuelta a Colombia bicycle race, very popular since the time it was first held in 1951.

The history of coffee in Colombia and of its economic institutions can be divided into three phases: (1) the rise of coffee, 1910–1940 (in the mid-1920s coffee was perceived as the motor of economic modernization in Colombia; (2) stagnation, from 1940 to 1975; and (3) reactivation 1975–circa 1994. Each stage has distinctive features determined by conditions of world demand, the social base and techniques of production, and geography. This chapter pays particular attention to the first phase.

First Phase, 1910–1940

Colombia entered the world market late. The establishment of coffee as a leading product, from about 1850, took nearly fifty years. The rise to dominance, 1910–1940, began with the rise of world prices after the prolonged depression that began in 1896. In these three decades the volume of exports increased by an average of 7.4 percent per year. In 1910–1915 the volume of Colombia's coffee exports only equalled those of Haiti in 1791 and represented only 3 percent of the world total. In 1994–1999 Colombian coffee exports accounted for 13 percent of the world total. In 1920 Colombia already was the second-largest producer in the world and the leading producer of mild coffees.

The recovery of prices in the decade of 1910 did not seem to guarantee Colombia's future as a coffee country. At this time Colombian elites were still looking for other possible options. In the Cartagena region, with the modernization of cattle-raising (new breeds and grasses, technical management of pastures), cattle were being exported to Panama and Cuba. Sugar was also being sent to Panama. These experiments, however, could not compete with Texas beef and Cuban sugar. Coastal cattle-raising ended up supplying growing domestic markets in the coffee regions of Santander and Antioquia.

Still, Colombia could rely on Antioquia's gold. Around 1910 Caldas became an important producer of gold. And there was new promise in the bananas of the United Fruit Company, which had arrived in the Santa Marta region at the end of the nineteenth century. Many Colombian farmers, large, medium-sized, and small, were growing bananas, although United Fruit monopolized their sale to world markets. Another promising product at this time was Amazonian rubber. It would take several years of high prices for coffee to be recognized as the best option.

Between 1918 and 1929 the economy grew at one of the fastest rates in its history. In these years Colombia's export income quintupled. In 1918 U.S. investments in Colombia represented only 1 percent of the U.S. total for Latin America. By 1929 U.S. investments in Colombia had tripled, reaching 6 percent of its Latin American total. This was the so-called "Colombian renaissance," the principal source of which was the coffee bonanza created by Brazil's schemes to raise international coffee prices by withholding part of its harvest. It has been calculated that, without Brazil's intervention, Colombia's coffee income would have been 60 percent lower in 1920–1934.

The coffee bonanza, the sustained rise of banana exports, and the promising takeoff of oil (the latter two produced in U.S. enclaves), along with the payment of 25 million U.S. dollars by the United States as an indemnity for the seizure of Panama, attracted the interest of lenders in New York. Some accounts have emphasized the importance of the U.S. indemnity and loans to Colombia's economic growth in the 1920s. But it should be noted that coffee income was triple the amount of the indemnity and the loans together. So coffee might be considered responsible in that proportion for the dynamism of Colombia's economy and the expansion of bank credit at this time.

The inflation of the 1920s stimulated a partisan debate. In calling these years the "dance of the millions," government critics seemed to think that the public debt was the only thing dancing. Behind the criticism was a struggle of competing regional interests to extract resources from a small but buoyant state. Until 1925 the hopes of the country revolved around the Panama indemnity. But then from 1926 to the first months of 1928 some 180 million dollars in loans were contracted, of a total of 214 million borrowed during the 1920s. Of these loans the national government took only 27 percent; Antioquia, Caldas, and the city of Medellín, the heart of the coffee economy, obtained 70 percent of the loans that went to departments, municipalities, and banks. In terms of economic sectors, railways, the channelling of rivers (principally the Magdalena), and improvements in the ports of Buenaventura, Barranquilla, and Cartagena took nearly half the loan money. Together with expenditures from the national budget, public investment in infrastructure reached 200 million U.S. dollars between 1922 and 1930.

The Great Depression reached Colombia in the latter half of 1928. First, external capital began to flow out of the country. Then world prices of coffee fell. Immediately Colombia's international reserves shrank; this led, between 1930 and 1932, to monetary contraction, diminished revenues, acute deflation, and unemployment. Nevertheless, the worst effects of the Depression were surmounted in 1933. Colombia's revival was aided by Brazil's destruction of 78 million sacks of coffee between 1931 and 1940, the equivalent of two years of total world production. Also rising demand for gold raised its price; consequently, gold rose from 3 percent of the value of Colombia's exports in 1925–1929 to 12 percent in 1930–1938.

Some internal conditions also helped attenuate the impact of the Depression. First, the peasant base of the coffee industry absorbed the cost of declining land prices and wages and responded to declining coffee prices by increasing production. Second, the peasants peaceably tolerated the redistribution of coffee income to the benefit of merchants and bankers. Further, in a way Colombia was aided by the modesty of its success as an exporter; exports represented only 24 percent of GDP in 1925–1935, which somewhat contained the cost of falling export prices.

Recovery also was aided by various monetary and exchange measures that helped to counteract the contraction of internal credit and the decline of government revenues. Two of these measures were the adoption of exchange controls and the devaluation of the peso as a consequence of the suspension of convertibility of the pound sterling by the Bank of England in 1931. These measures, and others more specific to the coffee industry, caused instability and brief panics but permitted the reactivation of the economy. Devaluation of the peso aided exporters and at the same time protected domestic industry. However, inflation also eroded the protective effects of the tariff; further, in 1935 Colombia, in order to get its coffee into the U.S. market untaxed, reduced the protection of Colombian industry from U.S. manufactures.

The Bank of the Republic, which since 1923 had acted as a modern central bank, aided the recovery by loaning funds to the national government.

But perhaps the thing that most contributed to the success of recovery was Colombia's conflict with Peru in the Amazon. The Amazon conflict justified increasing public expenditures and the internal debt, increased employment, and quieted social and party agitation. By the end of 1933 the deflationary cycle had come to an end and symptoms of economic recovery were evident.

During the period 1910–1940 the regional distribution of coffee production changed radically. As of 1900 it was mostly produced east of the Central Cordillera—in the two Santanders, Cundinamarca, and Tolima. But the coffee census of 1932 showed that a large part of western Colombia—Antioquia, Caldas, and the Cauca Valley—was now becoming the coffee belt. This land, cleared by colonists from Antioquia and the Cauca Valley, offered volcanic soil, abundant water, and a moderate climate.

According to the 1932 census, three-quarters of Colombia's coffee harvest came from 146,000 peasant farms (defined as having fewer than 20,000 bushes)—representing 98 percent of all producers. Surveys in 1955–1956 showed that this distribution had not changed much. The 1932 and the 1955–1956 data indicate, however, that two-fifths of these farmers could not be gaining their principal income from coffee. Either they were growing additional crops or were working on others' farms. Nonetheless, the existence of a large class of small coffee cultivators was exploited politically; with this supposed rural middle class, it was said, Colombian democracy had a stable base and its economy a promising future.

A Federation of Coffeegrowers survey during the mid-1930s in Caldas and Antioquia, the land of the "coffee middle class," found that an average family of seven people lived and slept in a single room; half of them lacked water, and none had running water; 97 percent lacked latrines, and those that existed were not hygienic; 93 percent did not grow garden vegetables; and the farms' average size was only 5.12 hectares (12.6 acres). The study concluded that "the route of tropical diseases is the route of coffee and the small cultivator without economic resources. Anemia and malaria have their setting in the geography of coffee." It was not comforting that the health conditions of tenants on the coffee haciendas of Cundinamarca, Tolima, Huila, and the north of el Valle were even worse.

Coffee's Second Phase, 1940–1975

In 1940 coffee exports began to stagnate, as prices fell because World War II closed European markets. This period of stagnation ended in 1975, when a coffee bonanza began. In the intervening thirty-five years, the volume of coffee exports increased at a rate of only 1.6 percent per annum. But while the volume of coffee exports did not grow much, the end of World War II did bring a compensatory rise in prices, which reached a peak in 1953–1954, after which prices dropped again.

Several factors contributed to the stagnation of 1940–1975: the fluctuation of world prices in a period of free or only partly regulated markets (1948–1963), competition from emerging producers in Africa, restrictions im-

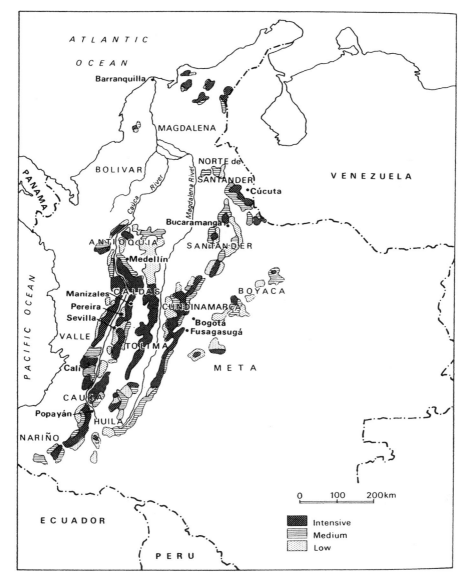

Map 7 Coffee-growing areas of Colombia (ca. 1930). From James J. Parsons, *Antioqueno Colonization in Western Colombia* (Berkeley, CA, 1968).

posed by international coffee accords, and a very grave internal problem, rural violence in the coffee belt (1954–1964). The Violencia, as it is known, brought the deterioration of coffee farms—the bushes were not maintained, and as they aged they were not replaced.

During the 1940–1975 period there occurred a marked change in the ideology of the Federation of Coffeegrowers. On the basis of the 1932 coffee census, the federation had exalted the small growers of the western coffee belt as a rural democracy, models of tenacity in their capacity to survive the adversities of the world market. The key, it was said, lay in the supposedly equal distribution of the land and in the interspersing of other crops among coffee bushes. However, a survey in the mid-1950s began to reveal the problems of the small grower. His productivity was low and his plots were being divided into unviably small units. The heroic small farmer now became the villain. Now the federation began to glorify the farmer who was able to break old routines and assume the risks of technological changes required to compete in the world market. The model coffee farmer now had to know how to administer his land efficiently and be a good client of the Banco Cafetero. This ideology justified the rise of an entrepreneurial, decidedly capitalist, coffee-grower and the displacement of many small cultivators, who became day laborers. Many of these new entrepreneurs, especially in the Quindío, may have begun as coffee-growers during the redistribution of land and harvests that occurred during the Violencia of 1946–1960.

The Third Phase of Coffee, 1975–circa 1994

In this phase the small producers of the western coffee belt declined as the federation directed a transition toward larger-scale coffee cultivation that was highly productive (in terms of kilos produced per hectare) but involved high costs. This development will be discussed in the next chapter.

THE ENCHANTED FOREST

If coffee was the center of the country, what was happening on its peripheries? As the twentieth century began, thousands of Colombians were clearing forests. Precious wood was being plundered in the Chocó and Urabá, and herons in the plains of Arauca were being hunted illegally for feathers much in demand by Paris fashion houses. The rise of the automobile spurred a demand for rubber, which prompted ruthless exploitation in the Amazon basin.

In more than half the territory of Colombia, a violent frontier society emerged of which the national state had little knowledge and over which it had even less control. In these years the eastern *llanos* were being colonized. White abuse of Indians was common, as was the exploitation by landowners of migrating peasants and poor *llaneros*. In the Guajira region Venezuelan contrabandists were enslaving Indians and sending them to Venezuela.

The rubber boom brought the most dramatic, and most publicized, frontier violence. Tomás Funes, a bloodthirsty Venezuelan caudillo, between 1913 and 1921 ruled an empire based on rubber and terror in the upper Orinoco, from which he dominated extensive areas of the Colombian Vichada. Similarly, during the first three decades of the twentieth century, a Peruvian, Julio

César Arana, operating from Peruvian territory, was the rubber king of Colombia's Caquetá and Putumayo. Arana's exploitation in the Putumayo was similar to that of Funes in the Vichada, described by José Eustacio Rivera in his novel *La Voragine* [The Vortex] (1924). Rivera describes the absence of government control, corrupt politicians, the vicissitudes of the rubber-gatherers, the spiral of violence that constantly threatened every aspect of precarious social relations, and the omnipresent magical and anthropomorphic hostility of the forest. Rivera's romantic vision makes the forest appear enchanted and supernatural. An investigation of the operations of Arana in the Putumayo by Roger Casement, the British consul in Rio de Janeiro, yielded a much less romantic description of conquest and repression of the indigenous population, slavery, debt peonage, and sexual exploitation of women. In June 1912 Pius X condemned Arana's exploitations. Arana's operation nonetheless survived British investigation, papal condemnation, and Peruvian criminal prosecution.

Development of plantations in Malaysia and Ceylon caused rubber prices to fall after 1915. But after World War I growth of the North American automobile industry renewed demand and exploitation in the Amazon basin. In 1924 Arana's rubber-gatherers again invaded the Putumayo, prompting street protests in Bogotá and Medellín. In 1932 Arana was a principal in Peruvian seizure of the Colombian town of Leticia, which provoked a brief war between Colombia and Peru.

THE NORTH STAR

After Colombian elites had accepted the loss of Panama as a fait accompli, they had to address the increasing importance of Colombia's commercial connection to the Colossus of the North. The Colombian writer José María Vargas Vila described the United States as "the unruly and brutal north that despises us"—synthesizing a generalized sentiment in the region.

The commercial interests of both Colombia and the United States required a diplomatic settlement of the Panama question. Nonetheless, agreement was delayed until 1922, amid intrigue and scandal that played a part in bringing down two Colombian presidents, Rafael Reyes in 1909 and Marco Fidel Suárez in 1921. The issue in Colombia was the size of the North American indemnity and how the funds would be divided among the country's regions.

The Panama indemnity became intertwined with the interests of U.S. oil companies seeking petroleum concessions in Colombia. In 1919, when the Colombian government decreed restrictions on the ownership of subsoil rights, American petroleum companies urged the U.S. Senate to hold up ratification of the indemnity in order to put pressure on Colombia to suspend the decree. After Colombia's Supreme Court cleared the way by removing some parts of the offending decree, American oil interests then supported the indemnity as a means of improving their competitive position as against

British petroleum companies. The U.S. payment of 25 million dollars to the Colombian government does appear to have helped the American companies' cause.

The bargaining position of the U.S. companies in negotiations with Colombia was further strengthened when it was learned during the 1920s that Colombia's oil potential was rather modest by comparison with Venezuela's. Then in the 1930s enormous deposits were discovered in the Middle East, further weakening Colombia's hand. The creation of the government's Empresa Colombiana de Petróleos (ECOPETROL), when one of the big concessions reverted to the state at the end of the 1940s, did not threaten North American interests. Rather, it fueled conflict among Colombian elites who wanted control of the concession.

There were recurrent tensions between the pressures of an aggressive imperialist power and the doctrine of the "polar star," or north star, enunciated by President Marco Fidel Suárez (1918–1921), which recognized North American hegemony in the hemisphere. In Colombia anti-imperialism tinted controversies over Panama, oil, coffee, and bananas. But with the payment of the Panama indemnity (1922–1926) and the flow of American loans and direct investments in the 1920s, the north star appeared to radiate a more benign light. Franklin Roosevelt's rhetoric of the "good neighbor" underlined the new amity. When the Cold War began, Colombian political and economic elites had fully accepted the asymmetrical relationship between the two countries: For Colombia, United States commerce and investments were of central importance, but to the United States Colombia was quite marginal.

Despite some ambiguities, anti-American sentiments were weakening. In the 1940s, Manuel Mejía, the chief executive of the Federation of Coffeegrowers, was called admiringly "Mr. Coffee." However, when the Truman administration in 1947 objected to the creation of a government-owned merchant fleet, the Flota Mercante Gran Colombiana, noisy anti-American demonstrations, encouraged by Colombian businessmen, occurred in Medellín. After that point, anti-imperialism was limited to the Liberal and Communist left and to rightist admirers of Francisco Franco—the latter soon changing their tune in the context of the Cold War.

The anti-imperialism of the left was not simply a matter of doctrine. It also stemmed from a history of social struggle of an emerging modern proletariate in the oil fields and banana plantations and in railway and river navigation companies. The absence of laws and a judicial apparatus to resolve labor conflicts, as well as the need felt by Conservative governments to maintain friendly relations with the United States, led to frequent strikes that the army ended up repressing. The years from 1918 to 1928 were a period of "heroic unionism," which in Colombia reached its greatest intensity between 1925 and 1928. This history is linked to the origins of the Communist Party, but it also involved ephemeral organizations of anarchists, freethinkers, and momentary revolutionaries. On the other side, at this time, well before the Cold War, an anti-communist ideology developed among army officers.

A milestone in this history is the massacre of the banana workers of United Fruit in the town of Ciénaga in December 1928. In October 1928 a union guided by the Revolutionary Socialist Party, a precursor of the Communist Party, declared a strike, and 25,000 members stopped cutting bananas. The movement was smashed two months later, in a series of massacres of strikers, their family members, and people considered suspicious. The day the strike began, the American manager of the banana company sent a message to the Colombian president, describing "an extremely grave and dangerous" situation. The president sent the army to keep "public order."

On December 5, 1928, some two thousand to four thousand strikers gathered at the railway station of Ciénaga, with the intention of marching to Santa Marta. The government declared a state of siege and imposed a curfew on the region. Troops arrived in Ciénaga with orders to disperse the workers. At 1:30 A.M. on December 6, the army commander read to the strikers the state of siege decree and the curfew order and ordered them to disperse in minutes. The strikers responded with "vivas" for Colombia, the strike, and the Colombian army. The bloodbath that followed came to be known as the "massacre of the banana plantations."

When these events became known, the country was disturbed, the government party became more divided, and the president lost still more prestige. From that time the massacre came to occupy a central place in the collective memory of Colombians—a memory in transformation that forgets, reinvents, changes the order of the facts, and reinterprets their meaning, particularly among the left and in the region where this drama occurred.

The publication of *One Hundred Years of Solitude*, the famous novel of Gabriel García Márquez, a native of a small town in the banana zone, further muddled that collective memory. In a British television interview in 1991, the author confessed the problem he confronted on discovering that three thousand people were not killed in the massacre. "There was talk of a massacre, an apocalyptic massacre. Nothing is sure but there can't have been many deaths. . . . It was a problem for me . . . when I discovered it wasn't a spectacular slaughter. In a book where things are magnified, like *One Hundred Years of Solitude*, . . . I needed to fill a whole railway with corpses."

The confession makes clear that it is a problem less for the novelist than for the historians that have been citing his work as a factual source. In the novel the magnitudes obey the evocative magic of that "interminable and silent train," loaded with cadavers placed "in the order and in the manner in which they transported the bunches of bananas" and in which José Arcadio Segundo, after surviving the massacre, awoke with "his hair caked with dried blood."

More important than establishing the number of victims is reconstructing the diverse meanings of the most traumatic episode, other than the loss of Panama, in the process of Colombians' adaptation to the gravitational force of the north star. This requires reconsidering the notion of enclaves. United Fruit had control of the conditions of production, of internal and maritime transportation, and of marketing the bananas in the consuming countries. This control permitted it to establish strategies of production comparing costs in its plantations in various countries or to decide to which port to send its ships, according to the prices in different markets.

But this dominant company was surrounded by a complex local and regional world, with its own life rooted in traditions and idiosyncrasies that preceded the arrival of United Fruit, although the company might modify them. Historians who have investigated the regional society find heterogeneity. Workers came from Antioquia, Santander, and various localities of the Caribbean coast; they had different kinds of contractual relations and diverse degrees of access to services the company provided and maintained different relations with the people living in the cities and towns of the zone.

Along with the company's plantations, merchants in Ciénaga and Barranquilla grew bananas, as did, on the margins, colonists on smaller plots. The merchants and colonists sold their bananas to the company or, eventually, looked for alternative markets. United Fruit, generally welcomed in the region, nonetheless lived in constant conflict with the Colombian planters over profits and marketing criteria, and it carried on a prolonged dispute with the departmental and national governments over control of the Santa Marta railway.

The banana zone had three principal towns: Santa Marta, the port from which the bananas were shipped and the site of the company offices, was a city dominated by a kind of aristocracy that looked down on the merchants of Barranquilla and Ciénaga, who were involved in the banana business. In the mental map of the Santa Marta elites and rich people in Ciénaga, Paris and Brussels were the capitals of universal civilization.

The way the strike was smashed and the union movement later broken up suggests a cultural undercurrent that, in various ways, reappeared during the Violencia of 1946–1960 and more recently in the military repression of demonstrations by coca growers in 1996. A spirit of conquest infuses the military when it imposes public order on regions "dominated by communism." The testimony presented by Jorge Eliécer Gaitán in debates in the Congress after the Ciénaga massacre offers a fragmentary but illustrative picture of how the "military regime" operated in the banana zone. The military's action suggests a pattern of reconquests of the land and of subduing strikers whom the officers considered enemies and those they believed to be accomplices. In the view of the military, the strikers had lost their nationality and had succumbed to anti-patriotic agitators. The military's allies were the landowning classes, whatever their nationality.

Perhaps because of this attitude in the army, in the denunciations of the massacre of 1929 the anti-imperialist theme became blurred and gave way to an attack on the military. In the background remained, vaguely, the idea of a wicked imperialist enclave. But rather than focus on the strike, that is, on the economic and labor system of the banana company, Liberal rhetoric criticized the government and army officers (rather than the army as an institution). Years later, the left and García Márquez, under the influence of the Cuban Revolution, rediscovered the threads of the anti-imperialist message.

United Fruit continued in the Santa Marta region until mid-century; the relations between the company and zone did not change fundamentally. During a strike in 1934 the Liberal government tried to manipulate the collective memory nationalistically, without much success. What ended United Fruit's fifty-year history in the zone was sigatoka disease, which by 1943 had devastated the banana plantations. Despite a recovery some years afterward, United Fruit sold its land in Santa Marta, later developing a new zone in Urabá under a different organizational scheme.

The 1920s, sometimes called "the dance of the millions," sometimes "the Colombian renaissance," was an outstanding period in diplomatic, commercial, and economic relations between the United States and Colombia. Nevertheless, a sample of the foreign missions invited to Colombia by the government indicates that Europe continued to be a fundamental point of reference.

Of the missions listed in Table 12.4, the one headed by a Princeton economist, Edwin W. Kemmerer, was the most important. It was not an official U.S. government mission, but it coincided with capitalist interests. Imbued with liberal economic principles, the mission reorganized the banking system, national accounting, and public administration in economic fields. For the first time there was monetary and banking stability and policies in accord with the aim of exporting. In 1931 the government again invited Professor Kemmerer, perhaps not so much to get his technical advice as to use his prestige to obtain loans in New York—in which it succeeded.

Table 12.4 Ten foreign missions in the 1920s

Country	Entity	Dates	Purpose
United States	Rockefeller Foundation	1917–1960	Public health
Germany	Julius Berger	1920–1928	Channel Magdalena River
United States	E. W. Kemmerer	1923	Monetary, banking, economic reforms
Germany	Pedagogic mission	1924–1926	Educational reform
Italy	Jurists	1926	Reform penal code
Switzerland	Army	1924–1933	Reform army
Switzerland	Hausermann mission	1926	Tariff policy
International	Council on highways	1929–1931	Highway plan
International	Petroleum experts	1929	Petroleum legislation
Germany	Army	1929–1934	Reform army

The tariff reform suggested in 1926 by the Swiss adviser, Hausermann, was quietly shelved; it contradicted Kemmerer's prescriptions and its protectionist bent would have damaged Colombian–U.S. relations. However, in 1931, amid the Depression, strong pressure from a Conservative majority in Congress obliged the Liberal government to turn toward agricultural protectionism, which incidentally also favored incipient national industry.

The mission of the Rockefeller Foundation beginning in 1917 revealed the obstacles to a public health mission in a society that still did not consider health a matter of public policy or a right of the people. The mission initially focused on eradicating such tropical diseases as yellow fever and hookworm, which infested the coffee zones. This effort tended to conflict with local powers, to whom it seemed dangerous to make an explicit connection between illness and nutrition and housing conditions. It also clashed with dominant ideologies, which privileged privately administered curative medicine over preventative public health. Furthermore, it exposed the lack of government administration in this field. However, the mission had an impact in teaching notions of hygiene. It also apparently affected the elites, who ultimately came to consider public health a social right. The creation of the Ministry of Health and Hygiene in 1947 owed something to the philanthropic action of the Rockefeller Foundation.

The modernization of the armed forces continued to be based on European prototypes. Four Chilean missions (1907–1915) brought Prussian patterns, which were reinforced by the German mission contracted in 1929. In 1921 the French were asked to organize a military aviation school. Behind these projects was the idea of forming a professional military standing above party divisions. But political partisanship, although somewhat attenuated, continued among the officers. After World War II the United States became the model for military organization. The underlying concept also changed: Now the focus was not on protecting the country's boundaries. The enemy now was within: international communism acting through its insidious native agents—"creole communism," as the press began to call it.

The German pedagogical mission, staffed by Catholics, was condemned by many Colombian educators—some Liberals, some clergy. But out of it came a new law affirming the legal responsibility of parents for the basic education of their children. The law left open the question of making primary education obligatory, to which the Church objected. The government adhered to Church views in rejecting university autonomy, which the Germans also had proposed. The vehemence of ideological and doctrinal conflict on educational issues in the 1920s anticipated that of the 1930s in a context of partisan polarization. In 1935–1936 the Liberal government again supported the ideas of obligatory education and university autonomy.

THE CHURCH

Until at least 1930 the Church acted as a complement to the State. But its activities were not evenly spread across the country. It gave preferential attention to the eastern highlands, the upper Cauca, and Antioquia, and its missions looked after the frontier regions. But the Church appears relatively to have neglected the Caribbean coast and the hot Magdalena and Cauca River Valleys. In ethnic terms, the Church focused more on mestizo populations and tended to overlook blacks and mulattoes. In electoral terms, the slighted regions and populations were Liberal. These regions inhabited by blacks and mulattoes also happened to be the axis of the new Colombian economy—the banana plantations, the oil fields, and the river transportation and railways that animated the life of cities along the Magdalena from Neiva to Barranquilla.

By contrast, Antioquia, a Conservative bastion, had a particularly close connection to the Church. Of thirty-four bishops in Colombia in 1960, fourteen were from greater Antioquia (Antioquia and Caldas). The Church appears to have been overrepresented in Pasto, Popayán, Tunja, and Bogotá, as well as in Medellín and Manizales—measured in terms of the ratio of clergy to population. In the nation as a whole, the number of clergy was not keeping pace with population growth, particularly between 1912 and 1938, ironically a period mostly dominated by Conservatives.

The lagging numbers of Colombian clergy were partially compensated by the arrival of foreign clergy, particularly from Europe. Between 1887 and 1960, eighty-six communities of nuns and twenty-eight of friars arrived. These foreign religious orders came during each of Colombia's political phases since 1886—the Regeneration (1886–1900), the Conservative Republic (1900–1930), and the Liberal Republic (1930–1946). But by far the largest number, more than 40 percent of the total, came during the Violencia and the state of siege (1946–1960). The concern of Pope Pius XII (1939–1958) to reevangelize Latin America in the context of the Cold War had much to do with the greater flow of foreign religious orders to Colombia after 1946.

During these same years (1887–1960), the proportions of secular and regular clergy changed dramatically. As Table 12.5 shows, in 1891 five-sixths of the clergy were seculars, mostly parish priests, and only one-sixth were fri-

Table 12.5 Proportions of secular and regular clergy, 1891–1960

Years	Secular Clergy		Regular Clergy	
	Number	Percent	Number	Percent
1891	607	84.0	116	16.0
1912	815	70.6	339	29.4
1938	1397	61.9	860*	38.2*
1960	2339	57.1	1,752†	42.9

*Data from 1944.
†36 percent were foreigners, 22 percent Spaniards.
Sources: 1891: S. Höeg Warming, "La Santa Iglesia Católica," Boletín Trimestral de la Estadística Nacional de Colombia (Bogotá, 1892). 1912–1960: Gustavo Pérez and Isaac Wust, La iglesia en Colombia: estructuras eclesiásticas (Bogotá, 1961).

ars. By 1960 the number of friars was not far below the number of secular clergy. While the secular clergy are fundamentally Colombian, as of 1960 36 percent of the friars were foreign, for the most part Spaniards.

Without the presence of these religious orders, the Church could not have had as much influence as it has had in education, hospitals, social welfare, and in the frontier and colonization areas. The religious orders evangelized in the eastern *llanos*; in the forests of the Vichada, the Putumayo, and the Chocó; and in the Guajira Peninsula and the Sierra Nevada of Santa Marta. In these regions they, at least in some ways, took the place of the state.

In the six decades from 1891 to 1950, the Roman Catholic Church in Colombia was governed by only two archbishops of Bogotá, Bernardo Herrera Restrepo (1891–1928) and Ismael Perdomo (1929–1950). To them fell the primary responsibility of interpreting the Vatican's efforts to adapt the Church to the modern world. The salient papal orientations of this period were those of Leo XIII (1878–1903), who emphasized the need for more understanding of and positive action on social questions, and of Pius XII, who brought a Cold War–influenced anti-communist orientation.

The political partisanship of the Church was evident. The hierarchy was quite open in its support of Conservatives and its hostility to Liberals. In 1913 the Eucharistic Congress in Bogota provided a platform for both Conservative candidates. And the Eucharistic Congress of 1935 in Medellín belligerantly expressed its opposition to the Liberal government of Alfonso López Pumarejo and came close to starting a religious war. At another level, partisanship was particularly evident among parish priests and missionaries. Both believed it imperative to take part in the electoral process and to help with the petitions of parishioners who needed some connection to power. In the religious orders' educational institutions in the cities political criteria influenced their decisions on the admission of students.

Was the Church a source of political legitimacy for the Conservative Party? Between 1905 and 1914 the Church was occupied primarily with its own internal reorganization. From 1914 to 1930, however, it was very actively involved in Conservative politics. Parish clergy indoctrinated the faithful with a partisan political catechism. In 1919 the parish priest of Málaga, in Santander, preached that "Saint Joseph was the first Conservative and Satan was the first Liberal." On the theme "Liberalism is a sin," the hierarchy proposed less rude formulas. And it tended not to become involved in local politicking. At a higher level, however, the hierarchy was a power in the Conservative Party and played a central role in the choice of its presidential candidates.

But secularizing forces were at work in the society, and the Church found that it could not control the opinions even of many Conservatives. In 1917 a "Progressive Coalition," including Liberals, Republicans, and Conservatives (the latter led by the later arch-conservative Laureano Gómez), supported the presidential candidacy of the Historical Conservative Guillermo Valencia, running against the Nationalist Conservative Marco Fidel Suárez.

The platform of the Progressive Coalition demanded that the history of Colombia be taught exclusively by Colombian professors. This clearly was a challenge to the secondary schools run by the religious orders, whose teachers were preponderantly foreign.

In 1922 the Liberal convention authorized the creation of the Universidad Libre, which became a bastion of Liberal politics. In addition to a law faculty, it opened a secondary school. In 1924 the Liberal convention urged supporters to withdraw their children from Church-run schools and to found educational institutions from which "clerical and sectarian influence" would be banished.

In 1925 the rector of a Church-run secondary school lamented that contemporary cultural changes were making it difficult to educate elite youths. The rector complained of "the changeability of their spirit, the yearning for diversions, the futility caused by the cinema . . . the rebelliousness that each day progresses more in the mass of undisciplined students, thanks to the socially destructive press."

Secularization was irresistibly invading the society. The Liberal press was beginning to recover after 1910. Theosophy societies, Masonic lodges, Spiritualists, and Rosacrucians, with their rites and periodicals, were appearing through much of the country, but principally in Liberal cities and towns. Even the Conservative press, increasingly attentive to the tastes and inclinations of its readers, imperceptibly was becoming secularized.

The society was beginning to adapt to modern currents. In public debates on crime and the death penalty, the family, marriage, and the Concordat (which obliged Catholics who wanted civil marriages publicly to leave the Church) emerged ideas about the legal equality of women and divorce.

The Church was beginning to confront such social realities as prostitution and alcoholism, which it viewed as issues both of moral welfare and health. They not only affected the morality of all classes but were also social problems that particularly hurt the poor. As a source of infectious diseases, prostitution was now controlled by municipal authorities, who regulated brothels and zones of tolerance. There was a notable stratification: for the poor, street walkers; for the more affluent, houses of prostitution. In the cities of the 1920s there was a palpable development of a bordello culture, which in Bogotá attempted to imitate supposed Parisian models.

In this environment the Church could no longer control the educational system. Among the upwardly mobile the motto "study and triumph" was a guiding rule. At least a few years of study in secondary school began to be considered a minimum requirement for social recognition. In provincial cities lay-controlled private secondary and commercial schools were proliferating. Run as family enterprises by former teachers, these schools were generally of low academic quality, in effect exploiting those aspiring to social ascent.

In 1929–1930, the hegemony of a Church-influenced Conservative Party came to an end. In the presidential election campaign of 1929, the Nationalist Conservative Alfredo Vázquez Cobo was pitted against the Historical Conservative Guillermo Valencia. Valencia was the candidate of the government and the Conservative Party machinery. But the Church hierarchy was for Vázquez, who had withdrawn as a candidate in 1925 only when Archbishop Herrera promised that he would be the candidate in 1930. Moreover, some clergy in traditionalist regions would not pardon Valencia for having been the candidate of the Progressive Coalition in opposition to Marco Fidel Suárez in 1917–1918. In their eyes Valencia, by courting Liberal support, had been an "ally of the Masons."

As the Church was in danger of internal division over the election, the Vatican prescribed neutrality. However, two weeks before the election, the Vatican responded to a cry for help from the incumbent president, the Conservative Miguel Abadía Méndez, and changed its position. Now the Vatican ordered Archbishop Perdomo, the successor of Archbishop Herrera, to support Valencia, the government candidate. However, eight bishops informed the archbishop that they would stay with Vázquez Cobo. The lower clergy also was disunited. With Conservatives and the clergy both divided between the two candidates, a moderate Liberal, Enrique Olaya Herrera, won the 1929–1930 election, the first Liberal to reach the presidency since the 1870s.

REDS INTO POWER, REACTIONARIES INTO OPPOSITION

The year 1930 marked a change of direction, not only in Colombia but also in the Western world. Political and economic systems entered into struggles exacerbated by extreme ideologies. With the Great Depression, the free market and political liberalism seemed to go into a spin. It was a time of strong leaders in the governments of the great powers (Roosevelt, Stalin, Mussolini, Hitler) and in some Latin American countries as well (notably Lázaro Cárdenas in Mexico and Getulio Vargas in Brazil).

In Colombia three strong leaders emerged, Liberal President Alfonso López Pumarejo (1934–1938 and 1942–1945), the extreme Conservative caudillo Laureano Gómez (president 1950–1953), and Jorge Eliécer Gaitán, Liberal populist candidate for the presidency in 1946. But these flamboyant leaders had their counterparts in quieter centrists, such as Liberal presidents Enrique Olaya (1930–1934) and Eduardo Santos (1938–1942) and Conservative President Mariano Ospina (1946–1950).

The four presidential periods from 1930 to 1946 are known as the "Liberal Republic." During these years there occurred an alternation between moderates and radicals, with López twice succeeding moderates, Olaya and Santos. López's radicalism synthesized the mystique of Liberal sectarianism with a search for adequate solutions for a society undergoing drastic economic change.

López had been the only Liberal leader in 1929 who insisted that the Liberals were ready to take power. His fellow Liberals did not listen to him, turning rather to the conciliatory Olaya. However, López's persistent activities with the base of the party faithful carried him to undisputed leadership and the presidency in 1934. His first two years in government were very active, particularly in his encouragement of labor organization. López referred to his administration as "la revolución en marcha" (the revolution on the march). This early start ended in a "pause" of two years. In his second term (1942–1945), he lost his radical luster, and his administration ended in a proposal for a bipartisan pact and López's resignation in 1945.

All four Liberal administrations revealed a formidable centralizing tendency. This was most evident in substantial increases in income taxes as a proportion of total revenue, reflected also in the marked decline of the proportion of government revenue deriving from customs duties. (See Table 12.6.)

The centralization began as a response to the Great Depression, with the Olaya administration's nationalization of the management of the public foreign debt, much of which had been contracted in the 1920s by various departments and municipalities. Olaya established exchange controls in 1931 as well as a system of controls on importations. And he intervened in bank interest rates and redesigned credit institutions. The military conflict with Peru (1932–33) enabled him to engage in deficit spending and in many respects strengthened the power of the presidency.

López, aided by labor laws passed under Olaya, became the supreme arbiter of worker-management conflicts by strongly supporting unionization. Under his aegis, the numbers of unions, of union members, and of labor demands all increased. Paternalist control of labor by the industrialists of Medellín was seriously challenged. Peasant agitation in coffee haciendas, which had been occurring in the 1920s, and the strikes of coffee harvesters in the Quindío, were now leading to unionization. Peasants and day laborers were obtaining better working conditions and in some cases ownership of plots of land.

President Eduardo Santos (1938–1942), in many ways a moderate man, and certainly more conservative than López on labor organization, proved much more adventurous in economic policy than López. His finance minister, Carlos Lleras Restrepo, announced that a government deficit was not necessarily a bad thing, that it could help to reactivate the economy. No pre-

Table 12.6 Changing proportions of revenue from customs duties and income taxes, 1910–1950

Years	1910	1920	1930	1940	1950
Customs duties*	77.9	54.7	45.3	29.3	19.2
Income taxes*	n.d.	n.d.	6.4	25.1	45.6

*As percentages of total revenue.

Source: Rosemary Thorp, *Progress, Poverty and Exclusion: An Economic History of Latin America in the 20th Century* (Baltimore, 1998), Statistical Appendix.

vious Colombian in charge of economic policy had dared utter such a Keynesian heresy.

Santos in various ways used the state to promote industrial development. In 1941 he created the Instituto de Fomento Industrial, or IFI (Institute of Industrial Development), to aid the establishment of industries that would reduce the country's dependence on imported manufactures. Through the IFI the State made direct investments in enterprises involving large investments of capital, slow maturation, and high risk—such as the steel industry and the production of basic chemicals. These enterprises, it was hoped, would come under private ownership when they became profitable.

IFI's investments of capital in the 1940s were disseminated among various regions of the country. The IFI backed a steelworks in Medellín (1941). It created a rubber factory (Icollantas) near Bogotá in 1942, with the raw material coming from the Guaviare and Vaupés regions of Colombia. It established a shipyard in Barranquilla (1943). And it initiated the largest of the state industries, the steel plant at Paz de Río in Boyacá, although that project came to completion under later Conservative and military governments.

State intervention in the economy under Santos also included the establishment of the Instituto de Crédito Territorial (ICT), whose mission was to encourage the construction of low-cost housing, and the Instituto de Fomento Municipal, whose function was to channel public funds into the construction of acueducts and sewers.

State intervention under the Liberals occurred on other fronts as well. For example, when radio news programs began to appear, the print press began to fear the loss of readers and advertising. Publishers began to cry alarm at the cultural decline that would occur if radio displaced newspapers and to ask for legal limits on radio news. In 1936 López's minister of government, Alberto Lleras Camargo, one of the most notable journalists of the time, urged state ownership of the radio industry, a proposal strongly opposed by broadcasters and the industrialists who already controlled radio broadcasting. Nonetheless, compromise solutions gave the state considerable control over radio news, which was broadened after strikes against President Ospina Pérez in 1946. From that time broadcasting news of strike movements was prohibited. From there it was but a step to the prior censorship imposed when Ospina carried out a coup against his own government in November 1949.

While the assertion of the authority of the national state was an important element of the Liberal years, we must not lose sight of the partisan features of the Liberal Republic, which also bore on political culture. The turning point was precisely the "revolución en marcha," which produced a constitutional reform that polarized the country between Liberals and Conservatives over the place that God ought to have in the preamble to the constitution. Two other issues had to do with the Liberals' assertion of the social function of property and the right of all children to education.

Up to that time property rights were considered to be in the realm of private transactions and were ruled by the civil code. To speak of the social function of property and expropriation for reasons of social utility was to Conservatives subversive and communistic. As for the legal guaranty of the right to education, the clergy objected on two grounds. First, the Church argued, the question of whether children should be educated was a matter for heads of families (i.e., fathers) to decide, not the state. Secondly, clergy considered educational obligations to be within the province of the Church. In the view of the clergy the intromission of the state in this area was intolerable. Thus, when the government sought to make schooling obligatory and to oblige educational institutions to receive students without any kind of discrimination, the Church reacted furiously. (The secondary schools run by religious communities did not accept "natural children.")

The ideological conflicts of the time in turn inspired a struggle to control the education of the elites. Liberals sought to strengthen the National University and explicitly Liberal universities such as the Universidad Libre. Conservatives for their part supported clergy-directed institutions; the Universidad Javeriana in Bogotá, refounded in 1931; and the Universidad Pontificia Bolivariana in Medellín, established by the archbishop in 1936.

López's manipulation of symbols served to inflame Conservatives. When he appeared on the presidential balcony flanked by Communist leaders in the May Day celebration in 1936, the right saw this as proof that Colombia was ruled by the Popular Front, the anti-fascist alliance proposed by Stalin in 1935. Despite López's radical gesture, however, the "pause" began a few months later.

López was aggressive on labor issues but rather conservative in economic policy. His ideas about financial management of the government were orthodox and he always avoided fiscal deficits. He believed in free trade in international commerce and in a commercial trade balance as the basis of sound money. He was critical of industrial protectionism because it would tend to concentrate privilege in large industries. In 1935 he had no difficulty signing a commercial treaty with the United States that reduced protection of Colombian industry in order to free Colombia's coffee exports from American taxation. López never proposed any measures to reform banking or to aid industry.

Already angered by López's intervention in labor disputes, Medellín's industrialists resisted his tax reform of 1935. To fight the tax reform they employed their radio stations in 1937 to organize one of the biggest demonstrations in the history of the city. This kind of incident gave López a radical image at the time and, to a considerable degree, still in historical perspective.

The sixteen years of the Liberal Republic began with a centrist coalition government that lasted three years (1930–1933). The Liberal Republic ended in the same way. López resigned in 1945, convinced that the country needed a bipartisan government. His successor, Alberto Lleras Camargo, governed under the banner of National Union, which Conservative President Ospina continued in 1946. This centrism was challenged both by Laureano Gómez on the right and Jorge Eliécer Gaitán on the left. The assassination of Gaitán in 1948 closed the way to centrist tendencies for a long time.

LABOR UNIONS

Several circumstances had eased the peaceful transfer of power from one party to the other in 1930. First, Olaya Herrera had created an alliance of moderates in both parties called the Concentración Nacional. Second, Conservatives dominated the Congress, the courts, the departmental legislatures, and city councils; they expected to overcome the internal divisions within their party and return to the presidency in four years. Third, the Church accepted the election result. Fourth, the army, despite its Conservative inclinations, had served since 1910 as the country's electoral police; in fulfilling that function over two decades it had become committed to ending the election-prompted civil wars of the nineteenth century.

Ideological controversy focused on labor questions; during the 1930s labor issues defined who was in the center and who was on the extremes. As a matter of party alliances, the unions were to the Liberals what the Church was for the Conservatives.

Labor legislation began to develop timidly in the 1920s, inspired by Catholic social doctrine and the legislative models proposed after 1919 by the International Labor Organization, formed as a complement to the League of Nations. The Liberals after 1930 broadened these laws, following more closely the Mexican labor system of 1931, which in turn was influenced by continental European legislation.

The norms formulated in the Colombian legislation of the 1920s had primarily a symbolic effect, as they were rarely fulfilled. The laws of that decade proclaimed the right to strike (except for workers in public services) if there had been been previous efforts at conciliation (1921); norms for hygiene and social assistance in work places (1924 and 1925); the establishment of work and hygiene rules in shops, factories, and other enterprises, with inspectors to ensure enforcement (1925); the right to rest on Sunday (1926); protection of child labor (1929); and hygiene regulations for haciendas (1929). In addition, the first steps were taken to establish institutions to deal with labor fights. The Oficina Nacional de Trabajo (1923) intervened sporadically in strikes in the principal cities and in some coffee haciendas. But it was absent from the biggest conflicts of the 1920s.

The change in relations between the state and workers in the sixteen years of Liberal government did not occur because of structural transformations in the mode of production. Rather, it stemmed from political mobilization in a country that was becoming more urban. The radical wing of the Liberal Party took over the issues of the left, thereby avoiding the formation of strong socialist or communist parties of the kind that developed in Chile.

Important impediments to labor organization were the small numbers and the geographic dispersion of the modern proletariat, who became absorbed by the political traditions of urban artisans. For the most part Liberals, the artisans allowed themselves to become engrossed in the conflict between the two traditional parties and in their own individualist dreams of social ascent.

Labor organization in the 1930s and 1940s reflected the weakness of modern industry and the slight weight of a stable proletariat within the working classes. The urban populace was a heterogeneous mix of operators of small grocery stores, owners of modest houses who rented out rooms, and artisans (tailors, dressmakers, carpenters, shoemakers, and bakers). Among the artisans were some who had shops with people working under them and some who elaborated their products at home for other artisans or other employers (putting out). Some were peasants recently migrated to the city who worked in the construction industry, in unmechanized shops and factories, and in services, including domestic service and prostitution. The 1938 census indicates that only 12 percent of the half million urban workers labored in what could be called modern factories of more than a hundred employees.

The unions were created, controlled, or co-opted by the two parties, the Church, and the Communist left. In the large textile factories of Medellín the owners themselves, along with clergy, organized the unions. The feeble unions represented the workers on wage and work conditions issues. They could not induce the workers to change their party loyalties or to vote one way or the other. Nonetheless, the memories of the confrontations and repressions at the hands of the army in 1925–1928, principally on the Magdalena River, the oil camps, and banana plantations, left traditions of rebellion and radicalism, which were constantly refreshed.

Given the ascendency of the Socialists and Communists in the unions and in general among the urban working classes during the 1920s, the Liberals' arrival in government created a kind of left alliance that provoked reactions from Conservatives and the Church. In this way the the party divisions were projected on the unions. Put in another way, the union question carried the seal of government paternalism and developed along party lines. In Medellín the paternalism was provided by the factory owners and the Church.

The Olaya government formulated legislation that guaranteed the basic rights of workers, with protection by a specific contractual relationship, and provided for collective negotiation. This legislation helped to end the unions' semianarchic confrontations followed by military repression that had been characteristic of the 1920s. The recognition of the unions and of the right to unionize, the establishment of the eight-hour day and the forty-eight-hour working week, and the specification of the legal responsibilities of employers won the Liberals popular sympathy. The labor reforms legislated under Olaya were made effective under López with a consequent strengthening of unionism.

The left (Liberal, Socialist, and Communist) came to dominate an important segment of unions through the Confederación de Trabajadores de Colombia (CTC), created after union congresses in 1936 and 1938. These were years of tension within the left, which ended during the Violencia of 1946–1960, when the Liberal left moved toward the center. Conservatives and the Church considered the CTC to be nothing more than a Liberal client organization. For their part, Conservatives did not succeed in creating their own union base. Rather, this role was assumed in the mid-1930s by the Church, which after a series of failed attempts in the 1940s formed the Unión de Trabajadores de Colombia (UTC).

The fear of popular and union mobilizations brought a clear majority of moderate Liberals to the Chamber of Representatives in 1937. Seeing himself in a minority position within his own party, President López offered his resignation, which was not accepted. But he was forced to propose a "pause" in his "revolution on the march."

In 1938, Eduardo Santos became president, with the support even of the Communist Party, despite his evident moderation. At the time the ideological spectrum in Colombia was being defined in part by events in the Spanish Civil War. On this Santos took a centrist position, supporting the Spanish Republican intellectuals in exile, while distancing himself from communism as well as Franco. The Communists' coup against the Spanish Republic, which had already been defeated militarily, to many Liberals demonstrated the deceitfulness of the Communists and proved Santos right. With arguments of this kind, moderate Liberals were able to discredit the young left-leaning Liberal ministers who had been in López's cabinet, widely known as "los muchachos comunistas" ("the Communist boys").

The Liberal-sponsored CTC included both Liberals and Communists in its leadership, and the two were frequently in conflict. The strongest union in the CTC, and in the country, was controlled by the Communists. This was the federation of maritime, river, air transportation and port employees (FEDENAL), which had organized workers of many kinds on the Magdalena River.

The relations between Liberals and Communists in the CTC worsened or improved depending on the latest policy line coming out of the Sovet Union. The German-Soviet pact of 1939 exacerbated Liberal-Communist hostilities in the union, but the German invasion of the Soviet Union in 1941 brought the two wings of the Colombian left together again. The reunified CTC was controlled by the Communists, although they left its Liberal leaders in visible positions. When the Communist International dissolved in 1943, the Communists in the CTC drifted away from the questions preoccupying Liberals, focusing more on their own sectarian issues. One wing of the Communists conceived of unions as the vanguard of the revolution. Jorge Eliécer Gaitán, the left Liberal labor minister in López's second administration, was not impressed with this formulation. Speaking at the opening of the CTC Congress in 1943, he pointed out that of four million Colombian workers, only 90,000 (i.e., 2.25 percent) were unionized. Where, Gaitán asked, was the revolutionary spirit of Colombian unionism?

But if the unions were far from "revolutionary," they were ready to defend democratic institutions. When a group of army officers held President López prisoner in Pasto in July 1944, the unions, joined by broader mass support, demonstrated in favor of constitutional government across the country. Under the state of siege that followed this attempted coup, López produced more advanced labor legislation, which established important principles in the individual rights of laborers and prohibited, for the first time, the use of strikebreakers to crush legal strikes.

During World War II the Communists won some tolerance and sympathy, which aided them in congressional elections in 1945, when they got the largest vote they ever received (3.2 percent). At this point the CTC and FEDENAL reached the height of their prestige and influence. This soon ended, however, with a massive strike by FEDENAL, prompted in part by factional conflict among its Communist leadership. The strike induced the centrist government of Alberto Lleras Camargo (who had been one of the "muchachos comunistas" under López in the 1930s) to remove the union's recognition as a juridical entity and to declare the strike illegal.

The end of FEDENAL showed the extreme vulnerability of the unions, subject as they were to changes in the temperament of Liberal governments. But divisiveness on the left also could be destructive. In 1946 the unions dominated by Communists decided to support the official (centrist) Liberal candidate, Gabriel Turbay, against the populist Liberal, Jorge Eliécer Gaitán, even though Gaitán was popular among union members. The Communist leaders were evening scores with Gaitán, who had tried to break the unity of the CTC when he attempted to found a new union organization which, ironically, evolved into the proclerical UTC.

The CTC, a creature of the Liberals while they governed, brought together many tendencies and could not adequately express the various interests of its affiliated unions. Its objectives were too broad. Its alliances with politicians were subject to the electoral uncertainties of the Liberals. It also was disrupted by the maneuvers of the Communists, whose actions were shaped by Soviet interests.

The CTC was a loose federation, without its own funds, which had difficulty controlling its member unions. Although unionization continued to increase, at the end of the 1940s membership did not reach 5 percent of the wage-earning population. Three-fourths of workers in manufacturing were not affiliated with any union. Barranquilla, however, was an exception. It was much more unionized than other cities and was one of the pillars of the radical wing of the CTC.

Another problem lay in the fact that the Liberals' labor legislation gave the unions the power to negotiate only within an enterprise, not in an entire industry. The only union with the power to represent workers in an entire industry was FEDENAL, which was destroyed in 1945.

Union organization, labor rights, and Liberal electoral support were all intertwined. Issues relating to the peasants and their access to land also formed part of the ensemble of Liberal-left concerns. Agrarian legislation on behalf of peasants, which began to gestate in the 1920s, was presented by the Liberals as a significant social reform. But its effects were very limited.

Even more than urban workers, peasants were dispersed geographically, worked under a great diversity of agrarian labor systems, and lived in varying local cultures. Despite the fact that a number of peasant protests occurred between 1920 and 1937, there really was not a peasant "movement." Moreover, divisions among the Colombian left (Liberal, Socialist, Communist) increased the fragmentation of peasant mobilizations.

In 1926 a decision of the Supreme Court created insecurity about land titles among landowners and expectations among peasant *colonos*, who claimed ownership of the land they were working. In 1932 Olaya took the initiative on this question and convoked a mostly Liberal group to prepare an agrarian reform proposal that would incorporate the most recent theories of French law on the social character of real property, as well as the agrarian principles of the Mexican Revolution and the Spanish Republic. The first government proposal, which had bipartisan support, established a presumption of state ownership of "all uncultivated land." In effect, public lands could be obtained by individuals only by working it.

It has never been explained how, when, and why this proposal lost its edge. After a complicated legislative process, it was reduced to the land law of 1936, which privileged the security of title of landowners over division of the land among peasants. The law strengthened the juridical position of large landowners, although it gave some relief to peasants who could prove good faith in the possession of their plots. That relief depended on the fate of their claims for recognition of improvements on the land. But the number of land judges created to deal with these conflicts was tiny. And they were not provided with instructions and regulations for more than a year, giving the landowners time to remove the *colonos*. Peasant protest was concentrated in the coffee zones of Tequendama and Sumapaz, which were dominated by the Communists, and to a lesser degree in the Santa Marta banana zone, the province of Vélez, the Sinú valley on the Caribbean coast, and the coffee-growing Quindío. The land law of 1936 served to resolve these conflicts by means that in reality had been employed since the 1920s—private or government division of large estates that were besieged by *colonos* and tenants and adjudicating public lands on a case-by-case basis.

Colonos and conflicts over colonization would continue to be a part of Colombian history in the second half of the twentieth century.

13

A Nation of Cities

Since the time of independence Colombian society had not experienced a change so charged with consequences as the partial capitalist modernization that occurred after World War II. This change manifested itself in a rapid increase and geographic redistribution of the population; substantial urban growth; the development of manufacturing of consumer goods, including consumer durables; the expansion of capitalist agriculture in some areas of the country; and, recently, deindustrialization and enlargement of the service sector. Change also came to the state, in the growth of state bureaucracies, a larger participation of state income and expenditures in the gross national product, and the reform of various institutions.

Poverty in various degrees has been the condition of most Colombians. Underemployment and poverty, which had characterized peasant society, moved to the city with the rural poor. Per capita income in Colombia ($U.S.2400 in 1998) continues to be low relative to the richer countries of the world. However, by comparison with other countries in Latin America, Colombia has done moderately well during the past hundred years. In the twentieth century, Colombia's gross domestic product (GDP) per capita grew at a rate slightly above the Latin American median. In 1950 Colombia's GDP per capita was tenth among Latin American countries; in 1995 it was eighth. This economic growth has permitted the rise of new urban middle classes.

At mid-century a national network of highways, designed in 1931, was about to be completed, better integrating the nation. Nonetheless, the country remained fragmented in four populated regions: the Caribbean coast, Antioquia, the Cauca, and the eastern zone.

Between 1945 and the 1970s the elites pragmatically pursued an economic policy that was a hybrid of industrial protectionism and free trade. Free trade, advocated by the World Bank and the International Monetary Fund, was favored within Colombia, particularly by coffee growers and exporters. But Colombia, while attempting in these years to diversify its exports, also pursued a policy of inward development, that is one of protected development of industry inspired by the Economic Commission for Latin America. The need for protected development of industry found particular justification with the end of the coffee bonanza in 1956, which brought increasingly negative terms of trade. The hybrid economic policy, with elements of protectionism and free trade, had important effects on the country's political drama of the years 1945–1957.

In the 1980s an important shift in policy began to occur. The problems

of the external debt and of economic adjustment, the subsequent globalization of markets, the high expectations created by oil income, and the impact
of the drug traffic brought to the fore an atmosphere of free trade dogma-
tism reminiscent of the middle of the nineteenth century.

The question is whether the State will fulfill the society's expectations
or, despite its increased revenues, expenses, and machinery, will draw back,
failing to maintain social peace. This chapter discusses the paradox of an expanding State that simultaneously was failing in such essential functions as
the provision of personal security and justice. In this failure perhaps may be
found one of the keys to the violence experienced in the second half of the
century.

Colombian democracy has been in some ways exceptional in Latin
America. The country has had a long tradition of two-party politics. With
the exception of a military government in 1953–1958, presidential succession
has occurred according to Western electoral rules. Nonetheless, between 1948
and 1958, the Colombian political system could not cope with problems created in part by the conflicting demands of capitalist modernization without
turning to dictatorial methods.

Some of New Granada's viceroys fretted, as did Simón Bolívar in his
last years, that the State was weak, and it continues to be so. In a liberal constitutional system the State ought to be a source of protection for individuals and for civility and social cohesion. But in Colombia, the fragility of the
State becomes evident when its social obligations as established by the constitution of 1991 are contrasted with its everyday performance.

The trajectory of politics and the State in the last half century falls into
three phases. First is the neoconservative order of 1946–1958. The term neoconservative emphasizes the intertwining of the old ideas, in Colombia commonly associated with the conservative order of the constitution of 1886,
with the rapid economic and social transformations that seemed to over-
whelm existing institutions at mid-century. Second is the period of bipartisan constitutionalism of the National Front (1958–1974), a formal pact that
sought to join together the neoconservative order with the civil politics of
the Liberal Republic of 1930–1946, followed by the *desmonte*, a gradual dismantling of the National Front (1974–1986). And third is an interregnum that
commenced in 1986 and still continues. The last fifteen years may be considered an interregnum, in that the effective sovereignty of the state has been
placed in question and the government has been unable to deal effectually
with national problems, as it confronts the powerful centripetal forces of
globalization and the conflictive encounters of narco-traffickers, guerrilleros,
paramilitaries, and politicians.

THE DEMOGRAPHIC TRANSITION

During the twentieth century the Colombian population multiplied tenfold.
In 1900 it amounted to only 4 million; in 2000 it was more than 42 million.
(See Table 13.1.)

Table 13.1 Colombian population, 1938–1993

Year	Population	Percentage of Annual Growth*	Births per 1000 Population	Deaths per 1000
1938	8,701,800	2.2	38.3	25.1
1951	11,548,200	3.3	43.0	22.1
1964	17,914,500	2.7	44.2	14.0
1973	22,973,900	2.1	36.0	10.1
1985	29,481,100	1.8	27.5	8.1
1993	37,664,700		24.2	7.0

*The annual growth rate refers to the period following the date. That is, the figure for 1938 represents the years 1938–1951.

At mid-century Colombia entered fully into a demographic transition, with a rapid increase of the population (1951–1973) followed by a decreasing rate of population growth. The transition alludes to the passage from a phase characterized by high levels of mortality and fertility and low life expectancy at birth to a phase in which mortality and fertility decrease and life expectancy increases. In Colombia, this demographic transition occurred rather quickly, even by comparison with the rest of Latin America, as Table 13.2 indicates.

In the first phase of the demographic transition, fertility remains high while mortality declines. As a consequence, the population increases. High levels of infant mortality are attributable to malnutrition, overcrowding, and illiteracy, which increase the risks of contracting infectious and parasitical diseases like tuberculosis, typhoid, and malaria. These diseases are reduced with the supply of potable water, increased vaccination, preventive medicine, and the spread of antibiotics. As infant mortality declines, the principal causes of death become cardiovascular disease and cancer. However, over the last two decades, homicide has been one of the chief causes of mortality for men between ages sixteen and thirty-four in Colombia's three largest cities (Bogotá, Medellín, and Cali).

Table 13.2 The demographic transition: Colombia and Latin America

	Fertility (Births per Fertile Woman)		Infant Mortality per 1000		Life Expectancy in Years	
Years	Colombia	Latin America	Colombia	Latin America	Colombia	Latin America
1950–1955	6.8	5.9	123.0	73.0	50.6	51.8
1990–1995	2.8	3.1	40.0	53.0	68.2	66.7

Source: Francisco Alba and José B. Morelos, "Población y grandes tendencias demográficas, in UNESCO, ed., Historia General de America Latina, vol. VIII, chapter X (Madrid, in publication).

In the second phase, fertility rates decrease, principally because of socio-economic and cultural changes, although family planning policies and programs can play an important role. Poverty is perhaps the principal socio-economic factor inhibiting the decline of fertility, as can be seen in the data for Bogotá in Table 13.3.

Rates of fertility varied greatly depending on the location of the mother in the rural-urban continuum and the region of the country. In 1946 Bogotá had a birth rate of 31.4 per 1000, but in Medellín, the largest city in Antioquia, a region historically characterized by early marriage and large families, it was 41.7. In the nation as a whole the birth rate in 1946 was 33 per 1000.

In traditionally Catholic societies the decrease in births implies an important change in values and attitudes of women. The field research of Virginia Gutiérrez de Pineda has revealed a breach between the type of traditional Catholic family that one might expect and the kinds of family that actually prevail in the various regions of Colombia. Even in markedly Catholic areas many women are heads of families because they have been abandoned or are widows; there also are many people living in free unions. Nonetheless, one must not underestimate the impact of the traditional views that predominated among the Colombian clergy in the middle of the twentieth century. Bishops and parish priests preached three rules of marriage: having children, observing the fidelity that spouses owe each other, and the indissolubility of the sacrament of marriage. And they kept watch from the confession box.

Although after much hesitation the Church accepted natural means of birth control, its use before mid-century was known only among the educated of the big cities. In other sectors of the society, clandestine abortions remained common. Since the 1960s, however, the use of various modes of contraception has spread with astonishing speed. An organized program to make birth control devices available through public clinics began in 1965; subsequently the use of contraceptives began to extend through urban networks until it reached rural regions. It is generally agreed that the degree of education of the woman is the most important determinant of acceptance of

Table 13.3 Fertility and infant mortality in Bogotá, 1985

Economic Condition	Fertility	Infant Mortality per 1000
Not poor	1.9	28.0
Poor	3.6	37.7
Destitute	4.3	48.1
Bogotá (total)	2.5	31.3

Source: Francoise Dureau and Carmen Elisa Flórez, "Dynamiques demographiques colombiennes: du national au local," in Jean-Michel Blanque and Christian Gross, eds., *La Colombie a l'aube du troisieme millenaire* (Paris, 1996), p. 155.

modern methods of birth control. In the 1970s Colombia was the Latin American country with the highest proportion of women who used contraceptives within the framework of family planning programs.

By permitting a clear separation between sexuality and procreation, the availability of modes of contraception opened the way to new values and social conduct in the relations between genders, in the sensitization of feelings, in the formation of couples and their life patterns, and in preferences as to the number of children. Women were more able to obtain higher levels of education and to work outside the home. All of this had an effect on the size of families, the care of children, and the greater acceptance of the social and legal equality of single mothers and of children born outside of marriage.

In the mid-1960s some in the National Front elite, particularly Liberals, began to make a concerted effort to foster an organized campaign for family planning, operating through both public and private networks. They also managed to secure from the Church tacit agreement not to subject the program to public censure. The Church hierarchy, for their part, had to mediate the conflict between papal doctrines condemning such programs and the concerns of many priests who ministered to poor parishioners and were conscious of the impact of having many children on the living conditions of the families, as well as on the life chances of the children. The Colombian hierarchy, in effect, began to treat decisions about procreation as a matter of private conscience. Although population policy was a matter of great importance to both Church and State and the fundamental principles shaping their views conflicted, ecclesiastical and political leaders were remarkably successful in reaching a peaceful modus vivendi.

During these years the Catholic Church was becoming visibly weaker. This could be seen in the declining numbers of priests in poor neighborhoods of the large cities, their almost total absence in regions of the country where the Church always had been weak, such as the Caribbean and Pacific coasts, and their marginal role in the colonization zones of the second half of the twentieth century—in contrast with their marked influence among Antioquia's colonizers.

URBAN GROWTH

Although urban growth in Colombia came later than in some other countries of Latin America, it followed the same patterns. In 1938 only 29 percent of Colombia's population lived in cities; at the end of the century the proportion was 70 percent. The rhythm of urban expansion was slow in the first decades of the century, began to accelerate in the 1930s, and reached maximum velocity in the 1950s. In 1940 no Colombian city contained a half a million inhabitants; in 1958 two cities had more than 2 million, and two more had more than 1 million. And another eight cities contained more inhabitants than Bogotá, the largest city, had in 1940. In less than fifty years a predominantly rural country had become a nation of cities.

A nation of cities—it is important to emphasize the plural. Each of the four more populated regions has a demographic and economic capital, along with a number of other cities of varying size and importance. As of 1970, some thirty cities composed a network distributed among the four populous regions. (See Table 13.4.)

The currents of colonization have created additional substantial regional centers, such as Florencia in the Caquetá, La Dorada in the Middle Magdalena, and Apartadó in Urabá. This ensemble of cities continues the development of an urban system that is more balanced than in most other countries in Latin America. In Colombia there is no overwhelmingly dominant city, as in the cases of Montevideo, Buenos Aires, Caracas, or Mexico City.

However, in Colombia there is a tendency for population to concentrate in the four large regional capitals—Bogotá, Medellín, Cali, and Barranquilla. As of 1938, 10 percent of the people lived in these four cities; at the end of the twentieth century the proportion was more than 25 percent. Bogotá in 1938 contained 4 percent of the national population, in 1998 nearly 15 percent. Of the four cities Bogotá grew the most rapidly after 1950, Barranquilla the most slowly. Over the forty-year period of 1950–1990, Bogotá has grown faster than most large Latin American cities. (See Table 13.5.)

The slower growth of some large cities in Latin America during the 1980s

Table 13.4 Urban hierarchy by region, circa 1970

Urban Hierarchy	Caribbean Coast	Antioquia	Cauca or Southwest	East
National metropolis	—	—	—	Bogotá
Regional capitals	Barranquilla-Soledad	Medellín-Itaguí-Bello-Envigado-La Estrella	Cali-Yumbo	Bogotá-Soacha
Primary regional cities	Cartagena, Santa Marta	Manizales-Villa Maria, Pereira-Santa Rosa	—	Bucaramanga/Girón/Floridablanca
Secondary regional cities	Montería, Ciénaga, Sincelejo, Valledupar	Armenia	Palmira, Pasto, Buena-ventura, Buga, Tuluá, Cartago	Cúcuta, Ibagué, Neiva, Girardot, Barrancabermeja, Villavicencio, Tunja, Sogamoso-Nobsa, Duitama

Source: Based on Departamento Nacional de Planeación, "Modelo de Regionalización," *Revista de Planeación y Desarrollo,* II, no. 3 (October 1970), pp. 302–339.

Table 13.5 Growth rates of principal Latin American cities, 1950–1990

City	1950–1960	1960–1970	1970–1980	1980–1990
Bogotá	7.2	5.9	3.0	4.1
Buenos Aires	2.9	2.0	1.6	1.1
Caracas	6.6	4.5	2.0	1.1
Lima	5.0	5.3	3.7	2.8
Mexico	5.0	5.6	4.2	0.9
Rio de Janeiro	4.0	4.3	2.5	1.0
Santiago	4.0	3.2	2.6	1.7
São Paulo	5.3	6.7	4.4	2.0

Source: Villa y Rodríguez, cited in Alan Gilbert, "El proceso de urbanización," in UNESCO, ed., *Historia general de América Latina*, vol. VIII (in publication).

occurred partly because of the closing of many factories and the reduction of government employment in a context of economic crisis and the opening to the global economy. In Colombia the external opening has come later, in the 1990s, and there has been less privatization. In any event, violence and insecurity in rural areas have forced continuing migration of displaced families to urban centers.

Medellín, the dominant center in Antioquia, offers a clear example of the impact of economic distress on urban life. After its industrial peak (1940–1956), Medellín has suffered a slow decline of economic activity, which, since the mid-1970s, has led to high unemployment, criminality, and insecurity of persons and property.

At the beginning of the 1970s, many in the political elite and the clergy were alarmed by the large-scale rural exodus to the cities, an alarm that increased after the results of the presidential election of 1970 suggested that the elites were losing control. The word "exodus," however, does not suggest the selectivity of this migration. Migrants to the cities come primarily for economic reasons and are people who have something to offer to urban markets. More women than men migrate to the cities, and young people with education and skills tend to predominate. Those who are older or unskilled tend to stay in the rural regions where they were born. While the migrants have something to offer, they also come in hopes of obtaining more education and better housing and health care. The migration of the last three decades also has coincided with a growth in the proportion of women in the work force. In Bogotá 36 percent of the work force were women in 1976; twenty years later, women constituted half of those working.

While the educational gap between the country and the city has increased, that between genders decreased, at least until 1985, as Table 13.6 indicates. However, there continue to be strong regional differences. The Caribbean coast tends to fall behind the rest of the country. The difference between primary and secondary enrollments, once very great, has dimin-

Table 13.6 Percentage of illiterates among those over 15 years of age, 1951–1993

	1951	1964	1973	1985	1993
Urban	21	14	11	8	7
Rural	50	41	33	26	23
Men	35	25	18	13	11
Women	40	29	19	14	17
Total	38	27	19	14	11

Source: Censos de población: 1951 (Bogotá, 1951); 1964 (Bogotá, 1963); 1973 (Bogotá, 1977); 1985 (Bogotá, 1986); 1993 (Bogotá, 1994).

ished. But much improvement remains to be made. In 1989 only 71 percent of the school-age population was receiving primary education, and only 57 percent of the children who began school were completing the primary program. Although the growth of primary instruction often is considered the responsibility of the state, research indicates that the patience and tenacity of mothers who want their children to study to improve their lives play a key role in getting youths into school and keeping them there.

The adaptation of migrants to the life of the big city is less traumatic than might be thought, in part because many previously pass through smaller cities. Although they may be better off than in rural areas, their lives remain difficult. Migrants generally are badly paid and usually have to endure long hours traveling to work. Few join unions, neighborhood associations, or other organizations. The cities do not offer the poor much in the way of diversions during their free time. Many men spend their weekends drinking and gambling in their neighborhoods, perhaps occasionally attending a game of soccer or a bicycle race; occasionally men and women use free time to visit their places of origin.

One of the principal objectives of migrants to the city is to own their

Table 13.7 Percentage of families owning their homes in some Latin American cities, 1947–1990

City	1947–1952	1985–1990	Increase
Bogotá	43	57	14
Medellín	51	65	14
Cali	53	68	15
Mexico	25	62	37
Guadalajara	29	60	31
Puebla	21	53	32
Rio de Janeiro	23	63	40

Source: Alan Gilbert, *The Latin American City* (London, 1994).

own home. The proportion of families who rent has diminished. As Table 13.7 indicates, circa 1950 home ownership was higher in Colombia's largest cities than in their counterparts in Mexico and Brazil; although the latter have since increased home ownership more dramatically, the levels in big cities in all three countries are now roughly similar.

The migrant poor in the cities generally live in large encampments in which the homes at first are little more than huts, without any urban services. Over time the residents turn these hovels into solid houses, often constructed of brick, of two or three stories, in neighborhoods with paved streets, sewers, piped water, electricity and telephones, schools, and health clinics and with connections to the rest of the city by public transportation. This process of home- and neighborhood-building, which takes ten to fifteen years, is powered by the migrants' strong desire to own good homes.

But government policies, and the actions of speculators and politicians, also shape it. As government plans for public housing fall behind demand, various kinds of associations emerge to meet it. Some migrant communities in large cities have been organized and aided by the Communist Party. But these have been the exception. The two traditional parties have obtained the greatest electoral and economic advantage from clientelistic involvement in urban community development.

A high proportion of migrant housing in cities is of illegal origin. Invasions of property, generally aided by politicians or organizations, are completely illegal; the invaders occupy private property and have no authorization to build. "Pirate urbanization," on the other hand, violates urban construction statutes, but the homes are built on property legally obtained by entrepreneurs, who generally are politicians or have purchased favor with the authorities and the police.

The new neighborhoods are generally as far removed as possible from residences of the upper and middle classes and their commercial centers. The migrants occupy land considered marginal by those developers who build homes for the middle class or create industrial zones. Often the migrant communities are located on eroded slopes or in places likely to be flooded. Thus frequent tragedies, reported by the press and television, afflict such poor neighborhoods as Ciudad Bolívar in Bogotá or La Comuna Oriental in Medellín. These vast barrios of the poor often contain as many people as many departmental capitals.

From the end of the 1940s to 1990 there were rent controls. Also in the 1940s the government sponsored programs for the financing and construction of housing for the poor and the middle class. These programs were expanded over the next three decades, but they began to be abandoned in the 1980s, in some cases because of financial insolvency of the builders or because of the rampant corruption of the politicians who controlled these projects.

Overcome by the massive scale of the new urban populations, both Colombian politicians and international development agencies concluded that the tenacity of the poor and the workings of the market would resolve the problem of urban housing for migrants. As a consequence the larger cities have developed as a series of segregated urban subworlds, with no sense of a common citizenship.

Practically all of the cities with populations of more than 200,000 attempted, with varying degrees of success, to amplify the urban infrastructure and public services, to regulate the use of land, and to engage in urban renewal. But in many cases the national government ended up paying much of the debt contracted by the cities for their local improvements.

Planning for these urban development projects has led to tensions between local politicians and the national and international bureaucrats who establish technical and financial guidelines for the projects and with the bankers who provide financing for them. The politicians' dependency on outside technical agencies may have had some benefits, in greater efficiency and transparency. But the requirements of these agencies have also led to rigidity in setting charges for public services, which at times has provoked violent protest movements.

POVERTY

In 1950 the first World Bank mission to Colombia succinctly analyzed poverty in Colombia. Most Colombians lived in the countryside in conditions scarcely above subsistence. High rates of infant mortality, generalized illiteracy, overcrowding in precarious housing, as well as the lack of public services, credit institutions, and agricultural instruction, and very low levels of energy consumption characterized most of the population. The World Bank report recognized the economic advances made by the country over the previous quarter-century. But it concluded that the improvement for most of the inhabitants was much lower than might be expected given the economic growth that had occurred. In other words, only the few had benefitted. In 1947, 80,000 people (0.72 percent of the population) were earning one-third of the national income. Unfortunately, comparable data do not exist for later periods.

Studies of poverty in Colombia have come to various conclusions. Some that focus on the degree to which people suffer inadequate housing, overcrowding, lack of services, lack of schooling, and a high degree of economic dependency have found that, although there remains an enormous gap between the urban and rural populations, notable improvements have occurred over the last quarter-century. On the other hand, a study of poverty as defined by the capacity to obtain an adequate supply of food, clothing, and housing has concluded that conditions have not improved significantly over the last twenty years and, as always, that the rural population is particularly poor. (See Table 13.8.)

Table 13.8 Percentage of population under the lines of indigence and poverty, 1978–1995*

Years	Country Towns	Rural People	Total
1978	49.6 (15.9)	76.0 (41.3)	59.1 (25.1)
1988	48.2 (15.9)	74.9 (43.3)	59.2 (27.2)
1992	47.5 (17.0)	74.5 (43.3)	55.9 (25.2)
1995	45.9 (12.9)	76.0 (37.2)	55.1 (20.3)

*Percentage of indigents in parentheses. Indigence here is measured by the capacity to obtain adequate food. The measure of poverty includes food, clothing, and housing.
Source: Departamento Nacional de Planeación-Misión Social, *Evolución de la pobreza en Colombia* (Bogotá, 1997).

ECONOMIC TRANSFORMATIONS

Since the colonial period, the cities have directed and coordinated the economy. But only in the middle of the twentieth century have urban activities become the principal sources of growth, as indicated by Table 13.9.

In 1951, when a little more than half the active labor force still worked in agriculture, that sector began to be perceived as a brake on economic development. Because of the low productivity of very small farmers, the diet of their families has been inadequate and especially poor in proteins. Further, their low income also has meant that they have provided little demand

Table 13.9 Contributions to gross domestic product by economic activity, 1945–1998*

Sectors	1945–1949		1976–1980		1993–1998	
	A	B	A	B	A	B
Agriculture	45.2	4.3	23.2	4.3	18.8	1.5
Mining/oil	3.4	4.1	1.3	−0.3	4.5	6.4
Industry	17.7[†]	9.4	22.8	4.6	18.1	1.2
Construction	5.2	−5.0	3.3	5.6	3.1	3.6
Services	28.5	9.9	49.4	6.4	55.6	5.3
GDP	100.0	6.2	100.0	5.4	100.0	3.7
State/GDP[‡]	9.7[§]	—	20.0	—	34.5	—

*A = percentage of participation; B = annual growth, in percentages.
[†]Sector includes factory industry (14.4 percent) and artisanal (3.3 percent).
[‡]Total expenditures of the State in relation to GNP.
[§]Data for 1950–1954.
Sources: 1945–1949. CEPAL, *El desarrollo económico de Colombia. Anexo estadístico* (Bogotá, 1957); 1976–1980 and 1993–1998: Alicia Puyana and Rosemary Thorp, *Colombia: Economía política de las expectativas petroleras* (Bogotá, 1998), p. 82.

for manufactured consumer goods. On the other hand, coffee-growing has generated a flow of foreign exchange without which the growth of cities and services, as well as of factory manufacturing, would have been inconceivable.

Fluctuations in the world coffee market deeply affected other aspects of the Colombian economy before 1980. The fall of coffee export earnings, not completely compensated by returns from other exports, as well as a decline in the formation of capital, tended to slow the growth of some other sectors (particularly construction and manufacturing). The service sector, which was less affected, unfortunately tends to have low productivity. (See Table 13.10.)

In the 1980s, the Colombian economy began to suffer the "Dutch disease" as a consequence of the dramatic growth of exports of narcotics and, to a lesser degree, of oil. The Dutch disease is so called because of the impact on the Netherlands of highly profitable gas exports in undermining agriculture and industry. In the case of Colombia, the narcotics trade and oil produced very high returns with relatively low employment costs. The profitablity of these two activities tended to discourage investment in other sectors, which became relatively less profitable. Further, narcotics and oil increased the supply of foreign exchange, which encouraged imports of manufactured consumer goods, further discouraging domestic industry. The relative contributions to GDP of agriculture, manufacturing, construction, and even services all declined. At the same time, oil production increased fiscal resources to the state, so that state expenditures expanded dramatically as a proportion of GDP, as seen in Table 13.9. Increased resources did enable the state to invest more in the development of infrastructure, health care, and education at all levels. As noted earlier, significant improvements occurred in indices of health and literacy and in the provision of clean water and sewer systems.

Table 13.10 Annual growth rates of variables in the Colombian economy, 1948–1998

Variables	1948–1956 Coffee Bonanza	1957–1970 Crisis	1970–1979 Recuperation	1980–1998 Dutch Disease
Exports of coffee	10.9	0.5	39.2	−3.1
All exports	9.9	2.2	35.3	8.9
Formation of fixed capital	11.4	4.5	6.5	−1.2
Agriculture	2.9	3.3	4.0	2.5
Manufacturing	7.3	5.7	5.4	2.7
Construction	12.9	5.3	5.1	1.0
Services	5.8	5.6	5.7	4.6
Real GDP	5.2	4.8	5.1	3.8

Sources: 1948–1970: Carlos F. Díaz Alejandro, "Tendencias y fases de la economía colombian y de sus transaccines internacionales, 1950–1970," in *Fedesarrollo* (Bogotá, 1972), Table 1; 1970–1998: Puyana and Thorp, *Colombia: Economía política*, p. 82.

BIPOLARITY IN THE COUNTRYSIDE

Over the last fifty years Colombian agriculture has resolved neither the problem of generating a better income for the majority of the rural population nor the need to increase efficiency in large mechanized commercial farms growing rice, cotton, sugar, and soy. On the contrary, these problems have become more acute.

Nearly forty years after the enactment of the first agrarian reform law, land in Colombia continues to be among the most concentrated in the world, according to a recent report from the World Bank. In 1988 a million peasant units, 62.4 percent of all agricultural properties, held only 5.2 percent of the area farmed; the mean size of their parcels was 1.2 hectares (not quite 3 acres). These small plots often are on sloping, eroded, and/or not very fertile land that produces little, requiring peasant smallholders to hire themselves out part of the year to try to sustain their families. At the other end of the scale, 1.7 percent of the properties occupied two-fifths of the land used for agriculture and ranching. Nonetheless, the importance of an intermediate group (5 to 50 hectares, or 12.4–124 acres), constituting an agricultural middle class, should be noted. (See Table 13.11.)

The concentration of land is most acute in extensive cattle zones on the Caribbean coast and in some of the most fertile valleys. Much land that could be used for farming is used less intensively to fatten cattle. By contrast, in coffee areas and in the highlands of the south (Nariño and Cauca) or the Eastern Cordillera (Cundinamarca, Boyacá, and Santander) small and medium-sized properties predominate.

The inequality of Colombia's land structure has changed little despite much legislation and many reports on agrarian reform. Redistributive policies, administered by the Instituto Colombiano de la Reforma Agraria (INCORA), were neutralized by other government policies favoring large

Table 13.11 Structure of land tenure, 1960–1988

Size	Percentage of Owners		Percentage of Area		Mean Size in Hectares	
	1960	1988	1960	1988	1960	1988
Less than 1 hectare	24.6	28.3	0.5	0.6	0.44	0.28
1–5 hectares	37.9	34.0	4.0	4.6	2.41	1.87
5–50 hectares	30.6	29.9	19.7	25.9	14.52	12.16
50–200 hectares	5.2	6.1	20.9	28.9	91.10	66.53
More than 200 hectares	1.7	1.7	54.9	40.0	730.59	214.90

Sources: A.E. Havens, William L. Flinn, and Susana Lastarría Cornhill, "Agrarian Reform and the National Front: A Class Analysis," in R. Albert Berry, Ronald G. Hellman, and Mauricio Solaún, eds., *Politics of Compromise: Coalition Government in Colombia* (New Brunswick, NJ, 1980), p. 358; Puyana and Thorp, *Colombia: Economía política,* p. 171.

landowners. The government encouraged increased productivity of large units by providing credit and machinery at subsidized prices and by undertaking costly irrigation projects. In this way, the value of large holdings was increased so much that they could not be expropriated with compensation. At the same time, government policies hurt peasant farmers by imposing controls on the prices of food. The legal and administrative restraints placed upon INCORA and a wall of juridical formalisms in the process of acquiring lands were additional impediments to a more equitable distribution of land.

In its first thirty years, the land reform benefitted some 63,000 families, to whom were distributed somewhat more than 1 million hectares. Confronting this mediocre record, the government turned to alternatives to dividing large properties into smaller ones. The government attempted to improve agricultural productivity and incomes, but these efforts were limited to a small proportion of peasants with sufficient and well-located land. A preference for capitalist entrepreneurs was evident. In the 1970s, for example, the government instituted programs for the dissemination of more productive, "green revolution" varieties of rice and maize. These improvements primarily benefitted large operators who were better able to adopt them.

Nevertheless, the history of coffee has revealed the entrepreneurial virtues and competitiveness of small and medium farmers. Recent technical studies have shown that these virtues can extend to producers of other crops. But here, again, powerful interests present obstacles, as the coffee industry itself shows. The elite-controlled coffee federation does not stimulate peasant production of coffee where there is appropriate land, abundant labor, and adequate transportation—as in southern Colombia (Nariño, Cauca, and Huila) and in the Eastern Cordillera—because this would hurt the interests of the established cultivators in greater Antioquia (Antioquia, Caldas, Risaralda, and the Quindío). The coffee federation continues subsidizing and protecting the cultivation of new coffee varieties that are highly productive over the short term but involve costs that are among the highest in the world. Without such aid from the federation, the established growers could not compete with peasant cultivators using older methods that are less costly and permit production over longer periods of time.

Throughout the last half century peasants generally have not been able to get bank loans. Even if they could obtain credit, their plots do not produce enough income to pay the debts they have contracted with INCORA to acquire their land. Because they lack access to credit, small farmers have difficulty buying seed, fertilizers, herbicides, and tools. They also lack the infrastructure for irrigation and access to education and health care.

In 1950 the World Bank mission to Colombia proposed a progressive land tax to encourage the division of large landholdings. Although such a tax would reduce the profitability of large properties and would discourage the purchase of land as a form of protection in an inflationary economy, it would not raise the price of small landholdings, nor would it improve the position of small farmers as borrowers from banks. Such a tax, although on occasion attempted by some Colombian administrations, has never been implemented.

COLONIZATION

As the modest program of redistribution has failed to change the structure of landholding significantly, Colombian peasants have attempted their own agrarian reform. The second half of the twentieth century has witnessed a dynamic colonization in eight zones, covering some 300,000 square kilometers of land—almost a quarter of the nation's territory. It has been estimated that some 375,000 were engaged in colonization in 1964, 1.3 million in 1990. Over the past fifty years they have cleared and settled some 3.5 million hectares.

Confronting the difficulties of redistributing land, INCORA has dedicated itself to providing titles to public land, developing programs that previously had been in the hands of other agencies since the 1940s. Most of these programs of *directed colonization* have occurred in the Caquetá, Ariari, Lebrija, Carare, and in the Alto Sumapaz. But very quickly *spontaneous colonists* have taken over. The programs in the Caquetá, for example, were designed for 1200 families displaced by violence from Huila and Caldas. But they soon were overwhelmed by some 20,000 families of spontaneous colonists, who ultimately controlled the settlement process.

The dominance of large numbers of spontaneous colonists has been repeated in other zones. In the Ariari River Valley party identities became a factor from the beginning. Conservatives got the land on the left side of the river; those on the right bank went to Liberals. And in towns in the region some streets are considered Liberal, others Conservative. Anyone transgressing these conventions could risk death.

Of the colonization zones the most dynamic and modern is that of Urabá, the center of a new banana enclave that has placed Colombia among the largest exporters of this fruit in the world. The industry developed originally as a replica of the model of the United Fruit Company's operations in Santa Marta from the 1930s to 1950. Before 1930 much of the fruit that United Fruit exported from Santa Marta was produced on its own land. But after the social and technical crises of the 1930s, United Fruit changed its system. It sold its land and provided technical assistance to Colombian farmers, from whom it bought the harvest for export. In the early 1960s the same approach was brought to Urabá. In the mid-1960s there were some 220 Colombian producers in Urabá, most of them Antioqueños.

Although Colombian planters grew the bananas, in the beginning foreign interests dominated exports abroad. By 1978, however, Colombians also played an important role in exporting. Two multinational companies controlled 54 percent of the fruit shipped, but the Union of Banana-growers of

Urabá exported the other 46 percent. Now Colombians export practically all of the bananas. But the business still is quite concentrated and the growers collaborate to control labor contracting. In 1987 20,000 workers, mostly blacks from the Chocó, were employed on 260 plantations.

As in other colonization zones, torrents of peasants flowed to the Urabá region in search of employment or vacant land, which was available north of the banana area. The Urabá also attracted merchants of all kinds, as well as prostitutes. Amid the avalanche of colonists, various social problems emerged—a lack of schools, health centers, police, and administration of justice. Social disorder led to political disturbances and these to the trauma of new forms of violence.

In these colonization zones social relations have been unstable because of individual mobility; property is insecure and peasant access to markets precarious. These things were also true of Antioqueño colonization in the nineteenth century. But in the middle of the twentieth century communications were better. Radio, and even television, bring the colonists in contact with news, opinions, and styles circulating through the country. Also aspiring politicians, Liberal and Conservative, in search of votes, were early on the scene. These politicians arrived before fragile public institutions were implanted, so that even before these institutions could be established they were already deformed by clientelism. In these frontier conditions, in which state functions have tended to be privatized and high levels of violence have prevailed, both guerrillas and networks of narco-traffickers have found an ideal niche. Whether allied or at war, guerrillas and narcos have operated in a complex environment that also has included new agricultural entrepreneurs, ranchers, military officers, police, and politicians.

If for the peasants the agrarian reform was frustrating, their spontaneous colonization has turned out to be a tragedy of biblical proportions. Thousands of families, trapped on a frontier between two fires or more (the army, the police, the guerrillas, and the narco-traffickers), have been forced to move to some new area of settlement and try, once again, to remake their lives.

BETWEEN PROTECTION AND FREE TRADE

Industrial protection, to encourage the manufacture of goods that otherwise would have to be imported, was the official policy beginning in 1950. This policy of import substitution prevailed, with minor alterations, until 1990. Postwar protection of industry in the developed countries, which only was modified in the 1970s, justified the protectionism of the developing ones.

Various factors encouraged the development of manufacturing. From the end of the nineteenth century reinvestment of coffee profits provided capital for manufacturing enterprises, particularly in Antioquia. Incipient industrialization before World War I was encouraged during the war by a scarcity of manufactured consumer goods formerly supplied by the industrial powers of Western Europe as well as by the United States. Colombian industries found further stimulus in the 1930s when Depression-forced devaluations and government restrictions cut the flow of imported goods. During World War II the absence of foreign goods provided further encouragement for factory manufacturing, as did the accumulation of reserves from coffee exports, which helped pay for imported machinery and raw materials. Urbanization made possible larger productive units, by making available modern services (electricity, telephones, banks, transportation), cheap and skilled labor, and concentrated markets for manufactured consumer goods. By the end of World War II industrialists were an established interest who pressed politically to obtain a protective tariff in 1950.

In addition to protectionist tariffs, the government used other means to subsidize or otherwise encourage manufacturing: preferential bank credit, subsidized rates for electric power, and tax advantages for investments in industry. In some basic industries deemed too risky for, or beyond the capacities of, private capital, the state founded government-managed enterprises, to which private funds were drawn through tax dispensations.

The government also aided manufacturing by, in effect, taxing coffee exports. Foreign currency earned from exports had to be sold to the government at below-market rates; the government then could sell these cheap dollars to manufacturers to lower their costs for imported machinery and raw materials. This policy was opposed by coffee interests, particularly in Caldas, but the coffee federation muffled this opposition in support of a consensus national policy.

Some other subsidies helped to keep labor costs low for industry, although they also benefitted the urban population in general and thus helped to sustain political support for the government. Government controls on food prices, subsidies of urban services and housing, and expansion of education and public health all provided support for industry as well as favoring the mass of the urban population. The pro-industrial program evidently gave economic policy a strongly urban bias.

In 1945 nearly 70 percent of industrial production occurred in the four largest metropolitan areas (Bogotá, Medellín, Cali, and Barranquilla). Since that time manufacturing has continued concentrated in these four metropolitan areas. There is some variation in the industrial profile of these cities. Medellín, for example, tends to specialize in consumer products, and Cali in intermediate goods, while Bogotá, which in 1950 was already the largest manufactering center, had a greater diversity of industries.

In the 1950s and 1960s more than two-thirds of industrial activity was in relatively light industries: food processing (including the processing of coffee), beverages, tobacco, textiles, clothing, and footwear. Such activities generally involved enterprises with simple technology, intensive use of labor, and little capital. Such an industrial structure is not surprising. Industrial activity was oriented to internal consumption, which was limited by the size of the market. From 1950 to 1970 Colombia's population grew from 11 to 21 million, but per capita income remained low, rising from $203 to

$281 in 1958 dollars. In part because of the concentration of income in the hands of a few, the purchasing power of the majority remained limited.

In the 1960s and 1970s there began to appear sectors with greater technological requirements: plastics, petrochemicals, metal-working, automobiles, and office and graphic arts machinery. The state contributed to this advance with schemes for regional economic integration, notably the Andean Pact, initiated in 1969. The pact aimed to make possible the export of manufactures that had limited internal demand and were not competitive in the international market. More technologically advanced manufacturing also was aided by investments from transnational companies seeking to produce within Colombia's protected market as well as an amplified Andean one.

The newer industries of the 1960s and 1970s relied heavily on imported equipment. These factories tended to be more mechanized than those in the first phase of industrialization and employed relatively few workers. Consequently, the second, somewhat more advanced, stage of manufacturing development absorbed less labor than advocates of industrialization had anticipated. Urban workers increasingly had to seek employment in the service sector, often in informal enterprises with low productivity.

Pro-industrial policy continued to the end of the 1960s without confronting serious challenges. In the postwar period the mystique of industrialization, if not also the influence of industrialists, was such that the choice between protected internal development, as opposed to export-led development, was easily resolved in favor of the former. At the same time, since coffee played a critical role in subsidizing industrial development, the coffee federation was able to increase its prerogatives, strengthen its financial and institutional resources, and ensure its central place in the formation of economic policy.

Around 1970 the limitations and disadvantages of import substitution industrialization became increasingly apparent. Colombian industry continued to be dependent on imported technology, machinery, and raw materials. The limited internal market did not provide a basis for industrial specialization. Because the market was small and protected, a few firms dominated, or monopolized, production in processed foods, tobacco, machinery, and electrical products. A protected market dominated by monopolies limited incentives for increasing manufacturing efficiencies. In a protected market, with high production costs and limited internal competition, prices to Colombian consumers were high and Colombian manufactured goods could not compete in international markets. International lending agencies argued that Colombian factories would become more competitive only if protective tariffs were lowered and manufacturing enterprises lost the special privileges of being able to borrow domestically and to buy dollars at government-subsidized, below-market rates.

With the arrival of the debt crisis of the 1980s, the government had to adopt an economic adjustment program, which terminated some of the privileges enjoyed by industrialists. The lowering of protective duties had to wait until the 1990s. As industrial protection declined, so also did investment in manufacturing; industrial growth slowed and its role in the economy lessened, as Table 13.10 shows.

ECONOMY AND DRUG TRAFFIC

At the end of the twentieth century, the economic dominance of coffee and the ideal of the republic of coffee were things of the past. When regulation of the world coffee market ended in 1989, Colombian coffee became more exposed to price fluctuations. However, a relative decline of coffee was compensated by the rise of nontraditional exports such as flowers, bananas, and such manufactured goods as textiles, ready-made clothing, shoes, tobacco, and processed food. In addition, exports of petroleum expanded in the 1980s.

However, even before 1980 illegal drugs already had became the country's dominant export sector. Although incomes from the drug traffic are difficult to calculate, the research of Roberto Steiner suggests that between 1980 and 1995, commerce in narcotics brought $U.S.36 billion into Colombia. This is equivalent to 5.3 percent of the country's GDP for this period, overshadowing coffee, which accounted for 4.5 percent, and petroleum (1.9 percent).

The emergence of cocaine and, to a lesser degree, petroleum, as new economic and political actors in the 1980s, in addition to generating foreign exchange, had an important effect in redefining politics and relations between regions. Regions that previously had been peripheral, such as the Arauca and the Caqueta, gained importance.

In addition, the great profitability of the drug traffic affected the rest of the economy in multiple ways. Because the flow of narco-dollars is incalculable and uncontrollable, and by definition impossible to include in macroeconomic variables, it introduced many uncertainties into economic policy. Nonetheless, the constant inflow of narco-dollars did help Colombian monetary authorities to keep down the cost of the dollar in relation to Colombian currency. However, a cheaper dollar also encouraged a greater flow of

Table 13.12 Income from drug exports compared to income from legal exports, 1980–1995 (percentages)

Years	Coffee	Nontraditional	Petroleum	Total Legal	Illegal Drugs*
1980–1984	50.1	40.4	9.5	100.0	65.4
1985–1989	38.8	48.1	13.1	100.0	40.3
1990–1995	17.7	63.9	18.4	100.0	30.6
1980–1995	31.2	52.4	16.4	100.0	41.4

*Percentage of exports of illegal drugs in relation to all legal exports.
Sources: For exports of illegal drugs: Roberto Steiner, "Los ingresos de Colombia producto de la exportación de drogas ilícitas," *Coyuntura Económica*, 1 (1997), pp. 1–33. For legal exports, Alicia Puyana, "Políticas sectoriales en condiciones de bonanzas externas," *Fedecafé* (Bogotá, 1997).

imports, which depressed domestic industries that competed with imported goods. This effect was intensified by contraband imports, the favorite mechanism for laundering drug money. Investments in urban real estate and construction and in ranches and farms have been other common means of laundering money. These had the effect of stimulating construction while boosting land prices in many areas. Meanwhile, drug traffickers became owners of immense tracts of land, among other places in the Urabá region and other parts of the Caribbean as well as on the eastern plains of Meta. Narco-traffickers also have acquired choice properties near the larger cities, particularly Bogotá, Medellín, and Cali.

As Colombia became increasingly important as producer of the coca leaf and poppies, peasants who had cultivated other crops migrated to the marginal territories where most the coca and poppies were grown. Workers who had lost their jobs because of commercial liberalization or because of declining prices of coffee, wheat, or barley also found employment on the drug frontier. The migration of workers to zones of narcotic cultivation helped to stop the fall of rural wages. By the same token, the profitability of nondrug crops declined.

Some of these effects, particularly the cheapening of the dollar, were reinforced by the surge of oil production that began in 1984. It has been estimated that between 1993 and 2005 income from Colombian oil (depending on the volume of production and oil prices) may amount to 4.25 billion dollars per year. This is equivalent to 20–25 percent of the total revenues of the government. This flow of money has brought a relaxation of restraints on public expenditures and government deficits have increased.

THE NEOCONSERVATIVE ORDER, 1946–1958

The passage from the republic of coffee to a nation of cities destabilized the political system, which had matured since the War of the Thousand Days. Constitutionalism could function as a means of legitimation as long as the elites of the two parties could agree on basic rules of coexistence, particularly after the direct election of the president, approved in 1914, increased the number of voters. Even in critically partisan moments, such as the presidential election of 1922, the change of party control of the presidency in 1930–1931, or the ideological polarization of the Revolution on the March in 1935–1936, although political violence increased, it was contained.

The system began to shake, apparently, with the populist challenge of Jorge Eliécer Gaitán in 1944–1948, intertwined with the partisan violence that accompanied the fall of the Liberal Republic in the presidential election of 1946. In this election there were two Liberal candidates, Gabriel Turbay, the official party nominee, and the dissident Gaitán. A divided Liberal vote permitted the Conservative candidate, Mariano Ospina Pérez, to win with only 41.4 percent of the vote. As president, Ospina confronted a Liberal majority in the Congress.

Gaitán's populist movement had its foundation in the urban growth and inflation of the 1940s, which provided conditions propitious for mass mobilizations and popular demands. Gaitán exploited the effects of inflation, condemned those who had become wealthy by hoarding food in time of scarcity, and attacked the ostentation of the rich. Gaitán's effectiveness in rallying mass support intimidated Conservatives and the upper classes in general.

Gaitán, the oldest son of a modest Bogotá family, began his political career while he was still in secondary school, in the electoral campaign of 1917. After becoming a lawyer, Gaitán traveled to Rome to become a disciple of Enrico Ferri, the father of the positivist school of penal law. In Rome Gaitán acquired an intellectual and professional discipline superior to most in his generation.

On his return from Europe in 1928 Gaitán won a seat in the Chamber of Representatives, where, in response to the massacre in the Santa Marta banana zone, he delivered one of the most memorable and devastating attacks against the Conservative regime. In the 1930s he served in the cabinet and as mayor of Bogotá, so that in the 1940s he was in a position legitimately to aspire to the presidency. In 1945 he took advantage of the political vacuum created by the resignation of President Alfonso López Pumarejo and began to speak of the people's hopes that had been betrayed by the Liberal Republic.

In a number of ways Gaitán's movement was comparable to the populist movements that occurred in Argentina, Brazil, Chile, and some other Latin American countries in the twentieth century. In these countries migration from the countryside to the cities created new urban middle and working-class constituencies, which became the bases of new parties demanding attention, in particular, to the needs and interests of the growing urban population. Typically these populist parties consisted of coalitions of industrialists, segments of the middle class, unions, and the popular masses, who, following middle- or sometimes upper-sector leaders, displaced from power older coalitions of landowners, merchants, and bankers tied to the export economy. The diverse elements of the populist coalition shared the goals of industrialization and a fervent economic nationalism. However, the populist coalitions were socially heterogeneous and unstable; often they were held together by a charismatic individual who became both leader of the movement and the chief of state.

The development of a populist movement under Gaitán was cut off by his assassination in 1948. At the time of his death, his movement had not yet achieved all of the dimensions of populist parties in some other places. Gaitán had a substantial following among the popular masses, rural and urban, as well as elements of the middle classes. However, he lacked significant support from industrialists. And, even had he lived beyond 1948, he may have found it difficult to win over the leaders of labor unions that since the 1920s and 1930s had developed in tight connection to the political parties. Furthermore, foreign corporations played a much less visible role in Colombia than in some other countries of Latin America, which limited the political potentialities of economic nationalism.

In addition, Gaitán's populism in some ways sounded conservative in tone, even for some ultra-conservatives. He called for "moral restoration." The word "restoration" appealed to Conservatives, and "moral" was perhaps the word most employed by the Conservative caudillo Laureano Gómez. Gómez himself had made businessmen frown when, in the tones of Falangist populism of Spain in the 1930s, he spoke of "the insufferable domination of the weakest by the strongest." The doctrinaire right noticed Gaitán's division of Colombian society into "the political country" and "the national country." From the perspective of the right this could be read as approximating the critique applied by the traditional monarchist Charles Maurras to French republicanism: the *pays légal* versus the *pays réel*. Gaitán's slogan even was echoed for some months in *El Siglo*, the principal Conservative newspaper in Bogotá, directed by Laureano Gómez. For this reason it was not inconceivable that the most doctrinaire Conservatives might court Gaitán. One consequence of this supraparty populism was that, when partisan violence began to occur, Gaitán's supporters were not hit as hard as were "official" Liberals.

However, while Gaitán's formula could appeal to Conservatives, it also could be interpreted as an expression of the popular tradition of the Liberal Party. The kernel of the "national country" was the working people, the quintessence of "the indigenous race of whom we are proud," from whom had been robbed the material, moral, and political bases of their dignity. The "political country" represented the marriage of the privilege of blood or wealth with the power of the state. The "national country" was composed of all those excluded by the oligarchy from the "political country." Accordingly, the "national country" also could include industrialists, farmers, merchants, and the small middle class, including independent artisans.

Local violence erupted in the elections of 1946 and 1947. It is estimated that in 1947 alone some 14,000 died. The killings increased in almost all of the municipalities that previously had been mentioned as sites of violence in reports of presidents Carlos E. Restrepo (1911) and Enrique Olaya Herrera (1931). In the elections of 1946 and 1947 the Liberal majority in the Congress decreased, and the change was even more pronounced in the elections of city councils. The Liberals lost more than a quarter of the municipal councils in which they had held majorities.

As a protest against the violence, some 100,000 supporters of Gaitán in February 1948 gathered in the Plaza Bolívar in Bogotá dressed in mourning black. By the imposing silence of this massive demonstration, Gaitán wanted to dramatize his power over the masses as well as the gravity of the political violence that had spread across the land.

On this occasion Gaitán said that peace depended on the conduct of the president. But the president could not act without taking local forces into account. Politicians and notables, bishops, local bosses, and parish priests directed the partisan conflict, inflaming or dissipating it depending on the circumstances. The increase of literacy and more numerous newspapers, as well as the telephone and radio, made it possible for national and departmental leaders to communicate more effectively with the municipal directorates of their parties; nonetheless, politics remained strongly local.

On April 9, 1948, Gaitán was shot to death by an unknown man in the center of Bogotá. The massive riots that this assassination prompted at first unified the political elites. But, once the populist leader had become a martyr, it was necessary to destroy his legacy. And, to do this, there was no alternative to reviving partisan antagonism. Thus, constitutionalism and party coexistence were destroyed.

In 1949 President Ospina did not hesitate to challenge the Liberals by closing the Congress, as well as changing the party composition of the high courts, which the Liberals had dominated. In doing this Ospina had the backing of the army. The U.S. ambassador also supported Ospina, and the Truman Administration in Washington turned a deaf ear to Liberal protests, possibly interpreting the partisan conflict in Colombia in the framework of the Cold War. The most doctrinaire wing of the Conservative Party spoke of the restoration of the Bolivarian principle of authority. Its leader, Laureano Gómez, won the presidency for the period 1950–1954, in an election from which the Liberals abstained.

After 1948 the idea that political mobilization represented a threat to the social system and to economic growth began to spread among political and business leaders. The dominant classes saw political authoritarianism and a limited economic nationalism as the programs that would get them through a minefield of unknown possibilities. Dictatorial forms of government emerged, inspired by the ethereal pair of Christ and Bolívar. From 1949 to 1958 the country lived under a state of siege. This period more or less coincided with years of notable economic growth. Although Liberals spoke of the dictatorship of the state of siege, they supported the first two years of the military government of General Gustavo Rojas Pinilla (1953–1957).

Under the extreme Conservatives, economic policies and institutions came down from above, without the oversight of Congress and without public discussion. Consequently conflict over economic policy primarily involved powerful economic interest groups, representing industry, commerce, coffee, and other aspects of agriculture.

These groups sought to have a national scope. But they tended to have rather diverse regional features, for in each region the business elites had distinctive profiles. In Cali, most of the industrialists emerged from the traditional landowning class, belonged to the Conservative Party, and participated actively in politics. By contrast, in Barranquilla the industrialists came from commerce and were more linked to the Liberal Party; further, the politics of the Caribbean coast were less partisan than in any other part of the country. While a number of manufacturing enterprises in Bogotá, Medellín, and Barranquilla had their origins between 1890 and 1910, those in Manizales, founded by coffee-growing and coffee-exporting families, had made their fortunes hoarding commodities during a crisis of food scarcity in 1942–1943. They all envied the Bogotá entrepreneurs not only for their proximity to high officials in government but also for their close connections with commercial banks, which were highly concentrated in the capital since the middle of the 1920s.

Rivalry among strong regional groups played a role in conflict between two of the most significant economic interest associations, the industrialists' Asociación Nacional de Industriales (ANDI), founded at the end of 1944, and the merchants' Federación Nacional de Comerciantes (FENALCO), created a few months afterward. ANDI initially represented a small group of manufacturing firms controlled by Antioqueño families. One of the early conflicts between ANDI and FENALCO was essentially a fight between the Echeverrías, a Medellín industrial clan, and Adolfo Aristizábal, a leading merchant in Cali, over how the Echeverrías were distributing the textiles produced in their factories.

Between 1945 and 1953 ANDI and FENALCO were pitted against each other in a struggle over the nation's economic policy. The ANDI, skilled in using the press and lobbying politicians and high officials, had a decisive effect in firming up Colombia's protectionist stance. It played an important role in preventing Colombia from joining the General Agreement on Trade and Tariffs (GATT) in 1949 and resisted a trade treaty with the United States.

The battles between ANDI and FENALCO at times had a partisan tint. FENALCO and the Liberal Party both supported free trade, while the Conservative government's protective tariff of 1950 aligned ANDI openly with the Conservative regime. Until 1953 the Liberal opposition declaimed that Conservative governments subordinated everything to "the fluctuations of the stock market and the aspirations of industrial capital." The Liberal convention of 1951 called the protective tariff of 1950 ignominious and attacked the formation of a new industrial oligarchy, the "oligarchy of the 175"—referring to the privileged rate of 1.75 pesos to the dollar granted to industrialists to buy imported machinery and materials, at a time when the dollar was selling on the black market at 3 pesos.

The strong leadership of Laureano Gómez also sustained the industrialist vision. An admirer of Franco's Spain, Gómez was convinced of the need for large-scale industry. But Gómez believed that industry should not expand without the embrace of the state. In 1953 Gómez declared that, while economic production was founded on freedom of enterprise and private initiative, it had to be exercised "within the limits of the common good." Gómez further asserted that the state could intervene, under the law, "to coordinate the various economic interests and to guarantee national security." He also said that the state would encourage enterprises to share their profits with their workers.

Gómez also wanted state-owned industrial enterprises, created at that time, along with the government's housing and social security agencies, to form the pivot of the new economy. He scorned the attacks levied on the new social security institute by both ANDI and FENALCO. The policies of the social security institute, he said, were consistent with the Christian traditions of Colombian business. Economic morality, he insisted, ought to recognize the heart of labor relations in the worker and his family; the state and economic enterprises both had to treat the worker and his family as a unit, going beyond the payment of mere wages, which tended to become nothing more than the price of dehumanized work. For this reason the prolific Catholic family received from the social security institute preferential attention through financial support for the education of their children. It is important to recognize, however, that when Gómez spoke of defending the family, he meant only the family constituted by marriage and in the Roman Catholic Church.

The beneficial role of the state in the economy and in social coexistence, of which Gómez's labor and social security legislation was an example, was emphasized by the ultra-conservative administrations. In addition, these regimes attempted to control inflation. Meanwhile they increased the political repression of unions and attempted to manipulate union bureaucracies the way that Liberals had in the 1930s. Calling a union communist was enough for it to be marginalized and its leaders proscribed. According to right-wing corporatist doctrines, workers were supposed to form a relationship of solidarity with their employers. Employers, however, disregarded the aspect of corporatism that called for solidarity with workers and sharing profits with them. Although labor costs were rising, businessmen could not complain about such a one-sided system.

The ultra-conservative governments paid no attention to the labor conditions of farm workers or sharecroppers, who, with few exceptions, continued to be tied to traditional arrangements beyond the reach of the law. Nor did they address the problem of the underutilization of the best land. They cast a blind eye on World Bank recommendations to tax landowners as a means of pressing them to use their land productively or sell it. Needless to say, the expropriation of land was not on their agenda.

The ultra-conservative order was constructed on four pillars: (1) the importance of industrialization for economic development and the strength of the nation state; (2) the control of unions through a combination of employer paternalism, social Catholicism, and repression; (3) electoral demobilization, to which Liberals contributed by abstaining from all elections from November 1949 to the plebiscite of December 1957; and (4) expanding electrification and the transportation and communications networks through loans from the U.S. Eximbank and the World Bank.

ROJAS

In 1953 the Conservative factions divided irrevocably. On June 13, two days before the National Constitutional Assembly was to meet, to ensure the continuity in power of his faction Gómez resumed the presidential functions he had relinquished because of illness in 1951. Disregarding the advice of various cabinet ministers, Gómez immediately removed the commander of the armed forces, General Gustavo Rojas Pinilla, and named a Gómez protégé as minister of war. Rojas without difficulty gathered the support of the military hierarchy. Encouraged by the Ospinistas, the Conservative faction rivaling that of Gómez, Rojas on the same night as his dismissal seized power in a coup d'etat.

Rojas's coup had rather general support, from Liberals as well as the Ospinistas, and from the chief interest group associations. The Church also turned against Gómez, blaming him in part for the political violence and finding his ideology too extreme. Rojas for the most part continued the established economic policy. In his second year, however, it was noticed that he was distancing himself from the "oligarchy." The former Liberal president, Alfonso López Pumarejo, for example, expressed his disquiet at the "new names" linked to the Rojas regime. But such reservations were obscured at first by Liberal euphoria and the fact that Rojas remained firmly under Ospinista tutelage.

Support for Rojas was bolstered by pacification of the eastern *llanos*, the coffee bonanza, successful control of inflation, and the flow of international loans. In August 1954 the National Constituent Assembly extended Rojas's rule to 1958. However, after the extension, Rojas began to free himself from the Ospinistas, to repress the Liberal press, and to govern according to his own judgment. Early in 1955 he announced that he would not end the state of siege. Inspired by Peronism, he tried to organize his own populist political movement, the Movimiento de Acción Nacional, with its own union organization, the Confederación Nacional de Trabajadores (CNT). Both parties saw these developments as a threat and at the end of 1955 formed an opposition "civil front." The Church hierarchy, which had objected to the Liberal-sponsored labor federation, the Confederación de Trabajadores Colombianos (CTC), seeing it as a front for communism, and which had supported a Church-linked union, the Union de Trabajadores Colombianos (1946), severely criticized the Rojas government for creating the CNT, in the view of the Church an imitation of Peronism. At this point Rojas tried to appease the Church hierarchy by intensifying his anti-Protestantism and launching an anti-communist crusade.

The Communist Party, at this point once again an illegal organization, attempted to strengthen its regions of peasant support. In 1949 it had decided to "respond to the violence of the Falangist bandits with organized violence of the masses." This became the "self-defense" policy. As the Communists explained in 1952, its guerrillas in the eastern *llanos*, Tolima, Antioquia, and elsewhere had not emerged as part of a "revolutionary plan," but rather as a "defensive action." The Communists denied responsibility for the actions of "adventurers" who undertook such aggressive acts as a failed assault on an air base near Bogotá.

The party recommended that its peasant base accept Rojas's offer of an amnesty, but at the same time it also sought to organize peasant "self-defense" better and to amplify the fight on agrarian issues. This was the strategy of the movement of Juan de la Cruz Varela, the veteran agrarian leader in Sumapaz since the 1930s. The defense of colonists and agrarian organizations was developed at that time in the coffee zone of Cunday, Villarrica, and Icononzo (all in Tolima). When Gaitán was assassinated in 1948, landowners in this region took this moment as an opportunity to destroy the peasant self-defense groups. The Conservative government collaborated with the landowners by using colonization programs to "sow Conservatives" around the Communist-dominated zones. This process in 1952 produced one of the worst peasant slaughters in the history of Tolima. Local Liberal leaders had to flee to Liberal-dominated towns in the region, while the peasants took refuge in the colonization of the Alto Sumapaz.

In 1954 the guerrillas of Juan de la Cruz Varela were accused of threatening hacendados, collecting "taxes" from them, and controlling sales of coffee. In 1955 the army launched an offensive, including aerial bombardment, against the town of Villarrica, scattering the peasant self-defense groups eastward to various parts of the Meta (the Ariari and Guayabero River Valleys, as well as the Sierra de la Macarena and el Pato). The peasant refugees in these places, with bitter memories of the massacre at Villarrica, became future nuclei of the Communist-linked Fuerzas Armadas Revolucionarias Colombianas (FARC).

The Liberal directorate responded to the army offensive against peasants in the Sumapaz by noting that while the Liberal Party was anti-communist, it did not believe that the fight against communism required "the physical elimination of the Communists" nor did it justify actions not authorized by law or against "the principles of Christian civilization."

During 1955 and 1956 economic as well as political elites began to turn against Rojas. Both were put off by his gestures toward a populist movement in the Gaitán vein, which had been encouraged by socialist advisers in his government. But these efforts, which for the most part did not go beyond propaganda, failed. To win worker support, Rojas raised wages of industrial workers. While this irritated industrialists, it could not provide the basis for a broad popular movement, since most in the popular classes, operating largely in an informal economy, gained nothing from measures that benefitted only factory workers. Rojas did not have an effective political apparatus, and, despite his repressive measures, the traditional parties remained strong. In June 1956 he held a mass meeting in the Bogotá soccer stadium to inaugurate a new Rojista party, the Third Force, which presented itself as a partnership of the people and the armed forces. In response the Church once again voiced its opposition and the new political movement never got anywhere.

The weak populist efforts of the Rojas regime and its moderately anti-oligarchic accent were accompanied by investments in public housing, health, and education; the construction of roads and highways in backward areas; and grants of public land to those harmed by rural violence. Rojas also sought to advance the position of women. He got the National Constituent Assembly to recognize full political rights for women, incorporated women into the police, and appointed the first woman governor and the first woman cabinet minister in the history of the country. Women voted for the first time in the whole country in December 1957, in the plebiscite that legitimated the National Front.

Despite the factionalism of the parties, a coalition of Liberals and Laureano Gómez came together in 1956 and 1957 to form the National Front, with the aim of removing Rojas and replacing him with a bipartisan government. Although this agreement facilitated Rojas's departure, he fell fundamentally because of economic crisis and a confrontation with the World Bank, which suspended credit to Colombia. At the beginning of 1957 the deterioration of the balance of payments, industrial and commercial recession, and an increase in the cost of living all favored the opposition to Rojas.

In this context Rojas was seeking to have himself reelected for a third term. Once again the Church led the opposition. The archbishop of Bogotá warned Rojas that the National Constituent Assembly did not have the authority to elect him. Rojas, nonetheless, hurried to have himself elected. However, when the interest group associations of the industrialists, merchants, and bankers responded with a strike, backed by university students in the principal cities, Rojas, rather than attempting to repress this broad-scale movement, resigned. Rojas left behind a military junta, which collaborated in peaceful transition to constitutional government.

TWO-PARTY CONSTITUTIONALISM AND THE *DESMONTE*, 1958–1986

The National Front was a pact between the majority factions of the Liberal and Conservative Parties, created in opposition to Rojas Pinilla in 1956 and 1957 and endorsed in a plebiscite in December 1957. The National Front established a sixteen-year period in which the presidency would alternate between Liberals and Conservatives and all positions in the three branches of government, throughout the country, would be distributed evenly between the two parties. This formula, which was to expire in 1974, was modified in various ways in a supplementary pact in 1968. One of the agreements of 1968 created what came to be called the *desmonte* (in this context translatable as the "dismantling"), an understanding of what would happen after the completion of the sixteen-year period. This provided that, while alternation of the presidency between the two parties and equal representation in the Congress and the rest of the government would be abandoned after 1974, "equitable" representation of the two parties in the cabinet would continue.

The National Front, in effect, attempted to create a synthesis between the Liberal Republic and the neoconservative order. The result was the nationalization of clientelism; that is, whereas local powers had been the chiefs of clientelist networks, under the National Front, the state to a greater degree became the source of patronage.

The National Front marked several changes from the previous regime. In the initiating pacts it was agreed that fulfillment of the constitution and the laws would be the source of legitimacy. The electorate was reactivated in some respects (particularly as Liberals once again began to vote). But the provision that only Liberals and Conservatives could be elected, and they in exactly equal proportions, rigidified the electoral process. As both parties had a specified allotment of seats in Congress and in the cabinet, political competition now became a matter less between the parties than between factions within the parties. One of the consequences was the trivialization of political discussion and factional maneuvers.

Further, the stipulation that only Liberals and Conservatives could hold office in effect denied political participation to those who preferred other political identities. This provided some justification for those on the left who began to operate outside the electoral system. Thus, the National Front pacified the country to the extent that it ended partisan fighting between Conservatives and Liberals; but, by excluding other groups from participation in normal political processes, it invited another sort of violence with which the system is still trying to cope.

Under the National Front most institutions and social groups underwent significant changes. The Church gave ground on education, and like all the established institutions, was overwhelmed by the process of urban growth. The hierarchy supported the government or did not oppose it openly even in matters like family planning. Liberation theology, in vogue in the 1960s and 1970s, did not affect the Colombian Church with the same intensity as in Brazil. Perhaps because liberation theology was relatively marginal in Colombia, the few clergy sympathetic to it became more militant, as in the case of Father Camilo Torres, killed in combat in 1966 fighting under the banner of the Ejército de Liberación Nacional (ELN). Between the traditionalism of the hierarchy and the radicalism of liberation theology prevailed the intermediary position of the Latin American Episcopal Conference in Medellin (1968). But the Church, with latent internal antagonisms, has been as fragmented as other social groups and institutions in the country.

The principal business interest groups firmly supported the various governments of the National Front and the successor *desmonte*. ANDI and FENALCO did not repeat their partisan skirmishes of 1945–1953. Rather, learning from the coffee federation, the interest group associations have become apolitical and bipartisan. Economic development under the National Front attenuated the regionalism of business groups. However, it still can be found in associations that present themselves as national, but in fact represent regional interests—as in sugar cane (dominated by the Cauca Valley), bananas (controlled by Antioqueños), and flowers (which Bogotá dominates).

Business interest groups as a whole developed more of a public profile under the National Front, but their influence diminished. During the 1960s and 1970s increasingly specialized interest group associations proliferated, making it possible for government officials to take advantage of the fragmentation and conflicts among multiple associations. Those who hold national office prefer to have the support of the interest group associations, but do not fear confrontation with them over specific points of policy. When the confrontation has important political implications, the interest groups lose. In 1996, when most of the interest group associations pressed for the resignation of President Samper in order to bring to an end the crisis stemming from accusations that he accepted narco-money in his campaign for election, they failed to budge him. In general, under the National Front and subsequent governments, there has existed a process of consultation between government officials and the interest groups in order to reach a consensus, although the consensus may be more fictitious than real. Lately the interest associations have presented themselves as speaking for the civil society, as they have done in the peace negotiations with the guerrillas.

Experts continue to rotate between the interest group associations and employment as government technocrats. But, as the state concentrates on macroeconomic management and leaves sectoral issues to the market, the connection between the state and the interest groups becomes more tenuous than was the case in the 1940s and 1950s.

The fall of real wages as a consequence of the coffee depression produced a wave of labor agitation between 1957 and 1966. Strikes by elements of the middle class multiplied, among them small entrepreneurs and drivers of city buses, as well as employees of AVIANCA. Bank employees formed an especially militant union. Marches of school teachers from the provinces to Bogotá, demanding back pay, proliferated. One of the most radical movements was the strike in 1963 of the workers of ECOPETROL, the government oil company; in this conflict the population of Barrancabermeja became mobilized, as did colonists around that city and university students. This strike influenced the origins of the Ejército de Liberacion Nacional guerrillas.

Although in 1960 the Liberals expelled Communists from the CTC, the Liberal-linked labor federation, the parties as such, with the exception of the Communists, have distanced themselves from the unions. The old identities of the unions, Liberal in the case of the CTC, Catholic for the UTC, have not disappeared, but the parties have not sought to reconstruct organic linkages with the unions.

During the National Front a number of labor conflicts were no longer noticed—because of the physical expansion of the cities, the proliferation of labor actions in many regions, the notable lack of interest of the parties of the coalition government, and the self-censorship of the the media.

During the strike wave, the leaders of the two established labor federations, particularly those in the CTC, were worn down. There emerged regionally based independent confederations, controlled by the left, especially the Communists. In the 1980s the guerrillas began to influence many unions of people working outside the big cities in the peripheral regions of the country.

From 1959 to 1965 the number of people in unions grew from 250,000 to 700,000. In 1990 there were nearly 900,000. As a percentage of the working population, union membership in these years rose from 5.5 percent to 13.4 percent and then declined to 8 percent. At present the rate of union membership is among the lowest in Latin America. In 1992, after twelve years of intricate fusions among diverse union federations, a single large Confederación Unica de Trabajadores was formed, incorporating the CTC and the UTC, the two oldest union federations, along with those controlled by the Communists and other left groups, as well as workers of the state. The unification has not increased the bargaining power of the unions. To the contrary, many of the gains of labor since the 1930s disappeared without much of a fight at the beginning of the 1990s, when the idea of making labor markets more flexible came into vogue.

In rural and peripheral regions the Juntas de Acción Comunal have grown considerably. These local community development committees were created by the first National Front president, Alberto Lleras Camargo, to organize, and co-opt, the urban poor. The program assumes that in any community there is likely to be a natural leader who can organize it and imbue it with a cooperative spirit. Aided by modest funds from the state, the community, with voluntary labor, constructs schools, health centers, streets, and sewers. Private organizations, national and foreign, also contribute funds to community action juntas. These juntas have been one of the favorite beneficiaries of clientelistic politicians through grants from the Congress. At the end of the National Front, in 1974, there were 18,000 community action juntas, with a little more than 1 million participants; in 1993 there were 45,600 juntas with 2.5 million participants.

One of the principal social causes of the National Front was agrarian reform. Agrarian reform legislation enacted under the administration of the Liberal Alberto Lleras Camargo (1958–1962) was disregarded by the successor government of the Conservative Guillermo León Valencia (1962–1966), to pacify opponents of the reform. Agrarian reform was reactivated in 1966, when its driving spirit, Carlos Lleras Restrepo, became president. Because a morass of legal formalism and bureaucratization posed formidable obstacles, Lleras decided to establish a mass movement to press for the reform from below—the Asociación Nacional de Usurarios Campesinos (ANUC), created in 1968. But this peasant pressure group did not achieve much, in part because it became divided between an official Armenia group and a radical Sincelejo group.

In 1971, during the last National Front government, the Sincelejo group organized peasant demonstrations and invasions of haciendas, cattle ranches, and public lands under dispute. The invasions had a momentary impact on the Caribbean coast, but soon disappeared. These efforts coincided with definitive abandonment of agrarian reform by the National Front coalition. But the failure of the Sincelejo group also was attributable to divisions within the Marxist organizations that tried to control it. Many peasant leaders were killed in repression by the state and large landowners.

Despite the peasant mobilization supported by Carlos Lleras, the agrarian reform proved to be poor as a political strategy. It did not much interest the populace as a whole, nor gain party support, nor did the program attain much institutional strength. Moreover, as already noted, state-subsidized capital investments in large landholdings made them too expensive to expropriate. Peasants were left with a sense of frustration and ultimately alienation, which for many found expression in abstention from voting or sympathy for guerrillas.

In 1971 INCORA suspended the distribution of land, and in 1972 the two parties agreed to abandon it entirely. As an alternative a tax on the presumed income of land, to encourage sales of unused land, was considered. President Alfonso López Michelsen made this part of his tax reform proposals. But an effective tax on land could not be carried out because there was no trustworthy land census, nor was there an accepted method of establishing a base for estimating income from land. A tax on presumed income on land was well accepted by the public, and for landowners it was a lesser evil than having their land divided. But landowners got the tax blocked by the Congress in 1979.

To mitigate the failure of the agrarian reform, the post–National Front governments embraced the World Bank's programs to fight rural poverty. Programs for nutrition and rural development were started to aid small farmers throughout the country, but with particular attention to places where peasants might be susceptible to guerrilla groups.

By the end of the National Front, fear of the Cuban Revolution had passed and promises of reform were abandoned. The governing class became oriented to favoring the accumulation of capital, leaving a fairer distribution of income for later. From experience with Rojas Pinilla's ANAPO, political leaders concluded that it was dangerous to mobilize the urban poor. Perhaps because the urban poor were disillusioned by the defeat of Rojas in the 1970 election, people in urban areas increasingly abstained from voting, and the big cities provided a decreasing proportion of the votes for the Liberal Party, previously the party that had depended most heavily on urban support.

The National Front demonstrated the strength of the two parties, upon which the populist challenge of Gaitán or the weak efforts of Rojas's third force had no permanent impact. But, following their tradition, the parties were divided, particularly the Conservatives. The agreements that formed the National Front were made with the Gómez faction. But the first elections of the new regime in 1960 were won by the Ospina faction in alliance with the followers of Alzate. So positions in the coalition government had to go to Ospinistas. Conservative factionalism was a burden that constantly threatened the continuity of policies. The faction of Laureano Gómez, whose leadership had passed to his son Alvaro Gómez Hurtado, was particularly a problem. Congressmen of the Gómez faction were decisive in torpedoing the Agrarian Reform and social reforms in general; in magnifying the counterinsurgency fight in 1964, when the guerrillas were still incipient and marginal; and ultimately in weakening the Conservative Party. Gómez Hurtado, vetoed as a possible president by the Liberals under the National Front, in the post–National Front years was a presidential candidate three times (1974, 1986, 1990), in campaigns that inflamed party divisions and finally relegated the Conservative Party to a distant secondary place.

By contrast the "official" Liberals were more successful in limiting internal opposition. The only Liberal opposition group was the Movimiento Revolucionario Liberal (MRL), headed by Alfonso López Michelsen, the son of President Alfonso López Pumarejo. The MRL had a short trajectory. It began by opposing the alternation of the presidency between Liberals and Conservatives. Its electoral support was in good part rural, particularly in the zones of violence, where some Liberal chiefs were not reconciled to the bipartisan framework of the National Front. Under the influence of the Cuban Revolution the MRL took on a more leftist hue. It reached its zenith in the 1962 election and then began to decline, divided into small doctrinaire factions. López, the "comrade chief," ended up negotiating his return to official Liberalism, and in 1968 was the first governor of the new Department of César. Thus he opened the way to his later election to the presidency.

During the late 1960s General Rojas Pinilla again became an important political force. Rojas had returned to the country in 1958 and in 1959 was tried before the Senate. Both his defenders and his accusers tried to convert the trial into a propaganda war; his defenders sought in vain to have the trial broadcast on radio and television. Rojas's defenders attacked the Gómez faction, accusing it of being responsible for the Violencia and the assassination of Gaitán. Rojas's accusers tried to reduce the issue simply to Rojas's enrichment of himself and his family. In the end he was charged with nothing more than engaging in contraband in cattle and collusion in some minor cases, for which he was sentenced to permanent loss of his political rights. The trial divided the Conservatives even more. The Ospinista newspapers opposed the trial and on more than one occasion President Alberto Lleras warned of Rojista plots and conspiracies. A few years afterward the Supreme Court annulled the verdict and returned to Rojas his political rights. The trial itself and the later treatment of the general, who was arrested every time there was a threat of a "military plot," turned him into a hero in the eyes of the common people.

Rojas initially hoped he could return to power by military coup, but when he concluded that the National Front had secured the loyalty of the armed forces, he turned to electoral politics. Like Gaitán, Rojas depicted himself as the champion of the people against the oligarchy, particularly emphasizing the effects on the people of the rising cost of living. Rojas claimed that he, not the National Front, had brought peace between Liberals and

Conservatives. He was sufficiently convincing that in many local Rojista offices former Liberal guerrilleros mixed in fraternal amity with former army sergeants of the period of the Violencia.

Rojas called for "socialism on Christian bases in the Colombian manner," free education for all, free medical and dental service for the poor, bank credit for small entrepreneurs, unifying all of the labor federations, and a new plan for housing for the poor. In economic policy with international ramifications, Rojas proposed to establish the Colombian peso on a par with the dollar, to limit foreign investment, and to end "tied" foreign aid—that is, foreign aid requiring that the money granted be used to purchase goods from the donor country.

In 1968 he also endorsed the papal encyclical of Paul VI opposing birth control, which gained Rojas the sympathy of many rural priests and those anti-imperialists who saw birth control as a North American instrument for subjugating Latin America. The common people, particularly those in the countryside, at this time were still uneasy about family planning. A campaign to eradicate malaria was denounced as aiming really to convince women to use birth control and to insert intrauterine coils known popularly as the *churrusco* (kinky hair).

In the late 1960s Rojas's movement, Acción Nacional Popular (ANAPO), became the most important Conservative electoral force in the country: Beginning with only 3.7 percent of the vote in 1962, in 1970 Rojas won 35 percent. The growth in Rojas's support reflected the inability of the National Front to win the mass of migrants to the city, the increase in urban unemployment in the 1960s, and the anger of many local politicians at the centralization of the state that occurred in the reform of 1968. Despite the strong showing of the Liberal Carlos Lleras Restrepo in the presidential election of 1966, electoral support for the National Front clearly was eroding. (See Table 13.13.)

In the election of 1970, the National Front coalition completely lost credibility. Hours after the polls closed, radio broadcasts were reporting the victory of General Rojas. That night the government cancelled transmission of

Table 13.13 The vote in favor of the National Front and electoral participation

Election	Percentage of Votes for National Front	Percentage of Those over Twenty-one Who Voted
1957 Plebiscite	95	73
Election of Alberto Lleras, 1958	80	48
Election of Guillermo León Valencia, 1962	62	28
Election of Carlos Lleras Restrepo, 1966	71	27
Election of Misael Pastrana, 1970	40	19

Source: Marco Palacios, *El populismo en Colombia* (Bogotá, 1971), p. 89.

Table 13.14 Distribution of votes among types of population centers: Comparison of General Rojas and Misael Pastrana, the National Front candidate, 1970

Urban Hierarchy	Rojas Pinilla		Misael Pastrana	
	Votes	Percentage	Votes	Percentage
National metropolis (Bogotá)*	251,456	16.7	236,303	14.5
Regional capitals	244,478	15.7	153,017	9.4
Primary regional cities	194,084	12.4	142,572	8.8
Secondary regional cities	152,024	9.7	110,671	6.8
Country towns	157,196	10.1	182,910	11.3
Rural communities	552,130	35.4	799,462	49.2
Total	1,561,468	100.0	1,625,025	100.0

*Includes votes from abroad: Rojas 3986, Pastrana 10,606.

Sources: Based on Registraduría Nacional del Estado Civil, Organización y Estadísticas Electoral, Bogotá, 1970, and Departamento Nacional de Planeación, "Modelo de Regionalización," Revista de Planeación, II, no. 3 (October 1970), pp. 302–339.

partial results and the following morning announced the victory of the official candidate, the Conservative Misael Pastrana. The next day President Carlos Lleras Restrepo confirmed this result and imposed a curfew in the big cities. Rojas acquiesced. A year later Rojas formally established ANAPO as a party at a massive rally in Villa de Leyva, in the heart of his native Boyacá. But, weakened by illness, he had to transfer leadership of the party to his daughter María Eugenia, after which ANAPO began to decline.

The 1970 election marks a change in Colombian electoral patterns. Now the electoral weight of the cities and, in particular, of the urban poor was even clearer than at the time of the vote for Gaitán in 1946 and 1947. Rojas's victory in the cities revealed a change in political culture. The rural-urban migration was producing a migration of voters from the traditional parties to new political forces. Table 13.14 indicates a stronger showing for Rojas Pinilla in cities than in rural areas. And much of Rojas's urban support came from neighborhoods of recent migrants to the city. By contast the vote for Misael Pastrana, the Conservative candidate of the National Front, was relatively weak in the cities and stronger in rural areas where traditional electoral mechanisms remained in place to some degree.

Before the dismantling of the National Front could begin, it was necessary first to to dismantle Rojas's ANAPO. Pastrana employed a rhetoric of socially enlightened conservatism. More concretely, he established a government agency to distribute subsidized food to poor neighborhoods where Rojas had strong support. Pastrana also announced, but understandably refrained from pursuing, a radical plan to expropriate property from urban residents who owned more than one home. Simultaneously Pastrana coopted many ANAPO leaders and denied financing to municipalities with Rojista majorities. After 1972, ANAPO was no longer a populist threat.

The political bosses of the period of the Violencia who later became prominent in the National Front were replaced toward the end of the National Front by a new generation of provincial politicians. These new regional "barons" and their political machinery provided electoral legitimacy to the state without having to manage social mobilization and conflict. This new generation proved much less deferential to established national party leaders.

The breach between political institutions and a large part of the population widened. Inflation worsened this malaise. While the annual rise in prices was 11.1 percent in the first twelve years of the National Front (1958–1970), during the next twelve the annual rate of price increases was 20.8 percent. And it reached 33.1 percent, the highest rate of the postwar period, in 1977, a year in which a national strike was followed by a degree of violent repression.

In the elections of 1974, the first in which the two parties were not guaranteed an equal number of seats, the Liberals overwhelmed the Conservatives—67 Liberals to 38 Conservatives in the Senate and 113 Liberals to 66 Conservatives in the Chamber of Representatives. By this time disaffection from the schlerotic electoral system of the National Front prompted many in the urban middle class to abstain from voting. When Alfonso López Michelsen, who as leader of the MRL once had postured as a "revolutionary," allied himself with a notorious machine politician, Julio César Turbay, many reformist Liberals were disillusioned. The López-Turbay alliance in 1973 defeated Carlos Lleras's bid to become the Liberal candidate for president, enabling López Michelsen, by a liaison with a political machine, to reach the presidency to which he surely felt destined by birth. It became Turbay's turn in 1977–1978, when in behalf of his presidential candidacy the alliance of López Michelsen and Turbay smashed Lleras's "democratization" movement, although the New Liberalism of Luis Carlos Galán afterward emerged from the ashes of that movement.

In a moment of intense social change, many people had become alienated from politics. It was becoming evident that the traditional parties were not serving as adequate expressions of social demands. The regime was operating by the clientelistic inertia inherited from the sixteen years of the National Front. The political insiders who had operated the National Front now knew from their experiences with the MRL and the ANAPO how easy it was for the government to co-opt and disrupt a challenge fueled by popular discontent. These insiders did not understand that a changing society required another kind of constitutional legitimacy. They imagined that simply winning elections would provide sufficient legitimacy, even if a tenuous one.

The dismantling of the National Front coincided with the crisis of import substitution industry. In the mid-1970s there began a slow turn toward economic liberalization. The government of López Michelsen (1974–1978) confronted ANDI, the representative of Colombia's industrialists, in an angry dispute over the costs to the nation of import substitution industry. López

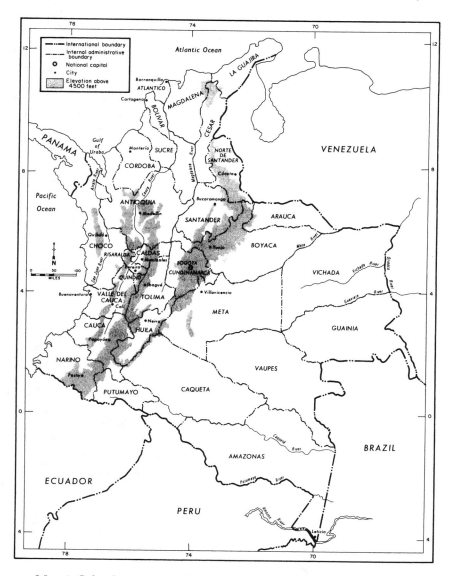

Map 8 Colombia, political divisions (ca. 1975). From *Area Handbook of Colombia* (Washington, DC, 1977).

argued that the government's continuing subsidies of Colombian manufacturers made them less efficient and competitive and also increased government deficits. In 1980 the Colombian government pledged itself to the movement toward freer trade by joining GATT. At this time the government also ended its economic planning (which in any case had been of a moderate sort, indicating goals for the economy rather than operating in a coercive or command mode). It also stopped establishing state-owned industries, as well as other forms of state entrepreneurship and investment in industry. In any case, the Colombian government had never gone as far down the path of establishing state-owned industries as did Mexico, Brazil, or Argentina.

During these years a process of financial liberalization occurred, with fewer restrictions on banks and other financial instituitons. Virtually unregulated financial manipulation led to clearly inappropriate practices (e.g., banks making loans to themselves) and an unprecedented concentration of capital in a few financial groups. The demands of two powerful financial groups led to an increase in the money supply and increased inflation. The activities of these groups created a major scandal during the Turbay government. This crisis aggravated divisions within the Liberal Party, permitting in 1982 the election as president of Belisario Betancur, a Conservative who projected a commitment to change that attracted many in a younger generation alienated by the sterility of the politics of previous decades.

In the 1980s there developed a consensus on the need to diversify the economy, gradually eliminating the protection of industry so that it might become more competitive and an effective exporter to external markets. The governments of both Betancur (1982–1986) and Virgilio Barco (1986–1990), in the context of a political crisis, focused more on social than economic policies. Under Betancur Colombia was hit by its version of the Latin American debt crisis. In Colombia's case, prudent policy had kept government borrowing abroad to relatively modest levels. But the debts of Colombian manufacturing enterprises, aggravated by the rise of interest rates in the international market, created an acute industrial crisis in Colombia, which was accompanied by a growing government deficit. The Betancur government had to agree to an IMF "voluntary adjustment," which required a drastic reduction in public expenditures and a substantial devaluation of the peso. The first measure brought a freeze of wages and of spending on education and housing for the poor. As in other economic adjustment programs, the poor bore disproportionately the burden of stabilization. The devaluation, in effect, protected domestic industry. But the current of economic policy was going in the other direction. President Virgilio Barco began to dismantle tariff protection of industry, a process completed in 1990–1992 by his successor, César Gaviria (1990–1994).

THE INTERREGNUM, 1986–PRESENT

Despite a widespread perception of the failures of the post–National Front *desmonte*, Betancur retained some of its features. Perhaps because his party was a minority in Congress, he did not dare to challenge the idea of a bipartisan cabinet. On the other hand, in other respects his government represented a "democratic opening," as he himself termed it—particularly in his efforts to seek peace with the guerrillas and in the constitutional reform that permitted election, rather than appointment, of mayors.

Table 13.15 Results of presidential elections, 1974–1986

Year	Liberal	Conservative	Other	Left	Participation
1974	López Michelsen, 56.2%	Gómez Hurtado, 31.4%	María E. Rojas, 9.4%	Echeverri, 2.6%	51.0%
1978	Turbay Ayala, 49.5%	Betancur, 46.6%	Valencia, 1.3%	Three candidates, 2.4%	41.2%
1982	López, 41.0%	Betancur, 46.8%	Galán, 10.9%	Molina, 1.2%	50.7%
1986	Barco, 58.3%	Gómez Hurtado, 35.8%		Pardo, 4.5%	n.d.

Source: Jonathan Hartlyn, *The Politics of Coalition Rule in Colombia* (Cambridge, 1988), p. 153.

The overwhelming victory of Virgilio Barco in the presidential election of 1986 (see Table 13.15) enabled him to abandon the last rule of National Front constitutionalism—the bipartisan cabinet. He offered Conservatives three ministries in a cabinet of thirteen, but in a way that obliged them to refuse. Barco then announced that he was going to govern with his party. Thus began the interregnum, which was supposed to end with the conclusion of the new constitution of 1991. But the constitution did not end the interregnum. For one thing, the underlying values and practices of informal politics continued shaping public life, irrespective of the constitution. As a Latin American proverb says, to enemies, one applies the law, to friends, favor. For another, the problems associated with the drug traffic and the guerrillas multiplied. And the discovery of new oil deposits in eastern Colombia worsened the symptoms of the Dutch disease. At this juncture, globalization struck with greater intensity the fragile structure of the Colombian state.

TOWARD A NEW CONSTITUTIONALISM

During the first government of the *desmonte* (López Michelsen, 1974–1978) fears of populism and social revolution evaporated. The misery of the new migrant neighborhoods in the cities did not impel the poor to rise up or to support urban guerrillas. The chief disorder in the cities originated with militants of the extreme left in the large public universities. After a while their demonstrations became a routine that, with some deaths and serious injuries, the police and army were able to control. (The private universities benefitted from this disorder. The middle classes already were pressing to enter private universities, believing that they were the route to success, an idea that appeared to be confirmed by the disruption of the public universities.) In the countryside the guerrillas were so weak that after the ELN was surrounded and defeated near Anorí, in Antioquia, President López in 1974 had to order that they not be annihilated.

Thus, it came as a surprise when a national civic strike occurred in September 1977. The strike led to violent repression, more improvised than calculated, which the media were scarcely able to hide. In this strike, more than in the various urban operations of the M-19 guerrillas at this time, symptoms of social discontent and alienation of broad sectors of society from the politicial regime were evident. The series of scandals involving financial and political corruption in the following years further eroded the prestige of the elites in the eyes of the middle classes.

President López's awareness of a growing alienation from the ruling system prompted him to propose a constitutional reform, but the Congress blocked this initiative. His Liberal successors, Turbay and Barco, who, like López had majorities in the Congress, also tried, fruitlessly, to start the process of constitutional reform. Only Betancur, a Conservative president without a majority in Congress, was able to obtain a partial reform, instituting the election of mayors. This reform in some places opened up politics and in others strengthened an already existing control by informal local powers.

Constitutional change came somewhat unexpectedly because of a crisis of public order in 1988–1991. The enemies on this occasion were the narco-traffickers who in 1988 began a ruthless terrorist war, against which the government seemed unable to take any effective measure. Of the many shocking terrorist acts of the drug lords, one of several that had major political impact on Colombian politics was the assassination in 1989 of the Liberal presidential candidate Luis Carlos Galán, in whose person many Colombians had come to place much of their hope for the future of the country. Galán, who had been active in Carlos Lleras Restrepo's "democratization" movement of the late 1970s, emerged in the 1980s as the leader of the New Liberalism. Under the banner of political moralization, Galán won strong support from the Liberal middle class, as well as a broad popular following. His assassination at a campaign event stunned the nation. Along with similarly shocking murders of other presidential candidates and hundreds of lesser public figures, this event seemed to signal the ultimate decomposition of Colombia as a functioning, civilized polity.

Confronting the political crisis of the end of the 1980s, political elites concluded that the only solution was to refound the state. From that understanding emerged a new constitution designed to legitimate the state through a system that was more participative and decentralized, more oriented to social justice, more transparent, and less corrupt.

The legitimacy and the legality of the constitutional process is open to question. There was no legal basis for convoking the Constitutional Assembly. And, in contrast with the 1957 plebiscite in which 90 percent of those eligible voted, in the 1990 election of delegates to the constitutional assembly 74 percent refrained from voting, the worst rate of abstention since the restoration of constitutional order in 1958. Less than half as many voted for the delegates than had cast ballots in congressional elections a few months before. Yet the delegates, on their own authority, without consulting the electorate, revoked the mandate of that same popularly elected Congress.

Just as the National Front was affected by the atmosphere of the Cold War, particularly the preventive reformism of the Alliance for Progress, so the constitution of 1991 expressed the themes of the post–Cold War era— emphasizing human rights, ecological concerns, a participative civil society, decentralization, and demilitarization.

There are other contrasts between the processes of 1957 and 1991. In 1957 the central economic policy of import substitution industrialization was widely embraced. In 1990, a decade behind some other countries in Latin America, an important element of the Colombian elite was prepared to embrace privatization and commercial and financial opening to the outside world. As these ideas had been preached, by some, since the industrial crisis of the 1970s, the ground was at least somewhat prepared. However, if there was little resistance to economic liberalization within the constitutional assembly, this new policy orientation was received with hostility by unions, particularly those in the public sector.

Whereas the plebiscite of 1957 created a two-party government from which all others were excluded, in the constitutional assembly of 1990, demobilized guerrillas of the M-19 were so strongly represented (seventeen delegates) that they formed one of the three major forces in the assembly, along with the Liberal Party (twenty-five delegates) and the Gómez faction of Conservatives, rebaptized as the Movement of National Salvation (eleven delegates). On the other hand, in 1990 as in 1957 the process was organized from above. The Liberal chiefs, particularly Alfonso López Michelsen, and Alvaro Gómez Hurtado on the Conservative side showed that in Colombia the established political families still were in command.

In a sense the constitution of 1991 buried the past. It was neither conceived nor presented with reference to any other previous Colombian constitution. Its points of reference were the new constitutions of Spain and Brazil, although its philosophical inspiration stemmed from the classic constitutionalism of the end of the eighteenth century.

The constitution presents recent visions of human rights and ecological law. It recognizes the ethnic plurality of the Colombian people. It affirms contemporary principles on fiscal decentralization and strengthens the judiciary. It restricts the government's power in monetary matters. And it limits even more than the constitutional reform of 1959 the conditions permitting a state of siege, now called a state of internal commotion. But it does not touch the delicate issue of the role of the armed forces in a democratic order.

Partly out of a sense of national desperation, not a few Colombians in 1991 hoped that the new constitution would somehow work miracles. The constitution specifically called for a reconciliation that would incorporate the guerrillas into the peaceful political process envisioned by the constitution. However, despite peace processes pursued by the various presidents since Belisario Betancur in 1982, such a reconciliation has not occurred. There also has been some disappointment that the constitution has failed to open up political competition, eliminate corruption, or strengthen modern parties. But a constitution alone could not work such wonders. Such fundamental objectives also require a changed political culture as well as alterations in the economic and social structure.

The leaders of the National Front, many of whom began their political careers in the 1920s and 1930s, have been replaced by new types of politician, whose perspectives are less national, more local and regional. The result is a fragmentation of politics, which is observable in elections—in the proliferation of many party slates, in which the parties and the candidates are of strictly local appeal. The mobilization of the poor by ANAPO and the emergence of short-lived middle-class civic reform movements decrying corruption have affected the electoral modes of the new generation of politicians that came to maturity in the 1980s, who both appeal to the popular classes and employ the rhetoric of anti-corruption.

The election of mayors was a decisive step in formalizing the fragmentation of politics. The constitution of 1991 consolidated this. It created different calendars, and therefore different campaigns, for the various offices. City councils, mayors, governors, and departmental assemblies have three-year terms; the Congress has four-year terms, with senators chosen at large in national elections and representatives elected by their departments. Furthermore, all of these elections are separated from the presidential elections, which have a second phase if no candidate obtains a majority of the votes in the first one.

With multiple elections occurring at different times, competition is increased and party electoral machinery is weakened. Nonetheless, the two traditional parties, particularly the Liberal Party, remain dominant. A new figure, the electoral micro-entrepreneur, has emerged. Television has become the most important medium of propaganda, and consequently campaigns have become more expensive.

In light of the high, and perhaps unrealizable, ideals proclaimed in the constitution of 1991, the 1990s have been particularly frustrating to Colombians. Urban unemployment, which in recent years has reached the highest levels since unemployment statistics have existed, contradicts the constitutional principle that declares the right to work to be fundamental. The assertion that the rights of children prevail over those of everyone else is not in keeping with increased denunciations of abuses of all kinds against children, nor with the growing inability of many municipalities to educate their children, particularly on the Caribbean coast. The difficult and increasing social problem of people displaced by violence, and often harassed by the armed forces, clearly contrasts with the constitution's protection of human rights.

Nevertheless, the protection of many rights of individuals and of labor have been advanced by a provision in the new constitution permitting individuals to bring complaints of denial of fundamental rights before judges, who can issue restraining orders. As a consequence of the exercise of this constitutional provision, Colombians are now exploring the frontiers of individual rights. For example, legal decisions have established that pregnant adolescents cannot be expelled from schools and that homosexuals cannot be discriminated against in the armed forces. Some of these conquests for individual rights involve moral issues so complex and troubling that many other societies have difficulty addressing them. In Colombia, for example, those who suffer terminal diseases may now legally request the assistance of a physician in the dignified termination of life. Another significant innovation has established the possibility of judicial decisions restraining economic measures of the state—for example, on the social equity of interest rates or anti-inflationary policies.

The legal development of the new constitution has remained in the hands of the same political class that had ruled before the constitution and, worse, of congressmen who have shown even greater defects than before. This was demonstrated in the congressional proceedings regarding donations from drug lords to the electoral campaign of President Ernesto Samper, in which the congressmen's own involvement with narco-traffickers made impossible an uncorrupted judgment. The fundamental problem has continued since the foundation of the republic: the distance between the dreams of constitutionalism and real social practices.

THE NEW POWERS: THE DRUG TRAFFIC AND PETROLEUM

In the globalization of the markets for illegal drugs, money, and guns, the United States plays a predominant role as the chief consumer of prohibited narcotics, the center of operations for illegal money, and an important perveyor of arms to Colombian black markets. The United States also unilaterally establishes the terms in which the source countries, like Colombia, must collaborate in the war against drugs.

Time magazine, on July 6, 1981, cited a study to the effect that, "Cocaine, like motorcycles, machine guns and White House politics, is, among many other things, a virility substitute. Its mere possession imparts status: cocaine equals money, and money equals power." These were times of permissiveness and high drug prices in the North American market. Shortly afterward, the U.S. media began to focus with greater seriousness on the plague of cocaine and even more harmful and addictive subproducts like crack—epidemics that affected public health and generated epidemics of criminality and the corruption of some police. Soon there formed a political consensus on a policy of "zero tolerance" and various programs for a war on drugs began that had an enormous impact on Colombia.

The strategy of the war on drugs defined the problem as lying primarily in the supply of narcotics, that is, in Bolivia, Peru, Colombia, and Mexico. Second, it assigned to the armies of these countries for the most part the job of suppressing the supply. In Colombia, however, the failure of the army, evident in the war against the drug lord Pablo Escobar, brought a change of strategy. The national police was reformed and replaced the army as the chief agent of repression.

The war on drugs was accompanied by the unilateral sanction of "de-certification." Washington also demanded the extradition of Colombians (and other Latin Americans) for trial in the United States. These policies pro-voked strong nationalist resentment. The threat of extradition led to an alarming terrorist campaign by the drug traffickers. Hundreds of witnesses, judges, and journalists were murdered. The end of the terror came only when the extradition of Colombians was prohibited in the new constitution of 1991. In 1997 the Congress, at the request of the president, who was under pres-sure from the U.S. government, reformed the constitution to permit the re-sumption of extraditions. Table 13.12 shows that the economic dynamic of the drug traffic has overwhelmed the logic of repression.

The drug traffic and the emergence of oil imply a massive transfer of re-sources to networks of cronies and to the guerrillas and also have brought corruption at the top. The scandal over the massive campaign donations of narco-traffickers, of which President Ernesto Samper was the focal point, was simply the most visible apex of an extended system of relations of pro-tection, complicity and bribery connecting the political class of both parties to the drug traffickers. Such relations date from the 1970s. Pressure from the United States and a change in Colombian public opinion tranformed what had been a more or less accepted, but discreet, practice into Colombia's biggest political scandal of the twentieth century. The financing of politicians by business had been long accepted. The industrialists' pressure group, the ANDI, had donated funds to politicians since the 1940s, and since the be-ginning of the National Front, practically all of the big companies financed campaigns. The narco-traffickers, however, in addition to being entrepre-neurs, were in an illegal business, and some of them directly managed crim-inal organizations.

The politicization of oil revenues also reinforced the patronage system. Under the precepts of fiscal decentralization, it was decided that 49 percent of the oil royalties would go to the departments and municipalities where the oil was extracted and through which oil pipelines passed, with the rest to go to the remainder of the nation. As oil exploitation occurs in regions with scanty populations, the result is a grotesque maldistribution of rev-enues. On a per capita basis the royalties going to Arauca are 362 times those received by Antioquia, 1300 times those going to Cundinamarca, and 8900 times those destined for Risaralda.

In addition, the new oil fields are located in frontier regions, which no-toriously lack established institutions and are ruled by patronage politics and extortionate guerrilla violence. In these places the huge oil royalties are spent on unnecessary, even absurd, public works, in gigantic contracts with illegal commissions attached. The guerrillas have such power that they are recognized intermediaries in these contracts.

The election of mayors, the obligatory transfer of revenues to the mu-nicipalities, and the neofederalist bent of the new constitution of 1991 together have changed the balance among the territorial units of the Colombian state, and adequate institutions to cope with this situation do not yet exist.

During the 1990s, an effort has been made to reduce the size of the national state. Between 1992 and 1998 the state sold into private hands government entities producing a variety of goods and services, in so doing freeing itself of a substantial financial cost. At the same time, studies were undertaken to rationalize the operations of state institutions, with the aim of reducing the bureaucracy, simplifying procedures, and becoming more accessible to citizens. The expected result was to make the state smaller, at once reducing its costs and improving its efficiency. But the reverse has occurred. Government expenditures have greatly increased. Why?

One fundamental reason is that, perhaps for the first time in the nation's history, because of increased oil production the state has revenues of such magnitude that politicians now are more autonomous in relation to the nation's business elites. The government can spend more without the political cost of increasing taxes. At the same time the private sector fights to capture some of the oil revenues, demanding tax exemptions, subsidized foreign exchange. and preferential interest rates on loans.

In only four years, 1995–1998, public expenditures rose from 32.2 percent of GDP to 36.9 percent. In a country with deficient infrastructure (highways, bridges, tunnels, ports), and unattended social needs, particularly in health and education, such an increase might be welcome. But 70 percent goes to current expenses, mostly to pay the bureaucracy and the military.

This imbalance between current expenses and public investment is a response to the incentives of the political game. The time horizon of the professional politician is short, generally limited to the four-year terms of the president and congressmen (or the three-year terms of the mayors and governors), while the positive effects of expenditures on education or road construction are seen only over a longer period. Given the dominance of patronage in politics, government salaries increased excessively—not only those of the central government but also those of the departments and municipalities, making use of revenues transferred from the national government by mandate of the constitution of 1991.

Moreover, the effort to repress the drug traffic and armed conflict with the guerrillas have required the government to make expenditures far in excess of its budgetary tradition. Military expenses increased from 1.6 percent of GDP in 1985 to 2.6 percent in 1995, and they continue to grow. But here also a substantial part of the increase goes to pay salaries, perquisites, and pensions of military personnel.

In these ways, the expansion of public expenditures generates a propensity to fiscal deficits and a permanent inflationary pressure. Given these patterns, it is hardly surprising that Colombians have conflicted attitudes toward the state. Although many businessmen and other citizens want the state to be more active in providing public improvements, they also distrust state enterprise as inefficient and corrupt.

CULTURAL CHANGE: HIGH CULTURE AND POPULAR CULTURE

The secularization of Colombian society is perhaps the salient cultural change of the second half of the twentieth century. Secularization has been a worldwide process, but its Colombian version had some particular features. In this period the authority of the Church was weakened considerably in matters of private and public morality, in educational policies, and in partisan politics. Urbanization, the expansion of education, the increase of literacy, and the development of cinema and television and new forms of popular culture, including sports, created new cultural patterns. Intellectuals, particularly writers in the print press, were becoming marginalized in their traditional role as shapers of opinion. The traumas of the Bogotazo and the violence that followed April 9, 1948, in the provinces fostered an alienation from politics. Peace under the National Front required submerging party ideologies, at least temporarily. Those who sought to exploit partisan ideologies were disdained as sectarian and anachronistic. In this context the ideological intellectual gave way to the intellectual as expert. And among experts, the jurist gave way to the economist. Now there is more of a balance between the two, but an assemblage of technical specialists in commercial and political markets has come to the fore.

Among the conditions providing a setting for the secularization process in Colombia, two may be noted here. First, indices of readership of books, magazines, and newspapers in Colombia since mid-century have been among the lowest in Latin America. Second, television arrived in the country in the mid-1950s under a regime of political and moral censorship, which also induced a prudent self-censorship, and these restrictions were particularly severe in radio and television. Important issues could not be directly and frankly addressed by the media. Instead soccer, bicycle races, and beauty contests distracted a depressed country. The hour of the newscasters and presenters of bland cultural programs began. Their polished voices and their speech without regional accents were adapted to the new public. The programs of greatest intellectual density consisted of quiz shows of an encyclopedic sort, in the charge of know-it-alls who made the radio listener or television viewer believe that he was being supplied with miraculous capsules of knowledge. Radio and television following North American commercial models tended to take the place of public education in shaping the national culture. Never, not even when the idea of an "Open University" was discussed in the 1980s, did Colombian leaders consider adopting a British or French model of public television that would raise the educational level of the people while entertaining them.

The retreat of ecclesiastical and lay elites as shapers and arbiters of culture became more evident in the 1990s, with the prevalence in the media of earthy talkers with strong regional accents, although they did not completely displace the most refined speakers. Andrés Pastrana's role as an elegant newscaster in the 1980s established him as a public figure on his way to the presidency. A contrasting example of the earthy element is Edgar Perea, who made his name as a rough-hewn sports commentator and on occasion was punished for inciting violence among soccer fans. Perea in 1998 became one of the republic's most important senators.

Colombia's two most popular national sports, soccer and cycling, became professionalized at the time of the political violence that began in 1948. In these sports the Colombian people found new heroes who represented the possibility of social ascent and recognition through effort and talent and also embodied the values of personal sacrifice, modesty, and attachment to authentic popular culture. The politicians were quick to exploit these new popular expressions. This pattern was evident in the creation by the Rojas Pinilla dictatorship of an armed forces' cycling team to compete in the national bike race, the Vuelta a Colombia. The team was made up of the most popular cyclists in the country, principally Antioqueños. It also has been said that the Vuelta a Colombia race of 1970 eased the tensions arising from the dramatic presidential election of that year.

Since the beginning of radio broadcasting in the 1930s, the concentration of ownership and control of communications media has been notable. Today the linkage among big businessmen, the media, and politics is notorious. Two of the biggest business conglomerates in the country, the Santodomingo group and the Ardila Lulle group, own the dominant private radio and television chains, as well as magazines aimed at the middle class. The Santodomingo group also recently acquired *El Espectador*, one of the two major Liberal newspapers in Bogotá. Both groups have become open patrons of one or another presidential candidate, as well as other politicians.

For a newly urban population, radio, phonograph records, films, and television shaped new tastes. Regional folk music was adapted to the urban audience. The public revealed a predilection for the Argentine tango, Mexican rancheras, the Cuban-Mexican bolero, and Afro-Caribbean dance music. Soap operas and humor programs from prerevolutionary Cuba became part of the texture of popular culture. But with time it became evident that North American culture had become the archetype of mass culture in Colombia. To the degree that popular culture in the United States purveys egalitarian values, as de Tocqueville early and perspicaciously noted, it offers a healthy counterweight to the high culture of the traditional dominant classes.

Consider, for example, the influence of North American popular culture in the soap operas of the last ten or fifteen years and in the incipient Colombian film industry. In the early 1990s the official acts of the Congress and of the president were scheduled so as not to conflict with a soap opera that had the highest ratings: *Café con aroma de mujer* (*Coffee with the Scent of*

Woman). The story revolved around a powerful coffee-growing family from Manizales during the bonanza of the 1970s. It offered a conventional miscellany of fraud in the export of coffee, boldness in social climbing, recycled virginities, and faked maternities. The narrative, unlike the shrivelled style customary in this genre, was dominated by a cynical and twisted point of view. But the program also was escapist. The most worrisome realities confronted by Colombian families—the tribulations of extortion, kidnapping, and common criminality—appeared nowhere in the program.

Some expressions of popular culture are notably upbeat. *La estrategia del caracol* (*The Strategy of the Snail*), one of the most popular Colombian films, narrates the vicissitudes of the ingenious tenants of a large colonial mansion in the center of Bogotá who are trying to elude a judicial order of eviction. Following Hollywood canons of the 1930s and 1940s, the pictures depict those who are powerful (the owner and his son) and their wily intermediaries (their lawyer, the judge, and the police) as ridiculous, while dignifying and ennobling the simple working people—and there is a happy ending.

Colombia's higher culture is now both more cosmopolitan and more Colombian at the same time. That is, the nation's higher culture has employed broader idioms of the Western world to describe and illumine Colombian idiosyncrasies. In the last fifty years the plastic arts, architecture, and the theater have experienced a golden age. And international recognition has consecrated the talent of Fernando Botero and Gabriel García Márquez, the color and power of whose imaginative art are extracted from the life and culture of the Colombian people.

14

Political Violence in the Second Half of the Twentieth Century

In the last decade of the twentieth century Colombians felt unprotected in life and property as at few times in the past. The indices of homicides, personal injuries, kidnappings, and forced displacement of families and neighborhoods are among the highest in the world. And they show no sign of declining.

The profusion of agents and forms of violence conflict dramatically with the postulates of a new constitution, drawn up in 1991, to remedy these and other injustices that Colombian society has been suffering. Why do Colombians live amid so much violence? How has the Colombian state arrived at such a degree of impotence? What is the relation between the lack of punishment of violence and the increase in violent crimes? Some answers can be found in the trajectory of the second half of the twentieth century.

This history begins with the Violencia, capitalized to indicate a specific period. Thus written, the term refers to a series of regional and local processes in a period from 1946 to 1964, although its greatest destructive force was released between 1948 and 1953. The variations in the statistical calculations offered, from 80,000 to 400,000 deaths, reflect differing partisan perspectives.

Seen as a national political process, the Violencia resulted from two interwoven causes: first, from an aggressive confrontation of elites of opposing parties seeking to impose through the national state a model of modernization, conforming to conservative or, contrarily, liberal norms; and, second, from a local partisanship that affected people of all groups, classes, and large regions of the country. In addition, the Cold War exacerbated the Liberal-Conservative division from the top to the bottom of society. Ultimately, however, the Violencia, by forcing many peasants off their plots, contributed to the flood of migration from rural areas to the cities. However, as more and more people migrated to the cities, they lost the local political loyalties, Liberal or Conservative, which had played a great part in the development of rural violence in the 1940s and 1950s, opening up the possibility of overcoming the long-established sectarian partisanship.

One of the suppositions of the seminal book of Monsignor Germán Guzman, Orlando Fals Borda, and Eduardo Umaña Luna, *La Violencia en Colombia* (1962), was that the worst had happened between 1948 and 1953 and was over after 1953. What followed after 1953 was viewed simply as an after-effect—very destructive, to be sure, in Caldas—that the forces of order could reduce and contain, which in fact occurred around 1964. The same assumptions were embedded in the defense of General Rojas Pinilla in his trial before the Senate in 1959.

Although there have been differences of interpretation of the various periods of violence, all later interpretations have used the same periodization. Referring to events after 1964, for example, the period of revolutionary or guerrilla violence appears in the mid-1960s, and the violence of narco-traffic erupts in the mid-1970s.

In recognizing the extraordinary multiplicity and confusion of forms, organizations, and settings that accompanied the escalation of homicides of the 1980s, a group of university researchers proposed speaking of violences (plural). The proposal, intelligently presented in *Violencia y Democracia* (1987) had extraordinary social influence and has served as a guide, as did the book of Guzmán, Fals Borda, and Umaña before it.

It is commonly said that Colombia has suffered a half-century of war, or of violence, as if it has been one continuous process. However, judging from the statistics, it is difficult to speak of a half-century of continuity. For example, if one groups all homicides together, without distinguishing between "political" and "common" killings, from the 1950s to the end of the 1970s the rates of homicide in Colombia were already the highest in Latin America—about 30 per 100,000. Nonetheless, although the rates were high, they were still within the range of the most homicidal countries of the world. But, early in the 1980s Colombian rates of homicide took off, and by the beginning of the 1990s had tripled over the levels of 1950–1980.

This chapter offers a historical description of Colombia's political violence, seen as a national process. This focus does not deny the validity of local and regional analyses. On the contrary, political violence is best understood as a galaxy of social conflicts, in which each case acquires its full significance in a history of local and provincial contexts, which may be unique. But these local conflicts, with all of their regional particularities, nonetheless occurred within a shared national political history.

It is always difficult to establish what connections there are between political violence and other forms of violence. Even so, in this chapter we offer a narrative sketch of political violence, describing four succesive phases, recognizing that some elements characteristic of one phase may be present in other phases.

1. *First phase.* This is the phase of violence of political partisanship that began in the electoral campaigns of 1945–1946 and ended in 1953, with the amnesty and programs of pacification offered by the military government of General Rojas Pinilla. This was a germinal period, covering much of the national territory, which sowed the field with myths, representations, and modes of behavior that would be harvested in later phases.

2. *Second phase.* From 1954 to 1964, the violence occurred through partisan and factional networks. But it operated by interfering with the supply

of labor on coffee farms and with coffee and land markets. Since this was a means of redistribution and social ascent, we may call it "mafia violence," following the interpretive suggestions of Eric Hobsbawm. This "mafia phase" was largely limited to the coffee slopes of the Central and Western Cordilleras, principally the northern part of the Cauca Valley and the greater Caldas region. But in this phase there also occurred armed struggles of an agrarian and Communist sort in southern Tolima and in the Sumapaz massif, some of which may be considered direct antecedents of the *guerrillero* period.

3. *Third phase.* A period whose signature is the guerrilla of the left, this phase started at the beginning of the 1960s, under the impact of the Cuban Revolution, and lasted until the end of the 1980s, when the Soviet system collapsed. Although the period is framed in these dates of the Cold War and the guerrillas identified themselves with Leninist, Guevarist, or Maoist postulates, the explanatory factors are really internal. One of the most important factors was the dynamism of the colonization process on eight frontiers. But the violent deaths that occurred in this process had an insignificant impact on the total number of homicides in the country.

4. *Fourth phase.* The fourth phase begins toward the end of the 1980s and still continues. It is characterized by a fluid combination of theaters of insurrectional war of low intensity and mafia wars. In this picture converge, variously in time and place, drug-traffickers, guerrillas, and paramilitaries. These are intermixed, in alliance or in conflict, with clientelistic politicians, cattle-owners, the military, and the police.

THE VIOLENCE OF PARTISANSHIP, 1945–1953

On the eve of the elections of 1946, President Alberto Lleras Camargo pointed out that

> the unleashed violence, is ordered, is stimulated, by remote control, [by people who are] free of risk. The most typical violence of our political struggles is that which atrociously makes victims of the humble people in villages and in rural areas, in the neighborhoods of the cities, as a product of the conflicts that alcohol illumines with the livid flames of insanity. But the explosives have been sent from urban desks, worked with cold unconcern, elaborated with guile, in order to produce their fruits of blood.

A commentary of the weekly *Semana* in January 1947, perhaps also from the pen of Lleras, showed how the partisan conflicts in the rural communities concealed private wars:

> The parties that furiously dispute the palm of martyrdom, contribute decisively to the fact that acts of violence are provoked, that those responsible escape punishment, that incidental criminality is covered with party banners, and that witnesses are found to protect the offenders or to shift responsibility to the innocent.

In high-risk regions partisan cleansing operations were carried out in settlements dominated by the minority party in the municipality. Almost immediate vengeance followed, particularly if a neighboring municipality was a traditional political rival. This pattern of propagating the violence became rapid and intense in the Eastern Cordillera, the Cauca Valley, the upper Cauca, and Nariño, as a consequence of the assassination of Jorge Eliécer Gaitán in 1948. In that year alone deaths by violence tripled over the three previous years.

Gaitán was assassinated on April 9, 1948, as he left his office in the center of Bogotá. Many have suspected that Gaitán was the victim of a plot—variously attributed to Conservatives, orthodox Liberals, or Communists. Convincing proof has not emerged of any of these possible conspiracies. But the multitudes who had placed their faith in Gaitán certainly believed there had been a plot from the moment they heard the news of his death. "They killed Gaitán:" They, the oligarchs; they, the Conservative government. The mass reaction produced one of the most destructive, massive, and bloody riots in Latin American history. Hundreds of government and religious buildings and private homes were demolished by mobs; hundreds of stores were sacked; the rioters burned the trolleys and automobiles that they found in their way. But they could not take the presidential palace. The next morning, when President Mariano Ospina Pérez announced to the country that he had reached an accord with the Liberals to form a bipartisan government, hundreds of cadavers already were piled in the capital's Central Cemetery. Most went into a common grave. Such rioting was replicated in many cities and towns. These episodes of April 9 mark a point of departure in Colombian politics and in the course of the Violencia. The bipartisan unity agreement fell apart in less than a year, amid exacerbated partisanship, and party violence ascended in a spiral.

The confrontation between the party elites reached a climax in the second half of 1949. The rise of the Conservative caudillo Laureano Gómez was one of the most important factors that destroyed the bipartisan agreement that President Ospina and the Liberals were seeking. An all-out party conflict became inevitable on October 12, 1949, when the Conservative Party launched the candidacy of Gómez for the presidential term of 1950–1954. In response, the Liberal Party decided to abstain from voting in order to delegitimize the new president and the Conservative regime in general. The Liberal abstention from the presidential elections of November 1949 marked a point of no return; it gave Ospina a pretext to close Congress and declare a state of siege.

In 1950 the geography, principal actors, and modes of organization of the Liberal resistance changed. While the departments of Nariño, the Santanders, Boyacá, and the Cauca Valley became somewhat pacified, the violence moved to the eastern slope of the Eastern Cordillera; to the eastern plains of Casanare and Meta; to the massif of Sumapaz; to the Antioqueño regions of Urrao, the Lower Cauca, and the Middle Magdalena; and to

Tolima. There it would rage for a long time, becoming joined by the most sinister violence, which took over Caldas and the northern part of the Valley of the Cauca in a wave that passed after 1954, and by the Communist guerrillas of Sumapaz and southern Tolima.

Now the Liberal resistance tried to organize itself better in guerrillas. At times, from 1950 to 1953, the violence seemed to lose its character of semi-anarchic wars of family vengeance within localities, becoming more of a generalized civil war. But this character of a violence more public than private, more national than local, was endorsed neither by the Conservative government nor by Liberal leaders. None of them wanted the conflict to be thought of as a civil war.

They chose early on to portray themselves as public-spirited citizens rather than as chiefs of the people in rebellion. To support the guerrillas openly would have meant giving pretexts to the government to maintain the state of siege and postpone the return to republican constitutional government. Some Liberal leaders must have profoundly distrusted the guerrillas, particularly as many of them originated as local revolutionary juntas that appeared in many places in reaction to the murder of Gaitán. The wing of Liberalism led by Alfonso López Pumarejo opted later, and with little success, to serve as mediator between the government and the guerrillas. The chief consequence was a break between the urban *Lopista* leadership and the Liberal guerrillas. The Conservatives also were deeply fragmented into three major factions, headed by Laureano Gómez, Mariano Ospina Pérez, and Gilberto Alzate Avendaño. Factions in both parties treated issues of war and peace as means of gaining tactical advantages within their party.

Thus, for example, when the Alzatista faction controlled the Conservative directorate, they made a peace pact with Liberal leaders, and for a time (October 1951–February 1952) the intensity of the armed confrontation lessened. But, when the Gómez faction gained control of the Conservative directorate, relations with Liberal leaders worsened again, particularly in the latter half of 1952. Partisan conflict reached one of its peaks after Conservative mobs, aided by the police, sacked and burned the buildings of the two leading Liberal daily newspapers, *El Tiempo* and *El Espectador*, as well as the homes of such Liberal leaders as former president Alfonso López Pumarejo and Carlos Lleras Restrepo.

Meanwhile, Conservative counterguerrillas, often called "guerrillas for peace," appeared. These were paramilitaries emerging from persecuted Conservative peasant communities, organized either by departmental political chiefs or directly by the police and the army. Among the more famous Liberal guerrillas were those in the Urrao region of Antioquia and in the eastern plains (*llanos*). In the south of Tolima there were both Liberal guerrillas, called *limpios* (i.e., the "clean" ones) and Communist guerrillas, called *los comunes*. *Limpios* and *comunes* ended up fighting each other.

The Liberal guerrillas in the eastern *llanos* came to be considered the model of Liberal resistance. But urban elites appear to have had only a dim understanding of what was happening in the rural wars. In March 1950 the weekly newsmagazine *Semana* featured an excursion into the *llanos* by a Jesuit in a Chevrolet. The priest concluded that, despite the horrific stories that were circulating in Bogotá, in the *llanos* there had passed a brief period of "uneasiness," but "calm returned . . . and the men, who now had forgotten those days, [had] returned to their tasks with new enthusiasm." It should not be surprising that this vision of the *llanos* from an automobile was limited. It is significant, however, that a national newsmagazine would take such a superficial report seriously. During that year some 50,000 people were killed in the country, and the eastern plains began to be transformed into the setting of a great guerrilla war.

The guerrillas were aided by sympathizers who provided them with arms, munitions, medicine, money, salt, sugar, and information. But a unified command with national authority did not exist. In any case the most organized, like those in the *llanos*, were able to collect taxes on cattle and to negotiate truces with the army, permitting the transportation of cattle for sale. The big Liberal landowners soon lost interest in the fate of their fellow party-members in arms. What really made the guerrillas effective was the underlying social organization—family relations, networks of friends, attachment to the land of their birth. In these local structures there emerged a new type of leader, whose personal courage, ability to command a following, and astuteness enabled him to attract the undivided loyalty of the local population.

Conservatives and officers in the army and police viewed the Liberal guerrilleros as bandits. In turn the Liberals tried to delegitimize the police by calling them *chulavitas*. The word referred to the fact that at the beginning of the Ospina Pérez administration (1946–1950), a number of police were recruited from the rural community of Chulavita, in a region of Boyacá that for many years had been predominantly Conservative. At the end of the 1940s Conservatives in this region made war against the Liberals of El Cocuy, forcing the latter to take refuge on the *páramo* (a high, cold, barren plateau). Liberal refugees from El Cocuy later joined the guerrillas of the *llanos*. When the *chulavitas* arrived in Liberal communities, they acted as an army of occupation. For this reason it was not rare for notable Conservatives to join Liberals in seeking to stop their incursions.

The army at first did not become involved in the depredations of the *chulavita* and therefore was viewed by many Liberals as relatively impartial. For this reason the appointment of military mayors for a time slowed the spiral of violence. But soon the army also lost its aura of fairness.

From the perspective of Bogotá the security of the state never really seemed to be threatened. However, as Liberal leaders feared, the existence of the guerrillas enabled the government to justify the indefinite prolongation of a state of siege and a two-year recess of Congress (November 1949–December 1951)—the longest interruption of meetings of the Congress in the history of Colombia. The copious legislation of the state of siege was the prelude to the "revolution of order," a peculiar version of the authoritarian regimes of Franco and Salazar in the Iberian Peninsula, imported by the ultra-conservative Laureano Gómez during his presidency (1950–1953).

The Cold War played a role in the authoritarianism of the period. As Pope Pius XII vigorously aligned the Church in the anti-communist camp, the hostility between Liberals and Conservatives was exacerbated. The Conservatives, with the support of many bishops, accused Liberals of being pro-communist. In addition, the Cold War distanced the upper classes still more from the poor and tended to unify the elite in the defense of the existing social order. Many labor unions, whose activism had been legitimated in Liberal political discourse since the 1920s, now were repressed high-handedly under the color of an anti-communism to which many Liberal chiefs were readily adapting.

The elites looked to the Cold War for signals to redefine the political order. Maintaining political hegemony became more risky as with increasing speed the modernization of the country transformed a social order based on family, neighborhood, party affiliation, and religiosity. The old order was being dissolved at a rapid pace by the growth and geographic mobility of the population, by the expansion of the cities with consequent increased criminality and secularization, and by increased schooling and the opportunities, real and illusory, of social mobility.

The first stage of violence ended in the latter half of 1953 with the demobilization of the guerrillas in response to an amnesty offered by General Rojas Pinilla. In the minds of the Liberal chiefs (many of whom were in exile), as well as the military government and the Conservatives, the surrender of the Liberal guerrillas of the *llanos* and some in Tolima closed the chapter of partisan violence.

THE PERIOD OF "MAFIA" VIOLENCE, 1954–1964

One of the distinctive features of the period 1954–1964 was the emergence of violence as a form of criminal economic enterprise. The bloodshed of these years grew out of the earlier years of partisan slaughter, in the sense that the participants had become socialized to murder as a social instrument during the first phase. Now, however, the principal aim of organized homicide was not political power but rather economic gain.

Violence as economic enterprise was particularly notable in greater Caldas, the Quindío, and northeastern Tolima, a coffee-growing zone colonized largely, although not exclusively, by Antioqueños during much of the nineteenth century and the first half of the twentieth. The pioneering work that helps to illuminate the historical background to the violence of the 1950s is Antonio García's economic geography of Caldas (1937), which brings out the conflictive nature of the colonization of the area. In the colonization process the possession of land was the key to the economic and social ascent of settlers, many of whom were of quite humble origins. In Caldas and the

Quindío there had been a long history of various kinds of conflict over land—confrontations between poor colonists and landowning companies, cases of colonists caught in the crossfire of disputes over boundaries between municipalities, and contention between middling colonists and large landowners. This was the drama that Alejandro López called "the struggle between the axe and stamped paper," that is, between the men who cleared the land and those who could manipulate legal decisions about property rights in their own favor.

These conflicts occasioned prolonged bargaining and some fighting, at times homicides. The process involved mayors, police, notaries, judges, shysters, and surveyors. But behind the scenes lurked two figures of local power, political bosses and parish priests, and two figures of local commerce, operators of mule trains and *fonderos*—the latter at once innkeepers, operators of country general stores, and coffee-buyers.

The participants in these conflicts sometimes saw themselves as fighting for the interests of a municipality; sometimes they proclaimed the agrarian populism of the juntas in charge of dividing public lands; in all cases they bespoke the desire for social mobility in conditions in which less and less public land was available to occupy. The violence sparked by conflicts over land was legitimated by local or regional political intermediaries. It also was symptomatic of the institutional weakness of the national state.

This was the legacy of coffee society in the middle of the twentieth century: a clearly delineated social stratification within the middle sectors, distance from the central state, and ferocious conflict among local political networks. Beyond this, property rights were fragile, as in the shadow of partisan violence local political bosses manipulated farmers into selling land by using threats and extortion. It was, as Carlos Miguel Ortiz said in his study of the Quindío, violence as a business.

The disorder of the partisan violence before 1953 was aggravated in the coffee belt with the appearance of armed bands, which, although linked to the struggle between the two parties and to local political bosses, established their own operations and their own rules. At first coffee stolen from farms whose owners had fled could be sold by farm managers or tenants to *fonderos* without armed bands playing a role. The business prospered wherever partisan pressure expelled Liberals, thus "conservatizing" rural communities. The armed bands emerged from the political confrontation between Liberals and Conservatives; later, many landowners, fearing being wiped out by their enemies, approached the latter, seeking to make a deal. Imperceptibly the farm owners became interlocked in the shady business, which was masked by the more visible conflict. Ortiz describes a kind of division of labor: While Conservative gangs dealt in stolen coffee, Liberal bands dedicated themselves to rustling cattle. But from stealing coffee and cattle the mafiosos went on to the purchase of farms, by subjecting the owners to extortion and forcing them to flee, in the process "Conservatizing" the land, or later "re-Liberalizing" it.

Coffee cultivation is compatible with civil wars that are prolonged and of low intensity. This has been shown in the history of Africa and also in Colombia's War of the Thousand Days. This is because coffee is a perennial plant and because of the seasonality of the Arabic variety traditionally cultivated in Colombia. The seasonality of the coffee harvest permitted exploitative armed bands to concentrate their extortions during a clearly delimited harvest period. By threatening to kill harvest workers or to drive them away, these rural mafiosos could bring landowners to their knees. Moreover, because coffee bushes are perennial, they go on producing no matter what social havoc transpires around them. Only after some years would it be noticed that the coffee farms were becoming less productive because of lack of care of the coffee bushes and the failure to replant new ones.

A characteristic of the coffee belt was the early consolidation of a tapestry of small cities and towns, well integrated into the commerce of coffee, and rather prosperous. In these towns and cities the business of the violence continued. Paid assassins, called *pájaros* (birds), originally operating in the northern part of the Cauca Valley in the first phase of the violence (1946–1953), reappeared in the Caldas region as enforcers for the mafiosos who sought monopoly control of local commerce by expelling their competitors. In some cities there operated a system that is now known to many inhabitants of Cúcuta or Medellín. Invisible lines are drawn in the street and anyone considered an enemy can cross them only at the risk of being murdered.

Gangs of bandits, local political bosses, and mafiosos on the rise converged, often accentuating the local power of one Conservative faction against the department-wide domination by a rival faction. During the 1960s, however, these local networks increasingly had to confront a reconstituted and resurgent national state under the National Front. The National Front often is described as if it were merely a convenient arrangement among national elites. But the National Front was seeking to extend the power of the national state into the localities traumatized first by the purely partisan, and then by the predatory economic, violence. With a more effective reassertion of the national state, armed bands and local political bosses had the alternative of demobilizing or confronting the state. Most bands demobilized and the struggle between factions continued through legal and constitutional channels. Liberal bands, as well as Conservative ones, had to give way before a more effective assertion of government authority. Some Liberal bands linked themselves to the MRL (Movimiento Revolucionario Liberal), the newly formed left faction within the Liberal Party. But these bands rapidly became isolated until they disappeared after a long series of confrontations.

The complex relations among parties, factions, local political bosses, and bandits are well described and analyzed by Gonzalo Sánchez and Donny Meertens for the same coffee region for the years 1958–1965. The questions that their analysis broaches are: Why did the armed bands become independent of the parties and political bosses that originally had supported them? Did the distance and weakness of the institutions of the national state before 1958 make possible the convergence of interests of armed bands and party bosses? And, was it pressure from the national government after 1958 that divided them and finally made them antagonists? The authors answer the last two questions in the affirmative.

The story of the gangs of emerald contrabandists in Boyacá in some ways parallels that of the armed bands in the coffee zone of the Central Cordillera. During the period of Conservative rule, the government tolerated the illegal activities of Efraín González because he was a Conservative bandit. With the National Front, however, Efraín González became identified clearly as a public enemy, whom the State moved, with some determination, to crush.

Could these bands acting as criminal economic enterprises transform themselves into revolutionary guerrillas, with more of a social program than a partisan agenda? Could these bands develop a less predatory and more altruistic ethos? Some new university-educated guerrilla leaders, moved by the example of the Cuban Revolution and its Sierra Maestra, thought so. This was the case of Antonio Larrota, who in the early 1960s went into the mountains, initiating the third period of political violence.

REVOLUTIONARY GUERRILLAS, 1961–1989

Just as the army was wiping out the last armed bands in the central cordillera, notably those led by Sangrenegra (Blackblood) and Desquite (Revenge), a new type of political violence was emerging. The period from 1961 to 1989 is usually called that of "armed conflict." That is, these were years of insurrectional struggle by guerrilla organizations whose aim was revolutionary transformation of the social order and the state that protects it and of reaction against the revolutionary movements by the military and paramilitary organizations. The two principal guerrilla organizations that survive today were founded in the 1960s. The ELN (Ejército de Liberación Nacional) dates from 1962. The FARC (Fuerzas Armadas Revolucionarias de Colombia), which had a prehistory in peasant organizations, was formally established in 1966.

In a broad perspective, two general types of guerrilla organizations may be distinguished—the agrarian-communist and the *foquista*. The FARC through most of its history has been agrarian-communist. Its origins were in the peasantry, and its aims for most of its history have essentially welled out of the peasantry. The FARC has supported the peasants' desire for land, for autonomous colonization (rather than colonization controlled by large landowners), for land reform to create a society of small property owners, and, where large plantations or haciendas continue to exist, for better working conditions for agricultural workers. The FARC's genesis in the peasantry is still reflected in the rural origins of its leader. Its perennial chief, now generally known by the name Manuel Marulanda, was born in 1928 in Génova, Quindío, in the Antioqueño-colonized coffee frontier. He has been involved in the armed struggle of the peasantry since the time of the "first Violencia," beginning in the south of Tolima in 1950–1951. In the early years he was known as "Tirofijo" (Sureshot), at the time his guerrilla nom de guerre.

In contrast with the FARC's foundation in the defense of the peasantry, the *foquista* guerrillas were inspired by the Cuban revolution and have tended to follow the revolutionary doctrines of Che Guevara. Guevara believed that revolution must be spearheaded by an armed vanguard, implicitly of urban origins. However, a successful revolution required vanguard leaders to move to the countryside to establish a revolutionary *foco* (focus) among the peasantry. Peasant support would expand the revolutionary base. At the same time, according to the theory, contact with the peasantry, and experience of life among them, would transform urban leaders, making them more truly revolutionary.

In Colombia the Cuban-influenced, *foquista* type of movement has been represented by the ELN and the 19th of April Movement (M-19), as well as by many smaller groups. The EPL (Ejército Popular de Liberación), also a creation of the 1960s, had both communist and *foquista* features, at least at first. Both the agrarian-communist and *foquista* groups had their bases in rural areas, especially frontier regions. Urban insurgency, in the form of terrorism, has been much less a part of their activities. The chief examples of urban insurgency were those of the ELN in its first years (1962–1964), the M-19 in the 1970s and in spectacular actions in 1980 and 1985, and the use of explosives in some towns in Urabá by the FARC in the 1990s.

The FARC

The FARC had its origins in peasant agitation, under the direction of the Communist Party, in the regions of Tequendama, Sumapaz, and the south of Tolima, from the 1920s to the time of the Violencia. In these struggles peasant self-defense organizations developed. Growing out of a tradition of struggle for land and for independent colonization, the self-defense organizations had proven their loyalty to the peasant population. At the beginning of the National Front (1958) they were located in Marquetalia, Riochiquito, El Pato, and Guayabero, remote places in a vast territory south of Bogotá, including portions of southeast Tolima, Huila, Meta, Caquetá, and the Cauca.

The self-defense organizations were more defensive than offensive. They were not given to sabotage or terrorism, nor to ambushes of the police or army. Nor did they defend themselves against the state. They protected peasant communities that obstinately cherished rivalries with other peasant communities that were also protected by clientelistic armed forces. This was a legacy of the battles between *limpios* and *comunes* in southern Tolima during the earlier Violencia.

In a second phase the group that later became known as the FARC moved from the peasant self-defense mode to that of a mobile and offensive guerrilla. This was a response to attacks by the state in 1964. In the context of the Cold War, after the most right-wing politicians in the National Front raised an outcry against the alleged existence of sixteen independent republics, the self-defense organizations became the target of a broad military offensive. Known as the "Laso Plan," the operation applied doctrines of counterinsurgency then being used by the United States in Vietnam.

These government attacks transformed the peasant self-defense organizations into revolutionary guerrillas. In the Second Conference of the Southern Bloc (1966), some peasant self-defense groups reconstituted themselves in the FARC. For a long time they remained under the tutelage of the Communist Party, which still was following the line of the IX Congress of 1961 of "combining all forms of struggle."

Influenced both by the Cold War and by the Sino-Soviet split, the pro-Soviet bureaucracy of Colombia's Communist Party viewed the FARC as their armed wing. However, when the FARC tried to establish itself in the coffee-growing Quindío, it was decimated. The FARC had made the mistake of engaging in what the Communist jargon of the time called "an adventurist action." This was an error they did not repeat. After recovering from these losses, the FARC grew slowly, consolidating its bases of peasant support.

In its third period, beginning in the 1980s, the FARC evolved from an armed force subject to the Communist Party to an independent guerrilla organization with its own political and military doctrine. At that time the FARC gained more public attention than before, and it underwent a metamorphosis that brought rapid growth, as well as its separation from the Communist Party. Several important factors led to the independence of the FARC in the 1980s. First, in a peace agreement with the government at La Uribe in 1984, the commanders of the FARC were recognized, in effect, as political protagonists, a status they had not had while under the tutelage of the Communist Party. Then, between 1985 and 1990, Colombia's Communist Party suffered two crushing blows. The Unión Patriótica had been established as a left political party in response to government promises of 1984 at La Uribe that aimed to bring the revolutionary left into peaceful political activity. But this proved a grave deception; the UP was literally annihilated as many of its leaders and hundreds of its candidates for office were murdered. At the same time the Communist Party of Colombia, like those elsewhere, was undermined by the collapse of the Soviet Union.

The development of the FARC in the 1980s also was affected in important ways by the entrance of narco-traffickers into cattle ranching, especially in the Middle Magdalena, Urabá, and the plains of Meta, Caquetá, and the Guaviare, all frontier zones where the FARC had established influence. The narco-traffickers found niches in some regions of spontaneous colonization as well as in frontier areas being settled under guerrilla influence. In these places both alliances and ruptures between the *guerrilleros* and the drug lords occurred. In 1987 a major break apparently took place. The paramilitaries of the Medellín cartel, in local complicity with the army, the police, landowners, and traditional politicians, attacked the left. But, since the guerrillas were not so easy to find and in any case were armed, the chief targets of the paramilitaries were not the guerrillas but rather peaceful and more or less unarmed people—the politicians of the Unión Patriótica and others in the civilian population that were deemed sympathetic to the guerrillas. Applying the guerrilla principle of preserving its own force, the FARC retreated, leaving its legal arm and the civilian population exposed.

Alienated from the peace process under the Barco government (1986–1990) and affected by the demoralizing slaughter of the Unión Patriótica, the FARC nonetheless participated with the ELN and a minority faction of the EPL in a series of peace dialogues from June 1991 to June 1992. When these failed, the FARC reconsidered its strategy and ended up adopting the *foco* approach formulated by Che Guevara. In the 1990s the role of the FARC as an armed vanguard became explicit.

In the 1990s the FARC became more firmly linked to the cultivation of plants usable in the production of narcotics. In the 1980s Colombia had been less significant as a cultivator of coca than as a site for refining and distributing cocaine. However, in the 1990s various factors encouraged the cultivation of drug crops in Colombia. One was the constriction of coca production in Peru. But conditions within Colombia were also important. The contraction of conventional agricultural production, increasing rural unemployment and the decomposition of peasant society, accelerated by the commercial opening of 1991–1992, found an escape valve in frontier cultivation of coca, marihuana, and poppies usable for heroin. Accordingly, the narcotic industry moved into the zones of colonization where the FARC had influence. Peasant cultivators of coca ended up forming a more solid social base for the FARC than any insurgent group has had in Colombia since the epoch of the Liberal guerrillas of the *llano* in 1950–1953.

The *Foquistas*: The Case of the ELN, 1962–1985

If the FARC originated in the first stage of the Violencia and in communist agrarianism, the ELN (Ejército de Liberación Nacional) and various other revolutionary groups that sprouted up in the 1960s were stimulated by the example of the Cuban Revolution. Most of these groups took as their guide Che Guevara's revolutionary doctrines, emphasizing the central role of the armed vanguard. According to Che, the first step was to create a clandestine urban front; then, however, it was necessary to establish a revolutionary camp or *foco* in an appropriate rural area.

Where to establish the camp was an important decision. In addition to geographical features favorable to the survival of the guerrilla, the social features and political traditions of the population in the zone had to be taken into account. The revolutionary dreams of the 1960s, based on the recent Violencia, imagined the existence of a supposed tradition of rebellion among the Colombian peasantry. Accordingly, the leaders of the ELN first established contact with former Liberal *guerrilleros*, seeking them out in their refuges. But, when these former *guerrilleros* could be found, they turned out to be operating among modest clientelistic networks of peasant families, in remote frontier regions. And they generally were sympathetic to the MRL.

The embryonic phase of the rural camp is one of great danger. Any information about it that might fall into the hands of the army could bring the annihilation of the movement. The simple tolerance of the local population is not a sufficient guaranty of safety. In the early years of Cuban-influenced *foquista* movements in Colombia (1961–1963), many revolutionaries suffered disasters—among them the MOEC (Movimiento Obrero Estudiantil Campesino) in the northern Cauca, as well as ventures of other groups in Puerto Boyacá in the Middle Magdalena, Turbo on the Gulf of Urabá, and the Vichada in the eastern plains. In the 1960s only the ELN and the EPL (Ejército Popular de Liberación) succeeded in consolidating camps, in which they indoctrinated the local population and from which they constructed fragmentary networks of supply, recruitment, and intelligence.

The ELN passed through four distinct phases. In the first period (1962–1964), groups of university students, mostly from the Youth of the MRL, under the influence of the Cuban Revolution, denounced the reformism and "parliamentary cretinism" of the Communist Party. In 1962 they supported Alfonso López Michelsen, the leader of the MRL, in his failed (and, in the view of the National Front, unconstitutional) candidacy for the presidency. Soon the students moved further to the left, proclaiming themselves Marxist-Leninists. Influenced by the FALN in Venezuela, some of the Youth of the MRL formed a clandestine nucleus that became one of the origins of the ELN. In mid-1962 the national press began to report minor terrorist acts committed by the ELN in Bogotá, Barranquilla, and Bucaramanga. Shortly afterward, the José Antonio Galán International Brigade was formed in Cuba, under the leadership of Fabio Vásquez Castaño. On returning to Colombia they established a rural base in the region of San Vicente de Chucurí in the Department of Santander. Elements of the Galán Brigade ended up controlling the ELN.

The second phase of the ELN began in 1965. After his return from Cuba, Fabio Vásquez, pressured by his Cuban mentors, led an assault on the small town of Simacota in Santander in January 1965. From this moment the focus of the ELN moved from clandestine urban activity to the effort to establish a rural guerrilla *foco*.

The theory of the *foco* developed from the Cuban experience in 1956–1959 supposed that rural guerrillas would have support from urban collaborators (though as Che later expounded it, the urban groups disappeared from the theory). The ELN looked for its urban support to the recently founded Frente Unido del Pueblo (United Front of the People) (FU), led by the priest Camilo Torres Restrepo. However, the ELN viewed the FU as *merely* a support group—as a consequence treating Torres and others with a carelessness that enabled the army to discover the clandestine urban network, forcing Torres to flee into the hills where he was killed in February 1966.

In this second period from 1965 to 1973 the ELN seemed to give much more importance to guerrilla military tactics than to political strategy. Not having clarified the relationship between their military activities and their political objectives, the ELN and its urban supporters suffered terrible punishment from the army. The ELN leadership also was riven by internal conflicts, stemming from ideological disputes or differing social origins, as well as personal rivalries—conflicts finally resolved in 1973 by ritual executions within the ELN itself. In 1973, after a series of defeats, the ELN neared extinction when the Colombian army decimated its most important column near Anorí, Antioquia. After this disaster its maximum leader, Fabio Vásquez, had to retire to Havana.

The third period of the ELN (1973–1985) began with the change of leadership in 1973, which did not end its political confusion or poor organization. Relations with peasants remained precarious and unsatisfactory and its urban support groups fragile, and the ELN continued ideologically dogmatic and politically isolated.

However, during the 1980s the ELN's logistical, ideological, and political weaknesses began to end, aided by the government's peace process, the discovery of oil in the Arauca, social agitation in northeastern Colombia, and the rise to leadership of the priest Manuel Pérez. Pérez stressed the need to develop a policy that would connect social movements to labor unions.

Other *Foquistas*

In the 1970s and 1980s a number of guerrilla groups emerged. Among them were dissidents of the FARC, the ELN, and the EPL. Of the smaller groups among the more interesting was the Movimiento Armado Quintín Lame, rooted in the indigenous communities of the upper Cauca. The Quintín Lame demobilized in May 1991; at the time it had 157 armed members. The efforts of the Quintín Lame on behalf of indigenous rights were among the factors leading to a provision in the constitution of 1991 that indigenes would have two elected representatives in the national Senate.

Of the various groups active in the 1970s and 1980s the M-19 became one of the more notable. Urban in origins, the M-19 initially was influenced by the urban focus of the Montoneros in Argentina and the Tupamaros in Uruguay. After the triumph of the Sandinistas in Nicaragua in 1979, however, the M-19 became more oriented toward the model of the rural guerrilla, while retaining its original interest in the possibilities of an eventual urban insurrection.

In 1980 the M-19 reached the zenith of its popularity when it seized the embassy of the Dominican Republic, holding many diplomats and other notables hostage. The M-19 also chagrined the Colombian army by taking substantial amounts of weapons from an urban arms depot and by the more symbolic act of stealing the sword of Simón Bolívar. These embarrassments to the Colombian military provoked a de facto coup during the government of President Julio Cesar Turbay, who agreed to permit the armed forces to bring civilians to trial before military tribunals.

In November 1985, however, the M-19 committed a gigantic blunder by seizing the Palace of Justice. The armed forces, in no mood to trifle with this outrage, assaulted the building with rockets, starting an inferno in which virtually the entire Supreme Court, many lawyers, and other citizens, as well as the attacking guerrillas, were killed. With this ill-conceived adventure, the M-19 lost much of its leadership and paid dearly in loss of popularity. Lacking intellectual clarity or any discernible ideology, and under severe pressure from the armed forces, the M-19 found it necessary to accept a government amnesty and demobilize in order to enter into conventional electoral politics. Despite some initial electoral success, the visible leaders of the M-19 continued to demonstrate a seeming lack of seriousness or intellectual coherence and has practically disappeared as a political force.

In addition to the M-19, a number of smaller insurgent groups that had emerged in the 1980s agreed to demobilize between 1989 and 1994. During these years more than 4000 *guerrilleros* laid down their arms. Many later joined other guerrilla groups, while others enlisted in the counterrevolutionary paramilitary forces. The former guerrillas who attempted to compete in conventional politics, with the exception of some individuals from the M-19, for the most part failed.

THE VIOLENCES OF THE 1990s

Homicide statistics give some insight into the character of the new violences of the 1990s. From 1960 to the end of the 1970s Colombia had very high rates of homicide, but in a range similar to those of other countries like Brazil, Mexico, Nicaragua, or Panama. But between 1980 and 1993 Colombia's rates of homicide tripled. Between 1960 and 1980, the rates varied in a range between 20 and 39 deaths per 100,000 people; however, by 1985 homicide rates had reached 57 per 100,000; in 1990 they were at 86, and in 1993 at 95.

In the mid-1960s, when the armed struggle seemed to polarize between the revolutionary guerrillas and the capitalist system, it could be said that revolutionary insurgency represented the greatest threat to the institutional order and the viability of liberal democracy in Colombia. Around 1985 such an affirmation was becoming increasingly questionable because the massive eruption of the drug traffic and organized criminality made it possible to demote guerrilla violence to the nebulous category of social violence. Although the connections among the diverse types of violence still have not been establised precisely, the most accepted hypothesis points to the drug traffic as triggering the upward leap of criminality in Colombian society.

In recent years nearly 70 percent of the homicides and murders in Colombia have been concentrated in Bogotá, Medellín, and Cali. Most of these crimes were perpetrated on the street or in bars, with firearms, in poor barrios, or in zones of social decomposition. And the apparent motives of the homicides were settling scores, fights under the influence of alcohol, or robbery. The victims of these common crimes are about 90 percent male, in their great majority under the age of thirty. But complaints of violence against women and children in the home are also increasing.

A more or less organized social murder also forms part of Colombia's portrait of homicide. In the middle of the 1970s there began in Pereira a process of "social cleansing," the killing of individuals thought to be a blemish on the face of society. Since that time squads of vigilantes in Cali and in other cities have been hunting down prostitutes, homosexuals, beggars, street people, and anyone else they consider to be an insult to the social order.

As for offenses against property, it is clear that organized crime plays a central role. Between 1991 and 1996 the crimes that increased most were armed robbery of trucks, bank robbery, and the theft of automobiles. Although calculations of the economic magnitude of the drug trade are imprecise, there can be no doubt that it has generated new behavior and codes of values (easy money), which have melded with old ones (*machista* honor, as well as the view that "life is worth nothing").

A glance at the statistics from a regional perspective confirms some aspects of the hypothesis of the drug traffic as a trigger of crime. The Caribbean coast, with the exception of some localities, was removed from the partisan violence of the 1950s. More recently, violence has most affected the Caribbean coast where it is touched by the drug trade—for example, in the the the Departments of Guajira, César, and Atlántico at the time of the marihuana bonanza (1977–1982). By contrast, other parts of the coast, such as Bolívar, Sucre, and Córdoba, have homicide rates well below the national median. This fact is particularly notable in the case of Córdoba, the epicenter of the bloodiest wars between narco-paramilitaries and guerrillas.

Antioquia was a Colombian region notably averse to warfare during the nineteenth century—although Colombians from other regions did note a marked tendency to personal violence among the popular classes. Today, Antioquia more than any other place in Colombia provides striking evidence of the impact of the drug trade in stimulating homicide and crime in general. Medellín for more than a century was a seedbed of the Colombian clergy and a center of private enterprise. What happened there since the end of the 1970s to make Medellín a seedbed of contraband, automobiile theft, and the most violent version of the drug traffic? Medellín in the 1980s and 1990s became the capital of homicide in Colombia. No other department has come close to the homicide rate of Antioquia in 1991: 245 homicides per 100,000 inhabitants.

Clearly the drug traffic has contributed to this mortality. But other underlying factors must be noted. Medellín has been particularly affected by the decline of manufacturing, which had been one basis of its prosperity for some seven decades. Large-scale unemployment, economic insecurity, and social marginality underlie the sinister turn of the drug trade in the enterprise of Pablo Escobar. For poor youths opportunities opened for employment as assassins. And as murder came to be seen a solution for a wide variety of problems, and indeed as a standard mode of employment, there emerged a subculture that considered violent death commonplace. This subculture as been treated masterfully in Fernando Vallejo's novel *La Virgen de los Sicarios* (The Virgin of the Assassins), in the crude testimonies collected by Alonso Salazar J. in *No nacimos pa' semilla* (Born to Die Young) and in the films of Víctor Gaviria, notably *Rodrigo D, no futuro* (Rodrigo D, No Future).

The New Guerrillas

In 1997 it was estimated that, as a consequence of guerrilla war, some 200,000 families, for the most part trapped in the crossfire between the guerrillas and anti-guerrilla forces, had been forced to abandon their homes and communities. In addition, between 1975 and 1995, the armed conflict produced some 11,000 deaths in combat and another 23,000 in murders and extrajudicial executions. These 33,000 deaths represent 10 percent of all the homicides committed in these two decades. At present, Colombia is the only country in the Americas in which guerrilla war remains a significant phenomenon.

In the 1960s there were never more than 500 combatants in Colombia's insurgent groups. And after that the numbers declined still more. However, in the decade 1986–1996, guerrillas increased more than in the previous thirty-two years. The FARC went from 3600 insurgents in thirty-two fronts in 1986 to about 7000 in sixty fronts in 1995. In 2000 its numbers were estimated at about 15,000. In the same period, the ELN went from 800 insurgents in eleven fronts to 3000 in thirty-two fronts. In 2000 it was thought to have about 5000 combatants.

These increases in the numbers of guerrillas have been accompanied by their geographic spread from marginal zones to richer, more populated areas and to places that are more strategically important for the economy and national security, including the borders with Venezuela, Panama, and Ecuador. The guerrilla has advanced from its original camps and now seeks to consolidate peasant support in colonization zones. But they are also advancing toward communities better integrated into the urban network. According to official sources, nearly 60 percent of Colombian municipalities experienced some form of guerrilla presence in 1996.

Of the tripod of Colombia's major exports since 1980, illegal drugs, oil, and coffee, the first two have contributed increased income to the insurgents. This is one key to their power and the spread of their forces. The expansion of cultivation of poppies in the southern frontier regions of Tolima, Huila, Cauca, and Nariño and of coca in the Caquetá, Meta, Putumayo, and Guaviare is in the hands of settlers over whom the FARC has strong control. It is said that the movement of coca cultivators in 1996 would not have reached the size, intensity, and influence that it had without the decided sup-

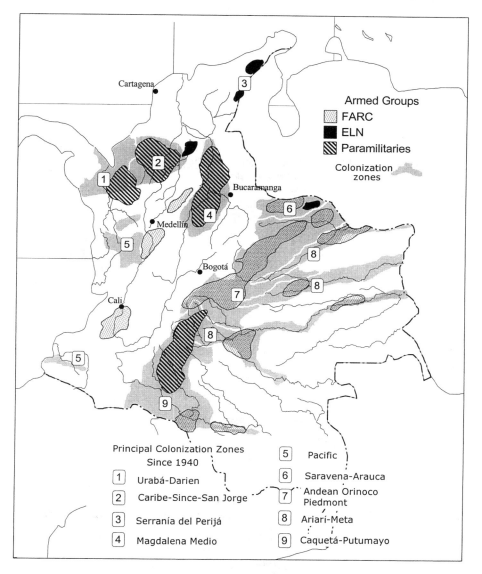

Map 9 Principal regions of colonization after 1940 and principal zones of guerrillas and paramilitaries, 1990–2000.

port of the FARC. The discovery and exploitation of new oilfields in the Arauca and the construction of oil pipelines has permitted the ELN to exact large-scale extortions, backed up by frequent dynamiting of pipelines.

The insurgents also have exploited the opportunities opened up by decentralizing political reforms, such as the election (instead of executive appointment) of mayors (1988) and governors (1991). Through their clients, they have been able to manipulate the substantial increase in the fiscal resources of the municipalities. In this way they have been able to consolidate their role as an alternative political class in such regions as the Arauca, Meta, Caquetá, or the Guaviare.

According to recent political analyses, the guerrillas do not have a national political plan. Rather, they are notable for their localism and a tendency to banditry. They no longer seek power to make a socialist revolution. Rather, they are dedicating themselves to the clientelistic control of many local governments in order to increase their control of territory, thus improving their negotiating position when the opportune moment comes to demobilize. The mentality in the ranks of the guerrilla also has changed. Once groups of altruistic peasants and university students seeking to accelerate social change, the present guerrillas now are a prosperous military enterprise with paid combatants.

In any case there are no objective signs that the FARC and the ELN are prepared to undertake a conventional war. Both continue to pursue a well-established routine that combines political work with its rural and urban popular bases and a hit-and-run war of attrition on the army, to which the physical and human geography lends itself. The FARC has not changed its mode of operations since 1982, when it added Ejército del Pueblo (Army of the People) to its name and established sixty fronts across the country. From experience they know that growth entails the danger of infiltration and difficulty in centralizing control.

In 1983 the FARC decided to become "an authentically offensive guerrilla movement," not waiting to ambush its opponents but going after them to besiege and attack them. Nonetheless, this remains the Guevara conception. The physical and social geography of the country makes the infrastructure (highways, pipelines, power lines) an easy military target.

The Paramilitaries

Despite having fought the guerrillas for a half century, the Colombian army has not changed its doctrines nor its forms of organization in any significant way. It still is largely organized for conventional warfare. For this reason, perhaps, the paramilitaries appear to the public to be the only truly effective counterinsurgency force. Of the various actors in the present armed conflict the paramilitaries are the most elusive. There is a tendency to conceive of them as responding in a reactive and stopgap way to insurgent actions. The paramilitaries began as self-defense groups, rooted in the traditional rural and frontier societies. With time some self-defense groups received the patronage of old lords of the land and new ones like the drug traffickers. They acquired sufficient mobility and offensive power so that, like the Castaño brothers, they now seek to project themselves on a national scale. But the image of the paramilitaries that these organizations project, at least since 1990, is that of legitimate self-defense.

To understand the trajectory and forms of action of the paramilitaries it is necessary to distinguish phases, zones, and contexts. If in the self-defense phase the common denominator was their reactive character, in time the paramilitaries developed more preventive tendencies. Thus the paramilitaries have become nuclei of an irregular war, the main objective of which is to prevent the increase of popular support for the guerrillas.

But the social features of the paramilitaries vary. Some may be purely local, groups of young men in the community, who, defending it from the guerrillas, maintain ambiguous relations with the army, local politicians, and landowners. But more frequently the paramilitary appears to be a combatant who does not belong to the community and arrives as a killer, as a part of a distant, hierarchically ordered organization—at times visible to everyone except the government and its security forces. The paramilitaries sally from their camps to find areas where it is presumed that the guerrillas have real or potential influence. The operative model for the paramilitaries copies the *guerrillero* model. In many cases a paramilitary is an ex-Communist or ex-*guerrillero* impelled by the passion of the converted. In Urabá and Córdoba a number of paramilitaries are former members of the EPL.

The chief regions of paramilitary strength, more or less in the order of establishment, have been the Middle Magdalena, Córdoba, Urabá, Meta, and Putumayo. Puerto Boyacá in the Middle Magdalena is typical. Puerto Boyacá is a colonization zone. During the Violencia, it was a refuge for Liberal guerrillas. In the 1960s the population viewed with some sympathy attempts to establish guerrilla camps; in 1960–1964 Puerto Boyacá voted for the MRL and in 1970 it voted for the dissident ANAPO. At that time the penetration of the Communist Party and the arrival of the FARC had become notable. Around 1977 the peasantry of the region began to resent increased exactions of the FARC. At this point the army arrived; it established check points, obliged the peasants to register and carry identity cards, kept a watch on the markets, and arrested peasants at will. These measures became more rigorous during the state of siege in the Turbay Ayala government (1978–1982).

In 1982 the government began to use civic-military brigades in a political war against the FARC and the Communist Party. In this effort the civilian population was mobilized in militia units. Under the umbrella of President Belisario Betancur's attempt at peace with the guerrillas, the army—with the support of Texaco, a committee of cattlemen, the Civil Defense, merchants, and local authorities—designed a plan to recover control of the Middle Magdalena. The complaints of peasants and in the press about excesses of the security forces (including murders of leaders of organizations such as the New Liberalism) culminated in February 1983 in a report of the Procurador General of the Nation (attorney general) on paramilitary activities. The report accused 163 persons of abuses, of whom 59 were active members of the armed forces.

The local and regional institutionalization of the self-defense units received public support from peasant marches. The counter-guerrilla mobilization culminated in the creation of the Asociación Campesina de Agricultores y Ganaderos del Magdalena Medio (Peasant Association of Farmers and Ranchers of the Middle Magdalena). Pedro Guarín, one of its principal leaders, had been a militant in the Communist Youth.

When the drug traffickers sought to protect themselves from the repression unleashed against them because of the murder of the Minister of Justice (April 1984), they found a sanctuary in the "independent anti-communist republic" of the Middle Magdalena. Quickly they discovered that the region offered promising investment possibilities. As the cattleowners of the region sold their properties in order to live in the cities, the narco-traffickers arrived with their capital and bought ranches. They also took control of the self-defense forces and changed their functions. To fight effectively on multiple fronts—against competitors in the drug trade, against state and international organisms charged with the repression of narco-traffic, and now against Communist subversion—the drug dealers newly become large landowners reorganized the self-defense units, equipped them, and trained them with the aid of local army batallions, as well as British and Israeli instructors. From 1986 to 1989 the narco-landowner-paramilitary leaders unleashed a campaign of extermination against political parties, unions, peasant associations, public functionaries, and journalists.

The paramilitaries now sought to project themselves on a national scale as a model of anti-communism. They also attempted to gain political status by actively opposing peace initiatives of the national president. And they tried to be represented in the municipalities that were receiving aid from the National Program of Rehabilitation, which had been created to solve social problems as well to repair the infrastructure of municipalities affected by the armed conflict. Simultaneously they endeavored to win the favor of national politicians and political organizations.

During the late 1980s, paramilitary units spread around the country. In 1987 the minister of government reported that there were at least 140 self-defense units dedicated to fighting left guerrillas and their civilian sympathizers. Applying the model of the Middle Magdalena, Córdoba was one of the regions where paramilitary activity was growing most rapidly. In Córdoba, between 1988 and 1990, paramilitaries carried out terrible massacres. By means of alliances of former illegal traffickers in emeralds with drug lords, the Puerto Boyacá model of paramilitary activity reached the eastern plains and from there was carried into the Putumayo.

The size of the paramilitary groups is a matter of conjecture. In 1993 it was said that there were twenty-four paramilitary fronts: nine in Córdoba and Urabá; five in the Santanders; two each in the Middle Magdalena, César, Meta, and Putumayo; and one each in Casanare and Arauca. These 24 fronts were composed of 80 paramilitary groups, who maintained some kind of activity in 373 municipalities. Recently it has been speculated that the paramilitaries number 4500–5000 armed men.

In their early years the paramilitary groups sought legitimation. Subsequently, having become accepted as public actors, they perpetrated waves of massacres. If broad sectors of the urban population repudiate the paramilitaries, they have obtained acceptance in regions like Urabá that are fed up with being caught in the crossfire between the guerrillas and their enemies. This explains why the paramilitaries in Urabá have been able to take territory that once was controlled by the FARC. In 1996, the Autodefensas de Córdoba y Urabá, the paramilitary group in the region, after a campaign of indiscriminate terror and cruelty, were able to force the FARC to move to the neighboring Chocó. As it has always done since its inception, the FARC retreated to save its armed force, leaving exposed the land and people that had been faithful to them.

The decline of the great drug mafias diminished the resources of the paramilitaries. Confronting this situation, they reorganized in the mid-1990s, retaining some self-defense groups at the local level, but now creating at the national level a centralized and mobile organization. Nevertheless, the current location of their camps suggests a continuing connection to the newer drug traffickers. As for the social base of the paramilitaries, a study of Fernando Cubides sustains that the paramilitaries, guerrillas, and drug traffickers all operate in localities with the same kind of socioeconomic profile. And the intensity of the violence in these places is greater when at least two of these three actors are present.

THE IMPACT OF THE VIOLENCE ON JUDICIAL POWER AND IMPUNITY

Over the last half century of rapid urbanization and social modernization, two key institutions of the modern state, the judiciary and the police, have been badly damaged by the violence and still have not recovered. In the 1950s the police developed, at least among Liberals, a reputation for brutality and incapacity that they have not been able to overcome completely, despite notable improvements in recent years, such as the expulsion of agents of doubtful conduct and the acquisition of the biggest fleet of helicopters in Latin America. These advances have permitted the dismantling of great networks of the narco-traffic and the capture of thousands of tons of drugs. For this reason they have received applause from Washington. But the common citizen continues to suffer the same insecurity. Kidnappings and robberies, rather than abating, have become more and more a part of the Colombian social fabric.

The judiciary has been marked by venality and partisanship; in addition there have not been enough judges in the frontier areas of the national territories. Furthermore the judiciary has remained subordinated to the executive. Only in 1945 was a Ministry of Justice created; for the preceding half-century judges were subject to the Ministry of Government, whose functions are much more political (such as relations of the national government with department governors and mayors of large cities). The waves of partisan violence impeded the development of an independent and trustworthy judiciary. Moreover, the Violencia of 1946–1964 contributed to an atmosphere of generalized disrespect for the law, which on the part of business elites found expression in a black market mentality, tax evasion, contraband, and illegal traffic in import licenses. This disrespect for the law was also favored by the coffee bonanza of 1945–1954, during which there occurred large speculative fluctuations in prices. Contempt for the law was further fostered, from 1949 to 1953, by the lack of political support for regimes that Liberal leaders condemned as illegitimate.

Over the last fifty years, the state has dealt with its enemies by applying justice under a state of siege. The judicial apparatus and penal legislation have been employed by the executive branch to strengthen and legitimate emergency powers, variously against the opposing party, the drug traffic, social protest movements, or the leftist guerrillas. Between 1950 and 1987, civilians accused of crimes against the security of the state were tried before military courts. Military justice, as slow and inefficient as other courts, had increased its jurisdiction to the point that in the 1970s nearly one-third of the crimes mentioned in the Penal Code could fall under the purview of military judges.

Justice administered under emergency powers fragments the action of various state organisms. For example, in 1995, with the alarming increase in citizen insecurity and under pressure from the press, politicians found it necessary both to toughen criminal penalties and to criminalize various kinds of "abnormal" social conduct, like student stone-throwing, which was likened to terrorism. The immediate result was an increase in the prison population, the overcrowding of prisons (most poor people cannot pay lawyers), and the politicization of prison riots. In 1999 there was talk of depenalizing some formerly criminal acts and of allowing a quarter of the prisoners to serve their sentences at home. We can expect a new wave of public indignation to begin the cycle again.

To this must be added the laxity shown toward powerful transgressors. At the same time that the penal system was being hardened against crimes of terrorism, including student stone-throwing, the government was providing a comfortable arrangement for the country's maximum terrorist, the drug king Pablo Escobar. In 1991, once a constitutional prohibition against the extradition of nationals had been obtained, the government negotiated what it called "the submission of Pablo Escobar to justice." Escobar was believed to have ordered a long series of major crimes, including the assassination of various presidential candidates, a minister of justice, and the nation's attorney general; the kidnapping of journalists and the relatives of people high in government; and the dynamiting of two major liberal newspapers, the administrative center of the nation's criminal investigative agency, and an airplane full of passengers while in flight. Nonetheless, with the aid of legislation providing for reduction of penalties, the government, in order to get Escobar to surrender, allowed the drug lord to dictate the terms of his captivity. Escobar determined the place where his prison would be constructed, approved the plans, wrote the prison's regulations, and in effect directed the prison himself. Since Escobar surrendered with his top aides, the "prison," which public opinion called the Cathedral, became a refuge from which he continued directing, now with state protection, both his drug traffic and his extortions of other narco-traffickers. Later, having fled his prison nest, Escobar carried on a ferocious fight against his enemies. He tried to neutralize the government by kidnapping hostages of political families and continued his war against his competitors in Cali, who had been able to carry on their narcotics trade peacefully in exchange for providing information and other help to eliminate the demonized Escobar.

In view of the drug traffickers' capacity to infiltrate government institutions and their power of extortion backed by a formidable private army, the government established special courts, in which both judges and witnesses remained unidentified—known as "justice without a face." Although this type of justice helped to make the threats of narco-traffickers against judges less effective, the system easily fell short of providing a fair trial. Furthermore, 90 percent of such trials were employed not in the cases of drug lords but rather in cases relating to civic or popular protests or involving military control of public order—at times making the system of justice openly complicit with violations of human rights. There are, nonetheless, pressures to have it continue. In 1987 trying civilians before military courts was declared unconstitutional, but such institutions as the faceless judges have continued serving to deny procedural guaranties to enemies of the state, whether drug traffickers or guerrillas.

Justice is also blocked by the juridical privileges of the military, which border on leaving them unpunishable. Since 1988 various army officers have been charged, along with civilians, with taking part in massacres of peasants suspected of aiding the guerrillas. In such cases some of the civilians are found guilty and penalized, but the military officers, brought before fellow officers in military courts, go unpunished and continue their careers.

The new constitution of 1991 has left the country with another juridical problem by creating the powerful Fiscalía General de la Nacion (office of the national prosecutor). The office, with full administrative and budgetary autonomy, revealed its flaws in 1995, when the fiscal (chief prosecutor) accused President Samper of complicity in the acceptance of funds from the drug cartel of Cali in the presidential campaign of 1994. With the prosecutor's office in the hands of a professional politician, and not a jurist, it carried out its investigation without being responsible to anyone. The prosecutor was unable to construct a solid case against the president, dedicated all his resources obsessively to removing the president, aligned himself very obviously with the political enemies of the president, and to top it off, resigned as prosecutor in order to put himself forward as a Liberal candidate for the presidency. The ease of bringing politics into the judicial system, and the use of the administration of justice as a political trampoline at the cost of a national crisis, ended up undermining still more national respect for the state as a guardian of justice.

But it is not all a matter of the state. One must also examine the so-called civil society, particularly in its laxity regarding another powerful transgressor: the guerrillas. Calling itself "the civil society," a group of leaders of interest groups, some notable journalists, and such public functionaries as rectors of public universities and the procurador general (attorney general) met in July 1998 with representatives of the ELN in the Door to Heaven, a Carmelite convent in Mainz, Germany. Those assembled signed a document that is supposed to serve as a starting point for new peace negotiations with the ELN. The tenth paragraph of this document, called the Agreement of the Door to Heaven, endorses kidnapping as a legitimate weapon for the ELN:

> 10. The ELN commits itself to end the holding or deprivation of the liberty of persons for financial purposes to the degree that by other means a sufficient disposal of resources is provided for the ELN, as long as during the peace process this organization is not weakened strategically. Also, from this day, the holding of minors and adults older than 65 will end and in no case will pregnant women be deprived of liberty.

In Mainz the soi-disant representatives of Colombian civil society, by in effect condoning the taking of hostages by the ELN, also have freed the FARC to admit that it takes hostages and to rationalize this conduct. The same could happen with the paramilitaries. Kidnapping opened up political possibilities for the M-19 in 1988 and served Pablo Escobar well some years afterward.

And this is what the leaders of the ELN have done to obtain from the government of Andrés Pastrana "equality of treatment" with the FARC in peace negotiations. To improve their negotiating position, the ELN in April 1999 seized an Avianca plane loaded with passengers, and several weeks afterward burst into a Sunday mass in an upper-class neighborhood in Cali, taking more than 150 persons hostage, including the parish priest.

With all of this it is difficult to think that, at the doorway of the twenty-first century, Colombians feel themselves to be at the door to heaven.

Selective Bibliographic Guide

General Works on the History of Colombia

In English, David Bushnell, *The Making of Modern Colombia: A Nation in Spite of Itself* (Berkeley, CA, 1993), particularly emphasizes the nineteenth and twentieth centuries. The *Cambridge History of Latin America* (Leslie Bethell, ed.) (11 vols., Cambridge, England, 1984–1995) deals with Colombia in the republican era in four chapters: two by Malcolm Deas, on Colombia, Ecuador, and Venezuela, from independence to 1930, in volumes III and V; and two by Christopher Abel and Marco Palacios, covering from 1930 forward in volume VIII. In Spanish, an excellent group effort by leading academic scholars in Colombia is Alvaro Tirado Mejía, ed., *Nueva historia de Colombia* (8 vols., Bogotá, 1989). Material in the initial volumes was published earlier in Jaime Jaramillo Uribe, ed., *Manual de historia de Colombia* (3 vols., Bogotá, 1976). More uneven is the mammoth multivolume *Historia extensa de Colombia* (41 volumes, Bogotá, 1964–), published by the Academia Colombiana de Historia.

Essays on Colombian History

Various combinations of essays by Jaime Jaramillo Uribe appear in *Ensayos sobre historia social colombiana* (Bogotá, 1968), *La personalidad histórica de Colombia y otros ensayos* (Bogotá, 1977), and *Travesías por la historia* (Bogotá, 1997). Also see Jorge Orlando Melo, *Sobre historia y política* (Medellín, 1979), and *Historiografía colombiana: realidades y perspectivas* (Medellín, 1996), and Malcolm Deas, *Del poder y la gramática y otros ensayos sobre historia, política y literatura colombianas* (Bogotá, 1993). See also Mario Arrubla et al., *Colombia Hoy* (Bogotá, 1978) and Jorge Orlando Melo, ed., *Colombia Hoy* (Bogotá, 1996), as well as Marco Palacios, *Estado y clases sociales en Colombia* (Bogotá, 1986) and *Entre la legitimidad y la violencia, 1875–1994* (Bogotá, 1995).

Pre-Columbian Cultures

Gerardo Reichel-Dolmatoff, *Colombia* (London, 1965), and his shorter piece in the *Manual de Historia de Colombia* I (1976) provide an excellent fundamental orientation. In Julian Steward, ed., *Handbook of South American Indians*, vol. II, (Washington, DC, 1946), leading scholars at the time contributed essays on various regions and cultural groups that remain worth reading, even though in some respects they are outdated. See Juan and Judith Villamarín, "Kinship and Inheritance among the Sabana de Bogotá Chibcha at the Time of the Spanish Conquest," *Ethnology*, 14 (April 1975), for a corrective. See also Sylvia Broadbent, *Los Chibchas: organización socio-política* (Bogotá, 1964), and Hermes Tovar Pinzón, *La formación social chibcha* (Bogotá, 1980). Pedro Cieza de Leon, *Travels*, vol. I (London, 1864), provides a first-hand view of cultures in western Colombia. Hermann Trimborn, *Señorío y barbarie en el Valle del Cauca: Es-*

tudio sobre la antigua civilización quimbaya y grupos afines del oeste de Colombia (Madrid, 1969), offers a provocative interpretation of the western cultures. See also Luis Duque Gómez, *Los Quimbayas: reseña etnohistórica y arqueológica* (Bogotá, 1970), and his general survey for the *Historia extensa*, vols. I–II (Bogotá, 1965).

Conquest and Early Settlement

Jorge Orlando Melo, *Historia de Colombia, I. La dominación española* (Medellín, 1977), provides an excellent account. José Ignacio Avellaneda inspects social features of the conquistadores and the conquest in *The Conquerors of the New Kingdom of Granada* (Albuquerque, 1995) and *Los compañeros de Federman* (Bogotá, 1990). Early chroniclers provide insight into sixteenth- and seventeenth-century mentalities: Joan de Castellanos, *Elegías de varones ilustres de Indias* [partly published 1589]; Fray Pedro de Aguado, *Recopilación historial* [1575]; Fray Pedro Simón, *Noticias historiales* [1627], and the ironic Juan Rodriguez Freyle, *El carnero* [1636–1638]. But, to get close to the grain, contemporary documents are recommended. See especially Juan Friede, ed., *Documentos inéditos para la historia de Colombia* (10 vols., Bogotá, 1954–1965), and *Fuentes documentales para la historia del Nuevo Reino de Granada desde la instalación de la Real Audiencia en Santafe* (8 vols., Bogotá, 1975–1976). Friede's *El Adelantado Don Gonzalo Jiménez de Quesada* (2 vols., Bogotá, 1979) also offers useful documents. Two early geographic descriptions of the Indies provide information of many kinds on early settlement: Juan López de Velasco, *Geografía y descripción universal de las Indias* [ca. 1570–1574] (Madrid, 1971), and Antonio Vázquez de Espinosa, *Compendio y descripción de las Indias Occidentales* [ca. 1622–1630] (Madrid, 1969).

Colonial Social and Economic History

Jaime Jaramillo Uribe, a founder of academic historical research in Colombia, published important essays on mestizaje and slavery among many thoughtful contributions. Jaramillo's seminar at the Universidad Nacional in the 1960s proved truly seminal in initiating the careers of students who transformed the economic and social history of Colombia in the colonial period. Germán Colmenares's *Historia económica y social de Colombia* (2 vols., Cali, 1973, and Medellín, 1979) is the landmark work, the first volume largely on the Eastern Cordillera (1513–1719), the second on Popayán (1680–1800); *Cali: terratenientes, mineros y comerciantes, siglo xviii* (Bogotá, 1980) followed. Others in Jaramillo's seminar have contributed to colonial history in ways too numerous to list in detail: Hermes Tovar Pinzón on demography, land and labor exploitation issues, and a host of other topics; Margarita González on the *resguardo*, the tobacco monopoly, and other economic institutions; and Jorge Orlando Melo on gold production, among other essays. See also Jorge Palacios Preciado, *La trata de negros por Cartagena de Indias (1650–1750)* (Tunja, 1973). Jaramillo's students have been followed by growing numbers of academically based historians. Beatriz Patiño, *Riqueza, pobreza y diferenciación social en la Antioquia del siglo xviii* (Medellín, 1985), is one outstanding example.

Urban history is well represented by Julián Vargas Lesmes, *La sociedad de Santa Fé colonial* (Bogotá, 1990) and Fundación Misión Colombia, *Historia de Bogotá* (3 vols., Bogotá, 1988). Colombians currently are doing interesting work on women and the family. The anthropologist Virginia Gutiérrez de Pineda offered a pioneering vision in *La familia en Colombia: trasfondo histórico* (Bogotá, 1963). Two examples of recent archivally based work are Pablo Rodríguez, *Seducción, amancebamiento y abandono en la colonia* (Bogotá, 1991), and Guiomar Dueñas Vargas, *Los hijos del pecado: ilegitimidad y vida familiar en la Santafé de Bogotá colonial* (Bogotá, 1996).

On colonial mining, see Robert C. West's masterful *Colonial Placer Mining in Colombia* (Baton Rouge, 1952). William Frederick Sharp, in *Slavery on the Spanish Frontier: The Colombian Chocó, 1680–1810* (Norman, 1976), deals with mining as well as slavery. Juan Villamarín's "Encomenderos and Indians in the Formation of Colonial Society in the Sabana de Bogotá, Colombia" Ph.D. dissertation, Brandeis, 1972) is a superb regional study of Spanish-Indian interactions. On elites in two regions, see Ann Twinam, *Miners, Merchants, and Farmers in Colonial Colombia* (Austin, TX, 1982), and Peter Marzahl, *Town in the Empire: Government, Politics, and Society in Seventeenth-Century Popayán* (Austin, TX, 1978).

The Bourbon Background to Independence

Hans-Joachim König, *En el camino hacia la nación: Nacionalismo en el proceso de formacion del Estado y de la Nación de la Nueva Granada, 1750–1856* (Bogotá, 1994), traces the development of national identity and consciousness from the Bourbon era to the middle of the nineteenth century.

Anthony McFarlane's *Colombia before Independence: Economy, Society, and Politics under Bourbon Rule* (Cambridge, England, 1993) is excellent on the Bourbon period. On particular topics, see Mark Burkholder and D. S. Chandler, *From Impotence to Authority: The Spanish Crown and the American Audiencias, 1697–1808* (Columbia, MO, 1977); Renan Silva, *Universidad y sociedad en el Nuevo Reino de Granada* (Santafé de Bogotá, 1992); Allan Kuethe, *Military Reform and Society in New Granada, 1773–1808* (Gainesville, FL, 1978), and Juan Marchena Fernández, *La institución militar en Cartagena de Indias, 1700–1810* (Seville, 1982); John Fisher, *Commercial Relations between Spain and Spanish America in the Era of Free Trade, 1778–1796* (Liverpool, England, 1985). John R. Fisher, Allan J. Kuethe, and Anthony McFarlane, eds., *Reform and Insurrection in Bourbon New Granada and Peru* (Baton Rouge, 1990), offers, among various useful essays, Marchena on the military, Lance Grahn on contraband, and Fisher on commerce.

On the Comunero rebellion, John Leddy Phelan, *The People and the King: The Comunero Revolution in Colombia, 1781* (Madison, WI, 1978), which deals primarily with elites and elite understandings, has been influential. Mario Aguilera Peña's focus on the popular bases of the rebellion in *Los comuneros; guerra social y lucha anticolonial* (Bogotá, 1985) provides a welcome corrective. Pablo Cárdenas Acosta, *El movimiento comunal de 1781 en el Nuevo Reino de Granada* (2 vols., Bogotá, 1960) is a solid traditional work. On the colonial Enlightenment, see Juan Manuel Pacheco, *La Ilustración en el Nuevo Reino de Granada* (Caracas, 1975). On connections to independence, see Thomas Glick, "Science and Independence in Latin America (with Special Reference to New Granada)," *Hispanic American Historical Review*, vol. 71 (May 1991). Practical and political consequences of the Enlightenment are visible in Pedro Fermín de Vargas, *Pensamientos políticos y memorias sobre la población del Nuevo Reino de Granada* [ca. 1790] (Bogotá, 1953); and in Manuel del Socorro Rodríguez's newspaper, *Papel periódico de la Ciudad de Santafé de Bogotá, 1791–1797* (7 vols., Bogotá, 1978), and the biography of its editor by Antonio Cacua Prada, *Don Manuel del Socorro Rodríguez*

(Bogotá, 1966). On Nariño, see Thomas Blossom, *Nariño: Hero of Colombian Independence* (Tucson, AZ, 1967). Documents providing a fuller understanding of the 1794–1795 crisis are printed in Eduardo Posada and Pedro M. Ibáñez, eds., *El Precursor* (Bogotá, 1903); José Manuel Pérez Sarmiento, ed., *Proceso de Nariño* (Cádiz, 1914); and Pérez Sarmiento, ed., *Causas celebres a los precursores* (2 vols., Bogotá, 1939).

Reports of viceroys are most amply compiled in German Colmenares, ed., *Relaciones e informes de los gobernantes de la Nueva Granada* (3 vols., Bogotá, 1989); reports of other officials are in Emilio Robledo, *Bosquejo biográfico del señor oidor Juan Antonio Mon y Velarde, Visitador de Antioquia, 1785–1788* (2 vols., Bogotá, 1954); Francisco Silvestre, *Relación de la Provincia de Antioquia* (David J. Robinson, ed.) (Medellín, 1988); Francisco Silvestre, *Descripción del Reyno de Santa Fé de Bogotá* [1789] (Bogotá, 1968); and *Indios y mestizos de la Nueva Granada a finales del siglo xviii* (Bogotá, 1985).

For the mental atmosphere circa 1800–1808, see the letters of Miguel Tadeo Gómez in Luis Martínez Delgado, *Noticia biográfica del procer Don Joaquín Camacho* (Bogotá, 1984); Sergio Elias Ortiz, ed., *Escritos de dos economistas coloniales: Don Antonio de Narvaez y la Torre y Don José Ignacio de Pombo* (Bogotá, 1965); and Francisco José de Caldas's *El Semanario de la Nueva Granada* [1808–1810] (Paris, 1849) and *Cartas de Caldas* (Bogotá, 1978).

Independence

José Manuel Restrepo, a participant, wrote the classic work, *Historia de la revolución de la República de Colombia* (6 vols., Medellín, 1969–1970). For modern analyses of the origins of independence, see Rafael Gómez Hoyos, *La revolución granadina de 1810: Ideario de una generación y de una época, 1781–1821* (2 vols., Bogotá, 1982); Sergio Elias Ortiz, *Génesis de la revolución* (Bogotá, 1960); and Javier Ocampo López, *El proceso ideológico de la emancipación en Colombia* (Bogotá, 1983). Among collections of documents are Eduardo Posada, ed., *El 20 de julio* (Bogotá, 1914) and Banco de la República, *El proceso del 20 de julio de 1810* (Bogotá, 1960) on the movement in Bogotá. Margarita Garrido, *Reclamos y representaciones: Variaciones sobre la política en el Nuevo Reino de Granada, 1770–1815* (Santafé de Bogotá, 1993), illumines local political processes outside the capital. Germán Colmenares et al., *La independencia: Ensayos de historia social* (Bogotá, 1986) focuses on the Cauca. For other regions, see Horacio Rodríguez Plata, *La antigua provincia del Socorro y la independencia* (Bogotá, 1983); Roberto M. Tisnes, *La independencia en la costa atlántica* (Bogotá, 1976); Manuel Ezequiel Corrales, *Documentos para la historia de la Provincia de Cartagena hoy Estado de Bolívar* (2 vols., Bogotá, 1883) and *Efémerides del Estado de Bolívar* (2 vols., Bogotá, 1889); and Alfonso Múnera, "Failing to Construct the Colombian Nation: Race and Class in the Andean-Caribbean Conflict, 1717–1816" (Ph.D. dissertation, University of Connecticut, 1995).

Maurice Brungardt uses tithe records to reveal economic trends before independence and the impact of the struggle: see "Tithe Production and Patterns of Economic Change in Central Colombia, 1764–1833" (Ph.D. dissertation, University of Texas, Austin, 1974).

Constitutions

Manuel A. Pombo and José J. Guerra, *Constituciones de Colombia* (5 vols., Bogotá, 1986). An earlier edition (1911) publishes constitutions 1810–1910 and commentaries; the 1986 edition contains amendments to 1986. On the 1886 constitution, Luis C. Sáchica,

La constitución colombiana, cien años haciendose (Mexico, D.F., 1982). On the constitution of 1991, Manuel J. Cepeda, *Introducción a la Constitución de 1991* (Bogotá, 1993); Carlos Lleras de la Fuente et al., *Interpretación y génesis de la Constitución de Colombia* (Bogotá, 1992). A critical view of Colombian constitutions: Hernando Valencia Villa, *Cartas de batalla. Una crítica del constitucionalismo colombiano* (Bogotá, 1987).

Colombia in the 1820s

The master work is David Bushnell, *The Santander Regime in Gran Colombia* (Newark, DE, 1954). Two of the better accounts by foreign visitors are Charles Stuart Cochrane, *Journal of a Residence and Travels in Colombia during the Years 1823 and 1824* (2 vols., London, 1825) and J. P. Hamilton, *Travels through the Interior Provinces of Columbia* (2 vols., London, 1827). Gaspard-Théodore Mollien, a French emissary, is most readily available in Spanish, *Viaje por la República de Colombia en 1823* (Bogotá, 1944), but an English edition exists (London, 1824).

José Manuel Restrepo, *Diario político y militar* (4 vols., Bogotá, 1954–1955) [index published with his *Autobiografía* (Bogotá, 1957)], gives insight into the entire period from 1819 to 1858. Also an important source: *Congreso de Cúcuta, 1821. Libro de actas* (Bogotá, 1971). Vicente Lecuna and Harold A. Bierck, Jr., *Selected Writings of Bolívar* (2 vols., New York, 1951), provides key letters in English translation. Two fuller collections are Simon B. O'Leary, ed., *Memorias del General O'Leary* (32 vols., Caracas, 1879–1888); Vicente Lecuna, ed., *Cartas del Libertador* (11 vols., Caracas, 1929–1948). See also Roberto Cortázar, ed., *Correspondencia dirigida al General Santander* (14 vols., Bogotá, 1964–1970); Roberto Cortázar, ed., *Cartas y mensajes de Santander* (10 vols., Bogotá, 1953–1956); and Guillermo Hernández de Alba and Fabio Lozano y Lozano, eds., *Documentos sobre el Doctor Vicente Azuero* (Bogotá, 1944).

Politics, 1830–1849

Two general political narratives: José Manuel Restrepo, *Historia de la Nueva Granada* (2 vols., Bogotá, 1952 and 1963); Gustavo Arboleda covers 1830 to 1860 in *Historia contemporánea de Colombia* (6 vols., Bogotá, 1918–1919, Popayán, 1930, Cali, 1933, 1935). General Joaquín Posada Gutiérrez gave his version of 1826 to 1853 in *Memorias historico-políticas* (3 vols., Medellín, 1971). See also Robert Louis Gilmore, *El federalismo en Colombia, 1810–1858* (2 vols., Santafé de Bogotá, 1995).

Biographies of conservative notables include Carlos Cuervo Márquez, *Vida del Doctor José Ignacio Márquez* (2 vols., Bogotá, 1917–1919); Angel and Rufino José Cuervo, *Vida de Rufino Cuervo y noticias de su época* (2 vols., Bogotá, 1946); and Ignacio Gutiérrez Ponce, *Vida de Don Ignacio Gutiérrez Ponce y episodios históricos de su tiempo (1806–1877)* (2 vols., London, 1900, Bogotá, 1973). See also Eduardo Posada and Pedro M. Ibáñez, *Vida de Herrán* (Bogotá, 1903); Estanislao Gómez Barrientos, *Don Mariano Ospina y su época* (Medellín, 1913); and Gabriel Henao Mejía, *Juan de Dios Aranzazu* (Bogotá, 1953).

The founders of the Liberal Party were less well served by admiring descendants. But more recent works are Pilar Moreno de Angel, *Santander* (Bogotá, 1989); Horacio Rodríguez Plata, *José María Obando, íntimo* (Bogotá, 1958); Andrés Soriano Lleras, *Lorenzo María Lleras* (Bogotá, 1958); Jaime Duarte French, *Florentino González: Razón y sinrazón de una lucha política* (Bogotá, 1971); and Gustavo Humberto Rodríguez, *Ezequiel Rojas y la primera república liberal* (Bogotá, 1984).

The best edited collection of letters, fundamental for the politics of the period, is J. León Helguera and Robert H. Davis, eds., *Archivo epistolar del General Mosquera: Correspondencia con el General Pedro Alcántara Herrán* (3 vols., Bogotá, 1972, 1978). Luis Martínez and Sergio Elías Ortiz, eds., *Epistolario y documentos oficiales del General José María Obando* (3 vols., Bogotá, 1973) and Gabriel Camargo Pérez, ed., *Archivo y otros documentos del Coronel Salvador Córdoba* (Bogotá, 1955), are also important for understanding the defining conflict of 1840. Among other useful collections of correspondence are those of Domingo Caicedo and Rufino Cuervo. See also José María Arboleda Llorente, *Vida del Ilmo. Señor Manuel José Mosquera, Arzobispo de Santafe de Bogotá* (2 vols, Bogotá, 1956).

The years 1845–1849 have been best studied in J. León Helguera, "The First Mosquera Administration in New Granada, 1845–1849" (Ph.D. dissertation, University of North Carolina, 1958).

Social interpretations of political alignments: Victor M. Uribe, *Honorable Lives: Lawyers, Family, and Politics in Colombia, 1780–1850* (Pittsburgh, PA, 2000) links political divisions in the early republican period to family social status in the late colonial period. Frank Safford, "Social Aspects of Politics in Nineteenth-Century Spanish America: New Granada, 1825–1850," *Journal of Social History*, vol. 5 (1972), also stresses "social location," but conceives of it a bit differently. José Escorcia persuasively analyzes the socioeconomic bases of political alignments in Cali in *Sociedad y economía en el Valle del Cauca, tomo III, Desarrollo político, social y económico, 1800–1854* (Bogotá, 1983). Maria Teresa Uribe de Hincapié and Jesús María Alvárez offer a broad socioeconomic analysis, *Poderes y regiones: problemas en la constitución de la nación colombiana. 1810–1850* (Medellín, 1987).

Politics, 1849–1863

Germán Colmenares, *Partidos políticos y clases sociales en Colombia* (Bogotá, 1968), is a spirited construction of the social formations in conflict circa 1848–1851. Works of young radicals of 1849–1853 include José María Samper's memoirs, *Historia de un alma* (Medellín, 1971), and his *Apuntamientos para la historia de la Nueva Granada* (Bogotá, 1853), and *Ensayo sobre las revoluciones políticas y la condición social de las repúblicas colombianas (hispano-americanas)* (Paris, 1861); Salvador Camacho Roldán, *Mis memorias* (2 vols., Bogotá, 1946); and Aníbal Galindo, *Recuerdos históricos, 1840 a 1895* (Bogotá, 1900). Manuel Ancízar, *Peregrinación de Alpha* (Bogotá, 1956), provides a description of the Eastern Cordillera and a window into the mind of a mid-century Liberal.

Gerardo Molina, *Las ideas liberales en Colombia, 1849–1914* (Bogotá, 1970), usefully delineates variants of Liberal thought. However, the commanding history of ideas in the nineteenth century is Jaime Jaramillo Uribe, *El pensamiento colombiano en el siglo xix* (Bogotá, 1964).

On artisans, see David Sowell, *The Early Colombian Labor Movement: Artisans and Politics in Bogotá, 1832–1919* (Philadelphia, 1992), and Carmen Escobar Rodríguez, *La revolución liberal y la protesta del artesanado* (Bogotá, 1990). Ambrosio López, *El desengaño* [1851] (Bogotá, 1985), expresses an artisan leader's disillusionment with the Liberals. On the Liberal Revolution in Cali, see Margarita Pacheco G., *La fiesta liberal en Cali* (Cali, 1992).

On the Melo revolution, see Venancio Ortiz, *Historia de la revolución del 17 de abril de 1854* [1855] (Bogotá, 1972); Alirio Gómez Picón, *El golpe militar del 17 de abril de*

1854 (Bogotá, 1972); see [Manuel Bosch?], *Reseña histórica de los primeros acontecimientos políticos de la Ciudad de Cali* (Bogotá, 1977). Anthony P. Maingot, "Social Structure, Social Status, and Civil-Military Conflict in Urban Colombia, 1810–1858," in Stephan Thernstrom and Richard Sennett, eds., *Nineteenth-Century Cities* (New Haven, CT, 1969), perceptively analyzes social status in the nineteenth-century military.

Politics, 1863–1886

Helen Delpar, *Red against Blue: The Liberal Party in Colombian Politics, 1863–1899* (University, AL, 1981), and James W. Park, *Rafael Núñez and the Politics of Colombian Regionalism, 1863–1886* (Baton Rouge, 1985), both provide important insights. See also Aquileo Parra, *Memorias de Aquileo Parra* (Bogotá, 1912). Some useful regional studies include Luis Javier Ortiz Mesa, *El federalismo en Antioquia, 1850–1880: aspectos políticos* (Medellín, 1985); Luis Javier Villegas, *Las vías de legitimación de un poder: la administración presidida por Pedro Justo Berrío en el Estado Soberano de Antioquia, 1864–1873* (Bogotá, 1996); and Alonso Valencia Llano, *Estado Soberano del Cauca: federalismo y regeneración* (Bogotá, 1988).

The Regeneration

Indalecio Liévano Aguirre, *Rafael Núñez* (Bogotá, 1944), depicts Núñez as an historical model for modern developmentalists. Charles Bergquist, *Coffee and Conflict in Colombia, 1886–1910* (Durham, NC, 1978), stresses the impact of fluctuations in international markets on Colombian politics. Darío Bustamante, "Efectos económicos del papel moneda durante la Regeneración," *Cuadernos Colombianos* 4 (1974), brings a modern economic perspective to the monetary policy of the Regeneration.

The Church and Politics

See Juan Pablo Restrepo, *La iglesia y el estado en Colombia* (2 vols., Bogotá, 1987); Jorge Villegas, *Colombia: Enfrentamiento iglesia-estado, 1819–1887* (Medellín, 1977); Fernán E. González, *Partidos políticos y poder eclesiástico: Reseña histórica, 1810–1930* (Bogotá, 1977); Russ T. Davidson, "The Patronato in Colombia, 1800–1853: Reform and Anti-Reform in the Archidocese of Santa Fe de Bogotá" (Ph.D. dissertation, Vanderbilt, 1978); and Miguel Aguilera, *Visión política del Arzobispo Mosquera* (Bogotá, 1954). On the contemporary Church, see Gustavo Pérez and Isaac Wust, *La iglesia en Colombia. Estructuras eclesiásticas* (Bogotá, 1961); Benjamin Haddox, *Sociedad y religion en Colombia* (Bogotá, 1965); Daniel H. Levine, *Religion and Politics in Latin America. The Catholic Church in Venezuela and Colombia* (Princeton, NJ, 1981) and *Popular Voices in Latin American Catholicism* (Princeton, NJ, 1992); and Oscar Maldonado, Guitemie Olivieri and Germán Zabala, eds., *Cristianismo y revolución* (Mexico, 1970), on Father Camilo Torres.

Education after Independence

See Frank Safford, *The Ideal of the Practical: Colombia's Struggle to Form a Technical Elite* (Austin, TX, 1976) on efforts to change social values through scientific and technical education. See also John L. Young, *La reforma universitaria de la Nueva Granada*

(1820–1850) (Santafé de Bogotá, 1994). For the twentieth century, see Aline Helg, *La educación en Colombia, 1918–1957: una historia social, económica y política* (Bogotá, 1987); Gonzalo Cataño, ed., *Educación y sociedad en Colombia* (Bogotá, 1973) and *Educación y estructura social* (Bogotá, 1989); Rodrigo Parra Sandoval, *Ausencia de futuro: la juventud colombiana* (Bogotá, 1985); and Ricardo Lucio y Mariana Serrano, *La educación superior: tendencias y políticas estatales* (Bogotá, 1992).

Economic History: General

The pioneering work, still indispensable, is Luis Ospina Vásquez, *Industria y protección en Colombia* (Medellín, 1955), the scope of which is much broader than the title suggests. Luis Eduardo Nieto Arteta, *Economía y cultura en la historia de Colombia* (Bogotá, 1942), on economic ideas, was influential to the end of the 1970s. Showing the mark of Nieto Arteta, but employing techniques of the New Economic History, is William Paul McGreevey, *An Economic History of Colombia, 1845–1930* (Cambridge, England, 1971), which prompted a critical symposium: *Historia económica de Colombia: Un debate en marcha* (Bogotá, 1979). Fedesarrollo, *Ensayos sobre historia económica colombiana* (Bogotá, 1980) and José Antonio Ocampo, ed., *Historia económica de Colombia* (Bogotá, 1987), present more recent Colombian perspectives. José Antonio Ocampo, *Colombia y la economía mundial, 1830–1910* (Bogotá, 1984), is authoritative on foreign trade.

Economy and Society, 1820–1850

Guillermo Wills, *Observaciones sobre el comercio de la Nueva Granada* [1831] (Bogotá, 1952), is informative. On Wills, see Malcolm Deas, *Vida y opiniones de Mr. William Wills* (2 vols., Santafé de Bogotá, 1996). J. Steuart, *Bogotá in 1836–7* (New York, 1838), is particularly good on the microeconomy. Isaac F. Holton, *New Granada: Twenty Months in the Andes* (New York, 1857), treats the early 1850s. Carl August Gosselman, *Informes sobre los estados sudamericanos en los años de 1837 y 1838* (Estocolmo, 1962), focuses on foreign trade. *Jeografía física i política de las provincias de la Nueva Granada por la Comisión Corográfica bajo la dirección de Agustín Codazzi* [1856] (4 vols., Bogotá, 1957–1959) provides information on interregional trade in the 1850s.

A good summary of the economy as a whole is Jorge Orlando Melo, "La evolución económica de Colombia, 1830–1900, in *Manual de historia de Colombia*, vol. 2, 135–207. Malcolm Deas focuses on a central difficulty in "The Fiscal Problems of Nineteenth-Century Colombia," *Journal of Latin American Studies*, 14 (November 1982). Frank Safford, "Commerce and Enterprise in Central Colombia, 1821–1870" (Ph.D. dissertation, Columbia, 1965), treats the regional economy of the eastern belt (manufacturing enterprise, exports, importing) and provides tables on freight rates (overland and on the Magdalena), interest rates, wages, and prices. For the depression of the 1830s and protectionism, see Safford, "Commercial Crisis and Economic Ideology in New Granada, 1820–1850," in Reinhard Liehr, ed., *América Latina en la época de Simón Bolívar* (Berlin, 1989).

Carl August Gosselman, *Viaje por Colombia, 1825 y 1826* (Bogotá, 1981), is excellent on conditions in Antioquia at the time. On the early economic reach of Antioqueño merchant capitalists, see Frank Safford, "Significación de los antioqueños en el desarrollo económico colombiano," in *Anuario Colombiano de Historia Social y de la Cultura* Vol. 2, no. 3 (1967). On Antioqueño colonization (and much else), see Antonio García, *Geografía económica de Colombia. Caldas* (Bogotá, 1937); James J. Parsons, *Antioqueño Colonization in Western Colombia* (Berkeley, CA, 1968); Alvaro López Toro, *Migración y cambio social en Antioquia durante el siglo diez y nueve* (Bogotá, 1970); Keith Christie, "Antioqueño Colonization in Western Colombia: A Reappraisal," *Hispanic American Historical Review*, 58 (May 1978); and, more recently, FICDUCAL, *La colonización antioqueña* (Manizales, 1989), and Roberto Luis Jaramillo, "La colonización antioqueña," in Jorge Orlando Melo, ed., *Historia de Antioquia* (Medellín, 1988). See also Albeiro Valencia Llano, *Manizales en la dinámica colonizadora, 1846–1930* (Manizales, 1990); Albeiro Valencia Llano, *Colonización: fundaciones y conflictos agrarios (Gran Caldas y norte del Valle* (Manizales, 1994); and Nancy Appelbaum, "Whitening the Region: Caucano Mediation and 'Antioqueño Colonization' in Nineteenth-Century Colombia," *Hispanic American Historical Review*, 79 (November 1999).

On slavery and abolition, see Eduardo Posada, *La esclavitud en Colombia* (Bogotá, 1933); Carlos Restrepo Canal, ed., *La libertad de los esclavos en Colombia* (Bogotá, 1938); Jorge Castellanos, *La abolición de la esclavitud en Popayán, 1832–52* (Cali, 1980). On Indians, primarily in the Eastern Cordillera, see Glenn T. Curry, "The Disappearance of the Resguardos Indígenas of Cundinamarca, Colombia, 1800–1863" (Ph.D. dissertation, Vanderbilt, 1981); and Frank Safford, "Race, Integration and Progress: Elite Attitudes and the Indian in Colombia, 1750–1870," *Hispanic American Historical Review*, 71 (February 1991). On Indians in the Cauca, Joanne Rappaport, *The Politics of Memory* (Durham, NC, 1998).

Economy, 1850–1900

Important contemporary sources include Salvador Camacho Roldán, *Escritos varios* (3 vols., Bogotá, 1892–1895), and *Notas de viaje* (Bogotá, 1890); Miguel Samper, *Escritos político-económicos* (4 vols., Bogotá, 1925–1927), and *La miseria en Bogotá y otros escritos* (Bogotá, 1969); Aníbal Galindo, *Estudios económicos y fiscales* (Bogotá, 1978); and Medardo Rivas, *Los trabajadores de tierra caliente* (Bogotá, 1946).

For comprehensive coverage of foreign trade, see Ocampo under Economic history, general. Luis F. Sierra, *El tabaco en la economía colombiana del siglo xix* (Bogotá, 1971), treats Colombia's first important tropical export.

Economy, Various

Entrepreneurial history: Carlos Dávila Ladrón de Guevara, *Historia empresarial de Colombia: Estudios, problemas y perspectivas* (Bogotá, 1991) and *El empresariado colombiano: Una perspectiva histórica* (Bogotá, 1996); Frank Safford, "National and Foreign Enterprise in Nineteenth-Century Colombia," *Business History Review*, 39 (December 1965).

Money and banking: Guillermo Torres García, *Historia de la moneda en Colombia* (Bogotá, 1987); Adolfo Meisel R. et al., *El Banco de la República: antecedentes, evolución y estructura* (Bogotá, 1990); Fabio Sánchez Torres, ed., *Ensayos de historia monetaria y bancaria de Colombia* (Bogotá, 1994); Adolfo Meisel R., ed., *Kemmerer y el Banco de la República: diarios y documentos* (Bogotá, 1994); Paul Drake, *The Money Doctor in the Andes: the Kemmerer Missions, 1923–1933* (Durham, NC, 1989).

Railways: Alfredo Ortega, *Ferrocarriles colombianos: resúmen histórico* (2 vols., Bogotá, 1920, 1923); Hernán Horna, "Francisco Javier Cisneros: A Pioneer in Transportation and Economic Development in Colombia" (Ph.D. dissertation, Vanderbilt,

1970); James Neal, "The Pacific Age Comes to Colombia: the Construction of the Cali-Buenaventura Route" (Ph.D. dissertation, Vanderbilt, 1971).

Various: Bernardo Tovar, *La intervención económica del estado en Colombia, 1914–1936* (Bogotá, 1984); René de la Pedraja, *Energy Policy in Colombia* (Boulder, CO, 1989); Fernando Botero, *La industrialización en Antioquia: Génesis y consolidación, 1900–1930* (Medellín, 1984); José Antonio Ocampo and Santiago Montenegro, *Crísis mundial, protección e industrialización: Ensayos de historia económica colombiana* (Bogotá, 1984); Eduardo Sáenz Rovner, *La ofensiva empresarial. Industriales, políticos y violencia en los años 40 en Colombia* (Bogotá, 1992); Gabriel Poveda Ramos, *ANDI y la industria en Colombia, 1944–1984* (Bogotá, 1984), Carlos Díaz- Alejandro, *Foreign Trade Regimes and Economic Development: Colombia* (New York, 1976); Albert Berry and Miguel Urrutia, *Income Distribution in Colombia* (New Haven, CT, 1976); Albert Berry, ed., *Essays on Industrialization in Colombia* (Tempe, AZ, 1983); Rosemary Thorp, *Economic Management and Economic Development in Peru and Colombia* (London, 1991); Miguel Urrutia, ed., *40 años de desarrollo: su impacto social* (Bogotá, 1990); Alicia Puyana, "The Campaign against Absolute Poverty in Colombia: An Evaluation of a Liberal Social Policy," in Christopher Abel and Colin Lewis, eds., *Welfare, Poverty and Development in Latin America* (London, 1993); Alicia Puyana and Rosemary Thorp, *Colombia: economía política de las expectativas petroleras* (Bogotá, 1998).

Foreign Relations

A comprehensive work (not exclusively on Colombian–U.S. relations) is Raimundo Rivas, *Historia diplomática de Colombia (1810–1934)* (Bogotá, 1961). U.S. treatments tend to focus on U.S.–Colombian relations: E. Taylor Parks, *Colombia and the United States, 1765–1934* (Durham, NC, 1935); J. Fred Rippy, *The Capitalists and Colombia* (New York, 1931); Richard Lael, *Arrogant Diplomacy: U.S. Policy toward Colombia, 1903–1922* (Wilmington, DE, 1987); Stephen J. Randall, *The Diplomacy of Modernization: Colombian-American Relations, 1920–1940* (Toronto, 1977) and *Colombia and the United States: Hegemony and Interdependence* (Athens, GA, 1992); David Bushnell, *Eduardo Santos and the Good Neighbor* (Gainesville, FL, 1967).

Colombian perspectives: Apolinar Diaz-Callejas, *Colombia-Estados Unidos: Entre la autonomía y la subordinacion. De la independencia a Panama* (Santafé de Bogotá, 1997); Jorge Villegas, *Petróleo, oligarquía e imperio* (Bogotá, 1969). On more recent periods: Gerhard Drekonja, *Retos de la política exterior colombiana* (Bogotá, 1983); Gerhard Drekonja and Juan Tokatlián, eds., *Teoría y práctica de la política exterior colombiana* (Bogotá, 1983); Martha Ardila, *Cambio de norte? Momentos críticos en la política exterior colombiana* (Bogotá, 1991).

On the drug trade: Juan Tokatlián and Bruce Bagley, eds., *Economía y política del narcotráfico* (Bogotá, 1990); Bruce M. Bagley, "Colombia and the War on Drugs," *Foreign Affairs*, 67 (1988) and "Colombia: the Wrong Strategy," *Foreign Policy*, 77 (1989–1990); Luis F. Sarmiento and Ciro Krauthausen, *Cocaina & Co.: un mercado ilegal por dentro* (Bogotá, 1991); Francisco Thoumi, *Economía política y narcotrafico* (Bogotá, 1994), Roberto Steiner, "Los ingresos de Colombia producto de la exportación de drogas ilícitas," *Coyuntura Económica*, #1 (1997).

Regional Studies

Some overviews: Ernesto Guhl, *Colombia: Bosquejo de su geografía tropical* (Bogotá, 1975). On regional expressions of the family, see Virginia Gutiérrez de Pineda, *Fa-*

milia y cultura en Colombia: Tipologías, funciones y dinámica de la familia (Bogotá, 1977). Patricia Pinzón de Lewin, *Pueblos, regiones y partidos* (Bogotá, 1989), is an introduction to political regionalism.

The East: Jane M. Rausch, *A Tropical Plains Frontier: The Llanos of Colombia, 1531–1831* (Albuquerque, NM, 1984) and *The Llanos Frontier in Colombian History, 1830–1930* (Albuquerque, NM, 1993); David Church Johnson, *Santander Siglo xix— Cambios socioeconómicos* (Bogotá, 1984); Alfred Hettner, *Viajes por los Andes colombianos, 1882–1884* (Bogotá, 1976); Orlando Fals Borda, *El hombre y la tierra en Boyacá: desarrollo histórico de una sociedad minifundista* (Bogotá, 1957) and *Campesinos de los Andes* (Bogotá, 1961).

The Caribbean coast: Adolfo Meisel Roca, ed., *Historia económica y social del Caribe colombiano* (Bogotá, 1994); Orlando Fals Borda, *Historia doble de la Costa* (4 vols., Bogotá, 1979–1984); Theodore Nichols, *Tres puertos colombianos* (Bogotá, 1973); Gustavo Bell Lemus, ed., *El Caribe colombiano* (Barranquilla, 1989); Eduardo Posada Carbó, *The Colombian Caribbean: a Regional History (1870–1950)* (Oxford, England, 1996) and *Una invitación a la historia de Barranquilla* (Bogotá, 1987).

On Antioquia: Jorge Orlando Melo, ed., *Historia de Antioquia* (Medellín, 1988), and *Historia de Medellín* (Medellín, 1996); Roger Brew, *El desarrollo económico de Antioquia desde la independencia hasta 1920* (Bogotá, 1977); *Memorias del Simposio: Los estudios regionales en Colombia: El caso de Antioquia* (Medellín, 1982); Ernesto Ramírez, *Poder económico y democracia política: El caso de la familia Ospina* (Bogotá, 1984),

On the Cauca: *Sociedad y economía en el Valle del Cauca* (5 vols., Bogotá, 1983)— five monographs covering the eighteenth century (Germán Colmenares), the independence period (Zamira Díaz de Zuluaga), socioeconomic configurations 1800–1854 (José Escorcia), credit and economy 1851–1880 (Richard Hyland), and the sugar industry 1860–1980 (José María Rojas G.). On later periods, see Oscar Almario G., *La configuración moderna del Valle del Cauca, Colombia, 1850–1940. Espacio, poblamiento, poder y cultura* (Cali, 1994). Alonso Valencia Llano, ed., *Historia del Gran Cauca: Historia regional del suroccidente colombiano* (Cali, 1994), provides essays on economy, society, and culture from pre-Columbian times to the present.

Cultural, Ethnic, and Literary Aspects

See Gerardo and Alicia Reichel-Dolmatoff, *The People of Aritama. The Cultural Personality of a Colombian Mestizo Village* (London, 1961); George List, *Music and Poetry in a Colombian Village: A Tri-cultural Heritage* (Bloomington, IN, 1983).

On indigenes: Juan Friede, *El indio en la lucha por la tierra* (Bogotá, 1946); Instituto Colombiano de Antropología, *Introducción a la Colombia amerindia* (Bogotá, 1987); Universidad Nacional de Colombia, *Colombia amazónica* (Bogotá, 1987); Ernesto Guhl et. al., *Indios y blancos en la Guajira* (Bogotá, 1963); Christian Gros, *Colombia indígena. Identidad cultural y cambio social* (Bogotá, 1991); Michael Taussig, *Shamanism, Colonialism and the Wild Man* (Chicago, 1988); Myriam Jimeno and Adolfo Triana, *Estado y minorías étnicas en Colombia* (Bogotá, 1985).

On Afro-Colombians: Aquiles Escalante, *El negro en Colombia* (Bogotá, 1964); Nina Friedemann, *Criele Criele son* (Bogotá, 1989); Peter Wade, *Blackness and Race Mixture: The Dynamics of Racial Identity in Colombia* (Baltimore, 1993).

Literary studies: Colcultura, *Manual de literatura colombiana* (3 vols., Bogotá, 1988); Antonio Curcio Altamar, *Evolución de la novela en Colombia* (Bogotá, 1975); Raymond Williams, *The Colombian Novel, 1844–1987* (Austin, TX, 1991).

Colonization

On colonization in general, see Catherine LeGrand, *Frontier Expansion and Peasant Protest in Colombia, 1850–1936* (Albuquerque, NM, 1986). In addition to works earlier mentioned on Antioqueño colonization, see James J. Parsons, *Urabá salida de Antioquia al mar: Geografía e historia de colonización* (Medellín, 1980). On more recent colonizations elsewhere, see Alfredo Molano, *Selva adentro. Una historia oral de la colonización del Guaviare* (Bogotá, 1987); Ronald L. Tinnermeier, "New Land Settlement in the Eastern Lowlands of Colombia" (Ph.D. dissertation, Wisconsin, Madison, 1965); Jaime Jaramillo, Leonidas Mora, and Fernando Cubides, *Colonización, coca y guerrilla* (Bogotá, 1986); José Jairo González, Roberto Ramírez, Alberto Valencia, and Reinaldo Barbosa, *Conflictos regionales. Amazonia y Orinoquia* (Bogotá, 1998).

Coffee

Robert C. Beyer, "The Coffee Industry in Colombia: Origins and Major Trends" (Ph.D. dissertation, Minnesota, 1947); Malcolm Deas, "A Colombian Coffee Estate: Santa Barbara, Cundinamarca, 1870–1912," in Kenneth Duncan and Ian Rutledge, eds., *Land and Labour in Latin America* (Cambridge, England, 1977); Mariano Arango, *Café e industria, 1850–1930* (Bogotá, 1977); Absalón Machado, *El café: de la aparcería al capitalismo* (Bogotá, 1977); Marco Palacios, *Coffee in Colombia, 1850–1970: An Economic, Social and Political History* (Cambridge, England, 1980); Bennett Eugene Koffman, "The National Federation of Coffee-growers of Colombia" (Ph.D. dissertation, University of Virginia, 1969); Michael Jiménez, "The Limits of Export Capitalism: Economic Structure, Class, and Politics in a Colombian Coffee Municipality, 1900–1930" (Ph.D. dissertation, Harvard, 1985). See also Michael Jiménez, "Travelling Far in Grandfather's Car: The Life Cycle of Central Colombian Coffee Estates, the Case of Viotá, Cundinamarca (1900–1930)," *Hispanic American Historical Review*, 69 (May 1989).

Agriculture: General

See Mario Arrubla, ed., *La agricultura colombiana en el siglo XX* (Bogotá, 1976); Jesús A. Bejarano, *El régimen agrario: de la economía exportadora a la economía industrial* (Bogotá, 1979); Salomón Kalmanovitz, *La agricultura en Colombia, 1950–1972* (Bogotá, 1975).

Agrarian Issues

Pierre Gilhodes, *Politique et violence: La question agraire en Colombie* (Paris, 1974); Darío Fajardo, *Haciendas, campesinos y políticas agrarias en Colombia, 1920–1980* (Bogotá, 1983); León Zamosc, *The Agrarian Question and the Peasant Movement in Colombia: Struggles of the National Peasant Association, 1967–1981* (Cambridge, England, 1981); Nola Reinhardt, *Our Daily Bread, The Peasant Question and Family Farming in the Colombian Andes* (Berkeley, CA, 1988); Luis Llorente, Armando Salazar, and Angela Gallo, *Distribución de la propiedad rural en Colombia, 1960–1984* (Bogotá, 1985). World Bank, *Colombia. A Review of Agricultural and Rural Development Strategy* (report no. 13437 Co) (Washington, DC, November 1994), provides data on concentration of land and income.

Urban and Rural Social Mobilization

See Miguel Urrutia, *The Development of the Colombian Labor Movement* (New Haven, CT, 1969); Ignacio Torres Giraldo, *Los inconformes* (5 vols., Bogotá, 1973) and *María Cano, mujer rebelde* (Bogotá, 1972); Daniel Pécaut, *Política y sindicalismo en Colombia* (Medellín, 1978); Judith White, *Historia de una ignominia: La United Fruit Co. en Colombia* (Bogotá, 1978); Mauricio Archila, *Barranquilla y el río. Una historia social de sus trabajadores* (Bogotá, 1987); Pierre Gilhodés, *Las luchas agrarias en Colombia* (Bogotá, 1970); Gonzalo Sánchez, *Las ligas campesinas en Colombia* (Bogotá, 1977) and *Bolcheviques del Líbano* (1976); Charles Bergquist, *Labor in Latin America: Comparative Essays on Chile, Argentina, Venezuela and Colombia* (Stanford, CA, 1986); Hernando Gómez Buendía, Rocío Londoño, and Guillermo Perry, *Sindicalismo y política económica* (Bogotá, 1986); Victor M. Moncayo and Fernando Rojas, *Luchas obreras y política laboral en Colombia* (Bogotá, 1973); Pedro Santana R., *Los movimientos sociales en Colombia* (Bogotá, 1989); Medófilo Medina, *Historia del Partido Comunista de Colombia*, tomo I (Bogotá, 1980).

Compare three visions of factory labor: Alberto Mayor Mora, *Etica, trabajo y productividad en Antioquia; Una interpretación sociológica sobre la influenca de la Escuela Nacional de Minas en la vida, costumbres e industrialización regionales* (Bogotá, 1984); Luz G. Arango, *Mujer, religion e industria: Fabricato, 1923–1982* (Bogotá, 1991); Ann Farnsworth-Alvear, *Dulcinea in the Factory: Myths, Morals, Men, and Women in Colombia's Industrial Experiment, 1905–1960* (Durham, NC, 2000).

Twentieth-Century Politics

See Fernán González, *Para leer la política: ensayos de historia política de Colombia* (Bogota, 1997); Patricia Pinzón de Lewin, *El ejército y las elecciones. Ensayo histórico* (Bogotá, 1994); Robert H. Dix, *Colombia: The Political Dimensions of Change* (New Haven, CT, 1967); Terence B. Horgan, "The Liberals Come to Power in Colombia, *por debajo de la ruana*: A Study of the Enrique Olaya Administration, 1930–1934" (Ph.D. dissertation, Vanderbilt, 1983); Javier Guerrero, *Los años del olvido: Boyacá y los orígenes de la violencia* (Bogotá, 1991); Alvaro Tirado Mejía, *Aspectos políticos del primer gobierno de Alfonso López Pumarejo* (Bogotá, 1981); Richard Stoller, "Alfonso López Pumarejo and Liberal Radicalism in 1930's Colombia," *Journal of Latin American Studies* 27 (1995); Alexander Wilde, *La quiebra de la democracia en Colombia: Conversaciones con caballeros* (Bogotá, 1982); Vernon L. Fluharty, *Dance of the Millions. Military Rule and the Social Revolution in Colombia, 1830–1956* (Pittsburgh, PA, 1966); Silvia Galvis and Alberto Donadío, *El jefe supremo: Rojas Pinila en la violencia y el poder* (Bogotá, 1988); Carlos H. Urán, *Rojas y la manipulación del poder* (Bogotá, 1983); John D. Martz, *Colombia: A Contemporary Political Survey* (Chapel Hill, NC, 1962); Jonathan Hartlyn, *The Politics of Coalition Rule in Colombia* (New York, 1988); Albert Berry, Ronald G. Hellman, and Mauricio Solaún, eds., *Politics of Compromise: Coalition Government in Colombia* (New Brunswick, NJ, 1980); Daniel Pécaut, *Crónica de dos décadas de política colombiana, 1968–1988* (Bogotá, 1989); Francisco Leal Buitrago and León Zamosc, eds., *Al filo del caos. Crisis política en la Colombia de los anos 80* (Bogotá, 1991); and Ana María Bejarano and Andrés Dávila, eds., *Elecciones y democracia en Colombia, 1997–1998* (Bogotá, 1998). Francisco Leal Buitrago and Andrés Dávila Ladrón de Guevara study Acción Comunal in *Clientelismo. El sistema político y su expresión regional* (Bogotá, 1989).

Urban Studies

See Alfonso Torres Carrillo, *La ciudad en la sombra. Barrios y luchas populares en Bogotá, 1850–1977* (Bogotá, 1993); Alan Gilbert and Peter M. Ward, *Asentamientos populares versus poder del Estado: tres caso latinoamericanos: Ciudad de México, Bogotá, y Valencia (Venezuela)* (Mexico/Bogotá, 1987); Medófilo Medina, *La protesta urbana en Colombia* (Bogotá, 1984); Jaime Carrillo, *Los paros cívicos en Colombia* (Bogotá, 1981); Alvaro Camacho and Alvaro Guzmán, *Ciudad y violencia* (Bogotá, 1990); and Alvaro Camacho Guizado, *Droga y sociedad en Colombia. El poder y el estigma* (Bogotá, 1988).

Public Health

See Christopher Abel, *Health Care in Colombia, ca. 1920–1950* (London, 1994) and "External Philanthropy and Domestic Change in Colombian Health Care. The Role of the Rockefeller Foundation, ca. 1920–1950," *Hispanic American Historical Review*, 75 (1995).

Crime and Political Violence

Germán Guzmán Campos, Orlando Fals Borda, and Eduardo Umaña Luna, *La Violencia en Colombia* (2 vols., Bogotá, 1962–1964), is the pioneering work. Paul Oquist, *Violence, Conflict, and Politics in Colombia* (New York, 1980), is a broad analysis of the first Violencia. Three studies of the Violencia in Tolima are Roberto Pineda, *El impacto de la Violencia en el Tolima: el caso de El Líbano* (Bogotá, 1960); James Henderson, *When Colombia Bled: A History of the Violencia in Tolima* (University, AL, 1985); and María Victoria Uribe, *Matar, rematar y contramatar. Las masacres de la Violencia en el Tolima, 1948–1964* (Bogotá, 1990).

Some suggestive interpretive studies of the origins, nature, and role of the Violencia in Colombian society and politics are Daniel Pécaut, *Orden y violencia: Colombia 1930–1956* (2 vols., Bogotá, 1987); and Malcolm Deas, "Violent Exchanges: Reflexions on Political Violence in Colombia," in David E. Apter, ed., *The Legitimization of Violence* (New York, 1997). Critical assessments of the state of research include Gonzalo Sánchez, *Guerra y política en la sociedad colombiana* (Bogotá, 1991); and Charles Bergquist and Ricardo Peñaranda, eds., *Violence in Colombia: The Contemporary Crisis in Historical Perspective* (Wilmington, DE, 1992).

Other important studies include Gonzalo Sánchez, *Los días de la revolución: Gaitanismo y el 9 de abril en provincia* (Bogotá, 1983); Herbert Braun, *The Assassination of Gaitán: Public Life and Urban Violence in Colombia* (Madison, WI, 1985); Gonzalo Sánchez and Donny Meertens, *Bandoleros, gamonales y campesinos* (Bogotá, 1983); Carlos M. Ortiz, *Estado y subversión en Colombia. La violencia en el Quindío años 50* (Bogotá, 1985); Darío Betancourt and Martha García, *Matones y cuadrilleros: origen y evolución de la violencia en el occidente colombiano* (Bogotá, 1990); Reinaldo Barbosa Estepa, *Guadalupe y sus centauros. Memorias de la insurrección llanera* (Bogotá, 1992); and Mary Roldan, "Genesis and Evolution of "La Violencia" in Antioquia, Colombia (1900–1953)" (Ph.D. dissertation, Harvard, 1992). See also Richard L. Maullin, *Soldiers, Guerrillas and Politics in Colombia* (Santa Monica, CA, 1973).

On guerrillas of the left, see Jaime Arenas Reyes, *La guerrilla por dentro. Análisis del E.L.N. Colombiano* (Bogotá, 1971); Eduardo Pizarro Leongómez, *Las FARC (1949–1966): de la autodefensa a la combinación de todas formas de lucha* (Bogotá, 1991);

Arturo Alape, *Tirofijo: las vidas de Pedro Antonio Marín, Manuel Marulanda Vélez* (Bogotá, 1989); José Jairo González Arias, *El estigma de las repúblicas independientes, 1955–1965* (Bogotá, 1992); Jacobo Arenas, *Cese al fuego: una historia política de las FARC* (Bogotá, 1985); and Congreso de Colombia, *El Palacio de Justicia y el derecho de gentes: la denuncia del Procurador ante la Cámara de Representantes y la reacción de la prensa: documentos* (Bogotá, 1986).

The collective analysis of Gonzalo Sánchez et al., *Colombia. Violencia y democracia. Informe presentado al Ministerio de Gobierno* (Bogotá, 1987), changed perspectives on the violence in Colombia. Studies exploring new themes include M. V. Uribe A., *Ni canto de gloria ni canto fúnebre. El regreso del EPL a la vida civil* (Bogotá, 1994); Alfredo Rangel Suárez, *Colombia: guerra en el fin del siglo* (Bogotá, 1998); Malcolm Deas and Maria Victoria Llorente, eds., *Reconocer la guerra para construir la paz* (Bogotá, 1998); Arturo Alape, *La paz, la violencia: testigos de excepción* (Bogotá, 1985); and Herbert Braun, *Our Guerrillas, Our Sidewalks. A Journey into the Violence of Colombia* (Niwot, CO, 1994). On the intense violence in Urabá, see Clara Inés García, *Urabá, region, actores y conflicto, 1960–1990* (Bogotá, 1996) and Carlos Miguel Ortiz Sarmiento, *Urabá: tras las huellas de los inmigrantes, 1955–1997* (Bogotá, 1999). On other forms of violence, see Ana María Jaramillo, *Milicias populares en Medellín: entre la guerra y la paz* (Medellín, 1994); and Carlos Medina Gallegos, *Autodefensas, paramilitares y narcotráfico en Colombia. Orígen, desarrollo y consolidación. El caso de Puerto Boyacá* (Bogotá, 1990).

The most recent studies show the complexity and the interaction of different forms of violence: Mauricio Rubio, *Crimen e impunidad. Precisiones sobre la violencia* (Bogotá, 1999); Jaime Arocha, Fernando Cubides, and Myriam Jimeno, eds., *Las violencias: inclusión creciente* (Bogotá, 1998); Fernando Cubides, Ana Cecilia Olaya, and Carlos Miguel Ortiz, *La violencia y el municipio colombiano, 1980–1997* (Bogotá, 1998). Ciro Krauthausen, *Padrinos y mercaderes. Crimen organizado en Italia y Colombia* (Bogotá, 1997), offers a suggestive comparison for an understanding of the violence of the 1990s.

On the peace process and more general political aspects, see Mark W. Chernick, "Insurgency and Negotiations: Defining the Boundaries of the Political Regime in Colombia" (Ph.D. dissertation, Columbia, 1991) and "Negotiated Settlement to Armed Conflict: Lessons from the Colombian Peace Process," *Journal of Interamerican Studies and World Affairs*, 30 (1988–1989); Mauricio García Durán, *De la Uribe a Tlaxcala. Procesos de paz* (Bogotá, 1992); Francisco Leal Buitrago, ed., *Los laberintos de la guerra. Utopías e incertidumbres sobre la paz* (Bogotá, 1999); Iván Orozco Abad, *Combatientes, rebeldes y terroristas. Guerra y derecho en Colombia* (Bogotá, 1992); Gustavo Gallón Giraldo, *La república de las armas: relaciones entre Fuerzas Armadas y Estado en Colombia* (Bogotá, 1983); Hernando Valencia Villa, *La justicia de las armas. Una crítica normativa de la guerra metodológica en Colombia* (Bogotá, 1993); and Alvaro Camacho Guizado and Francisco Leal Buitrago, *Armar la paz es desarmar la guerra* (Bogotá, 1999).

Chief Executives of Colombia (1819–2001)

Dates are of terms in office. Unless otherwise indicated, office-holders were elected in general elections. List does not include various short-term substitutions in office by vice presidents or *designados* [designates].

1819–1830	General Simón Bolívar (first elected by congresses; re-elected in general election of 1825)
1830	Joaquín Mosquera (elected by constitutional congress)
1830–1831	General Rafael Urdaneta (to power by military coup)
1831–1832	Vice presidents General Domingo Caicedo, General José María Obando, and José Ignacio Márquez (all elected by constitutional congresses)
1832–1837	General Francisco de Paula Santander (elected by constitutional convention 1832; confirmed by general election 1832)

"MINISTERIAL" GOVERNMENTS

1837–1841	José Ignacio Márquez
1841–1845	General Pedro Alcántara Herrán
1845–1849	General Tomás Cipriano de Mosquera

THE LIBERAL REVOLUTION

1849–1853	General José Hilario López
1853–1854	General José María Obando (removed by coup)
1854	General José María Melo (to power in coup)
1854–1855	Vice President José de Obaldia, constitutional vice president

divided authority during civil war of 1854

CONSERVATIVE INTERLUDE

1855–1857	Manuel María Mallarino, vice president, acting chief executive
1857–1861	Mariano Ospina Rodríguez

RADICAL DOMINANCE UNDER FEDERALISM

1861–1864	General Tomás Cipriano de Mosquera (provisional president 1861, as victor in civil war; 1863 elected by constitutional convention)
1864–1866	Manuel Murillo Toro
1866–1867	General Tomás Cipriano de Mosquera (removed by coup)
1867–1868	General Santos Acosta (seized power in coup)
1868–1870	General Santos Gutiérrez
1870–1872	General Eustorgio Salgar
1872–1874	Manuel Murillo Toro
1874–1876	Santiago Pérez
1876–1878	Aquileo Parra

END OF RADICAL DOMINANCE

1878–1880	General Julián Trujillo
1880–1882	Rafael Núñez
1882–1884	Francisco J. Zaldúa; 1882–1884 José Eusebio Otálora completed term as designate after death of Zaldúa in 1882

THE REGENERATION

1884–1894	Rafael Núñez
1894–1898	Miguel Antonio Caro (vice president, presided after death of Núñez)

CONSERVATIVE HEGEMONY

1898–1900	Manuel Antonio Sanclemente (removed by coup)
1900–1904	José Manuel Marroquín, vice president (to power by coup)
1904–1909	General Rafael Reyes (resigned 1909)

1909–1910	Ramón González Valencia (elected by Congress after Reyes' resignation)
1910–1914	Carlos E. Restrepo (elected by Congress)
1914–1918	José Vicente Concha
1918–1921	Marco Fidel Suárez (resigned 1921)
1921–1922	Jorge Holguín (as designate, completed Suárez term)
1922–1926	Pedro Nel Ospina
1926–1930	Miguel Abadía Méndez

RETURN OF THE LIBERALS

1930–1934	Enrique Olaya Herrera
1934–1938	Alfonso López Pumarejo
1938–1942	Eduardo Santos
1942–1945	Alfonso López Pumarejo (resigned 1945)
1945–1946	Alberto Lleras Camargo (finished term as designate)

THE VIOLENCIA

1946–1950	Mariano Ospina Pérez (Conservative)
1950–1953	Laureano Gómez (Conservative) (removed by coup)
1953–1957	General Gustavo Rojas Pinilla (to power by coup)
1957–1958	Military junta

THE NATIONAL FRONT

1958–1962	Alberto Lleras Camargo (Liberal)
1962–1968	Guillermo León Valencia (Conservative)
1966–1970	Carlos Lleras Restrepo (Liberal)
1970–1974	Misael Pastrana (Conservative)

THE "DESPEJE"

1974–1978	Alfonso López Michelsen (Liberal)
1978–1982	Julio César Turbay Ayala (Liberal)
1982–1986	Belisario Betancur (Conservative)

1986–1990	Virgilio Barco (Liberal)
1990–1994	César Augusto Gaviria (Liberal)
1994–1998	Ernesto Samper (Liberal)
1998–[2002]	Andrés Pastrana (Conservative)

Credits

Maps 1 and 4. From Anthony McFarlane, *Colombia before Independence* (Cambridge, England: Cambridge University Press, 1993). Reprinted with the permission of Cambridge University Press.

Map 2. From Warwick Bray, *The Gold of El Dorado* (London: Royal Academy of the Arts, 1978).

Map 3. Reprinted by permission of Louisiana State University Press from *Colonial Placer Mining in Colombia* by Robert C. West. Copyright by Louisiana State University Press.

Maps 5 and 7. From James Parsons, *Antioqueño Colonization in Western Colombia* (Berkeley, CA: University of California Press, 1968). Copyright © 1968 The Regents of the University of California.

Map 6. From Helen Delpar, *Red against Blue: The Liberal Party in Colombian Politics, 1863–1899* (Tuscaloosa, AL: University of Alabama Press, 1981).

Map 8. From *Area Handbook of Colombia* (1977).

Map 9. The map was drawn by Magda Hanna, Program in Geography, Northwestern University.

Index

Note: Page numbers followed by "m" indicate maps. Page numbers followed by "t" indicate tables.